www.wadsworth.com

wadsworth.com is the World Wide Web site for Wadsworth and is your direct source to dozens of online resources.

At *wadsworth.com* you can find out about supplements, demonstration software, and student resources. You can also send email to many of our authors and preview new publications and exciting new technologies.

wadsworth.com
Changing the way the world learns®

ABOUT THE AUTHOR

Howard Abadinsky was professor of criminal justice at Saint Xavier University/Chicago. He was an inspector for the Cook County Sheriff for eight years and a New York State parole officer and senior parole officer for 15 years. He is the founder of the International Association for the Study of Organized Crime and served as a consultant to the President's Commission on Organized Crime.

The author has a B.A. from Queens College of the City University of New York, an M.S.W. from Fordham University, and a Ph.D. in sociology from New York University. He is the author of several books, including *The Criminal Elite: Professional and Organized Crime; The Mafia in America; Probation and Parole*, Eighth Edition; *Law and Justice*, Fifth Edition; and *Drug Abuse*, Fourth Edition.

ORGANIZED CRIME

Seventh Edition

Howard Abadinsky

THOMSON
™
WADSWORTH

Australia • Canada • Mexico • Singapore • Spain
United Kingdom • United States

THOMSON

WADSWORTH

Senior Executive Editor, Criminal Justice: Sabra Horne
Acquisitions Editor: Shelley Murphy
Assistant Editor: Dawn Mesa
Editorial Assistant: Lee McCracken
Technology Project Manager: Susan DeVanna
Marketing Manager: Dory Schaeffer
Marketing Assistant: Neena Chandra
Advertising Project Manager: Bryan Vann
Project Manager, Editorial Production: Jennie Redwitz
Print/Media Buyer: Robert King
Permissions Editor: Stephanie Keough-Hedges
Production Service: Greg Hubit, Greg Hubit Bookworks
Text Designer: Burl Sloan

Photo Researcher: Meyers Art-Photo
Copy Editor: Donald Pharr
Cover Designer: Qi-Zhong Yu
Cover Image: Conference room sign by Ryan McVay;
    hundred-dollar bill and cocaine by C. Sherburne/
    PhotoLink; blackjack game by Kim Steele;
    businesspeople in crosswalk by Ken Usami; stack of
    international currency by Ryan McVay; skyscrapers
    and Hong Kong harbor by Annie Reynolds/
    PhotoLink; close-up of hands typing on a computer
    keyboard by Jonnie Miles.
Compositor and Illustrator: ATLIS Graphics
Cover and Text Printer: Phoenix Color Corp./BTP

For more information about our products, contact us at:
Thomson Learning Academic Resource Center
1-800-423-0563
For permission to use material from this text, contact us by:
Phone: 1-800-730-2214
Fax: 1-800-730-2215
Web: http://www.thomsonrights.com

Library of Congress Control Number: 2002102408

ISBN 0-534-55158-0

Wadsworth/Thomson Learning
10 Davis Drive
Belmont, CA 94002-3098
USA

Asia
Thomson Learning
5 Shenton Way #01-01
UIC Building
Singapore 068808

Australia
Nelson Thomson Learning
102 Dodds Street
South Melbourne, Victoria 3205
Australia

Canada
Nelson Thomson Learning
1120 Birchmount Road
Toronto, Ontario M1K 5G4
Canada

Europe/Middle East/Africa
Thomson Learning
High Holborn House
50/51 Bedford Row
London WC1R 4LR
United Kingdom

Latin America
Thomson Learning
Seneca, 53
Colonia Polanco
11560 Mexico D.F.
Mexico

BRIEF CONTENTS

CONTENTS

PART II ORGANIZED CRIME IN THE UNITED STATES

PART V FIGHTING ORGANIZED CRIME

CHAPTER 14

CHAPTER 15

PREFACE

In 1964, fresh out of college, I was sworn in as a New York State parole officer. Soon afterward, equipped with a badge and a .38, I was assigned to the waterfront section of South Brooklyn known as Red Hook. As I struggled to become familiar with the neighborhood, I noticed that my presence on certain streets seemed to generate a great deal of curiosity (I am six feet, one inch tall and in those days weighed an athletic 200 pounds) and, at times, activity (windows opening and closing, people on the streets suddenly melting into doorways or shops). I discussed Red Hook with my more experienced colleagues, and some of the naiveté faded.

Red Hook was dominated by a faction of one of New York City's five organized crime *Families*. Prior to my arrival, this faction had been involved in a conflict with the rest of the Family, and Red Hook had been the scene of a great deal of violence. A tentative truce was in effect when I appeared on the scene. I became familiar with such terms as "wiseguy" and "made guy," "capo" and "consigliere," and names like Crazy Joey, Blast, The Snake, Punchy, and Apples.

After 15 years as a parole officer and supervisor, I left New York for Western Carolina University and an academic career. My interest in organized crime continued, and I began to teach a course on the subject. However, a single text, one that was both comprehensive and accurate, was unavailable. Like so many others presenting courses on organized crime, I had students purchase the classics by Francis Ianni (1972), Donald Cressey (1972), Joseph Albini (1971), and Humbert Nelli (1976). Nevertheless, there were still gaps, particularly with respect to emerging organized crime and the statutes and techniques used in organized crime law enforcement.

The first edition of this book (1981) was the result of a need for a basic text that covered all of the important dimensions of organized crime and its control. But organized crime changed; hence, a second edition was published in 1985, when I was teaching at Saint Xavier University and becoming familiar with organized crime through contacts developed as a (part-time) Cook County deputy sheriff/inspector.

Ever dynamic, organized crime continued to change, with efforts to combat one aspect of the phenomenon, traditional organized crime, reaching new levels of prosecutorial success. Public officials and media presentations began to talk of the demise of traditional organized crime, while emerging criminal groups were becoming an even more serious threat.

A third edition of this book was published in 1991, a time when traditional organized crime was still being battered by federal law enforcement using the RICO statute. Since that time, the ranks of some organized crime units have been decimated; for all practical purposes, a few have ceased to function. According to some observers, the end is in sight—but is it? A number of crime Families have succeeded in recruiting new members and continue to be viable—and dangerous—entities. Meanwhile, emerging groups of criminals have become more sophisticated and more threatening, and additional crime groups have been added to the pantheon that we refer to as organized crime. This new edition reflects changes that have occurred and updates information and analyses of organized crime and efforts to deal with it.

To improve the ease of classroom use, chapters have been shortened and the book expanded into 15 chapters. A great amount of detail—particularly names and historical minutiae—has been trimmed to improve learning, with this edition concentrating on the "big picture" of organized crime on a global scale. Transnational organized crime—Italian, Latino, Russian, Asian—each has a separate chapter. Outlaw motorcycle clubs are examined in Chapter 1, which contrasts their bureaucratic style of organization with that of the American Mafia. Chapter 6 examines African-American, that is, domestic criminal organizations, and those from Nigeria and Jamaica. The curriculum format has been retained, and relevant Internet sites and review questions appear at the end of each chapter.

Acknowledgments

For their assistance, I would like to thank the New York Police Department's Organized Crime Investigation Division: (the late) Lieutenant John T. O'Brien, Lieutenant Gerard Pope, and Detectives Jerry Rosenberg, John Stebe, and Anthony Farneti. I would also like to thank Dr. Robert M. Lombardo, Deputy Chief of the Cook County Sheriff's Police Department; Thomas Bohling, Lt. Cook County Sheriff's Police Department; William Callaghan, Chief, Intelligence Bureau Organized Crime Division, Chicago Police Department; Don Herion, Director, Vice Detection Unit, Cook County Sheriff's Police Department; Wayne A. Johnson, Chief Investigator, Chicago Crime Commission; Tom Moriarity, Special Agent, Criminal Investigation Division, Internal Revenue Service; John J. O'Rourke, Special Agent, Federal Bureau of Investigation (ret.); Gregory Kerpchar, special agent, Pennsylvania Office of Attorney General, Bureau of Criminal Investigation; Raymond Risley, Commander, Organized Crime Division, Chicago Police Department; Al ("Wallpaper") Wolf, former special agent of the Prohibition Bureau, United States Department of the Treasury; Frank Cullotta, who is in the Witness Protection Program and agreed to telephone interviews; and numerous persons who preferred to remain anonymous. I would like to thank the following for their thoughtful reviews and suggestions, which helped make this a superior edition:

Frank Hagan, Mercyhurst College
William Hyatt, Western Carolina University
Stanley Jacobs, Villanova University
Mark Jones, East Carolina University
Debra Ross, Buffalo State College
Albert Sproule, DeSales University

My thanks to Sabra Horne, Senior Executive Editor at Wadsworth, for her interest in this project, Criminal Justice Editor Shelley Murphy, production editor Greg Hubit, and copy editor Donald Pharr.

The author welcomes comments on his work and can be reached at Saint Xavier University, 3700 W. 103rd Street, Chicago, IL 60655, or at abadinsky@att.net.

♠

C H A P T E R   1

ORGANIZED CRIME: ATTRIBUTES AND STRUCTURE

Organized crime is different from other types of crime: "The criminality of persons in organized crime differs from that of conventional criminals because their organization allows them to commit crimes of a different variety [labor racketeering, for example] and on a larger scale [smuggling planeloads of cocaine, for example] than their less organized colleagues" (Moore 1987: 51). In order to understand how these varied and large-scale tasks can be accomplished, we need to examine the structures that contemporary organized crime can manifest. In this chapter, we will consider two contrasting organizational models. The *bureaucratic/corporate* model and the *patrimonial/patron–client network* represent two ends of a continuum; criminal groups, if they are to be defined as *organized*, can be located somewhere along this continuum. In this chapter, we will apply these two models to outlaw motorcycle clubs and the American Mafia, sometimes referred to as *Cosa Nostra*. But, before we can begin, what is meant by *organized crime*?

DEFINING ORGANIZED CRIME

Attempts to define organized crime (OC) have met with only limited success, and no generally accepted definition has emerged. Donald Cressey (1969: 319) presented a definition that for many decades was used by the Federal Bureau of Investigation: "An organized crime is any crime committed by a person occupying, in an established division of labor, a position designed for the commission of crimes providing that such division of labor includes at least one position for a corrupter, one position for a corruptee, and one position for an enforcer." In 1970 the U.S. Department of Justice defined the term as "all illegal activities engaged in by members of criminal syndicates operative throughout the United States and all illegal activities engaged in by known associates and confederates of such members." In 1998 an international conference in Warsaw on the problem of organized crime used a definition offered by the host country: "Group activities of three or more persons, with hierarchical links or personal relationships, which permit their leaders to earn profits or control territories or markets, internal or foreign, by means of violence, intimidation or corruption, both in furtherance of criminal activity and to infiltrate the legitimate economy." This definition was followed by a list of "typical" activities (Jamieson 2000: 169).

Michael Maltz (1976: 76) points to a semantic problem, noting that we call a specific behavior or act organized crime, but when we refer to organized crime in the generic sense, we usually mean an entity, a group of people: "An organized crime is a crime in which there is more than one offender, and the offenders are and intend to remain associated with one another for the purpose of committing crimes." In its 1967 report, the Task Force on Organized Crime noted that these crimes typically involve the providing of "illegal goods and services" for which there is widespread demand: gambling, loansharking, and narcotics. The definition offered by the state of California adds theft and fencing, and no list of organized criminal activities would be complete without business and labor racketeering and extortion.

Although there is no generally accepted definition of organized crime—indeed, the federal Organized Crime Control Act of 1970 (discussed in Chapter 14) fails to define *organized crime*—there have been a number of attributes identified by law enforcement agencies and researchers as indicative of the phenomenon. Offering these attributes has a practical dimension: they provide a basis for determining if a particular group of criminals constitutes *organized crime* and, therefore, needs to be approached in a way different from the way one would approach other groups of criminals. Organized crime:

1. is nonideological
2. is hierarchical
3. has a limited or exclusive membership
4. perpetuates itself
5. exhibits a willingness to use illegal violence and bribery
6. demonstrates specialization/division of labor
7. is monopolistic
8. is governed by explicit rules and regulations.

Let us examine each of these attributes.

1. *Nonideological.* In attempting to understand and respond to a criminal organization, it is important to consider its *motivation*. An organized crime group is not motivated by social doctrine, political beliefs, or ideological concerns; its goals are money and power. While political involvement may be part of the group's activities, the purpose is to gain protection or immunity for its illegal activities. This distinguishes organized crime from groups of persons who may be organized and violating the law to further their political agenda—for example, the Ku Klux Klan or terrorist groups.

2. *Hierarchical.* An organized crime group has a vertical power structure with at least three permanent ranks—not just a leader and followers—each with authority over the level beneath. The authority is inherent in the position and does not depend on who happens to be occupying it at any given time.

3. *Limited or exclusive membership.* An organized crime group significantly limits membership. Qualifications may be based on ethnic background, kinship, race, criminal record, or similar considerations. Those who meet the basic qualification(s) for membership usually require a sponsor, typically a ranking member, and must also prove qualified for membership by their behavior—for example, willingness to commit criminal acts, obey rules, follow orders, and maintain secrets. There is a period of apprenticeship, which may range from several months to several years. If the OC group is to remain viable, there must be considerably more persons who desire membership than the OC group is willing to accept. Exclusivity of membership serves to indicate that belonging is indeed something to be valued.

While membership can refer to being part of a specific group, such as the Genovese Family or the Hell's Angels, it can also entail a more amorphous attachment to a criminal network, such as that which characterizes Russian organized crime in the United States (discussed in Chapter 9). In either event, ethnicity, a criminal history, the willingness to follow rules, and maintain secrets remain paramount.

4. *Perpetuates itself.* An organized crime group constitutes an ongoing criminal conspiracy designed to persist through time—that is, beyond the life of the current membership. Permanence is assumed by the members, and this provides an important basis for attracting qualified persons to the group, thus perpetuating the group's existence. The strength of this attribute often depends on the depth of the subcultural orientation (discussed in Chapter 2) manifested by the group. Cressey (1969: 263) states that in order for an organized crime group to survive, it must have "an institutionalized process for inducting new members and inculcating them with the values and ways of behaving of the social system."

5. *Willingness to use illegal violence and bribery.* In an organized crime group, violence is a readily available and routinely accepted resource. Access to private violence is an important dimension that allows the group to actively pursue its goals. When necessary, the OC group will resort to bribery in order to protect its operations or members. The use of violence or bribery is not restricted by ethical considerations but is controlled only by practical limitations.

6. *Specialization/division of labor.* An organized crime group will have certain functional positions filled by qualified members. Given the nature of an OC group, the position of *enforcer* is often crucial. This person carries out difficult assignments involving the use of violence, including murder, in a rational manner. The enforcer may use members or nonmembers to accomplish the assignment; he may also turn over assignments for murder to specialists.

If the group is sophisticated enough, it may have positions for a *fixer* and a *moneymover.* The fixer excels in developing contacts with criminal justice and/or political officials and, when appropriate, arranges for corruption. The moneymover is an expert at "laundering" illicitly obtained money, disguising its origin through a string of transactions and investing it in legitimate enterprises (discussed in Chapter 12). Certain OC groups—outlaw motorcycle clubs, for example (discussed below)—also have a position equivalent to *intelligence analyst.* Transnational criminal organizations, such as Colombian drug cartels, may have a rather elaborate division of labor that can include designees responsible for such matters as production, transportation, storage, and wholesale distribution—in addition to moneymovers and enforcers.

7. *Monopolistic.* An organized crime group eschews competition. It strives for hegemony over a particular geographic area (a metropolitan area or section of a city); a particular "industry," legitimate or illegitimate (for example, gambling, trucking, loansharking); or a combination of both (for example, loansharking in a particular area or the wholesale cocaine market in a city). A monopoly, of course, restrains "free trade" and increases profits. An OC monopoly is maintained by violence, by threat of violence, or by corrupt relationships with law enforcement officials. A combination of both methods may be employed.

Although an OC group may strive for a monopoly, this may not be possible given the nature of competing groups or the type of industry—for example, drug trafficking (discussed in Chapter 13). Moreover, territoriality is more closely associated with localness rather than the broader reach of transnational criminal organizations (Reuter and Petrie 1999). In Chapter 8, for example, we will examine Mexican organizations that, although they are associated with a particular geographic area—for instance, the "Juarez cartel"—do not expend resources defending geographic hegemony.

8. *Governed by rules and regulations.* An organized crime group, like a legitimate organization, has a set of rules and regulations that members are expected to follow. In an OC group, however, a rule-violating member is not fired but, more likely, fired upon. In a conversation with his brother-in-law (the son of a murdered mob boss and an attorney who had filed a lawsuit against his business partner in the Genovese Family), Salvatore Profaci, a *caporegime* in the Colombo Family, pointed

out that "Goodfellas don't sue goodfellas. . . . Goodfellas kill goodfellas" (FBI Surveillance Tape, 2 June 1992, from Anastasia 1998).

These attributes are arrayed in a structure that enables the organized crime group to achieve its goals—money and power. There are a number of criminal organizations that have many, if not all, of the attributes that have been discussed. Some are domestic, while most are transnational in scope or have important organizational or business ties overseas.

THE STRUCTURE OF ORGANIZED CRIME

The attributes of organized crime that we have examined can fit two contrasting organizational models: the *bureaucratic/corporate* model and the *patrimonial/patron–client network*. Each organized crime group approximates one of these models viewed as a continuum. Thus, while outlaw motorcycle clubs are clearly on the bureaucratic side of our continuum, the American Mafia is best understood according to the patrimonial/patron–client network model of organization. Criminal organizations discussed in later chapters can be located along this continuum—for example, Colombians tend to organize along bureaucratic (compartmentalized) lines, while Russians in the United States have a fluid structure that tends toward the patrimonial/patron–client network (see Figure 1.1).

The Bureaucratic/Corporate Model

The corporation, the police, and the military are examples of bureaucracies, that mode of organization essential for efficiently carrying out large-scale tasks. All bureaucracies are rational organizations sharing a number of attributes:

- a complicated hierarchy
- an extensive division of labor
- positions assigned on the basis of skill
- responsibilities carried out in an impersonal manner
- extensive written rules and regulations
- communication from the top of the hierarchy to persons on the bottom, usually in written (memo) form

Whenever an entity—club, business, crime group—continues to expand, at some point it will have to adopt the bureaucratic style of organization. For example, a "mom and pop grocery" need not have any of the attributes of a bureaucracy. The owners and workers are related, and the structure is informal and kinship based. If the business expands—the owners establish many groceries—a formal hierarchy becomes necessary, as do skilled persons and a division of labor; there will be extensive written rules and regulations, and directives will be via the hierarchy. Thus, the model of organization adopted by an entity—legitimate or criminal—will depend on the scope of its operations and the organizational experience of its leaders. In the example we will examine, the structure of the outlaw motorcycle club is best explained by the military experience of its early members—the military is *the* quintessential bureaucracy.

Outlaw Motorcycle Clubs

The outlaw motorcycle club is a uniquely American derivation, although several of these clubs now have chapters outside of the United States. They date from the years after World War II, when many combat veterans, particularly those residing in Cal-

FIGURE 1.1   *Structure of an Organized Crime Group*

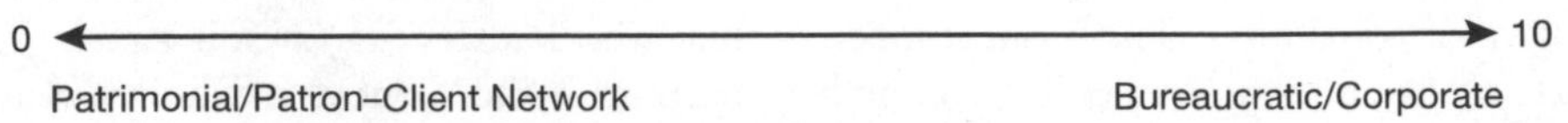

0 ←——————————————————————————→ 10

Patrimonial/Patron–Client Network   Bureaucratic/Corporate

The Outlaw Credo

"Outlaw bikers view themselves as nothing less than frontier heroes, living out the 'freedom ethic' that they feel the rest of society has largely abandoned. They acknowledge that they are antisocial, but only to the extent that they seek to gain their own unique experiences and express their individuality through their motorcycles. Their 'hogs' become personal charms against the regimented world of the 'citizen.' They view their club as collective leverage that they can use against an establishment that threatens to crush those who find conventional society inhibiting and destructive of individual character" (Wolf 1991: 9).

ifornia, sought new outlets for feelings of hostility and alienation. Some found release in riding motorcycles—military surplus motorcycles were plentiful—and in associating with others in motorcycle clubs. These clubs became a means of continued quasi-military camaraderie. At the same time, the motorcycle became a symbol of freedom from social responsibilities and restraints. Soon these new groups became a nuisance, if not a threat, to local communities in southern California.

Shortly after World War II, a group of California veterans formed a motorcycle club and called themselves the POBOBs, an acronym for "Pissed Off Bastards of Bloomington," a small southern California town 30 miles south of San Jose. By some accounts, the POBOBs were dedicated to mocking social values and conventional society through acts of vandalism and general lawlessness. Over the Independence Day weekend of 1947, following the arrest of a POBOB member for fighting in Hollister (south of Oakland), a reported 750 motorcyclists descended on the small community and demanded his release. When local authorities refused, the cyclists literally tore up the town, a scene that was later depicted in the 1954 Marlon Brando film *The Wild One*. The movie, based on a *Harper's* magazine story and originally titled *The Cyclists Raid*, also featured Lee Marvin and actual bikers—it helped fuel the outlaw biker phenomenon (Briley 1997).

Hunter Thompson (1966) reports a different version of this incident, which he states grew out of a July Fourth celebration that included motorcycle races sanctioned by the American Motorcycle Association (AMA). Around three thousand cyclists participated. The cyclists became unruly, and the seven-man police force was unable to handle the ensuing disorder. The cyclists were easily controlled when additional officers arrived, and the actual riot was timid compared with the film version. Daniel Wolf (1991: 4) states that about 500 unaffiliated bikers disrupted the AMA-sponsored event "by drinking and racing in the streets of the host town of Hollister. The ineffective efforts of a numerically insufficient seven-man police force, in conjunction with the sometimes provocative vigilante tactics of indignant local residents, caused the motorcyclists to coalesce as a mob." Bikers rode motorcycles into bars and broke windows with beer bottles. This unruly behavior ended 36 hours later after the arrival of additional police. At the center of much of the mayhem was "Wino" Willie Forkner of the Booze Fighters, who died of natural causes at age 76, shortly before he could lead a 50th-anniversary outlaw biker rally in Hollister (Associated Press 1997).

The Hollister incident gave rise to an important outlaw biker tradition—the annual July Fourth run; another traditional run occurs over the Labor Day weekend. In 1997, Hollister played host to the 50th anniversary of the incident that brought the small town fame, and it is now the site of an annual Independence Day biker rally. Bikers, outlaw and otherwise, also rally every August in the Black Hills of South Dakota, the "Sturgis Rally and Races." The 10-day event, which began in 1938 with less than two dozen bikers, now draws in excess of 200,000 persons to this town of 5,500. It

5

provides the outlaw clubs an opportunity to "profile," the biker equivalent of cruising. The obvious potential for violence requires an active presence of shotgun-wielding state police officers. (Hamilton 1998).

The word *outlaw* was first used by the sheriff of Riverside to distinguish southern California bikers such as the POBOBs from those motorcycle enthusiasts affiliated with the mainstream AMA. The lifestyles and traditions of the outlaw biker are promoted by a handful of magazines catering to both the hardcore outlaw subculture and the "wannabe" outlaw. Biker magazines "make it possible for a man to construct a biker identity and develop a sense of loyalty to that image without having met another biker" (Wolf 1991: 37).

In 1948, in the Fontana area of San Bernardino County, dedicated outlaws from the POBOBs formed a new group and adopted a name favored by fighter pilots and bomber crews in the world wars—Hells Angels: "A seamstress [sewed] their crest: a grinning, winged death's head wearing a leather aviator's helmet. The chapter name [was] shortened to 'Berdoo' to fit on the bottom of the rocker on the back of the jacket" (Lavigne 1987: 23).

In 1957 a 19-year-old former infantry veteran joined the Hells Angels. Ralph Hubert ("Sonny") Barger, Jr., had dropped out of the tenth grade to join the army; he completed basic training and advanced infantry training before being discharged for being too young. The 5-foot, 10-inch, 145-pound novice quickly rose in the biker ranks to become president of the club. He moved its headquarters to Oakland (the "mother club"). In 1967, Barger appeared in a film with Jack Nicholson, *Hell's Angels on Wheels*, which did not win an Academy Award but added greatly to the outlaw motorcycle club mystique.

There were three Hells Angels chapters, all in California, and a fourth had been established in (of all places) Auckland, New Zealand (Lavigne 1987). By 1965, police harassment of the Hells Angels in California had thinned their ranks to fewer than 100 members; the original Berdoo chapter was reduced to only a handful of diehards (Thompson 1966). Yves Lavigne (1987) reports that police ha-

rassment and legal fees left the club on the brink of extinction. However, the Hells Angels had been exposed to the drug subculture through a tenuous relationship with the counterculture movement— "hippies" and "flower children." Needing money to survive, they turned to a one-shot deal involving the sale of methamphetamine—"speed." The outlaw bikers eventually broke with the counterculture over the Vietnam War—the former military veterans were rabid hawks. But the easy money they had found in drugs eventually moved the Hells Angels beyond the biker subculture and into organized crime.

Until 1965, the Hells Angels were virtually unknown outside California. In that year, the state's attorney general unwittingly helped them score a publicity coup. In his annual report, he exaggerated their violent activities, and the California correspondent for the *New York Times* hyped the report for readers of "All the News That's Fit to Print." The result was a spate of articles on the Hells Angels in the national media, including *Time*, *Newsweek*, and the *Saturday Evening Post*. These articles led to radio and television appearances by club members, whose outrageous dress made for good "visuals." The exposure fueled interest in the Hells Angels and the outlaw biker phenomenon, helping to swell their ranks. At the time, Thompson states that most of the Angels were lawfully employed, and the publicity caused many of them to lose their jobs. In 1966 the Hells Angels were still confined to California (and New Zealand), but massive publicity and the Vietnam War soon changed this.

During the late 1960s and early 1970s, interest and membership in outlaw motorcycle clubs swelled because of the return of disgruntled veterans from the Vietnam war (Lavigne 1987). In some instances, entire outlaw motorcycle clubs were issued charters as Hells Angels. The club "expanded rapidly in the 1980s, taking over motorcycle gangs in countries all over the world" and "systematically set out to eliminate competitors through violence and intimidation" (Lavigne 1996: 50). Sonny Barger explains the process: "When we award charters in new states, it's always done by national vote. When a prospective club lets us know they

The Outlaw Motorcycle Club and OC

"In many ways all outlaw clubs are pre-adapted as vehicles of organized crime. Paramilitary organization lies at the core of their tightknit secret society. It is a society capable of enforcing internal discipline, including an iron-clad code of silence. . . . Uncompromising commitments of brotherhood generate cohesion, mutual dependence, and a sense of a shared common fate. The lengthy socialization required to become a legitimate 'biker' and the two years of proving oneself as a striker [probationary member] in order to become a member make the infiltration of a club by the police a virtual impossibility. The political structure of the club, the anti-Establishment attitudes and high-risk nature of the individuals involved, and the marginal social environment in which they operate have the potential to produce a clubhouse of crime" (Wolf 1991: 266).

want to become Hells Angels, we'll check them out to see if they're standup people. We'll send officers out to meet with them, and in return they'll send guys out to meet with us. We might invite them to a run or two, and likewise we'll send some of our guys to party with them. At some point—time varies—we'll vote on whether they can become prospects. Eventually we'll vote on their membership status. The same process that lets in individuals applies to entire new chapters as well" (2000: 35). The organization is international in scope, with about 85 chapters in 15 countries.

In 1973, Sonny Barger was convicted and imprisoned for the possession and sale of heroin, marijuana, and other drugs. He was released in 1977, but other indictments against Barger and the Hells Angels soon followed. The biker subculture had changed: "Some Hells Angels made big money in the drug business, and suddenly they had something to lose, something to protect. Their bank accounts came first and the brotherhood second. When a member threatened their income, they beat or killed him. The Hells Angels Motorcycle Club was no longer an organization that sheltered social misfits. It became an enclave for some of the underworld's most cunning drug manufacturers and dealers" (Lavigne 1996: 34). But the drug business breeds informants. In 1985, more than 100 Hells Angels across the United States were arrested in a major federal effort against the club's drug trafficking.

The development of the POBOBs from an outlaw motorcycle club (OMC) to a criminal organization was a model for other groups who wanted to emulate the Hells Angels. According to Allen ("Rod") McMillan, an expert on OMCs, these groups moved through four stages (personal correspondence):

1. The club shows rebellious and antisocial activity that is random and nonutilitarian.
2. A police response causes less committed members to drop out; members of weaker clubs either disperse or join stronger clubs.
3. The remaining clubs are better able to exercise discipline and control over their membership, particularly control over violence, which now changes from random and nonutilitarian to instrumental. The basic element shared by all members of outlaw motorcycle clubs is a penchant for violence; violence thus pervades the world of outlaw bikers. Rationally utilized, violence may be for the purpose of maintaining organizational discipline or defending hegemony.
4. The leadership uses organizational skills and intimidation in utilitarian criminal pursuits, and the group becomes a fully committed criminal organization.

From the fun-loving and hell-raising clubs of the immediate post-World War II era, a number of outlaw motorcycle clubs have developed into self-perpetuating, highly structured, disciplined organizations whose major source of income is from criminal activity. But not all of the estimated 500 outlaw motorcycle clubs are sophisticated criminal organizations. According to law enforcement officials, only four clubs actually fit the definition of organized crime: (1) Hells Angels, (2) Outlaws, (3) Pagans, and (4) Bandidos.

Hells Angels chapters are centered in California and the East Coast; the mother club is in Oakland.[1] The Outlaws trace their origins to the McCook (a rural county near Chicago) Outlaws Motorcycle Club, founded in 1935. But it was in the post-war years that the club grew, in 1950 changing its name to the Chicago Outlaws and moving to that city. In 1954 the club adopted its skull and crossed pistons logo. Outlaw chapters are scattered throughout the Midwest, Northeast, and several southern states. The mother club moved from Chicago to Detroit in 1984. The Pagans were founded in 1959 in Prince George's County, Maryland; chapters are centered on the East Coast. Although there are Pagan chapters in West Virginia and New Orleans, most are located in Pennsylvania. The mother club, which has no fixed location and often changes whenever a new national president is elected, has moved from Maryland to Pennsylvania to Suffolk County, New York. It is the only one of the "Big Four" that does not have international chapters, although it does have ties to outlaw bikers in Canada. The Bandidos were founded in 1966 in Houston. Chapters are centered in the far Northwest and in the South, particularly in Texas, where the mother club is located. Together, these four groups have a combined membership of about 4,000 white males.

The Bandidos have been allied with the Outlaws, while the Hells Angels and the Outlaws have been at war since 1974. These conflicts sometimes have international ramifications, such as the war between the Hells Angels and Bandidos in Scandinavia. With support from the California mother club, during the 1980s the Hells Angels organized in Denmark but were challenged by a local group that the Angels almost wiped out—13 were shot to death before the group disbanded in 1986. Rem-

nants joined a new club that eventually became a chapter of the Bandidos, renewing conflict with the Hells Angels, which in 1994 resulted more killings. During 1996 the conflict became even more violent, with the use of military weapons—hand grenades and antitank missiles—in Denmark, Sweden, and Finland. That year, the Copenhagen Hells Angels hosted a party for bikers from the Nordic countries at their headquarters, five buildings surrounded by a ten-foot wooden fence. An antitank grenade fired at the compound from the roof of a nearby building killed two and wounded nineteen, some seriously. Later that year, a jury in Copenhagen found two Hells Angels members guilty of murdering the leader of the Bandidos in an airport ambush. In 1997 the Norwegian headquarters of the Bandidos was obliterated by an explosion, killing a passerby and injuring four people, none of whom were bikers. Later, a rocket-propelled grenade was fired into a Danish jail in a failed attempt to kill an imprisoned Bandido leader. That same year, carloads of Hells Angels drove into a Bandido stronghold in a small resort town near Copenhagen and opened fire with machine pistols, killing one Bandido and wounding three more.

In 1997, when the Hells Angels opened their newest chapter in Stockholm, about 300 members from several countries gathered to celebrate: they were greeted by 300 police officers, who put a cordon around their new headquarters, searched all who entered the area, and even arrested one member for failing to wear a helmet (Ibrahim 1997). The authorities in Denmark have passed new laws that bar the bikers from having clubhouses in populated areas, and they have asked for assistance from the United States for a problem they see as originating in the states (Kinzer 1996a; Associated Press 1996; Reuters 1996; "Biker Club House . . ." 1997; "Bomb Kills 1 . . ." 1997; Moseley 1997).

In 1994 a similar situation arose in Illinois, where a local motorcycle club, Hell's Henchmen, was slated to become a chapter of Hells Angels, giving the international club an important presence in the Midwest. The Henchmen are headquartered in Rockford, 25 miles away from the Outlaws' headquarters in Janesville, Wisconsin;

---

[1]A struggle between the Berdoo chapter and Sonny Barger's Oakland chapter resulted in the mother club shifting to northern California (Lavigne 1996).

FIGURE 1.2   *National Organization Structure of the Pagans, the Outlaws, and the Bandidos*

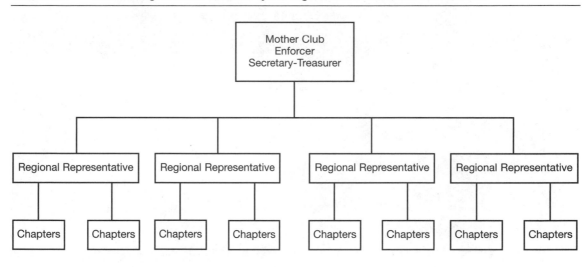

the Outlaws also have a clubhouse in nearby Chicago. The Outlaws expressed their outrage: a bomb went off in front of the residence of the Henchmen's president, and six hours later another destroyed the Henchmen's Chicago clubhouse (Thomas 1994a). Later, the Henchmen's president was gunned down at his Rockford residence. In response, 300 Hells Angels in full colors rode into Rockford for the funeral and a posthumous induction. The Outlaws answered with more bombings and shootings; in 1995 a Hells Angels member was shot to death while sitting in his car near the Chicago trucking company for which he worked (Thomas 1994b; Martinez 1995). In 1997, 17 members of the Outlaws from Wisconsin, Indiana, and Illinois were indicted for these and other acts of violence—listening devices had been planted in several clubhouses and in the home of one Outlaw who is said to have orchestrated several murders and bombings. One of those arrested became a government witness, and the violence stopped (Starks 1999). In 2000 the former head of the South Side Chicago Outlaw chapter was found guilty of racketeering acts that included the 1995 murder of a Hells Angels member (Daley 2000).

In Canada the Hells Angels have more than a dozen chapters as well as a number of affiliated outlaw clubs—"puppets" (Criminal Intelligence Service Canada 1998). In Montreal the Hells Angels successfully negotiated affiliations with several local motorcycle clubs—collectively they are referred to as *Les Hells*. When negotiations with a powerful local club—the Rock Machine—broke down in 1994, about 70 killings as well as dozens of bombings and arsons resulted as the conflict spread throughout Quebec. The Rock Machine is believed to have developed close ties to the Bandidos, and some reports (e.g., Fox 2001b) indicate that the Rock Machine was absorbed by the Texas-based club. By the end of 1998, the war between the Hells Angels and the Rock Machine had resulted in 103 homicides, 84 bombings, and 130 incidents of arson (Criminal Intelligence Service of Canada 1999).

Structure Consistent with their founders' background as military veterans, the Hells Angels and outlaw clubs that have copied them exhibit a bureaucratic structure (see Figure 1.2). Each has a written constitution and bylaws. While there are some minor variations, the Outlaws, Bandidos, and Pagans have a mother club that serves as the (inter)national headquarters. The Bandidos' mother club consists of a president and four regional vice-presidents. The national president has final authority over all club activities. The Outlaws

AP/Wide World Photos

Police in Plainview, New York, stand next to handcuffed participants in the "Hellraisers Ball" in February, 2002, after several people were shot during the motorcycle and tattoo expo. One person was killed in the melee, raising fears that this was not a one-time confrontation between the Hells Angels and other motorcycle clubs.

have a similar structure: the United States is divided into four regions; each has a regional president who reports to the mother club, which is ruled by the national president. The Pagan national president—head of the "Pagan Nation"—is not a supreme commander (Lavigne 1987). Instead, club activities are directed by a mother club of 13 to 20 former chapter presidents, who wear the number 13 on the back of their colors in deference to the original 13 founding members (Pennsylvania Crime Commission 1990). Membership in the mother club is a promotion based on skill and competence. Each member of the Pagans'

mother club has authority over chapters in specific regions. Their responsibilities include making decisions on all problems that the local chapters are unable to resolve and seeing to it that each chapter generates income, from which the regional head receives a portion.

The Hells Angels, reports Lavigne (1987), do not have a national president or national officers to give the club direction. Instead, the club is divided into East Coast and West Coast factions, with Omaha, Nebraska, as the dividing line: "East Coast Officers' Meetings (ECOMS) and West Coast Officers' Meetings (WCOMS) are held every three months in different chapters' areas. The faction officers and the president or vice-president from every chapter in the faction discuss only club business at the quarterly meetings: how to financially assist a chapter; should a new chapter be admitted; how individual chapters perform; how many new patches should be ordered; should the club issue a press release on the latest arrests of members. Drug deals and other crimes are not discussed" (Lavigne 1987: 66). The East Coast and West Coast factions also hold a meeting before their annual "USA Run," which each faction hosts in alternate years. The host faction president presides, and criminal activities are not discussed. In addition, special presidents' meetings may occasionally be called as needed (Barger 2000).

Any problems that involve a national outlaw club as a whole will usually be submitted to the mother club. The national secretary-treasurer is responsible for the club's finances, makes revisions in the club bylaws, and records and maintains the minutes and other club records. The national enforcer answers directly to the national president or to the mother club and may act as the president's bodyguard. In addition, he handles all special situations involving violations of club rules. There are some standard functional positions. Each of the four clubs has a national enforcement unit. Hell's Angels enforcers are adorned with Nazi storm trooper-like lightning bolts tattooed underneath the words "Filthy Few," the Outlaws have their "SS Death Squad," the Pagans have the "Black T-Shirt Squad," and the Bandidos have their "Nomad Chapter." Barger (2000) states that Hell's Angels no longer sport any Nazi symbols because they are banned in Germany; thus, their German chapter cannot wear them. Outlaw clubs also have at least one member responsible for "security/intelligence." He often travels under a variety of names, does not wear his colors, and is rarely if ever seen near the clubhouse (David 1988: 17). He "compiles photographs, descriptions, addresses, phone numbers, personal and financial information, vehicle descriptions, not only on rival gang members, but on police officers, reporters, lawyers, judges, public officials and witnesses. Dossiers include names and addresses of relatives,

girlfriends and boyfriends. Many of the newer members of the various outlaw motorcycle gangs have learned their intelligence skills in the military, where they also acquired the talent to use weapons and make bombs."

Each "Big Four" chapter has a president, vice president, secretary-treasurer, enforcer, and sergeant-at-arms (see Figure 1.3). The sergeant-at-arms is usually the toughest member and may also serve as an enforcer and executioner. There is also the road captain, who fulfills the role of logistician and security chief for club-sponsored "runs" or motorcycle outings. The road captain maps out routes; arranges for refueling, food, and maintenance stops en route; and establishes "strong points" along the route to protect the main body from police harassment or rival motorcycle clubs. Outlaw motorcycle clubs have several mandatory runs each year, and all members not otherwise incapacitated—hospitalized or imprisoned—must participate with motorcycles and full colors.

"Colors" are the official club insignia. A member typically wears colors on the back of a denim jacket with the sleeves cut off or, in colder climes, a leather jacket. The insignia consists of three separate sections, or "rockers." The top rocker carries the club name, the center rocker displays the club emblem, and the bottom rocker designates the club location or territory. Colors may also be worn as a tattoo—mandatory for Hell's Angels. Loss of colors can bring sanctions, including expulsion from the club (Wolf 1991). Also sewed or pinned on the jacket are other "authorized" patches, which are usually quite offensive to conventional society—for example, swastikas, 666 (sign of Satan), FTW ("Fuck the World"), and 1%: "Members of the outlaw motorcycle gangs refer to themselves as 'one percenters' in reference to an estimate advanced some years ago by the American Motorcycle Association that outlaw motorcyclists comprised less than one percent of the motorcycling population. Outlaw gangs immediately seized on the figure as a reflection of their belief that they are rebels, operating outside society's laws and mores" (PCOC 1986a: 61). Consistent with a military orientation, various offenses can result in the "pulling of patches." The clubs practice

FIGURE 1.3   *Chapter Organizational Structure of Outlaw Motorcycle Clubs*

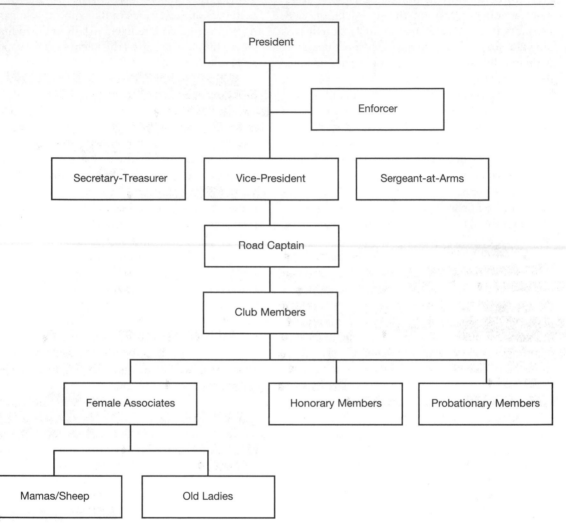

precision riding, and club runs are accomplished in a military-style formation (see Figure 1.4).

Outlaw clubs limit membership. Each chapter has prospective members ("strikers" or "prospects") who spend from one month to one year (striking period) on probationary status. Each prospect requires a sponsoring member who is responsible for the probationary member: "Gang members do extensive background checks on prospective members, often using female associates who have been placed in positions with public

utilities, government services, and law enforcement agencies to assist them" (PCOC 1986a: 65). Prospects must be nominated by a member and receive a unanimous vote for acceptance into provisional status. They carry out menial jobs at the clubhouse and for other members. Initiation ceremonies are frequently degrading and may involve felony crimes, acts that enhance solidarity while serving to keep out undercover law enforcement officers. Barger (2000) states that there has never been an initiation rite in the Hells Angels.

FIGURE 1.4   *Formation During a Run of an Outlaw Motorcycle Club*

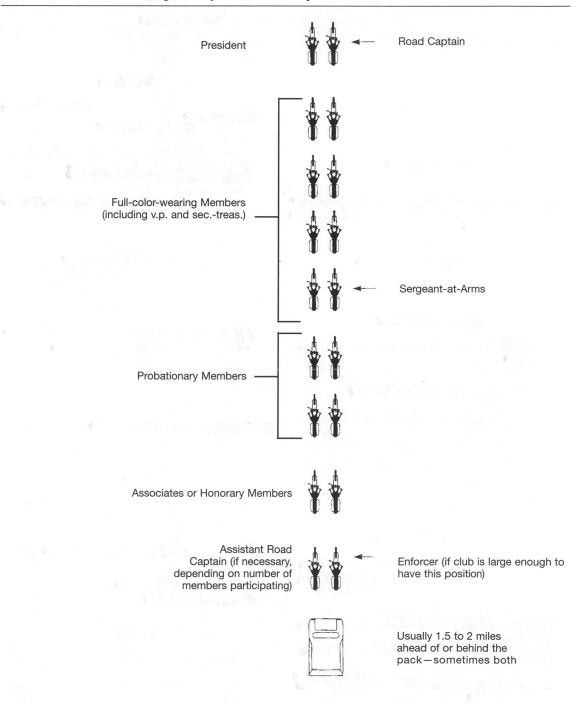

Note: The car at the bottom of the diagram carries supplies and disabled motorcycles.

FIGURE 1.5 *Pagan Motorcycle Club Constitution*

CLUB ORGANIZATION

The Pagan motorcycle club is run by the Mother Club. The Mother Club has last and final say so on all club matters. Any violation of the constitution will be dealt with by the Mother Club.

CHAPTER ORGANIZATION

Six (6) members needed to start a chapter. No new chapter may be started without approval of the Mother Club.

PRESIDENT

Runs chapter under the direction of the Mother Club. Keeps chapter organized, makes sure chapter business is carried out, inspects all bikes before runs and makes President meetings.

SERGEANT-AT-ARMS

Makes sure President's orders are carried out.

VICE-PRESIDENT

Takes over all President's duties when the President is not there.

SECRETARY-TREASURER

In charge of minutes of meetings and treasury. No members may change chapters without the Mother Club members permission in his area. All present chapter debts are paid and is approved by the president of the new chapter he wishes to change to. If a member has a snival, he must use chain of command, in other words, (1) His Chapter President, (2) Mother Club member in area, (3) President of Club.

MEETINGS

1. Chapters must have one organized meeting per week.
2. Chapter meetings are attended by members only.
3. Members must be of sound mind (straight) when attending meetings.
4. If a Mother Club member attends a meeting and a member is fouled-up, he will be fined by the Mother Club member.
5. Miss three (3) meetings in a row, and you're out of the club.
6. Members must attend meeting to leave club and turn in his colors and everything that has the name PAGANS on it. (T-shirts, Wrist Bands, Mugs, Etc.)
7. If a member is thrown out of the club or quits without attending a meeting, he loses his colors, motorcycle, and anything that says PAGANS on it, and probably an ass kicking.

8. When a member is traveling, he must attend meeting of the area he is traveling in.
9. If a vote is taken at a meeting and member is not there, his vote is void.
10. Member must have colors with him when attending meeting.

BIKES

1. All members must have a Harley Davidson 750–1200 CC.
2. If a member is not of sound mind or too fouled up to ride his motorcycle in the opinion of another member, his riding privilege may be pulled by said member until he has his head together.
3. All bikes must be on the road April 30th, or otherwise directed by the Mother Club.
4. All members must have a motorcycle license.

MANDATORIES

Two (2) mandatories, July 4, and Labor Day, Mother Club may call additional mandatories if need be.

FUNERALS

1. If a member dies in a chapter, it is necessary for all members in his chapter to attend funeral.
2. Chapter is in charge of taking care of all funeral arrangements, parties, police, procession, etc.

PARTIES

Pagan parties are Pagan parties only. Each chapter must throw (1) party or run a year.

RESPECT

1. Respect is to be shown to all Mother Club members, officer members, member's personal property, Bike, Old Lady, House, Job, etc. In other words, if it's not yours, "Don't Mess With It."
2. No fighting among each other is allowed, any punches to be thrown will be done by the Sgt.-at-Arms or a Mother Club Member.
3. No stealing from members.
4. Respect your Colors.

COLORS

1. President gets colors from Mother Club member in area when new member is voted in.
2. When a member leaves club, the president of his chapter turns over his colors to the Mother Club member in his area.
3. Respect your Colors, don't let anyone take them from you except the president of your chapter or a Mother Club member.

14

FIGURE 1.5 *(Continued)*

4. No colors are worn in a cage, except during funerals and loading or unloading a bike from a truck.
5. Nothing will be worn of the back of your jacket except your colors, Diamond, 13 Patch.
6. No Hippie shit on the front.
7. Colors are to be put on cut off denim jackets only.
8. The only member who may keep his colors if he leaves the club is a Mother Club Member.

OLD LADIES

1. Members are responsible for their Old Ladies.
2. Members my have more than one (1) Old Lady.
3. Members may not discuss club business with their Old Lady.
4. No Old Ladies allowed at meetings.
5. No property patch is worn on an Old Lady. So if you see a chick you better ask before you leap.

PROSPECTS

1. Prospect must be at least 18 years old.

2. Prospect must be sponsored by one member who has known him at least one year.
3. Sponsor is responsible for prospect.
4. Prospect must have motorcycle.
5. Prospect must ride his bike to meeting at time of being voted into club.
6. Prospect can not do any drugs.
7. Prospects can not carry weapons at meetings and Pagan functions, unless otherwise directed by the president.
8. No stealing from Prospects.
9. Prospects must attend all meetings and club functions.
10. Prospect must do anything another member tells him to, that a member has done or would be willing to do himself.
11. Prospect must be voted in by all members of the chapter and Three (3) Mother Club Members.
12. Prospect must pay for his colors before receiving them.
13. Prospects period is determined by the Mother Club Member.
14. Pagan's M.C. is a motorcycle club and a non-profit organization.

When a man is admitted to membership, he is allowed to wear the club's colors—the proudest possession of any outlaw club member and clearly parallel to being "made" in the American Mafia. The death's head emblem of the Hells Angels is copyrighted, although violations rarely result in litigation—the Hells Angels prefer to *settle out of court* (Lavigne 1987). (See Figure 1.5 for an example of a motorcycle club's constitution.)

A member's death's head tattoo must be crossed out if he leaves the group. A Hells Angels member who retires under "honorable" circumstances is permitted to keep the tattoo by adding the date of his separation from the club. While most outlaw biker chapters have headquarters,[2] the Bandidos meet instead in members' homes, which, like clubhouses, are usually heavily fortified and guarded by attack dogs.

Activities Outlaw motorcycle clubs usually exhibit racist attitudes, and in the United States no

known black males hold membership in the Big Four. There are predominantly black clubs with some white members, and Hells Angels has Jewish members. Women associated with a club are treated as nothing more than playthings—objects to be used, traded, and sold. "Old ladies" are the wives or steady girlfriends of club members. Sexual and other demands for their services can be made only by their husbands or boyfriends. "Mamas" and "sheep" belong to the gang at large and are expected to consent to the sexual whims of any club member. While women are not permitted to wear club colors, they may wear denim jackets with the inscription "Property of . . ." (with the club's name embroidered on it). Women often carry the gang's weapons and engage in prostitution or drug trafficking. Because of the freewheeling image of the outlaw clubs, teenage girls are often attracted to them. The girls are frequently gang raped, which bikers refer to as "training" or "pulling a train." They may also be photographed for blackmail purposes or transported to other states for employment in sex-oriented establishments, such as go-go bars and club-owned massage parlors.

---

[2]In 1999 the New York chapter of Hells Angels received $450,000 (plus the cost of legal fees) from the city of New York to settle a lawsuit arising out of a police raid on their Manhattan headquarters at 77 East Third Street (Weiser 1999b).

The outlaw clubs are involved in distributing automatic weapons, explosives, stolen motorcycles, and motorcycle parts; providing exotic dancers and prostitutes for various sex-oriented establishments; and trafficking in LSD, PCP, cocaine, and methamphetamine. They have been particularly successful in exerting control over the methamphetamine market. George Wethern (with Vincent Colnett 1978), a former ranking member of the Hells Angels in Oakland, states that because of their reputation for violence and anti-establishment attitudes, the Hells Angels are perfect middlemen for drug dealers. The wholesalers sell to the Angels, who then act as distributors for street-level operators. Any number of members also manufacture methamphetamine. Using violence, they were able to restrict market entry and monopolize the trade in parts of California. Other outlaw clubs have done the same elsewhere.

Their reputation for violence enabled the Pagans to extort $400 a week from topless dance clubs and other adult businesses throughout Long Island, New York. The protection racket was reportedly orchestrated by the president of a Long Island Pagan chapter who is also sergeant-at-arms of the national organization. In a federal indictment, the Pagans were accused of planning to murder a nightclub manager who resisted extortion efforts and who on several occasions beat up Pagan members; once he was stabbed five times while fighting off seven Pagans. They were also accused of plotting to kill members of the Hells Angels operating on Long Island (Draffen 1998; Kessler 1998, 1999). The indictments served to weaken the Pagans on Long Island and apparently encouraged the Hells Angels to claim the area by holding their "Hellraisers Ball" in Plainview. The event, at a catering hall, was attacked by ten van loads of bat-wielding Pagans, leading to the shooting death of one Pagan and the wounding of several others (Gootman 2002).

While most bikers operate along the lines of short-term hedonism, some profits have been invested in a vast array of legitimate businesses, often for profit and sometimes as fronts for illegal activities. The outlaw clubs have a reliable pipeline of members and chapters for the flow of illicit goods, and the members are highly mobile—they can find support and safety in any city that has a club chapter.

According to the President's Commission, if an outlaw motorcycle club has a discernible weakness, it is that members are easily identified by their colors: "However, there are growing reports that members are abandoning their outlaw image, wearing business suits and driving luxury cars; in essence, becoming an outlaw motorcycle gang without motorcycles. If so, that would complete the evolution that has been under way for more than 20 years, a period during which the Hells Angels developed from a collection of rowdy rebels into a genuine organized crime group" (PCOC 1986a: 65). In fact, the leadership of these outlaw clubs has become more conventional in appearance, leaving the more overtly subcultural dimensions to underlings.

Members of outlaw clubs have reportedly been involved in activities with traditional organized crime, providing muscle, firearms, bombs, or drugs. In Philadelphia, there was a great deal of friction between the Bruno crime Family and the Pagans. On one occasion, a Pagan attempted to shoot Philadelphia *caporegime* Harry ("Hunchback") Riccobene over a drug deal. He missed and wounded a former bodyguard for murdered Philadelphia crime boss Phil Testa (Pennsylvania Crime Commission 1989). Afterward, relations between the Philadelphia crime Family and the Pagans improved, leading to a variety of partnerships in the club's most lucrative activity, the manufacture and distribution of methamphetamine and phencyclidine (PCP, or "angel dust"). There continues to be a close relationship between the Philadelphia crime Family and the Pagans. The Philadelphia press reported a pact between ("Skinny") Joey Merlino, 40, boss of the Philadelphia crime Family, and his childhood friend, former police officer Steven ("Gorilla") Montevergine, 45, who is president of the local chapter of the Pagans. The Philadelphia crime Family interceded with New York crime bosses to keep the Hells Angels, who have ties to crime Families in New York, out of the New Jersey–Philadelphia area (Caparella 1999).

FIGURE 1.6 *Hells Angels California Bylaws*

1. All patches will be the same on the back, nothing will show on the back except the HELLS ANGELS patch. City patch is optional for each chapter. 1 patch and 1 membership card per member. Member may keep original patch if made into a banner. Prospects will wear California rocker on back and prospect patch left from where top of pocket is on a Levi jacket.
   FINE: $100 for breaking above by-law.

2. No hypes. No use of Heroin in any form. Anyone using a needle for any reason other than having a doctor use it on you will be considered a hype.
   FINE: Automatic kick-out from club.

3. No explosives of any kind will be thrown into the fire where there is one or more HELLS ANGELS in this area.
   FINE: Ass-whipping and/or subject to California President's decision.

4. Guns on CA runs will not be displayed after 6 PM. They will be fired from dawn until 6 PM in a predetermined area only. Rule does not apply to anyone with a gun in a shoulder holster or belt that is seen by another member if it is not being shot or displayed.
   FINE: $100 for breaking above by-law.

5. Brothers shall not fight with each other with weapons; when any HELLS ANGELS fights another HELLS ANGELS, it is one on one; prospects same as members. If members are from different chapters, fine goes to CA Treasurer.
   FINE: $100 for breaking above by-law or possible loss of patch.

6. No narcotics burns. When making deals, persons get what they are promised or the deal is called off.
   FINE: Automatic kick-out from club.

7. All HELLS ANGELS fines will be paid within 30 days. Fines will be paid to that chapter's treasurer to be held for the next CA run.

8. One vote per chapter at CA officer's meetings. For CA 2 no votes instead of a majority to kill a new charter and a charter goes below 6 they must freeze or dissolve on the decision of CA Officers' Meeting.

9. If kicked out, must stay out 1 year then back to original chapter. HELLS ANGEL tattoo will have an in-date and out-date when the member quits. If kicked out HELLS ANGELS tattoo will be completely covered with a 1/2 X through the tattoo.

10. Runs are on the holidays; 3 mandatory runs are Memorial Day, July 4th, and Labor Day.

11. No leave period except hospital, medical or jail.

Analysis of the Structure

As we have seen, the outlaw motorcycle club exhibits a number of characteristics that are bureaucratic. Given the military background of the founders and many members of the outlaw biker subculture, this is to be expected. There is a rather elaborate hierarchy, specialization, advancement based on skill, and extensive rules and regulations that are in written form (see Figure 1.6). There is general uniformity in style of dress, colors, and motorcycles—mostly large Harley-Davidsons. The secretary-treasurer records the minutes of meetings and collects and maintains dues. Each member contributes weekly dues to the chapter, and the chapter pays into the national treasury. The Hells Angels also maintain a multimillion-dollar fund to which members and chapters are occasionally asked to contribute. The fund goes for legal expenses and to help support the families of imprisoned members.

However, a criminal organization can exhibit a formal structure while its economic activities may actually involve small firms or partnerships among members and include nonmember associates. This is often the case with outlaw motorcycle clubs. Each member of the "Big Four" is reputed to have about ten associates and his own network of friends. For business purposes, each member is at the center of an action group that, although tied to every other member through the structure of the club, operates independently or in partnership. In other words, the formal structure of the motorcycle club is not necessarily the same as its economic structure. While there is a relatively clear hierarchy within each of the four outlaw clubs, income-generating illegal activities involve several smaller, operationally independent units. But members can call upon the muscle of the club in the event of conflict, making them formidable entrepreneurs. As Lavigne (1996: 246) notes, "The Hells Angels are truthful when they say they are not a criminal organization. Rather, they are an organization of criminals. They go out of their way to maintain a barrier between the Hells Angels as a club and the Hells Angels as a business. Criminal matters are discussed among members of many cliques within the gang." Thus, while the outlaw motorcycle club is clearly bureaucratic, its illegal business activities are not.

Patrimonial/Patron–Client Networks

The patrimonial organization is a characteristic of traditional societies that "centers around families, patrons and their clients, and other personalistic networks. The emphasis is on traditional rituals that demonstrate the emotional bonds among men." In contrast, personal ties in the modern bureaucratic organizations "are weaker, less ritualized, and emotionally demonstrative; in their place is the allegiance to a set of abstract rules and positions. The different class cultures in patrimonial and bureaucratic organizations are accordingly affected. Patrimonial elites are more ceremonious and personalistic. Bureaucratic elites emphasize a colder set of ideals" (Collins 1975: 65n).

Many aspects of bureaucracy are impractical for criminal organizations since they must be concerned with the very real possibility that communications are being monitored. The use of the telephone must be limited (often only to arrange for in-person meetings), and written communication is avoided. Information, as well as orders, money, and other goods, is transmitted on an intimate, face-to-face basis. Lengthy chains of command, characteristic of modern bureaucracy, are impractical for organized crime, and this limits the span of control. Randall Collins (1975: 293) points out that control is a special problem for patrimonial organizations. Bureaucracies develop, he argues, to overcome such problems: "Patrimonial organizations cannot be very well controlled much beyond the sight of the master." He notes that when the geographic range becomes too great, the organization collapses into feudalism. In organized crime, this can have deadly consequences: When Lucchese crime Family boss Vittorio ("Little Vic") Amuso of New York lost control of the New Jersey faction of his Family, he declared them outlaws and ordered the entire crew executed.

In fact, says Mark Moore (1987: 53), a highly centralized organization "tends to make the enterprise too dependent on the knowledge and judg-

ment of the top management, and wastes the knowledge and initiative of subordinate managers who know more about their own capabilities and how they fit into a local environment of risks and opportunities." But the very informality of organized crime can bring other dangers. In 1977, for example, Ruby Stein, a major loanshark for the Gambino crime Family, was murdered by the Westies, a group of Irish-American criminals from New York's West Side, because the Westies owed Stein a considerable sum of money. The murderers dismembered their victim and stole his "black book" containing records of Stein's loans. Because there were no duplicate or backup records, the Gambino Family was unable to claim millions of dollars in outstanding loans (English 1990).

Decentralization in a criminal organization can be advantageous for both business and security reasons, notes Joseph Albini (1971: 285). He points out that the bureaucratic model would be a relatively easy target to move against: "All that would be necessary to destroy it would be to remove its top echelon." Instead, Albini argues, the syndicate's real power lies in its amorphous quality: "If a powerful syndicate figure is incarcerated, all that has really been severed is his position as a patron to his clients." If it so happens that another individual is in a position to assume this role, the clients may continue in the enterprise. The alternative is to find a new patron—boss—or to develop their own enterprises. Albini's point is supported by the deputy administrator of the Drug Enforcement Administration, who notes that the bureaucratic structure of Colombian cocaine cartels makes them vulnerable. The need to exercise effective command and control over a far-flung criminal enterprise "is the feature that law enforcement can use against them, turning their strength into a weakness. The communications structure of international organized crime operating in the United States is, therefore, the prime target for drug law enforcement" (Marshall 1999: 5).

The American Mafia

A network consists of a collection of connected points or junctures. Every person is embedded in a social network, notes Jeremy Boissevain (1974: 24), "the chains of persons with whom a given person is in contact." Since contact can be through a chain of persons, an individual can send "messages" to far more people than he or she actually knows directly. These are the "friends of friends," a phrase that in Sicily refers to *mafiosi*: "Every individual provides a point at which networks interact. But not everyone displays the same interest in and talent for cultivating relationships with strategic persons for profit" (Boissevain 1974: 147). To be successful, each member of organized crime from the boss down to a soldier—just like Sicilian *mafiosi*—must display such interest and talent. This is done by acting as a *patron*.

When a social exchange relationship (see Homans 1961; Blau 1964) becomes unbalanced, we have a patron–client relationship. The patron "provides economic aid and protection against both the legal and illegal exaction of authority. The client, in turn, pays back in more intangible assets"—for example, esteem and loyalty. He may also offer political or other important support, thus making the relationship reciprocal (Wolf 1966: 16–17). The patron acts as a power broker between the client and the wider society, both legitimate and illegitimate.

The member of the American Mafia, acting as a patron, controls certain resources as well as strategic contacts with people who control other resources directly or who have access to such persons. The member-as-patron can put a client "in touch with the right people." He can bridge communication gaps between the police and criminals, between businessmen and syndicate-connected union leaders; he can transcend the world of business and the world of the illegitimate entrepreneur. He is able to perform important favors and be rewarded in return with money or power. There is a network surrounding the patron, a circle of dyadic relationships orbiting the OC member in which most clients have no relations with one another except through the patron.

The patron needs a great deal of time to manage his network adequately, develop and maintain contacts, provide services, enhance power and income, and keep well informed (Boissevain 1974).

Since organized crime members do not usually have to maintain conventional schedules, they are free to "hang around," to pick up and disseminate important information. An OC patron may dominate a particular geographic area or industry. He will have available a network of informants and connections—for example, with the police and other officials, as well as with specialized criminal operatives such as *papermen* (persons who convert stolen "paper," such as stocks, bonds, and checks, into cash), *torches* (professional arsonists), musclemen or legbreakers, and enforcers. He is in a position to fence large amounts of stolen goods—he can truly "get it for you wholesale"—or to lend out various amounts of money at usurious interest— loansharking. He will act as a center for information (providing targets for professional burglars, for example), "license" criminal activities (for example, enable a high-stakes dice game to operate), and use his position to assist criminals in linking up for specialized operations (for example, finding a driver for a robbery or hijack team). He can provide stolen firearms and autos and other items necessary for conventional criminal activity. Thus, despite their relatively small numbers, persons in organized crime can present a significant public threat—a single member can be at the center of, and act as a catalyst for, an extraordinary amount of criminal activity.

Criminal activities in his territory that are not under his patronage are "outlaw" operations whose participants act without his grace. If they are arrested, he will not intervene; if their activities conflict with those under his patronage, police raids or violence will result. When a member of the Genovese Family decided to deal with an independent bookmaker not under his patronage, he called upon a New York City Police Department detective (Manca with Cosgrove 1991: 129): "Later that day," the detective writes, "I drove down to Union Square. The bookie was so independent and small-time that he was running his own slips. I followed him into an apartment house, stuck a gun in his back, and forced him down to the basement. His knees were practically knocking. I grabbed this big manila envelope he was carrying, then handcuffed him to the boiler. He was begging me not to kill him. I emptied the envelope—money and slips fell out. There was about twelve hundred dollars. I scooped the money up, put it in my pocket. Then I picked up the betting slips and threw them in the boiler. The guy started to cry. I left him there, cuffed to the boiler."

When the Chicago Outfit crew headed by Rocky Infelise (discussed in Chapter 5) expanded into Lake County (just north of Cook County), gamblers were given a choice: pay street taxes, split the gambling business 50–50, turn it all over to the Outfit—or die. The body of one who failed to comply was found in the trunk of a car— "trunkin,'" as it's known in the Windy City, has been an Outfit favorite. Similar overtures were made to the proprietors of houses of prostitution and marginal businesses, such as bars with sex shows or adult bookstores throughout Chicago and nearby suburbs. A number of those who resisted became murder victims.

Independent criminal operatives may be forced to pay tribute for "protection"—protection from violence that the OC member can inflict or cause to be inflicted. Professional criminals who are not necessarily part of organized crime will often pay financial tribute to an OC patron, indicating *rispetto*—respect—a concrete recognition of his power. This enables criminals to secure vital information and assistance and ensures that other criminals will not jeopardize their operations: *respect* demands recognition of the immunity belonging not only to the member but also to everything that he has to do with or to which, explicitly or implicitly, he has given a guarantee of security.

Vincent Siciliano (1970: 55) provides an example. He and his gang held up a card game that was under the patronage of the Genovese crime Family in New York—a "connected" game. And he was summoned: "When we got to the cafe and those big shots started laying down the law and telling us we knocked over one of their games, butter wouldn't melt in my mouth. I told them I was careful to ask if the game has any connections, and the other guys agreed that nobody had any idea in the whole world that the game had any connections. The way we always put it (the way you still put it) is that we didn't know they were 'good peo-

ple,' which is like saying the guy is an American or an official something. Part of some organization. Not an outlaw." Then they made Siciliano give back the money.

At the center of the patrimonial/patron–client network model of organized crime is the boss— the *paterfamilias*—who may be assisted by an underboss (*sottocapo*) and counselor/advisor (*consigliere*). The boss is the "patron's patron." In a structure that resembles a model of the universe, the boss is surrounded by clients—for example, captains (*capiregime*), to whom he acts as a patron. The captains are surrounded by members or soldiers (*soldati*), to whom they act as patrons. This crime unit is tied together in a network that includes nonmember associates who are clients of each of the members, including the boss and captains (see Figure 1.7). In the American Mafia, each of the bosses is connected (by kinship, friendship, mutual respect) to every other boss. This structure represents what Richard Scott (1981) refers to as a *natural system:* members are not necessarily guided by their organization's goals, but they share a common interest in the survival of the system and engage in collective activities informally structured to secure this end. In organized crime as a natural system, the OC unit is more than an instrument for attaining defined goals; it is fundamentally a social group attempting to adapt and survive in a dangerous environment.

The basic unit within the American Mafia is the Family, or *borgata*. However, the actual name by which a group is known may vary. In New England, for example, it is the "Office"; in Chicago, it is the "Outfit." Groups in the New York metropolitan area are known as "Families." While any number of members may be related, the term *Family* does not imply kinship by blood or marriage. Each crime unit is composed of members and associates.

Membership In criminal circles, the importance of membership is revealed by the numerous terms and phrases to indicate membership status: "made guy," "wiseguy," "button" or "receiving his button," "being straightened out," "goodfella," "amico," and "friend of ours." And many share a simi-

FIGURE 1.7   *Patron–Client Network of Italian-American Organized Crime*

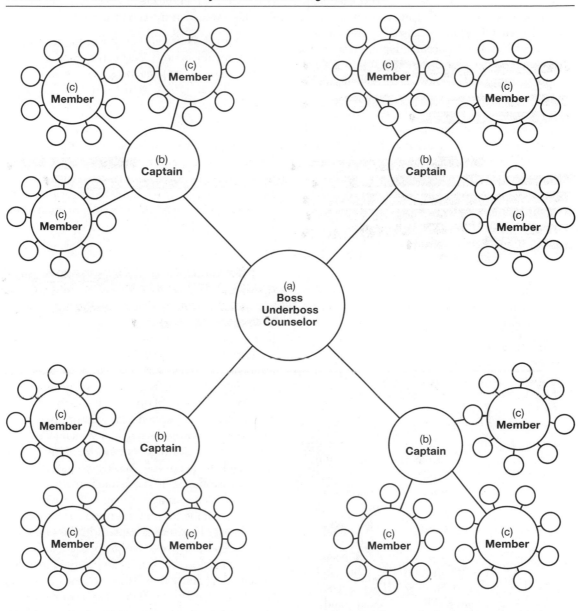

(*a*) At the center of each organized crime unit (*famiglia*: Family) is the boss (*capo*). He is assisted by an underboss (*sottocapo*) and a counselor (*consigliere*).

(*b*) Surrounding the boss are his clients, the captains (*capiregime*).

(*c*) Orbiting around each captain are his clients, the lowest-ranking members who have been formally initiated into the Family (*soldati*: "made guys").

The members act as patrons to nonmember clients.

Each unit is tied to other Families throughout the country by the *capo*, whose sovereignty is recognized by the other bosses.

lar initiation ceremony. Testifying before a Senate subcommittee ("Russian Organized Crime" 1996: 46), Anthony ("Gaspipe") Casso, imprisoned former underboss of the Lucchese Family, stated that "to become a 'made' member, you would have to be sponsored by a captain of the family, who would bring you to the boss of the family and sponsor you to become a 'made' member. They have a ceremony with the boss, the consigliere, and the underboss present at the time, and the captain who brings you in. They prick your trigger finger and make it bleed, and then they put a little piece of paper; they set it on fire and you burn it in your hand, and you repeat after them that you will never betray La Cosa Nostra, or you will burn like the paper is burning in your hand. And your life does not belong to you anymore; your life belongs to them."

At the 1992 trial of John Gotti, Salvatore Gravano recalled being made a member of the Gambino Family:

He [boss Paul Castellano] asked me if I liked everybody there. I told him yes. He asked me a few questions. One of the last questions he asked me was would I kill if he asked me to. I told him yes.

He told me what [sic] was my trigger finger. I pointed to my trigger finger. He pinched it [with a needle] and blood came out. He put it on the [picture of a] saint, and started to burn the saint in my hand. He said, honor the oath. He said to me that if I divulge any of the secrets of this organization that my soul should burn like the saint.

I kissed him on both cheeks. I kissed everybody. I went around the table and kissed everybody. I sat down. They got up. They locked hands. They unlocked hands. They made me get in the middle of it. They locked hands again and told me, at that point, I was part of the brotherhood. I was a made member and I belonged.

In 1989, two electronic eavesdropping devices were placed in the basement ceiling of a house in Medford, Massachusetts, a Boston suburb. The bugs recorded the initiation of four men into the crime Family then headed by Raymond Patriarca, Jr., who presided at the ceremony:

[Patriarca] We're all here to bring in some new members into our Family and more than that, to start maybe a new beginning. Put all that's got started behind us. 'Cause they come into our Family to start a new thing with us. . . .

The prospects were introduced to the gathered Family members, and the *consigliere* asked each to individually take an oath in Italian/Sicilian (translated): "I want to enter into this organization to protect my family and to protect all of my friends. I swear not to divulge this secret and to obey with love and *omertá*." He was then assigned to a *caporegime*.

Each candidate was then asked which finger he shoots with, and that finger was pricked to draw blood. A holy card with the image of the Patriarca family saint was burned. The prospect was told that he was required to keep secrets and could not leave the Family unless he was dead. Some details of mob protocol and rules were explained: to introduce other members as "a friend of ours" and associates as "a friend of mine"; if ordered, to kill anyone who betrays the Family, even if he is your brother; to respect the female relatives of other members—under penalty of death; to memorize the chain of command; to keep your *caporegime* informed of your whereabouts; to remember that all crime Families in America are related; and to avoid kissing other members in public—too conspicuous.

Michael Franzese, a captain in the Colombo Family, reports a two-stage process. First, he was formerly proposed: taken by an old-time member to meet the Family boss, who explained the rules: "After the meeting, my name, along with those of the other potential inductees, was circulated around the other four families" (Franzese and Matera 1992: 124). Franzese was then assigned to a *caporegime* for a probationary period of nearly a year. In 1975 he was formally inducted in a ceremony similar to those already described.

Former NYPD detective Ralph Salerno (with Tompkins 1969) reports that recruitment into OC involves the careful study of neighborhood youngsters by those who control membership. A potential recruit must exhibit a recognition of the authority of the organization and a willingness to perform various criminal and noncriminal functions (usually minor at first) with skill and daring and without asking questions. Robert Woetzel (1963: 3) points out that "the standards of the teenage gang from which the potential criminals come are the same as those of an adult conspiracy": a code of loyalty and exclusive "turf" (territory). The gang boy may also have a criminal record and an antisocial attitude, which indicate that he is a "stand-up" kid, the proper credentials for a career in organized crime.

Raymond Martin, a former ranking officer with the NYPD, describes why recruitment is made easy in certain Italian neighborhoods in Brooklyn (1963: 61):

> On so many street corners in Bath Beach, in so many luncheonettes and candy stores in Bensonhurst, boys see the mob-affiliated bookies operate. They meet the young toughs, the mob enforcers. They hear the tales of glory recounted—who robbed what, who worked over whom, which showgirl shared which gangster's bed, who got hit by whom, the techniques of the rackets and how easy it all is, how the money rolls in. What wonder is it that some boys look forward to being initiated into these practices with the eagerness of a college freshman hoping to be pledged by the smoothest fraternity on campus. With a little luck and guts, they feel, even they may someday belong to that splendid, high-living band, the mob.

The centrality of the neighborhood for providing a pool of OC aspirants cannot be overemphasized. In these areas there is a "romanticization of the mob"—young "wannabes" copy the styles of their notorious idols and are eager to ingratiate themselves with made guys. As one recruit, raised in the OC neighborhood of Brooklyn's East New York–Brownsville section, recounts, "At the age of twelve my ambition was to be a gangster. To be a wiseguy. To me being a wiseguy was better than being president of the United States. It meant power among people who had no power. It meant perks in a working-class neighborhood that had no privileges. To be a wiseguy was to own the world. I dreamed of being a wiseguy the way other kids dreamed about being doctors or movie stars or firemen or ball players" (Pileggi 1985: 13).

An undercover FBI agent describes the day an associate was "made"—initiated as a member of the Bonanno crime Family (Pistone 1987: 64): "When he came back, he was ecstatic, as proud as a peacock. 'Getting made is the greatest thing that could ever happen to me,' he said. 'I've been looking forward to this day ever since I was a kid.' . . . That night we partied together for his celebration. But now everybody treated him with more respect. He was a made guy now." After completion of his initiation, Jimmy ("the Weasel") Fratianno "was so excited that he could feel his legs tremble." Becoming a member of the Los Angeles crime Family of Jack Dragna "made him a special person, an inheritor of enormous power. It was something he had wanted for as long as he could remember" (Demaris 1981: 3).

To be eligible for membership, a young man (there are no female members) must be of Italian descent. As Gambino Family underboss Sam Gravano states, "Years and years ago, you had to be Italian on both sides. Then it became that you only had to be that on your father's side. Not your mother's. Because they say you are what your father is, you carry his name. Like John Gotti's wife is part Russian Jew. So his son, John Junior, got made, right? He's part Italian and part Russian Jew" (Maas 1997: 84). One source reports that this change in qualifications occurred in 1975 as a response to recruiting difficulties experienced by the New York Families (Volkman 1998).

The prospective member requires a sponsor and must have a long history of successful criminal activity or possess certain skills required by the group. For example, Jimmy Fratianno possessed an important "skill": the ability to execute persons in an efficient, impersonal, and dispassionate manner (Demaris 1981). However, every potential member is expected to participate in a murder—although not necessarily as the actual executioner.

Such participation serves to more closely bind the person to the ongoing conspiracy that is organized crime, and it precludes government agents from becoming members. Peter Maas (1997: 46) points that while committing a murder—making your bones—was not a prerequisite for induction into *Cosa Nostra*, more often than not, it would happen: "Murder was the linchpin of *Cosa Nostra*—for control, for discipline, to achieve and maintain power. For made members and associates, it was an everyday, accepted fact of life." Sam and Chuck Giancana (1992) state that in Chicago, a guy didn't necessarily have to kill someone to be made if he had powerful friends to protect him from such dirty work. There is also evidence that one can get credit for killing someone by assisting in the murder as opposed to carrying out the killing itself. An OC group is also interested in criminals who have proven to be moneymakers, "earners" who can increase the group's income. In 1988, the former underboss of the Cleveland Family testified before a congressional committee:

> My name is Angelo Lonardo. I am 77 years old, and I am a member of the La Cosa Nostra. I am the former underboss of the Cleveland organized crime family. I became a member of La Cosa Nostra in the late 1940's, but have been associated with the organization since the late 1920's. When I was "made" or became a member of La Cosa Nostra, I went through an initiation ceremony. I later learned that to be proposed for membership in La Cosa Nostra, you would have to have killed someone and stood up to the pressure of police scrutiny. Today, you do not have to kill to be a member, but just prove yourself worthy by keeping your mouth shut or by being a "stand-up" guy. However, if you are called upon to kill someone, you have to be prepared to do it.

In New York's five Families and others based on this model, each member is an independent operator, not an employee—he receives no salary from the group. Instead, the made guy or wiseguy has a form of "franchise": he is authorized by the group to make money by using the Family connections that come with membership, bolstered by the status (fear) that membership generates. While part of a particular crew, he is an independent entrepreneur, violent and aggressive, constantly on the prowl for moneymaking opportunities. In a typical pattern, a made guy, a franchised member, will attract nonmembers who are eager to associate with him, to become "connected," since an associate enjoys some of the status and connections that the crime Family enjoys. In a discussion with an associate, a new member of the Colombo Family reported on his recent change in status: "Since I got made I got a million fuckin' worshippers hanging around" (Iannuzzi 1993: 172). The member-as-patron thus sits at the center of a network of nonmember clients that constitutes an action-based unit for coordinated criminal activities. If the member is able to generate considerable income, he gains greater status in the Family and can become a candidate for advancement to *caporegime*. If successful associates are Italian, they become candidates for membership.

Because of their acquisitive and violent nature, members of organized crime can easily come into conflict with members of the same or another OC unit. The more members a group has, the greater the likelihood of conflict—too many made guys in search of too few moneymaking opportunities. Under such circumstances, members are more likely to become involved in high-risk ventures that can be a threat to the safety of the group. This dynamic serves to place natural limitations on membership. Furthermore, each new member is a potential threat to the security of the group—a potential informant—so new members are selected with caution and great care. A prospective member may have to serve the group for many years before achieving membership status.

According to FBI recordings released at the 1992 trial of John Gotti, in New York the "making" of prospective members requires passing the list around to other Families. But this is complicated by the very informality that characterizes OC—men are typically known only by their nicknames, which may not be precise enough to identify a particular person for such an important function as determining fitness for membership. In fact, just before a ceremony for the making of new members, Sam Gravano reported to *consigliere* Frank Locascio that "I don't have it right, Frank. I don't have their last names. I don't have the proper spellings. I ain't got the, the guys all down" (recorded January 4, 1990). In 1997, seven sheets of paper containing the names of 45 men whom the Bonanno, Genovese, and Lucchese Families had proposed for membership to replace members who died between 1983 and 1991 were found during a raid at a building owned by an associate of John Gotti. The lists were divided into "new" (proposed) and "old" (deceased) members, and each was identified by his given and surname and in some cases a nickname. At the trial of a Lucchese Family member—an admitted multiple murderer—the prosecutor produced a list of crime Family members that had been disguised as a wedding list with "Mr. and Mrs." salutations. According to testimony, the defendant was inducted into the Family in a prison bathroom ceremony at which underboss Anthony Casso presided (Capeci 1998a, 1998b).

According to Donald Cressey (1969), the "membership books" were closed in 1931, and since then new members have been initiated on a very limited basis and with the approval of the commission. Cressey states that this was an effort by the most powerful bosses, heads of the largest groups, to maintain the status quo. Michael Franzese states that "from 1955 to 1972, the Mob was a closed shop; virtually no one was inducted during that quarter century. . . . By 1972, with the ranks thinning by death, age, and imprisonment, the doors were opened" (Franzese and Matera 1992: 122–23).

Membership, as opposed to some type of associate status, provides rewards associated with being an "insider." As one member told me, "A made guy is considered more honorable," meaning that there is a greater level of trust—and respect. Only members will be allowed to attend certain important meetings and be privy to important conversations and information, and information is an important basis of power. The basic mechanism for resolving disputes is arbitration—a *sitdown* or *table*—and a nonmember needs a member to represent him. A nonmember associate in a dispute with a made guy is at a distinct disadvantage—a disadvantage that can be life threatening. This can become balanced if the associate is an "earner"—a source of substantial funds.

Considerable "psychic gain" accrues with membership. Within criminal and certain legitimate circles, being "made" conveys a great deal of prestige, if not fear. The President's Commission notes that although a soldier is the lowest-ranking member of the organization, "he is a considerable figure on the street, a man who commands respect and fear" (PCOC 1986a: 44). In testimony before the commission, a witness elaborated:

[Q:] How did you come to know that Greg Scarpa [soldier in the Colombo crime Family] is a "made" individual while someone in his crew is not "made"?

[A:] Conversation—you could just see the way that everybody answers to him; I mean, he has a club on 13th Avenue [in Brooklyn] and everyone comes up to him, and no one—they don't double park their car without getting his permission, so to say. In other words, no one does anything without getting his permission. So you could just see the respect he gets.

There are a number of otherwise legitimate persons who are attracted by the mystique that surrounds organized crime. Popular sources report that many young women are attracted to OC figures and to the bars and nightclubs that are owned or frequented by them. For similar reasons, young men may aspire to membership in OC—reasons that go beyond economic advantages—out of a desire to be part of the mystique reinforced by media representations such as the *The Godfather* trilogy, *Goodfellas*, and *The Sopranos*.

There are also important disadvantages associated with membership. Law enforcement agencies take great interest in a criminal if they discover he is a made guy. Any insult or assault on a member requires that he kill the offender. He is also required to obey the orders of his boss, even if this means participating in the murder of a complete stranger or perhaps a close friend or relative. But, of course, the member is protected by the boss, who will respond to any attack on one of his soldiers as a personal affront, a fundamental lack of respect, requiring mobilization of the group's resources for violence. It is the ready availability of private violence that makes the OC group a viable entity.

The continuation of traditional organized crime in the United States is dependent upon the ability of crime units to recruit new members, which, in turn, is dependent upon the availability of a pool of qualified applicants. For at least some Italian-American crime groups, this is becoming more difficult. On January 4, 1990, John Gotti, boss of the Gambino Family, was recorded by the FBI decrying the paucity of qualified candidates for membership to *consigliere* Frank Locascio: "And where we gonna find them, these kinda guys? Frank, I'm not being a pessimist. It's gettin' tougher, not easier. We got everything that's any good. Look around, ask your son someday, forget who you are, what you are. Talk to your son like his age. Put yourself in his age bracket, and let him tell you what good kids in the neighborhood other than the kids that are with you. Or good kids in the neighborhood other than with him. You know what I'm trying to say? I told you a couple of weeks ago, we got the only few pockets of good kids left." This issue will be examined in Chapter 2 in a discussion of "ethnic succession" in organized crime.

Crews Members and associates are organized into crews, semi-independent units nominally headed by a *caporegime*, a *capodecina*, a street boss, or even a soldier. Crews generate finances, which they share with their crew chief, who shares it with the *caporegime* or with the boss. These crews have been described in a number of popular books on organized crime. FBI agent Joseph Pistone (1987: 51–52),[3] in his undercover role, describes the crew of a soldier in the Bonanno Family, whose "headquarters" was the back room of a store stocked with expensive clothing—stolen merchandise: "Although these were lower-echelon guys in the mob, they always had something going. They always had money. They were always turning things over. They always had swag around. . . . You name it, they stole it. Jilly's crew would hit warehouses, docks, trucks, houses. . . . There wasn't one hour of one day that went by when they weren't thinking and talking about what they were going to steal, who or what or where they were going to rob. . . . The mob was their job."

The crew headed by Paul Vario,[4] a *caporegime* in the Lucchese crime Family, used a drab, paint-flecked storefront cabstand and dispatch office in Brooklyn as its headquarters. Nicholas Pileggi (1985: 35) notes that the Vario crew did most of the strong-arm work for the Lucchese Family: "At the cabstand there were always young tough guys ready to go out and break a few heads whenever Paul gave the order and killers who were happy to take on the most violent of assignments." The persons in Vario's crew "had always been outlaws. They were the kids from the neighborhood who were always in trouble. As youngsters they were the ones invariably identified as toughs by the police and brought into the precinct for routine beatings, whenever some neighborhood store burglary or assault moved the station house cops into action."

The crew headed by John Gotti, a *caporegime* and later boss of the Gambino Family, was headquartered at the Bergin Hunt and Fish Club, a (very) private storefront in the Ozone Park section of the New York City borough of Queens: "The Bergin men were good customers in the small cafes and stores operating on slim margins. Around his neighbors, Gotti acted like a gentleman; around him they acted as though he were a successful salesman. He began saluting the community with Fourth of July fireworks displays and barbecues; some residents began saluting him by alerting the club when men resembling undercover detectives were around" (Mustain and Capeci 1988: 112).

---

[3]Pistone's exploits became the subject of a book and movie, *Donnie Brasco*. The Bonanno Family captain who had permitted the agent's penetration was found murdered, his hands symbolically cut off.

[4]Vario, played by Paul Sorvino in the movie *Goodfellas*, died in prison while serving a 15-year sentence.

Frank (the Chessman) Cucchiara typified the "boss" of a traditional organized crime Family. He handled Family affairs and took orders from no one.

The Boss   Although he is at the center of the universe of an American Mafia unit, the boss does not have a complete overview of the decentralized activities of his members. In the past, the boss was usually a senior citizen—it takes many years to gain the respect of members and the knowledge and connections needed by the group. It is a sign of weakness that many of the current *Cosa Nostra* bosses are relatively young, as well as volatile and violent. In 1996, for example, Liborio Bellomo, acting head of the Genovese crime Family, the largest in the United States, was indicted on racketeering charges in New York—at age 39 (Van Natta 1996).

Typically, the boss operates out of a fixed location: a restaurant, a private club, or his own business office. Raymond Patriarca, the New England crime boss who died of natural causes in 1984 at age 76, operated out of his vending-machine business, the National Cigarette Service, in the Federal Hill section of Providence, Rhode Island. Vincent Teresa (and Renner 1973: 95) states that the entire area around Patriarca's headquarters was an armed camp: "It was impossible to move through the area without being spotted and reported." Throughout the day, Patriarca received visitors, sometimes legitimate persons asking for a favor, usually to resolve a dispute, but more frequently "a parade of the faithful bearing tithes, cold cash for the middle drawer in the dirty back room of a cigarette vending-machine business in a run-down section of Providence. It could be the receipts from a wholly owned subsidiary or rent from a franchise. In a complex maze of interests, he completely controlled some markets, especially those involving gambling, loansharking, and pornography, and dabbled in others such as truck hijacking and drug trafficking in which free-lancers negotiated fees to do business" (O'Neill and Lehr 1989: 43).

The boss of the Genovese Family in New York operated out of an Italian restaurant in lower Manhattan, to which he was driven every day from his home in Long Island by a chauffeur-bodyguard. In the back of the restaurant was a table reserved for him. Persons having business with the boss would come in all day long and sit at the table for varying periods of time. Strangers were not welcome in the restaurant, which was located in the heart of an Italian neighborhood dominated by the Genovese Family. There was no place to park; all parking spaces were taken by members of the Family or their associates. Anyone walking in the area who was not recognized would be reported to the Family members at the restaurant. If a stranger entered the restaurant, he or she was told that a reservation was needed—but the restaurant refused to take reservations (Abadinsky 1983). Joseph Colombo, whose crime Family bears his name, operated out of a neighborhood real estate firm, Cantalup Realty Co., in the Bensonhurst section of Brooklyn. He was on the books as a licensed real estate salesman—the licensing test was fixed (Cantalupo and Renner 1990). Gambino Family boss John Gotti operated out of the Ravenite Social Club on Mulberry Street in Manhattan's Little Italy; every Wednesday, Gotti would hold court at a gathering of Family captains. To avoid being electronically surveilled, Gotti would discuss business on the street or in an apartment upstairs from the club; however, the apartment was bugged by the FBI (Coffey and Schmetterer 1991).

A boss has a number of men who report directly to him. They carry messages and perform assignments as necessary; they also serve to physically protect the boss. In many crime groups, particularly those in New York, where five Families—and one from New Jersey—operate, most of the activities of Family members are not under the direct or indirect supervision of the boss. He often finds out about many of the activities of members only as the result of periodic briefings by the captains.

Crime boss Joseph Bonanno (1983: 157) describes how he operated as "Father" of his Family:

Internal disagreements between Family members were solved at the grassroots level by group leaders or by the consigliere. A Family member's personal or business problems were usually handled in this manner, and the problem rarely had to be brought to my attention.

On the other hand, if a Family member wanted to go into business with a member of another Family, such an association would need the approval of the Fathers of the respective Families. A Family member's relations with non-Family members was his own affair.

Other than meeting with other Fathers and meeting with group leaders within my Family on an ad hoc basis, being a Father took up relatively little of my time. Family matters were largely handled by the group leaders under me. Indeed, there were many Family members I never met. If I convened a Family meeting, I met only with the group leaders, who in turn passed the information to the people in their groups.

Peacekeeping, notes Bonanno, was his main responsibility as head of the Family. According to the PCOC (1985b), the Family boss is also responsible for making all important decisions on trial strategy when a Family member is the defendant. This responsibility is for the purpose of protecting Family interests during the trial.

Crime boss Carlo Gambino would often conduct briefings in a moving car to reduce the possibility of surveillance. Very important or sensitive operations, such as those that could result in conflict with other crime Families or attract undue law enforcement attention, are cleared with the boss in advance. And, as noted earlier, in all but the smallest units, the boss will be assisted by an underboss (*sottocapo*) and a counselor/advisor (*consigliere*).

The boss, like many other members of a crime Family, has investments in illegitimate and legitimate enterprises, often in partnership with other members of his own or other crime groups or with nonmember associates. He receives a portion of the illegal earnings of all of the members of his Family, roughly between 10 and 15 percent if he had no stake in the activities. With activities that he directs personally, the share will be considerably higher. A soldier will share his earnings with his captain, who will pass on a portion to the boss. Sitting in the back of his restaurant headquarters, the head of the Genovese Family would receive visitors who passed sealed envelopes filled with money to his bodyguard—their show of respect (Abadinsky 1983). As opposed to bureaucratic organizations, the money goes only in one direction—upward. When the boss gives someone money, it is for investments on which a substantial return is expected, or violence is guaranteed.

The boss demands absolute respect and total obedience. His working day is spent in exchanges with many people. With a word or two, a sentence, a shake of the head, a smile, or a gesture, he can set in motion a host of activities and operations involving dozens, if not hundreds, of persons. The boss is treated with a great deal of deference. People rise when he enters the room, and they never interrupt when he is speaking. If they are close, a kiss on the boss's cheek is considered an appropriate gesture of respect. If the boss rises, all rise. If the boss rises and embraces an individual, this is considered a great honor, often reserved only for other bosses.

The intensity of government surveillance and prosecution of organized crime during the last two decades has made the position of boss less desirable than in the past. As a result, filling the position may be difficult because those most qualified— men with good incomes and low profiles—may also be those who are most reluctant to undergo the law enforcement scrutiny that comes with the position. In such circumstances, the boss may be a relatively weak figure, with strength concentrated in the captains heading crews of earners.

The Commission All crime bosses are li rather informal arrangement known as the "commission," but only the bosses of the most powerful groups—particularly those in New York, Chicago, Buffalo, and Philadelphia—are considered actual commission members: "The national commission regulates joint ventures between families, intervenes in family disputes, approves the initiation of new members, and controls relations between the U.S. and Sicilian branches of La Cosa Nostra" (PCOC 1986a: 37). The commission, reports Bonanno (1983: 159), can arbitrate disputes. Having no direct executive power, however, it has to depend on influence: "It had respect only insofar as its individual members had respect. More than anything else, the Commission was a forum."

In addition to the "national commission," which is a body that rarely, if ever, meets as a group,[5] the bosses of the New York Families constitute a commission that serves to arbitrate disputes and deal with joint ventures between their Families. In 1986, in what became known as the "Commission Case" (*United States v. Salerno*, 85 CR 139, S.D.N.Y, 1985), a number of New York bosses were convicted of conducting the affairs of "the commission of La Cosa Nostra" in a pattern of racketeering that violated the RICO statute (discussed in Chapter 14). The case revealed the role of the commission in New York:

- Regulate and facilitate relationships between the five Families
- Promote and facilitate joint ventures between Families
- Resolve actual and potential disputes between Families
- Regulate the criminal activities of the Families
- Extend formal recognition to newly chosen Family bosses and resolve leadership disputes within Families

---

[5]According to Bill Bonanno (1999), until 1961, the national commission met regularly in odd years. He states that he was at a special commission meeting in 1962, which was called because of problems in the Profaci Family (discussed in Chapter 4).

Rules of the American Mafia

- Always show respect to those who can command it.
- Report any failure to show respect to one's patron immediately.
- Violence must be used, even if only of a limited type, to ensure respect.
- Never ask for surnames. (Underboss Sam Gravano testified that there were many people in his crime Family whose last names he did not know.)
- Never resort to violence in a dispute with a member or associate of another Family.
- Never resort to, or even threaten, violence in a dispute with a member of your Family.
- Do not use the telephone except to arrange for a meeting place, preferably in code, from which you will then travel to a safe place to discuss business.
- Avoid mentioning specifics when discussing business—for example, names, dates, and places—beyond those absolutely necessary for understanding.

- Keep your mouth shut—anything you hear, anything you see, stays with you, in your head; do not talk about it.
- Do not ask unnecessary questions. The amount of information given to you is all you need to carry out your instructions.
- If your patron arranges for two parties to work together, he assumes responsibility for arbitrating any disputes between the parties.
- The boss can unilaterally direct violence, including murder, against any member of his Family, but he cannot engage in murder-for-hire, that is, make a profit from murder. (The murder need not be related to business: Paul Castellano ordered his son-in-law murdered, believing his philandering responsible for the boss's daughter's miscarriage.)
- The boss cannot use violence against a member or close associate of another Family without prior consultation with that Family's boss.

Sources: Abadinsky (1981a, 1983); Coffey and Schmetterer (1991); transcripts from the 1992 trial of John Gotti.

- Authorize the execution of Family members
- Approve of the initiation of new members into the Families

The power of approving the initiation of new members keeps Family size stable and prevents wholesale initiation, which would be likely in times of intra-Family conflict. During the struggle to lead the Colombo Family (1991–1993), for example, the commission would not permit either faction to initiate new members and thereby gain an advantage over its opposition.

Rules An elaborate system of written rules and regulations is one of the important characteristics of a bureaucracy. While traditional organized crime does not have written rules, it has an elaborate set of norms that govern behavior. Francis Ianni (1972) argues that the rules of the American Mafia are actually standards of conduct based on

the traditions of southern Italy, particularly the concept of family loyalty. However, my research (Abadinsky 1981a, 1983) indicates that the rules are not traditional but quite rational and sometimes counter to southern Italian tradition. For example, loyalty to the crime Family supersedes loyalty to one's own blood family. According to the rules, if required by the boss, a member must participate in the murder of a relative (usually by helping to "set him up"). When Vincent Siciliano (1970: 74) discovered who had killed his father, he swore vengeance but later found out that the hit had been "authorized," the killers carrying out Family orders. Finding one of the killers at a restaurant, Siciliano told him: "Look, I came here to talk to you. I want to apologize about the noise I was making." His father's murderer responded: "Hey, don't worry about it. I know how you felt about your father. I understand. There are no hard feelings, Vinnie." In Philadelphia, Frank

("Chickie") Narducci was killed on orders of Family boss Nicky Scarfo, yet his sons, Philip and Frank, Jr., continued to work as enforcers for Scarfo (Anastasia 1991). After John Gotti had *caporegime* Thomas Gambino's uncle, Paul Castellano, murdered, Gambino continued to report and show respect to Gotti, who became boss of the Gambino Family.

This is all contrary to the southern Italian credo *sangu de me sangu* ("blood of my blood"), which actually means *famiglia* (family) above all: *o tortu o gridu difenni i to* ("right or wrong, defend your own" kin). In fact, the rules of traditional organized crime have succeeded in preventing the emergence of a violent southern Italian tradition: vendetta, the irrational blood feud that is bad for business. Since the 1930s, there have been no "wars" between traditional OC groups, although there has been a great deal of intragroup violence, such as the "Gallo–Profaci war" and the "Banana war" (to be discussed in Chapter 4).

Analysis of the Structure

The structure of the American Mafia that has been outlined here is rather fluid, similar to that of the real estate development business: "A great deal of illegal activity within the illegal industries is not routine production and distribution carried on under the auspices of a specific firm, but instead the result of many ad hoc deals and projects" (Moore 1987: 54). The firms (crews) in the New York model are not consistently in one business but are intermittently in several. They are organized not as a "production line" but as a "job shop." Annelise Anderson (1979) found that the formal organizational structure of the Philadelphia crime Family was not the same as its economic structure. There

was a relatively clear hierarchy within the Family—boss, underboss, captains, soldiers—but its income-generating activities were based on several smaller operationally independent crews involved in gambling and loansharking. This structure, notes Ronald Goldstock (Stone 1992: 29), former director of the New York State Organized Crime Task Force, is less like a corporation and more like a government: "In a corporation, people at the bottom carry out the policies and perform tasks assigned to them by the executives at the top. In the Mob, the people at the bottom are the entrepreneurs. They pass a percentage of their income upward as taxes in return for government-type services: resolution of disputes, allocation of territories, enforcement and corruption services." Anderson (1979: 46) argues that the most threatening aspect of this type of organized crime is the "group or organization's capacity for forming a quasi-government," giving it a competitive advantage.

Outlaw motorcycle clubs and the American Mafia share a common attribute—the structure of each is only loosely coupled to its criminal activities. However, there is also a fundamental difference. American Mafia groups are *criminal organizations*—their reason for existence is the business of crime. Outlaw motorcycle clubs exist to promote a subcultural "biker" lifestyle. The American Mafia attracts and selects hard-core criminals. Outlaw bikers were not necessarily in the business of crime before joining a club, and the club places a firewall between the organization and the criminal activities of its members. This also serves to insulate the group as an organization from Racketeer and Corrupt Organizations (RICO) prosecutions (discussed in Chapter 14).

In the next chapter, we will examine explanations for the existence of organized crime.

INTERNET CONNECTIONS

Cosa Nostra: **americanmafia.com**

Greater Toronto Area Combined Forces Special Enforcement Unit: **cfseu.org**

Royal Canadian Mounted Police Organized Crime Initiative: **rcmp-grc.gc.ca/organizedcrime**

Organized Crime Agency of British Columbia: **ocabc.org**

Organized crime links: **people.freenet.de/kvlampe**

New Jersey State Commission of Investigation: **state.nj.us/sci**

Hells Angels web site: **hamcsfv.com**

Outlaws web site: **outlawsmc.com**

Bandidos web site: **bandidosmc.com**

REVIEW QUESTIONS

1. How does the criminality of persons in organized crime differ from that of conventional criminals?
2. What are the eight attributes of organized crime?
3. What are the attributes of a bureaucracy?
4. What led to the development of the original outlaw motorcycle clubs?
5. What explains the rather bureaucratic structure adopted by outlaw motorcycle clubs?
6. In the organizational structure of outlaw motorcycle clubs, what are the functions of the mother club?
7. What aspects of outlaw motorcycle clubs are bureaucratic?
8. What are the similarities and differences between the American Mafia and outlaw motorcycle clubs?
9. What are the characteristics of a patrimonial organization?
10. What is the role of a patron in organized crime?
11. How can a member of organized crime act as a catalyst for a great deal of conventional criminal activity?
12. What is the primary role of a boss in the American Mafia?
13. What is the function of the "commission" in *Cosa Nostra*?
14. Why is the concept of "membership" important in the American Mafia?
15. What are the advantages and disadvantages of membership?
16. What are the basic qualifications for *Cosa Nostra* membership?
17. What is a "crew"?
18. How does the structure of outlaw motorcycle clubs and the American Mafia differ from the structure of their illegal business operations?

♠

CHAPTER 2

EXPLAINING ORGANIZED CRIME

Chapter 1 explores the issue of defining organized crime and presents the structures it can manifest. But what explains its existence? Organized crime has been subjected to only limited attempts at explanation. While sociologists have offered a number of theories to help explain crime and criminal behavior, rarely were these directed specifically at *organized* crime. Nevertheless, some theories of crime and deviance provide insight into organized crime, and they will be examined in this chapter.

ANOMIE

Building on a concept originated by the French sociologist Emile Durkheim (1951) back in the nineteenth century, in 1938 Robert K. Merton set forth a social and cultural explanation for deviant behavior in the United States. He conceived of organized crime as a normal response to pressures exerted on certain persons by the social structure. Merton points to an American preoccupation with economic success—*pathological materialism.* During the 1830s, a visitor from France, Alexis de Tocqueville, wrote that "It is odd to watch with what feverish ardor the Americans pursue prosperity and how they are tormented by the shadowy suspicion that they may have not have chosen the shortest route to get it" (1966: 536). According to Merton, it is the goal that is emphasized, not the means, which are at best only a secondary consideration: "There may develop a disproportionate, at times, a virtually exclusive stress upon the value of specific goals, involving relatively slight concern with the institutionally appropriate modes of attaining these goals" (1938: 673).

This being the case, the only factors limiting goal achievement are technical, not moral or legal: "[E]mphasis on the goals of monetary success and material property leads to dominant concern with technological and social instruments designed to produce the desired result, inasmuch as institutional controls become of secondary importance. In such a situation, innovation [such as organized crime] flourishes as the range of means employed is broadened" (Merton 1938: 673). Thus, in American society, "the pressure of prestige-bearing success tends to eliminate the effective social constraint over means employed to this end. 'The-ends-justifies-the-means' doctrine becomes a guiding tenet for action when the cultural structure unduly exalts the end and the social organization unduly limits possible recourse to approved means" (1938: 681). The activities of earlier capitalists, the unscrupulous "robber barons," exemplifies the spirit that Merton refers to as *innovation*. Taking advantage of every (legitimate and illegitimate) opportunity, these men became the embodiment of the great American success story. However, the opportunity for economic success is not equally distributed, and the immigrants who followed these men to America found many avenues from "rags to riches" significantly limited if not already closed.

Some immigrants recognized that the cards were stacked against them, and as a result, organized crime flourished. Writing several years before Merton, Louis Robinson (1933: 16) spoke of an American credo according to which "we dare not or at least will not condemn the criminal's goal, because it is also our goal. We want to keep the goal ourselves and damn the criminal for pursuing it in the only way he knows how":

> The methods which criminals use in attaining our common goal of wealth may, of course, differ from those which the non-criminal classes use. But this is to be expected. They are probably not in a position to employ our methods. We can think of a variety of reasons why a man without capital or without education or without industrial skill or without this or that advantage or handicapped by any one of several factors which anyone could easily name would be forced to seek the common goal by means differing from those employed by another man better situated or endowed. In other words, he would *play the game differently*. (1933: 15–16; emphasis added)

Anomie results when numbers of people are confronted by the contradiction between goals and means and "become estranged from a society that promises them in principle what they are deprived of in reality" (Merton 1964: 218). Despite numerous success stories, "We know in this same society that proclaims the right, and even the duty, of lofty aspirations for all, men do not have equal access to the opportunity structure" (1964: 218). Yet those with ready access to success ("born with a silver spoon") *and* those who are at a distinct disadvantage are constantly exposed to the rewards of "fame and fortune" by the mass media. For some, particularly the disadvantaged, anomie is the result. Merton states there are five modes of individual adaptation to this phenomenon: conformity, ritualism, rebellion, retreatism, and innovation. We are concerned only with the last adaptation—*innovation*—since it includes organized criminal activity for those who would *play the game differently*.

British sociologists Ian Taylor, Paul Walton, and Jock Young (1973: 97) summarize the anomic condition in the United States: "The 'American Dream' urges all citizens to succeed whilst distributing the opportunity to succeed unequally: the result of this social and moral climate, inevitably, is innovation by the citizenry—the adoption of illegitimate means to pursue and obtain success." However, "routine" pedestrian criminal acts do not lead to any significant level of economic success. Innovation, then, is the adoption of sophisticated, well-planned, skilled, organized criminality. A question remains: Why do some persons suffering from anomie turn to criminal innovation while others do not? Edwin Sutherland, the "father" of American criminology, provides an answer: *differential association*.

DIFFERENTIAL ASSOCIATION

According to Sutherland (1973), all behavior—lawful and criminal—is learned. The principal part of learning occurs within intimate personal groups. What is learned depends on the intensity, frequency, and duration of the association. When these variables are sufficient and the associations are criminal, the actor learns the techniques of committing crime and the drives, attitudes, and rationalizations that add up to a favorable precondition to criminal behavior. The balance between noncriminal and criminal behaviors is tipped in favor of the latter.

Learning the techniques of sophisticated criminality requires the proper environment—ecological niches or *enclaves* where delinquent/criminal subcultures (discussed later) flourish and this education is available. In a capitalist society, socioeconomic differentials relegate some persons to an environment wherein they experience a compelling sense of strain—anomie—as well as differential association. In the environment where organized crime has traditionally thrived, strain is intense. Conditions of severe deprivation are coupled with readily available success models and associations that are innovative, such as racketeers and drug dealers. This makes certain *enclaves* characterized by social disorganization and delinquent/criminal subcultures spawning grounds for organized crime:

> Various types of people tend to seek out others like themselves and live close together. Located within these distinctive clusters are specialized commercial enterprises and institutions that support the inhabitants' special ways of life. . . . Each distinctive group, along with its stores and institutions, occupies a geographic area that becomes intimately associated with the group. Through this linkage, areas acquire symbolic qualities that include their place names and social histories. Each place, both as a geographic entity and as a space with social meaning, also tends to be an object of residents' attachments and an important component of their identities. For example, people living in Little Italy or Chinatown think of themselves as Italian or Chinese, but their place of residence is also a prominent part of their self-concepts. . . . [The] enclave has some characteristics of a subculture, in which a group of people shares common traditions and values that are ordinarily maintained by a high rate of interaction within the group. (Abrahamson 1996: 1, 3)

SUBCULTURES AND SOCIAL DISORGANIZATION

Instead of conforming to conventional norms, some persons, through differential association, organize their behavior according to the norms of a delinquent or criminal group to which they belong or with which they identify. This is most likely to occur in environments characterized by relative social disorganization, where familial and communal controls are ineffective in exerting a conforming influence. In certain areas—enclaves with strong traditions of organized crime—young persons stand a greater chance of being exposed to criminal norms. In these areas, persons exhibiting criminal norms are often well integrated into the community, and such areas are the breeding ground for delinquent subcultures and entrants into organized crime (Kobrin 1966).

Culture refers to a source of patterning in human conduct: it is the sum of patterns of social relationships and shared meanings by which people give order, expression, and value to common experiences. The strength of a culture is determined by the degree of commitment of its members: culture is a valued heritage. A *subculture* "implies that there are value judgments or a social value system which is apart from a larger or central value system. From the viewpoint of this larger dominant culture, the values of the subculture set the latter apart and prevent total integration, occasionally causing open or covert conflicts" (Wolfgang and Ferracuti 1967: 99). "Subcultures are patterns of values, norms, and behavior which have become traditional among certain groups. These groups may be of many types, including occupational and ethnic groups, social classes, occupants of 'closed institutions' [for example, prisons and mental hospitals] and various age grades." They are "important frames of reference through which individuals and groups see the world and interpret it" (Short 1968: 11).

Central to the issue of culture versus subculture are *norms*, "group-held prescriptions for or prohibitions against certain conduct" (Wolfgang and Ferracuti 1967: 113). Norms are general rules about how to behave and expectations that are predictive of behavior. These rules and expectations are approved by the vast majority of a society, which provides rewards or punishments for conformity or violation: "The 'delinquent subculture' is characterized principally by conduct that reflects values antithetical to the surrounding culture" (1967: 110). Subcultural theory explains criminal behavior as learned; the subcultural delinquent has learned values that are deviant. Ideas about society lead to criminal behavior. A number of studies indicate that delinquent youths hold values that differ markedly from those of nondelinquents. Indeed, they may view their criminal behavior as morally wrong, but this is not the controlling attitude. Being right or wrong in terms of the wider society is simply not a guidepost for behavior. Nonconventional behavior is admired—the ability to fight, to win at gambling (Elliott, Huizinga, and Ageton 1985).

Clifford R. Shaw and Henry D. McKay, sociologists at the University of Chicago, used that city as a laboratory for their study of patterns of criminality during the 1920s and 1930s.[1] They found that certain clearly identifiable neighborhoods maintained a high level of criminality over many decades despite changes in ethnic composition. Thus, although one ethnic group replaced another, the rate of criminality remained constant. What was it about the environment of these neighborhoods that made them criminogenic?

According to Shaw and McKay (1972: 72), such neighborhoods are characterized by attitudes and values that are conducive to delinquency and crime, particularly organized crime:

> The presence of a large number of adult criminals in certain areas means that children there are in contact with crime as a career and with the criminal way of life, symbolized by organized crime. In this type of organization can be seen the delegation of authority, the division of labor, the specialization of function, and all the other charac-

teristics common to well-organized business institutions wherever found. . . .

> The heavy concentration of delinquency in certain areas means that boys living in these areas are in contact not only with individuals who engage in proscribed activity but also with groups which sanction such behavior and exert pressure upon their members to conform to group standards. (1972: 174)

A disruption of the social order is associated with high rates of delinquency in a community, the result of a breakdown in mechanisms of social control. In many U.S. cities around 1900, the social order was disrupted by the combined interactive effects of industrialization, immigration, and urbanization. Deviant traditions developed and competed with conventional norms; in some communities, deviant norms won out. Once established, these norms took root in areas that, according to Shaw and McKay, are characterized by attitudes and values conducive to delinquency and crime, thus creating a subculture of crime. The attitudes and values, as well as the techniques of organized criminality, are transmitted culturally: "Delinquent boys in these areas have contact not only with other delinquents who are their contemporaries but also with older offenders, who in turn had contact with delinquents preceding them, and so on back to the earliest history of the neighborhood. This contact means that the traditions of delinquency can be and are transmitted down through successive generations of boys, in much the same way that language and other social forms are transmitted" (1972: 174).

Back in the 1920s, John Landesco (1968) found that organized crime in Chicago could be explained by the prevalence of social disorganization in the wider society (during the period of Prohibition) and by the distinct social organization of urban slums from which members of OC emerge: "Once a set of cultural values is created and established—either because of economic factors or intellectual or moral transformations—they tend to become autonomous in their impact. From that point on, they can influence human relations inde-

---

[1]Despite the prominence of organized crime in Chicago during this period, the University of Chicago sociologists did not show any scholarly interest in the phenomenon (Reynolds 1995).

pendently of their original sources. And since they are, as a rule, accepted uncritically and through the most inadvertent process of socialization, they are regarded as normal and inevitable within each cultural system" (Saney 1986: 35).

In other words, the roots and culture of particular neighborhoods explain why gangsters come from clearly delineated areas "where the gang tradition is old" (Landesco 1968: 207) and where adolescents, through differential association, can absorb the attitudes and skills necessary to enter the world of adult organized crime. Indeed, in such neighborhoods, organized crime can provide a level of social control—limiting predatory crime, for example—that would otherwise be absent. At night, in an OC-dominated neighborhood in Brooklyn, a young woman did not realize she was being followed as she approached the door to her home. The young man following her did not realize that he was being watched. His attempt at a knifepoint robbery was foiled by several large men who quickly carried him up the stairs. As an observer recalls, "I could make out the small roof wall on the front of the building—it was made of brick—and then I saw the guy launched right over it into the air. He hung there for just a second, flailing arms like a broken helicopter, and then he came down hard and splattered all over the street" (Pileggi 1990: 40).

Inadequate familial socialization prevents some persons from conforming to the conventional norms of the wider society. Through differential association, some of these persons organize their behavior according to the norms of a delinquent or criminal subculture with which they identify or to which they belong. This is most likely to occur in environments characterized by relative social disorganization, where familial and communal controls are ineffective in exerting a conforming influence. In his classic study of Chicago street gangs, originally published in 1927, Frederic Thrasher (1968: 270) notes that "Experience in a gang of the predatory type usually develops in the boy an attitude of indifference to law and order—one of the basic traits of the finished gangster." As Thrasher (1968: 273) points out, "If the younger undirected gangs and clubs of the

Joe N. Gallo, New York City *consigliere* for the Gambino Family, at work in his Astoria, Queens, neighborhood. He is standing in front of Sperazza's Luncheonette. Due to the influence of gangsters such as Gallo and those preceding him, many delinquent boys in the area aspire to lives of crime.

gang type, which serve as training schools for delinquency, do not succeed in turning out the finished criminal, they often develop a type of personality which may well foreshadow the gangster and the gunman." In the Chicago of the Prohibition era, there was no hard-and-fast dividing line between gangs of boys and youth and adult criminal organizations (1968: 281): "They merge into each other by imperceptible gradations."

In order for an organized crime group to survive, it must have "an institutionalized process for inducting new members and inculcating them with the values and ways of behaving of the social system" (Cressey 1969: 263). Donald Cressey notes that "in some neighborhoods all three of the essential ingredients of an effective recruiting process are in operation: inspiring aspiration for membership, training for membership and selection for membership" (1969: 236). In his research, Gerald Suttles (1968) refers to areas from which members of organized crime have typically emerged as *defended neighborhoods:* recognized ecological niches whose inhabitants form cohesive groupings and seal themselves off through the efforts of delinquent gangs, restrictive covenants, and a forbidding reputation. Such neighborhoods have traditionally provided the recruiting grounds that ensure the continuity of OC.

In such communities, the conventional and criminal value systems are highly integrated. Leaders of organized criminal enterprises "frequently maintain membership in such conventional institutions of their local communities as churches, fraternal and mutual benefit societies, and political parties" (Kobrin 1966: 156). Formal and informal political, economic, and religious ties provide both illegitimate and legitimate opportunities. These leaders are able to control violent and delinquent behavior in their domain—they are effective instruments of social control. "Everyone," particularly would-be miscreants, "knows" not to "mess around" in certain neighborhoods. And those who do not "know" have suffered serious consequences—for example, selling drugs in one Chicago suburb resulted in mutilated corpses. In the Italian area of New York's Greenwich Village, "street corner boys" enforced the social order—made sure the streets were safe. And their self-appointed role was backed by the formidable reputation of the neighborhood's organized crime figures. For this, neighborhood residents reciprocated by providing "wiseguys" with a "safe haven" (Tricarico 1984).

Nicholas Pileggi (1985: 37–38) describes a defended neighborhood in Brooklyn:

In Brownsville–East New York wiseguys were more than accepted—they were protected. Even the legitimate members of the community—the merchants, teachers, phone repairmen, garbage collectors, bus depot dispatchers, housewives, and old-timers sunning themselves along the Conduit Drive—all seemed to keep an eye out to protect their local hoods. The majority of the residents, even those not directly related by birth or marriage to wiseguys, had certainly known the local rogues most of their lives. There was the nodding familiarity of neighborhood. In the area it was impossible to betray old friends, even those old friends who had grown up to be racketeers.

The extraordinary insularity of these old-world mob-controlled sections, whether Brownsville–East New York, the South Side of Chicago, or Federal Hill in Providence, Rhode Island, unquestionably helped to nurture the mob.

Recruitment into OC is made viable because "in the type of community under discussion boys may more or less realistically recognize the potentialities for personal progress in the local society through success in delinquency. In a general way, therefore, delinquent activity in these areas constitutes a training ground for the acquisition of skill in the use of violence, concealment of offense, evasion of detection and arrest, and the purchase of immunity from punishment" (Kobrin 1966: 156).

Robert Lombardo, a former organized crime investigator and ranking Cook County police official, points out that prospective members of OC "typically come from communities which share collective representations and moral sentiments which allow them to recognize the pursuit of a career in the underworld as a legitimate way of life" (1979: 18; 1994a). Young men from these areas dress in a certain style—"gangster chic"—and congregate in social clubs and night spots where they are able to associate with the men who have already been allowed entry into organized crime. They are ready—eager—to show their mettle by accepting assignments from "goodfellas." Even those who have moved to suburban locations—if they accept the "wiseguy" credo—gravitate back to the 'hood. In Chicago, this phenomenon has been referred to as the "suburbanization of the mob"—young men who have known only middle-class living conditions becoming part of organized crime. Like the members of outlaw motorcycle clubs discussed in Chapter 1, these young men are attracted to a subcultural lifestyle but not necessarily by the potential financial rewards offered by organized crime. For example, Salvatore ("Solly D.") DeLaurentis (b. 1938), who was raised in the Taylor Street neighborhood in Chicago, aspired to be a "gangster"—a term he uses to describe himself—since his earliest days. But his family moved out to suburban Lake County, and Solly D. found himself cut off from his career path: Lake County lacked the critical mass of older criminals and their young associates/wannabes. So DeLaurentis gradually made connections back in the old neighborhood and eventually became a member of the Infelice crew (discussed in Chapter 5) in charge of Lake County. (He is currently serving an 18-year sentence for a racketeering conviction.)

Even senior members of the Outfit who reside in suburban locations frequent the restaurants, nightspots, and social clubs back in the 'hood. James D. Antonio ("Jimmy D."), the ranking member of the Grand Avenue crew, resided in suburban Skokie. But until his death in 1993 from an auto accident, the 65-year-old operated a storefront social club in the Grand Avenue neighborhood, which even sponsored a boys' baseball team for neighborhood youths (O'Brien 1993).

According to Irving Spergel (1964), in such communities life in OC is considered acceptable and therefore a legitimate aspiration for young persons. While these communities provide an appropriate learning environment for the acquisition of values and skills associated with the performance of criminal roles, integration into OC requires selection and tutelage in the process of acquiring recognition—and only a select few are given recognition by those who control admission. Entry into organized crime is characterized by *differential opportunity*.

DIFFERENTIAL OPPORTUNITY

In agreement with Merton, Richard Cloward and Lloyd Ohlin (1960) note that American preoccupation with economic success, coupled with socioeconomic stratification, relegates many persons to an environment wherein they experience strain: "Many lower-class male adolescents experience extreme deprivation born of the certainty that their position in the economic structure is relatively fixed and immutable—a desperation made all the more poignant by their exposure to a cultural ideology in which failure to orient oneself upward is regarded as a moral defect and failure to become mobile as proof of it" (1960: 107).

Conditions of severe deprivation with extremely limited access to ladders of legitimate success result in collective adaptations in the form of delinquent subcultures. Cloward and Ohlin distinguish three types:

1. *Retreatist subculture:* Activities in which drug usage is the primary focus; the anomic condition leads the sufferer to reject the goal of economic success in favor of a more easily obtainable one—the "high."
2. *Conflict subculture:* Gang activities devoted to violence and destructive acting out as a way of gaining status. As with retreatists, the anomic condition leads to a rejection of economic success in favor of a more easily obtainable goal.
3. *Criminal/rackets subculture:* Gang activity devoted to utilitarian criminal pursuits, an adaptation that begins to approximate organized crime.

Anomie alone, note Cloward and Ohlin, is not sufficient to explain participation in organized crime: what is necessary is cultural transmission (Shaw and McKay) through differential association (Sutherland). However, Cloward and Ohlin point out that illegitimate opportunity for success, like legitimate opportunity, is not equally distributed throughout society (1960: 145): "Having decided that he 'can't make it legitimately,' he cannot simply choose from an array of illegitimate means, all equally available to him." In other words, access to criminal ladders of success are no more freely available than are noncriminal alternatives:

Only those neighborhoods in which crime flourishes as a stable, indigenous institution are fertile learning environments for the young. Because these environments afford integration of different age-levels of offender, selected young people are exposed to "differential association" through which tutelage is provided and criminal values and skills are acquired. To be prepared for the role may not, however, ensure that the individual will ever discharge it. One important limitation is that more youngsters are recruited into these patterns of differential association than the adult criminal structure can possibly absorb. Since there is a surplus of contenders for these elite positions, criteria and mechanisms of selection must be evolved. Hence a certain proportion of those who aspire may not be permitted to engage in the behavior for which they have prepared themselves. (Cloward and Ohlin 1960: 148)

Why do young men who have the opportunity not become contenders for positions in organized crime? *Social control theory* offers an explanation.

SOCIAL CONTROL THEORY

Social control refers to those processes by which the community influences its members toward conformance with established norms of behavior. Social control theorists argue that the relevant question is not "Why do persons become involved in crime, organized or otherwise?" but rather "Why do most persons conform to societal norms?" If, as control theorists generally assume, most persons are sufficiently motivated by the potential rewards to commit criminal acts, why do only a few make crime a career? According to control theorists, "delinquent acts result when an individual's bond to society is weak or broken" (Hirschi 1969: 16). The strength of this bond is determined by internal and external restraints. In other words, internal and external restraints determine whether we move in the direction of crime or of law-abiding behavior.

Internal restraints include what psychoanalytic theory refers to as the *superego* (Freud 1933): an unconscious, yet powerful, conscience-like mechanism that provides a sense of guilt. According to Sigmund Freud, conscience is not something that is a part of us from the very beginning of our lives. It is a controlling mechanism that develops out of the relationship with, and influence of, our parents. In the adult who experienced "healthy" parental relationships as a child, the superego takes the place of the controlling parental function. Dysfunction during early stages of childhood development, or parental influences that are not normative, result in an adult who is devoid of prosocial internal constraints; some refer to this as psycho- or sociopathology, or Antisocial Personality Disorder (ASP), characterized by a combination of antisocial behavior and emotional detachment.

"The most disturbing symptom of ASP often is aggression, expressed in shades from quiet intimidation to explosive violence. . . . His actions may be sudden and unpredictable, but more likely they are deliberate, purposeful, and designed for maximum impact" (Black 1999: 47). The psychopathic criminal is totally without conscience, capable of unspeakable acts, and shows no external signs of psychoses or neuroses. In his autobiography, Gambino crime Family underboss Sammy Gravano recalls his first murder—he shot a close friend in the back of the head on orders from the Colombo Family: "Am I supposed to feel remorse? Aren't I supposed to feel something? But I felt nothing like remorse. If anything, I felt good. Like high. Like powerful, maybe even superhuman. It's not that I was happy or proud of myself. Not that. I'm still not happy about that feeling. It's just that killing came so easy to me" (Maas 1997: 52).

The murderous behavior, devoid of remorse, engaged in by persons in organized crime can be explained according to this dimension. Whether they are conceived of in terms of psychology (Aichhorn 1963; Freud, 1933) or sociology (Hirschi 1969), internal constraints are linked to the influence of the family, an influence that can be supported or weakened by the presence or absence of significant external restraints.

External restraints include social disapproval linked to public shame and/or social ostracism and fear of punishment. In other words, people are

Organized Crime and Gratuitous Violence

"But you know, Paul, I think some guys just take so much pleasure from breaking heads that they'd almost rather not get paid"—*caporegime* Joe ("Piney") Armone to Gambino Family boss Paul Castellano (quoted in O'Brien and Kurins 1991: 243–44).

typically deterred from criminal behavior by the possibility of being caught and the punishment that can result, ranging from public shame to imprisonment (and, in extreme cases, capital punishment). In neighborhoods or among subcultural groups with moral sentiments favorable to organized crime, such public shame/social ostracism is ineffective. Only the threat of imprisonment can offer a deterrent.

The strength of official deterrence—force of law—is measured according to two dimensions: risk versus reward. *Risk* involves the ability of the criminal justice system to detect, apprehend, and convict the offender. The amount of risk is weighed against the potential rewards. However, both risk and reward are relative to one's socioeconomic situation. In other words, the less one has to lose, the greater the willingness to engage in risk. In the words of a Bob Dylan song ("Like a Rolling Stone"), "When you ain't got nothin', you got nothin' to lose." And the greater the reward, the greater the willingness to engage in risk. This theory explains why persons in deprived economic circumstances would be more willing to engage in criminal behavior. However, the potential rewards and a perception of relatively low risk can also explain why persons in more advantaged economic circumstances would engage in remunerative criminal behavior such as corporate crime.

ETHNIC SUCCESSION

As will be discussed in the next three chapters, during the decades following World War II, organized crime underwent considerable change. It became increasingly clear that OC was dominated mainly by Italians—the Irish, except for small pockets in New York and Boston, were no longer involved. And while the sons of Jewish immigrants played a vital role in organized crime, by the third generation, the Jews had moved out. As Jackson Toby (1958: 548) explains,

> Jews and Italians came to the United States in large numbers at about the same time— the turn of the century—and both settled in urban areas. There was, however, a very different attitude toward intellectual accomplishments in the two cultures. Jews from Eastern Europe regarded study as the most important activity for an adult male. The rabbi enjoyed great prestige because he was a scholar, a teacher, a logician. He advised the community on the application of the Written and Oral Law. Life in America gave a secular emphasis to the Jewish reverence for learning. Material success is a more important motive than salvation for American youngsters, Jewish as well as Christian, and secular education is better training for business and professional careers than Talmudic exegesis. Nevertheless, intellectual achievement continued to be valued by Jews—and to have measurable effects. Second generation Jewish students did homework diligently, got high grades, went to college in disproportionate numbers, and scored high on intelligence tests. Two thousand years of preparation lay behind them.

> Immigrants from Southern Italy, on the other hand, tended to regard formal education either as a frill or as a source of dangerous ideas from which the minds of the young should be protected. They remembered Sicily, where a child who attended school regularly was a rarity. There, youngsters

were needed . . . only to help on the farm. Equally important was the fact that hard-working peasants could not understand why their children should learn classical Italian (which they would not speak at home) or geography (when they would not travel in their lifetimes more than a few miles from their birthplace). Sicilian parents suspected that education was an attempt on the part of Roman officials to subvert the authority of the family. In the United States, many Southern Italian immigrants maintained the same attitudes. They resented compulsory school attendance laws and prodded their children to go to work and become economic assets as soon as possible. They encouraged neglect of schoolwork and even truancy. They did not realize that education has more importance in an urban–industrial society than in a semi-feudal one. With supportive motivation from home lacking, the second-generation Italian boys did not make the effort of Jewish contemporaries. Their teachers tried to stuff the curriculum into their heads in vain. Their lack of interest was reflected not only in low marks, retardation, truancy, and early school leaving; it even resulted in poor scores on intelligence tests. They accepted their parents' conception of the school as worthless and thereby lost their best opportunity for social ascent.

The pool of available candidates for membership in organized crime dwindled in Jewish communities. In Italian communities, it remained adequate enough; the large-scale organizations needed to profit from Prohibition were no longer necessary. During the height of Prohibition in Chicago, for example, Al Capone is reputed to have employed 700 gunmen for an organization that involved thousands of persons, while contemporary estimates of the size of the Chicago Outfit have ranged only as high as 130. The largest of the crime Families, the Genovese Family of New York, is estimated to have no more than 400 members. However, these core members have associ-

ates, and the total number of criminal actors participating directly or indirectly in a crime group's enterprises is many times the size of the core membership at any given time.

Peter Reuter (1983: xi) notes the small size of Italian-American crime groups and the absence of armed retainers: "My analysis suggests that the Mafia may be a paper tiger, rationally reaping the returns from its reputation while no longer maintaining the forces that generated the reputation." He theorizes that having established a dominant position, an unchallenged monopoly of force, the Mafia can depend on its fearsome reputation, an asset that can be substituted for personnel costs that would be incurred by maintaining armed forces. Reuter states that challenges to Mafia power in black and Hispanic communities have not "generated any effort by the Mafia to assert control through superior violence" (1983: 136; also 1995). Reuter theorizes that this may result from the lack of available force or simply from a cost–benefit analysis that militates against its use—excessive force attracts law enforcement attention and is bad for business in general.

Reuter notes, however, that challenges to the Mafia outside of black and Hispanic communities have not been noticeable. The structure of Italian-American OC groups provides an explanation. As noted in Chapter 1, business activities are typically decentralized, often franchised, while violence is not. The Mafia is often "invisible"; that is, members usually avoid directly operating illegal enterprises such as gambling or marginal businesses such as "topless bars" or "strip joints." Instead, they often finance or "license" such enterprises, sometimes receiving payments for restricting entry or competition, sometimes providing no service—simple extortion. How would a competing group set out to deal with this operation? The most obvious method would be a direct attack on its members. But they do not reside, meet, or otherwise assemble in significant numbers, and they may be unknown to anyone except persons intimately involved in the local criminal underworld. The decentralized nature of the organization would render a frontal assault unproductive.

While a number of members and associates could be killed here and there, the net effect would be analogous to punching an empty bag.

Any group with the temerity to undertake this challenge would require the resources necessary to sustain an "army in the field" for an indefinite period of time. Elderly members would probably head for condominiums in South Florida and Palm Springs, California, but remaining behind would be a cadre of assassins whose sole function would be to murder those mounting the challenge to the group's supremacy. They could be reinforced by executioners from other groups. As Reuter (1983: 133) notes, "Large numbers of young men in major American cities are willing to accept paid employment as violence disputants." Rational criminals with martial skill would be inclined to side with an organization with proven staying power—the Mafia—rather than take a chance with a seemingly reckless new group.

As Nicholas Gage (1971a: 113) points out in *The Mafia Is Not an Equal Opportunity Employer*, "No door is more firmly locked to blacks than the one that leads to the halls of power in organized crime." He states that Irish, Jewish, and Italian mobsters have tended to recruit and promote from within their own ethnic groups, while cooperating with one another. Organized crime is no less stratified than the wider "legitimate" society, and the dominant groups in both have always been white. This leads to the issue of *ethnic succession* in organized crime.

Daniel Bell (1964) refers to crime as an American way of life: "A Queer Ladder of Social Mobility." He points out that the "jungle quality of the American business community, particularly at the turn of the century, was reflected in the mode of 'business' practiced by the coarse gangster elements, most of them from new immigrant families, who were 'getting ahead' just as Horatio Alger had urged" (1964: 116). Francis Ianni (1974) notes that this "queer ladder" had organized crime as the first few rungs:

> The Irish came first, and early in this century they dominated crime as well as big-city po-

litical machinations. As they came to control the political machinery of large cities they won wealth, power and respectability through subsequent control of construction, trucking, public utilities and the waterfront. By the 1920s and the period of prohibition and speculation in the money markets and real estate, the Irish were succeeded in organized crime by the Jews, and Arnold Rothstein, Lepke Buchalter and Gurrah Shapiro dominated gambling and labor racketeering for over a decade. The Jews quickly moved into the world of business and the professions as more legitimate avenues to economic and social mobility. The Italians came next. . . . (1974: 13–14)

According to this thesis, each successive immigrant group experienced *strain* to which some members reacted by *innovating* in accord with a tradition that had been established by earlier American entrepreneurs—the "robber barons." Ethnic succession results when a group experiences success in crime, and legitimate opportunities thereby become more readily available. Strain subsides, and the group moves out of organized crime, creating an opportunity for innovation for the succeeding immigrant group. According to this thesis, persons involved in organized crime are not committed to a deviant subculture but are merely using available, albeit illegal, opportunity to achieve economic success.

Ianni states that ethnic succession is continuing, that "the Italians are leaving or being pushed out of organized crime [, and] they are being replaced by the next wave of migrants to the city: blacks and Puerto Ricans" (1974: 14). While they may not have been obvious to Ianni when he was conducting his research in New York during the early 1970s, today we would have to add other ethnic and national groups: Cubans, Chinese, Colombians, Dominicans, Jamaicans, Mexicans, Nigerians, Russians, and outlaw motorcycle clubs. According to the ethnic succession thesis, involvement in organized crime is simply a rational response to economic conditions.

Family Legacy

In the first edition of this book (1981b: 29), I theorized that "we may yet experience the Meyer Lansky Foundation and Carlo Gambino University." A decade later, Thomas Gambino, then 62, a graduate of Manhattan College and president of the Gambino Medical and Science Foundation, donated $2 million to Long Island Jewish–Hillside Medical Center and thousands more to Mount Sinai Medical Center in Manhattan. The Gambino foundation gives an average of $250,000 annually to Long Island Jewish Hospital, where a children's bone-marrow-transplant unit is named for the family ("The Smoking Gun" 1998).

Thomas Gambino is reputed to be a captain in the crime Family that bears his father's name. In 1992 he and his brother, Joseph, then 55, agreed to quit New York City's garment center and pay a fine of $12 million in exchange for not being imprisoned. The brothers had been accused of restraint of trade violations (Blumenthal 1992). In 1996, Thomas entered a federal prison to begin serving a five-year sentence for overseeing gambling and loansharking operations for the Gambino crime Family in Connecticut.

Bettmann/Corbis

In Brooklyn, many relatives and close friends, including top Mafia lieutenants, attended the funeral Mass for Carlo Gambino, patriarch of the Gambino Family and father of Thomas and Joseph. Gambino died of natural causes in 1974.

OC and the Media

Other theorists reject this one-dimensional view. Organized crime, they argue, provides important psychic rewards and meaningful social structures. Young Italian-American males from middle-class circumstances continue to be drawn by the allure of *Cosa Nostra*—a romanticization of the mob kept alive in certain neighborhoods (enclaves)—and reinforced by media representations. Being "connected" brings prestige, and in the social environment inhabited by wiseguys—bars, restaurants, nightclubs—a privileged status is evident. The "wannabe" outlaw is socialized into an exciting world where he eagerly adopts the attitude, behavior pattern, and even the clothing styles exemplified by wiseguys.

An example was the rise of a notorious gang of Italian-American hoodlums in the Pleasant Avenue section of Harlem, a Mafia stronghold. Dubbed the Purple Gang, apparently after the murderous Detroit (Jewish) mob of Prohibition days, they were used as "muscle" and executioners in many gangland murders, and their reputation for violence made them very useful to the Mafia leadership. The Purple Gang has been involved in numerous rackets, particularly drug trafficking, aided by their contacts with young men of other ethnic backgrounds who have access to importation quantities of heroin and cocaine. In his study of some members of the Purple Gang, Peter Lupsha (1983) found that they tend to have been born between 1946 and 1951 and to be third-generation Italian-Americans who are related by blood and marriage. While they come from the Pleasant Avenue neighborhood, most reside in the Bronx or suburban Westchester County: "They are now, like many New York suburbanite businessmen, commuters to the old neighborhood for work, money, and visiting rather than residents" (1983: 76). Many Purple Gang members have been "made"—inducted into membership in traditional OC Families in New York. Similar groups have been identified.

Journalist Mike McAlary (1998) has been following the exploits of a group of young Italian-Americans known as the "Tanglewood Boys"—they used the Tanglewood Shopping Center in suburban Yonkers, New York, as a hangout. Six of the post-adolescent gangsters had fathers who were members of New York's OC Families. The Tanglewood Boys committed armed robberies and murders, some for personal reasons, others for reasons related to business.

In Queens, the "Giannini crew" consisted of young men who worked for three of the New York City crime Families—their hangout is the Caffe Giannini on Fresh Pond Road in Ridgewood. They began their criminal careers in the late 1980s as a violent street gang affiliated with an older set of men, the Ridgewood Boys, some of whom had ties to organized crime. Federal officials describe the group as a "farm team" for organized crime. In 2001, when one of the Giannini crew, age 28, pled guilty to racketeering, he described several murders as if they were trips to the dry cleaners (Feuer 2001). During a recent visit to New York, an OC insider explained to this writer that while older wiseguys may try to hide OC affiliations from their offspring, the sons and daughters discover the truth during adolescence. He noted that without any encouragement—and even discouragement—from their fathers, some young men take advantage of their fathers' reputation to form crews of OC aspirants. Why? They are attracted by the allure of organized crime, the wiseguy lifestyle.

Entry into organized crime, states Lupsha (1981: 22), is not based on blocked aspirations—that is, on anomie or strain. Rather, it "is a rational choice, rooted in one perverse aspect of our values; namely, that only 'suckers' work, and that in our

The New Wiseguys

"These 'men of honor' who once swore a blood oath to live and die by the gun, now do their swearing from the witness stand while their agents negotiate book deals and peddle movie rights. Now the only people making offers that can't be refused are the authorities who run the Witness Protection Program and the producers who run Hollywood" (Anastasia 1998: 23).

society, one is at liberty to take 'suckers' and seek easy money." In fact, the term for a member of traditional OC, "wiseguy," exemplifies such an attitude. Nicholas Pileggi (1985: 20) presents Paul ("Paulie") Vario, a powerful *caporegime* in the Lucchese crime Family, as an example:

> Paulie was always asking me for stolen credit cards whenever he and his wife, Phyllis, were going out for the night. Paulie called stolen credit cards "Muldoons," and he always said that liquor tastes better on a Muldoon. The fact that a guy like Paul Vario, a *capo* in the Lucchese crime family, would even consider going out on a social occasion with his wife and run the risk of getting caught using a stolen credit card might surprise some people. But if you knew wiseguys you would know right away that the best part of the night for Paulie came from the fact that he was getting over on somebody.

With a great deal of insight, Pileggi (1985: 36) captures the wiseguy attitude toward society: "They lived in an environment awash in crime, and those who did not partake were simply viewed as prey. To live otherwise was foolish. Anyone who stood waiting his turn on the American pay line was beneath contempt." According to this view, OC comprises a deviant subculture to which members have a commitment that is not mitigated by the absence of strain. As one Gambino crime Family member told a reporter, "[W]e don't want to be part of your world. We don't want to belong to country clubs" (Brenner 1990: 181). Benjamin ("Lefty") Ruggiero of the Bonanno Family explained that "As a wiseguy you can lie, you can cheat, you can steal, you can kill people—*legitimately*. You can do any goddamn thing you want,

and nobody can say anything about it. Who wouldn't want to be a wiseguy?" (Pistone 1987: 330).

But while such young men appear to enjoy playing the wiseguy role—often outfitted with large pinkie rings and gold chains, and other symbols of gangster chic—many are neither bright nor tough.[2] As journalist George Anastasia notes, "they value form over substance" (1998: 25). The long, neighborhood-based apprenticeships through which OC chooses the cream of the "wannabes" are history. Those accepted into membership are often not the tough, street-smart, stand-up kids of yesteryear, but rather social failures and potential informants quick to play "I've got a secret"—to turn on their closest associates to avoid incarceration. As one knowledgeable Chicago detective explains, "the Outfit lacks quality control." Psychiatrists would point out that psycho/sociopaths have a weak sense of loyalty.

The relationship between certain insular—*defended*—neighborhoods and organized crime also appears to be undergoing change. For example, the traditional symbiosis was violated by the young, newly initiated members of the Nicky Scarfo group in South Philadelphia, who intimidated and abused neighborhood people who had once been cultivated with favors by the older criminals. In Bensonhurst, Brooklyn, young members of the Lucchese Family—perhaps hastily recruited because of the death and imprisonment of older members—set up a crack cocaine business that sold drugs to neighborhood youngsters (Kennedy 1996; Volkman 1998).

---

[2] However, some do have a college education. Two older "players," Thomas Gambino, son of boss Carlo Gambino and a *caporegime* in that crime Family, is a college graduate, as is Jack Tocco, boss of the Detroit crime Family.

Also Not Rocket Scientists

He was called "Frankie the Beast" because of his skill in using a baseball bat on victims. This enforcer for the Colombo Family spotted the concealed video camera and turned to a very fearful Vinnie, the informant who had led him into an elaborate FBI sting: "Hey, looks like a great [security] system you got here, Vinnie." His *capo*, he explained, was looking for a security system for his home. Vinnie had one installed, *gratis* (Bonavolonta and Duffy 1996: 148).

In New York, young men raised in comfortable middle-class circumstances have advanced into organized crime in a most violent way. For example, Roy DeMeo of Brooklyn, a second-generation American of Neapolitan heritage, became a loanshark while still in his teens. His uncle was a star prosecutor in the Brooklyn District Attorney's Office. But at age 32, in order to protect an extortion scheme run with his partner, a member of the Gambino Family, Roy committed his first murder—a solo job using a silencer-equipped pistol. He subsequently put together a crew of active criminals from the (middle-class) Canarsie section of Brooklyn. Their first murder victim, a car dealer who was testifying against them before a Brooklyn grand jury, was kidnapped, stabbed repeatedly, and dismembered. The medical examiner who handled the case, Dr. Dominick DiMaio, did not know that his cousin Roy DeMeo—his branch of the family spelled the name differently—was responsible for the murder. DeMeo was initiated into the Gambino Family, and his crew eventually killed and usually dismembered an estimated 75 persons; most of the bodies were never found. In fact, contrary to mob custom, Roy DeMeo added murder-for-hire to his repertoire, and against the edict of the Gambino Family boss dealt in cocaine. One of DeMeo's leading assassins was arrested and began providing evidence against the Gambino Family. Soon afterward, in 1983, at age 42, DeMeo was the victim of a volley of shots fired into his head at close range (Mustain and Capeci 1992).

Ianni (1972) described the "Lupollos," the Italian OC Family he studied, whose core members are all related by blood or marriage. In the fourth generation, "only four out of twenty-seven males are involved in the family business organiza-

tion. The rest are doctors, lawyers, college teachers, or run their own businesses" (1972: 193).

Ianni argued that ethnic succession continues (1974: 12): "We shall witness over the next decade the systematic development of what is now a scattered and loosely organized pattern of emerging black control in organized crime into the Black Mafia." Gus Tyler (1975: 178) did not find Ianni convincing, claiming that Ianni's evidence "consists of a pimp with a stable of seven hookers, a dope pusher, a fence who dabbles in loan sharking and gambling, a con man who gets phony insurance policies for gypsy cabs, and a numbers racketeer, etc." Tyler points out that although these activities are "organized," they are not in a class with white organized crime either qualitatively or quantitatively. Indeed, early in his (1974) book, Ianni reports that the brother and partner of the aforementioned "dope pusher," actually a large-scale heroin dealer in Paterson, New Jersey, was found sans genitals—a "message" from the "White Mafia." As for blacks and Latinos replacing Italians in OC, Lupsha (1981) argues that black and Latino groups have only succeeded in controlling markets that Italian-American groups have discarded because of poor risk-to-profit ratios. Lupsha (1981: 22) questions the "ethnic succession" thesis. He argues that despite Ianni's (1972, 1974) limited findings, Italian organized crime figures who have gained economic status are not leaving organized crime, and in many instances, their progeny have followed them into OC. This view certainly has empirical support—there are dozens of contemporary OC members whose children have followed them into "the life." A meeting between John Gotti, boss of the Gambino Family, and Vincent ("Chin") Gigante, boss of the Genovese Family, reveals their different attitudes toward offspring following them into organized crime. As Gambino underboss Sam Gravano reports, "One thing I'll never forget from that meeting, was John telling Chin in sort of a proud way that his son, John Junior, had just been made. Chin said, 'Jeez, I'm sorry to hear that'" (Maas 1997: 239–40). A journalist quotes Colombo Family *caporegime* Salvatore ("Big Sal"—350 pounds) Miciotta: "Only a real *gavone* [lowlife] wants for his kids what we got. . . . Idiots and wannabes are who's attracted to this life now" (Goldberg 1999: 27). The shrinking of Italian neighborhoods, notes Ronald Goldstock, former director of the New York State Organized Crime Task Force, "results in a lack of gangs, which means that there are no minor leagues to supply the majors" (Goldberg 1999: 71). A development affecting ethnic succession in OC is the arrival of relatively large numbers of southern Italian immigrants into the New York metropolitan area during the 1960s—"Zips."

Zips

The connection between the criminal organizations of southern Italy—Mafia, Camorra, 'Ndrangheta—and American organized crime are the *Zips*,[3] recent immigrants from the *Mezzogiorno*. Many are *mafiosi* fleeing intense pressure from Italian law enforcement and murderous factional conflicts between competing Mafia, Camorra, and 'Ndrangheta groups (discussed in Chapter 7): "Their entry to the United States was made particularly easy by the reversal of a restrictive immigration statute that had discriminated against southern and eastern Europeans" (PCOC 1986a: 53). Any number are related to members of traditional OC groups in New York. According to police sources in New York City, some of these Zips have been admitted to membership in traditional OC Families while many more are operating in their own associations independent of, but in cooperation with, traditional crime groups. They have been particularly active in heroin trafficking. Using drug profits, Zips have opened strip malls containing bakeries, tobacco shops, cafes, newspaper stands, and limousine service storefronts. They are essentially reproducing the small-scale neighborhood life in which organized crime has traditionally felt most comfortable.

Among Italian-American crime groups in the United States, there has been a demand for criminal labor, particularly in the highly rewarding but dangerous enterprise of drug trafficking. Southern Italy has provided a vast labor market for Italian-American drug trafficking organizations: "In southern Italy, *mafia* and *camorra* groups can rely on a 'reserve army' of individuals prepared to endanger their own—and other people's—lives in the execution of especially risky and violent tasks, because the problem of inner-city environment and youth unemployment are growing continually worse in the *Mezzogiorno*, so that the supply of criminal labour is continually increasing" (Arlacchi 1986: 194). In Naples and the surrounding Campania area, for example, the *Nuova Camorra Organizzata* of Raffaele Cutolo[4] recruited young boys, most under 14—the Italian penal code exempts them from punishment—to commit murders and deliver heroin: "For a child growing up in the slums of Naples, amid daily violence and where only the strong and cunning are admired, the Camorra bosses grow to idol stature" (Schmetzer 1985: 4).

Ties between traditional organized crime and the Zips were highlighted during the "Pizza Connection" case concluded in 1987. Former Sicilian Mafia boss Tommaso Buscetta was a prosecution witness in the trial of 22 defendants.[5] A Mafia group headed by Gaetano Badalamenti, then 64, an ousted *capomafioso* from Cinisi, Sicily, was found to have supplied heroin with a total value in excess of $1.6 billion to a group headed by Salvatore ("Totò") Catalano, then 46, a captain in the Bonanno crime Family of New York. Catalano[6] ar-

---

[3]The term is an allusion to the immigrants' rapid speech in Italian dialect.

[4]While Raffaele was in prison, his sister Rosetta ran his crime Family, one of the most important in Naples (Stille 1995a).

[5]For an exciting journalistic look at the "Pizza Connection" investigation, see Blumenthal (1988a) and also Alexander (1988).

[6]Catalano is serving a 45-year federal sentence.

rived in the United States from Sicily in 1961 and headed a crew of Zips in the Knickerbocker Avenue section of Brooklyn. The Sicilian defendants purchased morphine base in Turkey and processed it in Sicily. Pizza parlors in the United States owned by the defendants were used in the drug trafficking.

Two men implicated in the case were with Bonanno crime Family underboss Carmine Galente in a Brooklyn restaurant when he was shot down in 1977 (discussed in Chapter 3). Baldo Amato (born in 1952) and Cesare Bonventre (born in 1951), both Zips and cousins of Joseph Bonanno, for whom the Family is named, helped set up Galente's murder on behalf of Family boss Phil Rastelli.[7] Sicilian-born Gerlando Sciascia, 65, a major heroin dealer and Bonnano Family *caporegime* in charge of a crew of Zips, was shot at close range in 1999, and his body was dumped on a Bronx street (Capeci 1999b).

One of the important Zip drug organizations was led by several Sicilian cousins of Carlo Gambino and headquartered in Cherry Hill, New Jersey:

> Although related to the late crime boss Carlo Gambino of New York, the New Jersey Gambino drug operations are independent from the New York family. There are direct lines of communication and influence based on actual blood ties between the New Jersey Gambinos and other traditional organized crime families in New York. Gambino family members own significant interests in the pizza industry in South Jersey and parts of Pennsylvania. These businesses have been used for concealing illegal immigrants, for laundering money, and for storing drugs. They are known to have employed illegal aliens and other nonfamily members who were more experienced in drug trafficking to smuggle heroin into and transport it within the United States. (Permanent Subcommittee on Investigations 1983a: 134)

With permission from Philadelphia crime Family boss Angelo Bruno, several "Cherry Hill Gambinos" operated pizza shops, restaurants, and a disco in the city of Brotherly Love, including the brothers Giuseppe and Giovanni Gambino. Giovanni was a fugitive from an Italian conviction for heroin trafficking and a *caporegime* in the Gambino Family under John Gotti; Giuseppe is a soldier in that Family. A third brother, Rosario, is serving a 45-year sentence for heroin trafficking. In 1984, after a six-week trial, four Cherry Hill Gambinos were convicted in Newark federal court of marketing heroin in South Jersey. The 1993 trial of Giuseppe and Giovanni Gambino and two of their associates resulted in a mistrial. They were convicted of bail-jumping.

The Zips and their American counterparts "share similar customs, criminal philosophies and a common heritage. The prototype of the crime Family is identical in each system" (PCOC 1986a: 53). In criminal and law enforcement circles, however, their "Old World" ways have earned the Zips more fear and respect than their American counterparts. Just how many Zips are in the United States is not clear, but they are believed to be concentrated in the Northeast, particularly in the New York City area. Other groups are known to be located in Boston, Buffalo, Chicago, Philadelphia, Houston, and Dallas.

CONCLUSION

While *strain* can help explain why some persons from disadvantaged groups become involved in organized crime, it fails to provide a satisfying explanation for the continued existence of traditional organized crime. In other words, while poverty and limited economic opportunity can certainly impel one toward innovative activities, they do not explain why middle-class youngsters become involved in organized crime or why crimes by the wealthy and the powerful—for example, massive savings and loan industry fraud,[8] securities fraud,

---

[7]In 1984 the body of Bonventre was found stuffed into two barrels in a Garfield, New Jersey, warehouse.

[8]See Tillman and Pontell (1995).

insider trading, and collusive agreements—continue to be a problem in the United States. Perhaps the mind-set we are referring to as "wiseguy" transcends socioeconomic boundaries. In fact, organized criminal activity on a rather outrageous scale—for example, by robber barons—without necessarily being connected to conditions of *strain*, has been an important part of American history.

In recent years, however, the ranks of traditional organized crime have been thinned by successful federal prosecutions using the RICO statute (discussed in Chapter 14)—particularly the long, double-digit sentences typically handed down. Whether or not the Italian-American community and the Zips will be able to provide sufficient replacements to keep traditional organized crime viable in the years to come remains an open question. In the meantime, new criminal groups are emerging that may prove to be more powerful and difficult to combat than those of traditional organized crime. Gary Potter (1994) concludes that, historically, "ethnic succession" appears to be a dubious concept. Instead, he argues, new groups become part of organized crime, but they do not necessarily *replace* the older groups. This would appear to be the case with members of Italian-American organized crime, whose strong subcultural orientations have resisted changes in their economic status. In later chapters we will examine these emerging criminal organizations.

Prohibition was the turning point that allowed Jews and Italians to ascend the crooked ladder provided by participation in organized crime. In the United States, culture conflict between earlier and later immigrants created a demand from the latter for goods and services outlawed by the former. This led to the creation of gambling syndicates and the infamous criminal organizations of the Prohibition era. Today, alcohol and various forms of gambling are legally available in most areas of the country, while the outlawing of certain chemicals enjoyed by a large minority of the population provides continuing incentive and opportunity for criminal innovation. Though the Jews, largely in New York, were the next group to dominate organized crime, they quickly turned to business and the professions. Prohibition affected the Italian gangsters in a manner different than earlier immigrant groups. Prior to Prohibition, ethnic organized crime was restricted to the local community. Prohibition encouraged the creation of city- and region-wide criminal organizations that allowed Italian gangsters to consolidate their power and keep it longer.

The increasing scale and complexity of modern life have altered the social structure of urban communities. Greater social mobility has marked the end of many ethnically defined neighborhoods. Racket subcultures vanished as residents found jobs, became educated, and moved to the suburbs. While it may signal the beginning of the end of traditional Italian-American organized crime, it does not signal the end of organized crime as a method of crime or as a means by which members on the lowest rungs of the American ladder of social mobility achieve wealth. Italian-Americans are now being overshadowed by emerging criminal groups that are using the drug trade much as their organized crime predecessors did bootlegging. But these criminal groups lack the incubation provided by corrupt urban political machines and ineffective federal law enforcement, the focus of Chapter 3.

INTERNET CONNECTIONS

Crime theory: **crimetheory.com**

Organized crime history: **crimelibrary.com/gangsters**

REVIEW QUESTIONS

1. How does Robert Merton's theory of anomie explain organized crime?
2. How is differential association (Edwin Sutherland) relevant to explaining entry into organized crime?
3. How does cultural transmission (Shaw and McKay) explain the continuity of organized crime in certain neighborhoods?
4. What do Cloward and Ohlin (differential opportunity) say about organized crime?
5. What qualities of the delinquent subculture correlate well with the prerequisites of organized crime?
6. What is meant by the "defended neighborhood"?
7. How does social control theory explain the emergence of organized crime?
8. What is the theory of "ethnic succession"?
9. Why did Italians remain in organized crime so long? What factors explain the exit of Italian-Americans from organized crime?
10. How have the Zips affected ethnic succession theory?

♠

CHAPTER 3

THE HISTORY OF ORGANIZED CRIME IN THE UNITED STATES

It is virtually impossible to present an accurate history of organized crime in the United States. This is not for lack of material, which is abundant. But quantity cannot replace quality, and the latter is the problem. This chapter presents a history of organized crime in the United States and its historical antecedents. But first, we need to note the shortcomings—sources of information.

ORGANIZED CRIME: SOURCES OF INFORMATION

Writers on organized crime tend to rely on unsubstantiated accounts of informers or on the ideological preconceptions of law enforcement agencies (Block 1978). John Galliher and James Cain (1974: 69) point to the lack of scholarly material relating to organized crime, noting that the dominant literature is either journalistic, tending toward sensationalism, or consists of government documents: "There are two troublesome aspects to this reliance on such sources, one empirical, the other political. In arriving at conclusions and statements

of fact, the journalist or political investigator is not bound by the canons of scientific investigation as is the social scientist." They note the journalist's need to quickly produce exciting copy even at the expense of "careful accumulation and sifting of information characteristic of scientific investigation."

Organized crime reporting is an area of journalism that appears to lend itself to the use of dubious sources with a corresponding absence of corroboration. Jonathan Rubinstein and Peter Reuter (1978a: 57) state that "the difficulty the government had in obtaining accurate information on the reserves of energy-producing companies in the wake of the 1973 oil boycott should serve as a sober reminder of how difficult it is to collect accurate information even from legitimate organizations operating in a highly regulated environment. The challenges are immeasurably greater in collecting information about people who are consciously involved in illegal activities." The executive editor of the *New York Times* was troubled by information coming from law enforcement sources who request anonymity. We are "getting stuff out of law enforcement agencies who are letting that information out for reasons of their own or because of carelessness but are not prepared to take responsibility for it" (Rosenthal 1988: 9). Even a member of the President's Commission on Organized Crime (discussed later), at a briefing for reporters, insisted that information be attributed to an unnamed official ("Washington Talk" 1986). A specialist on organized crime who worked for the FBI for 20 years stated that the government regularly leaked false reports to the press in order to stir up dissension among organized crime figures (Villano 1978).

In one week in 1977, major news stories appeared in the *New York Times* (Franks 1977) and *New York* magazine (Meskil 1977) revealing that New York-born (in 1910) Carmine ("Lilo") Galente of the Bonanno Family was emerging as the new *capo di tutti capi*, "boss of all bosses." In 1962, Galente, then Bonanno Family underboss, was imprisoned in a drug case that also netted crime boss Vito Genovese. In 1977, Galente had been out of prison only a few months. Paul Meskil stated that law enforcement officials thought Galente's immediate goal was to bring all five New York crime Families under his direct control. According to these officials, he would succeed: "Soon, federal agents predict, Carmine Galente's peers on the Mafia Commission will elect him boss of all bosses" (1977: 28). As Lucinda Franks added, "Officials say that Mr. Galente is moving to merge the five New York crime families under his own leadership and aims to become a national chieftain who would try to restore the Mafia to a position of power it has not held in at least 20 years" (1977: 34).

Jerry Capeci (1978: 28), writing in *New York*, reported the *real* "godfather" to be Frank ("Funzi") Tieri, a 74-year-old Brooklyn mob leader. He stated that Carmine Galente was being proclaimed boss of all bosses as "the result of a well-planned 'leak' by the Drug Enforcement Administration of a 'confidential' report by its Unified Intelligence Division." Capeci added: "It now turns out that the report was based on quite old information and was leaked in self-interest by the drug agency." In fact, Galente was resented by other Family bosses for his extensive drug traffick-

ing enterprises. Instead of distancing himself from the trade, Galente directed his men to expand drug operations (Coffey and Schmetterer 1991).

On July 12, 1979, Galente was dining in the backyard of Joe and Mary's Restaurant, in the Bushwick section of Brooklyn, a Bonanno Family stronghold. As he pushed away his empty plate and placed a cigar in his mouth, "four Bonanno button men, including the father-and-son hit team of 'Sonny Red' and Bruno Indelicato, swung open the small wooden door leading from the restaurant and entered the backyard. Without warning they opened fire with shotguns and automatic pistols" (Coffey and Schmetterer 1991: 32).[1] The would-be *capo di tutti capi* was dead.

In 1974 a book by Martin Gosch and Richard Hammer, *The Last Testament of Lucky Luciano*, was purported to have been dictated by Luciano himself during the final months of his life. The book's introduction explains that in 1961, Luciano decided to provide the details of his life as a crime boss to Gosch. According to the introduction, the syndicate, acting on orders from Meyer Lansky, vetoed a movie that Gosch was producing: *The Lucky Luciano Story*. Luciano, who was living in exile in Italy at the time, was to be technical advisor, and now he was angry. However, according to Gosch, who died of a heart attack before publication, Luciano extracted a promise that his autobiography not be published earlier than ten years after his death; he died in 1962. The book earned more than $1 million before it was even published, and paperback rights were auctioned for an additional $800,000 (Gage 1974).

On December 17, 1974, in a front-page article, Nicholas Gage of the *New York Times* questioned the authenticity of the book, pointing to numerous errors of fact: "It is widely known that Mr. Gosch met on a number of occasions with Mr. Luciano on the aborted film project, and

---

[1]Bruno Indelicato was promoted to captain as a result of the Galente killing. In 1986 he was sentenced in federal court to 20 years for the murder and paroled in 1998 at age 51. He is married to Cathy Burke, daughter of the notorious Jimmy Burke, whose central role in the multi-million-dollar Lufthansa robbery was portrayed in the film *Goodfellas* (Rashbaum 2001a).

Organized Crime 101

Federal prosecutors hoped that the former Colombo associate would prove to be a credible witness in a racketeering case. But the imprisoned would-be informant needed information—about the inner workings of organized crime. He asked a fellow prisoner, an OC informant, for help. In response, that inmate wrote a six-page manual de- scribing crime Family structure, operational strate- gies, mediation of disputes, and so on. The docu- ment was full of such phrases as "hierarchy form of government" and "inborn Machiavellian guileful- ness" (Editorial, *New York Daily News,* January 18, 1993: 24).

presumably the gangster recounted some of his ex- periences during these meetings. But contradic- tions and inaccuracies in the book raise questions to the claim that Mr. Luciano told his whole life to Mr. Gosch and that everything in the book attrib- uted to Mr. Luciano actually came from him." For example, the book was incorrect on how and when Luciano gained the nickname "Lucky" and con- tained an alleged firsthand account about one event that actually occurred two years after Lu- ciano died.

The situation has been further complicated by the rash of "true crime" portrayals and the publicity-seeking activities of those peddling their stories (Pooley 1992: 45): "The thirst for reality- based entertainment has created an entertain- ment-based reality—book and movie projects about celebrated cases now become issues in those cases, as defense lawyers point to Hollywood money as a motive for cops to twist investigations or for witnesses to lie on the stand," and, as Eric Pooley notes, "just about every wiseguy entering the federal witness-protection program thinks about selling his memoirs."

Public policy with respect to organized crime is the result of the interaction of the news media, public opinion, and government. Government can influence the media by providing "anonymous sources," by leaking information, or by holding press conferences and public hearings. Investiga- tions by fact-finding bodies, congressional com- mittees, and presidential commissions have often provided the grist for news media mills, which in turn form public opinion about organized crime. This has led to increased allocations for investiga-

tive agencies and new laws for dealing with orga- nized crime. A symbiotic relationship exists among media representations, including fictional ac- counts such as *The Godfather,* public reaction, and governmental activity. One (or more) can trigger activity by the others.

The problem inherent in presenting an accu- rate history of organized crime is highlighted by a 1931 incident. On September 10, 1931, Salvatore Maranzano, the self-appointed American Mafia *capo di tutti capi,* was killed by gunmen dispatched by Meyer Lansky and Bugsy Siegel at the request of Lucky Luciano—a historic event in interethnic criminal cooperation. As Donald Cressey (1969: 44) reports, "On that day and the two days imme- diately following, some forty Italian–Sicilian gang leaders across the country lost their lives in battle." Fred Cook (1972: 107–108) refers to this episode as the "Purge of the Greasers": "Within a few short hours, the old-time crime bosses who had been born and reared in Sicily and were mostly il- literate—the 'Mustache Petes' or 'the greasers,' as they were sometimes called—were liquidated by the new breed of Americanized, business-oriented gangsters of the Luciano–Costello–Adonis school." Cook adds: "Beginning on September 11th and lasting through the next day, some thirty to forty executions were performed across the na- tion." A special publication of *New York* (Plate 1972) adds to the story: "During the bloodbath nearly 40 of the Old Guard were executed in vari- ous ingenious ways." In 1978 this episode was dubbed "the 'Night of the Sicilian Vespers' . . . be- cause Luciano had not only engineered the slaugh- ter of Salvatore Maranzano for the night of Sep-

Life Imitating Art

Robert Delaney, an undercover detective for the New Jersey State Police, testified before the Permanent Subcommittee on Investigations (1981b: 372):

Mr. Delaney: The movies *Godfather I* and *Godfather II* have had an impact on these crime families. Some of the members and associates would inquire of me, had I seen the movie? I said yes. They would reply that they'd seen it three and four times. One young man said he'd seen it ten times. At dinner one night at a restaurant, Patrick Kelly and I were with Joseph Doto, who is the son of Joseph Adonis [a powerful crime figure who was deported in 1953] and known as Joey Adonis, Jr. Joey Adonis, Jr. gave the waiter a pocketful of quarters and told him to play the juke box contin-

uously and to play the same song, the theme music from the "Godfather." All through dinner, we listened to the same song, over and over.

Senator [Sam] Nunn: In other words, you are saying sometimes they go to the movie to see how they themselves are supposed to behave, is that right?

Mr. Delaney: That is true. They had a lot of things taught to them through the movie. They try to live up to it. The movie was telling them how.

Gambino Family underboss Sam Gravano recalls seeing *The Godfather:* "I left that movie stunned. I mean I floated out of the theater. Maybe it was fiction, but for me, then, that was our life" (Maas 1997: 72). Indeed, Gravano was known to quote from *The Godfather* and loved to imitate Al Pacino.

---

tember 10, 1931, but had gone ahead and wiped out 40 of the 'Mustache Petes' across the country" (Capeci 1978: 26).[2]

In fact, there was no nationwide purge of "Mustache Petes"; only three murders, all occurring in New York and reported by that city's newspapers, could be traced to the Maranzano execution: "A careful examination of newspapers issued during September, October, and November of 1931 in twelve large cities . . . turned up evidence of only one killing that occurred at about the time Maranzano died and might have been [but apparently wasn't] linked to the death of the 'Boss of Bosses'" (Nelli 1976: 183). Thus, concludes Humbert Nelli, the "purge" applied only to New York, and the message was clear: "any oldtimers still permitted to live had better accept and adjust to the new order" (1974: 182). Nevertheless, the story continues to be presented in popular books on organized crime. *Mafia Dynasty* (Davis 1993: 42) tells us of the Luciano-ordered purge: "By the time it was over, sixty Maranzano loyalists had been killed."

---

[2]The source of this story appears to be a book (Powell 2000) originally published in 1939.

THE ROBBER BARONS

"Al Capone," notes Michael Woodiwiss (1987: 8), "was not the first ruthless entrepreneur to combine with thugs, gunmen, and government officials and carve out an illegal fortune. But the expression—'organised crime'—was not commonly used until the 1920s and the Prohibition era when academics and newspaper editors found it to be a convenient new label for an old phenomenon." While contemporary organized crime has its roots in Prohibition (1920–1933), unscrupulous American business entrepreneurs, such as Astor, Carnegie, Vanderbilt, Drew, Gould, Sage, Rockefeller, Stanford, and Morgan, provided role models and created a climate conducive to its growth. These earlier generations of predatory Americans with English, Scottish, Scandinavian, and German ancestry paved the way for later generations of Irish, Jewish, and Italian criminals who, in turn, are being emulated by criminals of Asian, African, Hispanic, and Russian ancestry. Rampant—that is, uncontrolled—capitalism, a feature of nineteenth-century America, is now being experienced by the former Soviet Union, and it too has spawned extensive corruption and organized crime.

(left and right) © Corbis

These late nineteenth-century cartoons reflect popular attitudes toward two of the most powerful and ruthless robber barons of the day. Railroad magnate Cornelius Vanderbilt (left) tightens his stranglehold on the American public, while oil monopolist John D. Rockefeller (right) balances the world in the palm of his hand.

We must understand that the United States, as the Eisenhower Commission[3] pointed out, is quite a violent country (see also Hofstadter and Wallace 1971). Important aspects of U.S. history have hinged on violence, both figurative (for example, "financial piracy") and literal (for example, the use of gunmen, thugs, private police, law enforcement agents, the National Guard, and the military), to further *private* ends. In Chapter 9 we will examine Russian organized crime, whose development in many aspects (including a class of

robber barons) appears to parallel that in the United States.

Lincoln Steffens, writing in 1902, noted that the "spirit of graft and of lawlessness is the American spirit" (1957: 8). With the western frontier closed, with the wealth of the "robber barons" institutionalized and their progeny firmly in control of the economy, there was only modest opportunity for the poor but ambitious adventurers of our urban frontiers. Among these later immigrants— Irish, Jewish, Italian—some have sought to innovate, not on the grand scale of the Vanderbilts, the Goulds, and the Rockefellers, but in a manner more consistent with available opportunity. Many found this opportunity in the politics and vice of

---

[3]National Advisory Commission on the Causes and Prevention of Violence (1969). See also Graham and Gurr (1969).

urban America beginning in the latter half of the nineteenth century.[4]

IMMIGRATION AND URBAN MACHINE POLITICS

Organized crime in America "is the product of an evolutionary process extending more than a century" (Tyler 1962: 89). The roots of organized crime can be found in the politics of urban America prior to Prohibition, in the exemplary patron–client network known as the political machine. The underpinnings of this phenomenon are found in immigrant America and in the role of the Irish.

Immigration into the United States, except for brief depressions, grew dramatically in the years from 1820 to 1850, particularly in urban areas. During those three decades, the population of cities in the East and West quadrupled—New York's population rose to half a million (Bennett 1988). Immigrants and their offspring constituted more than two-thirds of the population of the largest cities in the Northeast and more than three-quarters of the population of New York, Boston, and Chicago (Buenker 1973).

These urban immigrants found employment in the most dangerous, monotonous, and poorly paid industries; women and children often labored as well. They were forced into slum housing reserved for their own ethnic group. Their culture, customs, and religious beliefs and practices were subjected to virulent attack by Americans of earlier stock: "Beset by hostility and discrimination on virtually all sides, the immigrant gradually found that he possessed at least one commodity that some native Americans coveted: his vote" (Buenker 1973: 3). A new breed of broker—the political boss—emerged to channel these votes into a powerful entity known as the "machine."

The necessities of urban America required construction workers, street cleaners, police and firemen, and service workers of all kinds, thus providing the immigrant with his livelihood and the political boss with patronage (Hofstadter 1956). During the 1880s, for example, New York's Tammany Hall had more than 40,000 municipal jobs at its disposal (Erie 1988): "The immigrant, in short, looked to politics not for the realization of high principles but for concrete and personal gains, and he sought these gains through personal relationships. And the boss, particularly the Irish boss, who could see things from the immigrant's angle but could also manipulate the American environment, became a specialist in personal relations and personal loyalties" (Hofstadter 1956: 182).

The Irish

There are strong historical parallels between the repression suffered by Sicilian peasants (discussed in Chapter 7) and that endured by their Irish counterparts. In both cases, this helped shape their culture. Ireland fell under foreign domination in the twelfth century, although it was not until the latter half of the sixteenth century and the reign of Elizabeth I (1533–1603) that England tried to impose Protestantism on the largely Catholic Irish. England used the religious dispute to seize large tracts of the most fertile land in Ireland. Thousands of Protestant Lowland Scots (and to a lesser extent, English) were encouraged to settle in northern Ireland, and they soon owned most of the land. In the south, Oliver Cromwell crushed an Irish rebellion (1649–1650) and parceled out two-thirds of the land to his soldiers and followers (Shannon 1989). Ireland was reduced to a "country of peasants who were constantly oppressed by excessive rents, taxes, and tithes, and for whom poverty was a general condition" (Levine 1966: 5). Prior to Queen Elizabeth's rule, people of the island identified themselves as followers of a particular local chieftain; afterward, they called themselves Irish.

Paradoxically, this environment of misery gave rise to a culture of hospitality and openhandedness. The Irish looked forward to opportunities for social gatherings—even events as sad as death, which meant gathering for an "Irish wake." As in

---

[4]For information about the robber barons and their ilk, see Andrews (1941), Chernow (1990), Holbrook (1953), Josephson (1962), Klein (1986), Klepper et al. (1998), Lloyd (1963), Loth (1938), Myers (1936), O'Connor (1962), Rugoff (1989), Sinclair (1962), Swanberg (1959), and Zilg (1974).

southern Italy, a certain attitude developed: let outsiders, the government, and the world be damned (Shannon 1989). Finding no justice in the formal system of government imposed by the British, the Irish turned to informal mechanisms, bargaining and negotiating for favorable outcomes. The Irish resorted to secret and open organizations on local and national levels as part of their continuous efforts to deal with British oppression. When the franchise was extended to Ireland, the Irish were caught up in the corrupt politics fostered by the British, and they became a thoroughly politicized people (Levine 1966).

Two centuries of personal experience with Anglo-Saxon (British) Protestant government led to a disdain for law among the Irish and provided the knowledge and skill that enabled them to serve an important role in the rough-and-tumble politics of America's urban areas: "The Irish political personality was shaped by confrontation with British imperialism and colonialism. In their efforts to free themselves from anti-Catholic Penal Laws and to achieve national independence, the Irish learned to compete within the context of the Anglo-Saxon political system. They became particularly adroit in the techniques of mass agitation, political organization, confrontation, and liberal, democratic politics" (McCaffrey 1976: 8).

English policy reduced the Irish to abject poverty: "Unless an Irish labourer could get hold of a patch of land and grow potatoes on which to feed himself and his children, the family starved." When the Irish potato crop failed because of a fungus (1845–1847), there was widespread famine that resulted in the deaths of about 1.5 million people (Woodham-Smith 1962: 32). The workhouses, supported by taxes on landowners, were overflowing. The landlords encouraged and sponsored Irish immigration to the United States as a way of easing their tax burden (Wyman 1984).

Once in the United States, the Irish tended to settle in urban areas. Uneducated and often illiterate—the British had denied them educational opportunities—Irish immigrants secured employment as unskilled labor (McCaffrey 1976). But "Irish immigrants came to America with a live political tradition" (Shannon 1989: 15): They "were

the world's greatest experts in the art of warfare without confrontation. They could make alliances without formal conferences, agreements, or treaties that would leave a record. They could act in concert without giving commands but with a clear understanding of who was in charge. These were the lessons they had learned while living under repression. It did not take very long to learn how to apply their underground tactics to a democracy" (Reedy 1991: 22).

Between 1840 and 1844, about a quarter of a million persons from mostly Catholic districts in Ireland entered the United States (Bennett 1988). In a single decade, 1845–1854, almost 1.5 million Irish immigrants entered the United States, and from 1855 until the turn of the century, more than 3 million more arrived. They constituted the first large-scale immigration to the United States of a group since the arrival of Anglo-Saxon Protestants in the 1600s and 1700s. And "although generally peasants in their homeland, most of the new arrivals lacked either the resources or the desire to resume agrarian life. Arriving at a time when available land was scarce and agriculture mechanized, most sought work as unskilled laborers in the burgeoning industrial metropolises" (Buenker 1973: 2); only 6 percent would become farmers (Erie 1988): "By 1870, while only about 10 percent of the country's 29 million native-born whites lived in the big cities, 42 percent of the nation's 1.8 million Irish-born lived in the twenty-five cities with populations greater than 50,000" (Erie 1988: 25). By 1850, more than one-third of New York City's population was Irish (Shannon 1989).

In the United States, the Irish found themselves restricted from upward mobility, which was reserved for middle-class Protestants. In response, Irish immigrants remained in close-knit neighborhoods, where they joined the Democratic Party as an outlet for social and economic advancement. However, "instead of using politics as an avenue to integration into the middle class, politics enveloped the Irish, and the Irish social structure became an integral part of the process of recruiting other Irishmen into both the party and government. As the Irish swarmed into city politics, political office was recognized as the career among them, and politics became the secular extension of their essentially religious identity" (Levine 1966: 5).

Irish Catholic immigrants distrusted the public education system, which was dominated by Protestants: "Most Irish took a dim view of the usefulness of education and left its destiny in the hands of the clergy" (Levine 1966: 87). While Catholic parochial education promoted Irish solidarity, it did not encourage secular intellectual pursuits and higher education: "Before World War I, few Irish boys and girls went on to secondary schools and before World War II few of them enrolled in college" (McCaffrey 1976: 82).

Politics and government employment provided the most readily available road to social mobility. Irish success in politics coincided with a decrease in the substantial crime rate among Irish immigrants—that is, until Prohibition in 1920 suddenly offered a new fast track to economic—albeit crime-based—success: "The Irish, the most numerous and advanced section of the immigrant community, took over the political party (usually the Democratic Party) at the local level and converted it into virtually a parallel system of government" (Shannon 1989: 62). The Irish clan system welded the Irish into a community capable of acting in concert while disregarding the formal governmental and legal structure (Reedy 1991).

Irish success in politics was also advanced by their ability to speak English, their knowledge of government, and the timing of their arrival in the United States. They were also "community-minded, gregarious by nature, fond of visiting and talking" (McCaffrey 1976: 65); "the Irish have, in fact, been a highly social people, gregarious above everything" (Woodham-Smith 1962: 266). The Irish were also "neutral outsiders in the traditional ethnic antipathies and hostilities which the Central and East European ethnic groups brought to America from their homelands. 'A Lithuanian won't vote for a Pole, and a Pole won't vote for a Lithuanian,' according to a Chicago politician. 'A German won't vote for either of them—but all three will vote for a "Turkey," an Irishman'" (Rakove 1975: 33). And there was the Irish connection to the saloon, a refuge from overcrowded slum dwellings: "For many years the saloon was as

important a link in the communications process of the Irish social structure as was the parish church" (Levine 1966: 119). "Irish politicians used Catholic solidarity as a voting base, saloons as political clubs" (McCaffrey 1976: 140).

THE SALOON AND THE MACHINE

Throughout much of urban America, the saloon was a center of neighborhood activity, an important social base for political activity, and saloon keepers became political powers in many cities: "Part of the appeal of the saloon was due to the social services it provided. In saloons files of newspapers in several languages were available along with cigars, mail boxes for regular patrons, free pencils, paper, and mail services to those wishing to send letters, and information on employment. Saloons provided a warm fire in the winter, public toilets, bowling alleys, billiard tables, music, singing, dancing, constant conversation, charity and charge accounts, quiet corners for students, and special rooms for weddings, union meetings, or celebrations. No other institution provided such a variety of necessary services to the public" (Englemann 1979: 4).

City government was fragmented, and power was dispersed. The city was divided into wards or districts, which were both electoral and administrative units containing relatively small numbers of people. The police and police (lower) courts operated on the ward/district level (Haller 1990a). These wards/districts were divided into electoral precincts. In this environment, saloon keepers were in a position to influence their customers and their votes—they could deliver their precincts and thus control the wards or districts. It was only a slight exaggeration to jest that in New York, the easiest way to break up a meeting of Tammany Hall leaders was to open the door and shout "Your saloon's on fire!"

The Constitution does not provide for or even make mention of political parties. Indeed, the Founders perceived the political party as an unnecessary, if not divisive, element in the democratic process. As a result of this constitutional omission, political parties enjoyed the same degree of autonomy as any other voluntary association, despite the reality that a political party often determined the outcome of an election. Until the late 1880s, a political party was a private association and as such determined the method for nominating candidates. The methods used lacked state control; they were informal and often effectively disenfranchised the electorate.

Throughout most of the nineteenth century, each political party provided its own ballots and ballot boxes at the general election—previously, a voter stated his preference in a voice vote. Parties printed their own ballots, called "tickets," in different colors. Voters chose one and placed it in the ballot box under the careful eye of party workers. This system virtually precluded "split-ticket" voting and aided in the buying of votes, because party workers could readily see which ballot a voter cast.[5] This system enabled ward politicians, often with the help of street-corner boys and gangs that proliferated in urban ghettos, to deliver lopsided votes that helped the machine dominate a city. Politicians employed the gangs for legitimate purposes such as distributing campaign literature, hanging posters, and canvassing for votes. They were also used as "repeaters" (who voted early and often) and as sluggers, who attacked rival campaign workers and intimidated voters: "Elections were held at odd hours in odd places, including bars and brothels. Voters seldom were informed of their franchise, and there was frequent intimidation of voters whose loyalties were suspect" (Johnston 1982: 46). With a small following and a willingness to engage in "political hardball," machine politicians could easily win power: "Powerful ward chieftains were often rewarded with a share of the patronage commensurate with their district's share of the total party vote" (Erie 1988: 26).

---

[5]From 1888 to 1890, states began providing the ballots for general elections, placing party labels on these ballots. This made the ballot secret and gave formal recognition to political parties, but only the major political parties. Laws were enacted to restrict third-party access to the new ballot. The treatment of political parties as public entities provided legal justification for government control of the primary elections that followed: "By 1896 all states but one had statutory regulations for nominating candidates for elective office" (Epstein 1986: 166).

The machine politician was usually a popular figure who, in the days before social welfare programs, provided important services to loyal constituents—jobs, food, and assistance in dealing with public agencies, including the police and the courts. All that he asked for in return were votes and a free hand to become wealthy in politics. To the impoverished and powerless ghetto dweller, this was a small price to pay for services that would not otherwise be available. And even when such services became available through government agencies during the Great Depression, the loss of self-respect that this entailed discouraged many from applying. On the other hand, the precinct captain "asks no questions, exacts no compliance with legal rules of eligibility and does not 'snoop' into private affairs" (Merton 1967: 128).

Robert Merton points out that the "political machine does not regard the electorate as an amorphous, undifferentiated mass of voters. With keen sociological intuition, the machine recognizes that the voter is a person living in a specific neighborhood, with specific personal problems and personal wants. Public issues are abstract and remote; private problems are extremely concrete and immediate. It is not through the generalized appeal to large public concerns that the machine operates, but through the direct quasi-feudal relationships between local representatives of the machine and voters in their neighborhood" (1967: 128). "There is nothing satanic about the Chicago machine," notes one newsman. "The basis of its success has always been the machine's dedication to a policy of doing little favors for the people. If a humble householder is getting the runaround from City Hall when he complains about a crew from the Department of Streets and Sanitation smashing up his curbing, a ward committeeman who learns of this will instantly raise hell with 'somebody downtown' and get the curb fixed. The widow who is struggling to make ends meet will get a food basket delivered from the ward office" (O'Connor 1984: 114).

The very personal nature of the machine was noted back in 1931: "In the midst of the current depression, an Irish alderman named Moriarity distributed unleavened bread [matzah] to hundreds of Jewish families in his district, so that they might keep the feast of Passover. This will not cost him any votes" (McConaughy 1931: 312). A Tammany district leader in Manhattan at the turn of the century understood the business of being a political leader: "His job was to see that politics in his district were run efficiently for the purpose for which primarily politics existed. That purpose was to look after the welfare of individuals who resided in the district. . . . Almost any family was likely to want something. Perhaps the father had died and there was not money enough for the funeral. Perhaps one of the boys had been arrested, justly or unjustly. Perhaps a man who had a job on the police force had been dropped or moved to an undesirable location. Perhaps laborers had to be placed in the street cleaning department, or a transfer effected for one of his constituents from one department to another, or an increase in salary negotiated" (Hapgood and Moskowitz 1927: 41).

And when challenged, the machine could fight back with "hardball" tenacity: "Besides voter fraud, emerging machines used repression to weaken their opponents. Irish party bosses were famous for the ingenuity with which they systematically weakened labor and socialist parties. Machine-controlled bureaucrats and judges denied parade and meeting permits. The party's plug-uglies armed with brass knuckles waded into peaceful assemblies. Opposition leaders were frequently arrested on trumped-up charges. For insurgent Jews and Italians, the Irish machines specialized in rigorous enforcement of Sunday closing laws and in punitive denial of business permits" (Erie 1988: 11). By 1890, most big-city Democratic machines were controlled by Irish bosses.

UNDERWORLD AND UPPERWORLD

The machine leader was a master at keeping his ward/district organized, a broker par excellence who was in a key position to perform services for both the captains of industry and the captains of vice. The machine leader mediated among unorganized urban masses, the underworld, and the upperworld. The machine could deliver franchises, access to underdeveloped land sites, government contracts, tax abatements, and other special considerations (Steffens 1931). Once entrenched, the Irish machine bosses quickly built alliances with older-stock business interests (Erie 1988).

In Chicago, corrupt and inefficient government was promoted by business interests: "All factions, Republican and Democratic, were the handmaidens of the business interests" (Gosnell 1977: 8). "Populous and efficient as the underworld is, it could not wield the influence it does if it were not for its financial and political alliance with the inhabitants of Chicago's upperworld. . . . The deal is that the underworld shall have a 'liberal government' and a 'wide open town' and its upper world allies shall be permitted to plunder the public treasury and appropriate wealth belonging to the people" (Dobyns 1932: 8).

In most cities, particularly New York, Philadelphia, St. Louis, and Pittsburgh, "the rough and tumble ward and city bosses allowed the private utilities and favor-seeking men of wealth as well as the purveyors of vice to exploit the great mass of citizens" (Douglas 1974: ix; also Steffens 1957). Merton (1967: 135) notes the irony: "The supporters of the political machine include both the 'respectable' business class elements who are, of course, opposed to the criminal or racketeer and the distinctly 'unrespectable' elements of the underworld."

"Just as the political machine performs services for 'legitimate' business, so it operates to perform not dissimilar services for 'illegitimate' business: vice, crime and rackets" (Merton 1967: 132). In fact, the relationship between the racketeer and the machine was symbiotic: "Not only are the contributions from the underworld interests an important item in the campaign funds of the dominant party, but the services of the underworld personnel are also significant. When word is passed down from the gangster chiefs, all proprietors of gambling houses and speak-easies, all burglars, pick-pockets, pimps, fences, and their like, are whipped into line. In themselves they constitute a large block of votes, and they frequently augment their value to the machine by corrupt election practices" (Gosnell 1977: 42).

In Kansas City, a professional criminal (Audett 1954: 120) writes that he received his orders from gangster chief John Lazia, who was an important part of the Pendergast machine. He looked up vacant lots: "I looked them up, precinct by precinct, and turned them lists in to Mr. Pendergast—that's Tom Pendergast, the man who used to run Kansas City back in them days. When we got a precinct all surveyed out, we would give addresses to them vacant lots. Then we would take the addresses and assign them to people we could depend on—prostitutes, thieves, floaters, anybody we could get on the voting registration books. On election days we just hauled these people to the right places and they went in and voted—in the right places."

In return for "delivering the vote," the ward boss was rewarded with patronage and recognized as lord of his area in a system that resembled feudalism. He appointed, directly or indirectly, police officials in his area, so he was in a position to protect vice activity (gambling, prostitution, liquor-law violations), which he "licensed."

In Kansas City, James Pendergast began his political career as a saloon keeper. He became a dominant power in the First Ward, and his ability to deliver the vote enabled him to provide police protection for organized gambling. The police acted on his behalf, forcing independent operators to join the gambling combine or get out of business. Between 1900 and 1902, Pendergast named 123 of the 173 policemen on the Kansas City force. The Pendergast machine, under brother Tom, received the support of the gang bosses, and they in return secured police protection (Dorsett 1968). This led to the election day outrage of 1934. Despite an estimated 50,000 to 100,000 fake registrations, the machine was taking no chances (Steinberg 1972: 307):

In the streets that morning, long black limousines cruised slowly past voters on their way to the polls and created an atmosphere of fright, for none of the cars had license plates and their passengers looked like gang-

sters. One of the cars did more than cruise. When it rolled past the opposition's headquarters in downtown Kansas City, seven shots were fired through the big window, though miraculously no one inside the crowded office was hit by a bullet. Another car pulled up at the ninth ward center of the opposition, and its passengers rushed inside to beat several persons with blackjacks.

With repeat voters, the beating of opposition voters, and guns and baseball bats at polling places, the Pendergast machine won an overwhelming victory; four persons were killed and dozens beaten.

In Chicago, "the police department generally, and the [38] district stations in particular, were parts of the Democratic political machine. The department was a source of patronage jobs, while aldermen and ward committeemen controlled law enforcement in their districts. In effect, each alderman functioned as the mayor of a community, with the district captain acting as his chief of police. Aldermen would choose their own captains and controlled promotions, assignments, and transfers of personnel" (Bopp 1977: 91).

In New York, "in each district of the city, saloon keepers, owners of houses of prostitution, grocers who wanted to obstruct sidewalks, builders who wanted to violate the building regulations of the City, paid tribute at election time to the district leaders, who turned the money over to the general campaign fund of Tammany Hall. The organization collected not only from those who wished to violate the laws, but also from those who wished to live peacefully without having the windows of their shops smashed by the district leader's gang, or without being unnecessarily molested by the police" (Werner 1928: 293–94; Lardner and Reppetto 2000).

In Kansas City, Chicago, New York, and elsewhere, gambling operators paid heavily for protection, with the understanding that an occasional police raid would have to be staged "for appearances." The raiding squads were careful not to damage furniture or equipment, and policemen obligingly guarded the resort while the gambling operators and their customers made a brief, per-

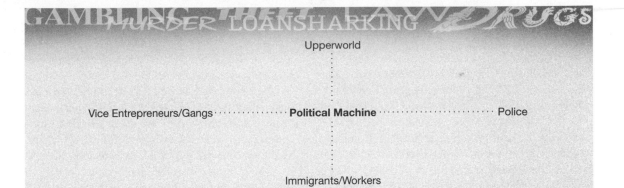

GAMBLING MURDER LOANSHARKING THEFT LAW DRUGS

Upperworld

Vice Entrepreneurs/Gangs · · · · · · · · · · · · · **Political Machine** · · · · · · · · · · · · · · · Police

Immigrants/Workers

The political machine organized and mobilized urban immigrants/workers into a political force through which it dominated city government. Control of government, in particular the police, enabled the machine to protect vice entrepreneurs and gang leaders, who reciprocated with financial and voting support. Control of government en- abled the machine to provide special favors to the captains of business and industry, who recipro- cated with financial support. Control of public and private sector jobs, and funds with which to pro- vide social services, strengthened machine sup- port among the urban masses.

functory appearance before a friendly magistrate before returning to the gaming house to resume play (Commission on the Review of the National Policy Toward Gambling 1976). An extraordinary Kings County (Brooklyn) grand jury, which sat for five years (1938–1942) investigating police corruption in that borough, found bookmaking and policy operations flourishing. Furthermore, the police had "a tendency to make unfounded arrests in order to create a record of apparent efficient law enforcement," and they had a "practice of presenting the evidence in such a manner that a conviction cannot possibly result." An "examination of the plainclothes policemen who were assigned to gambling cases in Kings County during the period covered by this investigation revealed that in all except a few cases the assignment to plainclothes work on gambling violations was accompanied by a distinct change in financial status" (Supreme Court of the State of New York 1942: 5–6).

A special grand jury in Philadelphia in 1928 found that certain members of that city's police department received a total of $2 million in bribes annually (Haller 1985b). As the National Commission on Law Observance and Enforcement concluded (1931: 45), "Nearly all of the large cities suffer from an alliance between politicians and criminals. For example, Los Angeles was controlled by a few gamblers for a number of years. San Francisco suffered similarly some years ago and at one period in its history was so completely dominated by gamblers that three prominent gamblers who were in control of the politics of the city and who quarreled about the appointment of the police settled their quarrel by shaking dice to determine who would name the chief for the first two years, who for the second two years, and who for the third."

REFORM AND NATIVISM

In cities dominated by machine politics, the same ones that would spawn organized crime, a pattern of corruption–reform–corruption–reform was often interspersed with investigations and widely publicized hearings. It is important to recognize the political motivation, and the not-insignificant degree of hypocrisy, behind many of these exposés and reform efforts. In New York, investigations were often initiated by upstate, rural, Protestant

Republican interests against downstate (New York City), urban, Catholic and Jewish Democrats. For example, in 1894 the New York State Senate appointed a special committee, five Republicans and two Democrats, headed by Senator Clarence Lexow of (heavily Republican) Rockland County, to investigate charges of vice and corruption leveled by the Reverend Charles H. Parkhurst. The hearings revealed a sordid tale of corruption. However, the recommendations of the committee, given its findings, were actually quite modest, since they were designed not to correct the problem but to enable Republicans to share in the rich patronage created by the Democratic machine (Fogelson 1977). The threat of investigation and public disclosure was often used to secure the support of city politicians for legislation favored by rural or big-business interests. Corruption was real and often rampant, but many of the efforts purporting to deal with it were just as corrupt—morally, if not legally.

Reform was typically fostered by business leaders for their own ends: "The machine leaders had to be paid to defeat legislation opposed by business interests: municipal ownership, labor legislation, adequate health regulations, better schools, new parks, decent housing, aid to the needy. . . . Businessmen in politics were eager without bribes to oppose anything that raised taxes or threatened private enterprise. They wanted to stop paying graft, but keep all the favors graft bought. They demonstrated that the perennial demand for business methods in government was as logical as a cry that penitentiaries ought to be run by criminals" (Loth 1938: 280).

In Chicago, dishonest, corrupt, and inefficient government was actually promoted by business interests: "All factions, Republican and Democratic, were the handmaidens of the business interests" (Gosnell 1977: 8). "Reform" was frequently a favorable label applied by newspapers to the efforts of two, sometimes overlapping, interest groups: businessmen and white, Anglo-Saxon Protestants, whose voting strength was in rural America: "Most immigrant voters realized instinctively that honesty, efficiency, and economy in government would do nothing to alleviate their condition and could severely cripple the system's ability to dispense favors" (Buenker 1973: 26).

Reformers were often part of the rampant *nativism* that at times intertwined with social Darwinism. Nativism helped tie urban dwellers—immigrants in general, Catholics (and often Jews) in particular—to the political machine. Attitudes of extreme religious prejudice have a long history in our country, dating back to the first colonists. Whereas settlers came to the New World in search of religious freedom, they sought only *their* religious freedom. Virulent anti-Catholicism was such an important part of Colonial America that in the seventeenth century, mass could not be publicly celebrated anywhere except in Pennsylvania. In 1834 a mob of Protestant workmen in Charlestown, Massachusetts, ransacked and burned a convent, the first fruit of Catholic educational enterprise in New England (Bennett 1988). Samuel Morse (1791–1872), distinguished painter, inventor of the telegraph, and son of a prominent minister, wrote that "we are the dupes of our hospitality. The evil of immigration brings to these shores illiterate Roman Catholics, the tools of reckless and unprincipled politicians, the obedient instruments of their more knowing priestly leaders"[6] (quoted in Bennett 1988: 40). In contrast, the machine politician "cultivated the immigrant's ethnic pride by defending him against nativist attack, observing his customs, and concerning himself with conditions in the homeland" (Buenker 1973: 5). The most successful campaign waged by nativist interests involved prohibiting the beverages most favored by immigrants.

PROHIBITION

The acrimony between rural and urban America, between Protestants and Catholics, between Republicans and (non-Southern) Democrats, between "native" Americans and more recent immigrants, and between business and labor reached a pinnacle with the ratification of the Eighteenth

---

[6]Morse was also a strong defender of slavery.

Amendment in 1919. However, efforts at limiting or prohibiting alcohol consumption date back to the earliest days of our Republic. Residents of the United States have traditionally consumed large quantities of alcoholic beverages. In 1785, Dr. Benjamin Rush, surgeon general of the Continental Army and a signer of the Declaration of Independence, wrote a pamphlet decrying the use of alcohol. The pamphlet helped fuel the move toward prohibition and inspired in 1808 the establishment of the first temperance society, whose cause was supported by Protestant churches throughout the country (Hamm 1995).

The temperance movement made great progress everywhere in the country, often accompanying the nativist sentiments that swept over the United States during the late 1840s and early 1850s. In 1869 the Prohibition Party attempted, with only limited success, to make alcohol a national issue. In 1874 the Women's Christian Temperance Union (WCTU) was established, and in 1893 the Anti-Saloon League was organized. Around the turn of the century, both groups moved from efforts to change individual behavior to a campaign for national prohibition. The WCTU was handicapped because its members lacked the franchise—women could not vote. After a period of dormancy, the prohibition movement was revived in the years 1907–1919 (Humphries and Greenberg 1981). By 1910, the Anti-Saloon League had become one of the most effective political action groups in U.S. history. It had mobilized America's Protestant churches behind a single purpose: to enact national prohibition (Tindall 1988). In 1915, nativism and prohibitionism fueled the rebirth of the Ku Klux Klan, which spread into northern states and exerted a great deal of political influence, including control of state politics in Indiana (see Tucker 1991). During World War I, anti-German feelings, already strong, were made more intense because brewing and distilling were associated with German immigrants (Cashman 1981).

Prohibition was accomplished by the political efforts of an economically declining segment of the American middle class: "By effort and some good luck this class was able to impose its will on the majority of the population through rather dra- matic changes in the law" (Chambliss 1973: 10). Andrew Sinclair (1962: 163) points out that "in fact, national prohibition was a measure passed by village America against urban America." We could add much of Protestant America against Catholic (and, to a lesser extent, Jewish) America: "Thousands of Protestant churches held thanksgiving prayer meetings. To many of the people who attended, prohibition represented the triumph of America's towns and rural districts over the sinful cities" (Coffey 1975: 7; Gusfield 1963). Prohibition reflected not only revulsion at drunkenness and contempt for the drinking immigrant masses but also an assault on the pleasures and amenities of city life (Bennett 1988).

Big business was interested in Prohibition as well: alcohol contributed to industrial inefficiency, labor strife, and the saloon that served the interests of machine politics. Workmen's compensation laws also helped stimulate business support for temperance. Between 1911 and 1920, 41 states had enacted workmen's compensation laws: "By making employers compensate workers for industrial accidents the law obligated them to campaign for safety through sobriety. In 1914 the National Safety Council adopted a resolution condemning alcohol as a cause of industrial accidents" (Cashman 1981: 6).

The Eighteenth Amendment to the Constitution was ratified in 1919, and ten months later, over a veto by President Woodrow Wilson, Congress passed the Volstead Act. The act strengthened the language of the amendment and defined as intoxicating all beverages containing more than 0.5 percent alcohol. Although prohibitionists believed that primary enforcement would come at the state and local level, the Volstead Act provided for federal enforcement, and the Prohibition Bureau, an arm of the Treasury Department, was created. Local enforcement was unenthusiastic and inconsistent, and the Prohibition Bureau soon became notorious for employing agents on the basis of political patronage (Hamm 1995).[7] This

---

[7]In 1923, New York repealed a statute that had incorporated Prohibition into state law, thereby placing the burden of alcohol law enforcement on federal agents.

patronage provision helped pass the act, and almost 18,000 federal jobs were exempted from Civil Service restrictions: "The clause had been passed by dry votes in Congress. The lobbyists who cracked the whip over the legislators later explained that Congress had insisted upon the exemption in return for passage of the Volstead Act" (Loth 1938: 346). The treasury agent who brought down Al Capone commented that the "most extraordinary collection of political hacks, hangers-on, and passing highwaymen got appointed as prohibition agents" (Irey and Slocum 1948: 5).

In addition to being inept and corrupt, Prohibition Bureau agents were a public menace: they ran up a record of being killed (by 1923, 30 had been murdered) and for killing hundreds of civilians, often innocent women and children. By 1930, the figure rose to 86 federal agents and 200 civilians killed. Prohibition agents set up illegal roadblocks and searched cars; drivers who protested were in danger of being shot. Agents who killed innocent civilians were rarely brought to justice—when they were indicted by local grand juries, the cases were simply transferred, and the agents escaped punishment (Woodiwiss 1988).

The bureau was viewed as a training school for bootleggers, because agents frequently left the service to join their wealthy adversaries. The Treasury Department was headed by the banking magnate Andrew Mellon (1855–1937), a man who had millions invested in the liquor trade before Prohibition and was not interested in enforcing the new law (Sinclair 1962). Neither were most local police agencies, and very little money was allocated to enforce the most sweeping criminal law ever enacted in the United States (Asbury 1950). Ten days after the Eighteenth Amendment went into effect, three Prohibition agents were indicted in Chicago for bribery and selling seized liquor to bootleggers. And it got worse. Prohibition agents escorted liquor trucks and helped smugglers unload cargoes: "On salaries averaging less than three thousand dollars a year, prohibition agents bought country homes, town houses, city and suburban real estate, speedboats, expensive automobiles, furs, and jewelry for their women, and fine horses; many reported to work in chauffeur-driven cars."

One agent had been a worker on a garbage truck before being appointed: "He worked three months as an agent and then took a six-month leave so that he and his wife could tour Europe" (Irey and Slocum 1948: 6).

Herbert Packer (1968: 263) reminds us that people do not necessarily respond to new criminal prohibitions by acquiescence. He points out that resistance can be fatal to the new norm; moreover, when this happens, "the effect is not confined to the immediate proscription but makes itself felt in the attitude that people take toward legal proscriptions in general." Thus, primary resistance or opposition to a new law such as Prohibition can result, secondarily, in disregard for laws in general: *negative contagion*. During Prohibition, a "general tolerance of the bootlegger and a disrespect for federal law were translated into a widespread contempt for the process and duties of democracy" (Sinclair 1962: 292). This was exemplified by the general lawlessness that reigned in Chicago:

> Banks all over Chicago were robbed in broad daylight by bandits who scorned to wear masks. Desk sergeants at police stations grew weary of recording holdups—from one hundred to two hundred were reported every night. Burglars marked out sections of the city as their own and embarked upon a course of systematic plundering, going from house to house night after night without hindrance. . . . Payroll robberies were a weekly occurrence and necessitated the introduction of armored cars and armed guards for the delivery of money from banks to business houses. Automobiles were stolen by the thousands. Motorists were forced to the curbs on busy streets and boldly robbed. Women who displayed jewelry in night clubs or at the theater were followed and held up. Wealthy women seldom left their homes unless accompanied by armed escorts. (Asbury 1942: 339)

Every year until Prohibition was repealed, the murder rate rose, going from 6.8 per 100,000 persons in 1920 to 9.7 in 1933 (Chapman 1991).

In the 90 days preceding the date when the Eighteenth Amendment became effective,

Changes in the Social Order

Pre-Prohibition	Prohibition
Machine Politicians	Gangs
Vice Entrepreneurs	Machine Politicians
Gangs	Vice Entrepreneurs

$500,000 worth of bonded whiskey was stolen from government warehouses, and afterward it continued to disappear (Sinclair 1962). Less than one hour after Prohibition went into effect, six armed men stole $100,000 worth of whiskey from two Chicago boxcars. In February of 1920, a case of whiskey purchased in Montreal for $10 could easily be sold in New York for $80 (Coffey 1975). In fact, the Canadians began making so much money from Prohibition that provinces with similar laws soon repealed them (Sinclair 1962). Almost immediately, stores sprang up selling hops, yeast, malt, cornmeal, grains, copper tubing, crocks, kettles, jugs, bottle tops, and other equipment for home distilling and brewing. Within one week of the onset of Prohibition, portable stills were on sale throughout the country (Asbury 1950).

Prohibition and Organized Crime

Until Prohibition, gangsters were merely errand boys for the politicians and the gamblers; they were at the bottom of a highly stratified social milieu. The gamblers were under the politicians, who were "kings" (Katcher 1959). Prohibition changed the relationship among the politicians, vice entrepreneurs, and gang leaders. Before 1920, the political boss acted as a patron for the vice entrepreneurs and gangs: he protected them from law enforcement, and they gave him financial and electoral support. However, the onset of Prohibition unleashed an unsurpassed level of criminal violence, and violence is the specialty of the gangs. Physical protection from rival organizations and armed robbers was suddenly more important than protection from law enforcement. Prohibition turned gangs into empires (Logan 1970).

Although America had organized crime before Prohibition, it "was intimately associated with shabby local politics and corrupt police forces"; there was no organized crime activity "in the syndicate style" (King 1969: 23). The "Great Experiment" was a catalyst that caused organized crime, especially violent forms, to blossom into an important force in American society. Prohibition mobilized criminal elements in an unprecedented manner. Pre-Prohibition crime, insofar as it was organized, centered around corrupt political machines, vice entrepreneurs, and, at the bottom, gangs. The competitive violence of Prohibition turned the power structure upside down. It also led to a new level of criminal organization.

The liquor business, licit or illicit, demands large-scale organization. Raw material must be purchased and shipped to manufacturing sites. This requires trucks, drivers, mechanics, warehouses, and laborers. Manufacturing efficiency and profit are maximized by economies of scale. This requires large buildings where the whiskey, beer, or wine can be manufactured, bottled, and placed in cartons for storage and distribution to wholesale outlets or saloons/speakeasies. If the substances are to be smuggled, ships, boats, and their crews are required, as well as trucks, drivers, mechanics, laborers, and warehouses. And there is the obvious need to physically protect shipments through the employment of armed guards: "As illegal entrepreneurs," notes Mark Haller (1985a: 142), bootleggers "also had to learn to use legal institutions to service their illegal enterprises, they had to learn banking to handle their money, insurance to protect their ships, and the methods of incorporation to gain control of chemical and cosmetics companies from which they diverted industrial alcohol. They also dealt with varied legitimate companies to purchase trucks, boats, copper tubing, corn sugar, bottles, and labels." Businessmen who had previously been involved in the legal liquor industry did not remain in business during Prohibition; this left the field open to opportunistic amateurs, often violent young men who had heretofore been left behind in the race for economic success. Bootlegging "was a relatively open field of endeavor and allowed ambitious young Italians and Jews (as well as some Poles and Irishmen) to catapult to quick success" (Haller 1974: 5).

Furthermore, Prohibition encouraged cooperation between gang leaders from various regions—*syndication*. Legal or illegal, the liquor business is international in scope. Smuggled rum and whiskey from Canada, the Caribbean, and Europe had to be moved across the Great Lakes or from the Atlantic onto beaches along the East Coast. Shipments then had to be trucked intra- and interstate to warehouses at distribution points. At each juncture, the shipment required political and physical protection. Only the criminal organization dominant in the local area could provide such protection. Syndication arose out of these needs, and a number of meetings between important organized figures have been documented: "Meetings were held for a number of reasons—to settle disputes, choose successors for slain or deposed leaders, divide local or regional markets, or discuss production, supply, and distribution problems. Some gatherings consisted of Italian criminals and limited their discussions to problems of interest to them. Others involved only Jews or Irish or some other ethnic group; still others were formed of members of a variety [of] ethnic syndicates" (Nelli 1976: 212).

With the onset of the Great Depression (1929) and the subsequent repeal of Prohibition (1933), the financial base of organized crime narrowed considerably. Many players dropped out; some went into legitimate enterprises or employment; others drifted into conventional criminality. Bootlegging, as noted earlier, required trucks, drivers, mechanics, garages, warehouses, bookkeepers, and lawyers—skills and assets that could be converted to noncriminal endeavors. For those

who remained in the business, reorganization was necessary: "When prohibition ended in 1933, bootleggers were still young men—generally in their 30's—yet with wealth and nationwide contacts that had grown out of their bootlegging enterprises. In addition to their liquor interests, they already had substantial investments in restaurants, night clubs, gambling, and other profitable businesses. In the 1930's and 1940's, then, they used their national contacts, diverse interests, and available capital to cooperate in a variety of entrepreneurial activities, legal and illegal" (Haller 1974: 5–6).

Some entrepreneurial bootleggers simply continued in the newly legitimate liquor trade. Sam Bronfman moved the main office of Seagrams from Canada to New York and paid $1.5 million in taxes that the United States said he owed on Prohibition-era shipments. Taking advantage of the start-up time that American distillers needed to get back into business, Seagrams flooded the country with Canadian whiskey (Allen 1998). Bronfman's bootlegging confederate, Lewis Rosenstiel, continued to operate Schenley Distillers Company. The Reinfeld syndicate—Joe Reinfeld and New Jersey crime boss Longie Zwillman—became Renfield Importers. Joseph P. Kennedy, father of a future president, moved from bootlegging to head Somerset Importers (Fox 1989).

Just prior to the end of Prohibition, gang leaders began meeting throughout the United States in anticipation of the new era. In 1932 the Chicago Police Department detained for questioning a number of gangsters, including Paul Ricca of the Capone syndicate, Lucky Luciano, and Meyer Lansky of New York. In 1934 the major leaders of OC in the East gathered at a New York hotel, with Johnny Torrio presiding. They came to an understanding: "Each boss remained czar in his own territory, his rackets unmolested, his local authority uncontested. In murder, no one—local or imported—could be killed in his territory without his approval. He would have the right to do the job himself or permit an outsider to come in—but only at his invitation. In fact, no lawlessness on an organized scale could take place in his domain without his sanction and entire consent, unless he was overruled by the board of governors." Now each mob leader "had behind him not just his own hoods, but a powerful amalgamation of all hoods. Every gang chieftain was guaranteed against being interfered with in his own area—and against being killed by a rival mobster" (Turkus and Feder 1951: 99).

"A second meeting was called in Kansas City to hear from the Western executives. The Capone crowd from Chicago and the Kansas City mob liked the idea. Reports came from Cleveland and Detroit that the Mayfield Gang and the Purple Mob wanted in. Boston and Miami, New Orleans and Baltimore, St. Paul and St. Louis—all flocked to the confederacy of crime, until it was nationwide" (Turkus and Feder 1951: 99). Hank Messick (1967: 32) adds that "the country was divided into territories. Wars ended between regional groups, between religious groups, between national groups." There are several significant indications of this cooperation: the founding of modern Las Vegas (discussed in Chapter 11), labor racketeering on a national level (discussed in Chapter 12), and the establishment and joint ownership of illegal casinos by Irish, Jewish, and Italian criminals from New York, Detroit, and Chicago (Haller 1990a).

By the end of World War II, it was becoming clear that organized crime was changing. Ethnic diversity was declining—Irish and Jewish communities were no longer providing candidates sufficient to replace aging and imprisoned gangsters. This was reflected in the first important congressional investigation of organized crime.

THE KEFAUVER CRIME COMMITTEE

The importance of organized crime as a national political issue was recognized by Tennessee Senator Estes Kefauver in 1950. The five-term member of Congress had been elected to the Senate in 1948 despite vigorous opposition from the political machine headed by notorious "Boss" Ed Crump of Memphis. On January 5, 1950, Kefauver introduced a resolution "to investigate gambling and racketeering activities" by a special subcommittee. The crime committee was established by Senate resolution but not without a fight. Bosses of big-city machines were concerned that an investigation might look into their activities. Further, the chairman of the Judiciary Committee, Pat McCarren of Nevada, was apparently worried about the impact of an investigation on his native state, so he held Kefauver's bill captive for several months. On April 6, 1950, Charles Binaggio, the gambling boss of Kansas City, Missouri, and one of his men were murdered in a Democratic Party clubhouse. This helped spur passage of the Kefauver legislation, and on May 10, 1950, Estes Kefauver became chair of the Special Committee to Investigate Organized Crime in Interstate Commerce, launching the first major congressional investigation into the phenomenon (Moore 1974). This was made all the more dramatic by a new element in public hearings—television:

> One factor, television, was largely responsible for fixing the public consciousness upon this one investigation. . . . For the first time millions of Americans (some 20 million by one estimate) observed the periodic outbursts of drama and boredom which comprised a congressional hearing as it unfolded. Americans gaped as the denizens of other worlds—bookies, pimps, and gangland enforcers, crime bosses and their slippery lawyers—marched across their television screens. They watched and were impressed by the schoolmasterish Estes Kefauver, the dignified Tennessean who was the committee's first chairman, as he condemned criminals and the system of ineffective law enforcement, graft, and popular apathy which permitted them to thrive. (Wilson 1975: 353)

The first hearing was conducted on May 26, 1950. Before Kefauver's term as chair ended on May 1, 1951, the committee heard more than 600 witnesses in 14 cities. This whirlwind of activity led to the committee to conclude:

> Crime is on a syndicated basis to a substantial extent in many cities. The two major

crime syndicates in this country are the Accardo–Guzik–Fischetti syndicate, whose headquarters are Chicago; and the Costello–Adonis–Lansky syndicate based in New York. . . .

There is a sinister criminal organization known as the Mafia operating throughout the country with ties in other nations in the opinion of the committee. The Mafia is the direct descendant of a criminal organization of the same name originating in the island of Sicily. In this country, the Mafia has also been known as the Black Hand and the Unione Siciliano [sic]. The membership of the Mafia today is not confined to persons of Sicilian origin. The Mafia is a loose-knit organization specializing in the sale and distribution of narcotics, the conduct of various gambling enterprises, prostitution, and other rackets based on extortion and violence. The Mafia is the binder which ties together the two major criminal syndicates as well as numerous other criminal groups throughout the country. (Kefauver 1951a: 1–2)

The committee reported that widespread corruption allowed the syndicates to flourish.

While the committee demonstrated extensive interstate contact and investments between gambling figures, notes Moore (1974: 101), "it failed to show extensive interstate control of gambling operations." However, Moore argues that the committee's conclusions about gambling had intellectual sincerity based on substantial if not always convincing evidence. Such was not the case with its conclusions about the Mafia: "Inadequate evidence and the necessity to reach some conclusion rushed the Committee into fuzzy and ill-founded statements that brought the senators sensational headlines but left an ugly popular misunderstanding in the country" (1974: 114). The Mafia, according to Kefauver (1951b: 19), is "the shadowy international organization that lurks behind much of America's organized criminal activity," a conclusion for which he credits the Federal Bureau of Narcotics. In fact, the com-

mittee's final report contained a great deal of nonsense.

According to Dwight Smith (1974: 85), there is an American preoccupation with alien conspiracy: "One of the conditions required for an alien conspiracy theory is a set of 'facts' or assumptions that can be constructed into evidence supporting a conspiratorial explanation. Such 'facts' often make fascinating reading; they sell newspapers, books, and magazines." Smith argues that the conspiracy theory provided the Federal Bureau of Narcotics with an explanation for failure: "The notion of total suppression of illegal narcotics use through importation control was a self-proclaimed mission, and it had not been attained. How better to explain failure (and, incidentally, to prepare the ground for increased future budgets) than to argue that, dedicated though it might be, the bureau was hard pressed to overcome an alien, organized, conspiratorial force which, with evil intent and conspiratorial methods, had forced its way on an innocent public?" In this era of McCarthyism, the search for alien conspiracies proved to be good politics.

Moore (1974: 211) concludes that the committee's "most constructive work had been the documenting of widespread corruption at the local and state level and the exposing of attempts by law enforcement officials to conceal their malfeasance or ineptitude behind a maze of conflicting, overlapping jurisdictional boundaries." Unfortunately, notes Moore, committee preoccupation with ethnic conspiracies detracted from these findings and some of its constructive policy recommendations. The committee tied organized crime and the Mafia inextricably, thereby equating Italians with organized crime.

THE MCCLELLAN COMMITTEE

In 1956 the Senate Permanent Subcommittee on Investigations (PSI) began an inquiry into the Teamsters Union, an effort that met with union recalcitrance (see Chapter 12). The Senate responded by establishing the Select Committee on Improper Activities in the Labor or Management

Field. The findings of the Select Committee led to the passage of the 1959 Labor–Management Reporting and Disclosure Act, usually called the Landrum–Griffin Act after its two sponsors. The Select Committee expired in 1960, but Senator John L. McClellan (D–Ark.) remained chair of the Permanent Subcommittee on Investigations (PSI). In 1963 the PSI held televised hearings on organized crime and introduced the public to its star witness, Joseph Valachi. Peter Maas (1968: 40) states that Senator McClellan visited Valachi privately at the District of Columbia jail just before the hearings began: "According to Valachi, the senator requested he skip any mention of Hot Springs, in McClellan's home state," which was notorious for its wide-open gambling operations.

Joseph Valachi   In 1962, Joseph Valachi, a convicted drug trafficker and member of the Genovese Family, was serving a federal sentence for drug trafficking when a fellow inmate accused him of being an informer for the Federal Bureau of Narcotics. His accuser was also a made guy, and this caused the accusation to be life threatening. Valachi was subsequently approached by an inmate he thought was an enforcer for the Genovese Family. He attacked the inmate with a lead pipe—the wrong man, as it turned out—and beat him to death. In 1963, Valachi was in Washington, D.C., appearing before the McClellan (PSI) Committee.

Valachi was inducted into the Maranzano faction during the Castellammarese war and had been a soldier for more than 30 years. The career criminal told of a secret society that insiders referred to as *Cosa Nostra*, replete with blood oaths and murders. He discussed the Castellammarese war and Luciano's murder of Joe Masseria, Salvatore Maranzano, and some 40 "mustache Petes." Valachi outlined the structure of each crime Family and explained how they were linked together through a national commission—the "Supreme Court of Organized Crime." Once the television lights were turned on, notes Maas (1968: 41), senators bombarded Valachi with questions designed to score points with the voters back home. For example, Nebraska Senator Carl Curtis asked about

organized crime in Omaha: "After a moment's reflection, the barely literate Valachi carefully cupped his hand over his mouth, turned to a Justice Department official sitting next to him, and whispered something. Those viewing the scene could be forgiven for supposing that Senator Curtis had hit on a matter of some import which Valachi wanted to check before answering. He was in fact asking, 'Where the hell is Omaha?'"

Valachi was a low-echelon soldier whose first-hand knowledge of organized crime was limited to street-level experiences. Much of the information attributed to him was obviously well beyond his personal experience. Virgil Peterson notes that some of Valachi's testimony was extremely vague, confusing, and inconsistent: "Not infrequently, it would appear, he either withheld facts that should have been known to him or deliberately lied" (1983: 425). Nevertheless, this did not prevent his disclosures from becoming the core of a chapter on organized crime in the final report of the President's Commission on Law Enforcement and Administration of Justice.

THE PRESIDENT'S COMMISSION ON LAW ENFORCEMENT AND ADMINISTRATION OF JUSTICE

In 1964, Lyndon B. Johnson was serving the remainder of John F. Kennedy's term and seeking election as president. The Republicans had nominated Senator Barry M. Goldwater of Arizona, who launched what has come to be known as a "law-and-order" campaign: the Republicans attacked the Democratic administration for being "soft on crime." Johnson won a landslide victory, but the issue of "crime in the streets" lingered on. In order to blunt criticism (and, Richard Quinney [1974] argues, to divert attention from the Vietnam conflict), Johnson launched his own "war on crime."

On March 8, 1965, in a message to the Eighty-Ninth Congress, "Crime, Its Prevalence and Measures of Prevention," President Johnson announced that "I am establishing the President's Commission on Law Enforcement and Administration of Justice. The commission will be composed of men and women of distinction who share my belief that we need to know far more about the prevention and control of crime." Nine different task forces were established, including the Task Force on Organized Crime, headed by Charles H. Rogovin, with Donald R. Cressey and Ralph Salerno serving as consultants. Cressey (1969) and Salerno (1969) extended the influence of the President's Commission by writing books on organized crime. In its report to the commission, the Task Force on Organized Crime (1967: 6) stated that "Today the core of organized crime in the United States consists of 24 groups operating as criminal cartels in large cities across the Nation. Their membership is exclusively men of Italian descent, they are in frequent communications with each other, and their smooth functioning is insured by a national body of overseers. To date, only the Federal Bureau of Investigation has been able to document fully the national scope of these groups, and the FBI intelligence indicates that the organization as a whole has changed its name from the Mafia to Cosa Nostra." The last statement was obviously based on the revelations of Joseph Valachi.

The task force continued what the Kefauver Committee had begun, equating organized crime with Italians. The only new wrinkle was a name change (Messick 1973: 8): "La Cosa Nostra was created [by the FBI via Valachi] as a public image. This simple device of giving the Mafia a new name worked wonders. Hoover was taken off the limb where he had perched for so long, and citizens had a new menace to talk about with tales of blood oaths, contracts for murder, secret societies." Hank Messick argues that this picture was 30 years out of date. More important, however, were the policy implications.

The task force recommended a witness protection program, special federal grand juries, and legislation permitting electronic surveillance— recommendations that were enacted into law. The task force noted the inadequacy of budgetary allocations devoted to dealing with organized crime and the lack of coordination among agencies charged with combating OC activity. Accordingly, budgetary allocations were increased to deal with the "new" menace, and in 1967 federal organized crime strike forces were established in each city with a *Cosa Nostra* Family. In 1968, the Omnibus Crime Control and Safe Streets Act was enacted, providing law enforcement agencies with legal guidelines for electronic surveillance. In 1970, Congress passed the Organized Crime Control Act, which contains the RICO provisions discussed in Chapter 14.

The task force concluded that the major income for organized crime is derived from gambling, with loansharking second. Little attention was given to other sources of income, in particular drug trafficking and labor racketeering. After the task force disbanded, the Permanent Subcommittee on Investigations remained the congressional committee most interested in organized crime, although it was eclipsed for several years by the President's Commission on Organized Crime. (In government, a committee is a legislative unit, while a commission is part of the executive branch.)

THE PRESIDENT'S COMMISSION ON ORGANIZED CRIME (PCOC)

The Reagan administration era was extraordinary with respect to organized crime. The man who welcomed the support of the International Brotherhood of Teamsters and who appointed its president, Jackie Presser (see Chapter 12), to his interim planning staff also issued Executive Order Number 12435 of July 28, 1983, creating the President's Commission on Organized Crime: "The Commission shall make a full and complete national and region-by-region analysis of organized crime; define the nature of traditional organized crime as well as emerging organized crime groups, the sources and amounts of organized crime's income, and the uses to which organized crime puts its income; develop in-depth information on the participants in organized crime networks; and evaluate Federal laws pertinent to the effort to combat organized crime." The commission was charged with advising the president on "actions which can be taken to improve law enforcement efforts directed against organized crime, and make recommendations concerning appropriate administrative and legislative improvements in the administration of justice." The commission was given 33 months and $5 million to accomplish these formidable tasks.

Controversy and discord were a dominant characteristic of the commission (Shenon 1986). Irving R. Kaufman of the U.S. Court of Appeals for the Second Circuit (New York) was appointed as chair. Judge Kaufman's sole connection to efforts against organized crime consisted of presiding at the 1959 conspiracy and obstruction of justice trial of some of the men who were arrested at the infamous "Apalachin Crime Convention" in 1957 (discussed in Chapter 4). The first executive director resigned before the commission began its work, reportedly because of a disagreement with Judge Kaufman. After a second candidate for executive director was rejected by the Justice Department, James D. Harmon, Jr., was selected and served until the commission completed its work. During the first year, there was a conflict with the Justice Department over the commission's independence and personnel. As a result, the commission was unable to fulfill its mandate to evaluate federal prosecutorial efforts. Finally, on July 17, 1984, the commission was given subpoena power.

Many important OC figures were subpoenaed. As expected, they invoked the Fifth Amendment or presented some novel arguments for their refusal to respond to commission questions. When he appeared on April 23, 1985, Teamster's Union president Jackie Presser invoked the Fifth Amendment in response to commission questions. One subpoenaed witness refused to testify after being granted immunity, and he was sentenced to one year of imprisonment by a federal judge in Miami—he was already serving a 62-year prison sentence for drug trafficking.

The seven public hearings held by the PCOC generated a great deal of media attention. They were denounced by some as mere publicity stunts, particularly when witnesses were produced wearing hoods to hide their identities. The commission highlighted the problem of money laundering and the continuing problem of labor racketeering, and drew attention to the problem of "mob lawyers." A staff study (PCOC 1985b: 3) "confirmed the existence of a small group of attorneys who have become integral parts of criminal conspiracies, using their status as sworn officers of the court to advance the criminal purposes of these criminal organizations. It is clear that traditional organized crime and narcotics traffickers depend upon and could not effectively operate without these attorneys."

While the commission revealed little that was new, it avoided an overemphasis on Italian-American organized crime and, instead, reflecting changes in organized crime, presented information on Colombian cocaine cartels and examined to a lesser degree other criminal organizations, including outlaw motorcycle clubs. In fact, there was so little attention paid to traditional OC that the commission failed to determine how many Mafia groups were actually operating in the United States—it used the number 24, which dates back to 1967 and the Task Force on Organized Crime.[8] The commission concluded that drug trafficking was the greatest moneymaker for OC. As opposed to its predecessor, the Task Force on Organized Crime, the President's Commission found existing laws generally adequate for dealing with OC, although it found significant deficiencies in carrying out the statutes. Whereas the Task Force on Organized Crime had great political impact, the President's Commission created hardly a ripple—new legislation was not forthcoming, nor did new initiatives result. The policy that was in place before the commission was established remained in place.

Now that we have completed an overview of the evolution of organized crime in the United States, in chapters 4 and 5 we will take a close-up look at the development of organized crime in New York and Chicago.

---

[8]So little information was gathered about traditional OC that just before the commission was to disband, I was asked to provide extensive information on the state of Italian-American organized crime and was given only 30 days to research and respond.

INTERNET CONNECTIONS

Organized crime links: **organizedcrime.about.com/newsissues/organizedcrime**

Nathanson Centre: **www.yorku.ca/nathanson**

Organized crime history: **www.crimelibrary.com/gangsters**

REVIEW QUESTIONS

1. What are the various problems with sources of information about organized crime?
2. What did the "robber barons" contribute to the development of organized crime?
3. What are the characteristics of "political machines"?
4. What explains the success of the Irish in American machine politics?
5. What was the relationship between the saloon and the political machine?
6. What was the relationship between the machine and big business?
7. Why did business interests often support reform politics?
8. How did nativism generate support for the political machine?
9. What was the conflict between rural and urban America that helped fuel the Prohibition movement?
10. How did Prohibition stimulate the development of organized crime?
11. How did Prohibition change the relationship between politicians and gang leaders?
12. How did Prohibition lead to criminal syndication?
13. How did the onset of the Great Depression affect organized crime?
14. How did organized crime change with the repeal of Prohibition?
15. What conclusions about organized crime were shared by the Kefauver Committee and the Task Force on Organized Crime?
16. How did the conclusions of the Task Force on Organized Crime differ from those of the President's Commission on Organized Crime?

♠

C H A P T E R 4

ORGANIZED CRIME IN NEW YORK

The history of organized crime in the United States encompasses cities in every region of the country.[1] A lack of space and a lack of detailed information prevent a historical review of them all. Instead, we will examine the phenomenon in New York and, in Chapter 5, Chicago. Organized crime elsewhere approximates that in New York and Chicago, the two cities with the strongest traditional organized crime groups.

In order to understand the development of organized crime in New York, we need to examine a most unique political organization—the Society of Saint Tammany, usually referred to as Tammany Hall.

TAMMANY HALL

The Society of Saint Tammany, named for a legendary Delaware Indian chief, began in 1789 as a fraternal and patriotic society with chapters in a number of states and quickly emerged as a full-fledged political organization in New York.[2] The guiding genius behind Tammany's rise to power was Aaron Burr (Peterson 1983), who in 1800 became vice president of the United States.[3] In 1836, Tammany leader Martin Van Buren was elected the eighth president of the United States (Connable and Silberfarb 1967). Tammany eventually became synonymous with the Democratic Party of New York City.

In post-Revolutionary War New York, only landowners could vote, an obvious handicap to an organization striving for broad-based support.

---

[1]Buffalo; Boston; Cleveland; Dallas; Denver; Elizabeth, New Jersey; Hot Springs, Arkansas; Kansas City, Missouri; Los Angeles; Miami; Milwaukee; Minneapolis; Newark, New Jersey; New Orleans; Newport, Kentucky; Phenix City, Alabama; Philadelphia, Pittsburgh, Pittston, Reading, and Scranton, Pennsylvania; Providence, Rhode Island; Rochester, New York; St. Louis; San Francisco and San Jose, California; Seattle; Springfield, Illinois; Tampa, Florida; and Youngstown, Ohio.

---

[2]At the time, the city of New York meant Manhattan; the five counties that now make up the city did not consolidate until 1898.

[3]In a duel in 1804, Burr killed former Secretary of the Treasury Alexander Hamilton.

Tammany responded with "collective property," in which the title to a house might be held by a number of persons, who would then be enfranchised as freeholders. Tammany established a system of district leaders and precinct captains in each assembly district and by 1838 had a reputation for dispensing favors and social services from funds extorted from vice entrepreneurs and a 6-percent kickback from all city employees. The tie-in between criminals and politicians was now firmly established.

During the latter part of the 1840s and early 1850s, large numbers of Irish immigrated to New York in order to escape famine and British repression. Despite nativist and anti-Catholic sentiment in Tammany, the Irish quickly rose to leadership positions and by the turn of the century clearly dominated "the Hall." The Irish immigrant spoke English and was quite at home in a saloon; his willingness to engage in fisticuffs made him a "natural" for the rough-and-tumble politics of that period. There was also an Irish genius for politics: "It is in close, warm, personal contact with local life that the Irish have excelled. That the Irish in New York have been almost altogether Democrats has been one element in making the character of the Democratic party in that city" (Hapgood and Moskowitz 1927: 43). The Irishman, because of his stature and ability to speak English, also dominated the city's police force, which was in effect an adjunct of Tammany Hall.

The Tammany Police

In 1844 the New York State legislature authorized the creation of a police force for New York City patterned after the London Metropolitan Police of Sir Robert Peel (from whom they get the nickname "Bobbies"). Whereas the London model centralized the police command, in New York the police in each of the city's wards were controlled by the alderman, who could hire and fire police officers: "Even after aldermanic appointment was formally discontinued, local politicians continued to exercise de facto control" (Repetto 1978: 41). Positions on the police force were sought after. The policeman's salary, compared with that of a skilled laborer, was good, qualifications for the job

were almost nonexistent, discipline was lax, and opportunities for graft were extensive: "Cops who chose not to take graft had to immerse themselves in areas of policing where they did not need to deal with vice—quiet precincts or special units such as the homicide squad—and to ignore any corruption they saw. To be a squealer in a predominantly Irish police force was a fate worse than death" (Repetto 1978: 75).

The police tended not only to be corrupt but also to be brutal toward the poor and the helpless. In response, the police received very little public support and were often subjected to abuse by Tammany-linked street gangs. To arrest a suspect, the officer frequently had to physically subdue him or her: "A tradition of police brutality developed out of this disrespect. Officers sought to gain with their billy clubs the deference to their authority that was not freely given" (Walker 1980: 63). The police manhandled and brutalized prostitutes, miscreants, and members of the underclass in general. In return, they were abused by the Tammany politicians. Police brutality was a "delegated form of vigilantism" tolerated by the respectable middle-class citizenry, who perceived a need to control the "dangerous classes" (Walker 1980: 63; Steffins 1957).

The Tammany Gangs

From the mid-1800s until World War I, old-style gangs were an important feature of the Tammany–criminal tie-in. By the 1920s, when they were disappearing, the *New York Times* could wax nostalgic about the "old breed" of gang with its twisted sense of valor, as compared with the current (1923) variety, which operated with "the calculation and efficiency of an industrial tool for breaking strikes or wrecking factories" ("New Gang Methods Replace Those of Eastman's Days" 1923: 3). The *Times* referred to the demise of the Shirt Tails, Dead Rabbits, Plug Uglies, Bowery Boys, Hudson Dusters, Cherry Hill Gang, Gophers, Five Points, and Whyos.

On election day, Tammany used these gangs as "repeaters" and "sluggers," which led the notorious, apelike Lower East Side Gang leader Monk

Eastman (born Edward Osterman in 1873) to utter: "Say, I cut some ice in this town. Why, I make half the big politicians" ("New Gang Methods" 1923). Gangs were so useful on election day that the politicians made natural alliances with them: "To keep gang members in funds between elections, the politicians found jobs for them in the off-season months" (Logan 1970: 56). They worked as lookouts, steerers, and bouncers—resident thugs for the gambling houses and brothels under the patronage of Tammany.

One of the more infamous of the Tammany gangs was the Five Points, with an estimated 1,200 members led by Paul Kelly, an ex-pugilist born Paolo Vaccarelli (it was not unusual for prizefighters or criminals to assume Irish names). Before he left for Chicago, Al Capone was a member of the Five Points Gang (Kobler 1971), as was Lucky Luciano (Powell 2000). The Five Points refers to a confluence of streets in a neighborhood on the city's Lower East Side, in what is today Chinatown (Anbinder 2001). One of the highlights of New York gang history is the feud between Kelly and his Italian Five Points Gang and the Jewish gang led by Monk Eastman over a small piece of Lower Manhattan real estate that each gang claimed as its "turf." When their political patrons insisted that they cease the bloodshed, Kelly and Eastman fought it out in a fracas that lasted two hours and ended in a draw when both combatants collapsed from exhaustion.

Eastman fell into disfavor with his Tammany patrons and was imprisoned for a 1904 robbery attempt. After his release in 1909, he was unable to reestablish himself as a gang leader. Enlisting under an alias, Eastman served with distinction in World War I, during which his gang faded. He received a full pardon from Tammany Governor Alfred E. Smith for his outstanding military service. Eastman was shot to death by an old crony after a petty quarrel that followed a Christmas Eve drinking bout. The friend, a federal Prohibition agent, escaped with a three-to-ten-year sentence by claiming self-defense—he thought the unarmed Monk was reaching for a gun (Lee 1963). Kelly eventually left the mayhem of lower Manhattan for Harlem, where he founded the Harlem Branch of the Paul Kelly Association. He became a labor organizer and, with the help of some of his Five Pointers, a vice president of the International Longshoremen's Association (a union discussed in Chapter 12).

Gambling and house prostitution in Manhattan were "licensed" by Tammany State Senator Timothy Sullivan,[4] with the support of the police chief. When a Tammany alderman opposed brothels in his heavily Irish district, Sullivan organized a primary election fight against him. He sent in the Kelly and Eastman gangs to beat and intimidate his opponent's supporters, while the Tammany police remained passive. Sullivan's candidate won by a margin of three to one (Connable and Silberfarb 1967).

Charles Murphy, a former saloon keeper, became Tammany boss in 1902 and remained in that position until his death 22 years later, amassing a personal fortune of $2 million (Van Devander 1944). Murphy changed Tammany operations: open gambling and prostitution were ended, and total immunity for gangsters was withdrawn. Murphy also moved to cut down the power of the police who had occasionally challenged Tammany (Katcher 1959). Murphy "concluded that the use of the police as major graft collectors was an antiquated concept" (Logan 1970: 340). Modern organization was needed—a conduit between the politicians and the gamblers, who, like the brothel owners, would be organized into a dues-paying trade association. That conduit was Arnold Rothstein—organized crime was beginning to evolve.

ARNOLD ROTHSTEIN AND JEWISH ORGANIZED CRIME IN NEW YORK

Under the czars, Jews were confined to life in the *stetls* of Russia's western territories—Latvia,

---

[4]Sullivan is best remembered in New York as the author of the "Sullivan law," which prohibits the carrying of concealed firearms without a permit. This law was enacted to enable Tammany to better control the behavior of their street gang allies. If they got out of line, gang members could be frisked by the police for firearms that could always be "found" (planted).

Lithuania, eastern Poland, Ukraine, and Belarus—or to a ghetto reserved for them in the cities of Minsk, Odessa, Vilnius, and Warsaw. The professions were closed to them, and their choice of occupations was severely limited. Poverty and persecution fueled immigration, and during the first two decades of the twentieth century millions fled to the United States, where they settled in areas already characterized by rampant criminality. These areas would serve as the breeding ground for Jewish organized crime.

In 1900 the Irish still constituted the dominant force in the dominant political organization, Tammany Hall. But in organizing gamblers and brothels[5] and in the emerging arena of labor–management conflict, Jews, toughened by the ethnic conflicts of urban America and endowed with a cohesion forged by centuries of antisemitism, began to gain a niche. By the second decade of the twentieth century, however, opportunities afforded by America released an entrepreneurial spirit that had been bottled up in the ghettos of Eastern Europe and gave free rein to the Jewish pursuit of education—the Jewish criminal was being pushed to the fringes of the past. Then came Prohibition, and the fast-track opportunities presented brought the Jewish criminal to the fore: "During Prohibition, 50 percent of the nation's leading bootleggers were Jews, and Jewish gangs bossed the rackets in some of America's largest cities" (Rockaway 1993: 5). In New York, they not only helped rationalize illicit activities but also provided a conduit between local crime personnel and Tammany. Among Jewish organized criminal operatives, Arnold Rothstein was the most important organizer and innovator.

Arnold Rothstein

The specter of Arnold Rothstein looms so large over organized crime in New York that it would not be much of an exaggeration to call him its "Godfather." As Jenna Joselit (1983: 143–44) states,

Arnold Rothstein, shortly before his death in 1928. His shadow looms so large over the New York OC scene that it would not be an exaggeration to call him its "Godfather."

© Corbis

Rothstein transformed criminal activity from a haphazard, often spontaneous endeavor into one whose hallmarks—specialized expertise, administrative hierarchy, and organizational procedure—correspond to the classic sociological model of a bureaucracy. Thus, Rothstein's illegal business had a definite administrative structure based on specific skills; competence and not ethnic pedigree determined one's rank and, of course, one's position in his outfit.

Rothstein's office . . . in the middle of the midtown business district employed a staff comparable to that of any large (and legitimate) commercial firm, replete with secretaries, bookkeepers, and legal counsel. . . . A decision to enter some new illegal venture tended to be based not on personal motives of revenge or power but on strictly commercial considerations: the amount of profit to be made and the length of time it would take to make it. Finally, by investing the money

---

[5]For a historical examination of Jewish involvement in "white slavery," see Bristow (1982).

he earned through illegal channels into legal enterprises such as real estate and the theater, Rothstein made it difficult to ascertain where the illegal enterprise left off and the legitimate one began.

"A. R." or "the Brain," as Damon Runyon called him, was born in New York in 1882 and served as the inspiration for Meyer Wolfsheim in F. Scott Fitzgerald's *The Great Gatsby* and for Sky Masterson in *Guys and Dolls*. His father, an Orthodox Jew born of immigrant parents, was a respected and successful businessman. Arnold was also respected and quite successful, but his business comprised gambling, bootlegging, drug smuggling, and labor racketeering (Katcher 1959). Rothstein is probably best remembered for his alleged involvement in the "Black Sox Scandal," the fixing of the 1919 World Series.

Rothstein also fenced stolen bonds and securities, and when Prohibition arrived he organized the importation of liquor from England and Canada. At the same time, diamonds and drugs, which took up very little space, were smuggled in on his whiskey ships, and he established an international drug-smuggling network. His buyers overseas shipped the drugs into the United States, where they were distributed to criminal organizations in several states.

"Rothstein set new and historic standards in the development of organized crime in America" (Lacey 1991: 50). He played the role of broker, not only between Tammany and the gamblers but also between two of New York's political-crime factions, one Italian, one primarily Irish and Jewish. Rothstein was tied to both factions and did favors for both—furnishing pistol permits and bail bonds, fencing stolen merchandise, and financing illegal operations. In 1929 it was publicly revealed that Rothstein had loaned nearly $20,000 to a Bronx magistrate who had helped Tammany get out the Italian vote (Mann 1965).

One Sunday night in 1928, Arnold Rothstein was found staggering into the service entrance of the Park Central Hotel, where he resided. He had been shot once in the abdomen with a small-caliber gun. At age 46, Rothstein died after refus-

ing to name the person who shot him, and the murder was never solved. It has been attributed to Rothstein's refusal to pay a gambling debt in excess of $300,000—he maintained that the card game was rigged ("Gamblers Hunted in Rothstein Attack" 1928). After his death, federal officials opened many of his safes and files. Papers found in his apartment linked Rothstein to what the U.S. Attorney called the largest drug ring in the United States ("Unger Indicted in Drug Conspiracy" 1928; "$4,000,000 in Narcotics Seized Here, Traced to Rothstein Ring" 1928). Rothstein left a public estate appraised at $1,757,572; his hidden assets, of course, are not known (S. Smith 1963).

Dutch Schultz

Arthur Flegenheimer—"Dutch Schultz"—provides an outstanding example of how the opportunities afforded by Prohibition turned street thugs into wealthy "beer barons." At the beginning of Prohibition, Schultz, a street tough, worked for a trucking company whose owner went into the beer business. In 1928, Schultz became a partner in a Bronx speakeasy. The partners soon bought trucks and garages and became major beer distributors, aided by a vicious crew of gunmen including Legs Diamond; the Weinberg brothers, Bo and George; and the Irish-born Coll brothers, Vincent ("Mad Dog") and Peter. Next, they began to expand into the territories of rival beer businesses. One unfortunate was kidnapped, severely beaten, hung by his thumbs, and eventually blinded—sending a message that was not lost on other recalcitrant beer distributors.

While Prohibition was in full swing, prominent gangsters did not pay attention to the numbers (illegal lottery), often referring to it derisively as "nigger pool" because many of its followers were African American. With Prohibition on the way out, however, Schultz began searching for new areas of profit. His attorney, who also represented some numbers operators, engineered Schultz's takeover of the business in Harlem from independent African-American, Hispanic, and some white numbers bankers. Schultz was able to offer political protection from arrest and physical protection from robbers as well as financing—several operators had had a costly run of bad luck: "Harlem numbers were not consolidated into a syndicate that pooled resources and assets; it was fragmented and lacked big layoff bankers who could handle a large 'hit' (win)" (Schatzberg and Kelly 1996: 79). By 1932, a combination of superior financing, force, and political power enabled Schultz to reduce independent operators to being his employees, and he centralized policy operations in Harlem (Sann 1971; Schatzberg 1993). Schultz also moved into labor racketeering, and in 1934 the *New York Times* reported an alliance between officials of the restaurant workers union and the Schultz organization ("Gang Linked to Union Charged at Trial" 1934).

In 1931 the Coll brothers rebelled against Schultz and began killing off the Dutchman's drivers and payoff men: the "band of killers would wake the Schultz employees in their homes at the dead of night and kill them in their own bedrooms" (Berger 1935: 17). In a five-month period in 1931, seven Schultz men were murdered ("Schultz Aide Slain; 7th in Five Months" 1931). Schultz responded by placing a $50,000 contract on Coll and began to return the gunplay ("Woman, 2 Men, Slain as Gang Raids Home in Coll Feud" 1932). It was during this feud that Vincent Coll received his nickname, "Mad Dog." Coll's men opened fire at a leader of the Schultz organization who was standing in the street near a group of playing children. He escaped injury, but a five-year-old child was killed and four other children were wounded. Coll was arrested as one of the shooters, but his attorney disclosed that the witness to the shooting had a criminal record and a history of providing false testimony. Coll went free (O'Connor 1958).

Another important Prohibition figure would soon play a role in the Schultz–Coll war. Owney Madden, born in England of Irish parents in 1892, began his career in crime as head of the Gophers, a notorious and widely feared gang that controlled an area of Manhattan's West Side appropriately called Hell's Kitchen. The gang's name was derived from their habit of holing up in basements

and cellars (Sante 1991). In 1915, Madden was sentenced to Sing Sing Prison for ordering the murder of one of his rivals. In 1923, he was paroled and began to hijack liquor trucks, including those of Vincent ("Bill") Dwyer, a major bootlegger. Instead of responding violently, Dwyer, ever the rational businessman, chose to make Madden part of his organization (Peterson 1983). Madden also became a partner with George Jean ("Big Frenchy") de Mange, a bootlegger and speakeasy owner who saw the need for the services that Madden and his Hell's Kitchen stalwarts could provide (O'Connor 1958).

In need of money to help finance his campaign against Schultz, Coll kidnapped de Mange and demanded ransom from Madden, who turned over $35,000 for "Big Frenchy's" return. Coll then tried to extort money from Madden by threatening to kidnap him. The outraged Madden joined forces with Schultz in an all-out war against Coll. They divided the city into zones and dispatched their gunmen to find the "Mad Dog." In the interim, Madden[6] fled to Florida, while Schultz barricaded himself in a bordello surrounded by bodyguards. In the end, Coll's bodyguards "fingered" him for Schultz. In 1932 the "Mad Dog" stepped into a drugstore phone booth and made a call. While he was busy on the telephone, his bodyguard discreetly left, and two men entered. One of the men carried a Thompson submachine gun. After ordering the customers to remain calm, he fired several bursts into the phone booth: Coll was almost cut in half by the barrage (O'Connor 1958).

With Coll out of the way, Schultz began to experience a new problem—the Internal Revenue Service. He went into hiding for 18 months. In

---

[6]As a result of his partnership with Bill Dwyer, Madden became a millionaire during Prohibition. He continued his operations until 1932, when he was arrested for parole violation and returned to prison. A year later he was paroled again and retired to Hot Springs, Arkansas, a town known for corrupt machine politics and illegal gambling. There, according to Stephen Fox (1989), he controlled the rackets, married, and lived out his days in comfort. In 1935, Lucky Luciano found temporary refuge from a New York indictment by hiding out in Hot Springs. On April 24, 1965, the front page of the *New York Times* reported that Madden, an "ex-gangster" who had given big contributions to charity, had died of emphysema.

1934 he surrendered and subsequently succeeded in obtaining a change of venue based on his notoriety in New York City. The case was moved to Syracuse, New York, where a mistrial (hung jury) resulted. The retrial was moved to the small upstate community of Malone. Schultz traveled to Malone in advance of his trial, bought candy and flowers for the children he visited in the hospital, held a grand ball to which he invited the entire town, and generally endeared himself to the good people of Malone. They acquitted Schultz, a verdict that outraged the presiding judge (R. N. Smith 1982).

Schultz could not safely return to New York; the federal government had several counts of the original indictment held in abeyance and, to avoid possible double-jeopardy problems, indicted Schultz for a series of misdemeanors. In addition, New York State had a warrant outstanding for income-tax evasion; Schultz owed the state $36,937 in back taxes. It was understood that if Schultz could be arrested in New York City, the authorities would be able to set a prohibitive bail and thus keep him in custody. Schultz traveled to New Jersey and surrendered to the federal charges; bail was set at an amount that enabled him to remain at liberty (Sann 1971). The Dutchman set up headquarters in a Newark tavern but faced threats from two sources: Thomas E. Dewey and Lucky Luciano.

Dewey, a special anti-rackets prosecutor, had successfully prosecuted gangster Waxey Gordon and was now after Schultz. Luciano and his colleagues expected Schultz to be convicted and imprisoned as a result of his trials in Syracuse and Malone. They were planning to move in on his numbers and restaurant rackets, and his acquittal presented them with a serious setback. The independent and violent Schultz, for his part, became even more unpredictable, personally murdering two of his own men. The Dutchman was also threatening to kill Dewey, an idea that had been rejected by a commission of the other leading gangsters in New York; they were fearful of the "heat" that would result (R. N. Smith 1982).

On the evening of October 23, 1935, Dutch Schultz entered the Palace Chop House and Tav-

On October 23, 1935, top enforcers working for Lepke Buchalter entered the Palace Chop House in Newark and gunned down Dutch Schultz and three aides. "The Dutchman" survived for almost a day. His deathbed ravings ranged from million-dollar deals to moralistic admonitions such as "Mother is the best bet" and "Don't let Satan draw you too fast."

ern in Newark, where he had established his headquarters "in exile." With him were his two bodyguards as well as the financial wizard of the Schultz organization. As Schultz entered the men's room, two men suddenly entered the tavern and opened fire with handguns and a shotgun; the Schultz men were mortally wounded. One of the gunmen entered the men's room and shot the Dutchman, who died about 20 hours later.

Lepke Buchalter

As a leading member of the syndicate "commission" in New York, Louis Buchalter—known as "the Judge"—"vetoed" the murder of Thomas E. Dewey (Turkus and Feder 1951), a decision he probably lived to regret. "Lepkeleh" (an affectionate Yiddish term for "Little Louis") was born on New York's Lower East Side in 1897. His father died when Lepke was thirteen, and his destitute mother sent him to live with his older sister. He had three brothers: one became a rabbi, another a pharmacist, and a third a dentist. Lepke took a different route. He was arrested and imprisoned for burglary several times. After being released from Sing Sing Prison in 1922, he teamed up with Jacob ("Gurrah") Shapiro (born in Russia in 1895), and the two began working as strong-arms for labor–industrial racketeer "Little Augie" Orgen, who worked for Arnold Rothstein.

In 1927 a labor dispute erupted in the painting trade, and the head of the painters' trade association gave Little Augie $50,000 to end the strike. Without consulting his lieutenants, Augie ordered the union to stop the walkout. However, the brother of one of Augie's top lieutenants was a friend of a painter's union official who had asked that the mob remain neutral. Augie's men demanded that he return the $50,000 retainer, but instead Augie contracted with Legs Diamond for help in breaking the strike: "At 8:30 P.M., on October 15, 1927, Li'l Augie and his new associate were walking along a lower Manhattan street. A black sedan picked its way through the pushcarts. Behind the wheel was Lepke. Next to him, pistol in hand, sat Gurrah . . . [who] hit the sidewalk yelling, 'Move over Diamond!' Legs fell back instinctively against the building. Li'l Augie, transfixed, was killed. Diamond got a bullet through his shoulder—for butting in" (Turkus and Feder 1951: 336–37).

After taking over the Orgen organization, Lepke and Gurrah revolutionized industrial racketeering: "Instead of using his sluggers and gunmen to terrorize labor unions during strike periods, Lepke worked them directly into the unions. By threat and by violence they controlled one local af-

ter another" (Berger 1944: 30). Manufacturers who hired Lepke to deal with the unions "soon found themselves wriggling helplessly in the grip of Lepke's smooth but deadly organization. He moved in on them as he had on the unions" (Berger 1944: 30). Until 1940, Lepke was the head of an organization that extorted wealth from New York's garment, leather, fur, baking, and trucking industries. His estimated income was between $5 million and $10 million annually—and this was during the Depression (Turkus and Feder 1951): "All through the Prohibition era, when other mobsters were splashing headily in alcoholic wealth and getting their names in headlines with a series of competitive killings that strewed urban and suburban landscapes with untidy corpses, Lepke went his quiet way" (Berger 1940: 30).

Special Prosecutor Dewey began to move against Buchalter and Shapiro, and by 1937 both were in hiding, leaving day-to-day operations to an aide. Shapiro surrendered the following year and was tried and convicted for extortion in the bakery industry (Joselit 1983); he died in prison in 1947. Lepke remained in hiding, and in an effort to eliminate all possible witnesses, he ordered a murder rampage—the number of killings at his direction is estimated at between 60 and 80 (Berger 1940). Despite his deservedly violent reputation, Lepke was a shy, slender man of about five feet, seven inches. In contrast to many of his more flamboyant colleagues, Buchalter preferred to spend most of his nonworking time at home with his English wife and stepson, occasionally playing a round of golf or basking on the beach at Miami (Tully 1958).

The murder binge backfired; the reign of terror turned loyal Lepke men into terrified informers seeking police protection (Turkus and Feder 1951). Law enforcement pressure against organized crime intensified in an effort to "smoke" Lepke out of hiding, particularly after one of his gunmen mistakenly killed an innocent music publisher. There was also a $50,000 reward on his head. In 1939, according to a prearranged plan, Lepke surrendered to J. Edgar Hoover and columnist Walter Winchell. Buchalter had been misled into believing that a deal had been arranged with the authorities and that he would only have to stand trial for federal (drug) and not state (murder) charges. In 1940, Buchalter was convicted in federal court of antitrust and narcotics law violations and sentenced to 14 years.

To Buchalter's dismay, he was subsequently turned over to New York authorities and prosecuted by Dewey for extortion, for which he received a sentence of 30 years to life. Then, in 1941, he was prosecuted for murder in Brooklyn. After a protracted legal battle, in 1944 Buchalter was electrocuted. He has the dubious distinction of being the only major organized crime figure to be executed by the state.

Meyer Lansky and Benjamin Siegel

Meyer Lansky was born in either 1902 or 1904 in Byelorussia, one of the fifteen republics of the former Soviet Union. Meyer, his brother Jacob, and his sister were brought to the United States by their parents in 1911. He attended school in Brownsville, Brooklyn, and on the Lower East Side, where he completed the eighth grade. At age 15, Meyer left school for a job as a tool and die maker. His first recorded arrest was in 1918. Until that time, various popular sources report, Meyer was an honest and hardworking apprentice craftsman. In that year, he was arrested for assaulting Lucky Luciano with a crowbar. According to Hank Messick (1973), Lansky was returning home from work, tools in his hand, when he came upon Lucky Luciano beating a woman in an alley, while the young (age 12) Ben Siegel feebly attempted to stop him. Meyer and his crowbar succeeded. They were all arrested, and Lansky was fined $2 for disorderly conduct. The judge is reported to have stated to Siegel and Lansky that "You boys have bugs in your heads." Messick notes that Siegel not only kept the nickname but also lived up to it. However, no one called Ben Siegel "Bugsy" to his face—a second time.

Lacey (1991) presents a different version of the first encounter between Lansky and Luciano. The young Sicilian, head of a gang that preyed on Jewish youth, encountered the physically unimpressive Lansky. Surrounded and subjected to threats and demands for money, Lansky reportedly told them to commit a physically impossible sex act. His pluck apparently provided the basis for a lifelong friendship.

Benjamin Siegel was born in 1906 and raised in the Williamsburg section of Brooklyn (just across the Williamsburg Bridge from the Lower East Side). He had four sisters and a brother, Maurice. Maurice became a respected Beverly Hills physician. Ben grew into a handsome and powerfully built young man who was quick to violence (Jennings 1967). The diminutive Lansky (five feet, four inches, 135 pounds) and his friend Ben Siegel were part of a gang of Jewish young men—Lansky the brains, Siegel the brawn.

In addition to his legitimate shop work, Lansky accepted assignments as a labor union strong-arm and protector of crap games (Lacey 1991). He and Siegel organized their own dice games. As they grew successful, the duo surrounded themselves with *starkers* (Yiddish for "tough guys"). At the onset of Prohibition, the pair were primed to take advantage of the new opportunities that would present themselves, and they found one in the transportation business. Lansky became an automobile mechanic. His reputation and mechanical ability soon led to his servicing and "souping up" of stolen vehicles for use by bootleggers. However, hauling whiskey was a very risky business, and the "Bug and Meyer Gang" was soon providing the *starkers* necessary to protect those valuable shipments from the likes of Legs Diamond.

Along with transportation and bootlegging activities, Lansky and Siegel continued their gambling operations. This eventually attracted the attention of Italian crime boss Joe Masseria, whose men tried to "muscle in." At this point, Luciano, who was working for Masseria, intervened and reconciled the differences between the Jewish and Italian gangsters. Throughout his career, Luciano was able to act as an intermediary between Jewish and Italian gangsters, enabling him to gain important stature in organized crime. The duo, often in partnership with Luciano, also initiated their own bootlegging business. By the end of Prohibition, Lansky and Siegel were major powers in organized crime.

In 1936 or 1937, Siegel left New York for the West Coast, sent by eastern gang leaders who were interested in exploiting opportunities in California (Turkus and Feder 1951). Syndicate units in Cleveland, Chicago, and New York sent men to join the Siegel operation on the West Coast. One of them was the notorious ex-boxer Mickey Cohen. Cohen, in his 1975 autobiography, confirms that he was sent to California by Lou Rothkopf, one of the leaders of the Cleveland syndicate. He reports (1975: 35) that Jack Dragna (born in 1891 in Corleone, Sicily), crime boss in southern California, was not running things too well: "The organization had to pour money on to help Dragna at all times. So Benny came out here to get things moving good."[7]

Siegel got things moving: he organized a coalition of the crime bosses in California, with himself at the top and crime boss Jack Dragna as his top lieutenant. His thugs forced bookmakers in California and Arizona to subscribe to the syndicate-backed wire service (which reported racing results throughout the country). He muscled in on gambling operations throughout the state, set up a narcotics pipeline through Mexico, and organized prostitution from Seattle to San Diego. Siegel also established offshore gambling on ships anchored beyond the three-mile limit, gained control of the union that represented movie extras, and extorted money from the movie industry. He was also the (hidden) owner of the California Metals Company in Los Angeles, which handled salvage metals during World War II (Reid and Demaris 1964).

Although he established himself in a host of rackets, Siegel is best remembered for his activities in Las Vegas. Beginning in 1946, with financial backing from Nevada-based gamblers and eastern gang leaders, Siegel built the first of the grand-style Las Vegas gambling casino hotels, the Flamingo. Upon opening, however, the not-quite-finished luxury hotel became a money loser because of a combination of bad luck, incompetent help, and a business downturn. Siegel reached out for more financing, but his activities apparently became more independent, which alienated him from Lansky and the other gang leaders. At midnight, June 20, 1947, Siegel was hit by a "fusillade of bullets fired through the living room of a Beverly Hills house [home of Virginia Hill] where he was staying" ("Siegel, Gangster, Is Slain on Coast" 1947: 1). Lacey (1991) states that it was Siegel's Las Vegas partners[8] who were behind his murder. In any event, they took over the Flamingo upon Siegel's demise.

During the 1930s, Lansky was able to arrange with the Cuban dictator Fulgencio Batista for the syndicate to control gambling in Havana. This domination was interrupted by World War II and Batista's postwar exile in the United States. A coup in 1952 brought Batista back to power, and Lansky returned to Cuba. Before he reassumed dominance in Havana gambling, the industry had been crippled by dishonesty and publicity about cheated tourists. Lansky put an end to this and turned the city into a gambling Mecca, until Fidel Castro booted both Batista and the syndicate out of Cuba (Lacey 1991). Lansky moved his gambling interests to the Bahamas and Haiti.

Despite his limited education, Lansky was known as a thinker and a reader—he belonged to the Book-of-the-Month Club—features of his personality that apparently brought kudos from his colleagues. His extensive gambling enterprises, many in partnership with Vincent ("Jimmy Blue Eyes") Alo, a boyhood friend from the Lower East Side and a partner of Lucky Luciano, reached from upstate New York to Fort Worth, Texas. Alo, a captain in the Genovese crime Family, provided the muscle for Lansky's operations (Lacey 1991). Lansky became known as the premier "money

---

[7]By the end of World War II, Mickey Cohen was well established (and notorious) in suburban Los Angeles, where he ran a large gambling operation. Jack Dragna had a number of Cohen associates killed and also attempted to kill Cohen in a secret but unsuccessful attempt to take over his gambling operations (Demaris 1981). The Los Angeles crime Family has long been considered weak and ineffectual—sometimes referred to as the "Mickey Mouse Mafia." During the 1980s, one mob associate—a strong-arm from Boston—was insulted by the offer of membership in the Los Angeles Family headed by Peter John Milano (J. Smith 1998).

[8]Gus Greenbaum, Moe Sedway, Davie Berman, Morris Rosen, and Willie Alderman.

mover" for organized crime, "washing" illegitimate funds and investing them in legitimate enterprises such as the jukebox business.

During World War II, Lansky registered for the Selective Service but was never called because he was above the draft age. In 1953 he served a brief jail term for running a gambling operation in Saratoga Springs, New York (just north of Albany). Afterward, Lansky moved to Florida and concentrated on investments in the southern part of that state. His operations were so lucrative that he is reputed to have kept a former bootlegger associate living in Switzerland as his full-time money manager (McFadden 1983). In 1970, fearing an indictment for income-tax evasion, Lansky fled to Israel, where he touched off a 26-month legal fight. Lansky claimed citizenship as a Jew under Israel's "Law of Return." He also reported that his efforts before the 1948 War of Independence resulted in badly needed munitions being smuggled out of East Coast ports to the Jewish underground in Palestine. The United States pressured Israel for his return, saying Lansky was a dangerous criminal. The case went to Israel's highest court, which in 1972 ruled that he was not entitled to citizenship because his past made him a "danger to public safety" (McFadden 1983).

When Lansky returned to Miami, he was immediately arrested and posted a cash bail of $250,000. He was ultimately cleared of, or ruled too ill to stand trial on, all the tax evasion, conspiracy, and Las Vegas "skimming" charges against him. Lansky spent his last years in seclusion in a Miami Beach condominium with his second wife. He died of cancer in 1983.[9]

INTERETHNIC COOPERATION: MURDER, INC.

The setting is the East New York–Brownsville section of Brooklyn, a Jewish neighborhood, and the

adjoining Italian neighborhood of Ocean Hill. The story begins in the spring of 1930, when Abe ("Kid Twist") Reles, Martin ("Bugsy") Goldstein, and Harry ("Pittsburgh Phil") Strauss decided to make some easy money by going into the pinball-machine business, renting the machines to candy stores and poolrooms. It was a good idea, but hardly original. In fact, the pinball business and organized criminal activities in that part of Brooklyn were controlled by the notorious Shapiro brothers—Irving, Meyer, and Willie. To deal with the anticipated problem, the boys from East New York–Brownsville teamed up with a crew of Italian criminals from Ocean Hill. Together they began to make inroads into the business controlled by the Shapiros, and with profits from the pinball machines they entered the loansharking business. The Shapiro brothers responded.

In 1930 a member of the Reles group was killed, and Reles and Goldstein were wounded. Meyer Shapiro then abducted Reles's girlfriend, whom he beat and raped. The Reles group struck back. During 1930 and 1931, eighteen attempts were made on the life of Meyer Shapiro—the nineteenth was successful. Brother Irving's demise followed, and Willie was abducted, severely beaten, and buried alive. The Reles group took over gambling, loansharking, and prostitution in the East New York–Brownsville sections, and they soon became involved in labor racketeering. However, their specialty became murder. Joselit (1983: 153) stresses the level of intergroup cooperation, noting that the Jewish and Italian members of the group "worked side by side on a daily basis, physically molesting tardy borrowers and stubborn union leaders." Moreover, they took orders from Albert Anastasia (discussed later).

The "Boys from Brooklyn" were used as staff killers by the newly formed confederation of organized crime leaders that emerged from Prohibition. In addition to their various criminal enterprises, the "Boys" received a retainer to be "on call" whenever the occasion arose—and it arose often. In a 10-year period, they murdered more than 80 persons in Brooklyn alone. They were so efficient that gang leaders from across the country made use of their services.

---

[9]Lansky's first marriage in 1929 ended in a divorce in 1946. The couple had two sons and a daughter. One of Lansky's two sons, Paul, is a graduate of West Point and a pilot with a master's degree in engineering who served a tour in Vietnam (Lacey 1991).

There were full-dress rehearsals; getaway routes were carefully checked. A "crash car" followed the stolen vehicle containing the actual killers in the event of a police pursuit. Guns were rendered untraceable, although ropes and ice picks were often the preferred weapons. One of the group's members describes the "contract system" (Berger 1940: 5): the killer ("trooper") is merely directed to take a plane, car, or train to a certain place to meet "a man." The man points out ("fingers") the victim for the trooper, who kills him when it is convenient. The trooper then leaves town immediately, and when local hoodlums are questioned, their alibis are perfect.

In 1940, several of the "Boys" were indicted for the 1933 murder of a nineteen-year-old who had been "convicted" of talking to the authorities. Quite to the surprise of the Brooklyn district attorney's office, one of the group's members agreed to become a government witness; he was reputedly the toughest of the "Boys." Abe Reles, upon being granted immunity from prosecution, began to disclose the sensational details of Murder, Inc. His information and subsequent testimony led to the conviction and electrocution of seven men. Before any case could be made against Albert Anastasia, however, Reles had an accident. On November 12, 1941, while under constant police guard, he fell out of the sixth-floor window of a Coney Island hotel. His death remains officially unexplained.

The Jewish role in organized crime was beginning to wane as the United States inched toward World War II. Restrictive immigration laws—the Johnson Act of 1921 and the Reed–Johnson Act of 1924—had cut off Jewish immigration, and the pool of available candidates for membership in criminal organizations was rapidly declining. By the end of the war, it was apparent that the Jewish role in organized crime had been eclipsed by Italians.

ITALIAN ORGANIZED CRIME IN NEW YORK

Between 1891 and 1920, four million Italians entered America, the overwhelming majority coming from the *Mezzogiorno*, the area south of Rome—in particular, Sicily, Naples, its surrounding Campania area, and the province of Calabria (Gallo 1981). Every important Italian-American OC figure has had cultural roots in the *Mezzogiorno*. These poor immigrants encountered an economy shaped by the Astors, the Rockefellers, and the Vanderbilts, in which powerless people had little opportunity. They faced enormous social and economic hardship exacerbated by ethnic prejudice. They "found work in the city's construction crews, laboring as ditch diggers, hod carriers, and stone cutters. As long as they had strong arms, it did not matter if they could not speak English or operate a complex machine" (1981: 44).

By early 1900, there were about 500,000 (mostly southern) Italians in New York City, living in the most deprived social and economic circumstances. Italian immigration "made fortunes for speculators and landlords, but it also transformed the neighborhood into a kind of human antheap in which suffering, crime, ignorance and filth were the dominant elements" (Petacco 1974: 16). The Italian immigrant provided the cheap labor vital to the expanding capitalism of that era. As with earlier generations of immigrants, a small number sought to succeed by bending and breaking both moral and legal codes. Being relative latecomers, they could not imitate the scions of earlier generations who had already, by "hook or crook," secured a place in society. Instead, they adapted their southern Italian culture to the American experience.

"Functional deficiencies of the official structure," notes Robert Merton (1967: 127), "generate an alternative (unofficial) structure to fulfill existing needs somewhat more effectively." Randall Collins (1975: 463) adds that "where legitimate careers are blocked and resources available for careers in crime, individuals would be expected to move in that direction." Thus, Collins notes, the prominence of Italians in organized crime is related to the coincidence of several historical factors: "The arrival of large numbers of European immigrants from peasant backgrounds who demanded cultural services that the dominant Anglo-Protestant society made illegal; the availability of a patrimonial form of military organization that could be applied to protecting such services; and the relatively late arrival of the Italians in comparison with other ethnic groups (e.g., the Irish) who had acquired control of legitimate channels of political and related economic mobility" (1975: 463).

"In order to beat rival organizations," notes Luigi Barzini (1965: 273), "criminals of Sicilian descent reproduced the kind of illegal groups they had belonged to in the old country and employed the same rules to make them invincible." Richard Gambino (1974: 304) concludes that although southern Italian characteristics do not predispose people toward crime, "where the mode of life has been impressed onto organized crime it has made it difficult to combat effectively the criminal activity" (1974: 297).

There were Mafia gangs in every American city that had a sizable Sicilian population, "feeding off the common laborer's honest toil and claiming to serve as a means of easing adjustment to American society" (Nelli 1976: 136). The Mafia "was imported by Sicilian immigrants, who reproduced it in the cities in which they settled, as a ritual brotherhood consisting of loosely linked but otherwise independent and uncoordinated 'families' organized hierarchically" (Hobsbawm 1969: 686). Mafia organizations "served important social as well as financial functions. The group produced a sense of belonging and of security in numbers. This function was at least in part through the use of initiation ceremonies, passwords and rituals, and rules of conduct with which members must abide" (Nelli 1976: 138). These groups of *mafiosi* were involved in the manufacture of low-cost, high-proof, untaxed alcohol, a business that prepared them well for Prohibition.

One of Francis Ianni's (1972: 57) informants describes a Mafia gang operating in Brooklyn in 1928: "All the old Sicilian 'moustaches' used to get together in the backroom of the club—it was a *fratallanze* [brotherhood] and they used to call it *Unione Siciliana*. They spent a lot of time talking about the old country, drinking wine and playing cards. But these were tough guys too, and they were alky cookers [bootleggers] and pretty much ran things in the neighborhood. They had all of

the businesses locked up and they got a piece of everything that was sold."

The *Unione Siciliana* emerged in late-nineteenth-century New York as a lawful fraternal society designed to advance the interests of Sicilian immigrants. Branches were established wherever new colonies of Sicilians expanded. With Prohibition, gangsters began to infiltrate and pervert the association. With an expanding criminal front, *Unione* leaders became natural catalysts for any racketeers seeking to widen their influence and profit potentials.[10] Membership included clannish old-world criminal types who stressed the maintenance of the cultural traditions of the Sicilian Mafia, and a younger Americanized faction anxious to increase operations through cooperative agreements even with non-Italians: "The *Unione* of the 1920s became the object of power struggles, with both orientations contending at local, regional, and national levels for more advantageous posts. This struggle terminated in 1931 in the Castellammarese war" (Inciardi 1975: 115).

The Castellammarese War

By 1930, there were two major factions in Italian organized crime in New York, one headed by Giuseppe ("Joe the Boss") Masseria, operating out of the Little Italy of East Harlem, and the other by Salvatore Maranzano, whose business office was in midtown Manhattan. Prohibition had enabled the Mafia gangs to break out of the bounds of "Little Italy" and operate in the wider society—booze-hungry Americans were not fussy about the source of their liquor. The struggle for domination of Italian-American OC in New York became known as the Castellammarese war because Maranzano and many of his supporters came from the small Sicilian coastal town of Castellammare del Golfo. The Maranzano group consisted mainly of Sicilians, especially the "moustaches," Old World types, many of whom had fled Mussolini's persecution of *mafiosi* (discussed in Chapter 7). After his

---

[10]In Italy, the Freemasons reportedly played a similar role: Mafia bosses became members to enhance their relationships with business and political leaders (della Porta and Vannucci 1999).

own escape, Maranzano helped smuggle many of his compatriots into the United States, and these supported their *padrone*. The Masseria group had both Sicilian and non-Sicilian members, including Lucky Luciano and Gaetano Lucchese (Sicilians), Vito Genovese (Neapolitan), and Frank Costello (Calabrian). Through ties developed by Luciano, they were allied with non-Italians such as Meyer Lansky and Ben Siegel. As the war turned against Masseria—the Maranzano forces were reinforced by a continuing supply of Sicilian exiles—five of his leading men, led by Luciano, went over to the other side. They failed to notify Joe the Boss.

On April 15, 1931, Masseria drove his steel-armored sedan, a massive car with plate glass an inch thick in all of its windows, to a garage near the Nuova Villa in the Coney Island section of Brooklyn. He then walked to the restaurant for a meal and a card game with Luciano. It was Masseria's last meal ("Racket Chief Slain by Gangster Gunfire" 1931). Luciano excused himself and went to the washroom: "Joe the Boss was shot as he sat at the table. As Masseria died, he still clutched the ace of diamonds, and that, in years to come, became a symbol of impending death to all good Mafia members" (Messick 1973: 54). The Castellammarese war was over.

It did not take long for Maranzano to irritate many of his followers, particularly the more Americanized gangsters such as Luciano. Joseph Bonanno, who was born in Castellammare del Golfo, was a staunch ally of Maranzano. In his autobiography, Bonanno points out that the new Mafia boss was out of step with the times: "Maranzano was old-world Sicilian in temperament and style. But he didn't live in Sicily anymore. In New York he was advisor not only to Sicilians but to American-Italians. Maranzano represented a style that often clashed with that of the Americanized men who surrounded him after the war. It was difficult, for example, for Maranzano even to communicate effectively with many of these men, for they only understood American street cant" (1983: 137–38).

On September 10, 1931, four men carrying pistols entered a suite at 230 Park Avenue, the Grand Central Building, in New York City: "One of them ordered the seven men and Miss Frances

Samuels, a secretary, to line up against the wall. The others stalked into the private office of Salvatore Maranzano. There was a sound of voices raised in angry dispute; blows, struggling, and finally pistol shots, and the four men dashed out of the suite." Maranzano was found with "his body riddled with bullets and punctured with knife wounds" ("Gang Kills Suspect in Alien Smuggling" 1931: 1). The killers are believed to have been Jews (who Maranzano and his bodyguards would not recognize) sent by Lansky and Siegel at the behest of Luciano. Because the killers flashed badges, Maranzano and his bodyguards apparently believed them to be federal immigration agents, who had visited him before as part of an investigation into the smuggling of Sicilians into the country. They attempted to kill him silently with knives, and when Maranzano fought furiously to save his life, they shot him.

In the aftermath of the Castellammarese war, five Italian-American crime Families emerged, and they continue to maintain distinct identities.

The Luciano/Genovese Family

Born Salvatore Lucania in western Sicily, in 1897, Luciano arrived in New York with his parents early in 1907. The family settled on Manhattan's Lower East Side. Although Luciano's conduct in school was satisfactory, his academic record was poor and made worse by chronic truancy. He left school when he was fourteen and secured employment as a shipping boy in a hat factory owned by Jewish man. The young Luciano became a member of the Five Points Gang and a heroin user and seller. In 1916 he was found guilty of possessing narcotics and sent to a reformatory for six months (Nelli 1976; Powell 2000).

With the advent of Prohibition, Luciano emerged as a leader in the Masseria crime Family. During the Castellammarese war, he was kidnapped, badly beaten, and left for dead. His survival has often been cited (incorrectly) as the source of his nickname, Lucky.[11] With the deaths

---

[11]Articles in the *New York Times* refer to Luciano as "Lucky" prior to this incident. The nickname is apparently derived from a shortening of Lucania to "Luc" and then "Lucky."

Charles "Lucky" Luciano on board a Sicilian train in 1949. Luciano rose to power in traditional organized-crime fashion. Arriving in Manhattan's Lower East Side from Sicily at age ten with his family, he soon became a member of a neighborhood gang and later was initiated into the Masseria crime Family. He emerged as a Family leader during Prohibition and, with the deaths of Masseria and Maranzano in the Castellammarese war, went on to become the most important Italian OC figure in New York.

of Masseria and Maranzano, Luciano became the most important Italian organized crime figure in New York, a status he would enjoy until 1935. In that year, investigators for Thomas E. Dewey discovered an extensive prostitution network that, although independent at one time, had been subject to extortion by a member of the Luciano Family. In a single raid, Dewey's investigators arrested prostitutes, madams, and "bookers" (pimps). They were pressured and cajoled into testifying against Luciano, who protested that he had no knowledge of or involvement in the extortion activities. Dewey charged that acting on behalf of Luciano, 200 bordellos and 3,000 prostitutes were orga-

nized into a $12-million-a-year business. In fact, the witnesses tying Luciano to prostitution were not credible, and this enterprise was not even a good money-maker for the syndicate (Powell 2000): "Dewey's argument seemed to be that Luciano was a prostitution overlord but even if he was not, he still was a menace to society" (Stolberg 1995: 128).

Luciano chose to take the stand in his own defense—a bad decision, as it turned out. Dewey was able to trap him in lies about his criminal record. In 1936, Luciano was found guilty of 61 counts of compulsory prostitution and sentenced to a term of 30 to 60 years in prison, despite an arguably weak case and a pervasive feeling that Luciano was actually convicted of being "notorious" (Powell 2000).

Luciano languished in Clinton State Prison at Dannemora, New York, while war raged in Europe and the Pacific. By 1942, German submarines operating in U.S. coastal waters had sunk 272 U.S. ships. It was suspected that information on American shipping was being leaked to the Germans by people employed in eastern ports.[12] It was also suspected, incorrectly, that German submarines were receiving supplies from American fishing boats. The specter of sabotage was raised when the luxury liner *Normandie*, which had been refitted as a naval vessel, rolled over in flames while harbored in the Hudson River. (In fact, renamed the U.S.S. *Lafayette*, the *Normandie* was accidentally set ablaze by workers using acetylene torches.)

With the help of the Manhattan district attorney, naval intelligence officials met with Joseph ("Socks") Lanza, the vicious criminal "czar" of the Fulton Fish Market, who was under indictment for conspiracy and extortion.[13] Lanza agreed to help but noted that his influence was limited; he suggested that the man to see was Lucky Luciano. Luciano was transferred to a prison closer to New

---

[12]Coastal cities such as New York, Atlantic City, and Miami, fearing a loss of tourist trade, refused to enforce blackouts, creating a neon shooting gallery for German submarines: "The U-boats nightly lay in the wait on the seaward side of the shipping lanes and picked off their sharply silhouetted victims at will" (Kennedy 1999: 68).
[13]Socks Lanza is discussed in Chapter 12.

York City to meet with naval intelligence officers. Through Meyer Lansky, the word went out. According to Rodney Campbell (1977), in addition to ordering port workers and fishermen to "keep alert," crime figures helped place intelligence operatives in key areas by supplying them with union cards and securing positions for them on the waterfront, on fishing boats, and in waterfront bars, restaurants, and hotels. They also provided another important service. At the request of naval officials, they prevented strikes and other forms of labor unrest that could interrupt wartime shipping. While Campbell provides documentation of Luciano's domestic role during the war, his data on Luciano's role in the invasion of Sicily are tenuous. According to Campbell, Luciano sent word to Sicilian *capimafiosi* to assist the Allied landing. However, *mafiosi* did not need encouragement from Luciano—their desire to rid the island of Mussolini's iron hand was incentive enough.

In 1945, Dewey, then governor of New York, received a petition for executive clemency on behalf of Luciano, citing his efforts during the war. The following year, Dewey announced that Luciano would be released from prison and deported to Italy. Luciano left the United States on February 9, 1946. Before the end of the year, however, he was in Havana, holding court with the elite of New York's underworld. The following year, U.S. pressure on Cuba compelled Luciano to return to Italy, where he died of a heart attack in 1962.

Frank Costello   With Luciano in prison and then deported to Italy, leadership of his crime Family was assumed by Frank Costello. Christened Francesco Castiglia, Costello was born in Calabria in 1891. Like several other Italian criminals (and boxers), he affected an Irish surname, which was certainly no hindrance in New York, where the Irish-dominated Tammany Hall ruled the city. In 1915, Costello served a ten-month sentence for carrying a concealed firearm. By 1923, he was a successful bootlegger working for Bill Dwyer, an ex-longshoreman turned rumrunner, who brought liquor from Canada across the Great Lakes in armored speedboats (Talese 1965). Costello moved into gambling and eventually became a successful

(and legitimate) real estate dealer. Known as the "King of the Slots," Costello operated an extensive network of "one-armed bandits"[14] in New York City until Mayor Fiorello La Guardia went on a highly publicized campaign to rid the city of "that bum." Many sources report that Costello was then invited to bring his slot machines to New Orleans by the political boss of Louisiana, Senator Huey P. Long.[15]

Costello was known for his political influence. In the 1940s, "Tammany's aging Irish chieftains turned to the Italian-controlled underworld for desperately needed funding." This "Mafia Plan" was not without risk: Costello and his colleagues "decided to install their own Italian district leaders in Tammany clubhouses" (Erie 1988: 122).

In 1951, Costello appeared before the Kefauver Committee (discussed in Chapter 3) and was exposed on national television as a major crime figure. However, only Costello's hands could be seen; his lawyer had insisted that Costello not be televised. The crime boss's evasive responses, coupled with a dramatic walkout, eventually led to an 18-month prison term for contempt of the Senate. In 1952 the government moved against him for income-tax evasion, for which in 1954 Costello received a sentence of five years' imprisonment. In 1956 his attorney proved that the conviction had been based on illegal wiretaps, and Costello was freed ("Frank Costello Dies of Coronary at 82" 1972: 21).

Costello routinely traveled without any bodyguards. In 1957 he had an appointment to meet a Family *caporegime* in charge of Greenwich Village. The restaurant meeting had been arranged by Vito Genovese, Family underboss, and Costello's

---

[14]The slot machines dispensed candy mints as well as tokens that were redeemable for money: "The purpose of this arrangement was to make it arguable before friendly judges that the one-armed bandits were actually vending machines" (Peterson 1983: 183).

[15]The Kingfish's biographer, T. Harry Williams (1969), questions Long's connection to Costello. Costello informed a federal grand jury that Senator Long had invited him into New Orleans to set up a thousand slot machines for a fee of $30 per machine. However, Williams argues that such a setup would require police protection in a city that in 1935 was controlled by Semmes Walmsley, a bitter enemy of the Kingfish.

movements were being monitored. A call was made to a pay phone where a double-parked car was waiting for word that Costello was on his way home. As Costello rushed to catch the elevator in his luxury apartment building, he ran by a large man wearing a fedora. The man yelled, "This is for you, Frank." As Costello turned, the man fired a revolver at Costello's face from a distance of six to ten feet. The bullet hit Costello in the head but caused only superficial damage. When questioned by authorities, Costello insisted he did not recognize his assailant, the easily recognizable Vincenzo ("Chin") Gigante, an ex-pugilist and Genovese gunman (who in 1985 would become boss of the crime Family). Several months later, in what is believed to have been a related incident, Albert Anastasia, Costello's close ally and boss of the Mineo crime Family, was murdered. Costello retired, leaving Vito Genovese as boss of the Luciano Family (Katz 1973).

Vito Genovese   The man who allegedly ordered the bungled attempt on Costello's life was born near Naples in 1897. At age fifteen, he arrived in New York and lived with his family in the Little Italy section of downtown Manhattan. Beginning as a street thief, Genovese graduated to working as a collector for the Italian lottery and eventually became an associate of Lucky Luciano. When his first wife died of tuberculosis in 1931, Genovese announced his intention to marry Anna Petillo— but she was already married. Twelve days later, Mr. Petillo was strangled to death, and Genovese married the widow Petillo. After twelve years of marriage, Anna Genovese sued him for support and denounced Vito in court as a racketeer with a huge income. The much-feared crime boss did nothing; reportedly, Genovese was too much in love with her to have her killed (Gage 1972).

During the 1930s, Genovese was already a power in organized crime, making huge profits in narcotics. In 1934, however, he was involved in a bungled murder and forced to flee to Italy to avoid prosecution; he took $750,000 with him. In Italy he is reputed to have become a confidant of Benito Mussolini. In 1943 a stridently anti-Fascist Italian newspaper editor in New York was shot to death "gangland style." The contract for his murder has been linked to Genovese's friendship with Mussolini (Peterson 1983). Nevertheless, during the American invasion, Genovese was able to gain the confidence of American military authorities, for whom he acted as an interpreter. This position enabled him to become a major black marketeer, until he was identified as an American fugitive and returned to the United States for trial. While awaiting trial, a key witness was poisoned while in protective custody, and Genovese went free.

In 1959, Genovese, along with 14 others, was convicted of conspiracy to violate narcotics laws. In 1969, while serving his 15-year sentence, Genovese died of a heart ailment. However, despite numerous changes in leadership, the group he headed is still referred to as the Genovese Family. Its operations extend into New Jersey, Connecticut, parts of Massachusetts, and upstate New York.

The Genovese Family is considered the most powerful in the United States. Under the leadership of Vincenzo Gigante, members kept a low profile and avoided the informant–eavesdropping combination that has crippled other Families. Discipline was rigorous, and members who failed to toe the line were beaten and, in at least two cases, killed. Nevertheless, in 1990, Gigante was indicted for conspiring to rig bids and extort payoffs from contractors looking to do business with the New York City Housing Authority and spent much of his time trying to avoid trial—his lawyers claimed that the ex-fighter was brain-damaged and incompetent. In 1993 he was indicted for approving six murders and plotting to kill John Gotti. In 1997, at age 69 and out on bail, Gigante was declared fit to stand trial. Later that year, a jury found him guilty of racketeering—but not murder—and he was sentenced to 12 years. In 2002, Gigante was indicted for continuing to run the Genovese Family from prison; his son Andrew, 47, was indicted for acting as his intermediary.

The Mineo/Gambino Family

Al Mineo was a close ally of Joseph Masseria and also a victim of the Castellammarese war—he was murdered in 1930. After the death of Masseria,

Frank Scalise, who had defected from the Mineo Family early in the war, was made boss of that Family. He became a close confidant of Maranzano and after Maranzano's death was replaced by Vincent Mangano. In 1951, after his brother Philip was murdered, Vincent Mangano disappeared, presumably murdered at the direction of Family underboss Albert Anastasia, who then became Family boss.

Albert Anastasia   Albert Anastasia was born Umberto Anastasio in Tropea, Italy, in 1902. He entered the United States in 1919 and reportedly changed his name to save his family some embarrassment as a result of his 1921 arrest for murdering a fellow longshoreman (Freeman 1957). His brother, Anthony ("Tough Tony") Anastasio, became the official ruler of the Brooklyn waterfront as head of Local 1814 of the International Longshoremen's Association (ILA). Albert became the unofficial ruler of these same docks. (A third brother, Salvatore, became a priest.) Albert was widely feared even among his associates and reportedly enjoyed the title "Executioner" (Berger 1957)—he issued the "contract hits" for Murder, Inc.

In 1923, Anastasia was sentenced to two years' imprisonment for possessing a firearm, although this did not prevent him from serving stateside in the U.S. Army during World War II. In 1955, he served a one-year sentence for income-tax evasion. Anastasia lived in a home along the Palisades in Fort Lee, New Jersey—a home with a seven-foot barbed wire fence, Doberman pinschers, and bodyguards. In 1957, Anastasia was in a chair at the Park Sheraton Hotel barbershop in midtown Manhattan. Two men walked in through the hotel lobby door. One walked up to Anastasia and fired a .38 caliber pistol. One bullet went into the back of Anastasia's head and lodged in the left side of his brain. Another went into his back at a downward angle, penetrating a lung, a kidney, and his spleen. The second shooter fired a .32 caliber pistol, and Anastasia staggered out of the chair and crashed to the floor—the "Executioner" had been executed. (In 1928 the Park Sheraton was known as the Park Central, the hotel where Arnold Rothstein was

shot.) Underboss Carlo Gambino, believed to have been in league with Vito Genovese and Joseph Profaci, became boss of the crime Family.

Carlo Gambino   Born in Palermo in 1902, Gambino arrived in the United States (an illegal alien) in 1921 and never became a citizen. He resided in Brooklyn, assisted by numerous relatives who had arrived earlier. In turn, he helped his brothers when they arrived in the United States. His boyhood friend from Palermo, Gaetano Lucchese, was already in the United States and rising in the ranks of organized crime, first under Masseria and then, as a defector, under Maranzano. He followed Lucchese into the Maranzano camp and after Maranzano's death moved into the ranks of the Mineo Family, eventually becoming a *caporegime* under Vincent Mangano. Gambino's son Thomas married Lucchese's daughter.

After Prohibition, Gambino continued in the bootlegging business and in 1939 received a 22-month sentence for conspiracy to defraud the United States of liquor taxes. Eight months later, the conviction was thrown out because evidence had been based on illegal wiretaps. World War II served to make Gambino a millionaire; it also prevented him from being deported to Italy. Joseph Valachi testified before a Senate committee that Gambino "made over a million dollars from ration stamps during the war. The stamps came out of the O.P.A.'s [Office of Price Administration] offices. First Carlo's boys would steal them. Then, when the government started hiding them in banks, Carlo made contact and the O.P.A. men sold him the stamps" (Gage 1975: 26): "Wartime rationing of gasoline, meat, and groceries opened a nationwide black market that the American public patronized as eagerly as it had once bought bootleg booze" (Meskil 1973: 58).

When Albert Anastasia became Family boss, he made Gambino the *sottocapo*. After Anastasia's murder in 1957, Carlo became boss. A strong family man, Gambino had one daughter and two sons who operated a trucking firm in the garment center. When Gambino became ill and his underboss, Aniello Dellacroce, was in prison for income tax evasion, he appointed his first cousin and brother-in-law, a powerful Brooklyn *caporegime*, ("Big") Paul Castellano, as acting boss (Maas 1997). When Gambino died of a heart attack in 1976, Castellano assumed control of the Family.

Castellano was born in Brooklyn in 1915, the only son of Sicilian immigrants. He dropped out of school after the eighth grade. After five years at the helm of the Gambino Family, Castellano withdrew from many of the day-to-day activities, preferring to spend most of his time with a mistress at his Staten Island mansion. In 1983, the mansion was bugged by the FBI for almost five months. In 1984, Castellano was indicted because of the activities of a murderous Gambino crew in Brooklyn (see Mustain and Capeci 1992). The following year, he was hit with more indictments, this time the "commission case" (discussed in chapters 1 and 14). On December 16, 1985, Castellano and his underboss, Thomas Bilotti, were heading to a meeting at Spark's Steak House in midtown Manhattan:

> Three men in trench coats, tipped off to Castellano's expected arrival by a confidant-turned traitor named Frankie DeCicco, loitered in the urban shadows of the early Christmas-season dusk. Thomas Bilotti turned his boss's black Lincoln onto Forty-sixth Street, and parked it directly in front of a *No Parking* sign; the car had a Patrolmen's Benevolent Association sticker on the windshield. As the two victims emerged, the assassins approached them, producing semiautomatic weapons from under their coats and loosing a barrage of bullets at close range. Castellano and Bilotti were each shot six times in the head and torso. . . . [O]ne of the killers then crouched over Castellano's body and delivered a *coup de grâce* through the skull. (O'Brien and Kurins 1991: 11)

At a meeting of Family captains called by the Family *consigliere*, John Gotti was "elected" boss (Gotti trial tapes).

John Gotti John Gotti is a career criminal whose media coverage has eclipsed that of all previous crime figures. He has been the subject of cover stories in *Time*,[16] *People*, *New York*, and the *New York Times Magazine* and of numerous television specials. As with Al Capone, also a man of Neapolitan heritage, notoriety aided his downfall.

Gotti was born in the South Bronx in 1940, to a poor first-generation couple. He was the fifth of thirteen children, seven boys and six girls, two of whom died in infancy and four of whom become part of OC. Raised in the East New York–Brownsville section of Brooklyn, of Murder, Inc., fame, he was a member of a neighborhood gang. Dropping out of high school at age sixteen, Gotti began working for a soldier in the Gambino Family. Later he became part of the East New York crew headed by Carmine ("Charley Wagons") Fatico, a hijacker and Gambino *caporegime*.

Gotti, a strong-arm ex-convict (for a hijacking conviction), moved to Queens when Fatico set up headquarters at the Bergin Hunt and Fish Social Club, two storefronts in Ozone Park, a quiet, working-class neighborhood. In 1973, in a poorly executed murder, Gotti and his close friend Angelo Ruggiero gunned down one of the kidnap-murderers (the head of an Irish gang from Hell's Kitchen) of Carlo Gambino's nephew. In a plea bargain, Gotti and Ruggiero received sentences with four-year maximums. Shortly after his release from prison in 1977, Gotti was inducted into the Gambino Family and became a confidant of Aniello ("Neil") Dellacroce, Gambino Family underboss. When Fatico came under intense federal investigation and became inactive, Gotti, despite his lackluster performance as an "earner"—his wife once sued him for nonsupport—was placed in charge of the Fatico crew by Dellacroce.

When Carlo Gambino died in 1976, succession should have gone to Dellacroce. Instead, Dellacroce and Castellano met at a private home in Brooklyn, and a deal was struck: Castellano would become boss, and in order to appease the Dellacroce faction, he would keep Dellacroce as

---

[16]Gotti kept a framed copy on the wall of his office at the Bergin Hunt and Fish Club (Maas 1997).

underboss, just as Gambino had appointed Del-lacroce underboss to placate Anastasia stalwarts. The loyal Dellacroce opposed any efforts to move against Castellano.

But the Family now had two factions, one headed by Castellano, the other by Dellacroce. The more sophisticated Castellano faction was im-mersed in labor and business racketeering, while the "thug 'n' drug" Dellacroce group engaged in hijacking, extortion, loansharking, gambling, and, in violation of a Castellano edict, drugs. (In 1989, Gotti's brother Gene, then 42, was convicted of drug violations and sentenced to 50 years' impris-onment.) In fact, before he became Family boss, drugs were the primary source of Gotti's income. When Angelo Ruggiero was indicted for drug traf-ficking, Gotti feared that he and Ruggiero would be killed by Castellano—Castellano had copies of government surveillance tapes proving the crew's involvement in drugs. Soon afterward, in 1985, Gotti's mentor, Dellacroce, died of cancer at age 71. Castellano, awaiting trial, failed to attend the funeral and replaced Dellacroce with a loyal aide who lacked real stature—Thomas Bilotti, a vicious 45-year-old enforcer. Two weeks later, both were dead.

Gotti named *caporegime* Frank DeCicco as his underboss for his aid in killing Castellano. In 1986, DeCicco was the victim of a remote-controlled car bomb—"Chin" Gigante, boss of the Genovese Family, was set on avenging the murder of a fellow boss and confidant. Gigante reportedly planned to murder Gotti and several Gambino captains in-volved in Castellano's death (Raab 1995b). A sol-dier from the Lucchese Family who was with De-Ciccio was mistaken for Gotti and badly injured, losing his toes in the explosion (Capeci and Mus-tain 1996; Maas 1997). The Gigante plot included a plan to install two Castellano loyalists as boss and underboss of the Gambino Family. In any event, FBI electronic surveillance uncovered the plot, and Gotti was warned by federal agents. Gotti and Gigante subsequently met to arrange peace, but treachery continued. Frustrated by his inability to kill Gotti, in 1990 and 1991 Gigante had two men close to Gotti killed—the first had been on the Castellano execution team; the second was Gotti's

driver/bodyguard. In response, Gigante's under-boss was shot in his car and a bag of rotting fish left on the body (Blum 1993; Capeci and Mustain 1996; LeDuff 1998).

As boss, Gotti's finances changed consider-ably. His underboss gave him more than $100,000 a month as his percentage of Gambino Family in-come (Fried 1993a). A compulsive gambler, Gotti lived in a modest home in Howard Beach, Queens. Nevertheless, he represented a distinctly different type of mob boss than his Gambino Family prede-cessors. A flashy dresser with a high public profile, Gotti appeared to take delight in his notoriety. This "Capone-like" trait made him an especially attractive target for federal prosecutors. However, it was the presence of an informant in Gotti's inner circle, who was later murdered, that made him the primary target of the FBI's Gambino squad (Maas 1997).

In 1990, Gotti was indicted for racketeering and murder. He had previously been acquitted at three separate trials in five years, earning him the sobriquet "the Teflon Don." Dexterity at avoiding conviction appears to have been aided by several factors: competition between Justice Department officials (Dannen 1992a), a detective on the New York City Police Department's Intelligence Unit (Lubasch 1992d) who in 1993 pled guilty to selling secrets, and jury tampering—one juror was con-victed of selling his vote. In 1992, Gotti was found guilty of 43 federal charges, including 6 murders, one being that of Paul Castellano. His acting un-derboss, Frank Locascio, age 59, was found guilty of racketeering and murder conspiracy charges. Both were sentenced to life imprisonment.

Gotti was betrayed by his hand-picked *con-sigliere* and (later) underboss Salvatore ("Sammy the Bull") Gravano and by his own careless com-munications. Although he suspected that his con-versations were being intercepted—he was taped warning others to be guarded in their conversa-tions—Gotti engaged in incriminating conversa-tions on the telephone. And bugs were placed in his headquarters at the Ravenite Social Club in Manhattan's Little Italy (Blum 1993). The FBI played the tapes for Gravano, who heard Gotti malign him. The tapes also revealed Gotti accusing Gravano of duplicity and blaming him for three murders that Gotti had ordered. Both had been indicted for these murders, and Gotti had selected Gravano's defense attorney. Gravano feared that his boss was planning to have him take the fall (Capeci and Mustain 1996). Gravano's testimony also led to the conviction of 36 other OC figures.

Gotti's son, John, Jr. (born in 1964), who was elevated to *caporegime* by his father in 1990, had reportedly been acting on his father's behalf during the senior Gotti's imprisonment—tradition dictates that a boss can be replaced only if he abdicates or dies (Raab 1996b). However, Junior lacked the stature and respect required by a boss, and the Family was actually run for a time by a panel of *capiregime*. Thus, mid-level management eclipsed the position of boss and underboss, weakening the Family's ability to deal with other crime Families, particularly the Genovese. Early in 1998, Gotti, Jr., at 35, was indicted on federal tax evasion and extortion charges. In 1999, on the eve of his trial, he pleaded guilty to racketeering and received a sentence of 6.5 years.

Despite the changes in leadership, the crime group is still referred to as the Gambino Family. Its operations extend into upstate New York, New Jersey, and parts of New England.

The Reina/Lucchese Family

Gaetano ("Tommy") Reina headed one of the five Families in New York City that "formed spontaneously as Sicilian immigrants settled there" (Bonanno 1983: 84). Bonanno reports that because of the power of "Joe the Boss" Masseria, Reina had to be careful not to offend him "and generally toed the Masseria line" (1983: 85). At the start of the Castellammarese war, however, Reina began talking (privately) against Masseria, and it was reported to the boss—in 1930, Reina was killed by a blast from a sawed-off shotgun. According to Bonanno, Masseria backed one of his own supporters to head the Reina Family. However, Gaetano Gagliano formed a splinter group and was joined by Thomas Lucchese, who became the underboss of the newly formed Gagliano Family. Gagliano emerged on the side of the victorious Salvatore

Maranzano. His leadership of the crime Family lasted until his death in 1953, at which time Lucchese became boss.

Lucchese was born in Palermo, in 1900, and came to the United States in 1911. In 1919 he lost his right index finger in a machine-shop accident. Lucchese's nickname, "Three-Finger Brown," was the result of a 1921 arrest for car theft—the policeman who fingerprinted Lucchese was a fan of Mordechai ("Three-Finger") Brown, a pitcher for the Chicago Cubs. He wrote that name down under the alias section of the fingerprint card. Despite the 1921 conviction, for which he served 13 months in prison, Lucchese became a naturalized citizen in 1943 (Reid and Demaris 1953; Volkman 1998).

Lucchese was active in gambling, particularly numbers and bookmaking, in Queens, New York. During the 1930s he dominated the kosher chicken industry in New York City, organizing a cartel that controlled prices and competition (Volkman 1998): "Police officials listed eight dress firms in New York City in which Lucchese was a part owner and he had similar holdings in Scranton, Pennsylvania." His firms in New York City were nonunion and "strangely free from labor troubles" (Peterson 1983: 403). Lucchese lived in a luxurious yellow-brick ranch house that he constructed in Lido Beach, Long Island. His son Robert is a graduate of the United States Air Force Academy and became an Air Force officer. His daughter Frances went to Vassar College and later married the son of Carlo Gambino. Lucchese died of natural causes in 1967, and the leadership passed to 53-year-old Anthony ("Tony Ducks") Corallo.

Corallo controlled the private waste hauling industry on Long Island and had a stranglehold on much of the city's construction business through his control over the pouring of concrete. He received the nickname "Ducks" because of his ability to escape ("duck") assassinations and convictions. In 1968 this "ability" failed: he was sentenced to three years for trying to bribe both a New York State judge and a chief assistant U.S. attorney. The case he was trying to fix involved the head of Tammany Hall.

After his release from prison, the cautious Corallo ran operations from his Jaguar to avoid electronic surveillance, but to no avail—in 1983 the New York State Organized Crime Task Force planted a bug in the car. The "Jaguar Tapes" were a central piece of evidence in the "Commission Case" (discussed in Chapter 1) that led to the 1986 conviction of Corallo; Carmine Persico, boss of the Colombo Family; and Anthony Salerno, boss of the Genovese Family. Defendant Paul Castellano, boss of the Gambino Family, was murdered before the trial ended. In 2000, at 87, Corallo died while serving a life sentence in federal prison.

In recent years, the Lucchese Family has been plagued by betrayal, rebellion, and prosecution. Family boss Vittorio ("Little Vic") Amuso of Bensonhurst, Brooklyn, lost control of the New Jersey faction, a very successful crew of about fifteen members headed by Anthony ("Tumac") Acceturro and his son, Tony, Jr. In response, Amuso declared them outlaws and ordered their execution. Some, including the Acceturros, fled while others were accepted back into the fold after pledging fealty. In 1993, Acceturro, Sr., and five other members of the New Jersey faction were convicted of murder and racketeering.

By 1990, Amuso was a fugitive from federal charges involving a bid-rigging scheme for the installation of windows at New York City housing projects. In 1992, he was found guilty on 54 counts, including 9 murders, and sentenced to life imprisonment. In what is becoming a pattern in traditional organized crime, leadership was assumed by a most violent *capo*, Anthony ("Gaspipe"—a nickname he hates whose origins are in dispute) Casso.

Casso was born in 1940 and has a criminal history dating back to his adolescence in the waterfront section of Red Hook, Brooklyn, where he developed a reputation as a marksman and a vicious street brawler. By age 21, Casso was an enforcer on the Brooklyn docks. A close associate of Vic Amuso, he subsequently became his underboss. Casso was known for a lavish lifestyle that included a $500,000 diamond ring and a $1-million house in Brooklyn. He bought $2,000 suits by the dozen, and restaurant tabs of $1,000 were not un-

common. In 1986, Casso was the victim of a parking lot ambush, although none of the four bullets that struck him injured a vital organ. The unauthorized attack was ordered by a captain in the Gambino Family involved in a business dispute with Casso; he went to prison for heroin trafficking before Casso could exact revenge. Two of the shooters was not so lucky: one was tortured and murdered; the other surrendered to police and died of a heart attack while in jail. A third victim, an innocent repairman, was killed by Casso in a case of mistaken identity.

With Amuso's imprisonment, Casso became acting boss, despite being a fugitive from racketeering and murder charges at the time—he had been tipped off about an impending indictment in 1990 by a law enforcement source. After being at large for 32 months, Casso was captured by FBI agents without a struggle at his hideaway, a home in suburban New Jersey. There, the FBI found $340,000 in cash and internal FBI documents. During his time as a fugitive, the increasingly paranoid Casso is reported to have ordered the murder of at least eleven persons, many of them long-standing, loyal members of the Lucchese Family (Raab 1992b, 1993; Weiss and Nolan 1993; Volkman 1998), and plotted with "Chin" Gigante against John Gotti (Capeci and Mustain 1996). One of Casso's intended victims, loyal hit man Peter Chiodo, survived being shot seven times and became a government witness. In response, in a violation of *Cosa Nostra* etiquette, Casso ordered Chiodo's sister killed, but the shooters managed only to wound her. They did kill Chiodo's uncle, who had no connection to organized crime. Alphonse D'Arco, who had been running the Family for his fugitive boss, was suddenly pushed aside by Casso for no apparent reason. Fearing that he too would become a murder victim, D'Arco became a government witness (Marriott 1992; Volkman 1998), sealing Casso's fate. In 1994, Casso pled guilty to murder charges as part of an attempt to win clemency by becoming a government witness. This effort failed when he was found to be lying to government attorneys. He is currently serving a life sentence.

Despite changes in leadership, this crime Family is still referred to as the Lucchese Family.

The Profaci/Colombo Family

Joseph Profaci was born in Palermo in 1897. An ex-convict, he came to the United States in 1922, when Mussolini was chasing *mafiosi*. In the United States, Profaci never served a prison sentence, a remarkable feat for the man who had a crime Family named after him. However, he did manage to owe the United States $1.5 million in income taxes. And he became the only mob boss to be arrested at OC conclaves both in Cleveland in 1928 and Apalachin, New York, in 1957 (discussed later—Neff 1989).

Profaci owned at least 20 legitimate businesses and as the "Olive Oil King" was the largest single importer of olive oil into the United States. In addition to his modest Brooklyn home, he owned a luxurious home in Miami Beach and a hunting lodge ("Profaci Dies of Cancer, Led Feuding Brooklyn Mob" 1962). His daughter Rosalie married Joseph Bonanno's son Salvatore ("Bill"), and another daughter is married to Jack Tocco, Detroit Family boss; his son Salvatore is a *caporegime* in the Colombo crime Family.

Although clean shaven, Profaci was clearly a "moustache," faithful to Old World traditions. He was a devoted family man, devoid of any apparent extramarital interests. His profession notwithstanding, Profaci was a faithful churchgoer, a friend of the priest, and a large contributor to church charities. One of the churches in the Bensonhurst–Bath Beach section of Brooklyn, where he lived, had a statue adorned with a crown of jewels worth several thousand dollars. Some reports indicate that Profaci contributed the crown. In any event, a local thief decided to steal the crown—an outrage that Profaci ordered "corrected." Although the crown was returned, the culprit failed to restore three missing diamonds. His body was subsequently found, and lest the reason for his murder be misinterpreted, a set of rosary beads was wrapped around his neck (Martin 1963).

The Gallo Brothers Profaci's traditionalism was viewed as despotic by some members of his crime

Family. He apparently demanded a big percentage of all their illegal profits, and he placed "blood" and friendship above business: relatives and old friends received larger shares of Family opportunities than did others in his ranks. In 1959 a numbers operator was murdered on orders from Profaci. The contract was carried out by Joseph ("Joe Jelly") Gioiello, a short, rotund, vicious killer, part of a Profaci crew headed by the Gallo brothers in Red Hook, Brooklyn. The Gallo brothers—Larry, Albert ("Kid Blast"), and ("Crazy") Joey—expected to receive a large share of the deceased victim's gambling operations. Instead, Profaci divided it up among friends and relatives. The Gallo crew fumed until February 1961. Then, in one 24-hour period, they abducted four of Profaci's closest associates, but the boss himself eluded capture. What transpired afterward would rival the Roman plots in the days of the Caesars.

Profaci agreed to be more generous with the Gallo crew. However, several Gallo men secretly went over to the Profaci side, and on August 20, 1961, they lured Larry Gallo to a lounge in Brooklyn. Early in the morning, before the lounge opened for business, Carmine ("Junior" or "the Snake") Persico[17] and Hughie ("Apples") McIntosh[18] placed a rope around Larry's neck and slowly began to squeeze the life out of him. A police sergeant came into the lounge only minutes before the victim would have expired—Gallo had already lost control of his bowels and bladder. The officer noticed Larry's feet sticking out from behind the bar, and he saw two men dash from the darkened room out a side door. His driver, a patrolman waiting outside, attempted to stop the two men and was shot in the face, suffering a wound in the right cheek. Larry survived the ordeal, his neck badly scarred.

Later that day, "Joe Jelly" was "put to sleep with the fishes"—his coat was dumped in front of the Gallo's South Brooklyn headquarters wrapped around several fresh fish. The "war" was on, but it

---

[17]In 1972, Persico became boss of the Colombo Family.
[18]In 1997, McIntosh, a longtime associate of Carmine Persico and a feared enforcer who wore a size 52 suit, died at age 70 while serving a sentence in federal prison.

was a rather one-sided affair. At least twelve men were killed, mostly Gallo loyalists. The Gallo group "took to the mattresses"—they sought refuge in their Red Hook headquarters at 49–51 President Street, a block away from the Union Street Seventy-Sixth Police Precinct House. A special squad of New York City detectives headed by Raymond V. Martin (whose book on the subject was published in 1963) was assigned to maintain surveillance of the area. The police probably saved the Gallo crew from being completely wiped out by Profaci gunmen. During this period, the Gallos were responsible for saving several neighborhood youngsters from a building fire; they joked to television reporters that the police would probably arrest them for arson. In any event, the Gallo boys became neighborhood heroes, and the news media reported extensively on their exploits.

Gang wars are expensive. It is difficult to earn money if one is in hiding or spending most of his time seeking out the enemy while avoiding being killed.[19] The financial condition of the Gallos grew worse. In 1961, in an effort to replenish his dwindling income, Joey Gallo attempted to extort money from the owner of several bars. The victim refused to pay, so "Crazy Joey" performed his best "Richard Widmark," explaining to the businessman that he could meet with an "unfortunate accident." It was no accident that two detectives were in the bar, and Gallo received a lengthy prison sentence. In 1968, Larry Gallo died of cancer.

Joseph Colombo   In 1962, Profaci died of natural causes, and his place was taken by Joseph Magliocco, his brother-in-law. Magliocco also died of natural causes at the end of 1963, and his place was taken by Joseph Colombo, Sr. In 1964, a truce was finally arranged with the Gallo faction. One condition of the truce was that several top Gallo men were "made," inducted as members of the Colombo Family (Salerno and Tompkins 1969). The Gallo crew was subsequently moved into the Genovese Family (Capeci 1999b).

While in prison, Crazy Joey continued to "raise hell." He so annoyed some of his fellow inmates in Attica that several of them threw him off a tier. Transferred to another prison, Joey befriended many black inmates, several of whom he recruited for his Brooklyn organization. In 1971, Gallo was released from prison, and the intrigue reached new heights.

There appears to be general agreement on how Joseph Colombo was chosen to succeed Magliocco as boss of the Profaci Family. A plot was afoot to kill two crime Family chieftains—Carlo Gambino and Thomas Lucchese—and Colombo informed Gambino of the plot. Some accounts say that the person who was supposed to effect the murders was Colombo, acting on behalf of Joseph Bonanno. One source (Salerno and Tompkins 1969) reports that Bonanno and Joseph Magliocco, underboss of the Profaci Family, were behind the plot. Another (Talese 1971) places responsibility on Magliocco, and Joseph Bonanno (1983) and his son Bill Bonanno (1999) deny any involvement. Instead, they blame their jealous cousin, Buffalo crime boss Stefano Magaddino, for "disseminating the story that Joe Bonanno wanted to kill Gambino and Lucchese" (1983: 235). In any event, Magliocco died, and Joseph Colombo was chosen by the "commission" to head the Profaci Family (Bonanno 1983).

In 1970, Colombo founded the Italian-American Civil Rights League and led in the daily picketing of the New York FBI headquarters, generating a great deal of media coverage. The league soon became a vehicle for protesting discrimination against and negative stereotyping of Italian-Americans. Colombo and the league succeeded in having all references to the Mafia or *Cosa Nostra* deleted from the scripts of *The Godfather* and the television series *The FBI*. U.S. Attorney General John Mitchell and New York's Governor Nelson Rockefeller ordered their employees to refrain from using such references.

The league raised large sums of money through dues and testimonial dinners and held an "Annual Unity Day" rally, which in 1970 drew about 50,000 persons to Columbus Circle in Manhattan. Nicholas Gage (1972: 172) notes that the

---

[19]For an interesting discussion of the preparations that are necessary for a gang war, see Bill Bonanno's (1999) discussion of his own experience during the "Banana war" (discussed later).

"rally conspicuously closed stores in neighborhoods controlled by the Mafia: New York's waterfront was virtually shut down . . . and almost every politician in the city joined" the 1970 celebration. There were articles in newspapers and magazines about Colombo and the league, and the boss began to portray himself as a civil rights leader who was simply misunderstood by the police.

Reports state that other crime Family bosses, particularly Carlo Gambino, did not look favorably on the activities of Colombo and the league, either because Colombo failed to share the financial fruits or because they resented the publicity—or both. At the second Annual Unity Day rally in 1971, only an estimated 10,000 persons were in attendance. While reporters and news photographers crowded around the podium, a lone black man wearing a camera and apparently presenting himself as a newsman approached Colombo, pulled out a gun, and shot him in the head and neck. The gunman, 24-year-old Jerome A. Johnson, was immediately shot to death: "Johnson's killer escaped as professionally as he had carried out his mission, shooting Johnson three times even as police clustered around" (Gage 1972: 171). Colombo remained paralyzed until his death in 1978.

Interest focused on Jerome Johnson. He was never connected to organized crime, although he had a criminal record and was known to be a violent person. Suspicion immediately centered on Joey Gallo, who had reason to dislike the Family boss and was known to have black criminals as associates. The day after Colombo was shot, the *New York Times* (Gage 1971b: 21) stated that "When Joseph Gallo was released in May from prison he was reported to have complained that the lot of his faction within the family had not improved much in his absence. He was also said to have questioned Colombo's involvement in the Italian-American Civil Rights League as drawing undue attention to the family."

With Colombo out of the way and acting boss Carmine Persico in prison, Gallo men began moving in on Colombo activities and completely took over the South Brooklyn waterfront (Goddard 1974). On April 7, 1972, Joey Gallo was celebrating his birthday with a late-night stop at Umberto's Clam House in Lower Manhattan, owned by a member of the Genovese Family and frequented by members of the Genovese and Colombo Families. With Joey's party was his new bride, her daughter, and his bodyguard. Three Colombo gunmen, who had apparently been quickly mobilized for the occasion, entered the restaurant and opened fire, killing Joey and wounding his bodyguard, who sought to return the fire (Diapoulos and Linakis 1976; Goddard 1974).

Despite the death of Joseph Colombo, the group he headed is still referred to as the Colombo Family, and intrafamilial violence continued. Persico, who is in prison serving combined sentences of 100 years, attempted to engineer a shift in leadership to his son Alphonse ("Allie Boy"), who was expected to be released from prison shortly. In the meantime, Persico chose Victor J. Orena to be acting boss. Before Alphonse was released from prison, Orena let it be known that he would not step aside for the much younger Persico—taking orders from Junior after being boss was apparently too much for Orena to accept.

Beginning in 1991, the two factions began shooting at each other's partisans. Persico loyalist Gregory Scarpa would drive past opponents' houses, and "one night he surprised a rebel who stood on a ladder, with his back turned, hanging Christmas lights on his house. Scarpa rolled down his car window, stuck out his rifle, and picked the man off with three shots" (Dannen 1996: 68). In 1992, in Queens, four men wearing masks jumped from a stolen van and opened fire at a car with shotguns and semiautomatic weapons. They killed the driver and wounded his two passengers. The victims were carpenter union officials associated with the Orena faction. Later that year, the 58-year-old Orena was convicted in Brooklyn federal court of RICO violations and murder. He received a life sentence. Nine days later, Gregory Scarpa[20]

---

[20]Scarpa, who was suffering from AIDS, the result of a blood transfusion in the wake of hernia surgery, pleaded guilty to murder and racketeering charges in 1993. He died in a prison hospital the following year. His bizarre role as an FBI informant is discussed in Chapter 14. Scarpa's son "Jr." is a made guy.

was ambushed near his Brooklyn home, receiving wounds in the face and left eye. Two associates were also wounded in the attack (Raab 1992c). The violence ended in 1993, both sides recognizing the futility and danger inherent in continuing the war. The imprisoned Persico picked his cousin, Andrew T. Russo (born in 1934), to be acting boss (Raab 1995b), and the Colombo Family resumed initiating new members to replace those killed or imprisoned—12 dead and more than 50 convicted of crimes related to the struggle. In 1998, Russo was convicted of federal charges, and Allie Boy, at 45, emerged as acting boss of the Colombo Family. In 2001, Persico pleaded guilty to racketeering, loansharking, and money-laundering charges in return for a 13-year sentence and a fine of $1 million.

The Bonanno Family

We know more about Joseph ("Don Peppino") Bonanno than about most other crime figures because he was the subject of a biography by Gay Talese (1971), he authored his own autobiography (with Sergio Lalli [1983]), and in 1999 a book by his son Bill was published. Bonanno states that his father, Salvatore ("Don Turridu"), was head of the Bonanno clan in Castellammare del Golfo and a "man of honor" (*mafioso*). Salvatore left Sicily for the United States with his wife and three-year-old son, Giuseppe, in 1908 to avoid prosecution (Bonanno does not say for what crime). In 1911, at the request of his brothers in Castellammare, Don Turridu returned home with his wife and child. He died there in 1915 of a heart attack.

Bonanno states that he was attending the nautical preparatory school when Mussolini came to power. He claims that his anti-Fascist activities forced him to leave, and he entered the United States in 1924. Bonanno quickly found help and refuge among friends and family from Castellammare. His cousin Stefano Magaddino was already a criminal power in Buffalo, and Bonanno eventually became involved in bootlegging with the Castellammare clan in Brooklyn under Salvatore Maranzano. During the Masseria–Maranzano conflict, Bonanno became an aide to Maranzano

and was seen as a leader of the Castellammare group arrayed against Joe the Boss. After Maranzano's murder, a meeting of Family members was held, and Bonanno was elected "Father" (a term he uses for "boss") of what became known as the Bonanno Family. Bonanno successfully parlayed income received as boss of his own Family into legitimate enterprises such as garment and cheese manufacturing.

In 1959 a federal grand jury indicted him for conspiracy to obstruct justice in the aftermath of the (in)famous meeting of crime bosses in Apalachin, New York, in 1957. In that year, events such as the attempt on the life of Frank Costello and the murder of Albert Anastasia sparked a top-level conference at Apalachin, New York.

The Apalachin Crime Conference In November of 1957, a New York state police sergeant became suspicious of the activities at the home of Joseph M. Barbara, Sr., boss of the Northeastern Pennsylvania crime Family. Barbara was from Castellammare del Golfo and had become the wealthy owner of a soda pop distributing business and a bottling plant outside of Endicott, New York. His estate in Apalachin was about six miles away. While investigating a bad check case at a hotel in the area, the sergeant discovered Barbara's son making room reservations. He later noted a number of expensive automobiles with out-of-state license plates parked at the Barbara estate. There was nothing the officer "could legally do about Barbara's visitors, but by Saturday, November 14, 1957, with what he figured to be as many as seventy guests assembled," he could not longer stifle his curiosity: "He organized what few deputies he had and conducted a raid on Barbara's house, one merely, as he explained later, 'to see if anything criminal was going on or if Barbara's guests were wanted on any outstanding warrants'" (Brashler 1977: 144): "Within minutes dozens of well-dressed men ran out of the house and across the fields in all directions" (Salerno and Tompkins 1969: 298). Using roadblocks and reinforcements, the police reportedly took 63 men into custody, although this figure is disputed. Joseph Bonanno was reported to have been at the meeting, and his driver's license was confiscated. However, he claims to have been elsewhere, attending a private meeting in a nearby motel.

The men were summoned to the sergeant's office, where they "gave their names and addresses, took off their shoes, emptied their pockets as troopers searched and watched" (Sondern 1959: 36). Those arrested included Joseph Profaci, Carlo Gambino, Paul Castellano, Vito Genovese, the Philadelphia crime boss and his underboss, and Russell Bufalino.[21]

In 1959, Bonanno and 26 other leading OC figures, after refusing to answer questions as to the purpose of the meeting in Apalachin, were indicted for conspiracy and obstruction of justice. Bonanno's case was separated from the others when he suffered a heart attack. After a three-week trial, a jury found 20 defendants guilty of conspiracy. However, the verdict was overturned in 1960 by the U.S. Court of Appeals; the court concluded that the people at the Barbara estate had been taken into custody, detained, and searched without probable cause that a crime had or was being committed: "[I]n America we still respect the dignity of the individual, and even an unsavory character is not to be imprisoned except on definite proof of specific crime" (*United States v. Bufalino et al.* 285 F.2d. 408).

In 1963 came the alleged plot against Gambino and Lucchese, and Bonanno sought, and was denied, Canadian citizenship. In February 1964, while Bonanno was still in Canada at a meeting of crime Family captains, his son Bill was chosen *consigliere*. The elevation of the young Bonanno was opposed from both within and without the Bonanno Family. This act, coupled with the plot against Gambino and Lucchese, resulted in a "summons" for Joseph Bonanno to appear before the commission, of which he was one of the nine members; Bonanno declined. On October 21, 1964, Bonanno and his attorney were standing in front of a luxury apartment house in Manhattan, where they had sought shelter from the rain. Bonanno describes what followed (1983: 260): "Two men grabbed me from behind by each arm and immediately forced me toward the nearby street corner. . . . 'Come on, Joe, my boss wants you.' . . . As they rushed toward the corner, I heard Maloney [Bonanno's attorney] shouting after us. He was saying something about my being his client and they couldn't take me away like that. A pistol shot pinged the sidewalk. Maloney retreated."

Bonanno reports that he was kidnapped by two of his cousins, the son and brother of Stefano Magaddino, and held in a rural farmhouse for more than six weeks. Federal officials call it a hoax, an effort by Bonanno to avoid appearing before a grand jury investigating organized crime. Bonanno states that following his release, he remained in hiding in his Tucson home for more than a year. In the meantime, a revolt broke out within the Bonanno Family led by *caporegime* Gasper DiGregorio, Bill Bonanno's godfather and best man at the wedding of Fay and Joseph Bonanno.

On January 28, 1966, in an effort to reestablish unity, Bill Bonanno and several Family members loyal to his father went to Troutman Street in Brooklyn to meet with DiGregorio. The unity meeting turned out to be an ambush, and the young Bonanno narrowly escaped in an exchange of gunfire. On May 18, 1966, Joseph Bonanno reappeared, and the revolt (dubbed the "Banana war") raged on. DiGregorio eventually withdrew, and the commission turned the Family over to an acting boss. Joseph Bonanno retired to his Tucson home, leaving a three-man committee to fill the leadership until the "loyalists" could select a new boss.

In 1979 a federal grand jury indicted Bonanno and a commodities dealer for obstructing justice. During the 14-week nonjury trial in 1980, the prosecutor maintained that Bonanno and his codefendant worked together to keep the records of several businesses from the grand jury. The FBI collected evidence by tapping Bonanno's telephone and retrieving his garbage for four years. The defense objected to the introduction of notes

[21]Russell Bufalino, who was born in Sicily in 1903, become Joseph Barbara's underboss. When Barbara died in 1959, Bufalino became boss of the Northeastern Pennsylvania Family. According the Pennsylvania Crime Commission, Bufalino retired, and his Family is no longer active.

in Sicilian fished out of Bonanno's garbage, contending that their translation into English was in doubt because there are no English equivalents to many of the terms used. Nevertheless, Bonanno was found guilty and sentenced to a term of one year. He entered the federal prison at Terminal Island at the end of 1983.

Despite Bonanno's retirement, the crime Family he headed is still referred to as the Bonanno Family, something that Bonanno decried: "It is improper for people to still refer to this Family as the Bonanno Family. It stopped being the Bonanno Family when I retired. In Sicily, a Family is sometimes likened to a cosca—an artichoke. The Family members are like the artichoke leaves and the Father is like the central stem on which they all hang. Remove the central stem and all you have is a lot of separate leaves. When I left New York to retire, all the separate leaves had to find themselves another stem" (1983: 292).

In 1977, Joseph Bonanno's underboss, Carmine Galente, was released from prison after serving 15 years for a narcotics conviction. Two years later he was murdered (discussed in Chapter 3). The Galente murder touched off another bloody struggle for control of the Bonanno Family, and Family fortunes waned. The decades of turmoil left the Bonanno Family so weakened that the FBI unit assigned to monitor its activities was disbanded. But under the leadership of Joseph C. Massino, 57 (in 2000), a former *caporegime* who took control after being released from prison in 1993, Family fortunes have rebounded. The Bonannos have avoided the indictments and convictions that have affected the other crime Families, and its membership went from 80 to about 110

(Raab 2000). The Bonanno Family has the closest ties with the Zips—Sicilian immigrant criminals discussed in Chapter 2. Joseph Bonanno died in Tucson in May 2002 at the age of 97.

THE FIVE FAMILIES

While the crime Families of New York have been subjected to intense investigation and prosecution, they have successfully recruited new members. Of particular importance is the ascendancy of the Genovese Family, both in members (approximately 300) and the strength of its money-making activities, at the expense of the Gambino Family. In 2001, however, more than 100 members and associates of the Genovese Family, including three captains, were indicted. The Colombo Family membership has suffered significant decline because the group has been devastated by deaths, imprisonment, and an inability to recruit new members—the commission would not allow initiations during the Family's internal struggle.

Reports (e.g., Raab 1998b) indicate that the commission of Family bosses has not been meeting because of fear of informants or because the use of acting bosses has created uncertainty as to who can actually speak for a Family. This has weakened the Families' ability to coordinate activities and, most importantly, resolve "beefs," disputes that, if they fester, can lead to unsanctioned violence. In any event, organized crime in New York remains unique—it is the only city with numerous traditional crime Families operating.

In the next chapter, we will examine organized crime in Chicago.

INTERNET CONNECTIONS

Organized crime history: **www.crimelibrary.com/gangsters**

New York crime Families: **ipsn.org/themob.html**

Gang Land news: **ganglandnews.com**

REVIEW QUESTIONS

1. What was the relationship among Tammany, the police, and vice entrepreneurs?
2. What was the relationship between Tammany and the gangs of New York?
3. How did Prohibition change the relationship between Tammany and the underworld?
4. Why was Arnold Rothstein so important for the development of organized crime?
5. What were the roles of Meyer Lansky and Bugsy Siegel in organized crime?
6. What led to the murder of Dutch Schultz?
7. How did organized crime in New York change after the repeal of Prohibition?
8. How does Murder, Inc., provide an example of interethnic cooperation in organized crime?
9. What was the broker role that allowed Lucky Luciano to become so important in organized crime?
10. What was the Castellammarese war?
11. What were the causes and outcomes of the Gallo–Profaci war and the Banana war?
12. What led to the Banana war, and what was its outcome?

♠

CHAPTER 5

ORGANIZED CRIME IN CHICAGO

In this chapter,[1] we will examine organized crime and its evolution in the Chicagoland area—Cook and the surrounding "collar counties." Traditional organized crime in Chicago presents a model of organization different from that of New York and most other areas with a Mafia Family, a model that developed out of the particular history of the Windy City—referring to its politicians, not its climate. There are also historical differences. While ethnic succession in New York and elsewhere saw the Italians take over from the Jews, in Chicago it was the Irish, not the Jews, who were important in organized crime prior to the final ascendancy of the Italians.

When Chicago was incorporated as a town in 1833, it was little more than an Indian trading post. Immigration, usually by steamship, increased with the breaking of ground for the Lake Michigan–Illinois River Canal in 1836. In the spring of 1837, however, a depression and banking panic caused the real estate market to drop, and the state of Illinois went bankrupt. It was not until 1845 that the city of Chicago began to boom again. The canal opened in 1848, and by 1852, the first train had rolled into Chicago. By 1855, Chicago was the terminus of ten railroad trunk lines and eleven branch lines and was the country's greatest meatpacking center and grain port (Asbury 1942). The boom naturally attracted adventurers, gamblers, pimps, prostitutes, and other undesirables.

The Civil War brought further prosperity to Chicago, but it also brought thousands of soldiers and the gambling establishments and brothels that were patronized by large numbers of unattached young men on military leave. It was at this time that Chicago became known as "the wickedest city in the United States" (Asbury 1942: 61). Even the great Chicago fire of 1871 would not change this. But it was not until Mike McDonald became established that vice in Chicago could be said to be truly *organized*.

---

[1] Unless otherwise cited, information on the Chicago Outfit is from court documents in *United States of America v. Carlisi*, 92Cr 1064 F2d 1990; *United States of America v. Damico et al.*, 94 Cr 00723 F2d 1994; *United States of America v. Infelise, et al.*, 90-Cr 0087 F2d 1990; *United States of America v. LaMantia*, 93 Cr 00523 F2d 1996; and *United States of America v. Rainone et al.*, 91 Cr 0727 F2d 1992.

MIKE MCDONALD

The origins of organized crime in Chicago can be traced to the mayoral election of 1873, in which Mike McDonald backed the victorious candidate for mayor (Nelli 1969): "McDonald, the gambling boss of Chicago, demonstrated that under effective leadership the gamblers, liquor interests, and brothel keepers could be welded into a formidable political power" (Peterson 1963: 31). At the time, there were 3,000 saloons in the city (Asbury 1942). The election pitted "reformers," who insisted on the enforcement of Sunday closing "blue laws," against a party, organized by McDonald, whose ranks were swelled by Irish and German immigrants (Flinn 1973).

"King Mike," as he became known, was born in Niagara Falls, New York, around 1840 and spent a great deal of time gambling, working the trains between New Orleans and Chicago. At the outbreak of the Civil War, McDonald organized a gang of bounty hunters who "recruited" men for the various Union regiments. In 1872, McDonald bought a bar in the heart of downtown Chicago. "Our Store" became the city's largest liquor and gambling house. The Store was frequented by politicians who used McDonald as a "bagman," an intermediary for the collection of bribes (Klatt 1983: 30): "Until McDonald opened shop, gambling had been rather unorganized in Chicago—and so were politics."

When his candidate won the election, "McDonald had Chicago in his back pocket" (Sawyers 1988: 10). From then until his death in 1907, McDonald controlled mayors, congressmen, and senators. His newspaper, the *Globe*, often influenced the outcome of elections, and he also owned the elevated railroad line in Chicago (Wendt and Kogan 1974). Any gambler who wished to operate outside of the red-light districts had to see Mike and arrange to pay over a large proportion of his income for division among the police, various city officials, and the members of McDonald's syndicate. As a close friend and chief advisor of mayors, and as a leader of the Cook County Democratic organization, McDonald was the boss of Chicago (Asbury 1942).

Reform hit Chicago in 1893 at a time when a rich and powerful McDonald had lost interest in maintaining his vast empire. His personal life had deteriorated.[2] In 1898, at age 66, McDonald renounced his Catholic faith and secured a divorce to marry a 23-year-old divorcée. He built a mansion for his bride, and they lived together until 1907, when she shot her lover, 15 years her junior, during an argument. She told the police of her affection for the deceased and of her dislike of her husband. McDonald never recovered from the shock of her revelations, and the gambling–political empire he ruled over fell apart. His political mantle was picked up by Michael Kenna and John Coughlin; gambling went to Mont Tennes. McDonald died in 1907 (Asbury 1942; Sawyers 1988).

"HINKY DINK" AND JOHN "THE BATH"

McDonald's Store was located in the Levee District of Chicago's notorious First Ward. With his backing, a "Mutt and Jeff" team became the political "Lords of the Levee": John ("Bathhouse" or simply "the Bath") Coughlin, a powerfully built six-footer, and Michael ("Hinky Dink" or simply the "Dink") Kenna, a diminutive organizational genius. Born in the First Ward to Irish immigrant parents in 1860, Coughlin began his political career as a masseur in the exclusive Palmer Baths, where he met wealthy and powerful politicians and businessmen. These contacts helped him when he opened his own bathhouse and soon other bathhouses. Among his customers were important politicians, and the Bath (a nickname he enjoyed) became a Democratic precinct captain and president of the First Ward Democratic Club.

In 1892, Coughlin was elected alderman from the First Ward, one of the 35 city wards. The First Ward, in addition to the Levee, contained the

---

[2]His wife shot and wounded a police officer who was snooping around the Store's third-floor living quarters. She was acquitted and ran off with a minstrel singer. She then took up with the Catholic priest whom McDonald had designated as her personal chaplain (Sawyers 1988).

city's central business district, "the Loop" (so-called because of the elevated train line circling the area). The city council that Coughlin joined was literally selling out the city of Chicago. The "boodles," schemes through which city privileges were sold, made the $3-a-meeting alderman's position quite lucrative: "The irksome aspect of the boodling was not only that the vicious system corrupted the whole of Chicago politics but that the city gained from the passage of boodle ordinances hardly a cent in compensation. Even the grafting aldermen . . . actually were being paid only a small fraction of the real worth of the privileges they were selling. Big business was the beneficiary of this system, for it needed such favors to expand and grow rich" (Wendt and Kogan 1974: 34).

Kenna was born in the First Ward in 1858. His nickname, "Hinky Dink," may have been a reference to his small stature or, some maintain, may allude to a water hole in which he swam as a young boy. After working as a newsboy for the *Chicago Tribune*, Kenna went to a booming mining town in Colorado, where he worked for two years as a circulation manager. When he returned home, Kenna became a successful saloon keeper (despite being a teetotaler) and, of course, a politician. He worked hard in First Ward Democratic politics as a saloon-based precinct captain and eventually became friendly with the Bath. With Kenna as the mastermind, the two men organized the vice entrepreneurs of the First Ward, established a legal fund, and forged an alliance with the mayor. Eventually they "found themselves in possession of a thriving little syndicate" (Wendt and Kogan 1974: 81).

After the mayor was murdered by a disgruntled job seeker, the Bath and Hinky Dink provided his successor with the margin of victory. When a depression swept the country in the winter of 1893, Kenna provided care for 8,000 homeless and destitute men, who did not forget this kindness. They registered in the First Ward and were brought back for each election. Coughlin and Kenna were also assisted by the police of the ward and by the Quincy Street Boys, who included some of the toughest and most feared hoodlums of the First Ward. In fact, notes John Landesco in 1929, the use of street gangs in politics became

widespread in Chicago (1968: 184–85): "The young of the immigrant group, beginning with the child at play in the street, were assimilated uncritically into all of the traditions of the neighborhoods in which they lived. Street gangs were their heritage, conflict between races and nationalities often made them necessary—conflict and assimilation went on together. The politician paid close attention to them, nurturing them with favors and using them for his own purposes. Gang history always emphasizes this political nurture. Gangs often became political clubs."

The ability of Coughlin and Kenna to deliver the vote was key to their power. Majorities in the First Ward were so overwhelming that they could affect city, county, and even state elections. And as their power grew, it became necessary to be "licensed" by Kenna and Coughlin to do business in the First Ward. In 1897 they skillfully engineered the Democratic nomination of Carter Henry Harrison, son of the murdered mayor. In the First Ward they delivered a vote of five to one, and Kenna was elected to the city council. However, Harrison eventually allied himself with reformers and moved against the Levee, which cost him the vital support of the First Ward and led to the 1915 election of Republican William Hale Thompson.

WILLIAM HALE THOMPSON

William Hale ("Big Bill") Thompson began his political career as a reformer in a successful race for alderman in 1900. His father was a wealthy real estate dealer, but the young Thompson (born 1865) preferred the life of a cowboy and spent much of his youth out West. Even as mayor, he often sported cowboy hats. Thompson was a gifted orator—to call him demagogic would not be an exaggeration—who vilified real and imagined enemies such as the British and the king of England. Such attacks gained him the support of German and Irish voters. In 1902 he was elected to the Cook County Board of Commissioners. His victory in 1915 was based on his demagogic appeals. In German neighborhoods he attacked the British, in German-hating Polish neighborhoods he at-

William Hale Thompson (center, with upraised reading glasses) awaiting results at his mayoral election-night headquarters in 1927 amidst a throng of supporters. Running on a pledge to let the liquor flow again in Chicago, Big Bill was swept back into office for a third term.

tacked the Germans, in Irish areas he attacked the British, and when addressing Protestant audiences he warned that a vote for his Catholic opponent was a vote for the pope. He promised the reformers strict enforcement of the gambling laws, and he promised the gamblers an open town. Thompson received strong support in the black wards, and many Harrison Democrats deserted the party to support the Republican.

"During the last few months of Mayor Harrison's final term Chicago was probably as free from organized vice as at any time in its history" (Asbury 1942: 309). With the election of Thompson, "the spoils system swept over the city like a noxious blight, and city hall became a symbol for corruption and incompetence" (Merriam 1929: 22): "Within six months he had violated every cam-

paign promise but one. He did keep Chicago wide open" (Kobler 1971: 57). Despite these excesses, Big Bill was reelected in 1919. In 1923, with Prohibition in full swing, and despite the support of Al Capone, Thompson was defeated by reformers. In 1927, running on a pledge to let the liquor flow again in Chicago, Thompson was swept back into office for a third term. In 1931, Thompson was defeated by Anton J. Cermak, the founder of what has since been called the Chicago Democratic "machine."

MONT TENNES

Mont Tennes inherited much of the gambling empire left by Mike McDonald. Writing in 1929, John Landesco (1968: 45) stated that "The complete life history of one man, were it known in every detail, would disclose practically all there is to know about syndicated gambling as a phase of organized crime in Chicago in the last quarter century. That man is *Mont Tennes.*" By 1901 Tennes dominated gambling on the city's North Side, and by 1904 he appeared as the backer of several hundred handbooks, becoming the major operator in Chicago racetrack betting (Asbury 1942). In 1907 he secured control of the wire service that transmitted the results of horse races throughout the country, and every bookmaker was dependent on the service. The wire service used operatives with binoculars whose instant reports on races were transmitted over phone and telegraph lines. Without the wire service, a bookmaker was vulnerable to "past-posting"—placing a bet after the race was already over and the winner determined. The swindler would set up a relay system to a confederate, who quickly placed a bet on a horse that had already won. The bookmaker would accept the bet because regular channels had not informed him that the race had even started.

When some bookmakers balked at paying Tennes for the service, he instigated an outbreak of violence and police raids. In retaliation, Tennes was attacked and badly beaten while walking with his wife. Tennes responded with stepped-up police raids and bombings. By 1909, he had absolute control over racetrack gambling in Chicago: "The Tennes ring at this time established systematic exclusion. Anyone wishing to enter the gambling business had to apply to the ring. The man and the location would be investigated, the leading gamblers in the city would be asked to approve the applicant, and if disapproved he would be placed upon the 'dead list'" (Landesco 1968: 54). Tennes controlled the wire service and paid politicians and the police; gamblers who paid Tennes received race results immediately and protection from police raids: "His combine had a grip on the police in twenty American cities and enforced its dictates with dynamite. Cities from New York to San Francisco and from Detroit to San Antonio paid for the Tennes wire service, which involved eighteen telephone and telegraph companies" (Landesco 1968: 59).

With the advent of Prohibition, the level of violence in organized crime increased dramatically, Tennes sold his service to both George ("Bugs"— for his sudden rages) Moran and his rival, Al Capone. In the end, Tennes became an associate of the Capone organization. He withdrew from this "shotgun marriage" and retired about 1927, a millionaire (Smith 1962).

FROM COLOSIMO TO TORRIO TO CAPONE

Like Mont Tennes, John Coughlin and Michael Kenna would soon feel the power of gangsterism in the First Ward. With Thompson in charge of city hall, the power of the Bath and Hinky Dink was reduced considerably. Political–police protection now had to be negotiated directly from "the hall"—individual Democratic aldermen had little or no influence with Big Bill. One of their precinct captains, a man who had aided Coughlin and Kenna in capturing the growing Italian vote of the First Ward, began to assert control over the Levee; that man was James Colosimo.

James ("Big Jim" or "Diamond Jim") Colosimo was ten years old when his father brought him to the United States from Calabria, Italy. He spent all but three years of the rest of his life in the Levee district of Chicago. Beginning as

a newsboy and bootblack, by the time he was eighteen Colosimo was an accomplished pickpocket and pimp. In the late 1890s, after several close brushes with the law, he obtained a job as a street cleaner and by 1902 had been promoted to foreman. Known as the "white wings" because of their white uniforms, sweepers were organized by Colosimo into a social and athletic club that later became a labor union. Kenna appointed Colosimo a precinct captain in return for delivering the votes of his club, a position that brought with it virtual immunity from arrest (Asbury 1942).

In 1902, Colosimo married a brothel keeper, and he began to manage her business. In 1903, he helped organize a gang of "white slavers," an operation that brought girls from many American and European cities, often as young as fourteen— turnover was good for business (Asbury 1942). Most were willing entrants to the business of house prostitution, but others were lured by false promises of domestic employment or some other duplicity, such as promises of marriage. Once in Chicago, the recruiters turned the girls over to specialists, who would drug, rape, and humiliate the girls for days. After being thus "broken in," they were sold as chattel to brothel keepers, who would restrict their contacts with the outside world.[3] Colosimo opened several brothels and a string of gambling houses. He also owned the nationally famous restaurant, Colosimo's Café, which attracted luminaries from society, opera, and the theater (Nelli 1969): "By the middle of 1915, Colosimo was the acknowledged overlord of prostitution on the South Side, and because of his political power was almost as important in other sections of the city" (Asbury 1942: 314).

Colosimo flaunted his success: "He wore a diamond ring on every finger, diamond studs gleamed in his shirt front, a huge diamond horseshoe was pinned to his vest, diamond links joined the cuffs, and his belt and suspender buckles were set with diamonds" (Asbury 1942: 312). All this attracted attention, some of it unwelcome. In 1909,

---

[3]The activities of white slavers led to the enactment of the Mann Act in 1910, making it a federal crime to transport females interstate for "immoral purposes."

Colosimo, like many other successful Italians, became the target of Black Hand[4] extortion threats. In response, he brought Johnny Torrio to Chicago. Some sources refer to Torrio as Colosimo's nephew, while others report that he was a distant cousin of Colosimo's wife.

Torrio was born near Naples in 1882, and his parents settled on New York's Lower East Side. Using brains rather than brawn, Torrio became leader of the James Street Boys, which was allied with Paul Kelly's Five Points Gang. He later moved operations to Brooklyn and entered into a partnership with Frankie (Uale) Yale, a member of the Five Points Gang who became a notorious gang leader in Coney Island. Although Torrio, a happily married man, did not smoke, drink, or consort with women, he was the right man for the job. Shortly after arriving in Chicago, Torrio lured three Black Handers into an ambush, where gunmen shot them to death. His Chicago career was under way (Schoenberg 1992; McPhaul 1970).

Torrio's usefulness extended to overseeing brothels and gambling operations for Colosimo. He bought a four-story building a block away from Colosimo's Cafe, which became known as the Four Deuces because of its address, 2222 Wabash Avenue. The first floor had a saloon and Torrio's office, protected by a steel-barred gate. The second and third floors had gambling rooms with solid steel doors; the fourth floor housed a bordello.

Back in New York, Frankie Yale hired a heavy-fisted member of the Five Points Gang to deal with obstreperous customers in his saloon. On one occasion, however, the young bouncer made an offensive remark to a young girl in the saloon, which led to a four-inch scar courtesy of her irate brother and his pocketknife. The young Five Pointer was prone to be overexuberant in carrying out his responsibilities. He was a suspect in two murders, and his third victim was on the critical list when

Yale thought it best that Alphonse ("Scarface") Capone leave for Chicago.

The Capones entered the United States from the Naples area in 1893 and were living in the Greenpoint–Williamsburg section of Brooklyn when Alphonse was born in 1899. A chronic truant, Al left school in the sixth grade at age fourteen. As a teenager, he held a variety of unskilled jobs and was a member of various youth gangs that proliferated in the area, eventually joining Paul Kelly's Five Points Gang. He arrived in Chicago at a fortuitous time, 1919, the year before Prohibition would go into effect. Capone went to work as a bouncer for Johnny Torrio at the Four Deuces. Meanwhile, Colosimo fell in love with a young musical comedy singer. In 1920 he divorced his wife and three weeks later married the young beauty. His new wife took much of Colosimo's time, so he left Torrio in charge of operations. Torrio began to give Capone important responsibilities (McPhaul 1970). Then came Prohibition.

PROHIBITION

With the coming of Prohibition, "the personnel of organized vice took the lead in the systematic organization of this new and profitable field of exploitation. All the experience gained by years of struggle against reformers and concealed agreements with politicians was brought into service in the organizing and distribution of beer and whiskey" (Landesco 1968: 43). However, Colosimo was fearful of federal enforcement efforts and wanted to stay away from bootlegging (McPhaul 1970). Torrio and Capone chafed at this reluctance; not only would it deny access to untold wealth, but it would also enable competing racketeers to grow rich and powerful. On May 11, 1920, Diamond Jim was found in the vestibule of Colosimo's Café—he had been shot to death: "After Colosimo's death, John Torrio succeeded to the First Ward based Italian 'syndicate' throne, which he occupied until his retirement in 1925. An able and effective leader, Torrio excelled as a master strategist and organizer and quickly built up an empire which far exceeded that of his

---

[4]*La Mano Negro*, or Black Hand, consisted of individuals or small gangs of extortionists preying on Italian immigrants who had achieved a level of financial success. Victims would receive a crude letter or note demanding money and signed with a skull or black-inked hand.

predecessor in wealth, power, and influence" (Nelli 1969: 386).

As an organizer and administrator of underworld affairs, Johnny Torrio is unsurpassed in the annals of American crime. Like Arnold Rothstein, he conducted his criminal enterprises as if they were legitimate businesses: "In the morning he kissed his wife good-by and motored to his magnificently furnished offices on the second floor of the Four Deuces. There he bought and sold women, conferred with the managers of his brothels and gambling dens, issued instructions to his rumrunners and bootleggers, arranged for the corruption of police and city officials, and sent his gun squads out to slaughter rival gangsters who might be interfering with his schemes." His workday over, "Torrio returned to his Michigan Avenue apartment and, except on rare occasions when he attended the theater or a concert, spent the evening at home in slippers and smoking jacket, playing cards with his wife or listening to phonograph records" (Asbury 1942: 320–21).

As in New York, Prohibition enabled men who had been street thugs to become crime overlords. Outside of the First Ward, various gangs ruled over sections of Chicago, where they pushed aside the local aldermen and parlayed crime and politics into wealth and power. On the North Side, the gang headed by Dion O'Banion controlled the Forty-Second and Forty-Third wards. O'Banion controlled the Irish vote much as Colosimo controlled the Italian vote in the First Ward. Despite his sordid background, including several shootings in public view, in 1924 a banquet was held in O'Banion's honor by the Chicago Democratic organization. It seems that O'Banion had decided to swing his support to the Republicans because the reform-minded Democratic mayor was insisting that laws against many of O'Banion's activities be enforced. Democratic officials made speeches in his honor and even presented O'Banion with a platinum watch—to no avail. O'Banion and the votes of the Forty-Second and Forty-Third wards went to the Republicans. O'Banion was a regular churchgoer and loved flowers. This led him to purchase a florist shop and become gangland's favorite florist (Asbury 1942; Landesco 1968).

The Torrio Organization

Late in the summer of 1920, Johnny Torrio held long conferences with the major gang leaders in Cook County and persuaded them to abandon predatory crime in favor of Prohibition-related activities. To simplify operations, the city and county were divided into spheres of influence. In each, an allied gang chieftain was supreme, with subchiefs working under his direction: "A few of these leaders themselves owned and operated breweries and distilleries, but in the main they received their supplies from Torrio and were principally concerned with selling, making deliveries, protecting shipments, terrorizing saloonkeepers who refused to buy from the syndicate, and furnishing gunmen for punitive expeditions against hijackers and independents who attempted to encroach upon Torrio territory" (Asbury 1942: 324–25).

Torrio also moved to extend the suburbanization of his business and by 1923 had expanded beer and bordello operations well beyond his South Side stronghold into towns west and southwest of Chicago. He toured the Cook County suburbs, and when a location was decided upon, the neighborhood people were canvassed. If they were agreeable, Torrio agents would provide rewards: a new car, a house redecorated or painted, a new furnace, mortgage payments. The local authorities were then approached and terms negotiated (Allsop 1968). Most of this was accomplished peacefully—but then there was Cicero.

When You Smell Gunpowder, You're in Cicero
Adjacent to Chicago's Far West Side is the suburban city of Cicero (current population about 55,000). In 1923 reform hit Chicago, and the mayoralty went to Democrat William E. Dever. He ordered the police to move against the rampant vice in Chicago, but corruption was too deeply ingrained to be easily pushed aside. However, with the Democrats in control of Chicago, the Republicans were fearful of a reform wave that would loosen their control of the suburban areas of Cook County. As a result, a local Republican leader made a deal with Al Capone while Torrio was on vacation in Italy. In return for helping the Repub-

licans maintain control in Cicero, Torrio would be given a free hand in that city (Allsop 1968).

In the election of April 1924, the Capone brothers, Al and Frank, led a group of 200 Chicago thugs into Cicero. They intimidated, beat, and even killed Democrats who sought to oppose the Republican candidates. Some outraged Cicero officials responded by having a county judge deputize 70 volunteer Chicago police officers, who entered Cicero and engaged the Capone gangsters. In one incident, Chicago police saw the Capone brothers, Charlie Fischetti (a Capone cousin), and a Capone gunman standing by the polls with guns in their hands ushering voters inside. In the ensuing exchange of gunfire, during which the police were probably mistaken for rival gunmen (Schoenberg 1992), Frank Capone was killed. In spite of this, the Capone candidate was overwhelmingly reelected mayor of Cicero (Kobler 1971).

Capone moved his headquarters from Chicago to Cicero, where he took over the Hawthorne Inn with a little help from his friends—they opened fire at the owner "while shopping housewives and local tradesmen threw themselves behind cars and into doorways in the horizontal position that was becoming an identifiable posture of Cicero citizens" (Allsop 1968: 62–63). At the Hawthorne Inn, Capone ruled with an iron hand. When the Cicero mayor failed to carry out one of his orders, Capone went to city hall, where he personally knocked "his honor" down the steps and kicked him repeatedly as a policeman strolled by (Allsop 1968). Today, Cicero continues to have political-corruption problems.

The Chicago Wars

The election of a reform mayor in Chicago had unexpected consequences. It created an unstable situation and encouraged competitive moves by various ganglords. When Thompson lost to Dever in 1923, the system of protection broke down, and in the ensuing confusion Chicago became a battleground. The most significant feud was between the Torrio–Capone syndicate and the forces headed by Dion O'Banion.

In 1924 the North Side O'Banion forces began to feud with the South Side Genna brothers. When his complaints about the Gennas were ignored by Torrio, O'Banion hijacked a load of Genna liquor. The Gennas bristled, but Torrio restrained them and attempted to negotiate a peaceful settlement. In that same year, O'Banion swindled Torrio and Capone out of $500,000, selling them his share in a brewery that he knew was going to be raided by the police. This indicated that Torrio had lost control of the police under Mayor Dever. Emboldened by the lack of a response from Torrio, and apparently mistaking caution for fear, O'Banion went around boasting about how he had "taken" Torrio: "To hell with them Sicilians" was a phrase O'Banion gunmen quoted when they told the story in underworld circles (Asbury 1942). This was a serious violation of *rispetto*, and the response was inevitable.

On November 10, 1924, Mike Genna and two Sicilian immigrants who worked for the Gennas entered the O'Banion flower shop on the Near North Side. O'Banion was busy preparing flower arrangements for the funeral of Mike Merlo, president of the *Unione Siciliana*, who had died of natural causes a few days earlier. What the florist didn't know was that Merlo had been exerting his influence to keep the Gennas and Torrio from moving against O'Banion. Merlo abhorred violence and also got along very well with O'Banion—but now he was dead (Kobler 1971). "Hello, boys, you want Merlo's flowers?" a porter told the police he heard O'Banion say to the three men. Torrio had placed an order for $10,000 worth of assorted flowers, and Capone had ordered $8,000 worth of roses. While shaking O'Banion's hand, Mike Genna suddenly jerked him forward and seized his arms. Before he could wriggle free and reach for any of the three guns he always carried, O'Banion was hit by five bullets. A sixth, the coup de grâce, was fired into his head after he fell to the floor. The war that followed took many lives and ended on St. Valentine's Day, 1929 (Asbury 1942; Kobler 1971; Allsop 1968).

The O'Banion forces, under the leadership of Earl Wajciechowski, a Pole better known as "Hymie Weiss," struck back. Torrio left Chicago one step ahead of Weiss gunmen, and early in 1925, Capone's car was raked with machine-gun fire. His driver was wounded, but Capone and his bodyguards were not hit. Capone began traveling in a specially built armored Cadillac limousine. Later that year, 12 days after his return to Chicago, Torrio was critically wounded while shopping with his wife. In the fall of 1925, he went to Italy for a visit, leaving his organization to Capone (Landesco 1968). As far as is known, Johnny Torrio never returned to Chicago.[5]

Weiss gunmen made a dozen attempts to kill Capone, and they nearly succeeded in 1926. The street in front of Capone's Cicero headquarters was filled with a lunch-hour crowd, and Capone was eating at a restaurant next door when "eleven automobiles filled with Weiss gangsters drove slowly past the Hawthorne Inn and began firing machine-guns, automatic pistols, and shotguns. After the roar of the attack had subsided, bullet holes were found in thirty-five automobiles parked at the curb. Inside the hotel, woodwork and doors had been splintered, windows shattered, plaster ripped from walls, and furniture wrecked in the office and lobby." However, Capone was uninjured, although one of his bodyguards was hit in the shoulder, and a woman sitting with her infant son was struck 30 times. Capone paid the physicians who saved her sight (Asbury 1942: 358–59).

Soon afterwards, two gunmen armed with submachine guns, who had been waiting for three days, opened fire on Hymie Weiss and his four companions as they approached their headquarters above the O'Banion flower shop. Weiss was

hit ten times. He and one of his companions died; the others survived. Weiss, at age 28, left an estate worth reportedly $1.3 million (Allsop 1968).

Gang wars are "bad for business," so in 1926, in the middle of the mayhem and murder, a truce was called. Weiss was dead by that time, and the O'Banion forces were led by George ("Bugs") Moran. The assembled gang chieftains divided up the city and the county, with the largest shares going to the Capone organization and the Moran gang.

In 1928, Capone clashed with Frankie Yale. Capone had discovered that Yale—his one-time Brooklyn boss and the person responsible for protecting Capone's liquor shipments as they were trucked west to Chicago—was actually behind a series of hijackings (Kobler 1971). A black sedan followed Yale's new Lincoln as it moved down a Brooklyn street. As the sedan drew near, shots were fired, and Yale sped off with the sedan in pursuit. The end came with a devastating blast of gunfire that filled Yale's head with bullets and buckshot ("Gangster Shot in Daylight Attack" 1928). He was 35 years old.

During the first few months of 1929, while a peace agreement was in effect (at least in theory), Bugs Moran had been hijacking Capone's liquor, owned jointly by Capone and the (predominantly Jewish) Purple Gang of Detroit. Capone gave orders and went off to enjoy the Florida sun at his palatial 14-room estate on Miami's Palm Island. On February 14, St. Valentine's Day, Capone entertained more than a hundred guests on Palm Island: gangsters, politicians, sportswriters, and show-business personalities. They all enjoyed a hearty buffet and an endless supply of champagne (Galvan 1982).

Meanwhile, back in Chicago, six of Bugs Moran's men and an optometrist who liked to associate with gangsters were waiting at a North Side warehouse to unload a shipment of hijacked liquor from Detroit. A Cadillac touring car with a large gong on the running board, similar to those used by detectives, stopped outside, and five men, two wearing police uniforms, entered the warehouse. Once inside, they lined up the seven men against the warehouse wall and systematically exe-

---

[5]Torrio emerged as part of organized crime in New York, where he apparently received some type of senior advisory status. He worked in partnership with a number of leading New York OC figures, including Dutch Schultz, with whom he was a partner in the bail bond business, and Frank Costello (Peterson 1983). He later received a two-and-a-half-year sentence for income tax evasion (Irey 1948). Some sources (for example, Messick 1967; Turkus and Feder 1951) credit Torrio with inspiring the formation of a national crime syndicate in 1934. Torrio suffered a heart attack while in a barber's chair in Brooklyn and died on April 16, 1957. His death went unnoticed by the media until May 8, when the *New York Times* ran a story: "Johnny Torrio, Ex-Public Enemy 1, Dies; Made Al Capone Boss of the Underworld." Torrio was described as a real estate dealer at the time of his death.

cuted them with Tommy guns. One of the victims lived nearly three hours with fourteen bullets in him but refused to tell the police who was responsible for the shooting. Bugs Moran was not in the warehouse at the time, even though the "St. Valentine's Day Massacre" had been arranged in his honor. He arrived late and, seeing the "police car," left. It was later learned that the killers thought Moran was among the victims; lookouts had mistaken one of the seven for the gang's leader (Koziol and Estep 1983). The killers were never caught; it was suspected that they were brought in from Detroit or St. Louis (where Capone had ties with "Eagan's Rats"). The affair was apparently arranged by South Side hit man and Capone bodyguard James Gebardi, better known as "Machine-Gun Jack McGurn."[6] For a long time it was generally believed that *real* policemen were the actual killers (Kobler 1971).[7]

While the wrath of Bugs Moran continued, his gang withered. The man who handled brothels and "immoral cabarets" for Moran was gunned down in 1930. Less than three months later, Moran's partner and president of the *Unione Siciliana*, Joe Aiello, met the same fate. Moran left Chicago and eventually returned to more conventional crime. In 1946 he was sent to prison for robbing a tavern employee of $10,000 near Dayton, Ohio. After ten years, he was released from prison and a few days later was arrested for bank robbery. On February 26, 1957, the *New York Times* reported that Moran died while serving his sentence in the federal penitentiary in Leavenworth, Kansas ("Bugs Moran Dies in Federal Prison" 1957: 59).

---

[6]The Moran gang had twice tried to kill McGurn, and on one occasion he was seriously wounded. Believed responsible for killing at least 22 people, McGurn used to place a nickel in the hands of his victims. He was responsible for the 1927 attack on comedian Joe E. Lewis, during which his vocal cords were slashed and his tongue lacerated. Lewis, then a nightclub singer, had left McGurn's club for employment at another speakeasy. The Lewis story was told in the Frank Sinatra motion picture *The Joker Is Wild*. Seven years after the massacre, on the eve of Valentine's Day, McGurn was machine-gunned to death in a Chicago bowling alley. The two killers left a comic Valentine card next to his ruined body.

[7]The old garage at 2122 North Clark Street was demolished in 1967. For many years, the site has sat vacant next to a retirement home.

Al Capone's Chicago

In May of 1929, after attending a national crime conclave in Atlantic City, Capone decided to go to jail to avoid the wrath of the Bugs Moran gang and any number of Sicilians who had vowed to kill him to avenge the vicious beating deaths of three of their countrymen, whom Capone suspected of disloyalty. He arranged to be arrested by a friendly detective in Philadelphia on a firearms violation. Although the maximum sentence was one year, Capone anticipated a sentence of about 90 days, enough time to let things cool down in Chicago. However, his arrest generated a great deal of media attention, and the judge imposed the maximum sentence; he was released in 1930, two months early, for "good behavior." While he continued to live with his family in a modest red-brick, two-flat house at 7244 South Prairie Avenue, the former saloon bouncer from Brooklyn was now the most powerful person in Chicago, thanks to Prohibition.

However, the Depression severely reduced the income of the Capone organization. New areas of profit were sought by the chieftains of organized crime, who had grown wealthy in gambling and bootlegging. Until 1929, business and labor racketeering was only a sideline for most top gangsters such as Capone. However, as liquor sales fell off with the onset of the Depression, gang leaders were faced with a restless army of young and violent men whom they were committed to paying anywhere from $100 to $500 per week (Seidman 1938). Capone also recognized by 1928 that Prohibition would probably last only a few more years; new sources of income would be needed.

During Prohibition, numerous forms of racketeering flourished in Chicago: the small businesses of the city were generally marginal and intensely competitive. To avoid cutthroat competition, businessmen formed associations to make and enforce regulations illegally limiting competition: "Many of the associations were controlled, or even organized by, racketeers who levied dues upon association members and controlled the treasuries; they then used a system of fines and violence to insure that all businessmen in the trade joined the association and abided by the

Gabby Hartnett of the Chicago Cubs autographs a ball for Al Capone, Jr. This picture was probably taken without the subjects' knowledge—"Scarface" Al rarely allowed himself to be photographed from the left side.

© Bettmann/Corbis

regulations" designed to keep prices uniform and high (Haller 1971–72: 225–26).

The Capone organization moved into racketeering on a grand scale and took over many of the rackets then prevalent in Chicago. In 1928 the Cook County state's attorney listed 91 Chicago unions and business associations under gangster control, and these gradually came under the thumb of the Capone organization—the gangsters who controlled racketeering in Chicago proved no match for the Capone forces (Kobler 1971; Seidman 1938). (It was the same in other cities. In Detroit, for example, the Purple Gang took over labor racketeering through a reign of terror.) The Capone organization

controlled a score of labor unions, most of them officered by ex-convicts, and as many protective associations. To build up this phase of the Capone syndicate operations, and to hold in line the businesses already conquered, bands of gunmen and sluggers hijacked and destroyed truckloads of merchandise, bombed stores and manufacturing plants or wrecked them with axes and crowbars, put acid into laundry vats, poured corrosives onto clothing hanging in cleaning and dyeing shops, blackjacked workers and employers, and killed when necessary to en-

force their demands or break down opposition. (Asbury 1942: 366–67)

Capone's Downfall   Not only did the Depression severely reduce the income of the Capone organization, but also a special team of federal investigators, headed by Elliot Ness and dubbed "the Untouchables," began to move against Capone distilleries, breweries, and liquor shipments. However, the most important event for Capone was a 1927 U.S. Supreme Court decision (*United States v. Sullivan* 274 U.S. 259) that upheld the Internal Revenue Service's contention that even *unlawful* income was subject to income taxes, the Fifth Amendment guarantee against self-incrimination notwithstanding. The tax-evasion case against Capone was initiated in 1929 by the Special Intelligence Unit of the Treasury Department. It was a low-key agency that avoided publicity. A nearsighted special agent who never carried a firearm was put in charge of the investigation. He brought Capone down with a pencil.

Capone stood trial for having a net income of $1,038,654 during the years 1924–1929 for which he failed to pay income tax. In 1931 he was found guilty of income tax evasion and received sentences totaling 11 years. In 1932, his appeals exhausted, Capone entered the federal prison in Atlanta. He was transferred to Alcatraz in 1934, where he was found to be suffering from syphilis. For several years, Capone refused treatment. Early in 1938, he began showing symptoms of paresis and was transferred out of Alcatraz. Capone was released in 1939, his sentence shortened for good behavior, but by then he was suffering from an advanced case of syphilis. He headed for his winter home on Palm Island, Florida, and, after living years as an invalid, died in 1947 of pneumonia following a stroke.

ORGANIZED CRIME IN CHICAGO AFTER CAPONE: THE OUTFIT EMERGES[8]

The Capone Organization "can best be described *not* as a hierarchy directed by Al Capone but rather as a senior partnership involving four men, who in turn entered into a variety of partnerships to run specific enterprises." These four—Al Capone, his brother Ralph, Al's boyhood friend Frank Nitti, and Jake Guzik, his accounting wizard—each received one-sixth of the income that they derived from their various enterprises. The rest was for the maintenance of their central headquarters and its personnel—mostly clerks and gunmen: "The senior partners, in turn, invested money and, when possible, provided political protection for an expanding and diverse group of enterprises" (Haller 1974: 11).

When Prohibition ended, Al Capone was in prison, and the country was several years into the Great Depression. These changes affected organized crime in Chicago. At the height of his power, Capone is reputed to have had 700 gunmen under his control (Palsey 1971). This expensive army was no longer necessary; the Capone syndicate, consolidated under what become known as the Outfit, had an unchallenged monopoly on organized crime in Chicago, maintained with minimal force and a great deal of political influence. The city's First Ward would remain at the center of the Out-

fit's political influence, which reached into the towns and villages of suburban Cook County. Frank Nitti ran the Outfit with the help of Capone's brothers Ralph and Matt, Capone cousins Charlie and Rocco Fischetti, Paul de Lucia (better known as Paul "the Waiter" Ricca), Anthony ("Joe Batters") Accardo, Jake Guzik, and Welchman Murray Humphreys. The Chicago Crime Commission points out that the Outfit "has been somewhat unique in its willingness to deal with and, indeed, grant considerable responsibility to non-Italians." For many years, Humphreys[9] was the Outfit's chief political fixer and troubleshooter, and he was succeeded by Gus ("The Greek") Alex ("Spotlight" 1981: 8).

Nitti was born in Sicily in 1889 and brought to the United States at two years of age. Known as "the Enforcer" for his role in dealing with internal discipline and external enemies of the Capone organization, Nitti began his career as a barber, fencing stolen goods on the side. Although physically unimposing, he had Capone's confidence and became his second in command (Schoenberg 1992). In 1943, Nitti, who had been in poor health, feared prosecution for a nationwide extortion scheme involving the motion picture industry (Demaris 1969), discussed below. On the day an indictment was handed down by a New York grand jury, Nitti committed suicide with a .32 revolver. He was not thrown off the roof of a building by Eliot Ness, as portrayed in Brian De Palma's movie *The Untouchables* (Koziol and Baumann 1987).

With the death of Nitti, Paul Ricca, born in Naples in 1897, became head of the Outfit. A noted political fixer, Ricca arrived in New York in 1920, fleeing prosecution for murder, and eventually settled in Chicago. There he secured employment with "Diamond Joe" Esposito, a major bootlegger and political power. He also worked in Esposito's restaurant, earning the nickname "Paul the Waiter." Ricca left Esposito to manage a theater in Little Italy and was hired by Capone to manage his World Playhouse Corporation. This theater

---

[8]For an interesting journalistic history of the Chicago Outfit, see Russo (2001).

[9]For a journalistic biography of Murray Humphreys, see Morgan (1985).

background provided the knowledge he needed to engineer the Browne–Bioff extortion scam.

The Browne–Bioff Episode

Willie Bioff was a Chicago racketeer who specialized in shakedowns of kosher butchers. He went into partnership with George Browne, a local official of the International Alliance of Theatrical Stage Employees (IATSE), whose members also included motion picture projectionists and other movie theater employees. The two began extorting money from theater chains under the threat of "labor trouble." With Prohibition ending, the Outfit was searching for new areas of profit, and Frank Nitti soon "muscled in" on the scheme, first as a 50-percent and eventually as a 75-percent partner. In 1932, Browne unsuccessfully ran for the presidency of the international union. In 1934, Nitti arranged for Browne to gain the support of major East Coast gangsters Lucky Luciano and Lepke Buchalter in New York and Longie Zwillman of New Jersey, and Browne was elected president of the IATSE (Nelli 1976). The convention that elected Browne was pervaded with "such an atmosphere of intimidation that opposition wilted" (Johnson 1972: 329).

Browne appointed Bioff to a union position, and the two increased their extortion activities, this time on a nationwide scale. They were able to extort money from Hollywood film studios such as RKO and Twentieth Century-Fox under the threat of closing down theaters throughout the country (Johnson 1972). The scheme came to an end in 1941, when the brother of the Twentieth Century-Fox chairman of the board was indicted for income tax evasion. In exchange for leniency, he disclosed the activities of Bioff and Browne. Bioff was eventually sentenced to ten years, Browne to eight. As a result of their cooperation, important members of the Outfit, including Ricca, were convicted.[10] Three years later, all were

---

[10]In 1955, living under an assumed name, Bioff left his Phoenix home and entered his pickup truck. A moment later, Bioff and the truck went up in a tremendous explosion—a dynamite bomb had been wired to the starter.

paroled in a scandal that rocked the administration of President Harry Truman.

When Ricca was imprisoned for his role in the theater scheme, Tony Accardo emerged as leader of the Outfit. One of six children, Accardo was born in Chicago in 1906 to Sicilian parents. His father was a shoemaker. Raised in the tough Grand Avenue neighborhood, an Italian area on Chicago's Near West Side, the future crime boss dropped out of school at age 14. He subsequently became a member of the Circus Cafe Gang (named after the site of its headquarters), a truck driver in the bootleg trade, and an enforcer and bodyguard for Al Capone, who gave him the nickname "Joe Batters" (or "J.B.") for his ability to wield a bat (Roemer 1995). While his arrest record dates back to 1922, and although he had been arrested about 30 times and was a suspect in at least two murders, Accardo could boast that he had never spent a night in jail. In 1955 the Internal Revenue Service expressed dissatisfaction with his tax returns: since 1940, Accardo had reported over 43 percent of his income as coming from "gambling and miscellaneous sources." The IRS considered this too vague, and prosecution was initiated for income tax violations. He was eventually convicted and sentenced to six years' imprisonment, but the conviction was reversed on appeal.

In 1955, fearing further federal prosecution as head of the Outfit, Accardo and his aging partner, Paul Ricca, looked for someone to take over the day-to-day operations of the Outfit. They turned to Sam Giancana (Peterson 1962; Brashler 1977).

Sam Giancana

Christened Momo Salvatore, Sam Giancana was born in Chicago in 1908 to Sicilian immigrants and raised in the notorious "Patch" of the Taylor Street neighborhood. Abused as a child, Giancana dropped out of school at age 14. Living mostly in the streets, he became a member of the "42 Gang"—a group that even other criminals of that day viewed as crazy. They specialized in truck hijacking and auto theft, becoming notorious for their level of violence (Landesco 1933; Giancana and Giancana 1992; Brashler 1977). Fellow members of the 42s would also gain prominence in the Outfit. While the gang was periodically involved in politics and union organizing as "muscle," its primary activity centered around conventional and often reckless criminality. Deaths, via the police or rival criminals, and imprisonment eventually brought an end to the 42s (Brashler 1977).

As an adolescent, Mooney served as a gunman for Al Capone in 1928. Arrested dozens of times, and indicted on several occasions for felonies, not a single case reached the trial stage—"friendly" judges are the explanation. In one murder indictment, the prosecution witness was murdered before the trial. In 1929, however, his "luck" finally ran out, and Giancana received a one-to-five-year sentence for burglary. Drafted by the army in 1943, Giancana was rejected for being a "constitutional psychopath" with an "inadequate personality and strong antisocial trends" (Demaris 1969: 8; Giancana and Giancana 1992).

Giancana's specialty for the 42s was being a "wheelman"—driving a getaway car. This eventually earned him a position as chauffeur for "Machine Gun" Jack McGurn and later Paul Ricca. However, his Outfit connection was no advantage in rural Garden Prairie, where Giancana was convicted of bootlegging in 1939. (The Outfit continued in the alcohol business after Prohibition, selling backwoods-still whiskey bottled as imported or as quality domestic brands to saloon keepers eager to improve their profits.) Giancana served three years in the federal prison at Terre Haute, Indiana, where he met Eddie Jones, a wealthy black numbers operator. Jones and his brothers were major gambling and political figures in Chicago's African-American areas. Jones, who had pled guilty to income tax evasion in 1939, told Giancana about the large amount of money that he and his brother George had made in this enterprise, which had been dismissed by leading white gangsters as "penny-ante." Since Prohibition, blacks had dominated the numbers business in Chicago (Haller 1990b). When Giancana was released from prison in 1942, Jones financed his entry into the jukebox racket and became his partner in a variety of gambling enterprises centered in the African-American areas of the city's South Side.

Giancana repaid his benefactor by advising Accardo of the lucrative black numbers operation and requested permission to take it over using his crew of 42s (Brashler 1977). After Jones's release from Terre Haute in 1946, he was kidnapped and held for ransom in Giancana's new suburban home in Oak Park. After a payment of $100,000 was made by his family, Jones was released and fled to Mexico with his brother, leaving Teddy Roe in charge of the business. Roe did quite well for six years—his income tax returns indicating an income of more than $1 million a year—but he was feeling heat from Giancana. After a campaign of intimidation, murder, beatings, and bombings, Roe became the last holdout from Giancana's takeover of the South Side numbers racket. Aiding Giancana's efforts were the police, who raided Roe's policy wheels. In 1952, Roe was ambushed and cut down by a shotgun blast. Sam Giancana had become a principal player in Chicago organized crime. Money from the numbers enabled Giancana to branch out into other enterprises, and his organizational skills and murderous crew allowed him to prosper. In 1955, Giancana was in charge of the Outfit's day-to-day operations (Brashler 1977; Giancana and Giancana 1992; Roemer 1995).

Giancana lived a high-profile social life, something that had become anathema to the now-modernized leaders of organized crime. He had a widely publicized romance with Phyllis McGuire (of the singing McGuire sisters) and a public friendship with Frank Sinatra. He even shared a girlfriend with President John F. Kennedy. Giancana generated a great deal of publicity when he secured an injunction against the FBI's intensive surveillance of his activities. In 1965 he was imprisoned for a year for contempt, refusing to testify before a federal grand jury after being granted immunity from prosecution (Peterson 1969). Following his release, Giancana sought refuge in Mexico. His daughter states that he was forced into exile by Ricca and Accardo (Giancana and Renner 1985). Giancana remained in Mexico until 1974, when Mexican immigration agents dragged him to a waiting car, drove him 150 miles, and pushed him across the border into the waiting arms of FBI agents. He was then brought to Chicago for grand jury investigations.

The organization was running smoothly without Giancana—Accardo[11] had apparently resumed active control—and his subsequent return to Chicago was apparently not welcomed by the Outfit leadership. In 1975, Giancana was shot to death at close range in his suburban Chicago home by someone he apparently knew and obviously trusted. Even in death, controversy about Giancana continued. It was disclosed that in 1960 the Central Intelligence Agency had contacted John Roselli, a Giancana lieutenant, to secure syndicate help in assassinating Fidel Castro. Syndicate leaders had reason to dislike Castro, and they also had contacts in Cuba and with exiles in South Florida. The plot apparently never materialized; in 1976, Roselli's body was found in an oil drum floating in Miami's Biscayne Bay.

In 1986, top leaders of the Outfit were convicted of skimming $2 million from gambling casinos in Las Vegas—portrayed in the book and motion picture *Casino*—except Accardo, who had assumed senior/semiretired status. A key witness at the trial was Angelo Lonardo, the head of organized crime in Cleveland.

Leadership was assumed by Joseph ("Joe Nagal") Ferriola. This former Outfit enforcer is alleged to have permitted members to involve themselves in drug trafficking, something that had heretofore been off limits. Ferriola died of natural causes in 1989, and leadership was assumed by Sam Carlisi (born in 1921) and John ("No-Nose"[12]) DiFronzo (born in 1928). In 1993, DiFronzo was found guilty of attempting to infiltrate an Indian reservation gambling operation in California for illegal purposes and sentenced to 37 months. That same year, Carlisi and seven members of his crew were convicted of racketeering and

related charges. Carlisi, at age 74, was sentenced to 12 years; he died of natural causes in 1997. DiFronzo successfully appealed his conviction and was released in 1994.

Outfit Street Crews

While New York has five separate families, the Chicago Outfit has traditionally been organized on the basis of separate street crews, each associated with a particular geographic area. There is evidence of criminal specialization among the various street crews, although it currently appears that various forms of gambling are a primary activity of each. The Grand Avenue specialty is burglary, while the Twenty-Sixth Street crew is noted for truck hijacking (cartage theft). The North Side/Rush Street crew is noted for its vice operations: prostitution, pornography, and liquor law violations. Many of these criminal specializations are related to ecological aspects of each area. For example, the North Side contains Rush Street, Chicago's adult night-club entertainment district, while the Twenty-Sixth Street area contains a large number of railroad yards and associated shipping and trucking terminals, providing the opportunity for cargo theft. Chicago Heights, located on the southern edge of the Chicago metropolitan area, has a reputation for automobile theft and chop shop operations, which became a major business for the Chicago Heights crew. This specialization did not prevent members of other crews from cartage theft: in 2001 the Chicago police uncovered an elaborate fencing operation whose source was goods stolen by members of the Grand Street and Elmwood Park crews from semitractor trailers parked in railway freight yards (Ferkenhoff and Vogell 2001).

Since Chicagoans refer to their neighborhoods in terms of South Side, North Side, and West Side (East Side is not used in Chicago), we need to explain their meaning. The city has baselines, with Madison Street, which runs east and west, and State Street, which runs north and south, intersecting at the zero point. Everything north of Madison is the North Side; everything west of State Street is the West Side. Buildings are num-

[11]Tony Accardo died of natural causes in 1992.
[12]As a young man, DiFronzo was a "smash-and-grab" thief—smash the window, grab the fur coat. On one occasion, before he could strip the mannequin and get back into his car, a jagged piece of glass took off part of his nose, which doctors were subsequently able to reattach.

bered with increases or decreases of one hundred, roughly equivalent to one city block. In order to provide greater specificity, locations may be given additional identifiers such as "Far" and "Near"— for example, the Near North Side is closer to the South Side, and the Far North Side is closer to the northern suburbs than to the zero point.

The Taylor Street Crew

The preeminent street crew is associated with the Taylor Street neighborhood contained within the Near West Side community area of Chicago. Poverty and overcrowding led to the establishment of Chicago's first settlement house by Jane Addams in 1889, and Mother Cabrini, the first and only American saint of the Catholic Church, also labored among the poor in this area until her death in 1917. The police precinct encompassing the area was referred to as the "Bloody Maxwell" district because of frequent gunfights between police and criminals (Longstreet 1973). Several urban renewal projects affected the area, including the Chicago campus of the University of Illinois in 1961. As they improved their lot, or were displaced by these massive urban renewal efforts, the early immigrants moved from the Near West Side to other growing areas of the city. By the end of World War II, except for the Italian enclave along Taylor Street, the Near West Side was made up largely of African-Americans who had recently emigrated from rural areas of the South.

The Taylor Street neighborhood served as the model for Gerald Suttles's (1968) original conceptualization of the *defended neighborhood* (discussed in Chapter 2), and the defended neighborhood concept accurately describes Chicago's inner-city racket neighborhoods. The Taylor Street neighborhood was also the setting for Solomon Kobrin's (1966) study of status criteria among street-corner groups. In describing the Taylor Street neighborhood, Kobrin writes that a firmly established integration of legitimate and illegitimate elements has existed in the community for some length of time. This integration of deviant and conventional lifestyles manifested itself in a locally acknowl-

edged alliance between the political leadership and the leadership of the Outfit.

Taylor Street's direct connection to the Outfit can be traced to the 1920s and the 42 Gang. Many members of the 42s were recruited during the 1920s by "Machine-Gun" Jack McGurn, who grew up in the neighborhood (Brashler 1977). Remnants of the 42s made up the core of what eventually became known as the Taylor Street crew. As already noted, gang member Sam Giancana rose through the ranks to head organized crime in Chicago.

Despite its history and formidable reputation, the neighborhood has changed due to the presence of the University of Illinois and rising property values brought on by the neighborhood's proximity to Chicago's central business district. However, perhaps out of feelings of nostalgia, Outfit wiseguys can still be found dining, meeting, and socializing in Taylor Street restaurants. Demographic changes have resulted in many Taylor Street stalwarts moving out to the western suburbs, and the crew identified with Taylor Street is sometimes referred to as the Cicero or Elmwood Park crew.

Rocco ("Rocky") Infelise   Until his death in 1989, Joe Ferriola of Cicero was street boss of the Taylor Street crew of about 20 persons and head of the Outfit. He was replaced as street boss by his top assistant, Rocco Ernest Infelise (born 1922), a paratroop combat veteran with an expensive home in upscale suburban River Forest and a vacation residence in Fort Lauderdale, Florida. Infelise paid $1,000 a month to the police chief of Forest Park to allow high-stakes dice games in the Chicago suburb. A major bookmaker for his crew, the Republican Party boss and town assessor of Cicero acted as a fixer and provided warnings of police raids. In 1993, a year after he pleaded guilty to gambling conspiracy charges, Frank ("Baldy") Maltese's wife was elected Cicero town president.

On orders from Ferriola, the Infelise crew participated in a massive effort to extort money from independent bookmakers and other gambling entrepreneurs in the Chicagoland area. Bookmakers were given a choice: pay street taxes, make an Outfit representative a 50–50 partner, go out of business, or be "trunked"—placing murder victims in car trunks has been an Outfit favorite. Operators of other types of gambling businesses—card rooms, for example—were ordered to pay a specific amount in taxes—or else. When the Infelise crew expanded into Lake County (just north of Cook County), they encountered recalcitrant gamblers; the body of one was subsequently found in a car trunk. In Lake County, similar overtures were made to the proprietors of houses of prostitution and marginal businesses, such as bars with sex shows or adult bookstores.

The crew included enforcers such as Harry ("The Hook") Aleman, William ("Butch") Petrocelli, and Gerald Scarpelli—experts at intimidation. Aleman (born in 1939), who has a Mexican father and an Italian mother, is Ferriola's nephew and is believed responsible for at least 15 homicides. His looks—five feet, eight inches, 145 pounds—belie a fearsome reputation, and the mob hit man fancies himself an artist; his canvases usually depict outdoor scenes. After high school, Aleman attended art school in Chicago. In 1997, in a historic trial, he was convicted of the 1972 murder of a Teamsters Union steward. Aleman had been tried for the same murder in 1977 and acquitted after a bench trial. It was subsequently revealed that the judge, since deceased, had taken a $10,000 bribe to fix the case. The appellate courts ruled that the special circumstances of this case did not violate the constitutional protection against double jeopardy (since there had never been jeopardy in the first trial). Aleman was sentenced to 100 to 300 years' imprisonment (Possley and Kogan 2001).

The five-foot, nine-inch, 220-pound Petrocelli, who spent a lot of time in the gym, grew up on Taylor Street. While an older brother became a Chicago police sergeant, Butch became a juice loan collector. He was known to sit across the table from a recalcitrant street tax victim, staring intently and in total silence. That was usually sufficient to gain compliance: "Those who somehow missed Butch's silent message, became corpses" (Brashler 1981: 152). He traveled all over the country, becoming a prime suspect in many gangland murders. In 1981, when he failed to turn

over $100,000 collected for the family of imprisoned Harry Aleman, Petrocelli was found dead in the backseat of his car. He had been disfigured with a blowtorch and stabbed several times. Petrocelli's mouth was taped shut, and he had died of asphyxiation.

Scarpelli was born in New York in 1938 and raised on Chicago's West Side. Arrested 17 times since 1960, he served prison sentences for armed robbery and counterfeiting. In 1989, while in federal custody, and after providing information to the FBI, Scarpelli committed suicide (Federal Bureau of Investigation 1988).

A typical ploy used by the trio involved associates making bets with unaffiliated bookmakers. If the bets were profitable, they would be collected; when a string of losses occurred, they would fail to pay. The bookmaker involved would demand a meeting and usually show up with one or more intimidating colleagues. They would find themselves face-to-face with Chicago's "fearsome threesome." With roles thus reversed, the unfortunate bookmaker would be ordered to pay a fixed amount in back taxes and to pay weekly street taxes.[13]

Crew members appear to enjoy their work. In a 1989 tape-recorded conversation, Infelise's second in command told William Jahoda, who was secretly cooperating with the government, about how much he enjoyed his work and the technique of putting on a turban: "I'm so busy. But I enjoy it. I enjoy my work. I wish I didn't have that sentence threatening over me all the time, but that's what it is. . . . Told him [potential competitor trying to engage in loansharking in Lake County], 'I'll put a turban on his head.' You break a guy's head, they got to wrap it." As a ranking intelligence officer told the author, "To a large extent they enjoy what they're doing; it's a game."

In the spring of 1975, an independent bookmaker and ex-Chicago police officer was told by

---

[13]A Los Angeles crime Family *caporegime* used a similar approach to extort bookmakers in that city: "His men bet into bookmakers across the city. When they won, they would collect. When they lost, they would stiff the bookies and remind them who they were dealing with and what right did they have to operate in this town?" (J. Smith 1998: 190).

members of the Taylor Street crew that he would have to pay street taxes. Harry Aleman became his business partner—a "forced marriage"—and directed the bookmaker to contact other gamblers on the North Side to tell them to pay street taxes; one was "A. R."

The ex-cop told A. R. that he represented "Harry," who on behalf of the Outfit was demanding 50 percent of his business. Unfortunately for A. R., he was not from Chicago and knew little about the Outfit. As the bookmaker responded, "Go fuck yourself and tell them guys to fuck themselves." After being told of his response, Aleman directed the bookmaker to try again. He did, with the same response. Subsequently, A. R. found out who "Harry" was and changed his attitude. But it was too late. An example was necessary, and Aleman told his "partner" to stay far away from A. R. On October 31, 1975, at 9 P.M., A. R., 34, entered a restaurant on the Far West Side and asked the cashier if anyone had been looking for him. When the response was negative, he ordered dinner. Shortly afterward, two men wearing ski masks entered the restaurant, one carrying a .30 caliber carbine, the other a short-barrelled shotgun. When the men approached, A. R. tried to rise but was pushed back into the booth. One masked man raised his carbine and fired four rounds into his chest. Blood spurted out, and the second masked man placed his shotgun against the bookmaker's head and fired two shots. Both men pointed their guns at patrons as they calmly exited the restaurant and entered a car, later found abandoned. Aleman's thumbprint was discovered on a warranty book in the car's glove compartment—dangerous does not necessarily mean smart. As part of an agreement, Aleman pled guilty in 1978 to home invasions in Indiana and Illinois and received an 11-year sentence; he was released in 1989. A. R.'s murder convinced most bookmakers and other gamblers to capitulate to Outfit demands, although there were exceptions.

In 1982 a bookmaker was lured to an illegal gambling casino in the suburb of Libertyville, where he was attacked and beaten to death. In 1984 the man in charge of the crew's Lake County activities demanded $6,000 a month in street taxes from successful bookmaker Hal Smith: "Or you're 'trunk music,'" alluding to the sound of flesh decomposing in the trunk of a car. Smith made a counteroffer: $3,500. Rocky Infelise was informed, and the counteroffer was obviously rejected.

William Jahoda, a successful bookmaker associated with the Taylor Street crew, told Infelise said he knew Hal Smith and arranged to meet him at Jahoda's suburban home. Before the meeting, the bookmaker's demise was rehearsed. Jahoda met Smith in a suburban tavern, where they had a drink. He told Smith that he had a couple of girls back at his house. When the two pulled into Jahoda's garage, Jahoda told Smith to go into the house while he checked the mail. Through the window Jahoda saw Smith walk into the kitchen, when suddenly a man appeared behind him. When Jahoda entered the house, Smith was lying on the kitchen floor with his back against a cabinet. Infelise later told Jahoda that the bookmaker had pulled a gun, but it had been taken away from him by one of Infelise's men. Smith's decomposing body was discovered in the trunk of his car. He had been severely beaten around the face and upper torso, and there were 13 incision-like marks around his neck; he had finally been strangled to death.

The Taylor Street crew also ran illegal gambling operations such as the Rouse House casino in suburban Libertyville, which offered dice and card games. As a natural extension of their gambling activities, the crew was heavily involved in loansharking. But Infelise also had significant expenses, aiding incarcerated members with legal fees and paying them part of the crew's profits. In a 1989 recording, Infelise complained that he was giving away $35,000 a month "for guys that are away, and the coppers. . . . We got seven guys away, [who] get $2,000 a month."

In 1992, Infelise and several members of his crew were found guilty of racketeering and murder conspiracy. The conviction was largely the result of testimony from Jahoda, who became an informant. At his sentencing hearing, Infelise castigated the judge and made a veiled threat against Jahoda, who was in the witness protection program. Infelice was sentenced to 63 years.

The Grand Avenue Crew

Grand Avenue is located within the West Town community area of Chicago. Anthony Accardo, the longtime elder of the Chicago Outfit, was born in 1906 on West Grand Avenue (Roemer 1995). His involvement with Capone is commonly believed to have been the beginning of the Grand Avenue street crew. Accardo began his criminal career as a member of the Circus gang, young toughs who frequented a tavern called the Circus. The Circus gang and another Near Northwest Side gang were subsidiaries of the Capone syndicate and served as counterforces to the O'Banion gang on Chicago's North Side. The headquarters of the *Unione Siciliana* was located within the Grand Avenue neighborhood, and Accardo was at one time the president of the organization.

The 1982 imprisonment of Grand Avenue boss Joseph Lombardo left the crew leaderless and without direction, causing a decline in their activities. Prior to his imprisonment, Lombardo and the Outfit played a role in the Grand Avenue community. A Chicago police officer familiar with the Grand Avenue crew reports, for example, that Lombardo would hold meetings in an old funeral parlor on Grand Avenue: "There, the old men came and told Joe their problems. If an old Italian told Joe that someone was speeding up and down his street and he was afraid kids would get run over, Joe would send someone to threaten the driver. The police couldn't do that, but the 'moustaches' can. It ain't right but the people got service that way." Lombardo was released from prison in 1995 and returned to the Grand Avenue neighborhood. He had been imprisoned as a result of his involvement with Allen Dorfman (discussed in Chapter 12).

Tony Spilotro   One of the most infamous members of the Grand Avenue crew, Tony Spilotro (whose activities have been portrayed in the book and motion picture *Casino*) was the son of Italian immigrants, small restaurant owners. Born in 1938, he grew up in the Grand Avenue neighborhood. An older brother became an air force captain and a dental surgeon, but Tony dropped out of

high school in his sophomore year. He associated with other dropouts, formed a gang, and earned a police record for various crimes. Although of small stature, Tony was widely feared because of his ferocity. This reputation earned him a spot with Chicago's most notorious loanshark, Sam ("Mad Sam," a former 42 gang member) DeStefano. A sadistic and violent individual who killed his own brother for using drugs, DeStefano was dubbed the "Marquis de Sade" of the Chicago Outfit. He was murdered in 1973 (see Kidner [1976] for a discussion of DeStefano).[14] At age 27, Spilotro took over his business, becoming the youngest loanshark in the Chicago Outfit. Tony also carried out executions for the Outfit leadership.

In 1964, Spilotro was sent to Miami, Florida, to assist Frank ("Lefty") Rosenthal, who was running gambling operations for the Outfit. In 1969, he was back in Chicago overseeing gambling operations and gaining a high profile because of his murderous activities. Two years later, apparently to let things cool off, Tony went to Las Vegas. There, Lefty Rosenthal was in charge of the Stardust Casino Hotel, where enormous sums were being skimmed off on behalf of organized crime bosses throughout the country. Spilotro brought with him a group of enforcers from the Windy City, and soon the tortured bodies of murder victims—wayward loansharks and cheating employees of mob-controlled hotels—began turning up. He extorted street taxes from local criminals and opened a jewelry store, which served as his headquarters. When his "Hole-in-the-Wall Gang" of burglars began looting homes, the store served as a fencing outlet.

In 1979, Spilotro's name was added to the *Black Book* of persons banned from casino hotels. In 1981, several members of the Hole-in-the-Wall Gang were arrested while engaged in a major burglary. One, believing he had been betrayed, became a witness against Spilotro in an old Chicago

---

[14]In 2000, DeStefano's nephew, Sam, who is the co-owner of a Chicago jazz club with Tony Spilotro's sister-in-law, was indicted for participation in a nationwide jewel theft ring allegedly headed by a former deputy superintendent of the Chicago Police Department (Barnum and Gibson 2000).

murder case. Spilotro was acquitted, but he had become infamous in Las Vegas, and his high profile disturbed the Outfit leadership, whose chief concern was maintaining their share of the "skim." Members of the Spilotro crew were dealing drugs, something that was anathema to the Outfit leadership, and in a serious violation of Mob etiquette, Tony was having an affair with Lefty Rosenthal's wife. In 1983, Outfit leaders and Spilotro were indicted for conspiracy related to the Las Vegas skimming. Spilotro claimed ill health—he had had a coronary bypass—and his case was severed from that of the other defendants, who were eventually convicted.

In 1986 a new boss was in charge of the Outfit's day-to-day activities, and Joe Ferriola blamed the trouble in Las Vegas on Spilotro. Tony was called back for a meeting in Chicago. His body and that of his younger brother Michael were discovered buried in an Indiana cornfield—they had been beaten to death (Roemer 1994; Pileggi 1995; and newspaper articles from Chicago and Las Vegas).

The Twenty-Sixth Street Crew

The Twenty-Sixth Street neighborhood is contained within the Armour Square community area of Chicago, named after the Armour Institute of Technology, the original name of the Illinois Institute of Technology. The Armour Square Community is truly an interstitial space in that it is a one-half-mile-wide strip of land bordered by a railroad yard and the Chicago River on the north and raised embankments of railroad tracks on two of the remaining sides. Just west of the neighborhood is the town of Cicero.

The neighborhood was the site of Al Capone's headquarters, the Lexington Hotel, and the Twenty-Sixth Street crew is considered a direct descendant of the original Colosimo–Torrio–Capone Syndicate, since many of the people who worked for Colosimo and later Torrio and Capone lived there. Much of the area has been replaced by an interstate roadway and public housing, reducing the size of the Italian enclave.

Twenty-Sixth Street is probably the strongest street crew neighborhood in metropolitan Chicago. Unlike Taylor Street, there have been no major urban renewal efforts in this Italian community; the homes are well cared for, and the neighborhood is stable. As reported by one organized crime investigator, "While guys from other neighborhoods have moved out, people from Twenty-sixth Street have remained in the neighborhood. They have such a base there. All of their people are right there. . . . Yeah, that neighborhood has been like time-frozen. It's like you go back to the [19]60s; it is still there. They still have the social club there." The presence of crime syndicate members in the Twenty-Sixth Street community is recognized by both community residents and government agencies.

The original boss of Twenty-Sixth Street was Bruno ("The Bomber") Roti, whose son became the chief deputy sheriff for Cook County in the 1980s; another became alderman of the First Ward and was later convicted of corruption. When The Bomber gave up his position, he was replaced by an assistant, who died in 1983 and was succeeded by Angelo LaPietra. In 1987, LaPietra was convicted in the Las Vegas skimming case—the government placed a court-authorized bug in the storefront headquarters of the Twenty-Sixth Street crew. The crew has extensive involvement in gambling and loansharking.

The North Side Crew

The North Side racket area is located within the Near North Side community, which includes the city's "Gold Coast" and downtown entertainment area. By the turn of the century, a portion of the Near North Side was already referred to as the "Gold Coast" because of the large number of luxurious homes that were built along the lakefront. The turn of the century also brought large numbers of Italians, particularly Sicilians, to the area, eventually replacing earlier immigrant groups. The "dark people," as they were called, soon dominated the area.

The natural clash between the well-to-do families of the eastern part and the immigrant families of the western portion of the Near North Side resulted in a central area that became progressively less desirable as a residential district. As a result, many of the wealthier families and businesses moved from the area. During the 1920s, many of the residential hotels and large homes that were left behind were transformed into boardinghouses in order to make them profitable. These rooming houses brought a large transient element to the area as well as a population of lower economic status. Soon the once-fashionable district became a center for dance halls, nightclubs, prostitution, and other forms of illegal activity and the beginning of the Clark Street and, later, Rush Street vice district in Chicago.

The North Side was the focus of Harvey Zorbaugh's classic community study *The Gold Coast and the Slum* (1929: 198), which described the North Side "as a community in the process of disintegration where church, school, family, and government have ceased to have any influence on community life." Existence there, he stated, "was without the law and without the mores of the larger society," a classic case of social disorganization. These findings were challenged by William Whyte (1961), who noted that portions of the North Side, particularly the Italian settlement, were highly organized. Citing one of the leaders of the Chicago Area Project Near North Program, Whyte argued that while the area was characterized by congested population, poor housing, and low family income, people there lived in family groupings and built up elaborate social networks reminiscent of Italian village life.

The connection between the North Side community and the Chicago Outfit can be traced to Prohibition, Al Capone, and the *Unione Siciliana*. In 1929, Capone's hand-picked successor to the leadership of the *Unione* was murdered by the Aiello brothers, allied with Bugs Moran. Capone responded by sending a cohort of men led by Frank Nitti into the area. They systematically bombed Aiello–Moran alky stills and speakeasies all over the North Side. The blasting continued until the St. Valentine's Day massacre of 1929 ended the Aiello–Moran axis forever and left the Capone syndicate firmly in control of Chicago's Near North Side.

Just as they had done in the Taylor Street area, the Capone organization turned to local Italian street toughs in the North Side community to find recruits for their criminal organization. Once the Capone organization had taken control of bootlegging activities on the North Side, it was a simple matter for them to dominate other vice activities.

The North Side was known as a "honky-tonk town," as saloons, cabarets, and rialtos marked every block on Clark Street from Grand Avenue to Division Street. The Chicago Crime Commission reported that by 1953, there were 165 "clip joints," burlesque bars, assignation houses, and gambling halls in the Clark Street area. Scantily clad "26-Girls" hustled drinks from out-of-town conventioneers and local men seeking a good time (Murray 1975). Today there is nothing left of the Clark Street rialto, though neighboring Rush Street contains numerous restaurants and upscale liquor establishments, and further north into the Forty-Third and Forty-Fourth wards are numerous night spots featuring blues and jazz, for which Chicago is famous. The North Side racket community no longer exists. Most of the members of the original Sicilian community moved away when the neighborhood was torn down between 1941 and 1962, during successive stages of the construction of the Cabrini–Green housing complex. Many North Side Italian emigrants resettled in the suburb of Melrose Park.

Lottery king Ken ("Tokyo Joe") Eto, born in 1920 of Japanese ancestry, paid thousands of dollars a month in street taxes to the North Side crew to remain in business. In 1983 he was convicted of operating an illegal lottery business that grossed nearly $6 million between May 4, 1980, and August 20, 1980. Facing imprisonment, he met with the crew's street boss, Vincent Solano, head of Laborers Union Local 1. Eto assured Solano that he could be trusted to be a "stand-up guy," but the street boss was apparently unconvinced. In 1983, Tokyo Joe was taken for a ride by two men, one a Cook County deputy sheriff, shot three times in the back of the head, and left for dead. But Eto survived. Later that year, the bodies of Eto's would-be assassins were found in the trunk of a car with multiple stab wounds—being "trunked" was apparently the Outfit's penalty for botching a murder. Eto went into the federal witness protection program. The North Side crew made headlines in Chicago during the 1990s, mostly as a result of the activities of Lenny Patrick.

Lenny Patrick Leonard Patrick was born in England (or possibly in Chicago to English parents, Jews who had somehow acquired Irish surnames) in 1913. He grew up in the Jewish community on Chicago's West Side, where he became a legend for his easy use of violence and strong defense of the neighborhood. His criminal record includes a seven-year sentence for a 1933 Indiana bank robbery. He has admitted committing two murders and ordering four others, all during the 1930s and 1940s. For decades he has been closely associated with Gus Alex, a major Outfit power and political fixer. With a crew of vicious enforcers, Patrick was responsible for gambling and loansharking operations on the North Side and northern suburbs. He also controlled several legitimate industrial laundering companies that rented towels, linens, and uniforms.

According to court records, the Patrick group extorted money from seven legitimate businesses: in each case, members of his crew approached the owners of the businesses and demanded payments of between $50,000 and $500,000. To back up their demands, they used threats and violence, routinely threatening to kill not only the primary victim but also family members. They extorted street taxes from bookmakers and other gambling operators and engaged in loansharking at rates up to 260 percent annually; those who were slow to repay were routinely beaten.

In 1992, after being accused of extortion from numerous legitimate firms and gambling operators, Patrick pled guilty and agreed to become a government witness. Gus Alex and the crew's primary enforcer were found guilty of extortion. Alex, at age 76, was sentenced to 15 years. However, Patrick's contribution to the success of the federal government is dubious. According to court records, "While Patrick purported to cooperate with the government beginning on November 6, 1989, his cooperation was at best halfhearted, and

he continued at the same time to participate in the conspiracy and to hide his participation from the FBI."

Chicago Heights

Chicago Heights was first incorporated as a city in 1901, its name based on the fact that the area is located 694 feet above sea level, one of the highest elevations in Cook County. The development of organized crime in Chicago Heights parallels the development of organized crime in Chicago. By 1908, this newly established city had a reputation for being overrun with gamblers, and many of the saloons also supported prostitution. That year, the mayor was arrested on gambling charges, and crime became a recurrent theme in Chicago Heights politics. During Prohibition, the city was famous for its bootlegging activities. Treasury Department officials declared that Chicago Heights was one huge distillery and that there was nothing in the United States equal to it. Conditions were so scandalous that in 1928 the chief of police was murdered in his own home—he had been scheduled to testify before a grand jury investigating two local bootleggers (Lanfranchi 1976; Schoenberg 1992).

During Prohibition, a struggle for control ensued between the three major gangland factions in Chicago Heights. One faction turned to Al Capone for assistance, and with his support, they eliminated all competition and became the undisputed lords of the Chicago Heights underworld. Al Capone made frequent visits to the city and was generally well regarded: at a 1931 baptismal reception at the Mt. Carmel School, as well-wishers filed past, Capone peeled off $1, $5, $10, and $20 bills—this was during the Depression—and passed them out to the guests (Candeloro 1981). Local underworld leaders held court at a bakery, where everything from domestic squabbles to territorial disputes among bootleggers was adjudicated.

During the early 1970s to the early 1980s, the Chicago Heights crew made news with a violent takeover of suburban area "chop-shops"—where stolen cars are dismantled for their parts, a multi-million-dollar business—around Chicago and into Lake County, Indiana. About 14 of those who resisted were killed (O'Brien 1988). One of the crew's enforcers attempted to parlay his success in the chop-shop business into other illegal activities, particularly drugs, without permission. In 1977 the former boxer was starting his Mercedes-Benz when a car with two men wearing ski masks pulled alongside. One of the men exited, carrying a twelve-gauge shotgun, which he fired into the victim's back. Badly wounded, he attempted to crawl to a nearby store entrance, but the gunman fired a second, fatal blast.

In 1978 a leader of the Chicago Heights crew was directed by the Outfit leadership to rein in the activities of his premier executioner, who was showing a streak of independence that was a threat to the Outfit. After refusing or failing to follow these orders, his bullet-riddled body was found in his Cadillac on Chicago's West Side. In 1980, after an extensive surveillance of the wayward executioner, a "work car"—whose ownership could not be traced—with two men inside followed him as he drove with his wife on a rural Illinois road. The work car radioed to a van and then pulled in front of the car and deliberately slowed down. The van pulled alongside the car, and Butch Petrocelli fired a .30 caliber carbine out of the passenger window, while Gerry Scarpelli opened fire with a twelve-gauge shotgun. The victim's car swerved off the road and crashed into a tree. Scarpelli exited the van and fired his shotgun several times into the bloodied body (FBI 1988).

In 1972, Al Pilotto, president of Local 5 of the Laborers Union, became street boss of Chicago Heights; at the time, his brother was the city's police chief. When Pilotto assumed senior status in the 1980s, his place was taken by Albert Ceasar Tocco. Tocco's 1989 federal conviction—a 200-year sentence—was devastating to the Chicago Heights crew. According to a federal agent who had participated in the Tocco investigation, the card rooms and social clubs that members of the Chicago Heights crew frequented are gone, and it is now difficult to locate organized crime figures in Chicago Heights.

The decline of the Chicago Heights crew has coincided with other changes that are taking place in the town. The post-World War II period saw the creation of new suburban areas and the development of regional shopping centers, which spelled the end of Chicago Heights' once bustling downtown business district (Candeloro 1981). In addition, the decline of railroads and the demise of heavy industry in the area have added to the deterioration of the town. This gritty, blue-collar town is also undergoing extensive demographic changes. Many of the children and grandchildren of the original Italian settlers have moved to other suburban areas. They are being replaced by African-Americans and Hispanics.

THE OUTFIT TODAY

The size of the Outfit today is markedly smaller than the version once ruled by Al Capone. Estimates of membership range from as low as 30 to as high as 130, revealing that it is still hard to determine who is and who is not a "member." (The FBI currently estimates 60 to 70 made members.) Nevertheless, outside of predominantly black and Hispanic neighborhoods, the Outfit has been able to maintain hegemony over gambling and related activities in an area ranging from southern Wisconsin to northern Indiana. They have been able to do this in recent years using considerably less violence. Perhaps this is to be expected from the nature of Outfit leaders who haven't "come up from the streets" and who seem to prefer competitive business strategies rather than intimidation.

The Outfit's political base in the First Ward has been destroyed.[15] From the 1870s to 1990, Chicago's First Ward remained a seemingly untouchable political link to organized crime. That changed in 1990, when indictments were announced against First Ward politicians and gangsters, most of whom were subsequently found guilty. The First Ward case was developed by the

---

[15]Nevertheless, corruption continues to infect the political process in Chicago, where dozens of aldermen have been indicted and convicted.

FBI through the use of a corrupt lawyer acting as a mole and the placing of an electronic bug in a restaurant frequented by First Ward politicians. In 1992, Mayor Richard J. Daley put an end to the long and sordid political reign of the First Ward. In redrawing aldermanic districts, the Loop—the central business district—and the Michigan Avenue shopping area were placed in the Forty-Second Ward, and a new First Ward was created from parts of neighboring wards to ensure the election of a Latino alderman.

In the past, aspiring Outfit members cut their teeth on theft, particularly from interstate truck and train shipments; today, gambling and its related activities—taking bets, collecting receipts, and servicing video poker machines—is the route to membership. Gambling is crucial to the Outfit; not only does it provide considerable income, but it also gives members something to do—they have considerable leisure time—while networking and socializing. The Outfit continues to be involved in the red-light districts that appear in certain suburbs, and through control of unions the Outfit is able to provide favored businessmen with a competitive edge, for example, by investing union funds. The most significant convictions involving members of the Chicago Outfit in the last few years have involved persons on the "heavy" side, those associated with violence. As a result, a decision to stay away from business operations most likely to require violence appears to have been made by the Outfit leadership. In recent years, there have been few OC-related murders—one in 1999 and another in 2001 involved the demise of two men with violent reputations who had been involved in loansharking.

Demographic changes have affected the structure of the Outfit. Because it did not have an Italian community base, the Outfit street crew on the North Side was captained by Lenny Patrick and reinforced from the ranks of the Taylor Street crew. With the demise of the Patrick crew, the North Side territory, which now includes the Grand Avenue crew and the suburbs of Elmwood Park and Lake County (just north of Cook County), is ruled by an "area boss."

The Structure of the Chicago Outfit

At the top of the structure is a boss, identified by most sources as John DiFronzo (born in 1928), assisted by Joe ("The Clown") Lombardo (born in 1929) and Angelo ("The Hook") LaPietra (born in 1929). The inability of law enforcement to definitively identify the boss of the Outfit contrasts with the rather high profile often exhibited by bosses in New York. Chicago also differs from the OC found in New York and other East Coast cities. The Chicago Outfit was always a cooperative venture with other groups, although the Italians were dominant. Outfit influence, if not hegemony, extends from northeast Indiana to Racine, Wisconsin, to Rockford, Illinois. Rockford has its own small crew with their own neighborhood leadership structure; however, they fall under the boss of the Outfit. There is an absence of independent entrepreneurs, and all important decisions are made at the executive level. Moving into a new business or new territory is determined at the top of a truly hierarchical organization. For example, when it was decided to get into the lucrative video poker machine business, an important question had to be answered: Should distribution be controlled centrally, or should each crew be allowed to distribute in its own territory? The boss, apparently in consultation with his advisors, decided on decentralization (Herion 1998).

The Outfit is led by a boss who at various times has actually been akin to a chief executive officer responsible to one or more persons constituting an informal board of directors. This was the case during the leadership of Sam Giancana, who reported to Tony Accardo and Paul Ricca. Ricca died in 1972, and until his death 20 years later, Accardo served as something analogous to a powerful president who appoints the prime minister. Assisted by his underboss and advisors—older and influential members of the Outfit who assume some type of senior status—the boss controls three area bosses. Each area boss has responsibility for a particular part of the Chicagoland area (the city and nearby counties). He oversees the activities of street bosses, who direct the day-to-day activities of crew members.

Each of the crews (discussed earlier) is associated with a particular geographic area, although these areas have undergone change over the years. In addition, there are subgroups nominally attached to crews. Thus, major gambling operations are the responsibility of a specialty crew whose members report to the Outfit hierarchy, not to a street boss. Further complicating the picture is the custom of referring to a crew by the name of its current street boss—for example, the "Carlisi street crew" or the "Ferriola street crew"—or the primary residence of the street boss—for example, the "Cicero crew"—by federal officials, the Chicago Crime Commission, and even Outfit members themselves. Members of the various crews are not necessarily familiar with members of the other crews.

Each street crew, for the most part, acts independent of the other crews, and each street boss, assisted by (two or more) lieutenants, is responsible for supervising the activities of his crew. The head of the Outfit settles disputes between the crews and is responsible for relations with those outside the organization such as corrupt public officials and organized crime groups in other cities. A street boss may also be involved in activities, such as labor racketeering, on an "industry" as opposed to a territorial basis. For example, Vincent Solano was boss of the North Side as well as president of Local 1 of the Laborers Union.

In Chicago, made guys are supervisors, and the people they supervise—associates—begin working for $500 a week in an entry-level position; an investigator (O'Rourke 1997) compared this to starting out as a ballplayer in the minor leagues. Salaries are kept on a par across crews, apparently to avoid competition and/or jealousy. Associates are assigned to activities for which they are equipped: for example, someone with numbers skills would work as a clerk for a bookmaker; someone with a tough-guy reputation would be assigned to collections. The clerk can earn additional income by recruiting customers and will even be allowed to have his own betters for whom he is responsible. If he becomes very successful, he will be allowed to start a bookmaking business of his own. The collector for a loanshark can earn half of the vigorish, 2.5 percent, of loans that he arranged. There is little crossover; for example, clerks would not be used as collectors or vice versa. There are also special people "kept on the shelf," provided with moneymaking opportunities in order to have them available for "heavy work"—murder (Moriarity 1998).

Outfit employment is not exhausting work, often requiring only a few hours a day. A worker may also hold a legitimate job—for example, employment with the city Streets and Sanitation Department or (in the past) with the county sheriff. Indeed, Outfit employment is often geared to keeping people busy so they remain tied to the Outfit—for some, crime may not pay (a great deal), but the hours are great! A successful bookmaker who also ran nightly gaming rooms (which were fixed—loaded dice, marked cards, magnetized roulette wheels) was asked why he did not give up the more time-intensive bookmaking for the time-limited and lucrative gaming rooms: "What would I do all day?" (Moriarity 1998; Herion n.d.). But every Outfit guy is on call: "It's worse than the FBI or the military. If they get a call at three in the morning: 'Go see Howard and collect some money; give him a whack or break his legs,' they can't say 'I'm tired.' They've got to do it." And they can be called to a meeting at any time: "Refusing to go to a meeting is a killing offense. It's the way they test loyalty. They call him in—call him in for 'a cigar,' where they get their ass chewed out by the boss. It's an easy way to set someone up for a murder. If you don't show up you got a problem; if you do show up . . ." (O'Rourke 1997).

Outfit Membership   Each crew is composed of made guys and associates who are said to be "connected" or "Outfit guys." The street boss and his lieutenants, if they are of Italian heritage, are made guys. Everyone else connected to the crew is an associate (although they are commonly referred to as "members" of a crew). It should be noted that there is some disagreement about the various terms used to describe positions within the Outfit. According to virtually all sources, the Outfit does not use terms common to the New York Families, such as *consigliere*, *caporegime*, or *Cosa Nostra*. And there is little evidence of an initiation ceremony involving oaths of secrecy and obedience, the drawing of blood, and the burning of a saint's portrait. To the extent that there is a ceremony, it appears to be more like a luncheon at which the person is introduced by the boss as a made guy. There is some evidence that the traditional ceremony was used by some in the past. In court testimony, a government informant related that the Taylor Street crew under Rocky Infelise made people "the old way." Such persons may have gone through two ceremonies, one with the Outfit boss and another with his street boss: "In Chicago, according to informants, they do not go through an old-country style initiation and they kind of laugh at that. If you talk to guys actually going out bombing places, collecting the tax, threatening people, someone like that is going to laugh and say 'We don't do that in Chicago.' You become a made-guy by being nominated by your boss because you have a history of making lots of money, a good earner. It's unclear if, like in the old days, you actually have to participate in a murder. Obviously, if you participated in a hit, either as the killer or getaway driver, you've made your bones and that helps your reputation" (O'Rourke 1997).

There are definite distinctions between being a made guy and being an associate. In the Chicago Outfit, made guys hold supervisory (or senior advisory) status; everyone else is a worker, with a few important exceptions. Persons who have proven their value to the Outfit have sometimes been given important responsibilities even in the absence of Italian heritage—for example, Gus Alex (Greek), Murray Humphries (Welch), and Lenny Patrick (Jewish). Being "made" also conveys important status: "Being a made guy grants certain rights and privileges that nobody else gets. You get a cut of the pie. You can order other people to do things. You get to work in a closed circle and you profit from it more so than everybody else. When you are a made guy, you are a guy that gets the money. All the rest of those guys get just a little shred. But there aren't that many made guys" (O'Rourke 1997). And there is considerable "psychic gain." Within criminal and certain legitimate circles, being "made" conveys a great deal of prestige, if not fear.

The requirement of being Italian has helped to prevent infiltration of the organization. It has also ensured that members of the Outfit share the same values. Many of the Southern Italian and Sicilian immigrants who were attracted to organized crime subscribed to the code of *omertá* and had lived under a Mafia-dominated social order, both of which aided their participation in organized crime. Today, the requirement of being Italian accomplishes a similar goal. Though the average recruit today has never been exposed to the Mafia, many have been raised in neighborhoods where the Outfit is part of the social structure, ensuring that potential recruits have been exposed to values supportive of organized crime.

However, many Italian-Americans, wiseguys among them, reside in suburbs where the critical core of street corner boys no longer exists. The traditional storefront social clubs are rare, often places where elderly Italians—Outfit guys among them—gather to talk, tell tales of the old days, and play cards or dominos. But certain traditions supportive of organized crime—cultural deviance (discussed in Chapter 2)—continue to exist among some families even in the suburbs: "Their time frame is short and dishonesty is something that someone else has defined. They don't see anything wrong, when they need a suit for the kid, when someone graduates from high school, they go down the street to see 'Louie' and take care of it. If someone gets into trouble, they know who to go to, who the fixer is" (Risley 1998).

The connection between cultural deviance and organized crime was revealed in an interview with an experienced investigator:

They saw the Outfit guys, and gave them deference. It's in the culture. They don't grow up to believe this is wrong; it's a perverted sense of values: Knockin' down an old lady to take her purse; killing the clerk at the store for a few bucks, that's wrong. But everything to do with organized crime is perfectly acceptable. They know it's illegal, but who cares. . . . There's one group, for example, who we first noticed in 1990, '91, who call themselves the "Boys in the 'hood." There are about fifty or sixty of them, many of whom are now associates of the street crews. We had some as young as sixteen, but usually eighteen, nineteen, and usually from Elmwood Park, Melrose Park, the Northwest Side of Chicago [a residential area with many Italian-Americans, and police officers and firefighters]. They were doing any scam that the Outfit would let them do—major burglaries, jewelry thefts, drug sales, credit card fraud. Many of them are relatives of Outfit members. Many of them now—they're in their twenties—work for the Elmwood Park [Taylor Street] crew. (Scaramella 1998)

Italian-American young men are being raised in more comfortable surroundings than their predecessors' ghetto experiences. A few—the Outfit does not require many replacements for its considerably streamlined operations—may still fantasize about being part of the "mob," being a wiseguy. If they have a connected relative, or perhaps a neighbor with whom they are close, they may be given an opportunity to be a clerk or a collector. While many members of the Outfit are related by blood and marriage, the sons of Outfit members are rarely found in the ranks of Chicago organized crime. As lawyers and accountants, they are sometimes found working for the same union locals traditionally associated with the Outfit, or they may be defense attorneys in Outfit cases.

A knowledgeable federal investigator points to an important difference between organized crime in the Big Apple and the Windy City: in New York, members faced with prosecution have frequently become government informants, something rare in Chicago, where there have been informants, but they have not been made guys (Moriarity 1998).

In the next chapter, we examine domestic African-American criminal organizations and black organized crime that operates in the United States but originates elsewhere.

INTERNET CONNECTIONS

Organized crime history: **www.crimelibrary.com/gangsters-outlaws-gmen.htm**

Chicago Crime Commission: **www.chicagocrimecommission.org**

Chicago Outfit: **ipsn.org/themob.html**

REVIEW QUESTIONS

1. What was the connection among corrupt politicians in Chicago, vice entrepreneurs, and big business?
2. What was the importance of the First Ward in the development of organized crime in Chicago?
3. How and when did this influence end?
4. What was the effect of Prohibition on Chicago politics, politicians, and vice entrepreneurs?
5. What effect did the election of a reform mayor have in Chicago during Prohibition?

6. How did the onset of the Depression and the end of Prohibition affect organized crime?
7. What happened to the Capone organization after the imprisonment and subsequent death of Al Capone?
8. What are the five traditional crews of the Chicago Outfit?
9. What is the current structure of the Chicago Outfit?
10. How does the structure of organized crime in Chicago differ from that in New York?

♠

CHAPTER 6

AFRICAN-AMERICAN AND BLACK ORGANIZED CRIME

African-American opportunity in organized crime has roughly paralleled opportunity in the wider legitimate community. There were important black criminal entrepreneurs operating in the early decades of the twentieth century. African-American criminals dominated the numbers (illegal lottery) racket in cities such as New York, Philadelphia, and Chicago until they were overpowered by violent white gangsters who had superior police/political connections (Schatzberg 1994). Until his death of natural causes in 1968, the organization headed by Ellsworth ("Bumpy") Johnson ruled over the black Harlem underworld in an alliance with the Genovese crime Family.[1] The civil rights/"black power" movements of the 1960s eventually made it impossible for white criminals to operate with the freedom necessary to continue dominating indigenous black criminal organizations.

A variety of black criminal groups exist throughout the United States; some are homegrown, such as the Gangster Disciples; others, such as Jamaican posses, are imported. There are important black criminal organizations in the heroin business, particularly in New York, Detroit, Chicago, Philadelphia, and Washington, D.C. While blacks have traditionally been locked out of many activities associated with organized crime (labor racketeering and loansharking, for example) by prejudice, *dope is an equal opportunity employer.* African-American criminal groups made important strides in the heroin business when the Vietnam War exposed many black soldiers to the heroin markets of the Golden Triangle—previously, black groups were dependent on organized crime Families for their heroin. As a result of their overseas experience, black organizations were able to bypass traditional organized crime and buy directly from

---

[1]Manhattan's Harlem neighborhood is informally divided into black/Latino/Italian sections. The Italian section, known by its major street—Pleasant Avenue—has been a stronghold of the Genovese crime Family.

suppliers in Thailand. The pioneer in this endeavor was Frank Lucas and his "Country Boys."

FRANK LUCAS

Frank Lucas arrived in Harlem from North Carolina as a teenager with a serious criminal history. He soon found work with Bumpy Johnson as a collector in the numbers business and also picked up heroin packages from "Pleasant Avenue." After Johnson died, Lucas had an inspiration, a way to bypass the Genovese connection—he decided to go to Southeast Asia: "Because the war was on, and people were talking about GIs getting strung out over there. I knew if the shit is good enough to string out GIs, then I can make myself a killing" (quoted in Jacobson 2000: 41).

Although he had never been to the Far East, the brazen, streetwise Lucas, traveling alone, quickly made contact with sources of heroin. A former Army sergeant, a North Carolina "homeboy" married to Lucas's cousin, was running a bar in Bangkok; together they organized a "military-homeboy" organization. They brought in a country carpenter from North Carolina who constructed copies of government coffins, but with false bottoms to hold six to eight kilos of heroin. Military personnel were bribed, and the Southeast Asian connection was complete (Jacobson 2000).

In a typical operation, a Lucas importer's agent left Kennedy Airport for Thailand carrying $600,000 in brand-new fifties and hundreds. In Bangkok, he would check into a hotel and telephone the overseas source's agent. The caller offered a password and was given instructions on where to deliver the money. At the money drop, the Lucas agent was informed of the shipping arrangements by an Asian. Shortly afterwards, 150 kilos of heroin with a 1974 retail value of more than $50 million was smuggled into Georgia in the footlocker and trunks of a soldier returning to Fort Gordon: "The heroin is transported into New York by automobile with two back-up vehicles fore and aft. In New York, it is secreted in one of the apartments rented throughout the city for this purpose. Lucas then arranges

for the cutting and distribution" (Langlais 1978: 14). The stateside Country Boys organization was restricted to blood relatives and friends from rural North Carolina, who actively trafficked the Lucas "Blue Magic" brand of heroin on Harlem's 116th Street. Two Lucas brothers, Shorty and Larry, operated in northern New Jersey and the Bronx, New York. Frank Lucas also supplied rings in Chicago, North Carolina, and Los Angeles (Langlais 1978). Lucas quickly became a multimillionaire, with a Cayman Islands bank account, office buildings in Detroit, apartments in Miami and Los Angeles, a string of gas stations and dry cleaning shops, and a several-thousand acre spread in North Carolina with 300 head of Black Angus cattle.

Like other major criminals before and after, Lucas had a fatal flaw. He enjoyed the public spotlight, and his high-profile drug-kingpin lifestyle—flashy diamond jewelry, a chinchilla coat, a retinue of bodyguards, women, and associates—eventually attracted law enforcement scrutiny (and apparently the ire of the Genovese Family): in 1975 a NYPD/DEA task force (acting on a tip from "Pleasant Avenue" sources) staged a surprise raid on Lucas's New Jersey residence. They recovered more than half a million dollars in small bills and keys to safe-deposit boxes in the Cayman Islands. Although he was eventually sentenced to a federal 30-year term, the sentence was subsequently reduced, and Lucas was released in 1983—he apparently provided the government with valuable information (Jacobson 2000).

While Frank Lucas could use his rural North Carolina ties to build a personalistic organization, African-American criminals have typically had to copy the structure of others or resort to a bureaucratic model. Francis Ianni (1974: 158) notes that for African-American criminals, "prisons and the prison experience form the most important locus for establishing the social relationships that form the basis for partnerships in organized crime." During the 1970s, in the Stateville (Illinois) Penitentiary, 30 black inmates from Chicago formed the Royal Family, patterning themselves after popular renditions of Mario Puzo's *Godfather*. They formed close ties with the Chicago Outfit, acting as "muscle" and contract executioners in Chicago and elsewhere (Brodt 1981a, 1981b).

The bureaucratic model was adopted by Chicago's best-known African-American organized crime group, the Gangster Disciples.

THE GANGSTER DISCIPLES[2]

The occupational opportunity structure of the United States has changed dramatically, characterized by a significant reduction in the number of good-paying jobs available to low-skilled workers. As such, the structural sources of mobility available to earlier immigrant groups have narrowed considerably. The deindustrialization of American society means that major cities are different places today than they were during the times of major European immigration. Advances in transportation and communication, industrial technology, and the global economy have transformed cities from centers of production and distribution to centers of administration, finance, and the exchange of information. In this environment, the blue-collar jobs that once provided a means of social mobility have vanished or moved to the Third World.

The congruent processes of social and spatial mobility that allowed earlier disadvantaged inner-city residents to succeed in society do not apply to large numbers of African-Americans today. As a result, we have witnessed the formation of an urban underclass made up of men and women who are excluded from participation in mainstream occupations. This structural entrapment denies people a method of maturing out of crime and has fueled the development of supergangs such as Chicago's *Gangster Disciples* (Robert M. Lombardo, personal correspondence).

The Gangster Disciples (GDs) were formed as the result of the 1969 merger of two South Side gangs, one headed by Larry Hoover (Supreme Gangsters) and the other by "King" David Barksdale (Disciples). The primary symbol of the GDs is the six-pointed "star of David" and crossed pitchforks; more-elaborate versions will include a heart. After Barksdale's death from kidney failure in 1974, leadership was assumed by Hoover, born in Jackson, Mississippi, in 1951. In 1973, Hoover was convicted of planning and ordering the murder of a man who had held up a GD drug house and has been incarcerated ever since, serving a 150-year sentence. Nevertheless, GDs remained active in selling cocaine and heroin throughout Chicago, a number of suburban areas, and in several states, including Wisconsin, Indiana, Missouri, Oklahoma, and Georgia. They also extort money from other drug dealers for the right to sell in areas in which the GDs assert control. Independent dealers who have achieved a level of success are typically approached by GD representatives and told to choose from three alternatives: (1) join the Gangster Disciples, (2) stop selling drugs, or (3) die.

Lower-ranking members who actually sell the drugs at the retail level keep most of the profit they make—they do not necessarily share it with higher-ranking members or the organization as a whole. Instead, the hierarchy makes considerable income from wholesaling drugs to these members. The GDs have been able to pool drug profits, street taxes, and membership dues to establish and operate legitimate businesses, including apartment buildings, sometimes for the purpose of money laundering and to serve as centers for illegal operations. As noted earlier, a criminal organization can exhibit a formal structure while its economic activities may actually involve small firms or partnerships among members and include nonmember associates—the formal structure is not necessarily the same as the economic structure. However, the size of the Gangster Disciples—about 6,000 members[3]—requires a corporate-style structure. (See Figure 6.1.)

---

[2]This section is based on information from O'Brien, O'Connor, and Papajohn (1995); Lehmann and McNamee (1995); Bey (1995); Papajohn and Dell'Angela (1995); O'Connor (1996a, 1996b); Martin (1996); Martin and O'Connor (1996a, 1996b); and a variety of public and private sources.

---

[3]According to one report (McCormick 1999), the GDs have 50,000 members in 35 states.

FIGURE 6.1   *Gangster Disciples Organizational Structure*

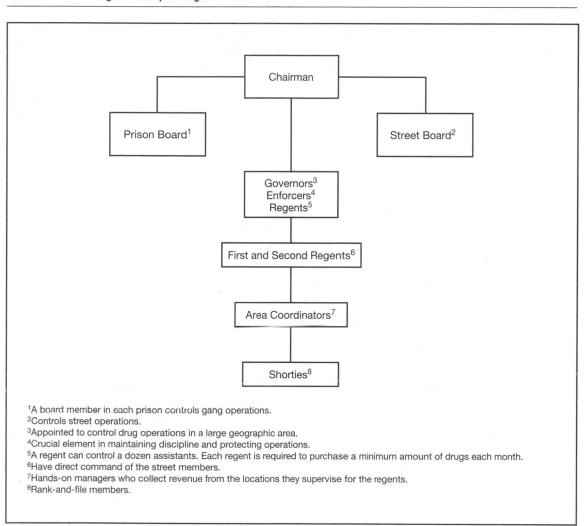

¹A board member in each prison controls gang operations.
²Controls street operations.
³Appointed to control drug operations in a large geographic area.
⁴Crucial element in maintaining discipline and protecting operations.
⁵A regent can control a dozen assistants. Each regent is required to purchase a minimum amount of drugs each month.
⁶Have direct command of the street members.
⁷Hands-on managers who collect revenue from the locations they supervise for the regents.
⁸Rank-and-file members.

Indeed, the size of the GDs requires a level of bureaucracy rarely seen in organized crime, serving to make the organization vulnerable to prosecution. A list is kept of all persons dealing drugs in GD territory so they can be forced to pay street taxes—one day's profit per week. In a 1995 raid on a GD front group—Save the Children Promotions, Inc.—federal agents found detailed records, including an organizational chart, a list of GD officers and their rank, a list of opposing gang leaders, the gang's pledge of allegiance, and its 16 "laws" that each members must memorize (Decker, Bynum, and Weisel 1998).

Inside prison, "legal coordinators" and "education ministers" indoctrinate new members with GD propaganda and assist fellow inmates in their appeals. Imprisoned members are instructed to complete their high school education and learn rudimentary principles of law, from law books available in prison. They are directed to strengthen their bodies in prison weight rooms.

There has been extensive political involvement by the Gangster Disciples, at least in part to aid in the parole release efforts of their imprisoned leader. Under the name of 21st Century VOTE, GDs have engaged in voter registration drives and have supported unsuccessful candidates for the city council. Support for Hoover's parole came from a former Chicago mayor and several state and local elected officials interested in the support of 21st Century VOTE. Most expressed dismay—if not remorse—when in 1995, Hoover and 38 GDs were named in an indictment charging 149 counts of criminal conduct involving their drug trafficking operations. Authorities devised a prison visitor's pass with a hidden transmitter, and Hoover was recorded passing orders to lieutenants who visited him at the Vienna Correctional Center. One of those indicted was a Chicago police officer who had been assigned to the Gang Crimes Unit—she received a 12.5-year prison sentence. Also convicted was a 30-year-old member of the "street board" (see Figure 6.1) who in 2000 was sentenced to 100 years (O'Connor 2000).

During the GD trials, it was revealed that the offices of 21st Century VOTE served as a drop-off site for street taxes collected by gang members. In 1997, Hoover and Gregory Shell, GD leader on the street, were convicted of 40 counts of drug trafficking (O'Connor 1997). Shell was sentenced to life imprisonment in 1998; Hoover was given six additional life sentences. Later that year, Darryl ("Pops") Johnson, then 33, who ranked second below Hoover, was sentenced to death for his role in the murder of two GD members who were suspected of being informants—Johnson rewarded the executioners with new cars. In 1999, three GD officers who had vied for gang leadership were sentenced to life imprisonment for supervising a multi-million-dollar cocaine operation (O'Connor 1999a). Following his additional convictions, Hoover was transferred to a federal supermax prison in Colorado.

As a result of the imprisonment or indictment of virtually its entire hierarchy and the conviction of about 100 members and associates, the gang is having difficulties maintaining discipline and thwarting encroachments by rival groups. Street taxes often go unpaid/uncollected, and since the 1995 indictments, several members have been killed by other GD members or rival gangs selling drugs where the GDs claim hegemony. In 1997 the 19-year-old who ran a drug territory on the South Side was recorded exhorting his juvenile drug sellers to carry firearms at their drug spots— he received a 24-year federal prison sentence. That same year, the government taped a meeting at which a leading GD board member exhorted members to join in a "war" to retake territory lost to rivals since the federal crackdown—in particular, to deal with the Black P. Stone Nation, which, as the El Rukns, was once Chicago's premier African-American gang.

EL RUKNS/BLACK P. STONE NATION

The best-known African-American organized crime group in Chicago is the El Rukns, headed by Jeff Fort. Born in 1947 in Mississippi, Fort was brought to Chicago by his mother in 1955. They settled in the poverty-stricken Woodlawn neighborhood. Fort left school after the fourth grade and remained functionally illiterate. Nevertheless, he emerged as leader of Woodlawn's notorious Blackstone Rangers, named after the intersection of Sixty-Fifth Street and Blackstone Avenue. With Fort at its head, the Blackstone Rangers fought a long and bloody gang war with a rival group. In 1965 the charismatic leader organized a coalition of 21 gangs into the Black P. Stone Nation, governed by a commission of gang leaders known as the "main 21," with Fort as the head. Through the efforts of some white clergymen and community activists who were seeking to channel gang violence into more constructive pursuits, the Black P. Stone Nation was given a federal grant of $1 million from the Office of Economic Opportunity for an elaborate grass-roots learning program. Mayor Richard M. Daley was outraged, and in 1968 and 1969 the grant was the subject of a United States Senate Investigation. In response to a subpoena, Fort appeared before the Senate Permanent Subcommittee on Investigations, introduced himself, and then walked out. In 1972 he was imprisoned for contempt of Congress and embezzlement of $7,500 in federal funds (Glab 1997).

While in prison, Fort founded the El Rukns, a "Moorish" religious organization, and dubbed himself Prince Malik. The Black P. Stone Nation headquarters at 3949 S. Drexel, a former theater, became the Grand Major Temple. After serving two years of a five-year sentence, Fort was paroled, and his organization began to dominate large areas of the black community. He purchased a home in Milwaukee for his wife and children but spent most of his time in Chicago's South Side, riding in a chauffeured limousine with several bodyguards. Fort, who was a thin teenager, grew into a physically imposing adult with a beard, braids, fur coats, and a Chinese coolie-type triangular hat. He granted no interviews and rarely spoke to anyone not part of his organization. In 1969, referring to the Black P. Stone Nation as a community group, President Richard Nixon invited Fort to his inauguration. In the 1983 mayoral race, the Cook County Democratic organization paid the El Rukns $10,000 to campaign in black wards and serve as poll watchers for Mayor Jane M. Byrne. In 1984, Reverend Jesse Jackson publicly praised them for their role in a voter registration drive on behalf of his presidential campaign (Shipp 1985).

In 1982, Fort was convicted of participation in a cocaine conspiracy and sentenced to 13 years' imprisonment. In 1987, Fort and four members of the El Rukns were convicted of plotting terrorist acts on behalf of Moammar Gadhafi of Libya; Fort was sentenced to 80 years. In 1988, Fort and three other El Rukns were convicted of the 1981 murder of a rival gang member who had failed to heed the El Rukn warning to share the proceeds of his drug dealings. With Fort in prison, the gang's headquarters were forfeited and destroyed, and a series of indictments and convictions followed. In 1989, 65 El Rukns were indicted, and by 1991, 19 had been convicted of drug- and murder-related offenses. In 1992, numerous El Rukn generals who had held the highest rank under Jeff Fort, all in their thirties and forties, received long prison sentences. In 1993, serious charges of prosecutorial misconduct resulted in the convictions of many El Rukn defendants being thrown out and new trials ordered. Many already convicted members were subsequently resentenced to significantly reduced terms.

Remaining El Rukns assumed their former name, the Black P. Stone Nation, and one faction ("Motown"), under the leadership of Jeff Fort's son, Watketa ("The Prince") Valenzuela, is estimated to have up to 2,000 members, holding sway in the Motown section of Chicago's South Side. The "Mos," as they call themselves, wear their hair in elaborate braids similar to those worn by the imprisoned Jeff Fort. In 1996 the young "Prince" and four other gang leaders were arrested and charged with running a major crack-cocaine network (Martin and O'Connor 1996a, 1996b). In 1997, Watketa, at age 26, received a 30-year sentence.

OTHER DOMESTIC AFRICAN-AMERICAN CRIMINAL ORGANIZATIONS

A variety of black street gangs have been expanding their operations and drug markets interstate, in particular the Crips and the Bloods of Los Angeles. The Crips, whose membership is reputed to be more than 10,000, have moved into Seattle and other large cities in the West and Midwest, as well as into smaller cities throughout California. Along with the Bloods, a smaller gang, members of the Crips have been slowly moving east, establishing drug distribution networks in Baltimore and Washington, D.C.

Bloods and Crips are heavily armed and quick to use violence. However, the Drug Enforcement Administration (1988: 11) points out that outside of Los Angeles, the Crips are "splinter groups composed of former gang members, ranging in age from their low to upper twenties, who utilize the gang names as a means of identifying their organization. These subgroups are independent entities, often operating in competition with one another." They are extremely violent: "Neither gang is rigidly hierarchical. Both are broken up into loosely affiliated neighborhood groups called 'sets,' each with 30 to 100 members. Many gang

Crip gang members, heavily armed and quick to use violence, have expanded to Seattle and other large cities in the West and Midwest.

Daniel Laine/Corbis

members initially left Southern California to evade police. Others simply expanded the reach of crack by setting up branch operations in places where they visited friends or family members and discovered that the market was ripe" (Witkin 1991: 51). In 1992 it was reported that the Crips, or perhaps older former members of the gang, had developed direct ties with the Medellín cartel ("FBI Says Los Angeles Gang Has Drug Cartel Ties" 1992).

In many areas of the country, particularly in New York and Los Angeles, the relatively stable neighborhood criminal organizations that have dominated the heroin and cocaine trade found new competitors: youthful crack dealers. Because it requires only a small investment to enter the trade, street gangs or groups of friends and relatives entered the market, often touching off an explosive level of competitive violence that frequently involves the use of high-powered handguns and automatic weapons. Some groups established direct connections to major Colombian traffickers.

Jerome Skolnick and his colleagues (1990) distinguish between two gang types. *Cultural gangs* are strongly grounded in a neighborhood identity, and members may be involved in crime, including drug trafficking. *Entrepreneurial gangs* are organized for the express purpose of distributing drugs. The first type is maintained by loyalty to the gang and the neighborhood; the second is based on continuing economic opportunity. In the cultural gang, involvement in drug use and dealing can serve as membership requirements; stature in the group may be linked to success in the drug trade. Unlike the entrepreneurial gangs, these groups define themselves in terms of brotherhood, are highly protective of their turf, and engage in non-utilitarian violence with other gangs. While the cultural gang is not organized expressly to sell drugs, "the gang organization facilitates that activity" (1990: 7). This can also be said of the outlaw motorcycle clubs. However, the low level of cohesiveness, loose organization, high member turnover, and unstable leadership typical of most street gangs militate against their being effective drug entrepreneurs (Klein, Maxson, and Cunningham 1991).

A number of other African-American criminal groups operate in urban areas throughout the country—for example, the Junior Black Mafia of Philadelphia and the Vice Lords of Chicago—but they have a limited degree of organization and longevity. Whether or not they will emerge as a "black Mafia" is a question to be answered in the future. In comparison with traditional organized crime, African-American criminal groups have an inherent weakness: confinement to the inner city "stymies the development of symbiotic community relationships that contribute to the survival of indigenous crime organizations." *Cosa Nostra* Families have traditionally generated "goodwill" by providing certain community services and by keeping the more predatory kinds of crime (e.g., drugs and prostitution) out of their own neighborhoods even while organizing it elsewhere in the city. African-American numbers operators cultivated considerable goodwill, but drug operators prey almost exclusively on their own people and thereby generate organized opposition from within their own community (Pennsylvania Crime Commission 1990). Furthermore, new laws, particularly RICO (discussed in Chapter 14), and effective law enforcement militate against the development and expansion of upstart criminals into self-perpetuating criminal organizations.

Section III examines international and transnational organized crime, but Nigerians and Jamaicans frequently interact with African-American criminals and so will be discussed in this chapter.

BLACK ORGANIZED CRIME: NIGERIANS

Nigeria, a former British colony where the official language is English, was granted full independence in 1960 but has been marked by civil wars and coups. In 1999, military rule ended, and a civilian government was elected. Nevertheless, there has been a great deal of unrest and violence, the result of northern states attempting to enforce Islamic law (*Sharia*) and southern ethnic groups demanding more autonomy and control of natural resources. About twice the size of California, Nigeria is Africa's most populous country, with about 100 million persons and 250 ethnic groups. Inefficiency and decades of corruption continue to hamper this oil-rich country—Nigeria is the sixth

largest oil producer in the world, but its per-capita income is about $1,000 a year. The country has an Atlantic coastline and a major port in its former capital city, Lagos. The Nigerian police are poorly organized and financed, and carry the baggage of British rule, during which the police served as an instrument of colonialism.

This climate proved fertile for the creation of crime syndicates that are active in drug trafficking as well as an array of sophisticated economic crimes such as bank, credit card, and insurance fraud. Nigerian criminal syndicates centered in Lagos, many of which have global networks, operate with virtual impunity in an environment of pervasive corruption. Their crimes sometimes turn violent. In the past few years, more than a dozen foreign businesspeople caught up in Nigerian fraud have been murdered in several countries. Nigerian criminal cells target banks and financial institutions through credit card fraud, check fraud, student loan fraud, and mortgage fraud; insurance companies through fraudulent claims for automobile accidents, personal injuries, and life insurance; and government entitlement programs through false or appropriated identifications. Nigerian criminals infiltrate major companies to obtain biographical data on company employees. Members apply for employment as security guards and cleaning personnel, positions giving them access to records during periods of minimal presence of legitimate company employees. Stolen data become the basis for securing false documents (*Afro-Lineal Organized Crime* 1990).

The most notorious of the Nigerian operations is the advance fee scam, in which thousands of unsolicited letters and faxes based on fraudulent representations are sent to businesspeople worldwide with the promise of great profits for an up-front cash investment. Simple investment schemes are set forth with promises of easy money, elaborate assurances, and extraordinarily low risk. They provide detailed instructions for establishing linked bank accounts and for exchanging authorization letters and account numbers, thus giving the appearance of legitimacy, then require various transaction fees before any moneys can be released. Victims of Nigerian fraud schemes may be strung along for months or years paying transactions fees and taxes before realizing they are being conned (*Nigerian Advance Fee Fraud* 1997).

Nigeria is an historical trading crossroads both on the African continent and along maritime routes between East and West. Accordingly, the international criminal operations of Nigerian syndicates are the legacy of a history of moving capital and commodities on a global scale. Nigerian involvement in international drug trafficking is remarkable since the country is not contiguous to a major drug producer or consumer state (Williams 1995a). Although Nigeria produces no precursor chemicals or drugs that have a significant impact on the United States, the country is a major trafficking hub and the base of criminal organizations responsible for a significant amount of heroin used in the United States.

Nigerian sea and airports are rife with corruption, and the country's borders are porous to criminals. As a result, Nigeria has become a major transshipment center for Golden Crescent heroin, and cocaine primarily from Brazil. In additional to drugs, Nigerian OC organizations are involved in collateral activities such as money laundering and document, immigration, and financial fraud (*International Narcotics Control Strategy Report 1999* [2000]).

Organized along familial and tribal lines, high-level traffickers seldom deal with outsiders (NNICC 1998). In Lagos, multi-millionaire drug barons rule vast organizations, at the bottom of which are drug couriers, who take most of the actual risks (Treaster 1992a). False birth certificates and passports are easy to obtain (Jones 1993), and Nigerian couriers based in Lagos travel to Pakistan to obtain heroin or to Brazil to obtain cocaine, then continue on commercial flights to their final destinations, or they return to Nigeria to repackage the drugs into smaller amounts for smuggling throughout the world. Nigerian students or poor residents of Lagos are used as mules; they receive a few thousand dollars a trip for bringing in 100 grams, usually by swallowing drug-filled condoms. Some Nigeria-based traffickers conduct

"training schools" that teach couriers how to avoid the suspicions of customs officials. Traffickers often place many couriers on the same flight. This tactic, known as "shotgunning," overwhelms customs officials when the flight arrives. Even if most of the couriers on the flight are caught, a number will inevitably get through during the confusion. The markups on heroin trafficking are so high that if only a small percentage of the product gets through, the traffickers will still reap huge profits. But as a result of increasing law enforcement pressure, Nigeria-based traffickers are beginning to switch from courier shipments to the use of express mail packages. In 1997, Nigerian organizations began using express mail services with shipments routed through European countries. Drugs can be mailed anonymously to fictitious persons or mail drops, which decreases the risk and cost associated with couriers (Drug Enforcement Administration information—hereafter, DEA).

Customs officials use X-rays of the digestive tract to discover the drugs. In 1991 a Nigeria–Chicago connection was uncovered that used the Philippines as a transshipment point. Asian women transported heroin from Bangkok to Manila, where Caucasian-American women received the drugs for transportation to the United States. This elaborate setup was designed to reduce the suspicion that would accompany Asian women flying from Thailand to the United States. Couriers carried between 4.5 and 6.5 pounds of heroin and were paid $20,000 plus expenses (Schmetzer 1991a).

In 1996, 34 persons in three countries were arrested for being part of a Nigerian drug ring that had been in business for 15 years. The group's leader, known as "the Policeman" for his ability to impose discipline, was living in Bangkok. While members operated out of London, Amsterdam, Pakistan, New York, and Detroit, most of those arrested were in Chicago, where the group was headquartered at an African women's boutique in the Edgewater neighborhood on the city's North Side. Heroin phone orders were delivered to Chicago by female couriers, who usually traveled with children from Bangkok, taking circuitous routes through Europe, Guatemala, and finally

Mexico, before reaching the United States (O'Brien 1996b; Martin and O'Brien 1996).

According to the Drug Enforcement Administration, Nigerians dominate the shipment of Southeast Asia heroin into the United States and Latin American cocaine into Europe (Dellios 1998). Nigerian wholesalers have developed close ties to street gangs in a number of urban areas, especially those with established Nigerian communities, particularly Chicago (NNICC 1998). But the Nigerian traffickers in the United States are finding it difficult to compete with Colombians, who with their own direct source of heroin have been lowering their prices to capture a greater market share.

JAMAICAN ORGANIZED CRIME

Jamaica, a Caribbean island south of Cuba, is slightly smaller than Connecticut, with a population of 2.6 million persons. Jamaica received its independence from Great Britain in 1962, but the island remained plagued by widespread poverty, particularly problematic in the capital city of Kingston. In the poorest sections of the city, criminals—known as *rankings*—are organized into gangs that have traditionally been supported and protected by the residents, among whom they foster a Robin Hood image. In a situation reminiscent of ties between big-city political machines and gangs in the United States (discussed in Chapter 3), those at the top of the rankings' food chain have strong political affiliations with one of Jamaica's two major parties, the People's National Party (PNP) and the Jamaica Labour Party (JLP). Both use these gangs to intimidate and attack opponents. Public housing projects were built for the partisans of each political party and their affiliated gangs, which are commonly known as *posses*. In addition to the name, posses developed their style and gunslinger ethos from American action movies, particularly the Westerns popular in Kingston. In Jamaica, a parliamentary democracy based on the British model, "a politician's political survival depends entirely on his or her ability to win repeatedly in his local constituency. One sure

method of ensuring repeated victory is to create what is called a garrison constituency: a pocket of housing erected with public funds, with carefully screened residents who will constitute the unbeatable core of the politician's voters" (Patterson 2001: 21).

When they lost their favored position with their political party patrons, the posses began trafficking in homegrown marijuana and imported cocaine. Profits from drug trafficking further unraveled political ties, and party leaders, menaced by an outlaw underworld that they could no longer control, turned the Jamaican police loose to imprison or execute their former allies. Like Mussolini's campaign against the Mafia (discussed in Chapter 7), this step drove posse members to the United States at an opportune time: Colombians were looking for street-level dealers to sell a new product, crack cocaine. Jamaicans quickly acclimated to the United States, where their language skills were an asset—the patois of Jamaica is a distinctly accented English. The posses also "brought with them a killer enthusiasm honed by years of warfare with one another and the police, and when they came onto America's mean streets, they were afraid of no one" (Gunst 1996: xv).

In the aftermath of the bloody 1980 election for president, more Kingston criminals began leaving the island for the United States, "transforming their island gang alliances into mainland drug posses" (Gunst 1996: xiv). By 1984, the Shower posse, with close ties to the JLP, had moved its base of operation to south Florida, followed by the rival Spanglers, affiliated with the PNP. Their Jamaica-based antipathy was transferred to the United States, a rivalry that led to many murders.

In the mid-1980s, Jamaican posses were heavily involved in the exploding crack-cocaine trade. Jamaica was a transshipment point for Colombian cocaine bound for the United States. This was the source of much of the cocaine hydrochloride that the posses used to manufacture and distribute crack cocaine. It was during the crack cocaine era that the posses gained a reputation as one of the most violent, sadistic group of criminals that ever operated in the United States. The Shower posse's chief enforcer would hold captive the family members of those who owed the posse money and repeatedly rape and sodomize the females until the debt was paid (Cardwell 2001).

Posse members are fascinated with firearms, particularly high-caliber weapons, and prefer always to be armed. Therefore, they avoid the use of commercial airplanes. Their favorite weapons include the Uzi, Mac-10, Mac-11, Intra-tec, MP-5, Browning Hi-Power, Berreta F-92, Smith & Wesson 9mm pistols, Glock 9mm, and Colt .45 semi-automatics. The Jamaican's typical method of operations includes multiple shots with multiple weapons, in a crowded public place. The most notorious, the 5,000-member "Shower posse," reportedly got its name for engaging in frenzied shootouts—*showering* gunfire (Witkin 1991). In one six-month period in the late 1980s, posse members were involved in 744 murders. Some of their victims were boiled alive; others were dismembered, with body parts shipped back to their families in Jamaica (DEA).

The Jamaican posses differ from other trafficking groups in that their members are importers, wholesalers, and distributors. They maintain control over the product during all its steps: acquisition of the cocaine powder close to the source; cutting, manufacture, and distribution; and street sales. Therefore, their profit margin is higher than traffickers who use middlemen: "A posse that controls 50 crack houses in one city can make $9 million a month. Other major importers of illegal narcotics, such as the Colombians and Cubans, are usually only wholesalers. They will turn profit on only one sale. The Jamaicans, on the other hand, never exchange any money until the narcotics are sold at the street level by members of the organization. The money is then funneled back up to the leaders" (McGuire 1988: 22).

At the national level, posses have one or more top leaders, sometimes called "generals." The first region of the country in which a posse operates may evolve into "headquarters" or base of operations from which the subsequent expansion of operations is directed. From headquarters, posse leaders may send "captains" or "lieutenants" to establish operations in new regions. They are responsible for recruiting supervisors to manage workers, frequently illegal aliens smuggled from Jamaica into the United States (Pennsylvania Crime Commission 1990).

Street-level operations are carried out by managers, couriers, sellers, lookouts, and steerers, most of whom are African-Americans or other minorities (*Crack Cocaine* 1994). In 1990, federal agents arrested 17 members of the Gulleymen—named after a neighborhood in Kingston, Jamaica—a posse that controlled crack houses in Brooklyn and Dallas and has been linked to at least 30 murders. As part of their business operations, the Gulleymen sold franchises to street-level dealers, providing them with crack and protection (McKinley 1990).

The demise of major posses, such as the Shower, was in large part a result of their predilection for violence, which helped undermine loyalty: "Loyalty was a scarce commodity within the posse ranks. And when the dons resorted to violence to discipline their troops, some of the soldiers started going to the police with information. . . . Once the cops were able to flip one or two gang members it was only a matter of time before they could rope the don" (Gunst 1996: 140). Although the Shower posse disbanded by the mid-1990s, those who remained active apparently abandoned much of the brutal practices that were their trademark and dropped the posse stigma, referring to themselves as "crews." Many also dropped out of the crack-cocaine trade and returned to marijuana. They reasoned that a conviction for selling crack would mean time in prison, while a conviction for selling small amounts of marijuana could generally result only in the payment of a fine. The source of supply for some ethnic Jamaican gangs has shifted, as well. Instead of acquiring marijuana from their counterparts in Jamaica, some groups have begun to purchase marijuana from Mexico-based criminal organizations in the southwest border area and then transport it back to eastern U.S. cities. The Mexican are also able to provide cocaine and heroin (DEA).

The tradition of gang-related violence continues in Jamaica, and in 2001, more than two dozen persons were killed when the police entered Tivoli

Gardens—a stronghold of the opposition Jamaica Labor Party—to confiscate firearms. Cynics note that when the bullets fly, it means an election is coming. The gangs "have their own source of funds, the sale of drugs, but the parties still provide political cover for gang support at polling time" (Borger 2001: 6).

Jamaican criminal groups have proven quite troublesome in the United Kingdom, where they are referred to as "Yardies." A crackdown in Jamaica has led to an increase in Jamaican emigration and in England "Yardie" activity—they have been linked to more than 20 killings in London in 2000. The Yardie phenomenon in the UK was first noted in the late 1980s and linked to crack cocaine. The rise of crack cocaine is mirrored by that of Yardie members who are linked mostly to drug and arms dealing, as well as robbery. Their lifestyle in England has been synonymous with violence—impulse shootings and gangland-style executions are used to sort out internal squabbles. There is no central control or brotherhood structure, so Yardies have few affiliations or loyalties. Gangs are very loose knit and often fall out with each other, sometimes violently.

While firearms are more difficult to acquire in England than in the United States, the Yardies have been using such automatic weapons as the "spray and pray," a Mach 10 submachine gun that can fire 1,200 rounds a minute. The Yardies have also spawned many imitators among black British youth ("Who Are the Yardies?" 1999; "Police Tackle London's Yardies 1999; Tendler 2000).

Increasing violence in Jamaica in 2001 led to an exodus of gang members, driven out by police and soldiers. They have been entering England with false passports and continuing their lethal feuds. As a result, London Metropolitan police officers were sent to the island to train their Jamaican counterparts and exchange intelligence (Leapman 2001).

Now that we have completed our examination of organized crime in the United States, in Section III we turn to international and transnational organized crime.

INTERNET CONNECTIONS

Chicago gangs: **sobs.org/chilocal/gangs/gnghome.html**

Nathanson Centre: **www.yorku.ca/nathanson**

Global Organized Crime Project: **csis.org/goc**

Drug Enforcement Administration: **www.usdoj.gov/dea**

REVIEW QUESTIONS

1. What led to the success of black criminal groups of the 1960s in the heroin trade?
2. Why are most black criminal organizations primarily, if not exclusively, involved in drug trafficking?
3. How was the organization of Frank Lucas organized?
4. What characteristic helped lead to his downfall?
5. Why is it necessary for the Gangster Disciples to have a bureaucratic structure?
6. What led to the downfall of the El Rukns?
7. Why has the introduction of crack touched off a new level of criminal violence?

8. What is so extraordinary about the Nigerian success in drug trafficking?
9. What are the Jamaican posses? How do they differ from other large drug trafficking organizations?
10. What is the connection between Jamaican politics and the posses?
11. What accounts for the Jamaican posse reputation for violence?
12. What factors mitigate against the development and expansion of upstart criminals into self-perpetuating criminal organizations?

♠

CHAPTER 7

ITALIAN ORGANIZED CRIME

In this chapter, we begin our examination of organized crime on the global scene, sometimes referred to as transnational organized crime. Our focus will be on criminal organizations that have affected, or have the potential to affect, the United States.

THE GLOBALIZATION OF ORGANIZED CRIME

The collapse of the Soviet Union was a pivotal historical event that intertwined with the rapid expansion of global markets: "money, goods and people have circulated with a rapidity and facility which were once unthinkable" (Violante 2000: x). And "Whether in the developed or in the developing world, criminal organizations' scope of action and range of capabilities are undergoing a profound change." Furthermore, note Roy Godson and William Olson (1995: 19), the decline in political order and deteriorating economic circumstances lead to a growing underground economy that habituates people to working outside the legal framework. Easy access to arms, the massive flow of emigrants and refugees, and the normal difficulties involved in accomplishing meaningful international cooperation are working to the advantage of criminal organizations. And the "rise of better-organized, internationally based criminal groups with vast financial resources is creating a new threat to the stability and security of international systems."

In Chapter 2, we saw how Prohibition acted as a catalyst for the unprecedented mobilization of criminal organizations and the cooperative ventures of syndication. The international trade in liquor altered the heretofore local scope of most criminal organizations, whetting the appetite for further innovative opportunities, such as the trade in heroin. The expanded capacity of contemporary criminal organizations derives from intensification of goods traditionally traded by organized crime—in particular, drugs, arms, and sex workers. In each case, the country of destination is different from that of its origins. Consignments travel across national boundaries and even oceans. As is the case with legitimate trade, arrangements need to be

Dangerous Liaisons

In 1994, French intelligence monitored a meeting of representatives of the Gambino Family, Japanese *yakuza*, and Colombian, Russian, and Chinese crime bosses: "The apparent purpose of the meeting was to subdivide Western Europe for drugs, prostitution, smuggling and extortion rackets." U.S. officials believe that other meetings have since taken place on chartered yachts in the Mediterranean (Jamieson 2000: 193).

made that involve the use of banks, finance houses, and customs formalities and that require ongoing relationships with criminal organizations of different countries: "These commercial necessities have created solid international relations between all the most dangerous criminal organizations" (Violante 2000: ix).

In this chapter, we will begin our examination of four of these criminal organizations—*Mafia*, *Camorra*, *'Ndrangheta*, and the *Sacra Corona Unita* (with its Albanian connection)—which have their roots in southern Italy, the *Mezzogiorno*.

THE *MEZZOGIORNO*

The southern Italian experience, which dates back more than a thousand years, led to the development of a culture that stresses the variables necessary for survival in a hostile environment. The southern Italian developed an ideal of manliness, *omertá*, which included noncooperation with authorities and self-control in the face of adversity, and the *vendetta*, which dictated that any offense or slight to the *famiglia* (family) had to be avenged, no matter what the consequences or how long it took. Neither government nor church was to be trusted. The only basis of loyalty was *famiglia*—"blood of my blood" (*sangu de me sangu*): "The *famiglia* was composed of all of one's blood relatives, including those relatives Americans would consider very distant cousins, aunts, and uncles, an extended clan whose genealogy was traced through paternity. The clan was supplemented through an important custom known as *comparatico* or *comparaggio* (godparenthood), through which carefully selected outsiders became, to an important (but incom-

plete) extent, members of the family" (Gambino 1974: 3).

The family patriarch, the *capo di famiglia*, arbitrated all ambiguous situations. The family was organized hierarchically: "One had absolute responsibilities to family superiors and absolute rights to be demanded from subordinates in the hierarchy" (Gambino 1974: 4): "The family, first source of power, had to be made prosperous, respected, and feared with antlike tenacity; it was enlarged (like dynasties of old) by suitable marriages, strengthened by alliances with families of equal status, by negotiated submission to more powerful ones, or by establishing domination over weaker ones. In the *famiglia*, physical aggression was rewarded and the strongest member of the domestic group assumed the dominant status" (Barzini 1977: 36).

The *Mezzogiorno* never enjoyed a Renaissance, remaining mired in feudalism and dependent on agriculture, a legacy of political, social, and economic repression and exploitation (Putnam 1993). A succession of foreign rulers ended in 1860 with a revolution against (Spanish) Bourbon rule that eventually united Italy. For the people of the *Mezzogiorno*, however, little changed. Instead of foreign repression, the *contadini* (peasants) were repressed by other Italians: "The political foundation of the new Italian state was an alliance between the northern industrial bourgeoisie and the southern landed aristocracy" (Chubb 1982: 16). The *Mezzogiorno*, with a population of about 20.5 million persons, continues to lag far behind northern Italy (and the rest of western Europe) in economic development, while its rate of unemployment remains high (Bohlen 1996d).

The South "was brought into the Italian nation dragging its feet as the new government issued edict after edict that affected the southerners adversely" (Mangione and Morreale 1992: xv). This history led to the development of three different types of criminal organization: "The volatile urban criminality of the Neapolitan Camorra was very different from the old rural mafia's activities in the Sicilian hinterland, and the Calabrian 'Ndrangheta was another thing again. But in each case a parasitic criminal class had inserted itself in the interstices between rulers and the ruled, exploiting both" (Robb 1996: 37). The Mafia— whose members refer to it as *Cosa Nostra*—and the *'Ndrangheta* "were an outgrowth of a section of the middle class which had been licensed to use violence by the ruling classes of the day and were founded on codes of honour, secrecy and silence." The Camorra was "an association of the poorest classes for whom crime was a means of survival and was neither secretive nor elitist." A fourth criminal organization, *Sacra Corona Unita*, is more recent, its expansion dating back to the 1970s because of "a desire by the other three criminal groups, at different times and for different motives, to have a consolidated criminal base on [the Italian] Apulia's long southeastern seaboard" (Jamieson 2000: 11).

THE SICILIAN MAFIA

The largest island in the Mediterranean Sea, Sicily lies almost at its center. As such, it was a bitterly fought over prize colonized by commercial powers: Greeks, Romans, Arabs, and Normans. In the twelfth century, rule passed to a German dynasty, then to the French, the Austrians, and, finally, Spain: "Until the nineteenth century, aristocratic families controlled Sicilian life more or less independently of whatever conqueror happened to be ruling at any given time" (Orlando 2001: 10). In 1860, Italy was freed of foreign rule and united by Giuseppe Garibaldi (1807–1882), but for the exploited Sicilians, little changed.

The government in Rome imposed a tax policy on the island that had the "overall effect of taking money out of Sicilian agriculture for investment in the north" (Finley, Smith, and Duggan 1987: 186). Landowners escaped heavy taxation, which fell disproportionately on the peasants (Catanzaro 1992). Eventually, the aristocracy collapsed, and the administration of their lands fell to middlemen called *gabelloti*, managers who had already gained the reputation of *uomi inteso*— "strong men" (Orlando 2001). The *gabelloto* ruled over the estate—*latifondo*—with brute force, protecting it from bandits, peasant organizations, and unions. He was assisted by *famiglia*, *amici* (friends), and *campieri* (lawfully armed mounted guards). The *campieri* were hired because they were *uomini di rispettu*, "men of respect," meaning they were quick to use violence and people feared them. An important—that is, widely feared—*campiere* could become a *gabelloto*. The *gabelloto* did not usually perform his overseer's functions in person—often he did not even show up on the estate that had been entrusted to his custody: "He simply allowed his name to be mentioned, with the declaration that the estate was under his protection" (Catanzaro 1992: 28).

The *gabelloto* was a patron to his peasants who labored on the *latifondo*; he controlled access to scarce resources—in particular, farming land—and he acted as a mediator between official power and government and the peasantry, a position he maintained by the exercise of force. In league with the landlords, he fought land reform, labor unions, and revolution (Servadio 1976). Peasants revolted in many parts of the *Mezzogiorno*, and an 1866 uprising in Palermo required an expeditionary force to quell it: "Such events soldered the alliance between the Mafia and aristocracy even more firmly" (Jamieson 2000: 12).

Along with their counterparts who provided protection in urban markets (for example, by policing monopolistic business practices), the *gabelloto* and the network of relationships surrounding him, *campieri*, *famiglia*, and *amici*, became known as the Mafia: "The mafia was outlaw, but tolerated, secret but recognizable, criminal but upholding of order. It protected and ripped off the owners of the great estates, protected and ripped off the sharecroppers who worked the estates, and ripped off the peasants who slaved on them" (Robb 1996: 48).

Explanations of the term *mafia* come from Sicilian historical and literary works that link its root and meaning to elements prevailing within Sicilian culture: "The word *mafia* is apparently Sicilian-Arabic derived from terms meaning to protect and to act as guardian; a friend or companion; to defend; and preservation, power, integrity, strength, and a condition that designates the remedy of damage and ill." In sum, *mafia* means "protection against the arrogance of the powerful, remedy to any damage, sturdiness of body, strength and serenity of spirit, and the best and most exquisite part of life" (Inciardi 1975: 112–13).

Thus, *mafia* is a state of mind, a way of life—not a secret criminal organization. An 1863 play describing prison life in Palermo, *I Mafiusi della Vicaria*, "gave national currency to a local dialect word that until then had lacked criminal overtones" (Finley, Smith, and Duggan 1987: 182). While a criminal organization known as the Mafia did not exist, there were most certainly *mafiosi* who exploited the gap left by an ineffective state and whose main function was to impose some form of rudimentary order on the anarchy of Sicilian life.

Luigi Barzini (1965: 253) separates *mafia* as a state of mind from Mafia as an illegal secret organization. The former (*mafia*) is shared by all Sicilians, the honest and the criminal: "they must aid each other, side with their friends, and fight the common enemies even when the friends are wrong and the enemies are right; each must defend his dignity at all costs and never allow the smallest slight to go unavenged; they must keep secrets and beware of official authorities and laws." The anti-Mafia Sicilian author Leonardo Sciascia notes the dichotomy: "When I denounce the *mafia*, at the same time I suffer, since in me, as in any Sicilian, there are still present and vibrant the residues of feeling *mafioso*. So by struggling against the *mafia* I also struggle against myself" (quoted in Siebert 1996: 57).

Barzini points out that the two (Mafia and *mafia*) are closely related, that Mafia could not flourish without *mafia*. Mafia represents a general attitude toward the state: "A *mafioso* did not invoke State or law in his private quarrels, but made himself respected and safe by winning a reputation for toughness and courage, and settled his differences by fighting. He recognized no obligation except those of the code of honor or *omertá* (manliness), whose chief article forbade giving information to the public authorities" (Hobsbawm 1976: 92).

In southern Italy, an ethos of mistrust and suspicion pervaded personal and business relationships—a dilemma the *mafioso* could overcome by offering himself as a guarantor (Putnam 1993). In Mafia areas, the issue was never who was "right" and who was "wrong." Instead, "preference tended to be given to whichever party proved victorious in the end, irrespective of the original conflict" (Arlacchi 1986: 13). Thus, in Mafia areas, at bottom nothing could really be unjust, and honor "was connected less with justice than with domination and physical strength": a Hobbesian world ruled by the credo "might is right." The *mafioso* brought order, albeit a conservative if not reactionary form, and dispensed primitive justice in a lawless society. *Mafiosi* were frequently not only tolerated by their communities but "respected to the point where they could parade as standard bearers of a more equitable system of justice than that provided by the state." Outsiders were baffled and governments frustrated by this phenomenon, leading to the development of a myth: that of a widespread secret criminal association, which they called the Mafia (Finley, Smith, and Duggan 1987: 157).

Every *mafioso* demands *rispetto*—indeed, is referred to as a *uomo di rispetto:* a man worthy of respect. American *mafioso* Bill Bonanno (1999: xiii) points out that this "respect has nothing to do with affection or even with a show of good manners. It is an acknowledgement of power" that Cesare Mori notes requires a concrete recognition of the prerogative of immunity belonging to the *mafioso*, not only in his person, but also everything that he had to do with or that he was pleased to take under his protection: "In fine, evildoers had to leave the *mafioso* severely alone, and all the persons or things to which, explicitly or implicitly, he had given a guarantee of security." As a man of respect, "the *mafioso* is in a position to provide protection where the state is unwilling or unable; to provide arbitration services superior to those available from local judges, especially to the poor person who cannot afford a lawyer, or for those whose justice is of a social, not a legal, nature—the pregnant daughter whose seducer refuses to marry." The *mafioso*, and in particular the *capomafioso*, can put it all right, and his services are speedy and final (Mori 1933: 69).

These "services" are the essence of *mafia*—the *mafioso* is a provider of protection broadly defined. For legitimate entrepreneurs, he provides insurance against otherwise untrustworthy suppliers and/or customers and will limit competition by restricting market entry. He acts as a guarantor so that persons who do not trust one another can transact business with a significant degree of confidence; this refers to legitimate entrepreneurs and, most particularly, the illegitimate, who cannot turn to the police or courts to remedy their grievances.[1] A *mafioso* engaged in a legitimate business enjoys advantages over other businessmen: potential competitors are likely to be deterred, and criminals will give his enterprise a wide berth (Gambetta 1993).[2]

"The constitutional state and elected parliament that accompanied Sicily's union with Italy provided a crucial step in the rise to power of the Mafia—Sicily's special kind of middle class" (Servadio 1976: 17): "With an electorate of little more than 1 percent, the landlords and their friends and employees [*mafiosi*] were often the only voters. If there were any doubt about the result of an election, intimidation was usually effective" (Finley, Smith, and Duggan 1987: 183). Because of its ability to control elections, the Mafia was courted by political powers in Rome. The "Mafia became the only electoral force that counted in Sicily and the government was realistic in acceptance of the fact" (Lewis 1964: 41). The situation remained unchanged until the rise of Benito Mussolini and the Fascist state.

Mussolini and the Mafia

Mussolini's rise to power in the 1920s had important implications for the Mafia and Italian-American organized crime. While the South was resistant to Fascism, "once it became clear that the Fascists would obtain a major share in national power, the entire south became Fascist almost overnight" (Chubb 1982: 25): "The mafia had always known how to cozy up to those in power" (Robb 1996: 48). The impact of the Mafia can be seen by comparing the elections of 1922, when no Fascist was elected to Parliament from Sicily, with the elections of 1924, when 38 Fascists were elected out of the 57 representatives from Sicily (Servadio 1976).

Mussolini visited Sicily in 1924 and was introduced to Ciccio Cuccia, a *capomafioso* who was also a local mayor. Don Ciccio[3] accompanied *Il Duce* on a tour and, after seeing the large number of police officers guarding him, is reputed to have said: "You're with me, so there's nothing to worry about" (Lewis 1964). To Don Ciccio, the large police escort indicated a lack of *rispetto*. When Mussolini declined to discharge the police contingent, the *capomafioso* arranged for the town piazza to be empty when *Il Duce* made his speech: "When Mussolini began his harangue he found himself addressing a group of about twenty village idiots, one-legged beggars, bootblacks, and lottery-ticket sellers specially picked by Don Ciccio to form an audience" (1964: 72).

A totalitarian regime does not tolerate pockets of authority that are not under its control, and Mussolini quickly moved to destroy the Mafia. Elections were abolished in 1925, depriving the Mafia of its major instrument of alliance with government and an important basis for its immunity from criminal justice. The other important basis was intimidation. However, "Fascist courts trying criminal cases in which members of the Mafia

---

[1] In later chapters, we will see instances of the crucial "service" role played by members of American organized crime in the private waste-hauling and construction industries, as well as in New York's major wholesale fish market.

[2] Inspiring fear without a direct threat is a valuable asset, one that was used quite successfully by the Gambino brothers in New York's garment center, discussed in Chapter 12.

[3] The appellation *Don* is an honorific title used in Sicily to refer to clergymen, government officials, and important *mafiosi*. It derives from the Latin *dominus*, "lord," and is used with the person's first given name.

Benito Mussolini is shown here leading a march of his troops in Italy. Mussolini was introduced to *capomafioso* Ciccio Cuccia during a trip to Sicily in 1924.

were implicated found it just as impossible to obtain convictions as it had been for the democratic courts of old" (Lewis 1964: 68). Mussolini responded by investing Prefect Cesare Mori of Lombardy, a career police officer, with emergency police powers and sending him after the Mafia. (Christopher Duggan [1989] stresses general lawlessness in western Sicily and a request by a delegation of war veterans as the bases for Mussolini's intervention.)

Mori assembled a small army of agents and set about the task of purging the island of *mafiosi:* "Under the jurisdiction of Prefect Mori, repression became savage. Many *mafiosi* were sent to

prison, killed or tortured, but also many left-wingers were called '*mafiosi*' for the occasion, and were disposed of. . . . In many cases the landowners provided Mori with information against the *mafiosi* they had so far employed, who had been their means to safeguard their interests against the peasantry. This was logical because they saw that the regime would provide a better and cheaper substitute" (Servadio 1976: 74). Thus, the Fascists replaced the Mafia as intermediaries and maintainers of Sicilian law and order.

Mori swooped down on villages and, with the free application of torture reminiscent of the Inquisition, was able to arrest hundreds of *mafiosi*.

He arrested Don Ciccio and other important *capi-mafiosi*. The *gabelloti* were required to be free of any police record, and in 1928, Mori declared that the Mafia had been destroyed. However, the reality was otherwise, and the Mafia began to reassert itself by 1941. When questioned by Allied officials at the end of World War II, Mori stated: "I drove the mafia underground all right. I had unlimited police powers and a couple of battalions of Blackshirts. But how can you stamp out what is in people's blood?" (quoted in Sciascia 1963: 6).

Many Mafia bosses assumed important positions within the regime, and the Fascists failed to significantly transform the social and economic conditions upon which the Mafia depended. When Mori began to investigate the connection between the Mafia and high-level Fascists, he was forced into retirement (Orlando 2001): "It was no surprise that the Mafia rapidly reemerged as soon as fascism fell" (Chubb 1982: 27). Many *mafiosi* awaited "liberation," which came in the form of the Allied landing in 1943. The campaign against the Mafia did succeed in driving some important *mafiosi* out of Sicily. They traveled to the United States at an opportune time, during the Prohibition era, and took up important positions in a newly emerging form of organized crime. The end of World War II led to a Mafia renaissance out of which the *Nuovo Mafia*—a "new" Mafia—emerged.

The *Nuovo Mafia*

World War II had negative consequences for southern Italy, blocking the northward migration of excess labor (Catanzaro 1992). The end of the war brought a Mafia renaissance in Sicily as a vacuum in local leadership was filled by former *capomafiosi*: "Not only were they respected local figures, but as victims of Mori's operation against the mafia they were also in a good position to pose as antifascists" (Finley, Smith, and Duggan 1987: 214). Many *mafiosi* became town mayors under the Allied military government, and they violently thwarted the efforts of trade unionists, socialists, communists, and land reformers (Catanzaro 1992; Robb 1996). A brief flirtation with separatism—se-

ceding from the mainland in favor of affiliation with the United States—was discarded in 1946, when the government in Rome announced Sicilian autonomy. In return, the most important *capomafioso*, Calògero Vizzini ("Don Calò"), the illiterate son of a peasant father, pledged support for the Christian Democratic Party. In return, *capomafiosi* were frequently accorded places of honor in the party, and "it was not uncommon for prominent politicians to appear as honored guests at the christenings, weddings, and funerals of major Mafia figures. In Sicily, being known as a friend of a *mafioso* was not a sign of shame but of power" (Stille 1995a: 20).

Born in 1877, Don Calò was imprisoned by Mussolini. He spent only a few days in prison before being released through the intervention of a young Fascist he had befriended. Vizzini was now a *gabelloto* and mayor of Villalba, and he "would hold court each morning in the small plaza of Villalba. People would approach him for favours, such as help with a bank loan or assistance with a court case—indeed anything in which 'authority' could be useful" (Duggan 1989: 67). As an "anti-Fascist," he possessed a special business license from the Allied military government. This allowed him to head up a flourishing black market in olive oil. In this endeavor, Vizzini worked with American expatriate Vito Genovese (Lewis 1964).

When Don Calò died of natural causes in 1954, he left an estate worth several million dollars (Pantaleone 1966). He was the last of the old-style *capomafiosi*, characterized by modesty in both speech and dress: "The old Mafia chief was a rural animal, holding sway over the countryside, dressed in shirt-sleeves and baggy pants: a multimillionaire who chose to look like a peasant" (Servadio 1974: 21). In fact, notes Pino Arlacchi (1986), the behavior of the old *mafioso* had power—*rispetto*—as its primary goal. However, the modern *mafioso* is a materialist for whom power is simply a means to achieve wealth, and he exudes conspicuous consumption. The "new" *mafioso* is not bound by the traditions of the rural *cosca*. He dresses like a successful businessman, sometimes a bit flashy, like the American gangster whose pattern he seems to have adopted—cross-fertilization. The New

Mafia—called *Cosa Nostra* by its members—has a distinctly American tint, the result of American gangsters being deported to Sicily, "where they immediately assumed leading positions in the Mafia hierarchy of the island" (Lewis 1964: 273).

Cosa Nostra resorted to robbery and kidnapping to accumulate the capital necessary to be a player in legal endeavors such as the construction industry and in the illicit heroin and cocaine marketplaces. Drug money changed the functioning and mode of organization of the Mafia, in which luxury and extravagant consumerism have become the norm (Siebert 1996). The New Mafia has also continued the *pizzo*, protection money extorted from large and small businesses (Cowell 1992e). But financial considerations reportedly play a secondary role in this enterprise, being primarily a Mafia way of maintaining territorial domination (Stille 1993): "While managing millions and operating on a grand scale, he [a *mafioso*] does not slacken his hold over the corner butcher's shop. Not so much for the sake of money perhaps, as to demonstrate the permanence of his power" (Siebert 1996: 123).

The contrast between the "two Mafias" is evidenced by a conflict between the *capomafiosi* of Corleone in the immediate postwar years. Michele Navarra was a medical doctor and (despite his education) a representative of the Old Mafia. Luciano Liggio (a police misspelling of his real name, Leggio), born in 1925, represented the New Mafia. At the age of 19, Liggio became the youngest *gabelloto* in the history of Sicily (his predecessor was murdered). Navarra was the inspector of health for the area and the head of the town's only hospital (his predecessor was also mysteriously murdered). In the tradition of Don Calò, he also trafficked in stolen beef and served as chairman of the local branch of the Christian Democratic Party. Luciano Liggio was his most violent assistant. Liggio and an associate hanged a trade unionist who was a threat to Navarra's power, and the murder was witnessed by a shepherd boy. In a state of shock after telling his story, the boy fainted and was taken to the hospital. There, an injection from the "good doctor" ended the boy's life (Servadio 1976). Navarra was convicted of the murder.

Although he was sentenced to five years' exile in Calabria, he returned home after a few months (Robb 1996).

With his followers, Liggio began to develop activities of his own. However, the Liggio group "had nothing in common with the organization presided over by Don Calò but its iron laws of secrecy and the vendetta" (Lewis 1964: 123). Liggio chose to control the supply of meat to the Palermo market rather than raising livestock. He drove out all of the tenant farmers on the estate under his protection, burning down their houses, and replaced them with day laborers. He recruited gunmen, and anybody who crossed him was summarily shot. From 1953 to 1958, there were 153 recorded Mafia murders in the Corleone area (Servadio 1976). According to one source (Mangione 1985: 147), Liggio was connected to organized crime in the United States and "had been a key contact man working closely with Joseph Profaci of the American Mafia."

The Old Mafia benefited from feudal conditions, living off control of the land and cheap labor. When a dam was proposed for the town of Corleone to harness the river water flowing to the ocean, Dr. Navarra vetoed it because he made money from the water pumped from artesian wells. *Cosa Nostra*, oriented toward capitalistic change, recognized the profits that could be earned from control over building projects, although this dam has yet to be built. While Navarra and his followers were living in the nineteenth century, Liggio was a man of the times. With Navarra in control, nothing would change, and the New Mafia recognized this reality (Lewis 1964). In 1958, 15 of Liggio's men ambushed Dr. Navarra's car; 210 bullets were found in his body. One by one, the remaining followers of Navarra were murdered, and Liggio became the undisputed *capomafioso* of the Corleonesi *cosca* (Servadio 1976).

During the 1960s, the emerging *cosche* engaged in a bitter struggle for dominance. The struggle between Mafia clans led to an emigration of *mafiosi* similar to that experienced during the reign of Mussolini. This proved to be quite beneficial as these overseas *mafiosi* provided the links for greater international operations. The Mafia

Economic Determinism

"A state relegated to purely economic functions has not only failed to produce a culture of legality, but has favored the culture of partiality, of doing favors for a friend, of trading interests, of ignoring the law—of promoting Mafia-type crime. In effect, the State in certain regions of Southern Italy is merely perceived as an economic entity, solely concerned with assistance and patron–client matters. All the institutions have been utterly relegated and no authority, even of a moral nature, attaches to them" (Argentine 1993: 21). Similar arguments could be made about the former Soviet Union.

connection to the cocaine trade is largely a result of this diaspora (Williams 1995a, 1995b).

In 1967, the Mafia war led to the trial of 114 *mafiosi*, and Luciano Liggio emerged as the most powerful *capomafioso* (Shawcross and Young 1987). In 1974, Liggio was convicted of the murder of Dr. Navarra and sentenced to life imprisonment (Schmetzer 1987, 1988). Liggio's right-hand man, Salvatore (Totò) Riina, became head of the Corleone *cosca*. A short, stocky man, the son of poor farmers with only a elementary school education, Riina is known as *La Belva*—"The Beast"—for ordering mass killings and personally participating in some of them. He formed private alliances with rising members of many *cosche*, planted his own men in others, and then with a reign of terror came to dominate the Mafia—at a cost of nearly 1,000 lives (Stille 1993, 1995a, 1995b; Robb 1996): "Rather than wage a street war like the previous Mafia conflict of the 1960s, Riina worked to peel away supporters from his rivals' forces, letting them see the inevitability of the Corleonesi" (Orlando 2001: 67). Many members of his *cosca* are close relatives, including his son and nephew.

After being tried in absentia and sentenced to life imprisonment for murder and drug trafficking, Riina became the most wanted man in Italy. He was able to avoid authorities for more than 23 years, partly because photographs of him were out of date. While living as a fugitive, Riina married the sister of a powerful *mafioso* in a ceremony performed by a Mafia priest (who was eventually defrocked), honeymooned in Venice, sired four children, and continued to oversee the activities of his Mafia clan (Robb 1996).

One of the victims of Riina's campaign to centralize and control the Mafia was *capomafioso* Tommaso Buscetta, who lost ten relatives, including two sons, a brother, a nephew, a son-in-law, and two brothers-in-law. (In 1995, another Buscetta relative, his 45-year-old nephew, was murdered in Palermo [Bohlen 1995d].) In 1983, Buscetta, who had escaped to Brazil, was arrested on an international warrant. He attempted to commit suicide with a strychnine pill. When he recovered, Buscetta agreed to cooperate with American and Italian authorities. In 1987, with the help of Buscetta and other informants, the Italian government convicted 338 *mafiosi* in the largest mass trial (452 defendants—referred to as the maxitrial) of its kind ever held in Italy.

Politics and the Mafia

Mafia voting strength is based on the circle of family and friends that each *mafioso* can deliver, 40 to 50 votes (Arlacchi 1993): in Sicily, at least 500,000 persons (out of a population of 5 million) are directly tied to the Mafia (Cowell 1992b). The Mafia is able to control votes because in the environment in which it operates, there is always fear of reprisals. Intimidation, surveillance of polling places, and sometimes rigged elections guarantee an outcome favorable to Mafia candidates. But frequently, outright intimidation is unnecessary. In the absence of political enthusiasm and voter passion, a cynical view prevails. Instead of signifying a preference among competing political ideas, the vote simply indicates support for a clientelistic group. The leveling of political traditions and an

Governing Italy

It is said that Italy's curse is to be the home of three world powers: the Italian government, the Catholic Church, and the Mafia, of which the government is the feeblest (Bohlen 1995b).

absence of ideology among the political parties lead voters almost naturally, without any forcing, to respect the "marching orders" given by the Mafia (della Porta and Vannucci 1999).

In 1987, angry over the government's maxi-trial, the fugitive *capo di tutti i capi* Totò Riina ordered a switch in votes: while the Christian Democrats increased their strength throughout the rest of Italy, only Mafia-backed candidates won in Palermo (Robb 1996). In 1992, the Mafia murdered the Sicilian head of the Christian Democratic Party in a Palermo suburb; it was his job to keep peace between the party and the Mafia: "This was the Mafia's way of announcing that it was 'renegotiating' its arrangement with the Prime Minister" (Kramer 1992: 112; Cowell 1992b). It appears that Totò Riina remained furious at the Christian Democrats for not intervening in the Mafia maxi-trial (della Porta and Vannucci 1999).

Since the end of World War II, the Christian Democratic Party (CDP) had ruled Italy, and "the party's bedrock . . . was the *mezzogiorno* and especially the *friends* in Sicily" (Robb 1996: 22). By 1993, increasing scandal and the collapse of European communism finally led to the demise of the CDP, which, despite its corruption[4] and ties to the Mafia, had been the only viable alternative to the Communist Party[5] (Stille 1993). The most powerful Christian Democrat in Sicily was Salvo Lima, the former *mafioso* mayor of Palermo who later became a deputy minister in Rome and a member of the European parliament. When Lima entered a restaurant in Palermo, people fell silent and kissed his hand. However, when scandal drove the Chris-

tian Democrats from power, Lima was no longer of use to the *friends*—he was gunned down by a man riding on the back of a motorbike (Robb 1996).

Vast government spending in the *Mezzogiorno*, often on useless building projects that provided patronage opportunities, became a vehicle for Mafia infiltration: "By corruption and physical intimidation, Mafia-controlled firms took their share of public contracts, either directly or through subcontracts and dummy companies." This approach has aided the spread of the Mafia phenomenon beyond its traditional areas "to towns and provinces that had once been free of organized crime. In many areas, democracy as we know it ceased to exist" (Stille 1993: 63). And the *mafioso* adds nothing of value to his environment: "Even in Medellin of the cocaine barons [discussed in Chapter 8], the Escobar clan and the Gavirias wanted an ultra-modern airport, a futuristic elevated metro system, and first-class hospitals. But in Cosa Nostra's Sicily, in the 'Ndrangheta's Calabria, in the Camorra's Naples, yesterday's ragamuffins turned into today's gang bosses exploit without putting anything back in except the frills and fancies of fly-by-night consumerism" (Siebert 1996: 81). Furthermore, fear of organized crime discourages business investment, and "although the Mafia's grip on Sicily has been visibly diminished, the island still suffers under the weight of poverty and unemployment" (Hundley 1998b: 5). And gangsterism increases the cost of credit—4 percent more than in northern Italy—which serves the business interests of Mafia loansharks (Bohlen 1997).

The Decline of the Mafia

As the political role of *mafiosi* changed, so too did their ability to act as brokers between peasant and

---

[4]For an examination of political corruption in Italy, see della Porta and Vannucci (1999) and Orlando (2001).

[5]In 1991 the Italian Communist Party, the most powerful in Europe, reorganized itself as the Democratic Party of the Left, social democrats seeking mainstream support (Burnett and Mantovani 1998).

American Versus Italian Mafia

"The American Mafia is a parasitic phenomenon operating at the margins of society. The Mafia of southern Italy plays a central role in almost every phase of economic and political life" (Stille 1993: 63).

officialdom. The *mafioso* was no longer *un uomo di rispetto* but simply an urban gangster in the American tradition—that is, a predatory criminal without popular roots or popular backing. The New Mafia reflects the emerging *Mezzogiorno*. The South is changing; modernization, fed by government-sponsored public works, is slowly encroaching on feudal ways. Above all, the mark of respect has more to do with one's wealth than with one's name or reputation. It was power, not wealth, that the traditional *mafioso* pursued: "The possession of wealth, regarded by the traditional *mafioso* as one among the proofs and results of a man's capacity to make himself respected, becomes, in the 1960s and 1970s, meritorious in itself." Family wealth, not family honor, is a reason for violence: "Wealth, in a word, becomes intrinsically honourable and confers honour on its possessors" (Arlacchi 1986: 60).

Since 1971, the *Nuovo Mafia* has assassinated investigative, judicial, and political officials, something that was anathema to the Old Mafia: "Offenses against symbols of authority were foreign to the methods of a Mafia that, considering itself an authority and surrogate for the state, wanted to preserve and respect certain values" (Kamm 1982a: E3). Indeed, "the *mafioso* customarily collaborated with the justice system. In fact, he would often appear before those who accused him of illicit activities as an honest citizen who helped bring the true outlaws to justice, claiming it was to his credit that order reigned in his community" (Catanzaro 1992: 24). As the Mafia was reduced to a marginal role in society, many *mafiosi* reacted in a manner similar to other marginalized persons, such as Jews during the early days of capitalism. They pursued wealth as the only way back to honor and power, and Mafia violence as a result of economic competition polluted the Sicilian political system (Arlacchi 1986; Catanzaro 1992). Across southern Italy, the government dissolved dozens of town councils because of their corrupt relationships with Mafia, Camorra, and 'Ndrangheta clans (Jamieson 2000).

As a result of the assassinations of government officials, the New Mafia lost the support of important elements of Italian society. In 1982, Salvatore Cardinal Pappalardo, the Sicilian-born archbishop of Palermo, led Sicilian priests "in a vocal campaign against the Mafia, reversing decades of church indifference toward and even tolerance of local dons"[6] (Withers 1982: 5). Later that year, while on a visit to the island of Sicily, Pope John Paul issued an attack on the Mafia. And since 1983, Palermo has elected and reelected an anti-Mafia mayor. In 1993 the Mafia struck back at its critics in the Church: a 56-year-old priest who spoke out against the Mafia was shot to death in front of his rectory in a Palermo slum[7] (Orlando 2001). And as part of its campaign of terror, the Mafia bombed two of Rome's most venerable churches, in addition to other bombings in Rome, Milan, and Florence that killed ten people and left dozens injured (Bohlen 1996b). In 1993 the Mafia bombed the world-famous Uffizi gallery in Florence, killing five persons and causing extensive damage (Bohlen 1995a).

In 1992 the prosecutor who helped gather evidence for the Mafia maxitrial, Judge Giovanni Falcone, was killed, along with his wife and three

---

[6]At times the Church–Mafia relationship was symbiotic, and some clergy were *mafiosi* (see, for example, Gambetta 1993: 48–52).
[7]In 1994 a priest who had spoken out against the Camorra was killed by two gunmen in his church north of Naples (Cowell 1994).

bodyguards, when a half ton of TNT was detonated by remote control on a road near Palermo.[8] The killers obviously had inside information about Falcone's movements. His murder led to an anti-Mafia demonstration by about 40,000 persons in Palermo, a remarkable occurrence for that city (Cowell 1992a). But it did not prevent the Mafia from striking again. Later that year, Paolo Borsellino, Falcone's replacement as Palermo's chief public prosecutor and head of a new anti-Mafia superagency, was killed along with five police bodyguards; 175 pounds of a Czech-made plastic explosive placed under a car was detonated while Borsellino was walking outside an apartment building where his mother and sister resided (Cowell 1992c).

The government responded by dispatching 7,000 troops to Sicily in a highly publicized anti-Mafia campaign, and Palermo reelected a crusading anti-Mafia mayor (Hundley 1998a). The soldiers were withdrawn in 1998: "Italy, which recently was admitted to the European monetary union, wants to shed the image of a nation that needs a peacekeeping force occupying its own territory" (Stanley 1998: 4). The day after troops were withdrawn, the police arrested scores of *mafiosi*, including 20 members of the Corleone *cosca*, whose boss was already in custody (Associated Press 1998a). And there have been dramatic results: murders in Palermo, which had averaged 130 to 140 annually, fell to fewer than 10 in 1997 (Hundley 1998a). As a sign of the Mafia's current weakness, in 1999 the president of Italy led an anti-Mafia demonstration in the notorious city of Corleone on a day dedicated to victims of the Mafia (Reuters 1999).

The violence that gained Riina his nickname also drove *mafiosi* to the authorities seeking protection from "the Beast" (Cowell 1992d, 1993b). In 1992, Italy enacted a witness protection law. The cooperation of *mafiosi* is believed to be behind the capture of the 62-year-old Don Totò, arrested in his car on a Palermo street at the beginning of 1993. He and his driver were unarmed. Later that year, Riina was ordered imprisoned for life by a Palermo court, and, like Palermo, his home city of Corleone elected an anti-Mafia mayor. Officials arrested other leading *mafiosi*, including the boss of eastern Sicily, Riina's heir apparent, who had been a fugitive for 11 years; the heads of the Camorra and 'Ndrangheta and hundreds of their followers were also arrested.

Bernardo Provenzano, boss of the Corleone *cosca* and the man convicted in absentia of the murder of anti-Mafia prosecutor Borsellino, is reputed to be the most important *capomafioso* in Sicily. He dropped out of school after the second grade and has been a fugitive for 40 years. Provenzano has reportedly been rebuilding Mafia ties with local politicians, business leaders, and the police—the police do not know what he looks like, and Provenzano operates through trusted intermediaries. His leadership has also reduced Mafia-related murders (Hundley 2001).

Excesses at home, the vigorous government response, and the increasing number of informers have weakened the Mafia. This fact and the emerging role of women in the *mezzogiorno* have led to the rise of women to prominent positions in organized crime, most notably in Naples but also in the Sicilian Mafia, where they have replaced their imprisoned husbands (Hundley 1998b; Stanley 2001).[9]

The Structure of the Mafia

At the center of the Mafia is the *padrino* or *capomafioso*, around whom other *mafiosi* gather, forming a *cosca*. The word *cosca* refers to the leaves of an artichoke, the *capomafioso* being the globe's heart. The structure consists of a network of two men that is patron–client oriented, relationships based on kinship, patronage, and friendship (Catanzaro 1992). The typical *cosca* rarely has more than 15 or 20 members, and at the center are four or five blood relatives (Arlacchi 1986). The *cosca* is devoid

---

[8]For an examination of his anti-Mafia activities and the events surrounding Judge Falcone's assassination, see Stille (1995a). For an analysis of anti-Mafia activities in Italy, see Jamieson (2000).

[9]For a discussion of the role of women in the Mafia and the 'Ndrangheta, see Siebert (1996).

of any rigid organization; it is simply *gli amici degli amici*—"friends of friends." The members are *gli uomini qualificati* ("qualified men"). Flexibility prevents the *cosca* from becoming bureaucratic: "The need continually to broaden the scope of the networks of social relationships reinforced the impossibility of creating stable organizational structures" (Catanzaro 1992: 40). The *mafioso* succeeds because he commands a *partito*, a network of relationships whereby he is able to act as an intermediary—a broker—providing services, which include votes and violence for the holders of institutionalized power. All he requests in return is immunity to carry out his activities (Hess 1973). The *mafioso* serves as a guarantor for price rigging and collusive bidding on building projects: "Any businessman who defects from the collusive agreement or refuses to take part in it, exposes himself to violent retaliation from a Mafia protector" (della Porta and Vannucci 1999: 229).

Standardized rituals around the Mafia developed in the 1870s (Hobsbawm 1976). *Carabinieri* (national police) reports from the early Mussolini era reveal that the "Mafia had already become a secret organization, structured in the form of clans or *cosche* and divided by sector or activity and geographical area" (Jamieson 2000: 14). Once initiated into the *cosca*, the *mafioso* became a *compadre*, a practice based on the custom of *comparático* (fictional kinship or godparenthood). The remnants of pre-unification power in western Sicily[10]— *gabelloti*, *campieri*, and in some instances clergymen—formed the *cosche* (plural of *cosca*). Each village has its own *cosca*, larger ones have more, and collectively they are the Mafia.

Barzini (1965) delineates four levels of organization that constitute the Mafia. The first, the *famiglia*, constitutes the nucleus. Some families, he notes, have belonged to the *società degli amici* for generations, each *padrino* bequeathing the family to his eldest son. The second level consists of a group of several families who come together to form a *cosca*; one family and its *padrino* are recog-

nized as supreme. The *cosca* establishes working relationships with other *cosche*, respecting territories and boundaries. The third level is achieved when *cosche* join in an alliance called *consorteria*, in which one *cosca* is recognized as supreme and its leader is the leader of the *consorteria*—*capo di tutti capi*, the boss of all bosses: "This happens spontaneously . . . when the *cosche* realize that one of them is more powerful, has more men, more friends, more money, more high-ranking protectors. . . . All the *consorterie* in Sicily . . . form the *onerata società*, a solidarity that unites all *mafiosi*; they know they owe all possible support to any *amico degli amici* who needs it . . . even if they have never heard of him, provided he is introduced by a mutual *amico*" (Barzini 1965: 272).

The New Mafia has a membership in excess of 5,000, each with his own network—a circle of dozens of relatives, friends, associates, and employees—divided into about 180 *cosche* (Stille 1993; de Gennaro 1995; Jamieson 2000). Each *cosca* is held together by a core of blood relatives and encompasses a membership of 25 to 30 persons (Arlacchi 1986; Argentine 1993). The *cosche* form alliances that are sealed through marriage: "Such is the strategic significance of marriages for the structure of the criminal organization and the arrangement of alliances between the different cells, that by following the trail of weddings, christenings and confirmations, the judges [in the 1986–1987 Mafia maxitrial] managed to gather information about internal changes within the organization" (Siebert 1996: 29).

Capomafioso-turned-informer Tommaso Buscetta describes the *cosca* as hierarchical, with elected leaders[11] and precise decision-making processes. Each *cosca* takes its name from the territory under its control and is composed of *uomini d'onore* ("men of honor") in numbers varying from 10 to 100. They are organized into groups of 10 (*decina*) headed by a *capodecina*. Above the *capidecina* is the *capofamiglia*, who has a deputy and a few advisors. Three or more families with adjoining territories

---

[10]The eastern half of the island did not have a Mafia Family until 1925 (Arlacchi 1993).

[11]Catanzaro (1992) discounts the "electoral procedure" because it is not used to decide between two or more contenders, but simply to confirm the single contender for leadership.

The Unchanging Mafia

The Mafia phenomenon, whatever its regional tongue, is always the same: a feudal-style hierarchy, involving a strictly defined system of relationships, with reciprocal rights and duties, is cemented throughout by close links or personal devotion, by a code of conduct, by alliances and agreements with rival bodies and, above all, by a common combination against civilized society (Spadolini 1993).

are represented by *capimandamenti*, who are members of the *cupola*, or *commissione*. This central directorate of the Mafia, headed by a *capocommisione*, oversees the activities of the organization on a provincial level. More-recent reports (e.g., Jamieson 2000) indicate that the Mafia has become less hierarchical and more impermeable, with small, tightly structured cells that, like those of Colombian organizations (discussed in Chapter 8), have a membership that is unknown to all but a few persons. There is greater internal secrecy and selectivity in recruitment and an increased tendency to favor family members to reduce the likelihood of informants, a strategy long favored by the *'Ndrangheta*.

According to a *capomafioso* turned *pentiti* (repentant—an informer), "men of honor become such in large part through heredity, but not in the same way as the aristocracy, where the father leaves his title to his son. In the *mafia* it's more complicated. There's observation, a study of the best young men by the oldest ones. The most senior *mafiosi*—friends of the father, relatives of the mother—watch the young ones, some of whom come to stand out from the others. . . . When one of them distinguishes himself because he's clever, determined, and ruthless, he is cultivated, encouraged by adult men of honor who teach and guide him, and if he follows them they start to let him do a few things" (quoted in Arlacchi 1993: 21). Despite its weakened condition, the pool of Mafia prospects remains strong, the result of an unemployment rate approaching 60 percent among the young of Sicily (Stanley 1998).

THE NEAPOLITAN CAMORRA

Whereas the Mafia began as more of an idea than an organization, and whereas it evolved along cultural lines in western Sicily, the Camorra was deliberately structured as a criminal society. The term *camorra* is believed to have derived from the Castillian *kamora*, meaning "contestation," and to have been imported into Naples during the years of Spanish domination (Serao 1911a). Ernest Serao reports that the forebears of the Neapolitan Camorra were the Spanish brigands of the Sierras known as the *gamuri* (1911a: 723): "Not a passerby nor a vehicle escaped their watchful eye and their fierce claws, so that traveling or going from one place to another on business was impossible for anyone without sharing with the ferocious watchers of the Sierras either the money he had with him or the profits of the business that had taken him on his journey."

While there are several versions of how the term *Camorra* came into being (Walston 1986), it seems clear that the Camorra as an organization developed in Spanish prisons during the Bourbon rule of the Two Sicilies (the *Mezzogiorno*) early in the nineteenth century. The members of this criminal society eventually moved their control of the prisons into Naples proper. They were "rather tightly, centrally, and hierarchically organized" (Hobsbawm 1959: 55). The Camorra "was organized as openly and carefully as a public school system, or an efficient political machine in one of our own cities. Naples was divided into twelve districts, and each of these into a number of sub-districts. Although burglary and other remunerative felonies were not neglected, extortion was the principal industry; and the assassination of an inconvenient person could be purchased by anyone with the price. In the case of a friend in need, a murder could be arranged without any charge—a simple gesture of affection" (McConaughy 1931: 244). As one English diplomat in Naples during the 1860s observed,

> There was no class, high or low, that did not have its representatives among the members of the Society which was a vast organized association for the extortion of blackmail in every conceivable shape and form. Officials, officers of the King's Household, the police and others were affiliated with the most desperate of the criminal classes in carrying out the depredations, and none was too high or too low to escape them. If a petition was to be presented to the Sovereign or to a Minister, it had to be paid for; at every gate of the town Camorristi were stationed to exact a toll on each cart or donkey load brought to market by the peasants; and on going into a hackney carrosel in the street, I have seen one of the band run up and get his fee from the driver. No one thought of refusing to pay, for the consequences of a refusal were too well known, anyone rash enough to demur being apt to be found soon after mysteriously stabbed by some unknown individual, whom the police were careful never to discover. (quoted in Hibbert 1966: 181–82)

The Camorra was "more efficiently organized than the police, and set up a parallel system of law in the typical southern Italian style" (Ianni 1972: 22). In contrast with the Mafia, the Camorra was highly organized and disciplined (Serao 1911a: 724):

> There is a *capóntrine*—a sectional head—and a *capo in testa*, or local head-in-chief of the Camorra, a kind of president of the confederation of all the twelve sections into which Naples is divided and which are presided over by the *capíntrini*. The lowest or entry

level of the Camorra is the *picciuotto*, which requires an act of daring often simply a bloody deed, including "very dreadful crimes committed against very peaceful and quiet people." The *picciuotto* has no share in the social dividend. If he wishes to live on other people's money, he must do the best he can by stealing, cheating, or swindling whom he can, giving, however, to his superiors of the Camorra proper *shruffo* or proportionate percentage. (Serao 1911b: 781)

Below the *picciuotti* were specialized associates of the Camorra, such as the *batista*—a person who could plan burglaries because of his access to the homes of wealthy persons. The Camorra had its own authorized fences, usually dealers in secondhand goods, who arranged for the auction of stolen articles.

The Camorra welcomed Garibaldi and his "Red Shirts" in 1860, and after his success, their power increased. Upon the proclamation of the constitution in 1860, *camorristi* were freed from the prisons in Naples, and the new prefect used the Camorra to maintain order: the Camorra constituted not only the *de facto* but also the legally constituted police power in Naples (Walston 1986). Devoid of a political ideology, the Camorra continued to act as mercenaries in the various struggles for power (Behan 1996). At the peak of their power, from 1880 until 1900 (Gambino 1974), "if they so decided, there would not be, in some regions, a single vote cast for a candidate for the Chamber of Deputies who was opposed to their man" (Ianni 1974: 246).

The Camorra differed from the Mafia in the style of dress and comportment of their members. While even a *capomafioso* exuded an air of modesty in both dress and manner of speaking, the *camorrista* was a flamboyant actor whose manner of walking and style of dress clearly marked him as a member of the *societá*. In the United States, the public profile of important Italian-American organized crime figures with a Neapolitan heritage have tended toward Camorra, while their Sicilian counterparts have usually been more subdued. For example, Al Capone and, in more recent years,

John Gotti, boss of the Gambino crime Family, are both of Neapolitan heritage.

In 1912, in the "Cuocolo Case," a key witness allowed the *Carabinieri* to prosecute the entire Camorra hierarchy (Walston 1986). Given its highly formal structure, this was devastating to continuity. The old Camorra did not survive Mussolini because, like the Mafia, it required weak government control (Ianni 1972). One source (McConaughy 1931: 248) writes that the Camorra welcomed the Fascists as they had Garibaldi; after that, there was not a Camorra: "They are all Fascists, and everything they do is legal." Fascism brought an end to Camorra influence in the city of Naples; the few remaining members were incorporated into the Fascist power structure, and Camorra gangs in the countryside were used by the Fascists to intimidate antigovernment peasants (Behan 1996).

While there are still criminals operating in Naples identified as being part of the Camorra, Francis Ianni (1972) argues that they have no direct links to the criminal society of the past. Vincenzo Ruggiero (1993: 143) reports that the last boss of the traditional Camorra died of natural causes in 1989 "after having acted for years as an informal 'justice of the peace' in one of the most crowded areas of the city. He settled disputes and, it is said, helped the poor." In an interview shortly before his death, "he mourned an end of an era—that of the men of honour who succored the people—and condemned the present, dominated by cruel, greedy and unscrupulous individuals."

Indeed, postwar Naples has been plagued with violence attributed to these "unscrupulous individuals." Suspected but not convicted, Sicilian *mafiosi* were forced into "internal exile"—obliged to leave Naples. In collusion with local criminals, they began to expand illegal opportunity. In the countryside, Camorra gangs began to emerge as soon as the Allied forces withdrew. They asserted control over agriculture and cattle markets. Slowly, they began to move into the urban areas of Naples to further their control over these markets, dictating prices and acting as brokers between sellers and buyers. They subsequently moved into and expanded upon the Naples contraband industry—from cigarettes to drugs. An estimated three-quarters of the cigarettes sold in Naples, where about one-third of the inhabitants are unemployed, originate in the black market[12]—Italy has very high cigarette taxes. In 1997, more than two dozen murders were blamed on a feud between two Camorra groups (the Mazzarella and Contini clans) for control of the contraband cigarette business (Hundley 1997). Gambling, and especially extortion from illegitimate and legitimate enterprises, round out Camorra activities (Schmetzer 1982; Kamm 1982c; Walston 1986; Argentine 1993; Behan 1996).

When government reconstruction programs were initiated in the Campania region, the Camorra, much like their Mafia "brothers" in Sicily, soon found a new source of income, and their ability to provide jobs gained them political influence (Behan 1996). The earlier versions of Camorra were not directly involved in politics, but during the 1980s the new Camorra began to penetrate the local political scene, and some members now hold local elected offices. In Campania, dozens of town counsels have been dissolved because of Camorra influence (de Gennaro 1995).

Government redevelopment was a failure—a testament to political patronage and corruption. This was repeated when an earthquake devastated Naples in 1980, claiming almost 3,000 lives and leaving 300,000 homeless. A huge program of reconstruction was effectively hijacked by corrupt politicians, government bureaucrats, and the Camorra, which diversified its wealth from drug trafficking by moving into the construction industry. Their ability to intimidate workers thwarted union pressures and ensured lower costs, allowing

---

[12]In 1994, when the government threatened a crackdown on this practice, hundreds of street vendors for whom the contraband is their only source of income took to the streets in demonstrations (Tagliabue 1994). The largest American tobacco companies have been accused of cooperating with smugglers, and in 1998 an RJR Nabisco subsidiary pled guilty to federal criminal charges stemming from a scheme to smuggle cigarettes into Canada through an upstate New York Indian reservation (Bonner and Drew 1997; Drew 1998).

Camorra firms a competitive advantage (Behan 1996).

A growing population and rampant poverty led to the development of new Camorra gangs that operated for many years without direct conflict with their older and more established brethren, who often had Sicilian Mafia ties.[13] A "New Camorra Organization," *Nuova Camorra Organizzata* (NCO), was organized by the leader of one of the important Camorra groups, Raffaele Cutolo. Born in 1941, Cutolo had been running his group while serving a 24-year sentence for murder and extortion. Consistent with the Camorra's historical origins, Cutolo did much of his recruiting among the violent young men in Neapolitan prisons: "Cutolo protected these kids in jail, looked after their families outside and guaranteed a job on release. In return he got an oath of loyalty to the Nuova Camorra Organizzata" based on eighteenth-century Camorra rituals (Robb 1996: 165).

Naples had been divided into zones by the older established Camorra groups, but Cutolo shattered the arrangement—and the peace—by attempting to bring all Camorra groups under his NCO. In 1980 and 1981, there were 380 murders attributed to the "Camorra war." Cutolo's opponents formed their own *Nuovo Famiglia* and received help from their Sicilian Mafia allies (Robb 1996). In the end, the NCO attempted takeover failed, and Cutolo was moved to a maximum-security prison on an island near Sardinia. With Cutolo and his NCO no longer a threat, both the NCO and the *Nuovo Famiglia* fell apart into competing and often feuding Camorra groups (Argentine 1993; Behan 1996; Robb, 1996).

As opposed to its predecessors, the modern Camorra "has a 'fragmented' and widespread structure, made up of a number of gangs [over one hundred] which easily band together and then split up, sometimes peacefully, but more often after bloody wars" (de Gennaro 1995: 36). At the center of a typical Camorra group is a boss whose group is known by his surname, such as the *Alfieri* headed by Carmine Alfieri[14] in Nola. A high turnover has resulted in members and leaders who are younger than those of other southern Italian criminal groups, and the Camorra is less structured and less family based than the Mafia. There is a general absence of rituals, although the NCO used a century-old ceremony to initiate members. Camorra membership is about 7,000.

To the Camorra, territorial control is crucial. Although extortion from legitimate businesses provides a relatively low return for the amount of effort and risk involved, it is a way of asserting domination over a geographic area; it also provides an opportunity for those on the lower rungs to prove themselves and thereby move up in the Camorra ranks. Camorra groups dominate illegal gambling and usury within their territorial hegemony, although some of their gambling operations reach northern cities such as Rome, Florence, and Milan. Territorial control extends to local politics and is enhanced by the Camorra's ability to provide employment where unemployment rates are consistently high. While the need to maintain power and influence through territorial control limits the extent of the Camorra's international connections, members have forged links with Sicilian *mafiosi* who operate internationally (Behan 1996; Robb 1996).

In stark contrast to the Sicilian Mafia, the *Secondigliano Alliance*, a collection of some of the most ruthless Camorra clans in Naples, is ruled by Maria Licciardi. The short, fiftyish woman is the daughter of a respected *camorrista* and has three *camorrista* brothers, whose imprisonment cleared the way for her to ascend the Camorra hierarchy. After being a fugitive for two years, hiding out in Eastern Europe, she was arrested in 2001 by a special Neapolitan police squad that had been tracking her for eight months (F. Kennedy 2001).

---

[13]One of the most important Camorra groups, headed by the Nuvoletta brothers, had important links to the powerful *capomafioso* Luciano Liggio, discussed earlier in this chapter.

[14]Alfieri was known as first among equals and able to maintain discipline and territorial integrity among the more than 100 Camorra clans. In 1992 he was arrested and subsequently became a government informer. This led to a breakdown of Camorra order and an upsurge in feuds and murders (Hundley 1997).

THE 'NDRANGHETA

The province of Calabria is located in the far south of the Italian "boot." It encompasses about 6,000 square miles, of which more than 90 percent are hills or mountains. Italy's poorest province, Calabria has a population in excess of 2,000,000 people; the capital city, Reggio di Calabria, is home to about 200,000. Lacking the charm of historical sites and world-class art, tourism is almost nonexistent. Much of the housing stock was built illegally by criminal groups, the fearsome *Onerate Societá* ("Honored Society") or *'Ndrangheta* ("Brotherhood").

In Calabria, the term *'ndrangheta* is used to indicate a high degree of heroism and virtue as embodied in the *'ndranghetisti*, men who are governed by *omertá* (Arlacchi 1986; Paoli 1994). The word *'ndrangheta* derives from the Greek *andra gateo*,[15] meaning to behave like an *able* man. There is a Mafia-type hierarchy in each *andrine* or *'ndrina*—equivalent to a *cosca*—and members take a blood oath (Argentine 1993).

Originally several bands that grew because of government repression, the *'Ndrangheta* gained popular support because of its political stance against the central government: "In 1861, the new Italian government sent troops to police Calabria. The old economic order had collapsed under the strains of national unification, and the number of gangs had increased. Because of the government's deliberate policy of favoring the North over the South of Italy in its programs of economic development, and because of its ignorant and arrogant insensitivity to the customs of the South, the Calabrians soon grew to hate the new government in the North. They naturally turned to the gangs" (Gambino 1974: 289).

These gangs mixed political insurrection with banditry and were supported and romanticized by the repressed peasantry. But the *'Ndrangheta* had no positive program; its sense of social justice was basically destructive: "In such circumstances to as-

sert power, any power, is itself a triumph. Killing and torture is the most primitive and personal assertion of ultimate power, and the weaker the rebel feels himself to be at bottom, the greater, we may suppose, the temptation to assert it" (Hobsbawm 1969: 56).

The *'Ndrangheta*, sometimes referred to as the "Calabrian Mafia," consists of 85 (Paoli 1994) to 144 (Snedden and Visser 1994) to 160 (de Gennaro 1995) *andrine*, some exceeding 200 members, with a combined membership of 5,000 to 6,000. Each group—*'ndrina*—exerts its influence over a well-defined geographic area generally corresponding to a town or village, although the *'Ndrangheta* now operates in northern Italy's cities and throughout much of Europe, wherever Calabrians have settled. They are particularly strong in Canada and Australia (Paoli 1994). In the larger areas such as Reggio, two *'ndrina* could be located in one area, but the criminal functions will be divided either by "turf" or by function. For example, one may control extortion while another will control drugs (Snedden and Visser 1994). The *'Ndrangheta* also collaborates with Sicilian and Neapolitan counterparts. Unlike these groups, however, *'Ndrangheta* groups are based on blood ties, allowing for a high degree of internal cohesion, which protects against informants. *Omertá* remains strong, and there are few cooperating witnesses of Calabrian origin (de Gennaro 1995; Bohlen 1996d). Their violence is reminiscent of the cruel Colombian practice (see Chapter 8) of *no dejar la semilla* (don't leave the seed): known as *fida*, all members of a victim's family, including women and children, are killed (Snedden and Visser 1994).

At its core, a *'ndrina* is composed of one or two biological families and their network of artificial kinships: "In order to strengthen the cohesion of the inner nucleus, the practice of intermarriage between first cousins is strongly encouraged and marriages are also used to cement alliances with other groups in the immediate neighborhood" (Paoli 1994: 215). Loyalty is further promoted through the use of initiation ceremonies similar to those of the American *Cosa Nostra* (see Chapter 1). *'Ndrangheta* women frequently play important roles, maintaining family traditions and running

---

[15]The Greek derivation may be from the word *andragaqos*, "brave man" (Paoli 1994).

family enterprises. Like its Sicilian counterparts, *'Ndrangheta* has established a commission that recognizes territorial hegemony and mediates disputes in an effort to reduce the high level of violence for which the Calabrians are noted. In 1999 the *Carabinieri* captured the man reputed to be the most powerful *'Ndrangheta* boss; Giuseppe Piromalli was convicted of murder in absentia and had been a fugitive since 1993. He was arrested inside a secret apartment located in what appeared to be an uninhabited old hut, but it contained highly sophisticated "James Bond" type electronic equipment (Reuters 1999).

The organization exhibits its criminal skills mainly in kidnapping, vast-scale international arms and drug trafficking, extortion from almost all profit-making activities, and control of public contracts (de Gennaro 1995). Extortion inhibits legitimate investment and plays a significant role in the backwardness of the region. During the 1980s, ransom kidnappings provided capital for entry into large-scale drug trafficking. Many of these kidnappings were collaborative efforts among *'Ndrangheta*, Camorra, and Mafia groups (Siebert 1996). Ready access to the sea makes drug, as well as arms and cigarette, smuggling relatively easy. Drug profits led to the purchase of large tracts of land and the opening of legitimate businesses, such as supermarkets, although not necessarily in Calabria (Paoli 1994). The growing of cannabis has become part of the organization's portfolio, and marijuana plantations have been discovered in western Calabria (Snedden and Visser 1994).

SACRA CORONA UNITA AND THE ALBANIAN CONNECTION

The Puglia (Apulia) region at the heel of the Italian boot forms an elongated peninsula on the Adriatic and Ionian seas. The *Sacra Corona Unita* (SCU), Sacred United Crown, evolved in the region already noted for Camorra and *'Ndrangheta* activities. As the name suggests, the SCU uses a great deal of Roman Catholic imagery as part of its rituals. At the end of the 1970s and early 1980s, lo-

cal criminal gangs began patterning themselves on their elder Mafia and Camorra colleagues, eventually coalescing into the SCU. The origins of the SCU are traced to Giuseppe Rogoli, who reportedly established the organization as a ritual brotherhood on Christmas day in 1983, while a prisoner serving a life sentence for murder. The SCU is organized horizontally, with a series of about 45 autonomous clans accountable to the common interests of the organization (Hess et al. 1999: 387). Total membership is estimated at about 2,000, and women often play important roles in the business operations. The SCU has close ties to the Balkans, particularly Albania, located just across the Strait of Otranto from Puglia. During World War II, Albania was occupied by Mussolini's Italy.

Albania, a primarily Muslim nation with a population of about 3.5 million, is slightly smaller than Maryland. A mostly mountainous country with small plains along its long coastline on the Adriatic Sea, Albania is noted for its strong sense of familial and clan ties. Albanian criminal groups have much in common with their southern Italian colleagues, including concepts of *omertá* and *famiglia*. Albanian tradition includes absolute loyalty to the extended family and clan, known as *fare*, and the notion of *bessa* requires total respect for oral promises.

Once the most isolated country in Europe, Albania became a haven for local and foreign criminal groups after the collapse of its Stalinist regime in the early 1990s. The opening of the country's borders and political disarray have allowed Albania to become a primary alternative to traditional Balkan smuggling routes through the former Yugoslavia that were disrupted by the breakout of ethnic fighting in the early 1990s. Taking advantage of a weak central government and a great deal of political chaos, SCU clans were quick to establish a presence in Albania, linking up with local criminal groups.

Being a rather recent phenomenon not as strong as the Mafia or Camorra, *Sacra Corona Unita* leaders apparently decided to join forces rather than run the risk of a conflict with Albanian OC groups, which are known to be extremely violent. As a result, in certain areas of Italy, the market for cannabis, prostitution, and the smuggling of illegal immigrants is run mainly by Albanians, whose situation has been strengthened as a result of the Kosovo crisis: "As the Albanian gangs continue to proliferate, the SCU has been there to support them in joint venture opportunities such as the trade of weapons and drugs" (Hess et al. 1999: 390). The SCU is behind the smuggling of thousands of Albanians into Italy, including Albanian women sold into prostitution. Macedonia, which borders on Albania, has become a major center of the European sex trade (Gall 2001). A crackdown in Italy led to the relocation of hundreds of *mafiosi* to the Albanian coastal town of Vlore, while their Albanian counterparts are found throughout Italy (Cilluffo and Salmoiraghi 1999). Albanian criminals frequently reside in Calabria, indicating ties to the *'Ndrangheta*, and in 1999, police in the coastal Albanian city of Durrës, with Italian assistance, arrested one of the godfathers of the *Sacra Corona Unita*.

With its strategic position on the Adriatic, the SCU is able to provide smuggling services to the Mafia, Camorra, and *'Ndrangheta*. It routinely uses Albania's long and now virtually unguarded coastline as a staging area for smuggling drugs—Southwest Asian heroin, hashish, and, to a lesser extent, cocaine—arms, and other contraband across the Adriatic Sea to Italy. There are also ties among the SCU, Colombian cartels, and Russian, Southeast Asian, and Southwest Asian criminal groups. Albanian organized crime groups are hybrid organizations, often involved both in criminal activity and in political activities, mainly relating to Kosovo-based organizations.

Albanian criminals are also involved in the traffic of illegal immigrants to Western Europe, transporting Albanians, Kurds, Chinese, and people from the Indian subcontinent. Albanian groups are mainly responsible for the crossing of the Adriatic Sea from the Albanian coast to Italy. From Italy, illegal immigrants are transported by allied criminal groups such as the SCU. Immigration is not only a source of income, but important in creating networks in foreign countries, bridgeheads for the Albanian Mafia abroad. Reports indicate that some of the people admitted into Western European or North America as refugees during the Kosovo conflict had been carefully chosen by the Albanian Mafia to stay in the host country and act as a future liaison for the criminal networks (Hess et al. 1999; National Security Council and Interpol information).

Now that we have examined the criminal organizations of Italy and Albania, in the next chapter we will cross the Atlantic to Latin America.

INTERNET CONNECTIONS

U.S. Department of State: **state.gov/index**

Global Organized Crime Project: **csis.org/goc**

International links: **people.freenet.de/kvlampe/oclinx01**

Centre for Sicilian Documentation: **centroimpastato.it/index.php3**

Le Mafie: **www.fionline.it/mafie**

International Organization for Migration: **www.iom.int**

United Nations criminal justice: **uncjin.org**

REVIEW QUESTIONS

1. What is the parallel between Prohibition and the expanded capacity of contemporary criminal organizations?
2. How did Mussolini affect the Mafia and the Camorra?
3. What led to the reawakening of Mafia power at the end of World War II?
4. How does the "New Mafia" differ from the "Old Mafia"?
5. How do Mafia, Camorra, and 'Ndrangheta differ?
6. How does the structure of the old Camorra differ from its contemporary manifestation?
7. Why is there a close relationship between the *Sacra Corona Unita* and Albanian crime groups?
8. How do the *Sacra Corona Unita* and Albanian crime groups cooperate?

CHAPTER 8

LATINO ORGANIZED CRIME

A common element that characterizes most of the criminal organizations examined in this chapter is extensive—sometimes exclusive—involvement in drug trafficking: "Narcotics and drug traffic have the same pattern of relationship which surrounded alcohol and bootlegging during the prohibition era" (Ianni 1974: 320). If anything positive can be said for the drug business, it is that it has become an *equal opportunity employer* (Durk and Silverman 1976). As noted in Chapter 1, a criminal organization can exhibit a formal structure while its economic activities may actually involve small firms or partnerships among members and include nonmember associates. This is often the case with outlaw motorcycle clubs and the American Mafia. In contrast, for Latino organized crime groups, income-producing activities are typically integrated into a bureaucratic structure—it is their sole *raison d'etre*—and are devoid of the subcultural traditions that distinguish the Sicilian Mafia and outlaw motorcycle clubs.

In the United States, most Latino organized crime groups import their criminal organizations along with the drugs they sell.[1] Most prominent among them are groups based in Colombia and Mexico.

THE CUBAN–COLOMBIAN CONNECTION

When Fidel Castro overthrew the corrupt dictatorial regime of Fulgencio Batista early in 1959, he expelled American gangsters who operated gambling casinos in Havana. Many of their Cuban associates fled to the United States, along with

---

[1]This is not to say that Latinos are not involved in other areas of organized crime: ("Spanish") Raymond Marquez, a Puerto Rican, is/was a (perhaps *the*) major numbers operator in Harlem. In 1997 he announced his retirement, but a year later, at 68, Marquez was arrested with 24 others and charged with handling more than $6 million in bets annually. He resides in a $1-million home in Great Neck, New York. José Miguel ("El Padrino") Battle, a Cuban, controls numbers operations in parts of Florida, New York City, and New Jersey. Both men have ties with Italian-American crime groups.

narcotraficantes who had distributed cocaine in Cuba. They settled primarily in the New York, New Jersey, and Miami areas and began to look for new sources of income. Many Cubans who fled with, or soon after, the Batista loyalists were organized and trained by the Central Intelligence Agency in an effort to dislodge Castro. After the Bay of Pigs debacle in 1961, members of the CIA-organized Cuban exile army were supposed to disband and go into lawful businesses. However, as Donald Goddard (1978: 44) points out, "They had no lawful business." Elements of these exile groups (they often overlapped) began to enter the cocaine business. At first, they imported only enough cocaine to satisfy members of their own community, but by the mid-1960s, the market had expanded way beyond the Cuban community, and so they began to import the substance in greater quantities.

Until the early 1970s, the importation of marijuana and cocaine into the United States was largely a Cuban operation, although the suppliers were Colombians. During the second half of the 1960s, Colombians began emigrating to the United States in numbers sufficient to establish communities in Miami, Chicago, Los Angeles, and New York. Many were illegal immigrants who entered the United States through the Bahamas, carrying false documents such as phony Puerto Rican birth certificates and forged immigration papers of high quality.

The Colombian traffickers became highly organized both in the United States and at home. By 1973, independent foreign nationals could no longer "deal drugs" in Colombia. In 1976, the Colombians became dissatisfied with their Cuban agents in the United States, who were reportedly making most of the profits and shortchanging the Colombians. Enforcers, often young men from Colombia's version of the "Wild West," the Guajira Peninsula, or from Barrio Antioquia, the slums of Medellín, were sent in and systematically executed Cubans in Miami and New York. By 1978, Cubans remaining in the cocaine business had became subordinate to the Colombians. Then the cocaine wars began between rival Colombian gangs, bringing terror to South Florida.

COLOMBIA

Control of most of the world's cocaine industry remains in the hands of Colombian organizations. A nation of about 26 million, Colombia is the only South American country with both Pacific and Caribbean coastlines. It is a nation that has been torn by political strife, with civil wars in 1902 and 1948. In 1948 the leftist mayor of Bogotá was assassinated in the street before thousands of his supporters. The assassin was immediately lynched. Three days of rioting ensued, setting the stage for a civil war. *La Violencia*, as the civil war of 1948–1958 is known, cost the lives of about 300,000 persons (Riding 1987a). It ended when the Liberals and the Conservatives formed the National Front, but several Marxist insurgencies continued to threaten the stability of the central government. Not only was murder frequent, but the methods used were also often sadistic, such as the *corte de corbata*—the infamous "Colombian necktie"—in which the throat is cut longitudinally and the tongue pulled through to hang like a tie. Another practice, *no dejar la semilla* (don't leave the seed), includes the castration of male victims and the execution of women and children (Wolfgang and Ferracuti 1967): "In Colombia, it wasn't enough to hurt or even kill your enemy; there was a ritual to be observed." Rape had to be performed before family members: "And before you killed a man, you first made him beg, scream, and gag . . . or first you killed those he most loved before his eyes. To amplify fear, victims were horribly mutilated and left on display. . . . Children were killed not by accident but slowly, with pleasure" (Bowden 2002: 14).

In Colombia, drug traffickers exemplify a lack of belief in the legitimacy of the country's political and economic institutions: "Breaking the law—any law—is justified, and not just for the usual economic reasons that criminals favor. For traffickers, the law, law-enforcement officials, U.S. drug operatives, and drug-control organizations all represent the traditional elite, international imperialism, or other international competitive economic interests, none of which has any historical moral standing in their eyes. Therefore, moralistic arguments about restraining violent behavior do not capture these people's attention . . . [and allow] traffickers to garner enthusiastic support in some areas" (Tullis 1995: 66).

"At the root of Colombia's easy violence is an extraordinary indifference toward death" (Romoli 1941: 37). The homicide rate is eight times higher than that of the United States. Murder is the leading cause of death for Colombian males aged 15 to 44 (Schemo 1997a). The country has the highest child murder rates in the world—street children kill one another, and hundreds are murdered by vigilante groups as part of their campaign of "social cleansing" (Luft 1995a).

In this sociopolitical atmosphere, bandits have roamed freely, engaging in a combination of brigandage, terrorism, and revolution. In the northern cities of Barranquilla and Santa Marta and in La Guajira, smuggling (*contrabandista*) groups have operated for decades. Bandits, *contrabandistas*, and Guajiran Indians, often backed and financed by businessmen in Bogotá, emerged as crime Families, or *narcomafia*. Members are often related by blood, marriage, or *compadrazgo* (fictional kinship), and in many important respects the core groups resemble those of the Sicilian Mafia. Colombian groups are sometimes headed by women. In a country where drug barons act as a state within a state, dozens of well-armed paramilitary groups "ply their murderous trade in the cities and countryside, sometimes selling themselves to the highest bidder as outmanned and intimidated judges and government officials feel helpless to stop them" (de Lama 1988b: 5; Duzán 1994). These paramilitaries are sometimes allied with—sometimes fighting against—the drug traffickers, and they receive financial backing from wealthy landowners.

Colombian Drug Trafficking

The Colombians have been able to control the cocaine market for a number of reasons. The President's Commission on Organized Crime (1986c: 78–79) notes that "Colombia is well-positioned both to receive coca from Peru and Bolivia and to export the processed drug to the United States by air or by sea." (See Figure 8.1.) And "the country's vast central forests effectively conceal clandestine processing laboratories and air strips, which facilitate the traffic." The Colombians "have a momentum by benefit of their early involvement in the cocaine trade. And, there is a Colombian reputation for violence that serves to maintain discipline and intimidate would-be competitors" (PCOC 1986c: 78–79). The propensity to use violence led to domination of potential Bolivian and Peruvian rivals in the cocaine business. It permitted Colombian cartels to face down attempts at intimidation by other criminal organizations. On several occasions, the Sicilian Mafia tried to acquire the monopoly of the European cocaine market, challenging the Colombians with the threat to kill their independent couriers. That Colombian cocaine couriers continue to pour into Italy "is good enough proof of the fact that the Mafia received a negative answer to its demands" (Rey and Savona 1993: 75).[2]

The economic modernization of Colombia failed to bring about a corresponding respect for government. Delegitimization of government and *La Violencia* "left legacies which have worked to permit, if not encourage, the development of the cocaine industry" (Thoumi 1995: 84). Delegitimization spurred the development of smuggling, particularly the export of products out of Colombia and into Venezuela and Ecuador—cattle, emeralds, coffee—providing experience in the contraband trade and money laundering: "Aside from their disdain for Colombian institutions and their long criminal records, Colombian traffickers share other characteristics. They appear to be great believers in fate and providence and seem unmoved by normal considerations of personal danger. It is a perspective unaltered by normal law-enforcement efforts and one that makes dealing with or trying to control them such a dangerous enterprise" (Tullis 1995: 67). Speculative capitalism and a focus on very high short-term profits—a feature of Colombia's financial elite—provided the

---

[2] For an insider's look at the relationship between the Medellín cartel and the Sicilian Mafia, see Gately and Fernandez (1994).

FIGURE 8.1   *Latin America and Colombia, Center of the World's Cocaine Trafficking*

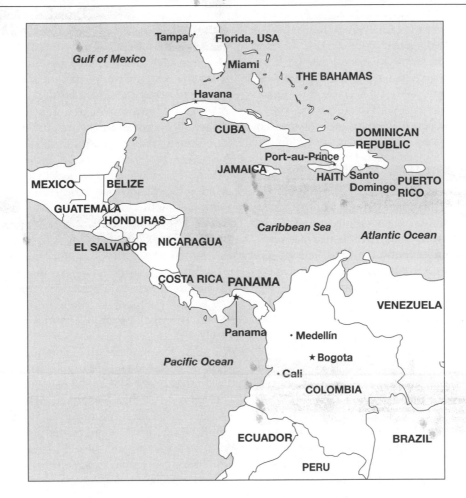

resources for the development of a cocaine industry (Thoumi 1995).

Colombia is a relatively large country, and many regions have only a weak federal presence: "While Colombian authorities built suburbs and major highways between cities, they ignored vast sections of the country; much of rural Colombia is isolated by hilly, trackless terrain" (Duzán 1994: 63). Three steep Andean ranges run the length of Colombia, and impenetrable jungle covers the South: "The government didn't lose control of this half of Colombia; it never had it" (Robinson 1998a: 39). The vacuum left by the central government has proved ideal for coca cultivation and co-

caine manufacture because it left areas where only local officials had to be bribed, a cheaper and less risky action (Thoumi 1995).

In the remote jungle areas where coca is cultivated, there are powerful Marxist guerrilla forces protecting the crops and levying taxes on the drug business. They have been effective against Colombia's mostly poorly trained and motivated conscript military (Robinson 1998b). And members of the Colombian military, often those trained by the United States, have been involved in widespread human rights abuses that often generate support for the rebels and drug traffickers (Schemo and Golden 1998). Attempts to eradicate the crop have encountered stiff opposition from the subsistence farmers, for whom coca is an economic lifeline ("Anti-Drug Efforts Encounter Resistance in Colombia" 1995). At the end of 1998, in an effort to advance peace negotiations with FARC (Revolutionary Armed Forces of Colombia) guerrillas, the Colombian government evacuated its security forces from a swath of Colombia the size of Switzerland (Schemo 1999). In 2002, frustrated by the lack of progress in peace talks, the Colombian armed forces invaded the rebel zone.

The major Colombian trafficking organizations are structured to control each intermediate step required in processing and exporting cocaine. An organization contains various sections, each with a separate function, such as manufacturing, transportation, distribution, finance, and security. This bureaucratic structure not only promotes greater efficiency but also serves to protect the organization: "Few members of one section are aware of the others involved, and the loss of one member or even a whole section does not threaten the stability of the entire organization" (PCOC 1984a: 562). In fact, at the lower levels of organization there are many workers who move between one organization and another, and are often unaware of which organization they are working for at any given time. At the highest levels, members are well insulated from the physical operations of their organizations: "The money generated by the wholesale cocaine transaction is maintained for the organization by financial experts familiar with international banking and investing drug profits, and for assuring that a portion of the drug profit is returned to Colombia for reinvestment in the organization's cocaine enterprise. The cartel's own financial experts are supported by a complement of bankers, lawyers and other professionals in the United States, who play a crucial role in facilitating these transactions" (PCOC 1986c: 82). (See Figure 8.2.)

In the United States, cocaine cartel representatives act as brokers to coordinate deliveries, usually 100 kilos at a time, to the various drug networks, franchising others, particularly Dominican organizations (discussed later), and, to a lesser de-

gree, Jamaican posses (discussed in Chapter 6) to distribute drugs. Colombian cocaine distribution networks are informally structured and operate in a fluid, transactional manner. Often, a network will develop solely to distribute a single shipment of cocaine. The network may operate from six months to one year and then dissolve. Although structurally independent of the cartels, these distribution networks are symbiotic and in regular contact with their cartel sources: "While the main organizers are hand-picked by the Colombian traffickers, individual members of the same network seldom know one another and usually deal with one another on a single occasion. Each drug transaction is conducted separately and each part of the network is compartmentalized. Inventories are stored in hidden locations. After raids or arrests, the cartels conduct internal investigations to assure that their employees were loyal, security measures were followed, and lessons were learned to improve the operation" (Comptroller General 1989: 14).

The sheer volume of Colombian drug transactions makes them vulnerable to sophisticated law enforcement efforts: "While most drug traffickers conduct financial transactions in cash, the volume of business conducted by the Colombian traffickers requires sophisticated record-keeping to track expenses and sales. Modern methods of monitoring inventories and deliveries are used; advanced communication centers arrange for the arrival of smuggled drugs, their distribution, the movement of cash proceeds, and other logistical matters. Distributors are instructed to keep accurate records, and many use facsimile machines to keep track of sales and to relay information to Colombia" (Comptroller General 1989: 19). However, infiltrating a Colombian group is nearly impossible. A prospective wholesale buyer must establish his bona fides at an audience with top management in Colombia: "If he is approved, he is not required to pay cash up front. He will send the cartel payment after he resells the drugs to middlemen. The wholesale buyer must put up collateral, cash or deeds to real property, as insurance if he is caught. He must also provide human collateral in

FIGURE 8.2   *Compartmentalized Colombian Drug Organization*

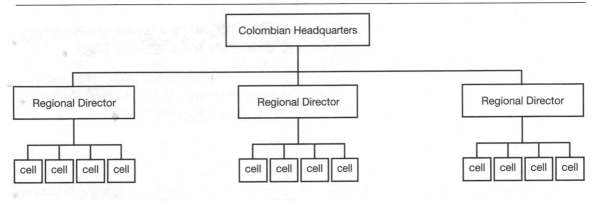

Colombian Headquarters: The drug lord oversees operations through designates who are responsible for regional directors. He will also have a staff responsible for Colombian operations, including production, transportation, distribution, finances, and enforcement.

Regional Director: Responsible for overall operations of the several cells within a region, the regional director reports via cell phone, fax, or e-mail to a designate in Colombia. The regional director has discretion in the day-to-day operations, but ultimate authority rests with the leadership in Colombia.

Cells: Compartmentalization involves cells of 10 or more members, each operating independently—members of one cell typically do not know members of other cells. Upper echelon and management levels of these cells are normally composed of family members or longtime close associates who can be trusted because their family members remain in Colombia as hostages to the cell members' good behavior. Operating within a geographic area, each cell specializes in a particular facet of the drug business, such as transport, storage, wholesale distribution, or money laundering. The head of each cell reports directly to a regional director.

Source: Based on Ledwith (2000) and Constantine (1999b).

the form of his family in Colombia, who will pay with their lives if he ever turns informer" (Shannon 1991: 32). The most notorious of the Colombian cartels are those of Medellín and Cali.

The Medellín Cartel

Medellín, an Andean industrial and tourist city of about 1.5 million persons in the province of Antioquia, has been the home of some of Colombia's most notorious drug traffickers. Antioquia and neighboring provinces bore the brunt of the civil war violence of 1948–1958. Long before cocaine emerged as an important commodity, Medellín had a long-standing reputation for smuggling and as a school for pickpockets. It is known as a place where assassins are trained in such techniques as

the *asesino de la moto:* a passenger on a motorbike uses an automatic weapon—usually a .45 caliber machine pistol. The murder rate in Medellín is nearly nine times that of New York City. It is virtually free of any American diplomatic personnel. The city served as the headquarters for drug-trafficking organizations known in Colombia as *Los Grandes Mafiosos* and in the United States as the Medellín Cartel, whose founders include Pablo Escobar, the Ochoa clan, and Carlos Lehder-Rivas.

Lehder-Rivas was indicted in 1981 by a Jacksonville, Florida, federal grand jury for drug trafficking and income tax evasion, and in 1983 the United States requested his extradition. Lehder-Rivas went underground, emerging back in Medellín denouncing the United States for imperialism. He threatened to join forces with the Marxist revolutionary group known as M–19. In a 1987 shootout, Lehder-Rivas was arrested by Colombian authorities and extradited to the United States. The following year, Lehder-Rivas was convicted of shipping 3.3 tons of cocaine to Florida and Georgia in 1979 and 1980, and sentenced to life without parole. In 1991 he appeared as a U.S. government witness in the trial of General Manuel Noriega, who, he stated, provided enormous help—and sometimes double-crossed—the cartel. Lehder-Rivas alleged that Noriega had sold the cartel an arsenal of Uzi submachine guns as well as photographs and addresses of DEA agents but had also seized their cocaine and, after being praised by the DEA, sold it back to the traffickers (Rohter 1991a).

Pablo Escobar   The most notorious member of the cartel was born in 1949; his father was a farmer, his mother a schoolteacher. Pablo Escobar (Gaviria) received a high school education but was too poor to attend college. He embarked upon a career in petty crime, later rising to bodyguard-enforcer for an electronics smuggler. By 1976, Escobar headed a small group of "mules" who transported raw coca paste and base from the south into Colombia, where it was processed into cocaine. In that year, he was arrested with five other men and charged with attempted bribery—they had attempted to smuggle a 39-pound shipment of cocaine inside a spare tire. After three months, the case was dropped on a technicality. The records of the case subsequently disappeared, and the two officers who had arrested Escobar were murdered.

As the market for cocaine in the United States increased dramatically, Escobar invested much of his profits in a fleet of planes. He was now able to deal directly with source countries (Peru and Bolivia) for his coca paste and coca base and to ship the finished cocaine directly to the United States. As his wealth grew, his lifestyle changed accordingly. Escobar purchased several large ranches, houses, and apartments in and around Medellín, and he invested in legitimate businesses. In 1980 he purchased a $762,500 Miami Beach mansion and, the following year, the King's Harbor Apart-

ments in Plantation, north of Miami, for more than $8 million.

In 1982, Escobar was elected as an alternate Colombian representative in Envigado, a *barrio* outside Medellín. There he cultivated a Robin Hood image, building 500 small houses for slum squatters and financing the construction of 80 soccer fields for the young men. His newspaper, *Medellín Civico*, was a public relations piece that promoted Escobar as an up-from-the-slums statesman. As a representative, he enjoyed immunity from arrest, until this was removed by the government of Colombia and a warrant was issued for his arrest for having smuggled an assortment of African wildlife into the country for his own personal zoo (Eddy, Sabogal, and Walden 1988; Gugliotta and Leen 1989). Escobar shared a trait with Al Capone and John Gotti—he enjoyed being in the public spotlight, even hiring publicists to advance his image (Bowden 2001).

In 1984 the minister of justice responsible for a major seizure of Medellín cocaine labs was murdered, creating a public backlash against the Medellín cartel. This was followed by the murder of more than 30 judges who had been considering extradition requests from the United States for cartel members. In a communiqué from the "Extradictables" printed in Colombian newspapers, Escobar warned anyone who supported extradition to the United States. With his high public profile, Escobar bore the brunt of a campaign to bring cartel members to justice. In an effort to mollify the police, he tipped them off to the whereabouts of Carlos Lehder-Rivas (Bowden 2001). But the pressure continued, and Escobar's carefully crafted public persona was abandoned for a more instinctive reaction: he orchestrated a campaign of increasing terror. In 1989 his men executed the favored candidate for president of Colombia because he had pledged to bring the *narcotraficantes* to justice. Three months later, in an effort to kill his successor, Escobar had a bomb planted on an Avianca airliner—110 passengers died when the plane was blown out of the sky.

In response to the intensive police campaign to apprehend him, Escobar offered a bounty of $4,200 for each police officer killed. In the following month, 42 police officers were murdered (Brooke 1990). In 1990, some 250 police officers were murdered. The police responded by killing dozens of major traffickers and their enforcers as well as many innocent civilians (Marx 1991). Escobar operatives were tortured with electric shocks and thrown out of helicopters (Bowden 2001).

In 1990, Escobar began indicating that he would surrender. In an effort to dictate the terms of the surrender, he went on a bombing campaign that terrified the public, and his men kidnapped ten journalists—two were eventually killed (see Márquez [1997] for an intimate look at these kidnappings). In 1991, ten hours after the constitutional assembly voted to ban extraditions, Pablo Escobar, then 41, surrendered to authorities. He was accompanied by a popular television priest who had helped negotiate the surrender, and placed in a specially built jail overlooking his hometown of Envigado. It was in Envigado that Escobar assisted in the construction of a hospital and sports stadium and endeared himself to the people with jobs and lavish gifts.

The jail was a converted mountaintop ranch with many amenities—a Jacuzzi, waterbed, bar, wood-burning fireplace, sophisticated electronic equipment that included a computer with a modem, 60-inch television set, and cellular telephone. The guards were assigned by Envigado's mayor, and several aides to Escobar also surrendered to provide him with companionship and security while he awaited further legal action. He also enjoyed female companionship. On July 22, 1992, the Colombian government attempted to transfer Escobar to a more secure prison, a site where he would (in theory, at least) be unable to continue overseeing the drug trade. The result was a furious gunfight during which Escobar and nine of his aides escaped.

After his escape, the police began tracking and killing his men; Escobar responded by killing police officers. Early in 1993, bombs began destroying property linked to Escobar, and the bodies of his associates began turning up in Bogatá and Medellín—the work of two extended families whose members, former Escobar associates, had been killed by the drug lord. They called them-

Pablo Escobar, the most notorious member of the Medellín drug cartel, was killed in a rooftop shootout with Colombian police and soldiers in December, 1992.

selves *Los PEPES*, an acronym in Spanish for "People Persecuted by Pablo Escobar." Information targeting the victims of *Los PEPES* reportedly came from Colombian law enforcement who were privy to the results of high-tech monitoring by American operatives in Colombia—monitoring that eventually led to Escobar himself (Brooke 1993; Bowden 2001). On December 2, 1993, the drug lord was killed in a rooftop shootout with police and soldiers while attempting to escape "capture"—as Escobar probably realized, there was no chance he would be taken alive. He was making a cellular call to his family when his whereabouts were determined by the use of telephone tracking equipment contributed by the United

States (Brooke 1992a, 1992b; Treaster 1991c; Christian 1992; for a detailed look at the hunt for Escobar, see Bowden [2001]).

The Ochoa Family   The class and social backgrounds of the Ochoa clan differ from that of their Medellín colleagues. The *paterfamilias* of the Ochoa clan, Fabio Ochoa Restrepo, owns a country estate with herds of cattle and horses, *La Finca de la Loma* ("The Ranch on the Hill"), in Medellín. Nearby is a bullring in which he has invested; his family business is inextricably tied to bullfighting. Don Fabio, as he is known locally, heads a wealthy and close-knit clan of old-line cattle breeders and landowners. They claim to have descended from the second wave of settlers to Colombia from the Basque region of Spain who founded Medellin in 1616. These Spaniards enslaved and annihilated the native Indians they found.

During the early 1970s, Fabio Ochoa experienced financial difficulties that forced him to sell off some horses in Venezuela. At the time, his middle son, Jorge Ochoa (Vasquez), lived in Miami, where he headed an import–export firm that imported cocaine for Jorge's uncle, Fabio Restrepo Ochoa. A narrow escape from the DEA caused Jorge to flee to Medellín, where he informed his father, Don Fabio, of the demand for cocaine in the United States (Eddy, Sabogal, and Walden 1988). Fabio Restrepo Ochoa was mysteriously murdered in Miami shortly after his nephew returned to Colombia (Gugliotta and Leen 1989).

Jorge Ochoa, born in 1949, owns large tracts of land in Medellín, where he raises horses for bullfighting. He also owns a horse-breeding farm near Bogota and a bullfighting arena near Cartagena. He was a frequent traveler to Panama, where his assets are in secret accounts, to Brazil, where he has important investments, and to Spain. In 1984, Jorge Ochoa and his associate Rodriguez Orejuela, of the Cali cartel, were arrested while living under assumed names in Spain; they were reportedly setting up a Colombian cocaine network in Europe. After two years in a Spanish prison awaiting extradition to the United States, they were instead extradited to Colombia. Meanwhile, Spain emerged as a major consumer and transshipment point for cocaine.

In Colombia, Jorge Ochoa was convicted of illegally importing bulls—it turned out that they had hoof-and-mouth disease and had to be destroyed. Although serious drug charges and a U.S. extradition request were outstanding, Ochoa was released pending appeal. While the judge who released Ochoa lost his job, he remains alive and is rumored to be quite wealthy. The Colombian extradition treaty with the United States was subsequently declared unconstitutional.

In response to the release of Jorge Ochoa, the U.S. Customs Service increased inspections of all cargo, passenger luggage, and passengers arriving from Colombia. However, these reprisals have caused strong feelings of nationalism and generated anti-U.S. sentiment that is exploited by Colombian left-wing political groups, who often denounce the United States as "imperialistic." Colombian officials chide the United States for not providing enough material support for Colombian efforts against the *narcotraficantes* and for not doing enough about the demand for cocaine in the United States.

In 1981, Lehder-Rivas was kidnapped. He escaped, but not before being wounded by the Marxist revolutionary group 19th of April, known as M–19 (Gugliotta and Leen 1989). That same month, M–19 kidnapped Jorge Ochoa's 28-year-old sister, Marta Nieves, from the campus of the University of Antioquia in Medellín and demanded a ransom of $1 million. In response, the Ochoa family called a meeting of traffickers—223 attended. Leaflets later announced that each had contributed to a common fund to establish a special enforcement section, *Muerte a Secuestradores* ("Death to the Kidnappers"—MAS), for the "immediate execution of all those involved in kidnappings." The leaflet warned that those who escaped would simply leave their families and friends liable for retribution. Soon afterward, dozens of persons believed connected to M–19 were tortured and murdered (Kerr 1988b): "Ten M–19 guerrillas were kidnapped and tortured, and two of them—who were on the Colombian army's 'most wanted' list—were handed over to the military commanders amidst widespread publicity. In Medellín, MAS invaded homes and shot suspected guerrillas—but also trade unionists, old ladies, young children, horses, pigs, and chickens. Mere sympathizers of M–19 were abducted from the university, tortured, and, if they were lucky, sent home in their underwear. After a few weeks of this . . . Marta Nieves was released unharmed"[3] (Eddy, Sabogal, and Walden 1988: 289).

During the 1980s, conflict between leftist guerrillas and the *narcotraficantes* intensified as the drug barons purchased huge tracts of land, an estimated 2.5 million fertile acres, and emerged as a powerful political force in the countryside, where they are backed by private armies of gunmen (Riding 1987b). Families displaced by this upheaval have drifted into coca and poppy cultivation (Schemo 1998). For the traffickers, a Marxist government would bring an end to their lucrative business, if not their lives. In fact, guerilla activity, particularly extortion, has left many cattlemen eager to sell their ranches, often to the *narcotraficantes,* who are the most willing buyers and whose private armies are able to keep the guerrillas at bay (Weisman 1989). The rancher-traffickers invested their resources in organized peasant bands that were turned into fighting units. A U.S. congressional committee revealed that the private armies had been trained by British and Israeli mercenaries under the guise of helping Colombian ranchers fend off leftist guerrillas.

While Colombian officials were busy with Pablo Escobar, Jorge Ochoa responded to a government offer of amnesty for major traffickers. He surrendered, confessed, and was sentenced to eight years. In 1996, after serving five and one-half years, the Ochoa brothers, Jorge, Fabio, and David, were released from prison for "good behavior." They were whisked away in a bulletproof

Mercedes-Benz, rich men who continue to own farms and other valuable properties. The United States protested their release, but an extradition law passed at the end of 1997 does not affect any prior cases. In 1999, Fabio Ochoa was one of 31 persons arrested in Colombia for drug trafficking and money laundering. In 2001, Colombia's Supreme Court ordered him extradited to the United States, and he arrived in Miami shortly afterward (Leitsinger 2001).

The Cali Cartel

The drug boom inspired a competing cartel in Cali, a city of 1.5 million persons located about 250 miles south of Medellín. It is second only to Spain in the number of Spanish-language books it publishes each year, and advanced printing technology has also made the city a center of counterfeiting, mostly of U.S. currency (Brooke 1991a). The Cali cartel refers to a loose alliance of five major trafficking groups with preeminence shared by the kinship/crime families of Gilberto Rodriguez Orejuela ("the Chess Player"), his brother Miguel, and José Santacruz Londono ("Don Chepe") (*Intelligence Bulletin Colombia* 1995). Gilberto Orejuela and one of his brothers, an attorney, own several banks, a national chain of 150 drugstores, television stations, and a leading soccer team (Treaster 1989a; Lupsha 1990). His seven children have been educated at U.S. and European universities (Moody 1991). He controls taxi companies whose 1,500 drivers provide intelligence information for the traffickers (Brooke 1995c). Santacruz Londono was trained as an engineer. When he was refused membership in a local club, Londono had a replica built in an exclusive suburban neighborhood (Brooke 1991b).

In 1991 the Orejuela brothers and 42 others were indicted in the United States for allegedly laundering $65 million per year in drug profits from Miami, New York, and Los Angeles. In 1995, Gilberto was apprehended in a secret compartment at a luxurious house in Cali. Miguel was arrested two months later. The brothers confessed to drug trafficking in order to secure leniency. In

---

[3]In 1990, M–19 disarmed its fighters and formed a political party, whose leader was appointed the Colombian minister of health. However, a small group of members returned to insurgency. Along with three other major revolutionary groups, they remain Latin America's longest and largest insurgency (Brooke 1995d).

1997, Miguel and Gilberto received sentences of 9 and 10 years, respectively; they are eligible for a 50-percent reduction in their sentences for good behavior. The Orejuela clan owns many legitimate businesses—a supermarket chain, for example—that are run by the adult children of Miguel and Gilberto (who are alleged to be continuing their drug operations from prison). In 1995, Santacruz Londono was indicted in the United States and subsequently arrested in Colombia, only to slip out of a maximum-security prison in 1996. Two months later, he was killed in a shootout with police.

Members of the Cali cartel favored bribery over violence—cartel members were taped talking about millions of dollars in contributions to the successful presidential bid of Ernesto Samper[4] in 1994. They took a percentage of the profits from shipments by smaller organizations and, in return, provided transportation, distribution, and enforcement services. Despite their reputation for preferring diplomacy, enforcement services could be quite violent—suspected informants were immersed in barrels of acid. The cartel's chief of enforcement, known as "the Scorpion," launched a year-long reign of terror against unionists and guerrilla sympathizers who threatened his way of life as newly landed gentry[5]—in 1991, 107 persons were tortured and killed, most dismembered with chain saws (Brooke 1995a).

Organized in a patriarchal manner, the Cali cartel stressed discipline and loyalty. Leaders operated compartmentalized organizations (see Figure 8.2) so that the loss of any one section does not destroy the enterprise. In Cali, there was a chief executive officer whose executives were responsible for acquisition, production, transportation, sales, finance, and enforcement (Shannon 1991). There were also dozens of overseas branches.

Cali operations in the United States were headquartered in the Elmhurst–Jackson Heights area of Queens, New York, home to about 30,000 Colombians, a section known as "Little Colombia" because of the numerous ethnic restaurants and businesses owned by Colombians.[6] Close to LaGuardia Airport and within easy distance of Kennedy Airport, the neighborhood provides cover and financial outlets for the group's activities. The neighborhood houses an excess of travel agencies and wire services that help with the movement of drug money to Colombia—very little is invested in legitimate businesses in the United States (Fisher 1993).

In 1995, as a result of arrests of Cali cartel leaders, the price of cocaine in New York increased dramatically at both the wholesale and retail levels (Krauss 1995). The tensions created by the arrests in Colombia also led to an increase in drug-business-related murders in Queens, believed caused by an eroding of organizational discipline due to a leadership vacuum (Brooke 1995b). The 1995 crackdown on the Cali cartel also had a noticeable impact on the Colombian economy—it helped fuel a devaluation of the peso as U.S. dollars became scarce ("Drug Crackdown Said to Sap Colombia's Economy" 1995). For Cali, successful efforts against the cartel led to a doubling of unemployment to 15 percent and a significant downturn in the city's economy (Schemo 1996).

The Evolution of the Colombian Drug Business

Government success against the Medellín and Cali cartels has caused a balkanization of the cocaine trade in Colombia. A multiplicity of smaller organizations is filling the vacuum, and they maintain lower profiles in Colombia and the United States than did their cartel predecessors. And while the

---

[4]In 1996 the Clinton administration revoked Samper's entry visa to visit the United States. Several officials of the Samper campaign team have been sentenced to imprisonment for taking money from the drug traffickers. In 1998 the man who had accused Samper of accepting drug money, Andrés Pastrana, was elected president—he defeated the candidate who had defended Samper.

[5]Drug traffickers have become Colombia's largest landowners.

[6]It was in Jackson Heights that in 1992, a Colombian journalist who had written articles about the Cali cartel was shot to death. The gunman, wearing a hooded sweater, walked calmly into a restaurant and fired two shots from a 9-millimeter pistol into the brain of Manual de Dios Unanue. The gunman, 16 years old at the time, was subsequently convicted and sentenced to life imprisonment.

fragmentation reduces efficiency, combating this multiplicity requires even more personnel and greater intelligence-gathering efforts.

Independent traffickers who worked in the shadows of the major cartels have joined forces, and the cycle continues (NNICC 1998). In the absence of powerful drug lords, the drug trade has become more decentralized. Power swiftly passed to experienced traffickers who are now seizing opportunities to increase their own share of the drug trade. These enterprising traffickers come primarily from two areas: the northern Valle del Cauca region, of which Cali is the capital city, located on Colombia's southeast coast, and the Caribbean North Coast. The Drug Enforcement Administration anticipates that Colombia-based cocaine trafficking organizations will remain the dominant players in the international cocaine trade well into the twenty-first century. They continue to control the supply of cocaine at its source, have a firm grip on Caribbean smuggling routes, and dominate the wholesale cocaine markets in the eastern United States and in Europe. They are also aggressively increasing their share of the U.S. heroin market.

Colombia began to emerge as a poppy grower during the late 1980s; by 1999, Colombians had become major heroin wholesalers. They often sell cocaine and heroin to wholesalers as part of a package deal (Navarro 1995). However, it appears that the major cocaine traffickers have not been involved in the heroin business, which is run by small, independent organizations (Schemo 1997b). They typically use "swallowers" to get the drug into the United States: poor Colombian women are recruited to swallow heroin packed into the cut-off fingers of surgical gloves. The $10,000 salary entails risks to life (the packets will disintegrate, causing a massive overdose if she does not arrive at her destination quickly enough) and liberty—being intercepted by customs officers using drug-sniffing dogs and body scanners (Wren 1999a).

MEXICO

Mexico is a nation of about 91 million persons, 75 percent of whom live in urban areas. Indepen-dence from Spanish rule in 1821 was followed by a series of revolutions, rigged elections, and general turmoil. There was a war with the United States in 1848 and a French invasion and occupation from 1863 to 1867. In still another violent overthrow, Porfirio Diaz came to power in 1876 and ruled Mexico for 35 years. Out of the revolution that ousted Diaz emerged Mexico's dominant political party, known as the PRI (rhymes with free)—*Partido Revolucionario Institucional.*

In the Mexican culture, "people are not treated alike; strangers, those outside the circle of family and close friends, are not wholly to be trusted. One is much safer giving one's confidence only to friends of long standing or family members. Thus, as in Southern Italy [see Chapter 7], societal focus is on the interests of the immediate and extended family, not the wider interests of a more impersonal societal good" (Shelley 2001). This effect is visible in Mexican political life, where each political leader has his intimate circle of contacts, relatives, and friends from childhood, "whom he protects and appoints to key positions as he moves up the career hierarchy. These *camarillas*, or cliques of friends, are in some ways the basic unit of Mexican politics" (Needler 1995: 51). Patron–client relationships, political patronage, and endemic corruption provide the backdrop against which Mexican organized crime is to be understood.

For decades after its founding, the PRI "was a tool of successive presidents using authoritarian methods to insure one-party rule" (Dillon 1999b: 1). The police forces—federal, state, and local—that evolved out of this atmosphere were deployed not to protect but to control the population. Furthermore, police officers have been poorly paid, and it is understood that they can supplement their pittance with bribes as long as they remain loyal to the government (Dillon 1996e). Using tactics reminiscent of the political machines discussed in Chapter 3, the PRI ruled Mexico for more than 70 years without any strong opposition, during which corruption became endemic. When Carlos Salinas became president in 1988, his brother Raúl was given a low-profile government post from which he reportedly played a central role in protecting

Corruption in Mexico

"For nearly a decade, American officials have been haunted by the spectacle of Mexican officials' be-ing linked to illicit activities soon after they are embraced in Washington" (Golden 1999b: 10).

the flow of drugs from Mexico into the United States. This enabled him to deposit more than $130 million in Swiss bank accounts (Golden 1998c, 1998d). In 1999, Rául Salinos was sentenced to 50 years for masterminding the assassination of a rival politician. In 1998, it was revealed that an elite Mexican drug enforcement unit trained by the Federal Bureau of Investigation and Drug Enforcement Administration had been compromised by members with ties to drug traffickers (Golden 1998b).

With the assistance of foreign advisors, many of whom also advised the former Soviet Union, in the 1990s Mexico embarked on an ambitious program of privatization. As in Russia, this was done in the absence of a free and vigorous press in a system that lacked grounding in the rule of law. The lack of sufficient safeguards accompanying this economic transformation led to the acquisition of valuable assets—banks, communications, food sectors—by families whose source of capital was gambling and drugs, "thereby facilitating the infiltration of organized crime into the larger Mexican economy" (Shelley 2001: 218).

In 1997 an emerging opposition party that has been critical of the PRI-inspired corruption won control of the lower house of Congress. In 1999, in an effort to change its image, the PRI voted to hold a national primary to select its presidential candidates; previously, the sitting president was allowed to choose his successor. In 2000, in a major political upset, the PRI candidate for president was defeated by Vicente Fox of the National Action Party.

Nevertheless, Mexico is in an economic crisis, crime has skyrocketed, and the criminal justice system is in an advanced stage of deterioration. Corruption extends into the banking system: in 1998, in the culmination of a three-year sting operation,

U.S. authorities arrested more than 130 people in the largest drug-laundering case in American history. They included 22 bankers from 12 of Mexico's largest banking institutions—who had been lured into the United States—charged with laundering drug profits for the Cali cartel of Colombia (discussed earlier) and the Juárez cartel (discussed in following sections) of Mexico; $35 million, two tons of cocaine, and four tons of marijuana were seized as part of the operation (Van Natta, Jr., 1998).

Mexican Drug Trafficking

The popular culture of Mexico is infused with songs and *corridos* (ballads)—*narco-corridos*—glamorizing drug trafficking. Major *narcotraficantes* are celebrated, along with their subculture of violence (Edberg 2001). Many songs contain references to an outlaw code of behavior, and their music videos depict violence, including torture and the murder of police officers (Dillon 1999a).

In the early 1990s, Mexican criminal organizations struck a deal with the Colombians whose cocaine they were moving from Mexico into the United States on a contract basis: for every two kilograms of smuggled cocaine, the Mexicans would keep one kilogram as payment in kind (O'Brien and Greenburg 1996; Wren 1996). The Mexicans had attempted to convert Peruvian coca paste into cocaine in Mexico-based laboratories. However, the end product had the odor of kerosene, and the effort had to be abandoned in favor of buying the product from Colombians or acting as their shipping agents in return for half the load (McMahon 1995). Both sides benefited from the new arrangement. The Colombians had an abundance of cocaine, and the Mexicans had a distribution network in the United States that they had been using for heroin. This arrangement was aided by the North American Free Trade Act, which further opened the already porous borders with Mexico. The benefits to the Mexican traffickers were significant: profits increased 5 to 10 times. In 1998, officials in Chicago seized 2,800 pounds of cocaine and $5 million at a West Side produce company being used to store drugs from Mexico (O'Connor 1998). There was also a dramatic increase in payments to public officials to protect their lucrative business (Golden 1997a). As a consequence, Mexico traffickers control a substantial proportion of wholesale cocaine distribution throughout the western and midwestern United States. They also provide money-laundering services for Colombian clients and direct delivery to wholesale-level customers on behalf of the major Colombian-based cocaine groups (Marshall 2001).

In 1998, there was a resurgence of heavy smuggling from the Bahamas and a corresponding drop-off on the southwest border, an indication of Colombian concern that Mexicans are becoming their competitors in the cocaine business. Indeed, in 1997, 29 persons working for the Juárez cartel were arrested as they competed with Colombians over drug distribution in the northeastern United States (Wren 1997; Navarro 1998). With the weakening of the major Colombian cartels, particularly the one centered in Cali, Mexicans have formed direct links to coca leaf farmers and processing laboratories in Bolivia and Peru (P. Smith 1999).

The relationship with the Colombians also led to structural changes, with some Mexican drug groups modeling their organizations along Colombian lines—compartmentalized units operating independently of one another but controlled hierarchically (see Figure 8.2). The leading syndicates "are highly and efficiently organized. Often led by family members at the top, they involve hundreds of individuals with specialized roles—from security chiefs to hired guns to marketing agents, accountants, financial consultants, and money-laundering specialists. They make regular use of sophisticated technology, countersurveillance methods, and state-of-the-art communications devices" (P. Smith 1999: 198). Financial re-

wards and intimidation serve to maintain strong internal discipline. Although they may be big businesses, Mexican drug organizations remain family-run operations with a correspondingly high degree of personal trust (P. Smith 1999).

Mexican heroin smuggled into the United States is transported to metropolitan areas in the western and southwestern states with sizable Latino populations. Mexican heroin is also transported to primary markets in Chicago, Denver, and St. Louis. Attempts to find markets for black tar heroin in East Coast cities such as Boston and Atlanta have failed (Marshall 2001).

Better organization and an extensive drug portfolio have enabled Mexican organizations to diversify, dividing operations into heroin, cocaine, marijuana, and now methamphetamine units. Mexican involvement with methamphetamine apparently began when the Hells Angels turned to them in order to avoid the hazards posed by the drug's manufacture: it is explosive, the chemicals are caustic, inhalation can be fatal, and the strong odor can alert law enforcement. Eventually, the Mexicans improved on the methods learned from the bikers, and now it is the latter who typically buy for distribution from the Mexicans (Arax and Gorman 1995: 1): "Once the domain of outlaw biker gangs [discussed in Chapter 1], the nation's meth trade has been taken over by Mexican drug families in the rural belt from San Diego County to Redding. Operating from Sinaloa and other Mexican states deep inside Mexico, these families oversee teams of cookers dispatched to orchards, cotton fields, chicken ranches, and abandoned dairies north of the border."

Mexican national trafficking organizations now dominate wholesale methamphetamine trafficking, using large-scale laboratories based in Mexico and the western and southwestern United States. Outlaw motorcycle clubs are still active in methamphetamine production but do not produce the large quantities distributed by Mexican groups (Marshall 2001). Mexican-based methamphetamine trafficking organizations have ready access to the necessary precursor chemicals on the international market. These chemicals have fewer controls in Mexico and overseas than in the United

Mexican police examine confiscated drugs that were being smuggled across the border into the United States.

States. The Mexican-based organizations have capitalized on this advantage by producing huge quantities of high-purity methamphetamine in clandestine laboratories in both Mexico and southern California (Keefe 2001a). Rounding out the portfolio of Mexican criminal organizations is the smuggling of immigrants, especially young girls and women to work in brothels, particularly those catering to migrant workers (Shelley 2001).

The Amezcuas (Colima) Cartel

Methamphetamine provides Mexican organizations an opportunity for profit that does not have to shared with others, as does cocaine with Colombians. And the profits are substantial, usually a tenfold return on an investment (Arax and Gorman 1995). In 1998, Luis and José de Jesús Amezcua-

Contreras, leaders of Mexico's major methamphetamine organization based in Guadalajara and wanted in the United States for drug trafficking and murder, were arrested by Mexican authorities. They were transported to the same prison that holds their brother Adan (arrested in 1997). Among other properties, the brothers owned drugstores in Tijuana that were used in the importation of precursor chemicals to manufacture methamphetamines. These chemicals are shipped to gangs in California that operate methamphetamine labs (Constantine 1999c). José de Jesús was subsequently cleared of money-laundering charges in Mexico, and in 1999 a Mexican judge turned down a U.S. extradition request.

In less than ten years, their cartel grew from a low-level cocaine trafficking group to the most prolific methamphetamine and precursor chemi-

"The Independent Republic of Dope"

About 450 miles south of the U.S. border, in a remote corner of Sierra de Durango, armed Indians question strangers and demand photo identification. There are vast fields of marijuana farmed by Indians for drug cartels in Durango City that move the product by plane and mule train. Marijuana, the basis of the local economy, enriches the cartels and leaves little more than subsistence for the impoverished Indian population: a hidden sweatshop industry. Army patrols rarely enter the largely roadless region (Salopek 1998).

cal trafficking organization in North America (Labaton 1997; Dillon 1998a). While working with Colombian organizations, the Amezcuas learned the lessons of marketing and structuring the drug trade as an international business. They also learned from the mistakes made by other organizations, avoiding violent clashes for territory and markets. By 1992, the Amezcuas had established their own international chemical contacts in Switzerland, India, Germany, and the Czech Republic. With their drugstore fronting for the business, they were able to exploit the legitimate international chemical trade. They were traffickers in their own right and as such kept 100 percent of all profits, providing the freedom to expand their trade and territory. The success and longevity of the organization have been promoted by the group's insular structure. The brothers recruited relatives and longtime friends, who then recruited a second tier of operatives to engage in the dangerous cooking of methamphetamine, as well as the risky activity of smuggling either chemicals or methamphetamine into the United States (DEA press release, June 2, 1998).

The Herrera Family

For many years, trafficking in Mexican heroin was dominated by the Herrera Family, whose operations began shortly after World War II. From their first laboratory in Mexico, the Herreras shipped heroin to relatives who had moved to Chicago. Actually a cartel of six interrelated family groupings, the Herrera Family has been headed by the sometimes imprisoned Jaime ("Don Jaime") Herrera-Nevarez (born 1924 or 1927), a former Mexican state judicial police officer. (The judicial police are similar to the Canadian Royal Mounted Police in jurisdiction.) Headquartered in Durango, a city of about 200,000 in the state of Durango (with a population of about one million), the organization is estimated to have around 5,000 members, about 2,000 of whom are related by blood or marriage.

Since key members are tied by blood, marriage, or fictional kinship (godparenthood), the group has proven to be very difficult to infiltrate on both sides of the border. In the United States, the Family operates out of Chicago. From Chicago, Mexican heroin and marijuana are wholesaled to groups in New York, Philadelphia, Boston, Detroit, and Louisville. Organizational management is maintained by some two dozen executive-level directors and a vast array of field representatives in a number of American cities. The network is held together through the Herrera organization's U.S. headquarters in Chicago and through communications and trips back to the organization's headquarters in Durango. Don Jaime lives the life of a *padrone*, giving to the poor, befriending the rich, and playing godfather at weddings and baptisms: "In the village of Santiago Papasquiaro, where many of the opium farmers lived, the clan built the water system, installed streetlights, and created a town square. Three hospitals benefited from the clan's philanthropy" (Shannon 1988: 59). The Herreras did not buy off the power structure in Durango—they *are* the power structure.

By the 1980s, the Herrera Family had established cocaine contacts throughout Latin America. In fact, Colombians have now married into the Herrera Family. In 1985, federal judicial police

FIGURE 8.3   *Mexico and the Southwest United States*

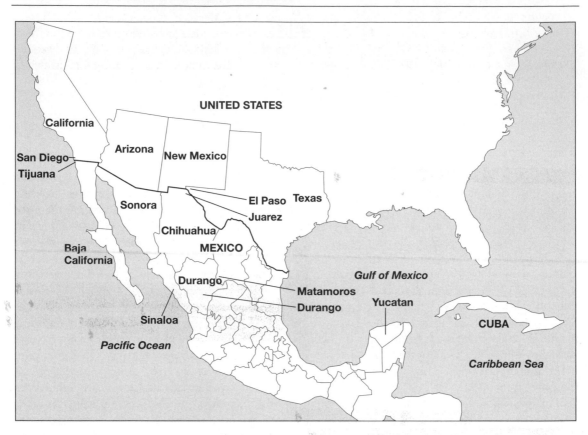

arrested Don Jaime's son for cocaine trafficking. His case was subsequently transferred from Mexico City to Durango, where he was ordered released by a local judge for lack of evidence. In that same year, 135 persons constituting eight separate Herrera-related distribution rings were indicted in Chicago. By 1987, the Herrera Family was reeling under a continuing federal investigation in the Chicago area that resulted in more than 80 convictions, and dozens more became fugitives. By the end of 1988, however, those who had been convicted and those who were fugitives had been replaced. Herrera Family operations in both heroin and cocaine surged, but other drug chieftains were coming to the fore.

By 1995, it became apparent that Mexican drug trafficking was dominated by about a half-dozen *padrones* (bosses), leaders of cartels that were sometimes allied, sometimes in competition, and sometimes in violent conflict, although gun battles have been infrequent. They are often referred to by their geographic location, such as the "Gulf cartel." While they operate out of discrete sites in Mexico, their stature "comes not from controlling territory so much as from the international scope of their contacts and their ability to operate across Mexico with Government protection" (Golden 1995b: 8). Thus, the leader of the infamous Juárez cartel in the state of Chihuahua, Amado Carrillo-Fuentes, resided in Culiacan, in the neighboring state of Sinaloa, which is actually the home of another cartel by that name. We will examine the most prominent of the Mexican drug cartels. (See Figure 8.3.)

The Sinaloa Cartel

Sinaloa is an agricultural state that, with U.S. encouragement, grew poppies for morphine during World War II. Drug dealers are legendary in the state, where they are memorialized in ballads. In 1989 the entire police department of Culiacan, a city of 700,000 and the capital of Sinaloa, was taken into custody by the Mexican army. Also arrested was the assistant director of the antinarcotics program in Sinaloa, who confessed to receiving $23,000 a month to keep an infamous drug boss informed of police activities against him (Rohter 1989b).

In 1993, Joaquín Guzmán, 45, known as "El Chapo" or "Shorty"—he is five feet, six inches—was arrested for murder and cocaine trafficking. He was sentenced to 20 years, but his Sinaloa cartel remained intact and continued to smuggle tons of cocaine each month into the United States. Indeed, they built a 1,500-foot concrete-reinforced, air-conditioned tunnel between Tijuana and a town near San Diego, Otay Mesa. In 2001, Guzmán escaped from Mexico's toughest prison—two guards for each inmate, isolated cells, and sophisticated video surveillance. A few years earlier, Guzmán's colleague, Palma Salazar, was arrested, and 34 police officers, his private protection force, went to jail with him. Guzmán is wanted in the United States, and his escape occurred a day after Mexico's Supreme Court ruled that he could be extradited (Weiner 2001).

The Gulf Cartel

Juan Garcia Abrego was born in 1944 into a notorious smuggling family—his uncle is Juan N. Guerra, the legendary "godfather" of crime in Matamoros, Mexico (Dillon 1996d). Abrego eventually emerged as a leader of the Gulf cartel, controlling drug trafficking throughout northeastern Mexico and along the Gulf of Mexico. The chubby, curly-haired drug czar, called "the Doll" or "Dollface" by his subordinates, borrowed organizing techniques from the Cali cartel, including compartmentalizing his organization into cells

(Dillon 1996a, 1996b). He is reputed to have pioneered the Mexican role in cocaine trafficking and in over a decade built an empire estimated to be worth $15 billion (Eskridge 1998). Rather than pay cash for moving Cali cartel cocaine into the United States, Abrego decided to take cocaine as payment in kind: "He would guarantee delivery anywhere in the United States for 50 percent of the load. He would assume all risks" (Lupsha 1995: 90): "Instead of being paid $2,000 to move a kilo [2.2 pounds] of cocaine, Garcia Abrego allegedly would turn it into $16,000 or more by selling the drug in Houston, Dallas, or New York, his three main markets" (McMahon 1996: 4). Abrego paid millions of dollars in bribes and headed a private army—whose members included law enforcement officers—that slaughtered dozens of people (Bohlen 1996; McMahon 1996; Dillon 1996c). In 1996 it was disclosed that the deputy attorney general in charge of Mexico's federal judicial police and its entire counternarcotics program had accumulated $9 million by protecting Abrego's organization (Dillon 1996g).

Abrego was indicted in the United States in 1990, and in 1996 he was arrested in Monterrey by Mexican authorities. He was quickly flown to the United States, where a reward of $2 million had been offered for his capture. While Mexico refuses to extradite its citizens for drug charges, Abrego holds U.S. citizenship and was technically expelled from Mexico. About 60 members of Abrego's organization are already serving time in U.S. prisons, increasing the power of competing cartels in the Mexican cities of Juárez and Tijuana (Katel 1996).

At the time of his arrest, Abrego's power was waning: his Cali suppliers had cut him off because of the notoriety he had attracted, and his most influential government protectors were out of office—he became a victim of Mexico's need to show progress in dealing with drug trafficking (Dillon 1996f). The primary witness against Abrego was a Mexican-American FBI agent who, by pretending to be corrupt, had infiltrated his organization. Abrego's place was taken by Oscar Malherbe, who is allied with the Carrillo-Fuentes organization of Juárez.

The Juárez Cartel

Ciudad Juárez, in the state of Chihuahua, is just across the Rio Grande from El Paso, Texas, and has a population of 1.5 million. The city is racked with poverty and lacks a sewage treatment facility but is home to one of Mexico's richest drug cartels. The Juárez cartel is the result of a mid-1980s consolidation of various drug rings accomplished by Rafael Aguilar Guajardo, a notoriously corrupt commander of a local unit of the federal judicial police, and his brother Rafael Muñoz Talavera. A 1989 raid on a Los Angeles warehouse uncovered 21 tons of cocaine, which was traced to Muñoz Talavera. After considerable U.S. pressure, Mexican authorities arrested Muñoz Talavera, and he was held for trial. In 1993, Guajardo was murdered on the orders of Amado Carrillo-Fuentes, who took charge of the organization (Puente and de la Garza 1999).

The son of a mechanic from the state of Sinaloa, Carrillo-Fuentes proved to be a man gifted with organizational skills. The nephew of one of Mexico's drug trafficking pioneers, he started his career in the early 1980s as a drug mule for his uncle and built his own organization in the late 1980s, developing important ties to the Herrera Family and the Cali cartel. He spent lavishly to gain protection from government at all levels. By 1993, Carrillo-Fuentes and his brothers were in control of the Juárez cartel and the owner of a fleet of Boeing 727s, from which he derived his nickname "Lord of the Skies" (Brant 1997a). Estimates of his wealth reached $25 billion, and the head of Mexico's antidrug agency was on his payroll—police and military forces[7] were used on his behalf in efforts against rival drug organizations, in particular the Tijuana cartel (Dillon and Pyes 1997a; Golden 1998a). Responsible for as many as 400 drug-related murders, Carrillo-Fuentes nevertheless contributed heavily to the church (de la Garza 1997a). In 1997, at age 41 or 42—neither his birth date nor his face is known to the police—Amado Carrillo-

Fuentes died of heart failure after undergoing eight hours of plastic surgery at a posh maternity hospital in Mexico City (Brant 1997b).

In 1996, Muñoz Talavera was cleared of the charges against him—extensive bribery was later revealed as the reason—and launched a violent campaign to regain control of the Juárez cartel from the Carrillo-Fuentes brothers. In the struggle, dozens of people died. In 1997, his gunmen sprayed a popular Juárez restaurant, killing a top Carrillo-Fuentes lieutenant and five bystanders. Several months later, in 1998, at age 46, Muñoz's body was discovered in Juárez, bound and with several bullet wounds (de la Garza 1998; Dillon 1998b).

The Carrillo-Fuentes organization (CFO) continues to flourish, reputedly under the leadership of brother Alcides Ramon Magaña, a former judicial police commander and bodyguard for Carrillo-Fuentes. Magaña moved the operations eastward along the Gulf Coast and into the Yucatán Peninsula. Nicknamed "El Metro," Magaña had quick success in Quintana Roo state, home of Cancun, a popular vacation spot. In very little time, he took what had been Colombian traffickers' territory and made it his own. In the process, he reputedly bought the state's governor, who disappeared a few days before leaving office in 1999 and hasn't been seen since. A U.S. investigator reports that the Juárez cartel turned Quintana Roo into a *narcostate* and its highest elected official into a *narcogovernor* (LaFranchi 1999).

The organization "maintains drug transportation and distribution cells in U.S. cities such as Los Angeles, Houston, Chicago and New York," from which it distributes cocaine to Nashville, Miami, Detroit, Raleigh, Houston, Newark, Philadelphia, San Antonio, Tulsa, and Los Angeles, cities where it is sold to domestic organizations (Constantine 1999c: 10). The scope of the CFO was revealed by "Operation Impunity," a two-year U.S. federal investigation culminating in 1999 with the arrest of 93 persons and the seizure of over $19 million in U.S. currency; another $7 million in assets was seized, as well as over 27,000 pounds of cocaine and over 4,800 pounds of marijuana ("Press Release" 1999).

---

[7]Patrick O'Day (2001) argues that in Mexico, the military is part of the drug problem.

The Tijuana Cartel

A city of more than one million persons just across the border from San Diego, Tijuana is the home of a drug cartel led by the Arellano-Félix family, seven brothers and four sisters. Noted for their level of violence—brother Ramón is a suspect in more than 60 murders—they literally shot their way into control of drug smuggling along the Mexico–California border (Preston and Pyes 1997). But they have not overlooked bribery: in 1998, two members of an elite Mexican drug enforcement unit working undercover were arrested by federal and state police acting on behalf of the Tijuana drug cartel (Dillon 1998d). Mexican police are reputed to have supplied the cartel with a steady flow of stolen vehicles, while members of the military arranged for the purchase of assault weapons and machine guns. Using brokers, the brothers provide money to politicians and struggling businesspeople (Golden 2000a).

Like their Colombian counterparts, the Tijuana cartel has intimidated and murdered journalists who have reported on their activities, and victims also include law enforcement officers (Dillon 1997; DEA "Fact Sheet" n.d.). In 2000, Arellano-Félix gunmen tortured and murdered three Mexican drug agents, one of whom was an expert on the Arellanos and their chief pursuer. The three were returning to Tijuana from San Diego, where they were living for security reasons. They were intercepted shortly after crossing the border and before they could retrieve their weapons—there is a dispute between Mexico and the United States over whether agents of one country working in the other can carry weapons (de la Garza 2000; Golden 2000b). On the U.S. side of the border, the cartel employs California street gang members to carry out murders (de la Garza 1997b).

In 1999, ten men believed to be overseeing operations for the Tijuana cartel in Southern California were arrested. They were in possession of 1,100 pounds of cocaine and 4 pounds of heroin; one of those arrested also had $100,000 in cash in his home (A. O'Connor 1999). In addition to heroin and cocaine, the cartel deals in methamphetamine and marijuana. In 2000, DEA agents arrested more than 80 persons in the United States who were involved with selling 117 tons of Tijuana cartel marijuana to Jamaican traffickers. Among those arrested were employees of the FedEx parcel service who had arranged to ship the drugs from California to the East Coast (Sniffen 2000).

The Tijuana cartel is allied with the Sonora cartel, and they have been feuding with the Carrillo-Fuentes/Juárez cartel. In 1998, Arellano-Félix gunmen entered a suburb of the city of Ensenada in Baja California, 60 miles south of California. Reportedly high on alcohol and cocaine, they rounded up and shot to death at least 19 men, women, and children from three families with ties to the Tijuana cartel. The primary target was the head of a group that specialized in guiding drug planes to desert airstrips (Eskridge 1998; Sandoval 1998; Golden 1998c; Dillon 1998e).

"The Arellano-Felix family, headed by Benjamin, has evolved into one of Mexico's most powerful criminal drug enterprises for smuggling multi-ton quantities of drugs yearly. While Benjamin manages the multi-million dollar business, his brother Ramon heads security-related operations." His functions include recruitment of enforcers and killers from the streets of San Diego and Tijuana (Constantine 1999: 8). In 2000, Ramon and Benjamin Arellano-Félix were indicted by a federal grand jury, and the U.S. Department of State offered a $2-million reward for their capture. The brothers are also wanted in Mexico. That same year, Mexican police and soldiers who went to arrest the cartel's second in command were met by gunfire. He later surrendered. In 2002, Ramon Arellano-Félix, 37, carrying a gold-plated handgun and fake federal police identification, was reportedly killed in a shootout with police. Before a positive identification could be made, his body was claimed by two unidentified persons and cremated. Several days later, Mexican authorities arrested Benjamin Arellano-Félix, 49, who confirmed his brother's death. At about the same time, in the United States, federal authorities arrested 22 suspected members of the Arellano-Félix organization in Minnesota, Colorado, California, and South Dakota (Weiner 2002).

The Danger from Mexico

"Unlike the American organized crime leaders, organized crime figures in Mexico have at their disposal an army of personnel, an arsenal of weapons and the finest technology that money can buy. They literally run transportation and financial empires and an insight into how they conduct their day-to-day business leads even the casual observer to the conclusion that the United States is facing a threat of unprecedented proportions and gravity." Thomas A. Constantine, director of the Drug Enforcement Administration, before the U.S. Senate Drug Caucus, February 24, 1999.

The Sonora Cartel

The state of Sonora borders Arizona and is ideal for drug trafficking: it is a sprawling region—Mexico's second largest state in size—of cattle ranches, desert landing strips, and isolated roads that lead north to the border (Dillon and Pyes 1997b). The Sonora cartel was founded by Miguel Angel Felix-Gallardo, imprisoned since 1989 for the 1985 torture-murder of a U.S. DEA agent. Though wanted by both the Mexican and American governments, Gallardo was able to remain at large for more than a decade. He is a second cousin of the Arellano brothers (Golden 2000a).

The Sonora cartel is now run by the Caro-Quintero brothers, Rafael, Miguel, and Genaro. Like Feliz-Gallardo, Rafael Caro-Quintero is imprisoned for his role in the murder of the aforementioned DEA agent. Miguel, who heads the organization, was indicted in the United States and arrested in Mexico in 1992, but the charges against him in Mexico were dismissed under questionable circumstances. While his organization specializes in cultivation, production, and distribution of marijuana, like the other major drug organizations, it is polydrug in nature, transporting and distributing cocaine and amphetamine as well. Since 1992, Miguel has operated freely throughout northwestern Mexico and runs his drug smuggling activities from the city of Caborca in Senora (Constantine 1999b, 1999c). In 1999, the Mexican Supreme Court ruled that if he is arrested by Mexican authorities, Miguel can be extradited to the United States. In 2001, Mexican authorities arrested Miguel for the purpose of extradition to the United States. Later that year, however, the Mexican Supreme Court ruled that Mexican citizens could not be extradited to the Unites States if they faced either the death penalty or life imprisonment.

THE DOMINICAN REPUBLIC

The Dominican Republic, with a population of eight million, occupies about two-thirds of the Caribbean island of Hispaniola, which it shares with Haiti. The Dominican Republic is a major transit country for cocaine moving to the United States. It serves drug smugglers as both a command-and-control center and transshipment point. Increasing amounts of designer drugs, especially "ecstasy," are being moved through the Dominican Republic from Europe to the United States and Puerto Rico. (See Figure 8.4.)

The movement of drugs is aided by the existence of structured and integrated criminal organizations of Dominicans, Puerto Ricans, and Colombians that operate in Santo Domingo as well as in New York, Boston, Providence, and other cities. The Colombians are generally in charge of control and supply in the Caribbean and begin the first phase of the transport. Later, Dominicans become the primary transporters (U.S. Department of State 2001).

Although the Dominican Republic is not as depressed as Haiti, in the mid-1960s political unrest and economic upheavals caused many residents to seek their fortunes by going north. In New York City, Dominicans who have legally entered the United States number about 350,000;

FIGURE 8.4

The Dominican Republic and Environs

thousands more are illegal aliens. Some of these immigrants, legal and illegal, have entered the drug trade. Known as Dominican-Yorks, the traffickers keep a low profile in the United States, returning their profits to cities in the Dominican Republic such as San Francisco de Macoris, conspicuous for its wealth in a country where the per-capita income is less than $1,000 a year.

The center of the Dominican wholesale trade in crack is the uptown Manhattan neighborhood of Washington Heights. In recent years, some of the leaders have slipped out of New York and are running operations from their homeland, where corruption is endemic among airport officials and law enforcement. Until 1998, the Dominican Republic refused to extradite its citizens for crimes committed in the United States. In that year, two notorious traffickers were sent to New York, where they were wanted for drug trafficking and murder.

Dominicans have demonstrated the necessary talent for moving large amounts of heroin and crack cocaine at the wholesale and street level. They purchase directly from Asian and Colombian importers, sharing a common language and entrepreneurial values with the latter. Dominicans have apparently applied their well-known skills as tradesmen and merchants to become New York City's top traffickers and have also captured markets in Pennsylvania (Pennsylvania Crime Commission 1990). As well, they control a significant portion of the cocaine trafficking in New England (Drug Enforcement Administration 1991b). Do-

minicans generally provide top-quality, uncut drugs at competitive prices, avoiding the common practice of diluting the product as it passes through the distribution chain. Often operating out of grocery stores, bars, and restaurants in Latino neighborhoods, they employ a variety of marketing gimmicks to move their product. In Philadelphia, they sold heroin packets with lottery tickets attached that a winner could use to claim an additional twelve packets (Pennsylvania Crime Commission 1990).

The structure of Dominican drug-trafficking organizations is based on familial or regional loyalties:

The organizations are *vertically integrated*, with the family maintaining control over several consecutive stages of the operation. They obtain uncut heroin and cocaine from Colombian and Chinese sources on the supply end in New York and then distribute the drug to street-level dealers who may be Dominican, Black, Puerto Rican, white, or someone of other ethnic origins. Activities of the group are directed by the leader through a number of "lieutenants," who may include brothers, sisters, cousins, and friends from home. Lower level workers—largely Dominican nationals, and often illegal aliens—will travel a circuit taking them between New York City and various communities in eastern and central Pennsylvania (and sometimes New Jersey), performing various specialized tasks as they are directed, serving as couriers, security for stash houses, cutters and packagers, lookouts, street dealers, and enforcers. Women often serve as "mules" or couriers, carrying kilo packages on their persons. When riding public transportation, these women may appear to be unaccompanied. Actually they are being shadowed by a group member who can provide protection if needed. (Pennsylvania Crime Commission 1990: 267–68, edited)

Dominicans developed a reputation as reliable dealers who promptly paid their suppliers and avoided violence to muscle in on others or maintain exclusive control of a particular market. Instead, they usually competed on the basis of efficiency and pricing, allowing them to avoid high-profile violence (Pennsylvania Crime Commission 1990). However, while "early Dominican gangs were known for keen marketing techniques . . . their successors in the 1990s mark out their territories" and use violence to maintain hegemony (Kleinknecht 1996: 260–61). Indeed, several Dominican groups have become noted for their excessive violence, both to maintain internal discipline and to deal with competitors. In one instance, "The Company," a Brooklyn-based Dominican gang, even lured a police officer to his death (Wren 1998a).

Dominicans have come to dominate the middle echelon between the Colombians and the street dealers of cocaine and heroin in the New York City area and into New England (Wren 1998a; Rohter and Krauss 1998b). In part, this is a result of Colombian dissatisfaction with their Mexican counterparts. By 1995, major Colombian organizations had established themselves in the Dominican Republic to coordinate activities with their Dominican partners: "While the bulk of Colombian cocaine and heroin continues to move through Mexico, the Colombian traffickers have in the last few years come full circle, returning to the Caribbean as a base of operations." And the influence of drug money on the island has been pervasive: "Office buildings, hotels and shopping centers are springing up in Santo Domingo, Santiago,

and San Francisco de Macoris—often in the gaudy style that some describe as narcodeco" (Rohter and Krauss 1998a: 6). Police corruption is widespread and often coordinated with law enforcement counterparts in Colombia.

The Dominicans and their Colombian partners have made Haiti, which (along with the Dominican Republic) lies roughly between Colombia and Florida, the fastest growing transit point for cocaine being shipped to the United States. Haiti has proven attractive to the traffickers because it is the poorest country in the hemisphere, making it relatively cheap to find criminal labor and bribe officials. The police had to be created from scratch after the old force was abolished in the wake of the American troop landing in 1994; they have limited training and resources. The Haitian coast guard consists of ten boats, only half of which are operating at any given time (Rohter 1998a).

THE MEXICAN MAFIA

Prison-based gangs have been gaining prominence as organized criminal groups, most notably the Mexican Mafia. Found in at least nine state prison systems and reputed to be the most powerful of the prison organized crime groups, the Mexican Mafia (also known as *la M*—pronounced *la emay*—is composed primarily of Mexican-American convicts and ex-convicts from the barrios of East Los Angeles. Like many other prison gangs, as well as their street counterparts, the Mexican Mafia has a "blood-in-blood-out" credo: murder or the drawing of blood is a prerequisite for membership, and those seeking to resign will be killed.

Its origins are traced to the Deuel Vocational Institute in Tracy, California, where, in 1957, 20 young Mexican Americans from the Maravilla area of East Los Angeles began the Mexican Mafia as a self-protection group. They soon "began to control such illicit activities as homosexual prostitution, gambling, and narcotics. They called themselves the Mexican Mafia out of admiration for *La Cosa Nostra*" (PCOC 1986c: 73). Attempts by the Department of Corrections to diminish gang power by transferring members to other institutions only helped spread their influence. Vigorous recruiting occurs among the most violent Mexican-American inmates, particularly those housed in adjustment centers for the most dangerous and incorrigible. In 1967, Mexican Mafia reliance on wholesale violence increased, and in that year members attacked the first Mexican American outside their group. This attack on an inmate from rural northern California led to the formation of a second Mexican-American gang, *La Nuestra Familia*, with whom the Mexican Mafia has been feuding ever since.

By the mid-1960s, the Mexican Mafia had assumed control over prison heroin trafficking and numerous other inmate activities. In 1966 it started to move its operations outside the prison and is reputedly attempted to organize Hispanic gangs into a confederation to confront black Los Angeles gangs for control of the drug trade (Mydans 1995). The gang, which has a membership of about 400, asserts control over drug trafficking by Hispanic street gangs and collects "street taxes" in exchange for the privilege of staying in business and protection against encroachment by other gangs. In 1998, 12 members of the Mexican Mafia were convicted in a federal court in California of RICO violations (discussed in Chapter 14): directing a terror campaign from their prison cells to control drug trafficking by street gangs (Associated Press 1998b).

In the next chapter, we will discuss the most recent organized crime threat, the "Russian Mafiya."

INTERNET CONNECTIONS

Drug Enforcement Administration: **www.usdoj.gov/dea**

National Criminal Intelligence Service: **www.ncis.gov.uk**

Nathanson Centre: **www.yorku.ca/nathanson**

Yahoo organized crime links: **dir.yahoo.com/society_and_culture/crime/organized_crime**

CSIS Global Organized Crime Project: **csis.org/goc**

Narcotics Control: **state.gov/g/inl/narc**

REVIEW QUESTIONS

1. What is the relationship among Cuban exiles, Colombians, and cocaine trafficking?
2. What variables account for the Colombian success in the cocaine business?
3. Why has it been so difficult for Colombia to eradicate its cocaine trafficking organizations?
4. Why has it been difficult for the United States to respond to the Colombian cocaine trafficking organizations?
5. What is the relationship between cocaine trafficking and politics in Colombia?
6. What are the characteristics of Mexican organized crime?
7. What is the relationship between Colombian and Mexican criminal organizations?

8. How has the political climate of Mexico aided in the development of criminal organizations?
9. What are the unique characteristics of Dominican criminal organizations?
10. What is the relationship between the Dominicans and the Colombians?
11. According to the degree to which their criminal activities are integrated into the organizational structure, how do outlaw motorcycle clubs differ from Colombian cocaine cartels?

♠

CHAPTER 9

RUSSIAN ORGANIZED CRIME

In contrast to the criminal organizations discussed in chapters 4 and 5, many emerging groups are flourishing in the United States in the absence of the corrupt political machines that provided a protective incubator for the Irish, Jewish, and Italian criminal organizations of an earlier era. Unlike these earlier groups, which in their infancy tended to be local in their operations and ambitions, emerging organized crime often has a great range of influence and action on an international level. This is exemplified by Russian organized crime (ROC).

Unlike the farmers and unskilled laborers who composed the majority of earlier immigrations to the United States, "Russian émigrés are generally urban in origin, well-educated, and industrially and technologically skilled." Despite a language barrier (although many have learned some English in Soviet-era schools), "they have marketable skills and have not been closed off from the legitimate ladders of upward mobility." Thus, Russian-émigré crime in this country did not grow out of the same cultural alienation and economic disparity experienced by other immigrant groups. Fur-

thermore, Russian criminals did not begin their criminal careers as members of adolescent street gangs in ethnic ghettos, as did most of the criminals discussed in chapters 4 and 5 (Tri-State Joint Soviet–Émigré Organized Crime Project 1997: 9–10).

THE ROOTS OF RUSSIAN ORGANIZED CRIME

"In the decade since the collapse of the Soviet Union, the world has become the target of a new global crime threat from criminal organizations and criminal activities that have poured forth over the borders of Russia and other former Soviet republics such as Ukraine" (Finckenauer and Voronin 2001: 1). With a land mass that stretches from Europe to Asia, "Russian" does not necessarily reflect the ethnicity or nationality of many identified as part of organized crime. Thus, while they may speak Russian and come from regions that have been dominated by Russia, many ethnic and groups and nationalities "do not regard themselves nor do Russians regard them as Russians" (Finckenauer and Waring 1999: 132). Therefore, *Russian organized crime* encompasses any ethnic or national group—e.g., Armenian, Chechen, Georgian, Jewish, Latvian, Lithuanian, Tatar, or Ukrainian—from the territory of the former Soviet Union. Some analysts also include Albanians (discussed in Chapter 7).

In the former Soviet Union, law enforcement resources have been inadequate to deal with the menace of organized crime. Many poorly paid officers are on gang payrolls, while others have left the service to work for the gangs full time (Gallagher 1992a; Hockstader 1995): "Parliamentary bodies are riddled with de facto criminal syndicate representatives, who diligently block or water down any significant anti-crime legislation" (Voronin 1997: 57).

While in Italy the word *Mafia* signifies discreet criminal organizations with strict hierarchical structures, "in Russia it has come to mean much more. Here it embraces the noxious blend of crime, politics and business that has engulfed Russia since the lifting of Communist control" (Bohlen 1999: WK 6). Although there is no universally accepted definition of organized crime in Russia—in major part because Russian law (like U.S. law) provides no definition (Finckenauer and Voronin 2001)—researchers have distinguished three levels (Foglesong and Solomon 2001):

1. *Gruppirovki:* Mainly gangs of extortionists, thieves, swindlers, and narcotics traffickers who exhibit a rudimentary and episodic structure.
2. *Prestupnaia organizatsiia:* This middle level involves relatively large formations with connections to authorities at the regional level.
3. *Soobshchestvo:* The highest level has influence extending to multiple regions of the country, often with international ties.

The breeding and training ground for ROC was established during the Communist era, and it is against this background that we must understand the variety of Russian organized crime. Citizens of the former Soviet Union (FSU) were deprived of a work ethic—"We pretend to work; they pretend to pay us"—and schemed to survive. For the average Russian, the consequence of honesty was deprivation (Rosner 1995: vii): "In Russia, governments both under the rule of the Tzars and that of the Communist state represented totalitarianism in one form or another where individual freedom was suppressed. As such, like the invading foreigners of Sicily, the internal government system of Russia has made the Russian, like the Sicilian, distrustful of government" (Albini et al. 1995: 222). And like Sicily, the common method of social interaction, lawful and unlawful, is the patron–client relationship.

The sudden onset of a market economy gave rise to unrestrained aspirations—the classic condition that Emile Durkheim refers to as anomie (discussed in Chapter 2). Although first revealed in 1897, Durkheim's concept of anomie fits the situation of present-day Russia: "The collapse of the previous system brought in fundamental changes in social and political order which shaped the personal lives of individuals in the most profound way. Several years of market reforms which changed the nature of the country's economy also brought with them hyperinflation, a sharp rise in unemployment and an overall drop in the standard of living" (Frisby 1998: 27). In 1991 the Soviet Union broke into 15 independent states, with Russia dominant. Russia is struggling to establish a modern market economy and achieve strong economic growth. The economy has actually contracted despite the country's wealth of natural resources, its well-educated population, and its diverse—although increasingly dilapidated—industrial base. Concomitantly, rapid social transformation resulting from market reforms created fantastic wealth for the few *nouveau riche*. Ironically, most of those who had power under Communism not only retained their material status but very often improved it considerably.

Russia remained estranged from the European Enlightenment ideal of the rule of law, and this did not change with the advent of the Soviet Union (Shelley 2001). Since the collapse of Communism, the legal system has failed to keep pace with these changes, and law enforcement institutions have become fragmented. Lacking coordination, they have been unable to cope with the sheer volume of work in processing mountains of information. The turnover of investigative staff has been high and technological provision low. Without professionalism, morale declined and corruption increased rapidly. People, particularly vulnerable businessmen, began relying on the suddenly increasing private protection services, a large number of which operate without proper registration or licenses. Many resorted to taking justice into their own hands, often with assistance from the criminal fraternity. As a result, a kind of "shadow justice" appeared, dominated by criminals (Frisby 1998). The line between the private security forces and organized crime is often very narrow or nonexistent. With their high-level security training and knowledge of advanced military tactics and weapon systems, Russian military officers are in demand to organize and lead private security forces. Former special forces are in particular demand (Center for Strategic and International Studies 1997).

During the Soviet era, three tiers of organized crime developed: "The first tier was high-level government and party bureaucrats; the second was shadow economy operators who produced goods off the books; and the third was professional criminals, including the vory v zakone" (Finkenauer and Waring 2001: 3).

THE *VORY*

While the former Soviet Union did not have organized crime in the pattern of the American racketeer, it did have an extensive professional underworld—the *vory v zakone*, "thieves with a code of honor." In the tradition of the Neapolitan Camorra (see Chapter 7), and unlike the Sicilian Mafia, the *vory* developed among hard-core prison camp inmates. One source (Friedman 2000) states that this occurred during the reign of Peter the Great (1682–1725) and quickly spread through the entire Russian prison system. A more credible source argues that a secret criminal society in the form of the *vory v zakone* did not exist in Czarist

Russia but is a product of the Soviet system. In any event, a member (*vor*) today is less likely to have joined while in prison.

Their strict conspiratorial code forbade any involvement in politics or collaboration with the state. Conflict between those who agreed to collaborate and those who refused presumably gave rise to the term *vory v zakone*, applied to those who remained true to the strict code of the criminal *vory* fraternity. Since it was believed that only very strong and "honorable" thieves could resist the pressures of the authorities, the name became a title of honor and status in the criminal community. During World War II, the *vory* split into two factions; one (patriots) supported efforts to defeat the invading Nazis, while the other (traditionalists) remained aloof. By 1953, the patriots had been driven out of the "thieves' world" for their disloyalty to its traditions (Chalidze 1977; Friedman 2000).

Emblazoned with tattoos, including giant eagles with razor-sharp talons on their chests, they developed a coded language decipherable only by other members of the criminal fraternity. *Vory* members often sport elaborate tattoos that reveal their status in the organization's hierarchy and even their criminal specialty. The title *vor* is bestowed at special initiation ceremonies at which the novice (*malyutka*) pledges fealty and is given a new name—a rechristening. *Vory* membership requires three sponsors and a ceremony with an oath of allegiance to abide by 18 rules—if a rule is broken, the offense is punishable by death. In particular, forsake all relatives, help other *vory*, and never work (at legitimate employment); never insult or raise your hand against another *vor* (unless sanctioned by a *vory* court). Prospects have to be free of involvement with conventional aspects of society, such as regular employment, paying taxes, or military service (Frisby 1998; Varese 2001).

Vory organizations are conspiratorial and hierarchical. They include representatives of the administration of various enterprises who, during the Soviet era, were often party members with high positions who lived double lives. Organized into tight networks, "from their cells, crime bosses planned and organized their operations across the country . . . [while] lieutenants, often called *brodyagi* (vagabonds), conducted formal dealings with the outside" (Handelman 1995: 209). The criminal society has a form of insurance: "*obshchak*—derived from members' contributions and fines for violating the thieves' code, that is used to bribe officials inside and outside of prison, to provide amenities to imprisoned members and to help support their families. After leaving prison, members are expected to repay the *obshchak*" (Finckenauer and Waring 1999: 107).

The *vory* is exclusively male, and women, even wives, lack respect. Indeed, attachment to a spouse is seen as a weakness—undermining loyalty to the *vory*—as is faithfulness. A wife is not permitted to socialize outside of the thieves' world, and she is never permitted to leave. Paternal bonds lack emotional attachment, and it is assumed that the children of a *vor* will follow him into the fraternity, although this often does not happen (Varese 2001).

Under Communism, managers of state-owned enterprises became unofficial entrepreneurs. In order to meet the quotas set by the regime, they established informal networks to ensure the provision of supplies from other state-owned enterprises. There were rationing and price controls and, as a consequence, a divergence between market values and administrative controls. This led to the development of an underground economy whereby commodities were diverted to informal markets where they could be sold at higher prices. Managers reserved their most valuable goods for the *vory*, who paid premium prices that the managers did not report and, subsequently, embezzled. Managers were unwilling to provide scarce goods to ordinary citizens, exacerbating existing shortages. The *vory*, taking advantage of the managers' inability to turn to law enforcement for protection, extorted money from their erstwhile partners in the black market. Subsequent privatization and legalization of joint ownership meant that state enterprises were handed over to corrupt managers and their *vory* partners through worker buyouts. The strategic use of intimidation and violence then allowed criminals to infiltrate the banking industry. All this occurred at a time when the law enforcement apparatus was considerably weakened. The law en-

forcers, employees of state justice and security agencies, acted informally as private enforcers or resigned and joined private protection companies. Many became partners with violent entrepreneurs in the racketeer gangs (Volkov 2000).

Gang wars broke out as criminals struggled to claim state enterprises and property, leading to informal agreements that defined territories and functional boundaries. In industries owned or extorted by criminals, the result was higher prices passed on to consumers by industry-wide cartels. Criminals were now deeply entrenched in the Russian economy (Tomass 1998).

Nascent capitalism, a relaxation of the totalitarian law enforcement apparatus, and liberalization of travel provided a fertile environment for these criminals schooled in a system rife with corruption and an underground economy. In a situation paralleling that of the "old" and "new" Sicilian Mafia discussed in Chapter 7, a new *vory* has adapted the thieves' code to the new reality and has largely replaced the old. Steeped in ritual and custom with a rigid code of honor, the old *vory* has been eclipsed by one whose ideals are more economically driven (Rawlinson 1997).

With the collapse of the Soviet Union, *vory* groups emerged as an important element in Russian organized crime. Each is headed by a *vor v zakonye*, who is recognized by all others as the authority in his territory. A *vor v zakonye* is chosen at a meeting of members and requires the recommendation of at least two other bosses—the more recommendations, the more prestige. By 1992, the most powerful bosses had divided the country into 12 regions, where they interact with bureaucrats and industrial managers. Dressed in leather coats and driving flashy cars, they eat openly with government officials in restaurants that they often control (Handelman 1995).

The most powerful of these criminal groups is the Moscow-based *Solntsevo* (or *Solntsevskaya brigada*), with about 9,000 members active in several countries. The organization, which takes its name from a Moscow suburb, is both hierarchical and flexible. At the top of the hierarchy is a supreme council consisting of 12 people who are the leaders of individual crews and who meet regularly to discuss matters of importance to the organization. The council manages a joint fund (*obshchak*) to which all brigades allocate money on a regular basis (Varese 2001).

Now in his forties, Sergei Mikhailov, boss of the *Solntsevskaya*, once held Russian, Israeli, and Costa Rican passports—he had legitimate business interests in these countries, as well as in Hungary and Belgium. More than 15 years ago, Mikhailov was employed as a waiter in a Moscow hotel. In 1984 he was imprisoned for collecting insurance on his motorcycle, which he had fraudulently reported stolen. Prison contacts helped lay the groundwork for a flourishing criminal career (Bohlen 1999). In 1998 he was accused of illegally buying property in Switzerland, where he lived in a village outside of Geneva with his wife and children. He had Swiss bank accounts totaling $2 million (Kaban 1998). At the end of 1998, Mikhailov was acquitted by a Swiss court: "If he were an Italian being tried in Italy, he might well have been found guilty under a 1982 law that makes 'mafia association' a criminal offense" (Bohlen 1999: WK 5).

In a pattern that parallels that of the Chicago Outfit (see Chapter 5), "the *vory* ritual now marks the entry of powerful crew leaders into the 'governing body' of the biggest criminal groups in Moscow"; that is, being "made" indicates a management position reserved for the leaders, rather than being a requirement for each group member (Varase 2001: 177).

New criminal groups devoid of the traditions of the *vory* have also emerged, and in the competitive spirit of capitalism their leaders—*avtoritet* (authority)—have challenged the *vory*.

THE RUSSIAN *MAFIYA*

Some observers report two levels of Russian organized crime. The first is inhabited by street thugs, basically low-level muscle who extort payoffs from small businesses for "protection" (Voronin 1997). The second level is more reminiscent of the robber barons than of Al Capone, where organized crime and government are symbiotic, criminals and bureaucrats forming a network "that is highly organized, stratified, meticulous in planning, highly efficient in execution and well disciplined" (Serio 1992a: 130; Stanley 1994). In most countries, organized crime thrives primarily through the provision of goods and services that happen to be illegal. In the former Soviet Union, by contrast, "organized crime flourishes well beyond these areas—it wields power over all the economy" (Voronin 1997: 55–56). In the important Asian port city of Vladivostok, 6,000 miles from Moscow, the criminal underworld merges with local government and a shadow economy whose benefactors can be seen driving luxury automobiles and sailing yachts (Witt 1994; Spector 1995). This shadow economy is pervasive throughout the country, a result of onerous taxes and licensing requirements imposed by the central government (Hockstader 1995).

Some ROC groups—the Russian *Mafiya*—emerged from the pastimes of many Russian young men: participation in sports clubs and fitness centers. In the Soviet Union, sports were a major priority of the state because they expressed its might and socialized its youth. But in different circumstances, sports, especially fighting sports and martial arts, can supply all that is needed to create a racketeer gang: fighting skills, willpower, discipline, and team spirit. When the state withdrew sponsorship, the constraints of a rule-governed nonviolent competition also ended, and this situation was enough to launch a dangerous process whereby sportsmen started to look for an alternative career. Powerful gangs emerged from the gyms and sports clubs of the former Soviet Union. In Moscow and its suburbs, at the city markets, the first flowering of free trade and private entrepreneurship, the former sportsmen discovered a way for their physical assets to be turned into cash—offering protection for a regular fee. The market and the gym were at the origin of a peculiar local capitalism: small business provided the economic base for new gangs supplying protection (Volkov 2000).

The *Mafiya* and the *vory* extort (offer *krysha*—literally a "roof" that provides protection) from both legitimate and illegitimate entrepreneurs: "*Mafiozy* approach businesses directly, visiting in

The New Russian Authoritarianism

"Post-Soviet organized crime represents a new form of non-state based authoritarianism. Citizens still live in fear but are now intimidated by non-state actors in the form of organized crime groups. . . . Traditional authoritarianism is based on total state control. The authoritarianism of organized crime represents abnegation of the state's obligations to its citizenry and reflects its inability to protect them from threats against their life, livelihood, or economic security" (Shelley 1997: 122–23).

groups of three or four. One of them speaks in a friendly manner, warning the directors that they must pay dan'—15 to 20 percent of their company's gross earnings—or suffer violence at the hands of unnamed gangs. If the *mafiozy* operate under the guise of a security agency, they may insist that the director sign a contract." Businesses refusing to pay, something rare, are subjected to a campaign that begins with verbal threats and escalates to bullets, bombs, and the torture of family members (Tayler 2001: 38). These groups can also provide services such as restraining competition: "If competition with lower prices or better goods appear[s] on the scene, fires, theft, murder, and other bedlam can be arranged" (2001: 38). Russian organized crime groups have excelled at restraining trade and controlling pricing in a variety of arenas, including airport taxis and farmers' markets. Businessmen do not necessarily wait for the inevitable "visit." Instead, they may seek out the most effective "roof"—the one able to provide protection from competing ROC groups and predatory criminals (Varese 2001).

In the manner of southern Italy, OC bosses provide a viable alternative to a formal justice system that is ineffective, if not corrupt. Instead of hiring lawyers to settle contract disputes, Russians engage *Mafiya* bosses. Businessmen keep them on retainer to avoid shakedowns or to ensure that they have representation in the event of a business dispute (Gallagher 1995a; Witt 1996). In a country where contract law and the tradition of property rights are weak, the Russian wiseguy, like his Sicilian *mafioso* counterpart, acts as a guarantor so that persons who do not trust one another can transact

business with a significant degree of confidence: "The introduction of private property in Russia has led to a demand for protection which the state has been unable to meet—and that organized crime is meeting instead" (Williams 1997: 6). ROC also provides services to banks experiencing problems collecting debts. Resorting to the courts for such service is time-consuming and runs the risk that the debtor will declare bankruptcy (Varese 2001).

Note the transition made by the *uralmashevskaya*—whose name derives from a district in the industrialized Ural Mountains city of Ekaterinburg—from gang to "financial–industrial enterprise." Formed around young toughs from the local sports clubs, they produced illegal alcohol and provided *krysha* to area businesses. Assets from these activities were invested in businesses experiencing a need for cash. As their enterprises expanded, the *uralmashevskaya* began to conflict with a similarly ambitious *vory*. Violence broke out in 1992–1993, and the *vory* were outmatched by their more ruthless opponents, who were better disciplined and schooled in the use of force. After eliminating their rivals, the *uralmashevskaya* expanded their business interests and entered the political arena, financing candidates and having members run for elected office. They completed their transition by establishing institutionalized relations with the regional government (Volkov 2000).

In a scenario that parallels that of American organized crime after the repeal of Prohibition and the onset of the Great Depression, Russian criminals have ready access to investment capital in a society where sources of financing are scarce:

An OC-related double homicide in Moscow. Russian law enforcers tend to attribute the common occurrence of this kind of violence to *rasbourkas,* illegal street trials designed to settle major business claims. Each of the parties involved may be backed by fifty to two thousand infantry on call from protection organizations.

© Anthony Suau/Getty/Liaison Agency

"Even apparently legitimate entrepreneurs find it difficult to muster the necessary capital for new enterprises and all too frequently must borrow funds from mobsters at extortionate rates of interest" (Voronin 1997: 56). And many criminals have "displayed a surprising knowledge and expertise in the workings of the market" that is rare in post-Soviet society (Rawlinson 1997: 46).

And they have proven to be very violent: machine-gun fire, car bombs, public assassinations, and onlookers who remember nothing have become common (Bohlen 1993; Spector 1994). As a result of the disintegration of the Soviet military and the breakdown in arms control at weapons plants, high-quality automatic weapons are available throughout the country (Hersh 1994; Hockstader 1995). Members of the military constitute an important element in Russian organized crime: "poorly paid, badly housed, and demoralized, Russian military forces at home and abroad are deeply immersed in criminal activities conducted for personal and group profit. Smuggling crimes of all types (particularly drug and arms trafficking), the massive diversion of equipment and materials, illegal business ventures, and coercion and criminal violence, all fall under the umbrella of military organized crime" (Turbiville 1995: 63; Gordon 1996). And there are close links with organized crime groups outside the military.

An undetermined number of banks have fallen under the effective control or ownership of organized crime groups that use them to launder and embezzle money. Bank records provide information for selecting businesses from which to extort protection money (Bohlen 1994). The Russian banking system is grossly unregulated, which aids money laundering, not only for Russian criminals in the United States but also for Colombian cartels and Mafia *cosche* (Friedman 1996). The Russians provide money-laundering services for the Colombians, while the latter provide cocaine for distribution among the elite of the former Soviet Union ("Russian Organized Crime" 1996—hereafter "ROC" 1996).

Moving into more risky spheres of criminal behavior, such as bank fraud and drug trafficking, these new groups command wealth beyond the dreams of the old *vory* (Handelman 1995). Russian gangsters have been involved in the production and sale of methadone and similar synthetic narcotics, such as trimethyl phentanyl, often called 3MF. There is also extensive trafficking in military

Tort Action, Russian Style

Traveling way above the village speed limit, the luxury car hits a German shepherd and drags the body about 100 feet. The driver is enraged. He grabs the dog owner and demands $300 for the damage to his car. After a tussle, the driver leaves, but not before promising to return. That evening, four four-wheeled vehicles arrive at the village and stop in front of the dog owner's house. Men with shotguns emerge and open fire, terrorizing the villagers. The dog owner seeks help from a policeman friend, who arranges for a representative of the gang's boss to come to the village. Driving a BMW and accompanied by men in an Audi, the representative "explains" that the dog owner must pay $300 for the damage to the car—"or else." The dog owner pays (Kalfus 1996).

weapons, which frequently wind up in areas of ethnic conflict (Hersh 1994). There is fear that this could extend to nuclear devices.[1] Ransom kidnappings are also part of the repertoire. While some of the gangs in the Russian *mafiya* are local, "others span the entire former Soviet Union, and more and more are establishing links abroad" (Elliott 1992: 52). In 1993 a ton of cocaine was seized by officials near St. Petersburg, Russia (Hanley 1993), and there have also been reports (such as Friedman 1996) of meetings between Russian and Sicilian mobsters in Europe and documented connections between Colombian drug traffickers and Russian *mafiya* in South Florida (Navarro 1997).

One of the more nefarious activities associated with Russian organized crime is trafficking in women for the sex industry. Women in the former Soviet Union often face chronic unemployment, forcing them to look abroad for work, making them vulnerable to exploitation. The road leading to the sex industry typically originates with a newspaper ad or an unexpected meeting on the street, a proposition to work abroad as maid, secretary, showgirl, nanny, or waitress. The victims are often well-educated and answer advertisements for positions in service industries for which they are overqualified—such is the state of the Russian economy and job market. Women are usually trafficked in Europe—Belgium, the Netherlands, Poland, and Switzerland—and Asia—China, Japan, and Thailand (Stocckers 2000).

Criminals can supply their victims with services such as fraudulent travel documents, transportation, guided border crossings, accommodations, and job brokering. Upon their arrival at a foreign destination, the women are informed that the job no longer exists, but they are still indebted to the agent for the trip, which usually costs them between $5,000 and $20,000. Women who refuse to cooperate are subjected to physical and sexual abuse; sometimes they are murdered. One victim who refused to have sex with potential customers was taken into a country field, and while other women were forced to watch, her throat was cut. Having lived in a society ruled by an oppressive government, Russian émigrés tend to be inherently distrustful of government and reluctant to speak with or seek assistance from law enforcement (Zalisko 2001).

CHECHENS

Members of various ethnic groups have also moved into *mafiya* activity. Organized around feudal clan and tribal relationships, literally "crime families," these groups are well suited to take advantage of dislocations in post-Soviet society. One of these groups originated in the Central Asian region of the Caucasus Mountains. The Chechen

---

[1]In 1995 it was revealed that 4.4 tons of beryllium—a critical element for building nuclear warheads—141 kilograms of which was radioactive, seized by police in Lithuania was from an experimental reactor in Russia (Zimmermann and Cooperman 1995). That same year, Chechen separatists buried a vial of low-level radioactive cesium in a Moscow park, apparently as a scare tactic ("Editorial" 1995).

Politics, Russian Style

In 1998 a leading liberal politician and defender of Russia's democratic reforms, Galina V. Starovoitova, 52, was gunned down by a submachine gun and a silencer-equipped pistol. She was a candidate for governor of the region just outside St. Petersburg, a major city that has been the site of number of politically related OC-style killings in recent years (Bohlen 1998).

national homeland is located due north of the Georgian Republic, on the western shores of the Caspian Sea. Largely Muslim, historically hostile to Moscow, and legendary warriors, the Chechens were subjected to massive deportations in 1944 by Stalin, who falsely accused them of collaborating with the Nazis during World War II; they returned to the region in 1957. Known for strong family loyalties and a sense of personal honor, Chechens, like Sicilians, are governed by the concept of *omertá*—*adat* requires vengeance to uphold family honor ("A History of Antagonism" 1994; Gallagher 1995b). And the Russian attitude toward Chechens parallels that of northern Italians toward Sicilians.[2]

In 1991, Chechen leaders declared their independence, and they have been locked in violent conflict with the Russian military ever since. Independence leader Dzhokar Dudayev is reported to have turned Chechnya into the "Chicago of the twenties": "Chechen mafiosi engaged in some of the most spectacular criminal scams Russia has ever known. With Dudayev's police looking the other way (or, more likely, cooperating at every turn), Grozny [the capital] became a center of illegal trade. The city's airport served as a hub for unsanctioned flights hauling contraband and outlaws. . . . The flights—from the Middle East, Turkey, central Asia, and elsewhere—brought in huge amounts of narcotics and 'duty free' goods, and a succession of bandits in hiding. Mafiosi were also in the habit of robbing cargo trains travelling through Chechen territory" (Remnick 1995: 53).

Vast supplies of arms were left in Chechnya by the Russian military; arms trafficking and the counterfeiting of currency and financial documents are important parts of the Chechen crime portfolio. Chechen crime groups operate in many areas of the former Soviet Union, including Moscow, where there are about 1,500 active members: "The group is more structured than most. Most important for them is the strict hierarchical arrangement of their clan relationships. It is a closed organization, recruiting only from among their own people. Chechens actively recruit juveniles from the Chechen regions where unemployment is high. This ensures a degree of 'purity' in the membership, making it difficult for law enforcement agencies lacking personnel that speak Chechen to infiltrate the group. . . . Each group has a clear structure: leader, senior advisors, soldiers, and associated members" (Serio 1992b: 5).

Chechen gangs are quite violent and much feared. Protection rackets, enforcing restraint of trade agreements, and narcotics trafficking are all part of the Chechen crime repertoire. In 1993 a group of well-armed gangsters drove to a building across the Moscow River from the Kremlin to extort money from a local businessman. They were met by the businessman's protectors, Chechens, who opened fire, killing the gangster boss and four of his men (LeVine, McKay, and Lebedeva 1993). Members of Chechen groups have been found throughout Eastern and Western Europe and have sent members to New York to set up operations. Some have entered the United States for contract crimes—murder, extortion, fraud—after which they return home before authorities can detect and apprehend them.

---

[2]For a discussion of Chechnya and the conflict with Russia, see Gall and de Waal (1998) and Lieven (1998).

RUSSIAN ORGANIZED CRIME IN THE UNITED STATES

Russian criminals enter the United States with backgrounds for excelling in organized criminal activity without moving through the more traditional routes, which typically include street gang delinquency and apprenticeship under adult criminals: "Unlike their ethnic predecessors in crime, Russian émigrés do not have to go through any developmental or learning process to break into the criminal world in this country. They are able to begin operating almost immediately upon their arrival" (Tri-State Joint Soviet–Émigré Organized Crime Project 1997: 185). They typically have military experience, and many are college-educated: "Many of today's foremost Russian mobsters have Ph.D.'s in mathematics, engineering, or physics, helping them to acquire an expertise in advanced encryption and computer technology" (Friedman 2000: xviii).

These criminals have established themselves in a number of U.S. cities where Russian immigrants have settled—Boston, Chicago, Cleveland, Dallas, Miami, New York, Philadelphia, Portland, San Francisco, and Seattle. Although known by their fellow Russians as the *organizatsiya* (the organization), the actual degree of organization appears limited. What has not been limited is the exploitation of the Russian émigré community. In Brighton Beach, a major Russian émigré community in Brooklyn, Jewish criminals from the former Soviet Union, working in small gangs, have systematically extorted money from legitimate businesses (Friedman 2000).

Robert Friedman (2000) argues that in the United States, Russian criminals are well organized and pose a threat more serious than that of Italian-American criminal organizations. Unfortunately, he provides virtually no information on the structure of the Russian groups, although he reveals that they are in awe of their Italian-American counterparts. Friedman also uses terms such as "member" and "cartel" when referring to Russian organized crime but provides no explanation of their meaning. The Tri-State Joint Soviet–Émigré Organized Crime Project (1997) concludes that

Russian criminals in the United States have neither the critical mass nor the criminal sophistication to create a major local or regional threat, much less a national or international one.

It appears that Russian crime groups in the United States are typically fluid, and membership is transient, comprising 5 to 20 persons. Their pattern has been compared to that of the Zips, discussed in Chapter 2 (Mitchell 1992; Finckenauer and Waring 1999). Loosely structured, without formal hierarchy, groups are usually formed on the basis of regional backgrounds or built around a particular enterprise. One group may be composed mainly of immigrants from Kiev, while another may consist mainly of Georgians. Or a group may organize to extort money from local merchants or to operate a gasoline-tax-evasion scheme. Many group members are professional criminals; after their experience of criminal life in the Soviet Union, where police were feared and treatment of lawbreakers harsh, they view the United States as a haven. They engage in extortion, insurance fraud, Medicaid scams,[3] securities-related fraud,[4] con games, counterfeiting, tax fraud, and narcotics trafficking.

The Tri-State (New York–New Jersey–Pennsylvania) Joint Soviet–Émigré Organized Crime Project (1997—hereafter, Tri-State) states that the Russian-émigré criminals in the United States typically mistrust one another. There is generally little or no personal loyalty based upon common ethnic or cultural backgrounds, even though some of the criminals knew one another in the former Soviet Union. Their network structure is usually an ad hoc group of specialists teamed for specific criminal enterprises. They form opportunistic partnerships, which are sometimes based on referrals by other Russian criminals. After the criminal objective is attained, the specialists may split up or may move together to other criminal ventures. There are also professional criminals with a propensity for violence who form small criminal groups to commit extortion or engage in drug traf-

---

[3]See, for example, Finkelstein (1998).
[4]See, for example, Eaton (1997).

Good News, Bad News

"While criminal cells or networks now operating in the United States have been called, among other things, 'the Russian mafia,' unlike the traditional mafia, Russian organized crime is relatively unstructured; there is no well-established criminal hierarchy or firm chain of command. This absence of what has typically been an identifying feature for international criminal syndicates frequently makes it difficult for law enforcement agencies to tie specific criminal activities to Russian organized crime" (George Weise in "ROC" 1996: 11).

ficking. These groups often center around one or more dominant individuals, and the composition of the group is subject to frequent changes. Colombo Family captain Michael Franzese, who worked closely with Russian crime groups, states that "I did not find the Russian criminals to be a very structured group in comparison to the Italian La Cosa Nostra. They were very clannish, however, and the most financially successful Russian was looked up to by his comrades as their leader or boss. The boss was given a lot of courtesy and respect and in return provided the members of his group with opportunities to work for him and make money" ("ROC" 1996: 39).

Moreover, "One way to contrast La Cosa Nostra and Russian-émigré criminal organizations is to view the former as having a structure—a distinct, definable crime family—that is supported by criminal activities. The structure is continuous, and crime is used to carry out its objectives and maintain its strength and vitality. Russians, however, create floating structures on an as-needed basis to enable them to carry out particular crimes. The criminal opportunities come first, and the necessary structure to take advantage of those opportunities follows" (Tri-State 1997: 24).

The Fuel Oil Scam

An example of the types of activities in which Russian criminals are involved in the United States, and their relations with traditional crime Families, involves the fuel oil scam. Michael Franzese, born in 1951, son of the infamous underboss of the Colombo Family, John ("Sonny") Franzese, testified before a congressional committee ("ROC" 1996) on how the scheme transpired.

In 1987 a major Italian-American independent gasoline wholesaler approached Franzese for protection: he was involved in a massive tax evasion scheme and was being extorted by some mob figures. In return for his help, Franzese became a partner in the business. Later, some Russian gasoline dealers using the same scheme approached Franzese for help in collecting some debts. Through his contacts, Franzese also helped them hold and obtain the wholesale licenses needed to keep their business in operation. In both cases, the scheme was similar: using a "daisy chain with a vanishing point," gasoline was transferred on paper from one bogus company to another. Taxes are due when the fuel is finally sold to retailers, but the last company receiving the gasoline existed only on paper, as revenue investigators discovered. By the time auditors and investigators would unravel the series of transactions to determine the tax liability, the "burn" company had disappeared without a trace of records or assets. The taxes were skimmed when the fuel was actually sold at discount prices to dealers (Van Duyne and Block 1995). The wholesalers need to be able to purchase fuel tax free, and this requires an IRS excise tax certification of exemption. The certifications were obtained by buying out registered companies or by falsifying the documents of legitimate companies.

In response to these schemes, Congress in 1993 moved the point of taxation on gasoline from the wholesale distributor to the distribution terminal. Unable to divert the excise tax, the Russians moved to a new scam. Using numerous dummy firms, they purchased home heating (diesel) oil, which is tax free. The diesel oil was then transferred through fake companies and sold as diesel fuel, which is subject to federal excise taxes, and the Russians pocketed the tax money. Franzese recalls that "it was not unusual for me to receive $9 million in cash per week in paper bags" from the combined operation ("ROC" 1996: 38), estimated to have cost the government $140 million (Levy 1995). Legislation enacted in 1994 requires that only fuel dyed red—diesel fuel is typically yellow or green—can be tax exempt and can be used only for off-road purposes such as home heating or in tractors. The dyed fuel is easily spotted by IRS inspectors or state tax agents who check truck stops or set up road checkpoints. The Russians responded by purchasing fuel in low-tax states and shipping it to high-tax states, a maneuver that can produce a 12-percent advantage.

As a result of this successful collaboration, Franzese was involved in numerous lucrative deals with Russian criminals involving loansharking and insurance and securities fraud.

Anthony Casso, who later become involved with the fuel scam on behalf of the Lucchese Family—eventually four crime Families became involved, each working with different Russian groups—notes that the unstructured Russians needed the organizational experience of the Italians: "It is putting it together, because like Marat [Balagula, one of the key Russians], he owned a couple of hundred gas stations. So when we put the cartel together, now no one else was going to go into his stations to sell gas a little cheaper, just sell the gas, and they start fighting amongst themselves again. So we held peace, and, you know, protection goes more than one way" ("ROC" 1996: 48). The Lucchese Family also took care of a problem Balagula was having with the violent boss of a Russian gang—they shot him to death as he left a Brighton Beach restaurant. The FBI and IRS set up their own petroleum company to compete with the "bootleggers." The response by OC figures to

this competition led to the breaking up of the petroleum cartel.[5]

In 2000 an investigation in the ports of Newark and Elizabeth, New Jersey, revealed a massive smuggling operation orchestrated by Russian criminals. At the behest of Russian criminals in the United States, a number of American distilleries were disguising millions of gallons of their product—192-proof grain alcohol—by adding dye and shipping it in giant containers marked windshield-wiper fluid, cologne, mouthwash, and cleaning solvent. Once the product was in Russia, the recipients used a formula provided by the distillers to remove the dye, dilute the alcohol with water, and add vodka flavoring. The product was then distributed by Russia-based criminal organizations, evading millions of dollars in import duty and taxes. The smuggling was encouraged by high Russian tariffs designed to protect domestic alcohol production (Rashbaum 2000b).

Vory in the United States

Vory members are given special status—*respect*—in the Russian-American underworld. In 1991, Vyacheslav Kirillovich (*Yaponchik*—"Little Jap") Ivankov, a high-ranking *vor v zakonye* with the *Solntsevskaya* gang (discussed earlier), was released early (political influence/bribery is suspected) from a 14-year prison sentence for robbery, aggravated assault, and extortion. After his release, he went on a campaign of extortion, often torturing victims, and was responsible for ordering many killings, including those of journalists and police officers. His murderous campaign against Moscow's powerful Chechen crime groups further

---

[5]In 1986, Michael Franzese pleaded guilty to the massive fuel-tax fraud and received a 10-year sentence. He was released in 1989 and ordered to pay the government back more than $14 million—which was never paid. That year, under a grant of immunity, he admitted that he was a member of the Colombo Family. Franzese produced low-budget movies and wrote a book in which he portrayed himself as the "yuppie Don." In 1991, he received a four-year sentence for violation of probation.

Vyacheslav Ivankov, a high-ranking boss in the Russian mob, center, is escorted by FBI agents after his arrest in New York in 1995.

raised Ivankov's profile to a liability: the *vor* leadership's "Circle of Brothers" banished him to America (Friedman 2000).

Shortly after his arrival at Kennedy Airport, Ivankov was given a suitcase with $1.5 million by an Armenian *vor*. He established his headquarters in Brighton Beach and recruited Russian combat veterans with a $20,000-per-month retainer. They were sent out to extort money from legitimate businesses worldwide and to assassinate his rivals. Fear permeated the Russian émigré community, and its major criminal operatives were soon allied with Ivankov—or they were dead (Friedman 2000).

Ivankov's reign as the reputed leading Russian crime boss in the United States did not last long: in 1995 he was arrested for Hobbs Act violations (see Chapter 14), attempting to extort millions of dollars from two immigrant businessman—both embezzlers—who had been kidnapped at gunpoint from a Manhattan hotel (Myers 1995; Dubocq and Garcia 1997). Ivankov had become personally involved in the plot and was recorded on a wiretap giving instructions on how it was to be carried out; he also threatened the two businessmen, who, unbeknownst to him, were cooperating with the FBI. While in custody awaiting trial, Ivankov so alienated his codefendants that two of them became cooperating witnesses against him (Friedman 2000). The following year, Ivankov and three codefendants were convicted of extortion; he received a nine-year sentence (Finckenauer and Waring 1999).

One of his business partners, Semion Mogilevich, 55, is a Ukrainian-born Jew with a college degree in economics. Originally part of a Moscow crime group during the Soviet era, Mogilevich made his first fortune by defrauding fellow Jews who were fleeing to the United States. Holding Israeli and Hungarian citizenship—his wife is Hungarian—Mogilevich heads an organization of about 250 persons, many of whom are relatives, whose operations transcend national boundaries. In the Czech Republic, they tortured and murdered businessmen who resisted their extortion efforts; at Moscow's international airport, they control smuggling; in Hungary, Mogilevich owns nightclubs and a major portion of the Hungarian arms industry; and in the United States, his operatives have been involved in money laundering and contract murders—supplying weapons and spiriting the killers out of the country after their assignment is complete (Friedman 1998). According to Friedman (2000: 239), Mogilevich built a "highly structured criminal organization in the mode of a 'classic' American Mafia family," with a clearly defined chain of command, specialization, and division of labor. While he may have indeed built such an organization, as noted in Chapter 1, the bureaucratic attributes that Friedman describes are not the mode of a "classic American Mafia family."

In 1999 it was revealed that Mogilevich, who is an undesirable prohibited from entering the United States, set up a magnet manufacturing and importing company in suburban Philadelphia. YBM Magnex had a blue-ribbon board of directors and was audited by two prominent American accounting firms. Before YBM pled guilty to securities fraud, Mogilevich and his associates had made millions of dollars from selling inflated shares of the company's stock (Bonner 1999). He was subsequently linked to a major money-laundering operation in which billions of dollars were channeled through the Bank of New York. Some of the money from the account reportedly went to pay contract killers, and some went to drug barons (Bonner and O'Brien 1999).

Many of the criminals, *vor* and non-*vor*, are Jews. Unlike Jewish immigrant groups that took part in organized crime in the past (discussed in Chapter 4), the Russians are relatively well educated and adept at exploiting weaknesses in American society. Jewish émigrés—many from the Ukrainian seaport of Odessa, noted for its criminal subculture—have settled in the Brighton Beach section of Brooklyn ("Little Odessa"), and the New York police department has been handicapped in dealing with the protection rackets and loansharking activities in the community by a lack of Russian-speaking officers.

THE FUTURE OF ROC

While they come with a great deal of education and marketable skills, "the new immigrants arrive from a social system where beating the system is a normal practice." They "are skilled in behavior needed for living in a particularly corrupt system of acquiring and dispensing goods and services" (Rosner 1986: 43, 126). And they have proved to be able and willing to engage in the type of violence that typifies organized crime in general (Raab 1994a), although they prefer financial accommodations to violence—they are essentially ruthless businessmen rather than gangsters. In other words, as the immigrants become economically successful and acculturated, their progeny are unlikely to be found in the ranks of organized crime. The same cannot be said of the *vory*, whose subcultural orientation belies political and economic changes. Will these criminals eventually emerge as the twenty-first-century version of American organized crime? Only the passage of time will allow this question to be answered. According to James Moody, a ranking official with the FBI, "I anticipate, based on 25 years in organized crime, that we are going to continue to see them evolve and build more structured organizations, and that a lot of the organizations that we see today will fall by the wayside; they will either be destroyed in fights for territory, or they will be absorbed by some of the stronger groups. And as they become more structured, they will set up various coordinating mechanisms, like the Cosa Nostra, here in the United States" ("ROC" 1996: 27).

In the next chapter, we will look at Asian contributions to organized crime.

INTERNET CONNECTIONS

Organized Crime in the Baltic region: **www.balticseataskforce.dk**

Global Organized Crime Project: **csis.org/goc**

Nathanson Centre: **www.yorku.ca/nathanson**

International Organization for Migration: **www.iom.int**

United Nations criminal justice: **uncjin.org**

REVIEW QUESTIONS

1. Why do Russian criminals come to the United States well prepared for a life in organized crime?
2. What are the problems experienced by Russia that promote organized crime?
3. What are the different groups that make up Russian organized crime?
4. What are the types of activities engaged in by Russian organized crime in the former Soviet Union?
5. What is the *vory*?
6. What are the similarities between the old and new *vory* and the old and new Sicilian Mafia?
7. What is the structure of Russian organized crime groups in the United States?
8. How do members of Russian organized crime groups in the United States differ from members of previous immigrant groups?
9. How does organized crime in Russia differ from that in the United States?
10. What have been the criminal activities of Russian crime groups in the United States?
11. What can we predict about the future of Russian organized crime in the United States?

♠

CHAPTER 10

ASIAN ORGANIZED CRIME

*A*sian is a rather imprecise term that can include many diverse groups. In the United States, for example, Asian communities are made up of 34 distinct ethnic groups, including Chinese, which itself has several different groups, such as Cantonese and Mandarin (Song 1996). A number of unrelated Asian groups are involved in organized crime. Some, such as the *Yakuza*, are more of a problem in Japan, although there is a potential for expansion overseas. Others, such as the Triads, have been an international problem for many years.

YAKUZA

Most Americans have heard of the Mafia, Lucky Luciano, Al Capone, and their "soldiers"—but what about the Yamaguchi-gumi, Kazuo Taoka, Hideomi Oda, and their *yakuza*? The Yamaguchi-gumi (*gumi* means "group") is a criminal organization that dominates the industrialized, densely populated region extending from Kyoto through Osaka to Kobe, as well as Tokyo and most other major centers in Japan. They are the largest *bo-*

ryokudan ("violent groups"), organizations that constitute Japanese organized crime. These organizations have been in existence for about 300 years and have their roots in the Tokugawa period (1600–1850), when Japan united under a central system of government. With the end of Japanese feudalism, *samurai* (knights) lost their role in life, and many roamed the countryside as free-lance mercenaries (Rome 1975). The *yakuza*—masterless *samurai*, unscrupulous itinerant peddlers, professional gamblers, and common criminals—eventually formed structured groups: *boryokudan*.

Under the leadership of their *kumi-cho* (boss), they were able to exert control over sections of Japan's urban areas. By adhering to rules of conduct that preclude violence against the police and innocent civilians, *yakuza* syndicates have been able to operate openly, with high-profile headquarters. Yoshinori Watanabe, the head of the Yamaguchi-gumi, the largest *boryokudan*, who is in his late fifties, resides in a home in Kobe, a city about 275 miles southwest of Tokyo that also serves as the group's headquarters. The heavily guarded residence takes up a full city block in an

Quid Pro Quo, Japanese Style

In 1995, two members of the Yamaguchi-gumi walked into police headquarters crying and begging for forgiveness—they had killed a police officer after mistaking him for a member of the rival Aizukotetsu. The group subsequently announced that 12 members who had been peripherally involved in the killing had been expelled from the Yamaguchi-gumi (Andrews 1995).

upscale neighborhood. Steel doors are illuminated with floodlights and monitored by video cameras; bodyguards are quick to challenge unknown visitors. Watanabe is reputed to get $1 million a month in tithes from his top aides and has been moving the group into areas of legitimate business such as construction (Kristoff 1995b; Agence France-Press 1997; Talmadge 1999).

"The *yakuza* were largely local crime rings that controlled neighborhood card games and brothels. As Japan grew into the world's second-largest economy, the *yakuza*, too, grew increasingly sophisticated and business-minded. A handful of super syndicates expanded nationwide, gaining political access and influence over the entertainment and construction industries" (Kaplan 1998: 46). They are widely reputed to control Japan's busy ports (Sanger 1997) and, in cooperation with violent Chinese "snakehead" gangs, traffic in amphetamines smuggled in from the People's Republic (Jordon and Sullivan 1999). In some areas, such as Tokyo's Kabukicho entertainment district, gambling and prostitution are controlled by the snakehead gangs, which are considered more ruthless than their *yakuza* counterparts (Kristoff 1999). They are particularly active in the smuggling of Chinese immigrants into Japan and the United States (Chin, Zhang, and Kelly 1998).

Present-day *yakuza* view themselves as modern *samurai* and maintain exotic rituals, including extensive tattooing that often covers their bodies from necks to ankles, and clipped fingers that have been self-amputated with a short sword in a ritual—*yubizume*—that serves as a sign of contrition for mistakes. The amputated top of the smallest digit is placed in a small, alcohol-filled bottle with the person's name written on it; it is sent to whomever one is asking forgiveness. While not obligatory, the tattooing indicates the ability to withstand pain and commitment to the *yakuza* life. Resignation or expulsion is accomplished with a *homojo* or "red letter" to all members of the *boryokudan*, which signals that the person is no longer a member (PCOC 1984b).

There are more than 80,000 identified *yakuza* members in Japan; about 17,000 belong to the three most powerful syndicates: Yamaguchi-gumi, Inagawa-kai, and Sumiyoshi-kai (National Police Agency of Japan 1996; Kaplan 1998; Talmadge 1999; Sims 2000a; French 2001). *Yakuza* share similar backgrounds. In sharp contrast to Russian organized crime and reminiscent of the early days of American organized crime, *yakuza* are typically lower-working-class high school dropouts, with one or two parents of Korean or Chinese extraction—marginalized persons with a history of juvenile delinquency (Seymour 1996).[1] They are also the most loyal consumers of American automobiles, particularly Cadillacs, although in more recent years they have taken to European luxury cars.

The term *yakuza* "is derived from an old card game . . . whose object was to draw three cards adding up as close as possible to 19 without exceeding it," similar to our game of "21" or blackjack: "*Ya-ku-za* represents the Japanese words for 8, 9, 3, which total 20, a useless number. Basically, *yakuza* means 'good for nothing'" (Haberman 1985: 6). Like many of their American counterparts, the *yakuza* "were born into poverty and

---

[1] An estimated 75 percent of the Yamaguchi-gumi are ethnic Koreans or *burakumin*, descendants of outcasts—Japanese "untouchables"—who have been subjected to generations of discrimination because their families are associated with "dirty" occupations: butchers, tanners, and grave diggers (Kristoff 1995c). In Japan, organized crime is an equal opportunity employer.

A Japanese *yakuza* gang member being tattooed. While not mandatory, the extensive tattooing is a sign of the members' ability to withstand pain and of a commitment to the *yakuza* life.

© Horace Bristol/Corbis

graduated from juvenile delinquency into organized crime" (Kirk 1976: 93). The Al Capone of Japan, Kazuo Taoka, was, like Capone, born into a poor family. He began his criminal career as a bouncer in Kobe, much as Capone filled this capacity in Brooklyn before going to Chicago. Taoka, like Capone, played a major role in the gang conflicts of the day, and both men rose to prominence because of their penchant for violence and talent for organization. In 1981, Taoka, 68, died of a heart attack. His funeral was attended by more than 1,200 *yakuza:* "Taoka's friendships and contacts extended to the highest levels of government, with two former prime ministers . . . among his friends. That kind of relationship reflected not only Taoka's personal success but also historic ties between gangsters and prominent government figures" (Kirk 1981: 17).

Similar ties were forged by Susumu Ishii, boss of Japan's third-largest crime group, the Tokyo-based Inagawa-kai. Before he died of natural causes in 1991, Ishii was involved with the world's largest brokerage houses, from which he received $2.3 billion in loans and loan guarantees (Kaplan 1998). He had invested heavily in real estate and stocks: his portfolio was estimated to be worth more than $1 billion. Four thousand persons attended his funeral. In 1992 it was revealed that one of the most powerful political figures in Japan, a high-ranking governing (Liberal Democrat) party official, had business and political ties to Ishii; the politician's parliamentary colleague is, in fact, a former *yakuza* member (Sanger 1992; Sterngold 1992b). Executives of Japan's most profitable retailer paid gangsters (*sokaiya*) to ensure that the firm's stockholder meetings would not be disturbed—this is a standard, albeit now illegal, practice in Japan (Sterngold 1992c). A police raid on the offices of Mitsubishi Motors found evidence of a continuing relationship between *sokaiya* and the company (Lev 1997).

In contrast to most organized crime groups (see the attributes of organized crime in Chapter 1), the *yakuza* have a distinct ideological orientation—ultra-nationalistic and conservative on matters of foreign policy, and vigorously anti-Communist. This has endeared them to many right-wing politicians, and *yakuza* are intimately involved in the politics of Japan. The relatively low rate of street crime in Japan is in large part the result of a symbiotic relationship between the *yakuza* and the police (Kaplan and Dubro 1986). The police share the political views of the *yakuza* and historically have done little against them—police raids are often publicity stunts. The *yakuza* reciprocate by keeping *disorganized* crime under control. In 1995, when leaders of the Pacific Rim countries met in Osaka, the Yamaguchi-gumi, like others concerned with the city's image, explained their position through a spokesman: "All members of our group want to do our part for our country. So we agreed to exercise self-control over our businesses" (Kristoff 1995a: 6).

The *yakuza* are also concerned about their public image: when famed Japanese film director Juzo Itami (*Tampopo, A Taxing Woman*) portrayed them in an unflattering manner in film, he became the victim of a knife attack by assailants who slashed his neck and face (Goozner 1992; Sterngold 1992a). In 1995, when a devastating earthquake hit Kobe and killed 5,500 people, the relief efforts established by the Yamaguchi-gumi proved superior to those of the government. This was seen as a way of blunting the high-profile police campaign against the group (Sterngold 1995). The earthquake also provided a vehicle for Yamaguchi-gumi-controlled construction firms to increase their wealth: they threatened rivals so that they did not submit lower bids and collected "greetings fees" as insurance against construction site disruptions (Kristoff 1995b).

In 1994 it was revealed that the *yakuza* have close financial ties to the banking industry, which provided funds for the gangsters to invest in real estate. When property values deteriorated as a result of a market downturn, financial institutions found themselves holding many bad loans; efforts to collect proved dangerous—one banker was shot to death, and firebombings and cut telephone lines became frequent. In 1997 a securities executive was slashed to death as he walked home (Hirsch and Takayama 1997; Kaplan 1998; Sterngold 1994; WuDunn 1996). Banks in Japan frequently designate certain employees to deal with the *yakuza*, and the *yakuza* have played havoc with efforts to clean up the banking mess that is at the heart of the Japanese economic downturn. Fear is widespread, making it difficult for banks to collect bad loans. American companies buying distressed Japanese firms often have written clauses that nullify contracts if they discover *yakuza* involvement (Jordan and Sullivan 1999).

Japan has a serious drug problem, particularly the abuse of amphetamines, which the *yakuza* produce in clandestine laboratories in Japan, the Philippines, and Korea. In 1994 a *yakuza* subgroup boss pleaded guilty in a Hawaii federal court to importing and distributing methamphetamine and was given an 11-year sentence. At times, the *yakuza* have been big news in Hawaii because of their involvement in methamphetamine trafficking, gambling, and prostitution on the islands. More recently, they have been linked to the importation of cocaine, which is growing in popularity in Japan.

The *yakuza* are also at the center of an international trade in sexual slavery: females, often children, bought and sold throughout Third World countries. They helped popularize the Southeast Asian "sex tours" (*Kisaeng* parties) favored by Japanese businessmen. These women and children also serve in the *yakuza*-dominated sex entertainment centers of Tokyo. Rounding out their criminal activities are extortion from both legitimate and illegitimate entrepreneurs and the intimidation and eviction of people from their homes on behalf of real estate developers. Automobile accident victims will sometimes hire *yakuza* to retrieve damage payments on a contingency basis (Weisman 1991): "Japanese courts are notoriously slow

Colombian Ties

"Colombian traffickers import cocaine into Japan and then sell the drug to the *yakuza* groups, which manage retail distribution. Working relationships, dating back to 1992, exist between Colombian traffickers and *yakuza* groups operating in Tokyo's Shinjuku District. . . . Moreover, cocaine trafficking and distribution no longer are limited to Tokyo. Colombian night club hostesses, working in *yakuza*-controlled entertainment districts in several Japanese cities, provide a convenient link between the Colombian traffickers and the *yakuza*" (*Cocaine in Japan* 1994: 2).

and indifferent to the complaints of individuals. Essentially, the *yakuza* have taken on the role of lawyers-cum-negotiators" (Seymour 1996: 202). Similarly, most Japanese bankruptcies are handled informally by *yakuza*-backed "adjusters," and the police are reluctant to intervene in what they consider civil matters. Bankers sometimes dispatch *yakuza* to bankrupted businesses to confiscate property ahead of unsecured creditors (Hirsch and Takayama 1997; Kaplan 1998).

The *boryokudans* "form closed societies in their individual groups, but the groups are interlinked through a widespread underworld syndicate" (Takahashi and Becker 1985: 3):

> *Boryokudans* distinguish between members (*kumiin*) and associates (*jun-kumiin*) who have not been initiated into the secrets of the organization by way of an elaborate sake ceremony, and are therefore at the bottom of the *yakuza* world. Rising in the ranks depends on the amount of money sent up to superiors in the organization, and one's share of profits is in order of rank, with the boss getting about half. There are a variety of ranks and titles in the various *yakuza* groups; these establish the status and power hierarchy and the order of authority within the family group. On occasion when a follower reaches a certain status in the hierarchy, he is given permission to train his own followers and become a small boss. He announces the name of his own family and, in accordance with his prestige, he is permitted to call himself either the boss of "a branch of the family" or boss of "a whole family." (Iwai 1986: 216–17)

A low-ranking member may be called upon—actually directed—to take the place of a boss (*oyabun*) who has been implicated in a crime, even if this means a prison sentence (Seymour 1996).

The self-image of the *yakuza* stands in contrast to that of their American counterparts. For example, the Yamaguchi-gumi is listed in the telephone book and publishes a membership newsletter, and its headquarters are clearly marked for all to see. Group members typically wear lapel pins that designate their *boryokudan*. For instance, the logo of the Yamaguchi-gumi, a golden diamond-shaped design, appears on their headquarters building in Kobe, on lapel pins, and on members' business cards. Movies that portray *yakuza* as noble gangsters are popular in Japan, and the *yakuza* are influential in the Japanese movie industry. In 1981, when Masahisa Takenaka was installed as the head of the Yamaguchi-gumi, the event was seen on national television. His funeral in 1985 was also telecast—Takenaka was gunned down by rival members of his *boryokudan*. When a rival for leadership seceded from the clan, he announced it at a news conference at one of Kobe's leading restaurants (Haberman 1985). With 18 top lieutenants, he formed the 3,000-member Ichiwa-kai. In 1999, Tokutaro Takayama, 71, godfather of the Aizu-Kotetsu *boryokudan*, was interviewed by reporters at his private office just outside of Kyoto, surrounded by surveillance cameras and bodyguards with missing pinkies. He decried the state of *yakuza* in present-day Japan: "Today, they don't care about obligations, traditions, respect and dignity. There are no rules anymore" (Jordon and Sullivan 1999). Similar sentiments could be uttered by the elders of America's organized crime Families.

The rebellion of the Ichiwa-kai against the mainstream Yamaguchi-gumi resulted in a great deal of violence, and it caused headlines in Hawaii. While Yamaguchi-gumi loyalists had numerical superiority, the Ichiwa-kai had seized most of the organization's arsenal. Desperate for firepower, Masashi Takenaka (brother of the slain leader and his replacement as head of the Yamaguchi-gumi) and two of his ranking officers attempted to exchange large quantities of amphetamines for military arms in Honolulu, but they were caught in a Drug Enforcement Administration undercover sting. A DEA agent told Takenaka that the weapons would be delivered to Japan aboard a U.S. Air Force plane in order to avoid scrutiny by Japanese authorities—Japan has strict gun-control laws (Yates 1985). By the end of 1988, the gang war had left 25 dead and 70 injured and led to a significant increase in Yamaguchi-gumi membership. According to Japanese law enforcement officials, tough police crackdowns "may have worked to the syndicate's benefit, putting many smaller gangs out of business or forcing them to seek Yamaguchi-gumi protection" (Talmadge 1988: 2). An anti-*yakuza* law enacted in 1992 designates the seven major *yakuza* syndicates as dangerous entities whose members have diminished legal rights. *Yakuza* have held public demonstrations against these laws, but the police have been emboldened (Seymour 1996).

Police crackdowns on *yakuza* business interests and a downturn in the Japanese economy have affected organized crime. When the easy money was plentiful, *yakuza* "stuck closely to their own turf and honored hierarchy as if it were life itself. Things were so simple, in fact, that using a little muscle often meant little more than, say, depositing a dead cat on the doorstep of a landlord being pressured into selling a coveted property" (French 2001: 4). With business expense accounts slashed, *yakuza*-controlled bars and nightclubs are hurting, and the gangsters have become more competitive and more violent (Talmadge 1999). Members are having a more difficult time paying monthly honorariums to their leaders, and discipline has lapsed. Public bombings and shootings—traditionally anathema to the image-conscious *yakuza*—have

become more frequent (Sims 2000a, 2000b). In 1997 the Yamaguchi-gumi second in command was shot to death at a Kobe hotel by four gunmen (Agence France-Press 1997). In 2001, at a Sumiyoshi-kai funeral in Tokyo, two men laying white chrysanthemums on the altar suddenly pulled out handguns and killed two of the *boryoku-dan* bosses. Two days later, another ranking member of the Sumiyoshi-kai was shot to death in the doorway of his flat (Whymant 2001).

In a situation that closely parallels that of the "old" and *Nuovo* Mafia in Sicily (see Chapter 7), a new breed of gangster—*keizai yakuza*—is emerging. These "economic mobsters" are abandoning *yakuza* traditions, such as amputating fingers, in favor of pure materialism (French 2001).

TRIADS, TONGS, AND ASIAN GANGS

Secret societies have a long history in China, some dating back to the beginning of the common era (Fong 1981; Chin 1990). An important part of these societies is the Triads and their American offshoots—tongs and Chinatown gangs. Before we can understand the qualities of these groups, we need to explore the unique cultural dynamics of Chinese society, in which loyalty to family and friends is a moral imperative (Liu et al. 1998).

Any member of the Chinese community is part of a "latent organization" because of the existence of *guanxi*, a phenomenon that parallels *partito*, discussed in Chapter 7: "Chinese are born into a hierarchically organized society in which they never see themselves or others as free individuals, but as bound to others in an ever expanding web of social relations hearing mutual obligate bonds of varying strength." The Chinese *guanxi* "embraces many concepts, some familiar to Westerners, such as connections, networks, and patron–client relations." They are built upon "a series of dyadic relationships, some that are naturally present and others which must be acquired, cultivated, and maintained" (Myers 1995: 3).

The Chinese concept of *qinqing* parallels that of the southern Italian *famiglia*. Family, the primary and most important group to a Chinese individual, "serves as the crucible for formation of the ideals of harmonious social relations and the model for social interaction. It is an association composed of parental and filial bonds carrying the strongest obligations of mutual reciprocity (*qin-qing*)." All family resources "are pooled and shared according to apparent or expressed need. Each member is obligated to contribute to the family as able and the family is obligated to provide each member with the resources for living" (Myers 1995: 4). The pooling of familial resources has advanced the business interests of overseas Chinese in the many communities where they have settled.

In this cultural setting, notes Willard Myers (1995), law is marginalized, relegated to a position well below mediative mechanisms within a particularistic social order of human relationships. Like *famiglia* and *partito*, these cultural manifestations, while not ipso facto criminal, lead to criminal organization. Of particular interest are persons of Cantonese and Fukienese heritage,[2] who as immigrants throughout the world were subjected to pernicious discrimination; they responded by relying on cultural attributes that provided great advantages in business, both legal and illegal. And *guanxi* is global, providing a dynamic for international business, both legal and illegal. The Triad phenomenon is a natural extension of these cultural attributes.

Triads

The term *triad* refers a common Chinese symbol: an equilateral triangle representing the three basic Chinese concepts of heaven, earth, and man. Triad members are assigned numbers based on their position. For example, enforcers or "Red Poles" are assigned number 426; an ordinary member is a 49; a leader or "Hill Chief" is 489. Based on ancient occult numerology, assigned numbers always begin with a 4 (Booth 1990). These groups, based in Hong Kong and Taiwan, engage in highly ritual-

ized dress and behavior—secret hand signs, passwords, and blood oaths are used in elaborate initiation ceremonies. The initiation ceremony includes the recital of the Triads' 36 oaths, each of which ends with the death penalty for its violation. For example, "If I am arrested after committing an offense, I must accept my punishment and not try to place blame on my sworn brothers. If I do so, I will be killed by five thunderbolts" (Carter 1991b). The ceremony may take six or seven hours (Booth 1990). In contrast, the man who would later emerge as head of the powerful Big Circle (discussed below) recalls his initiation into the Green Gang (Triad) in a Bangkok hotel room in 1969. There was no elaborate ceremony. Instead, in the presence of his Green Gang mentor, Johnny Kon handed a cup of tea and an envelope containing $108 to a ranking member and said in Shanghai dialect, "If you accept me, I'll be very happy." The man placed the envelope in his jacket and responded, "Never tell secrets. Never betray anyone. If ever your brothers need help, never refuse them." "Thank you, master," Johnny responded, and they adjourned to a celebratory meal at a Chinese restaurant. However, his subsequent admission into another (Red Gang) Triad, in addition to the ceremonial $108, was replete with 36 oaths, the decapitation of a live chicken, and the drawing of blood from his finger (J. Sack 2001).

The Triad phenomenon is believed to have originated in opposition to the Ch'ing dynasty established by the conquering Manchus in 1644 (Fong 1981). The Ch'ing dynasty ended in 1911 with the success of Dr. Sun Yat-sen (1866–1925), who had been a Triad member. With their political role no longer relevant, many Triad members turned to criminal activities: gambling, loansharking, extortion, and trafficking in opium from the Golden Triangle of Southeast Asia. This trade was strengthened considerably by the activities of Chinese Nationalist forces in the Golden Triangle (discussed in Chapter 13). Chiang Kai-shek, himself a Triad member, is reputed to have used Triads in his war against the Communists and labor unions. Triads were suppressed with a great deal of violence on the mainland by Mao Tse-Tung when his Communist forces defeated Chiang's National-

---

[2]Competition between members of these two groups, in both licit and illicit spheres, has led to violence in a number of American cities (Myers 1995).

ist Army in 1947. Triad members who fled to Taiwan with Chiang Kai-shek were tightly controlled by the Kuomintang, the Nationalist Party, and were unable to expand their criminal operations on the island (Chin 1990).

Thousands of other Triad members fled to the British colony of Hong Kong, linking up with local Triads that dated back to the early twentieth century. The indigenous Hong Kong Triads began as guilds and benevolent societies. They extended into criminal activities and actively collaborated with the Japanese during Japan's World War II occupation of the colony. In the postwar era, Triads emerged as powerful criminal societies (Chin 1990, 1995).

While most Triad societies are based in Hong Kong, Taiwan, or Macau, their influence spans international boundaries, with members located in virtually every country that has a sizable Chinese community. Triads, which collectively have an estimated worldwide membership that exceeds 100,000, are fluid associations of ethnic Chinese criminals and quasi-legitimate businessmen involved in an array of criminal enterprises. Most Hong Kong Triads have evolved into loose-knit groups operating and cooperating with one another on the basis of personal introductions and mutual interests. Triad leaders do not dictate to members what criminal activities they should pursue and generally do not receive monetary benefits unless they are directly involved with the actual criminal enterprise. The major Triads like 14K and Sun Yee On, both based in Hong Kong, and the United Bamboo, based in Taiwan, have autonomous branches extending worldwide that help in transnational criminal activities. In the 1990s, Hong Kong Triads strengthened their presence and relationships in Western countries by making various investments in legitimate businesses, a hedge against the political, economic, and law enforcement uncertainties of Hong Kong's reversion to China in 1997. The 14K and Sun Yee On have made substantial property investments in Canada, where the 14K is reportedly the fastest growing Triad.

The reputed leader of the United Bamboo is a wanted man in Taiwan who served several prison terms in the United States for drug trafficking.

Nevertheless, he resides in Shenzhen, China, just north of Hong Kong. While his activities might be anathema to officials in Taiwan and even in Beijing, in Shenzhen his ties to Taiwan and to potential deal makers and smugglers abroad make him a potential ally to the rich and influential. His politics—reunification of Taiwan with China—make him an attractive ally to Beijing. His presence in China highlights the of ties between organized crime figures and the Communist Party (Pomfret 2001).

It is not unusual for different Triads to work together where there is a specific opportunity for mutual profit. However, the Hong Kong police maintain that there is no international Triad network or centralized control over cross-border activities, such as drug trafficking or alien smuggling, between mainland China and Hong Kong. They state that most cooperation in such criminal enterprises is more ad hoc. Criminal groups from mainland China, typified by the Big Circle (*Dai Huen Jai*) and the Fuk Ching, have cells operating in countries around the world that cooperate with one another on an ad hoc basis to conduct far-reaching criminal schemes. These criminal cells typically operate autonomously, with no known central authority controlling them. Cell leaders use their extensive connections to arrange complex criminal operations that require a high degree of organization and planning. The coordinated efforts of members in various countries enable them to carry out international drug trafficking, arms trafficking, and alien smuggling operations, as well as a variety of more sophisticated financial frauds.

The Big Circle has its origins in Communist China's Red Guard, Mao's personal militia established to enforce the "Great Cultural Revolution." When the revolution was called off three years later, many Red Guards fled to Hong Kong but maintained camaraderie as the Big Circle—from their red armbands—and engaged in well-planned robberies, particularly of jewelry stores. As a result of their relationship with a leading Triad member in Hong Kong, the major bosses of the Big Circle were initiated into the Gang of Tranquil Happiness (Triad), and in a short time they became one of the most active Asian criminal organizations in

Coast Guard officers stand guard over several hundred Chinese immigrants found during an attempt to smuggle them into the United States, an activity associated with "snakehead gangs," criminal organizations in China that specialize in people-smuggling.

AP/Wide World Photos

the world. By the early 1990s, the Big Circle had established criminal cells in Canada, the United States, and Europe. It is extensively involved in drug trafficking, alien smuggling, vehicle theft and trafficking, and various financial, intellectual property rights, and high-tech crimes. Big Circle cells are also highly sophisticated in their use of technology to thwart law enforcement. Known primarily for the manufacture and distribution of counterfeit credit cards and other documents, this group has also been involved in drug trafficking, extortion, prostitution, and gaming offenses (National Security Council and Criminal Intelligence Service of Canada information).

The drug trafficking Triads expanded their operations during the Vietnam War, when thousands of GIs were attracted to the potent heroin of Southeast Asia. When the Americans withdrew from Vietnam, Triads followed the market and internationalized their drug operations. Since many soldiers were stationed in Europe, a major Triad marketplace developed there, with operations headquartered in Amsterdam. The powerful 14K society is reputed to have as many as 30,000 members in Hong Kong (the former colony has a population of 5.6 million) and about 10,000 in Taiwan. In the nearby former Portuguese colony of Macau, population over 500,000, 45-year-old Wan Kuok-koi ("Broken Tooth Koi") heads the local 14K. When the colony was under the Portuguese, he directed a violent conflict to control the lucrative gambling business that accounted for more than 40 percent of the enclave's economy. Wan financed a film on his exploits and in a promotional interview promised to wipe out an opposition group. Less tolerant than their Portuguese predecessors, the People's Republic imprisoned Wan Kuok-koi in 1999 (Sly 1999).

Triad membership requires a sponsor who is a ranking official of the society. Many of the younger members are involved in the martial arts; martial arts schools are often controlled by Triads. In British Hong Kong, membership in a Triad was a criminal offense. In the Hong Kong controlled by the People's Republic, there have been reports of ties between Triads and members of the Communist Party, and Triads have moved beyond Hong Kong into several mainland cities (Sheridan 1997).

Triads have been producing martial arts action ("chop socky") movies that, despite requiring little capital investment, are extremely popular in Asia (Dannen 1995: 31–32): "The only thing that matters is the cast. Indeed, many Hong Kong films are shot without a script. Anyone—literally anyone—who can persuade a popular performer or two to appear in his movie can make the movie with little or no investment." Triad persuasion techniques frequently "compensate for their ignorance of film technique."

Fenton Bresler, testifying before the President's Commission on Organized Crime (1984b:

42–43), points out that each Triad has its own triangular flag and territory: "If I want to become a new Triad head, I have to ask the original guy back in Hong Kong or Taiwan to give me a flag which means I can bring it over and that means this is my territory. . . . It authorizes for me to go to the new town and organize my branch." Although each Triad affiliate boss is theoretically independent—has his own flag—he is really only semi-independent. Spiritually, he is linked with the old country.

The typical structure of a Triad lodge is presented by Martin Booth. Each has a hierarchy that determines its activities (1990: 33–35, edited):

The leader is called the Shan Chu, and there is a deputy leader, the Fu Shan Chu, to assist. Below them come the Heung Chu, or Incense Master, and the Fin Fung, or Vanguard. These two officers administer the lodge rituals and have the power to invest, initiate, and order retribution against the members. Beneath them are a number of departmental heads responsible for the everyday running of the society and of any sub-branches, each of the latter having an internal structure similar to that of the main lodge except for the Incense Master and Vanguard. These are only found in principal lodges and their presence is a sign that a lodge has reached maturity and achieved power in its own right. Sub-branches are controlled by a leader, the Chu Chi, and his deputy, the Fu Chu Chi. Some lodges also have a treasurer, but this is comparatively rare. All Triad officers are appointed for fixed periods and are elected by lodge members.

Initiate members are required to pay an entrance fee. They must also obtain a sponsor, to whom further fee is payable—often far in excess of the entrance fee. This is a private arrangement and is reached only after the initiate's credentials have been thoroughly checked by the Incense Master and the Vanguard. A sponsor must also be found, and paid for, when a member seeks promotion within the lodge. All monies earned by an individual society, from whatever source, are deposited in the central lodge fund. Embezzlement is not uncommon and has caused major rifts in some societies, sometimes leading to violence.

Within each society there are four ranks of officials. The first is the Hung Kwan, or Red Pole, who is a fighter and is responsible for discipline. The Paz Tsz Sin is also known as the White Paper Fan and occupies a position similar to the *consigliere* in the Mafia. The Cho-Hai or Messenger is a liaison officer who acts as a go-between in lodge affairs and as a representative in its dealings with the outside world or with other lodges.

As in Italian-American crime Families and outlaw motorcycle clubs, Triads have an associational hierarchy that does not exert vertically integrated control over the members' criminal enterprises. Instead, leaders "devote their time to advancing the influence of the organization for the benefit of themselves and their members. When control is exercised it is to mediate a dispute or ensure the loyalty of a member." Furthermore, "Triad members are not solely dedicated to criminal pursuits and are found in virtually every occupation and profession in the society" (Myers 1995: 12). At the international level in drug trafficking, Chinese syndicates, whose members do not necessarily belong to a Triad, will come together for a particular enterprise and then reconfigure at a subsequent time for a new venture (Hopton 1996).

Tongs

The term *tong* means "hall" or "gathering place." Tongs were first established in San Francisco in the 1850s as benevolent societies (Chin, Kelly, and Fagan 1994). Some Chinese immigrants, like Sicilian immigrants who had been *mafiosi*, were Triad members at home. In the United States, they engaged in organized criminal activities, particularly opium trafficking, prostitution, gambling, and extortion. In a pattern similar to that of the *Unione Siciliana*, discussed in Chapter 4, many of these men joined tongs that were able to transcend the worlds of legitimate business and crime. At the turn of the century, "fighting tongs" controlled large-scale vice operations—gambling and prostitution—in urban areas with significant Chinese populations.

While most tongs were business, fraternal, or political in character, the "fighting tongs" licensed illegal businesses and were part of a tight-knit nationwide alliance. Therefore, a purely local dispute between fighting tongs "could and often did precipitate a fight between affiliates in every U.S. Chinatown" (Light 1977: 472). During the last decade of the nineteenth century and the first two decades of the twentieth, tong wars occurred on both the east and west coasts. In New York in 1909, a tong war between the On Leong ("Peaceful Dragon") and Hip Sing ("Prosperous Union") claimed an estimated 350 lives (Sante 1991). As the importance of gambling and house prostitution in Chinatowns declined following World War I, vice entrepreneurs discovered the profitability of tourist enterprises, and restaurants replaced the brothels and gambling halls. Nevertheless, the struggle between the On Leong and Hip Sing to control vice operations in New York's Chinatown continued into the 1930s. Contemporary tongs such as the Hip Sing and the On Leong have dropped the term from their names because of its association with "tong wars" (Chin 1990).

Nevertheless, these tongs continue to be associated with illegal gambling. In 1988, for example, federal agents raided the Chicago headquarters of the On Leong, where they found evidence of extensive commercial gambling, including more than $320,000 in cash and records indicating extortion from local Chinese merchants. A 1990 indictment accused the Chicago On Leong and affiliates in New York and Houston of being a key part of a gambling operation that netted $11.5 million. Gambling, in particular *Pai Gow*, an ancient Chinese domino game, was available from 9:30 A.M. to 7:00 P.M., seven days a week, at the On Leong Chicago headquarters, which was subsequently forfeited to the government. In 1994, Chicago On Leong officers were found guilty of running gambling operations, making payoffs to the police, and paying street taxes to the Outfit.[3] They also bribed a state judge to fix a murder case involving three members of a New York Chinese gang brought to Chicago to kill a troublemaker (Hayner 1990; O'Connor 1994a, 1994b).

Asian Gangs in North America

Many contemporary tongs are national in scope, particularly the Hip Sing, On Leong, and Tsung Tsin, and some are connected to Chinatown gangs such as the Ghost Shadows and the Flying Dragons in New York, Chicago, Boston, and San Francisco. The gangs date back to 1965, the year that new immigration laws resulted in a large influx of youths from Hong Kong: "During the late 1960s and early 1970s, the gangs transformed themselves completely from self-help groups to predatory groups" (Chin, Zhang, and Kelly 1998: 131). A number of young Chinese immigrants became alienated from school, found little economic opportunity, and were beyond family control (Kelly, Chin, and Fagan 1993). The result was an upsurge of violent street crime in communities that heretofore had been relatively crime free: "They terrorized the community by demanding food and money from businesses and robbed illegal gambling establishments. When the youth gangs began to 'shake down' merchants and gamblers who were themselves tong members, the tongs decided to hire the gangs as their street soldiers to protect themselves" (Chin, Zhang, and Kelly 1998: 131). Youths involved in these gangs are sometimes as young as thirteen, although established gang leaders—often martial arts masters—would normally be in their thirties. Each gang typically has 20 to 50 members.

As opposed to outlaw motorcycle clubs (discussed in Chapter 1) and Mafia groups, Chinese street gangs make great efforts to attract potential members and sometimes coerce others into joining: "Sometimes the *dai lo* [street boss] stages an incident in which he appears to be rescuing an innocent teenager from a gang beating, earning the victim's gratitude and admiration. This is followed by gifts and exposure to attractive women and the promise that no one will ever dare to bother the victim again if he joins the gang. He will have instant respect on the streets" (Kleinknecht 1996: 97): "Once a youth decides to join the gang, he goes through an initiation ceremony that is a simplified version of the Chinese secret societies' recruiting rituals. The youth takes his oaths, burns yellow paper, and drinks wine mixed with blood in front of the gang leaders and the altar of General Kwan, a heroic figure of the Triad subculture" (Chin 1990: 124). Members often dress in black outfits and sport exotic tattoos—dragons, serpents, tigers, and eagles. The gang becomes a substitute for the member's family: "They are not youth gangs in the usual sense but, rather, a young form of organized crime" (Dannen 1992b: 77).

Some gangs form around a tong member, typically a martial arts master who helps train the members (Chin 1990), and they may be used by the tongs to provide security for gambling operations: "The On Leong Merchants Association utilizes the services of the Ghost Shadows street gang; the Hip Sing Tong is allied with the Flying Dragons; and the Tsung Tsin Association is connected to a gang called the 'Tung On Boys'" (Pennsylvania Crime Commission 1988: 22). In some instances, Chinatown gangs have become inseparable from certain tongs, being linked through certain tong members and gang leaders. If a tong needs help from its affiliated gang, the message will be conveyed to the *Dai Dai Lo* ("Big Brother") by the *Ah Kung* ("Grandpa"). A *Dai Dai Lo* may also be an officer of the affiliated tong. Likewise, the highest leaders of the gangs have served as officers of the affiliated adult organizations (Chin, Kelly, and Fagan 1994).

A 1995 federal indictment revealed that New York's Chinatown, the largest Chinese community in the United States, was divided into fiefdoms

---

[3]In 1991 a former national On Leong president from Pittsburgh testified that at his request, the Pittsburgh crime Family arranged a deal with the Chicago Outfit to permit the On Leong to operate a gambling casino in that city. The On Leong paid $12,000 per month to the Outfit's 26th Street crew—Chinatown is in their territory—$4,000 of which was given to the Pittsburgh Family (O'Connor 1996c).

under the domination of tongs aided by their affiliated gangs: the Tsung Tsin and Tung On tongs
with the Tung On Boys,[4] the On Leong tong with
the Ghost Shadows, and the Hip Sing tong with
the Flying Dragons. Through this arrangement,
protection money was collected from virtually
every Chinatown business, legal or illegal; the latter include 24-hour-a-day gambling dens. In addition to the tong leaders, two Chinese-American
police officers were indicted for providing information about police investigations and planned
raids on gambling houses and brothels; they also
engineered raids on competing casinos (English
1995a; Faison 1995a, 1995b; Frantz and Toy 1995;
Fried 1995; Kleinfield 1995; Sexton 1995). In
1996, in a scenario reminiscent of recent traditional crime Family betrayals, the four top leaders
of the Ghost Shadows became government witnesses, all but demolishing the gang.

In San Francisco, a researcher (Joe 1992: 10)
found that a majority of Chinese/Vietnamese
street gang members in the nine groups he studied
knew little or nothing about the tongs and Triads.
Ties that existed between the two groups were
based on associations between individuals, not organizations—that is, gang members were connected to particular tong members. Another researcher (Toy 1992: 655) points out that certain
tongs need gang members "to ensure the smooth
operation of the gambling houses; they needed
guards, escorts for gamblers with large sums of
money, lookouts for police raids, and especially
people to collect gambling debts." The tongs "do
not have direct control of gangs nor are the
arrangements permanent. Tong members often
use certain respectable gang leaders as liaisons between the tong and the gangs in order to carry out
specific criminal activities. More often than not,
the average gang member is not aware of the par-
ticulars of this connection" (1992: 656).

While these gangs draw upon the traditions of
the Triads, particularly the ceremonial aspects of
initiation, they have many members who are Vietnamese (of Chinese ancestry); the latter are apparently favored because of their reputed ability with
firearms. There are also mixed gangs of Vietnamese and Chinese-Vietnamese (*Viet Ching*, ethnic Chinese born in Vietnam), who are usually
heavily armed. They operate mainly in California
but also reach into Vietnamese and Chinese communities in other locales. One such gang was
founded by a member of Chinatown's Flying
Dragons, David Thai, who was born in Saigon in
1956 and arrived in the United States in 1976.

As a Vietnamese, Thai was consigned to a
smaller unit known as the Vietnamese Flying
Dragons. Dissatisfied with his lesser status among
Chinese criminals, Thai attracted adolescents who
were recent immigrants from Vietnam, offering
them a place to live and work, slowly forming his
own gang, which became known as the Canal
Boys—their headquarters was on Chinatown's
Canal Street. They asserted their territoriality by
extorting money from the local Canal Street
merchants.

In 1989, Thai formed a confederation of Vietnamese gangs in the New York City metropolitan
area and adopted the name Born to Kill (BTK), a
slogan that often appeared on the helmets of
American GIs. Thai was the leader, *Anh hai*, and
the constituent gangs were headed by a *dai lo*. Each
BTK member signed a paper agreeing to abide by
the group's rules, which included a vow of secrecy
and a requirement to clear all planned criminal activity with his *dai lo*. Members were tattooed with
the initials BTK, a coffin, and three candles, signifying that they did not fear death (Lorch 1990;
English 1995a).[5]

Because they were viewed as interlopers and
left out of the criminal power structure in Chinatown, there was nothing to restrain the members
of the BTK, who victimized massage parlors, bars,
and tong gambling dens. In broad daylight and in

---

[4]In 1995, Clifford Wong, the head of the Tung On tong, was found
guilty of murder and sentenced to life imprisonment. He had ordered
the Tung On Boys to assault the Ghost Shadows in retaliation for the
murder of a Tung On Boys member. The attack left a 17-year-old
honor student with no gang affiliations dead ("Chinatown's New Enforcer" 1995).

[5]The BTK gang had many non-Vietnamese associates, some of whom
were non-Asians, who participated in their robberies. However, the
leaders and core members were all Vietnamese.

Vietnamese Gangs in Germany

There are more than 100,000 Vietnamese in Germany; many are illegal immigrants. In recent years, a unified Germany has experienced a serious problem with Vietnamese gangs, particularly in Berlin, where about a half-dozen operate, each with about 150 members. Turf wars between them have resulted in dozens of murders; some victims have been beheaded with samurai swords. Funds accumulated through cigarette smuggling have enabled the gangs to move into gambling, prostitution, and video pirating; using intimidation, they have taken over many Chinese restaurants. The police are handicapped—they have no officers of Vietnamese origin, and gang leaders typically operate out of Czech or Polish border villages (Kinzer 1996b).

front of numerous witnesses, two Flying Dragons who had insulted David Thai were shot to death. BTK members subsequently killed two Ghost Shadows at their hangout, and, on orders from David Thai, a BTK member blew up a police van in front of a NYPD precinct house (English 1995a). However, the ultimate insult was Thai's 1990 refusal to meet with Chinatown's "godfather," the venerable Benny Ong,[6] leader of the Hip Sing tong. This loss of face brought swift retribution—Thai's closest associate was gunned down, and at the funeral gunmen sprayed automatic fire at the mourners. Shortly afterward, three BTK members were slain execution style. This did not stop the BTK from committing a string of armed robberies in New England, the South, Canada, and anywhere else that Asian businesses could be victimized. In Georgia, they seriously wounded a jewelry store owner who had resisted. The arrest of a BTK member involved in the Georgia robbery led to an extensive interagency investigation and the successful prosecutions of the gang's leadership (English 1995a).

The Vietnamese avoid the territoriality that characterizes other similar crime groups, a lesson they learned from the Vietcong, who routinely changed their unit designations to confuse American intelligence (Okada 1992). In California, Vietnamese gangs, whose members often sport round, deep cigarette burns or blue dragons tattooed on

their forearms, have been active in the armed robbery of computer chips, which are often smuggled to the Far East only to wind up back in computers lawfully imported into the United States (Webster 1994).

Founded in 1987, the Green Dragons, a Chinese gang based in Queens, are enemies of the BTK. The group is made up mostly of recent immigrants from Fukien Province on China's southeastern coast. Their leader was ambushed in 1989 by rivals and subsequently returned to China. Day-to-day leadership was assumed by Taiwan-born Chen I. Chung, who was barely out of his teens. The Green Dragons had a clearly defined hierarchy that exacted complete obedience from subordinates. An order to kill would be carried out even in the absence of an explanation. Without any ties to the tongs, and with only about two dozen members, the Green Dragons successfully moved the extortion practices of Chinatown into Queens. They were a particularly vicious group of criminals, murdering rivals and innocents alike. A joint NYPD–FBI investigation using wiretaps led to arrests of the gang leadership in 1990. They were prosecuted at the same time and in the same federal courthouse in Brooklyn as the Born to Kill defendants. On another floor, John Gotti was being tried; his trial garnered the media attention. Like Gotti, Chung and six of his Green Dragons received life without parole (Dannen 1992b; English 1995b).

As with almost all organized criminal groups prior to the onset of Prohibition, Asian criminal organizations typically exploited only their own

---

[6]Benny Ong died of natural causes at age 87 in 1994.

According to the FBI

"No single Triad, tong, or street gang dominates the heroin trade, and membership in a Triad or tong is not a prerequisite to involvement in these illegal activities. Their members, however, have been identified as significant participants in international heroin-trafficking networks. Indeed, such membership can be important—in terms of criminal networking and determining who can be trusted" (speech by Louis J. Freeh, Director of the FBI, March 6, 1995: 4).

countrymen and were therefore able to avoid serious law enforcement efforts. In recent years, however, the extensive heroin networks of Chinese organizations have drawn intensive investigative efforts, particularly by the Drug Enforcement Administration. In 1989, for example, Johnny ("Onionhead") Eng, head of the Flying Dragons, was arrested in Hong Kong and extradited to the United States for masterminding the importation of 400 pounds of heroin. At the end of 1992, Eng was convicted in Brooklyn federal court, and in 1993 he was sentenced to 24 years in prison and fined $3.5 million. However, the efforts of the DEA have been hampered by a lack of Chinese-speaking agents. In New York, Chinese organizations—not necessarily tied to Triads or tongs—sell their highly potent Southeast Asian "China White" directly to wholesalers from black and Latino groups.

Chinese crime groups are involved in smuggling illegal aliens for employment in garment-manufacturing sweatshops, particularly in New York and California. The aliens are treated as indentured servants—forced to work at below minimum wages to pay back their benefactors for getting them into the United States. Women are sometimes forced into brothels. In 1993, as a result of the seizure of a steamer with almost 300 Chinese aboard, it was revealed that the Fuk Ching gang is a major player in the smuggling of illegal aliens. The leader of the Fuk Ching, Guo Liang Chi ("Ah Kay"), 27, often relayed orders to New York by telephone from his fortress-like headquarters in China's Fujian province. He was eventually arrested in Hong Kong as a fugitive from a murder charge in the United States (Treaster 1993b; Faison 1993).

In the next section, we will examine the business of organized crime, beginning with gambling and loansharking.

INTERNET CONNECTIONS

Yakuza: **officer.com**

Yakuza: **dir.yahoo.com/society_and_culture/crime/organized_crime**

Yakuza: **organizedcrime.about.com/newsissues/organizedcrime**

Nathanson Centre: **www.yorku.ca/nathanson**

Global Organized Crime Project: **csis.org/goc**

Japan Today News: **japantoday.com**

REVIEW QUESTIONS

1. Who are the *yakuza,* and how are they organized?
2. How do the *yakuza* differ from the American Mafia?
3. What are Triads, and how do they operate?
4. What is the relationship between Triads and tongs?
5. What is the relationship between tongs and Chinese street gangs?
6. Why have the Triads had a great deal of success in international heroin trafficking?
7. How are the tongs similar to the *Unione Siciliana*?

♠

CHAPTER 11

THE BUSINESS OF ORGANIZED CRIME: GAMBLING, LOANSHARKING, THEFT, FENCING, AND SEX

The business of organized crime has been described as providing goods and services that happen to be illegal. According to the Task Force on Organized Crime (1967: 1), "the core of organized crime activity is the supplying of illegal goods and services—gambling, loan sharking, narcotics, and other forms of vice—to countless numbers of citizen customers." Translating morality into a statute backed by legal sanctions does not provide for greater morality; it merely widens the scope of the law and creates both temptation and opportunity for a particular set of social actors (Packer 1968). As in any business, the better organized are usually the more successful, and organized crime is basically a business enterprise. However, the business of organized crime (OC) often includes activities that are neither "goods" nor "services" but are clearly parasitic.

GOODS AND SERVICES OR EXTORTION?

Thomas Schelling (1971) states that organized crime has a relationship with the purveyors of ille-

gal goods and services that is extortionate: *the business of organized crime is extortion, and those criminals who provide goods and services are its victims.* Thus, Schelling points out, a bookmaker operating in an area dominated by an OC unit will be required to pay for the "privilege" of doing business—or suffer from violence (or perhaps a raid by corrupt police). The OC unit merely "licenses" the business, and the bookmaker or other criminal purchases a "license" through the payment of "street taxes" to avoid being beaten or killed (or subjected to police harassment). Edward Hegarty, former special agent in charge of the Chicago office of the FBI, pointed out that while persons in organized crime do not get involved in the theft of automobiles, they extort money from those who do: "Many of the murders which have been committed in the Chicago area in recent years arose from automobile theft and chop shop activity. Generally these murders resulted from a failure, inability, or cheating by lower level organized crime figures on their La Cosa Nostra superiors. They were cheating on the street tax which is imposed on criminal cartels of the lower strength, the lower power base, that you have in and around the Chicago area" (Permanent Subcommittee on Investigations 1983b: 33–34).

During the 1970s, the Outfit began "taking over" (collecting regular street taxes) from the owners of chop shops around Chicago and into Lake County, Indiana. About 14 of those who resisted were killed (O'Brien 1988). A 1990 federal indictment revealed the Outfit's response when their hegemony over gambling was challenged: three men from the street crew of Sam Carlisi forced their way into a Chicago apartment at gunpoint, taking money and jewelry from the persons running a high-stakes card game. There were threats of physical harm and a demand for $2,000 from each. The operators agreed to turn over 50 percent of the game's profits to Carlisi, who subsequently became the head of OC in the Chicagoland area. Games in Cicero were similarly raided because the operators had not been paying street taxes. As noted in Chapter 5, unaffiliated gambling entrepreneurs in the Chicagoland area were routinely given the choice of paying street taxes or being "trunked."

The boundary between providing a good or a service and being parasitic is not clearly delineated. For example, while professional gamblers may be required to pay street taxes to operate in a particular area, in return the OC group may limit market entry—competition—and provide collection and/or arbitration services that are vital in such enterprises. Chapter 10 notes that Chinese and Vietnamese gangs typically engage in extortion from legitimate Asian businesses. But the gangs affiliated with tongs also provide protection and collection services for tong-operated gambling establishments. Jonathan Rubinstein and Peter Reuter (1978a: 64) note a distinctive service provided by Italian-American OC—arbitration: "In an economy without conventional written contracts, there is obviously room for frequent disagreements. These are hard to resolve. Many bookmakers make payments to 'wise-guys' to ensure that when disputes arise they have effective representation." As noted in Chapter 1, traditional OC operates as a shadow government, providing policing and judicial services to a vast underworld, thereby increasing efficiency and coordination in an otherwise anarchic—Hobbesian—environment. The effectiveness of traditional organized crime is grounded in its power to provide illegal services to its own members and, for a price, to other racketeers and legitimate businesspeople: "Among the more valuable services are mediation of disputes with other criminals, criminal enterprises, and ventures; allocating turf to Cosa Nostra and other criminal groups; fending off incursions by others into these territories; providing financing, muscle, or a corrupt contact wherever necessary to the success of a criminal venture" (New York State Organized Crime Task Force 1988: 73).

The concept of *rispetto* (discussed in Chapter 7) enables a made guy to act as an arbitrator. If, at the request of an aggrieved party, an *uomo di rispetto* is asked for assistance, he can summon the accused to a "sitdown" or "table," an informal hearing over which he presides. Robin Moore (Moore and Fuca 1977: 64) points out that "anyone in the community, mob-connected or not, who had a legitimate complaint against someone else was entitled to ask for a Table hearing" and that "any ranking Mafioso or man of respect could be prevailed upon to preside at a Table." To refuse to appear or to disregard a decision made at a table would indicate disrespect, with attendant life-threatening consequences. In Chicago, crime boss Joey ("the Clown") Lombardo reveled in his role as an arbitrator for all types of neighborhood disputes. As noted by Reuter (1983) and Abadinsky (1983), the arbitrator receives a fee for this service when the disputants are criminals.

A successful bookmaker in New York told me that he always kept a wiseguy on the payroll at a cost of several hundred dollars a week. This was insurance—it prevented other criminals from placing bets and then refusing to pay, using their status as made guys to protect them. It also kept other criminals from trying to "shake down" the bookmaker. The wise guy can also assist in the collecting of debts. The amount he keeps as a "commission" varies, but it can be as high as 50 to 100 percent. In northwestern Indiana, Ken ("Tokyo Joe") Eto, the lottery kingpin, paid thousands of dollars a month in street taxes to the Outfit in order to remain in business.

The Mafia needs victims who cannot easily hide, states Schelling (1971: 648), persons with fixed places of business: "Even if one can find and recognize an embezzler or jewel thief, one would have a hard time going shares with him, because the embezzler can fool the extortionist if he can fool the firm he embezzles from, and the jewel thief needn't put his best prizes on display." Schelling underestimates members of organized crime, who spend a great deal of time on the prowl for information and opportunity. Bartenders, fences, prostitutes, and a host of legitimate and illegitimate persons are often eager to provide the wiseguy with information to be on his "good side." They may owe him favors or money, or may simply seek to ingratiate themselves for any number of reasons. Salvatore ("Sally Crash") Panico of the Genovese crime Family found out about upscale brothels operating in Manhattan by perusing sex-oriented publications in which the owners usually advertised. Each location was then visited by Panico and his men. Guns, threats, and robbery soon brought the brothel into line. The scheme ended when Panico appeared on closed-circuit television threatening an FBI agent who was playing the role of bordello manager (Post 1981).

Albert Seedman (1974: 70–74), former chief of detectives in New York City, taped a conversation between "Woody," who had swindled $500,000 from Mays Department Store in Brooklyn, and Carmine ("the Snake") Persico, an enforcer for the Profaci Family and subsequently boss of the Colombo Family. In this edited conversation, Woody wants to know why he is being "asked" to pay a rather large share of the money he had stolen to Persico, who had played no part in the scheme:

PERSICO: When you get a job with the telephone company, or maybe even Mays Department Store, they take something out of every paycheck for taxes, right?

WOODY: Right.

PERSICO: Now why, you may ask, does the government have the right to make you pay taxes? The answer to that question, Woody, is that you pay taxes for the right to live and work and make

money at a legit business. Well, it's the exact same situation—you did a crooked job in Brooklyn [in the territory of the Profaci crime Family]. You worked hard and earned a lot of money. Now you have to pay your taxes just like in the straight world. Why? Because *we* let you do it. We're the government.

The jewel thief deals in expensive merchandise, and he needs a fence who can provide large sums of cash on very short notice. Some jewel thieves fence their jewels the same night they are stolen (Abadinsky 1983). A fence connected to organized crime can be relied upon to have, or to be able to raise, large amounts of cash on short notice. Dealing with a "connected" fence also provides insurance for the thief. It guarantees that he will not be "ripped off" by other criminals (since this would indicate a lack of *rispetto* and raise the ire of the crime unit). Thus, dealing with *Cosa Nostra* can provide an umbrella of protection to independent criminals who might otherwise be at risk from other criminals. Marilyn Walsh (1977) notes that although fencing is basically a sideline for the OC entrepreneur, the organized crime connection "is particularly helpful to the vulnerable good burglar who needs a somewhat amorphous affiliation with the criminal superstructure to protect him from some of its less genteel elements" (1977: 132). She provides an example:

Greg and his three associates had successfully executed a residence burglary, netting a substantial amount of expensive jewelry, one item in particular being an $8,000 bracelet watch. A few days after the theft the following series of events evolved.

A local enforcer in the area decided he wanted the bracelet. Determining who had stolen it, he and two associates proceeded to the apartment of the youngest of the thieves involved and took him "for a ride," explaining that the thieves and the bracelet would be expected to appear the following day at a private club in the city so that he might bargain for the purchase of the bracelet. When the thief returned from his ride, he called Greg and explained the situation. Smelling a shakedown, Greg got in touch with the bodyguard of one of the big syndicate men in the city. He offered to sell the bracelet to the latter individual at an extremely low price and asked for help. It was given.

The next morning only the bodyguard and Greg made the appointment at the private club. On entering it was obvious that Greg's evaluation of the situation had been accurate. There sat the enforcer with nearly ten others waiting for the burglars. The appearance of the bodyguard startled them. This latter individual said only three words, "Joe's getting it," and the whole charade was over. (1977: 108–109)

Because of the extensive network that is traditional organized crime, a connection can provide a professional criminal, such as Chicago's Frank Hohimer, with invaluable information (1975: xvii–xviii): "The outfit knows them all: Palm Springs, Beverly Hills, Shaker Heights. . . . You name the state and the Mob will give you not only the names of the millionaires and their addresses, but how many people are in the house, a list of their valuables, and where they keep them and when they wear them. . . . Their information is precise, there is no guess work. It comes from insurance executives, jewelry salesmen, auctioneers of estates. The same guy who sold you the diamond may be on the corner pay phone before you get home."

Information of value to conventional criminals operating in and around Kennedy Airport in New York comes from cargo handlers and persons holding similar positions. In one instance, a cargo supervisor in debt to OC-connected gamblers provided information to a Lucchese Family crew that led to the largest cash robbery in U.S. history—$6 million from Lufthansa Airlines: "He had methodically worked out the details: how many men would be needed, the best time for the heist, how to bypass the elaborate security and alarm system" (Pileggi 1985: 203).

For Vincent Teresa (Teresa and Renner 1973), an associate of the New England crime Family of Raymond Patriarca, what started out as a "service"

ended up as an extortion scheme. Joseph Barboza, a vicious ex-fighter, was an unaffiliated criminal operating in Massachusetts with his own band of thugs. One evening they were at the Ebbtide, a legitimate nightclub in the Boston suburb of Revere, when they beat up the owners and threatened to return and kill everybody. The owners went to Teresa for help. Teresa went to Patriarca's underboss, Henry Tameleo, who agreed to help—for a price. Acting on Tameleo's behalf, Teresa found Barboza: "Henry Tameleo wants to see you." When Barboza hesitated, Teresa explained the alternatives: "You want to come, fine. You don't want to come, you don't have to, but he'll send someone else to see you" (Teresa and Renner 1973: 123). After being "called in," Barboza agreed not to bother the Ebbtide—it was now a "protected" club. This gave Teresa an idea: "We sent Barboza and his animals to more than twenty nightclubs. They would go into these places and tear the joints apart. . . . These people would come running to us to complain about Barboza, to ask for protection" (1973: 123–24).

Sometimes the approach is less subtle but more lethal: in 1987, Gambino Family member Michael ("Mike Rizzi") Rizzitello, operating out of Los Angeles, decided "to pay a visit to Mustang topless bar owner Bill Carroll. Rizzi had met Carroll while in prison in 1970 and had been attempting to acquire a piece of the club for months. He had warned Carroll repeatedly to come up with part of the $150,000 the Mustang generated each month. Carroll refused. 'This is for not letting us eat,' Rizzitello said as he pumped three bullets into Carroll's head" (J. Smith 1998: 203).

When it comes to "goods and services," then, the picture is mixed. Many of those who provide gambling and other goods and services such as loansharking have a relationship with organized crime that is forced upon them. Others find the OC connection useful to their enterprise, and sometimes the made guy is a bookmaker, numbers operator, or (more frequently) a loanshark.

In order to understand the business of organized crime, we need to consider the degree to which a crime group's business activities are integrated into its organizational structure. In

Chapter 1, we note the rather loose coupling between the structure of New York's crime Families and the business activities of their members, but in Chicago the fit is quite close. Outlaw motorcycle clubs (OMC) have a bureaucratic style of organization, but their (illegal) business activities are not under the control and direction of the organizational hierarchy. Instead, members engage in crime in association with other members—persons in whom they have trust—and use their OMC membership for purposes of intimidation and networking. Thus, while an OMC may not be a criminal organization, it aids the criminal activities of its members. At the other end of this structure/business spectrum are the Colombian cocaine cartels, whose business structure and organizational structure are one and the same.

With this in mind, let us review the "goods and services" of organized crime. In this chapter, we will examine gambling, loansharking, theft/fencing, and commercial sex. In Chapter 12, we will examine organized crime in labor and business, and in Chapter 13, we will look at the business of drugs.

GAMBLING

Gambling includes a wide array of games of chance and sporting events on which wagers are made. Some of these are legal—for example, state-licensed horse- and dog-racing tracks and government-operated offtrack betting parlors. Most states operate lotteries, and dozens license casino gambling. State, county, and municipal governments earn a great deal of money from these authorized gambling activities. At the same time, there are unauthorized (illegal) gambling operations whose control is the responsibility of these same governments. In such an ambiguous environment, it is easy to understand why gambling enforcement may not generate a great deal of public support. The estimated amount of illegal betting increased tenfold between 1983 and 1995, while arrests for illegal gambling declined significantly, particularly in urban centers. Although 123,000 persons were arrested for illegal gambling

in 1960, by 1995 that number was down to about 15,000 (McMahon 1992; McGraw 1997).

The low priority given to gambling enforcement adds to its attractiveness to organized crime. Although profits from drug trafficking are quite substantial, so are enforcement activities and penalties, while sentences for illegal gambling are minimal. Lack of enforcement resources due to competing demands for police services, combined with advanced telephonic communications—for example, the mobile phone and the Internet—explain why enforcement has declined. There is an absence of public pressure to improve gambling enforcement.

Bookmaking

Bookmakers "book" bets on two types of events—horse and sometimes dog races and sporting events such as football, basketball, baseball, and boxing. In earlier days, "horse parlors" or "wire rooms," neighborhood outlets, were often set up in the back of a legitimate business. Results coming in over the wire service were posted on a large chalkboard for waiting bettors. Today, most bets are placed by telephone directly or through a roving "handbook," "runner," or "sheetwriter" who transmits the bet to the bookmaker. To maintain security, some bookmakers change locations frequently, often monthly, and/or they may use cellular telephones. Many use a "call-back" system. The bettor calls an answering service or answering machine and leaves his or her number. The bookmaker returns the call from a variety of locations, and the bet is placed.

Bets are written down and may also be tape-recorded by a machine attached to the phone. This helps avoid any discrepancies over what arrangements were actually made over the phone. The bookmaker usually employs clerks and handbooks, runners, or sheetwriters. The clerks handle the telephone, record the bets, and figure out the daily finances. The runners call the clerks and are given the day's totals for the bets they booked. Based on this information, they either collect or pay off. The runners receive a portion of the winnings, usually half, and they must also share in the losses (Rubinstein and Reuter 1977).

FIGURE 11.1   *Common Wagers as Recorded by a Bookmaker*

Win—choose the horse that will finish first.

1 NY JOEY' BOY 2//
6 L# 85-0-0

(First race, New York [e.g., Aqueduct], $2 to win on Joey Boy
(Sixth race, Laurel horse with post position 8. $5 to win)

Place—choose the horse that will finish first or second.

4 GS MARY MARY X-10-X

(Fourth race, Gulfstream, $10 to place on Mary Mary)

Show—choose the horse that will finish first, second, or third.

9 S/A 65/3

(Ninth race, Santa Anita, horse #6, $5 to show)

Combo (Across-the-Board)—a single bet encompassing equal amounts for win, place, and show.

B 6 2 2/2/2

(Sixth race, Bowie, horse #2, $2 to win, $2 to place, $2 to show)

Horse-Race Wagering[1]   The oldest of the major bookmaking activities, illegal horse-race wagering ranks behind sports wagering. This discrepancy has increased with the advent of legalized offtrack betting in places such as New York, Connecticut, and Illinois. The typical bettor is middle-aged or older, and wagers are usually modest. Information on the horses running at each track on a given day may be obtained from a local newspaper or a guide such as the *Daily Racing Form*. Voluminous data are available in the *Daily Racing Form*, which provides information on the time and nature of each race, the jockeys, the post positions, the weights carried, the probable odds, and the handicapper's estimates of the horses' finishing positions. This information is the basic data needed by the bookmaker in handling wagers.

Payoffs at the track are the basis for a bookmaker's profits (a net of between 10 and 15 percent), except where a bookmaker's limits are reached. The bookie's cut is obtained in the following manner: before the track makes a payoff under the parimutuel system (in which the track acts as a broker to pay the winners from the money it collects from the losers), it deducts for taxes and operational expenses. The bookmaker, by keeping the allocation of wagers roughly equal to the track's, realizes a profit from the portion that at the track goes to expenses and taxes. Since this deduction is generally from 15 to 20 percent, there is comfortable room for maneuvering. A bookmaker who has booked too much money on one horse, vis-à-vis the track, lays off the excess. This layoff process continues wherever a lack of balance exists until it reaches the top layoff operation, which has its agents stationed near major tracks. Upon being given their orders, the agents make an ultimate layoff by placing large wagers at the track's parimutuel window. In the event that the wager is a winning one, money to assist in making payoffs comes from the track winnings. Also, by placing large wagers at the track, the track's payoff, and consequently the bookmaker's, is reduced because the odds are determined by the amount of money bet on each entry.

The bookmaker cannot, of course, know precisely what percentage of money will be wagered on each horse at the track. However, information supplied by the *Daily Racing Form* is generally an acceptable guide. In the event of a high track payoff, the bookmaker invokes limits: generally 15 or 20 to 1 for a "win" bet, 6 or 8 to 1 for a "place" bet, and 3 or 4 to 1 for "show"; for multi-horse events such as the "daily double," it will usually be 50 to 1.

The wagers shown in Figure 11.1 are

[1]Unless otherwise cited, material in this section has been adapted from Boyd (1977).

Sports wagering—being done legally here—has surpassed horseracing as the most important source of illegal wagering.

AP/Wide World Photos

commonly recorded by a bookmaker: the information includes a bettor's identity (often in code), the racetrack, the identity of the horse, the type of wager, and the amount of the wager. The name of the track is almost always abbreviated (either by name or location). The identity of the horse may be written out fully or represented by its post position or its track program number.

Sports Wagering   From a gross dollar volume standpoint, sports wagering is the king of bookmaking, although the net profit for the bookmaker is typically less than 5 percent. As in other forms of bookmaking, the sports bookmaker seeks to act as a broker, not a gambler. In order to achieve equality between teams, one that the bookmaker hopes will attract like sums of money on each contestant, a handicapping process takes place through the use of a *line* or *spread*, the expected point difference between the favored team and the underdog:

> The line theoretically functions as a handicap to balance relative strengths of the opposing teams. It consists of points either added to the underdog teams' final scores

or subtracted from the favorite teams' final scores. Then again, theoretically having balanced the relative strengths of the teams, wagers are accepted by bookmakers usually at eleven to ten odds. Thus, for instance, if a bettor desires to bet $500 on the Washington Redskins at −6 (meaning Washington is favored by 6 points and, thus, 6 points are subtracted from Washington's final score to determine the result of the wager), he would actually risk $550 to the bookmaker's $500.

> The line is only theoretically a balancing of the strengths of the teams. However, as a practical matter, the line is really a number of points, either added to the underdogs' scores or subtracted from the favorites' scores, which the bookmakers feel will tend to attract relatively even amounts on wagering on both sides of the contest. If the bookmaker achieves an even balance of wagering on a game and he has no gamble or risk, his profit is assured of being 10 percent, the "juice" or "vigorish" of the losing wages. (Harker 1977: 2)

That is because bookmakers build in a profit by requiring a bettor to risk $11 to win $10—the $1 is called *vigorish*. Thus, in order to break even, a bettor would have to win 52.38 percent of the time. In the case of the Washington Redskins bet, if the Redskins won by more than 6 points, the bookmaker would pay out $500. He would receive $550 from someone who bet that amount on the losing team—a profit of $50, or 10 percent.

To make any necessary line changes, major booking operations continuously track changes in the Las Vegas line by computer. Sports betting and the use of the point spread (line) are illegal except in Nevada. Professional gamblers—who bet for income, not fun—also track line changes in an effort to "middle": they shop around for the most advantageous lines and bet opposite sides of a contest, thus ensuring that the only possible loss is vigorish, while possible earnings will be many times that amount. The bookmaker's profits depend on an ability to alter the point spread so that bets keep coming in for both teams. While the bookmaker sets the opening line, it shifts largely in response to what bettors do. Too much money on one team, and the vigorish is endangered, and the bookmaker becomes a gambler—unless he can lay off his out-of-balance bets (discussed below).

When there are attempts to fix the outcome of sporting events, the approach is to have key players "shave points."[2] That is, their play will reflect the need to keep the score within the point spread favored by the fixers. The National Football League has been extremely outspoken in its opposition to the legalization of sports betting. As former NFL commissioner Pete Rozelle (quoted in Tuite 1978: B21) stated, "The league believes legalized gambling on professional sports will dramatically change the character of the fan's interests in the sports. No longer will sports fans identify their interests with the success or failure of their favorite teams, but with the effect of their team's performance in the winning or losing of bets." The NFL's real fear, of course, is that legalized gambling will greatly increase the security problems confronting professional sports. In fact, the incomes of professional athletes makes the fix more likely in college sports.[3]

When the state of Delaware experimented very briefly with football wagering in 1976, the NFL sued that state but lost the suit. The league's chief security officer explained why the suit was brought: "We are not naive. We are not unaware of the fact that there is a great deal of gambling going on, but we don't think that the state or any governmental authority rightfully should come in and impose a gambling situation on our game" (Marshall 1978: 21). Delaware gave up football wagering "after it found out that state officials were less adept at setting odds than the underworld. Professional gamblers realized they could take advantage of Delaware's inexperience in bookmaking and collect a lot of easy money" (Marshall 1978: 21).

How difficult is the bookmaking business? An experienced investigator responds: "Well, you have day games and night games. So you're bookin' from twelve to one during the day, and five-thirty to six-thirty at night—we're talkin' maybe four hours. Then if you use voice mail, you're not even bookin', you're at the golf course. So at night you call up and get all your bets. . . . Where's the work? There's not much. All you have to worry about is who's winnin' and who's losin'. You pay someone $500 a week to take care of the collecting and payouts. He should set it up where he has a pattern, where he meets the guys at a set time. They usually get retired guys to do this, and these guys don't think they're doing anything wrong. You can't even arrest him—for what, for givin' someone money?" (Herion 1998). See Figure 11.2 for an example of the "latest line."

---

[2]For a discussion of point shaving, see Whalen (1995). If a bookmaker suspects a fix—experiences an influx of bets ("smart money") on a particular underdog, for example—he may "circle" or "scratch" the game. A circle means that he will limit the amount any one bettor can wager; a scratch means that he will accept no further bets.

---

[3]For an inside look at the effect of gambling on college basketball, see Rosen (1978), Cohen (1977), and Hill (1981).

FIGURE 11.2   *Sports Betting Lines*

Latest Line
Sports Features Syndicate Inc.

College Basketball Tonight Preseason NIT Quarterfinals					
Favorite	*Pts.*	*Underdog*	San Jose St.	3	at Nevada
At Arkansas	1 1/2	Arizona	Southern Miss.	6	at SW Louisiana
At Georgia Tech	3	Oklahoma	At Stanford	9	California
At Michigan	10 1/2	Weber St.	Tennessee	25 1/2	at Kentucky
College Football Tomorrow			At Texas	17 1/2	TCU
			Texas Tech.	19	Ohio
Favorite	*Pts.*	*Underdog*	At Utah St.	9 1/2	Pacific
At Baylor	15	Rice	At Virginia	4	Virginia Tech
At BYU	5 1/2	Utah	At Washington	13 1/2	Washington St.
At Brown	7 1/2	Columbia	At W. Michigan	8	C. Michigan
Cincinnati	4 1/2	at Tulsa	At Wisconsin	7	Iowa
Clemson	4	at S. Carolina	At Wyoming	4 1/2	Fresno St.
At E. Carolina	13	Memphis			
E. Michigan	13 1/2	at Kent	**NBA Tonight**		
At Florida	42	Vanderbilt			
At Illinois	6	Minnesota	*Favorite*	*Pts.*	*Underdog*
Kansas	9 1/2	at Oklahoma St.	At Boston	4 1/2	Washington
At LSU	1 1/2	Arkansas	At Atlanta	3 1/2	Miami
At Louisiana Tech	3 1/2	N. Illinois	At Chicago	14	New Jersey
At Louisville	26	N. Texas	Dallas	4 1/2	at LA Clippers
At Miami (Fla.)	12	W. Virginia	At Denver	1	New York
At Miami (Ohio)	30 1/2	Akron	LA Lakers	7 1/2	At Vancouver
At Missouri	3 1/2	Iowa St.	Minnesota	1 1/2	at Toronto
At Navy	6 1/2	Tulane	At Philadelphia	3	Cleveland
At UNLV	6 1/2	New Mex. St.	Phoenix	3	at Sacramento
New Mexico	13	at UTEP	Seattle	1 1/2	at Charlotte
At N. Carolina	15	Duke	Utah	4	at Detroit
N.C. State	6	at Wake Forest			
Northwestern	4 1/2	at Purdue	**NHL Tonight**		
At Ohio St.	32 1/2	Indiana			
At Oregon	16	Oregon St.	*Favorite*	*Gls.*	*Underdog*
At Penn	5	Cornell	At Anaheim	1-1 1/2	NY Islanders
Princeton	1 1/2	at Dartmouth	Colorado	1-1 1/2	at Calgary
Rutgers	3	at Temple	At Dallas	1 1/2-2	San Jose
San Diego St.	8 1/2	at Hawaii	Detroit	1/2-1	at Edmonton
			NY Rangers	E-1/2	at Winnipeg
			Pittsburgh	E-1/2	at Washington
			E-Even		

Organized Crime and Bookmaking   In an earlier period, bookmaking was an important source of income for organized crime. OC units ran the operation directly or "licensed" syndicate bookmakers, and the wire service that provided instant race results was an important source of organized crime control over bookmaking. However, most illegal wagering today involves sports, as opposed to horse racing, and bets are made by telephone—or over the Internet. Payoffs are made the day after the event, so the prompt results provided by the wire service are no longer relevant. The almost exclusive use of the telephone provides greater security and has reduced the need for police protection, often an important syndicate service.

Bookmakers (and numbers operators) frequently find their bets sufficiently unbalanced to require that they be layed off (or else the bookmaker becomes a gambler, not a broker). The bookmaker may use legal bookmakers in Las Vegas to accomplish this layoff, or he may contract with a layoff service. The layoff service is actually a bookmaker's bookmaker, accepting bets nationally and thereby better able to balance teams from different cities. For example, if a New York team is playing a Chicago team, bookmakers in New York are likely to have too many bets on the hometown favorite. The layoff service can balance those bets with excess ones from Chicago, where bookmakers have the same hometown-team problem. Because of its scale, the layoff is typically a service provided by organized crime.

Bookmaking involves many transactions and generates a great deal of paperwork. The wagers are recorded when received, and clerks have to review their receipts to determine winners and losers. In 1995, police raided a major bookmaking operation—estimated gross $65 million, net of 20 percent—where they found all data entries on computers using a custom-made sports betting program. The computers were also linked to an on-line service from Las Vegas that provided the latest line on sporting events. The operation was connected to the Colombo and Gambino Families (Raab 1995g).

Technical changes have also made it harder to find bookmakers, who have insulated themselves by the routine use of mobile telephones, pagers, and call-back services. A gambling investigator explains:

> I've been trying to find a guy [bookmaker]. An informant would give me this phone number. I would check it out and it [the address] would be a vacant lot; the bill would go to a Post Office box in some other county. Suppose you're the bookmaker. You pay me $500 a week. You give me the phone and people call up. I don't know who they are, they all have [ID] numbers. So a guy would call up and say, "Give me $2,000 on the Bulls minus two" . . . whatever. I write it down, but I don't know them. You're in the background and you're the only one who knows. But you are not involved in bookmaking. You're the bookmaker, but you're not involved in the actual booking itself. You just figure out who

won and who lost, and pay or collect. So you meet him [the bettor]. But, if you're real sharp, you have another guy meet him. Now you just meet your guy on a street corner and he hands you an envelope. You meet the guy in a different place all the time. You call him on the phone and give him ten minutes to meet you. Now how am I [as a gambling enforcement officer] supposed to find you? (Herion 1998).

Competition is difficult to control because bookmaking can involve operations outside the United States. Bookies frequently advertise in sports publications and on radio programs. Allegedly, the nation's biggest bookmaker, Ron Socko, has set up operations in the Dominican Republic, where gambling is legal; an 800 number provides a link to bettors in the United States. And, despite their dubious legality in the United States, the Internet is replete with gambling sites, up from 6 in 1996 to more than 600 in 2000, many of them legal in their country of origin—Costa Rica, for example. Internet gaming includes casino gambling, sports betting, and the lottery. A bettor opens an account by sending a cashier's check, money order, or wire transfer to a licensed bookmaker in the Caribbean; a minimum balance of $500 is usually required. Each bettor is given a personal identification number, bets are placed on a special long-distance toll-free number or on the Internet, and money is added or subtracted from the account. A bettor can withdraw money, receiving his or her winnings in the mail via check or wire transfer (Financial Crimes Enforcement Network 2000; Dretzka 2001). The use of credit cards encourages Internet gambling, but credit card companies often refuse to process payments for Internet gambling, which is an industry that accounts for $3–4 billion per year (Richtel 2002).

While it is a violation of federal law to use the phones for gambling across state lines or international boundaries, the business is legal where it is licensed and bookmakers are outside of U.S. jurisdiction. But if they enter the United States, they could be in trouble. In 1998 the federal government charged the executives of 14 offshore betting firms with illegally using interstate phone lines for betting purposes. Three of the defendants were subsequently found visiting the United States and arrested (Weiser 1998b). In 2000 a man who operated a sports betting business on the Internet was convicted by a federal jury in what is believed to be the first case of its kind to go to trial. He headed an operation based in Antigua and was among 22 defendants charged with operating offshore companies that took bets from Americans via the Internet or toll-free telephone numbers. He was sentenced to 21 months, and a federal appeals court subsequently upheld his conviction (Neumeister 2000; "Man Loses Federal Appeal in Internet Gambling Case" 2001).

Lotteries/Numbers The American colonies were floated with lotteries: "In 1612, King James I authorized a lottery to promote the colony of Virginia. The colonies themselves used lotteries, and such outstanding men as George Washington bought and sold lottery tickets." The lottery was used (unsuccessfully) to help finance the Revolutionary War. Many of America's outstanding institutions of higher learning were supported through the use of lotteries—Rhode Island College (now Brown University), Columbia, Harvard, the University of North Carolina, William and Mary, and Yale (Chafetz 1960: 20–21).

During the nineteenth century, lotteries under state license or control were found throughout the United States. Because of the negative publicity surrounding problems with the Louisiana lottery, in 1890 the United States enacted legislation prohibiting lotteries from using the mails and even prohibited newspapers that carried lottery advertisements from using the mails (Chafetz 1960). This prohibition opened the way for the illegal exploitation of the desire to bet on lotteries through such devices as "numbers" or "policy" betting.

Policy is based on drawing numbers from 1 to 78 by spinning a wheel. Twelve to fifteen numbers are drawn, and players bet that from one to four numbers in various sequences will be among those drawn. Bets are typically small, but when a policy operation is controlled by a syndicate, the total profits can be quite large. In the past, bets were placed in "policy shops" or, in more contemporary times, through runners. "Dream books" are sold to help players choose their lucky numbers.

During the 1920s, *numbers* were introduced as competition for policy. In numbers, a player selects one, two, or three digits from 0 to 9 with the odds of winning running from 10 to 1, 100 to 1, and 1,000 to 1. For a single-digit ("single action") play, the payoff is 6 or 7 to 1; for two digits ("double action"), the payoff is between 50 and 64 to 1; for three digits, the payoff is between 550 and 600 to one. On certain popular combinations (for example, 711), the payoff may be reduced to 500 to 1 or even lower. A player can also "box" numbers—bet all the possible three-digit combinations. While this increases the chances of winning, it also lowers the payoff to about 100 to 1.

There are a variety of elaborate schemes for determining the winning numbers—for example, using the amounts for win, place, and show of the first race at a particular racetrack or the last three digits of the racetrack's "handle" (total gross receipts)—figures that are readily available in the daily newspapers. In some games, the numbers are selected before an audience of bettors at a central location. Today, in states having a legal lottery, the illegal lottery will often use the same numbers as the state lottery, although the odds in the illegal lottery may be higher than those offered by the state. In the Chicagoland area, while the legal lottery pays $500 for each dollar wagered on a three-number bet, the illegal lottery pays $600; payment for a four-number bet is the same as the state's, but winners are paid in cash, and no taxes are withheld.

The structure of the illegal lottery requires a great deal of coordination and is labor intensive, providing many jobs for unskilled individuals, making it an important source of employment in poor communities. At the bottom of the hierarchy are those who accept wagers directly from the bettors, such as writers, runners, and sellers. These are generally individuals with ready access to the public, such as elevator operators, shoeshine boys, newspaper vendors, bartenders, and waitresses.[4]

---

[4]The proliferation of small grocery stores in some neighborhoods is explained by the illegal lottery.

Exploitation

"Any government that exploits the weakness of its citizens to enrich itself cheapens its own charac- ter and thus damages the public interest" (Russell Baker 1996: 11).

Customarily they are paid a percentage of the wagers they write (unlike sports bookmaking, numbers wagering is done on a cash basis), usually from 15 to 30 percent, and are frequently given a 10-percent tip by winning bettors.

It is essential that wagers reach trusted hands before the winning number or any part of it is known. Sometimes this is done by telephone; other times, wager records (commonly known as work, action, or business) are physically forwarded to a higher echelon by a pickup man. In a small operation, the wagers may go directly to the central processing office (commonly called the bank, clearinghouse, or countinghouse). More often, in large enterprises they are given to management's field representative (known as the field man or controller), who may be responsible for making a quick tally to determine the existence of any heavily played numbers that should be layed off. At such levels of operation, one frequently finds charts consisting of 1,000 spaces numbered 000 to 999, where tallies can be made for only certain wagers meeting minimum dollar values.

Near the top of the hierarchy is the *bank*, where all transactions are handled. During the collection process, the bank will be making decisions as to whether or not to lay off certain heavily played numbers.[5] After the winning number is known, the bank will meticulously process the paperwork to determine how much action has been written, how many hits are present, and the controllers and/or writers involved. (For a look at the details of the numbers game and its historical relationship to organized crime, see Liddick 1998.)

Decreasing organized criminal opportunity was one argument for the legalization of certain types of gambling, in particular the state lottery, beginning in New Hampshire in 1964 and followed by New York in 1967. However, the first financially successful lottery was the fifty-cent weekly established by New Jersey in 1971 (Gambling Commission 1976). Most lottery states have a variety of games: instant winners, daily drawings, weekly drawings, and multistate lotteries with payoffs in the millions of dollars. This form of gambling was originally offered as a way of reducing the income of the illegal lottery—numbers—and capturing those monies for public use, particularly education. Without a doubt, the lottery has added billions of dollars to the public coffers without generating the political heat that raising taxes would, about $12 billion annually (from wagers of about $35 billion).

However, there is no evidence that the legal lotteries have diminished the revenues of their illegal counterparts. In fact, publicity may have actually increased illegal revenues along with those of state lotteries. The introduction of a legal lottery serves to educate persons who heretofore did not know the intricacies of numbers gambling (Blount and Kaplan 1989). Illegal operators typically provide better odds and do not report the winnings to tax officials. Furthermore, the daily lottery provides illegal operators with a winning number in which bettors have confidence and offers a free layoff service so that numbers banks can always balance their bets. However, the illegal lottery does not encourage people to gamble by an unseemly spate of advertising (about $375 million a year). In America's poorest communities, "the [legal] lottery is a dominant force and many poor and modest-income residents are devoted to an endless search for winning numbers in an

---

[5]In games using state lottery numbers, the layoff can be accomplished by purchasing large quantities of lottery tickets, although illegal operators will have to absorb some loss on the transaction, because they usually pay winners more than the state does.

The Role of Government

"It is the state governments—the same entities that for years outlawed gambling—that are now leading the way in building widespread acceptance of gambling across the country" (Brett Pulley 1999: 12).

unswerving belief that a jackpot waits for them" (Pulley 1999: 12).

Almost three decades ago, a federal commission warned that "the availability of legal gambling creates new gamblers." Therefore, "a government that wishes merely to legitimize illegal wagering must recognize the clear danger that legalization may lead to unexpected and ungovernable increases in the size of the gambling clientele" (Gambling Commission 1976: 2). In the constant quest for new revenues, states such as New York have introduced new forms of lottery; an example is Keno, an electronic game in which bettors pick one or more numbers and win if the computer comes up with their numbers. Instead of a weekly or daily drawing, Keno picks a new number every five minutes—the compulsive gambler's nightmare.

Offtrack betting (OTB) in New York has been less than a resounding success and is struggling to cover its expenses, although it has created plenty of patronage jobs. OTB did succeed in reducing illegal betting on horses, for few bookmakers in New York accept bets on horse racing. As in a number of other states, OTB in New York is considering the introduction of sports betting. Some fear that the introduction of sports betting will serve to educate more persons on the intricacies of gambling. Since illegal operators typically provide better odds (their overhead is significantly lower), do not report the winnings to tax officials, and accept bets on credit and over the telephone, legalized sports betting may succeed in recruiting new bettors for the bookmakers.

Casino Gambling and Related Activities

Casino gambling (with a wide array of games of chance, including roulette, chuck-a-luck, black-jack, and craps) requires a great deal of planning, space, personnel, equipment, and financing. In the past, casino gambling was available in "wide-open towns" such as Newport, Kentucky, and Phenix City, Alabama,[6] and on a more discreet level in Saratoga Springs, New York, and Hot Springs, Arkansas. Some cities have a tradition of holding "Las Vegas Nights," events often run under the auspices of, or with the approval and protection of, an organized crime unit, using the legitimate front of a religious or charitable organization. The operators provide gambling devices, personnel, and financing, and they share some of the profits with the sponsoring organization.

OC operatives may also organize or sponsor card or dice games, taking a cut out of every pot for their services. These may be in a permanent location such as a social club or veterans' hall, or, for security reasons, may "float" from place to place. The games may be operated in the home of a person in debt to a loanshark as a form of paying off the loan. In certain cities, gambling activities not operated under OC protection, "outlaw games," run the risk of being raided by the police or being held up by independent criminals or robbery teams sponsored by an OC unit. As Vincent Siciliano (1970: 50), an armed robber with OC connections, reports, "The organization knows there is this game and when some friend in the police needs an arrest, to earn his keep as a protector of the people against the bad gamblers, the organiza-

---

[6]On June 15, 1954, Albert L. Patterson, a Phenix City reformer who had been nominated Alabama attorney general, was murdered. His son Gordon was subsequently elected governor of Alabama. He declared martial law in Phenix City and sent in the National Guard to "close it down." These events inspired the movie *The Phenix City Story* (Wright 1979).

tion guy tells the police and off they go with sirens wailing." During the raid, Siciliano notes, the police can also help themselves to much of the game's proceeds. He points out that even the dumbest thief knows which are syndicate games and recognizes the consequences of disregarding the OC connection. A career armed robber expresses concern with the possibility of "knocking over" a "connected" operation: "I don't think the Mafia'd read me my rights and let me go consult with an attorney. And I said [to my partners], 'Is this thing connected?' I said, 'Look, if this is the Mafia's money I don't want any part of it. I don't want some guys to come gunnin' for me'" (Greenberg 1981: 93).

Las Vegas and New Jersey   In 1931 the state of Nevada, desperate for tax revenue during the Great Depression, legalized gambling and established licensing procedures for those wishing to operate gambling establishments. Las Vegas "served principally as a comfort station for tourists fleeing the desert heat" (Reid and Demaris 1964: 12). Then came Bugsy Siegel, the first important criminal to recognize the potential from legalized gambling in Nevada. Operating out of California, "from about 1942 until the time of his death, Siegel controlled the wire-service in Las Vegas through Moe Sedway, an ex-convict, gambler, and longtime associate of many New York mobsters, who Siegel brought to Las Vegas. Through control of the wire service, Siegel controlled the operations of all handbooks operating in Las Vegas. He refused wire service to any book unless he or his agents operated and managed it" (Kefauver 1951a: 91).

With financing from OC leaders throughout the country, including Frank Costello, Meyer Lansky, Tony Accardo, Longie Zwillman of New Jersey, and Moe Dalitz of the Cleveland syndicate, Siegel built the Flamingo Hotel, the first of the elaborate Las Vegas gambling establishments. Up until then, gambling consisted of a "few ancient one-armed bandits and a couple of homemade crap tables," and most of the action was at the poker table (Reid and Demaris 1964: 12). The former bootleggers were ideally suited to exploit Las Vegas: they had available capital that they were used to pooling, expertise in gambling, and business acumen developed during Prohibition. "Without the ex-bootleggers to found and staff the first generation of hotel casinos," argues Mark Haller (1985a: 152), "Las Vegas might not have been possible."

After Siegel's murder in 1947, the Flamingo and a number of plush hotels were controlled (through hidden interests) by OC units. Typically, funds were "skimmed" before being counted for tax purposes, and the money was distributed to OC bosses in proportion to their amount of (hidden) ownership. According to federal officials, from 1973 to 1983 at least $14 million was skimmed from just one hotel, the Stardust. In 1983, several Stardust employees were prosecuted, and the owners (of record) were forced to sell the hotel. The Stardust was originally licensed to Moe Dalitz. In 1983, two Kansas City, Missouri, OC figures and an executive of the Tropicana Hotel-Casino were sentenced to long prison terms for skimming operations (Turner 1984). As noted in Chapter 5, the top leaders of organized crime in Chicago, Kansas City, Cleveland, and Milwaukee were sentenced to prison in 1986 for skimming the profits of Las Vegas casinos (depicted in the book and movie *Casino*).

Las Vegas is no longer a mob-controlled playground—casinos are major corporate entities—and OC has been moved to the fringes of the Las Vegas scene. In 1998, for example, federal agents arrested six men from the Gambino Family for planning to use violence against several "out-call" operators. The intended victims provide nude dancers for hotel room sessions (prostitution, while legal in some parts of Nevada, is illegal in Las Vegas/Clark County). The operators were competing with OC-affiliated services, and, as one of the Gambinos told an undercover agent, the competing firms were being sent an "aspirin"—an enforcer known as "Vinnie Aspirins." Mr. Aspirins is known for using a cordless power drill to bore holes in victims' heads; he was arrested in Las Vegas with a former military mercenary, an expert on explosives.

In Atlantic City, New Jersey, the second state to authorize casino gambling, there were intensive efforts to keep organized crime out of the casinos. The New Jersey State Police, which has extensive experience in dealing with OC, and the New Jersey Casino Control Commission, were put in charge of overseeing casino operations to prevent OC infiltration: "While it may be true that mobsters haven't yet found their way into the casino counting rooms—as they once did in Las Vegas—almost anywhere you look in the city you'll find a wiseguy or one of his associates. The mob is on the floor of every casino in the city. It's in the restaurants and the casino lounges. It controls the labor unions whose workers make the big casino-hotels go" (Anastasia 1991: 163). In Atlantic City, OC has been able to influence the purchase of goods and services through control over key unions, particularly Local 54 of the Hotel Employees and Restaurant Employees Union. Local 54, which represents 22,000 casino hotel employees, has long been dominated by the Bruno Family of Philadelphia. In 1990 the federal government, under provisions of the Racketeer Influenced and Corrupt Organizations (RICO) statute, sued to have Local 54 placed in receivership. In 1991 the government reached an agreement with the union, and Local 54 was placed into receivership. Its leaders accepted voluntary "banishment" (Sullivan 1991).

There is increasing evidence that the easy availability of legalized gambling is attracting young persons at an alarming rate. Lottery scratch cards contain cartoon graphics, video poker machines resemble the video games that many have grown up with, and video arcades on the Atlantic City boardwalk feature slot machines for children that dispense prizes instead of money. Casino operators encourage parents to bring their children, and they sponsor amusement parks to keep the children busy while their parents gamble. The entry of underage gamblers into casinos without detection continues to be a problem (Pulley 1998).

Miscellaneous Gambling

Bingo is legal in 46 states. Although played purportedly to raise funds for charitable causes, bingo is also a source of profits for OC. They may run the operations for the front (charity) or merely be connected through "licensure." In a number of localities, coin-operated video poker machines are very popular, often a staple in many bars or taverns. These machines operate like slot machines but are legal because they do not dispense money. Payoffs are provided by the proprietor (or bartender) surreptitiously. In Chicago, the Outfit provides the machines and splits the profits, which can be several thousand dollars per week per machine. Net profits from the poker machines are typically split 50–50 between the distributors of the machine and the proprietor, and each machine can generate $2,000 per week. In the Chicagoland area,

They're all over the place. And the poker machines themselves are not illegal. . . . Mostly snack bars, blue collar places. Let's say the owner hears about the money you can make. He contacts a guy and the guy explains that they will be partners. He will put a machine in, maybe more. "Whatever you net for the week we'll split down the middle." He can't lose. The machine will take up to $20 at a time; its got different slots for different denominations. You get so many units for a winning hand. They're not supposed to pay out in cash, but the rule of thumb is every forty units is worth $10. You wave over the clerk or the bartender and he pays $10 for every forty points. The machine adds it up and you can add units by adding more money. . . . The distributor can set it to pay out whatever he wants. There's no skill, strictly chance. When they first put in the machine, they will maybe set it to pay out up to 80 or 85 percent [of the times]. Then they get people hooked and the distributor reduces the payout. [And the profits?] Some places, like a truck stop I know, they had ten machines and were making $100,000 a month. Some mom and pop operations couldn't stay open without the machines. They've taken seats out of restaurants so they could make room for more of these machines. (Herion 1998)

As a sheriff's investigator reports, "About five months ago our vice unit hit a truck stop somewhere in the Calumet City area [just south of Chicago], an oasis just off the Calumet Expressway. They brought in ten or twelve machines that had been running for two days, and there was $8,500 registered on them. I think a lot of mom and pop type taverns in the city are probably paying their overhead with the income from the machines" (Scaramella 1998). In 2002, the former mayor of suburban Stone Park was sentenced to 18 months' imprisonment for taking bribes from the Chicago Outfit to protect video poker machines in the town's taverns.

Although there is no evidence of any attempts to restrict market entry—competition—video poker appears to be totally an Outfit business. People know how to contact Outfit guys, and in many neighborhoods, the owners of small businesses would rather do business with the Outfit than someone unknown to them (who could be an undercover officer).

LOANSHARKING (USURY)

The generally negative view of money lending is highlighted in the Bible, which on three separate occasions cautions against charging interest—*neshek* (to "bite"): "If thou lend money to any of My people, even to the poor with thee, thou shalt not be to him as a creditor; neither shall ye lay upon him interest" (*Exodus* 22: 24); "And if thy brother be waxen poor . . . thou shalt not give him thy money upon interest nor give him thy victuals for increase" (*Leviticus* 25: 36–37). However, "Unto a foreigner thou mayest lend upon interest [for business investment purposes]; but upon thy brother thou shalt not lend upon interest." Thus, the Hebrews could not charge interest on a loan to another Hebrew.[7] Later, the Church adopted a similar interpretation: Christians could not charge interest on loans to other Christians. This prohibi-

tion created problems for commercial enterprises and led to a paradoxical situation.

Within organized Jewish communities, the Hebrew Free Loan Society developed to loan money to Jews without interest, while laws and regulations restricting the ability of Jews to purchase land and enter guilds resulted in Jews becoming moneylenders to Christians. William Shakespeare's character Shylock, in *The Merchant of Venice* (1596), is based on this historical irony. Shakespeare depicted the unsavory Shylock as a money-lending Jew demanding a pound of flesh from a hapless borrower as repayment for a delinquent loan. At the time Shakespeare was writing, there were no Jewish moneylenders in England—all Jews had been expelled from that country by Edward I in 1290, and they did not return until the 1650s. The name "Shylock" reportedly became slurred by illiterate criminals into "shark," and the word *loanshark* was born. As noted earlier, the Hebrew term for interest is *neshek*, to bite, something for which sharks are noted.

Between 1880 and 1915, a practice known as "salary lending" thrived in the United States. This quasilegal business provided loans to salaried workers at usurious rates. The collection of debts was ensured by having the borrower sign a variety of complicated legal documents that subjected him or her to the real possibility of being sued and losing employment. Through the efforts of the Russell Sage Foundation, states began enacting small-loan acts to combat this practice. Massachusetts was the first in 1911. These laws, which licensed small lenders and set ceilings on interest, eventually brought salary lending to an end; credit unions, savings banks, and similar institutions began to offer small loans. However, this also led to the wholesale entry of organized crime into the illicit credit business (Goldstock and Coenen 1978).

Loansharking embodies two central features: "The assessment of exorbitant interest rates in extending credit and the use of threats and violence in collecting debts" (Goldstock and Coenen 1978: 2). As noted in chapters 4 and 5, as Prohibition was drawing to a close, and with the onset of the Great Depression, persons in organized crime began searching for new areas of profit. These criminals

---

[7]According to the Talmud (*Baba Metzia* 5: 4), while charging interest on personal loans is prohibited, Jews can lend money to other Jews for business purposes and receive an equity stake in the enterprise.

Payday Loans

The current form of salary lending, frequently known as "payday loans," takes advantage of people who are willing to pay high interest rates to get small, short-term loans, which many banks no longer offer. The payday lender accepts a postdated check, which is deposited after a specified period, usually two weeks. In states that do not have caps on interest, rates can be in excess of 500 percent annually. However, most borrowers repay the loans in one or two weeks. In Chicago, which has hundreds of payday loan outlets, the common rate is $10 per week for every $100 borrowed—it would be cheaper to borrow from a New York loanshark, whose rates are typically 2 to 5 percent a week. Although the typical payday loan is less than $500, some persons become dependent on the loans or take out too many from several outlets at one time (Wahl 1999c, 2000). Some states have caps on interest rates—in New York, it is 25 percent a year or 16 percent on person-to-person loans.

found themselves in the enviable position of having a great deal of excess cash in a cash-starved economy, which gave them an important source of continued income: "Contemporary loansharking is marked by the dominance of organized crime. This pervasive influence is hardly surprising. Syndicate access to rich stores of capital allows the underworld to pour substantial amounts of cash into the credit market. The strength and reputation of organized operations lends credence to threats of reprisals, thus augmenting the aura of fear critical to success in the loansharking business. Moreover, organized crime's aversion to competition militates strongly against successful independent operations" (Goldstock and Coenen 1978: 4).

Persons in organized crime may insulate themselves from direct involvement in loansharking by using nonmember associates. For example, Gambino Family soldier Tony Plate (Piatta) employed—actually, funded—his associate Charles ("the Bear") Calise. Calise, in turn, employed others as lenders and collectors. The connection with Tony Plate gave the whole operation an umbrella of protection from other criminals and credibility to debtors. Without this connection, a borrower who is a "made guy" or an associate of a crime Family could easily avoid paying back the loan, and violence used to collect the debt could bring retaliation from the Family.

Many loansharks provide loans to other criminals: "There is strong evidence for specialization by loansharks. Some deal with legitimate businessmen only, some with illegal entrepreneurs. One medium-level loanshark specialized in fur dealers, though he might make loans to other small businessmen. Some specialize in lending to gambling operators" (Rubinstein and Reuter 1978b: Appendix 3–5). Genovese Family soldier Joseph Valachi (Maas 1968) worked as a loanshark and reported that most of his customers were themselves involved in illegal activities such as numbers and bookmaking. Loansharks "frequently provide capital for a bookmaker who is in financial difficulty" (Rubinstein and Reuter 1978b: 53).

Individual gamblers may also borrow from a loanshark who stays around card and dice games or accepts "referrals" from a bookmaker. In Chicago, the street crew headed by Sam Carlisi "would require that delinquent debtors obtain a juice loan at an interest rate of 5 percent per week to pay off the gambling debt" (*United States of America v. Samuel A. Carlisi et al.* 1990). In one New York case, a young gambler borrowed from a loanshark to pay his bookmaker. He continued to gamble and borrow and was eventually unable to pay his loanshark. As a result, he embarked on a series of illegal activities that led to a prison term. He ran high-stakes poker games, at which his wife played hostess, and secured fraudulent loans from numerous banks. On one occasion, he decided to use some of this money to continue gambling and missed his loanshark payment. He was severely beaten in a parking lot, leaving him with two black eyes and a broken nose. (The loanshark obviously has methods of collection not typically employed by other lending institutions.) When a debtor fell behind on his juice payments to Joseph DiFronzo, brother of Chicago mob boss John DiFronzo, he was given an offer he could not easily refuse: grow marijuana. DiFronzo, in 1998, at age 63, was arrested for overseeing the largest indoor marijuana growing operation ever discovered in Illinois.

The case of Louis Bombacino, a collector for the Chicago Outfit's Twenty-Sixth Street crew, who routinely carried a firearm, vividly reveals the intimidation involved in loansharking. The government intercepted a telephone conversation between Bombacino and a debtor who indicated he could make no further payments. The debtor said he was afraid of the federal government because he had engaged in criminal activity to pay back the loan. Bombacino introduced his associate, known as "Pete," and told the victim, "Pete can be ten times worse than the 'G' [federal government]. The 'G' could only put you in jail; Pete could destroy your whole family." He then put Pete on the phone. Pete made threats of violence against the debtor and his family, then returned the phone to Bombacino: "I'm glad you talked to this guy, [because] this will be the same guy that'll probably come looking for you. . . . You know I love you like a brother. You know what? I don't need no more kids to adopt and you got three beautiful daughters. And I really love 'em, that's why I keep protecting you."

Debtor: What, I, I, what are they gonna do? They gonna kill me for that [paying late]?
Bombacino: Yeah, yeah. Ya know why?
Debtor: Why?
Bombacino: It ain't the money; it's the principle. The money don't mean a fuckin' thing.

In 1997, Bombacino, 54, pleaded guilty to racketeering and received a 12-year sentence.

However, loansharks are not in the "muscle" business; they are in the credit business, so "they lend money to customers whom they expect will pay off and eventually return as customers again. The loanshark is not attempting to gain control of the customer's business" (Rubinstein and Reuter 1978b: Appendix 3–4). A loanshark obviously has the money to be in a legitimate business. However, loansharking requires very little time and can be engaged in by those with limited intelligence and ability. While some persons in organized crime are obviously very bright, many others would lose an argument with a fire hydrant.

But sometimes a loanshark finds himself involved with a debtor's business. Joseph Valachi lent money to a legitimate businessman, the owner of a dress and negligee company, and became a partner when the loan could not be repaid. With Valachi's financial backing, however, and his ability to keep labor unions from organizing the factory, the business prospered (Maas 1968). Research into loansharking in New York revealed that collection rarely involves violence or even the threat of violence: "Loansharks are interested in making credit assessments in the manner of legitimate lenders. Often they secure collateral for the loan, though it may be in an illiquid form. Sometimes a borrower will have to produce a guarantee. In many cases the loan is very short term, less than a month, and collection is simply not an issue. Repeat business is the backbone of those operations we have studied. A good faith effort to make payments will probably guarantee the borrower against harassment, particularly if he has made substantial payment of interest before he starts to have repayment problems" (Rubinstein and Reuter 1978b: Appendix 4).

There are two basic types of usurious loan: the *knockdown* and the *vig*. The knockdown requires a specified schedule of repayment, including both principal and interest. For example, $1,000 might be repaid in fourteen weekly installments of $100. The vig is a "six-for-five" loan: for every $5 borrowed on Monday, $6 is due on the following Monday. The $1 interest is called *vigorish* or *juice*, and loansharking is frequently referred to as the "juice racket." If total repayment of the vig loan, principal plus interest, is not forthcoming on the date it is due, the borrower must pay the interest, and the interest is compounded for the following week. Thus, for example, a loan of $100 requires repayment of $120 seven days later. If this is not possible, the borrower must pay the vig, $20, and this does not count against the principal or the next week's interest. The debt on an original loan of $100 will increase to $120 after one week, to $144 after two weeks, to $172.80 after three weeks, to $207.36 after four weeks, and so on.

The insidious nature of the vig loan is that the borrower must keep paying interest until the principal plus the accumulated interest is repaid at one time. It is quite easy for the original loan to be repaid many times without actually decreasing the principal owed. The loanshark is primarily interested in a steady income and is quite willing to let the principal remain outstanding for an indefinite period.

THEFT AND FENCING

Members of *Cosa Nostra* do not usually engage directly in theft, burglary, or robbery, although many have criminal records for such activities that typically precede their entry into organized crime. However, members will provide information and financing, arrange for necessary firearms or stolen cars, and help link up criminals to carry out more predatory crimes such as payroll robberies, large-scale commercial burglaries, hijackings, and thefts of stocks and bonds. They will finance frauds, swindles, and any conventional criminal activity that can bring in a profit substantial enough to make the effort worthwhile. They will help market stolen merchandise such as securities, checks, and credit cards. Members of organized crime are in a unique position to provide these services. Their widespread connections to both legitimate and illegitimate outlets provide a link between conventional criminals and the business world. Organized crime serves as a catalyst for a great deal of "disorganized" crime. In 1997, for example, an FBI sting resulted in the videotaping of members and associates of a Gambino Family crew in Canarsie, Brooklyn, disposing of $6 million worth of stolen merchandise, much of it hijacked over a two-year period (Raab 1997b).

Stolen Securities

The late 1960s and early 1970s saw a dramatic increase in the volume of securities being traded, which provided a lucrative source of income for organized crime. Because of the large volume of trade, security grew lax. Paperwork began to back up, and brokerage houses and banks were frequently totally unaware that hundreds of thousands of dollars worth of securities were being taken from their vaults. Thus, the securities were not even reported as missing for several months. The securities industry employs a great many persons—clerks and runners—whose pay is relatively low. Employees with gambling or loanshark debts or those merely seeking to supplement their incomes found a ready market for such "paper." All that was needed was an OC connection. In some cases, armed robbery or "give ups" (faked robberies) of messengers were used.

Although many people may have access to valuable securities, few can put stolen securities to immediate use. Organized crime groups serve as the intermediate link in the criminal enterprise. Bookmakers and loansharks who may have exerted the pressure that induced the thief to take the securities frequently serve as the conduit by which the stolen securities get into the hands of other organized crime figures. Passing through the network of organized crime, the stolen securities will eventually reach the hands of someone who does have the expertise, the capital, and the personnel to effect a profitable disposition.

The bull market of the late 1990s led to another addition to the dynamic repertoire of organized crime, the "pump and dump." High-ranking members of the Bonanno and Genovese Families cooperated in a scheme that duped investors in seven states of millions of dollars. The crime Family members bribed a group of brokers to use high-pressure tactics to sell shares of stock owned by the conspirators, who then dumped the inflated securities before the prices plummeted. In 1999, several members of the conspiracy were sentenced to imprisonment for their role in the scheme (Weiser 1999).

Fencing

The fence provides a readily available outlet for marketing stolen ("hot") merchandise. He thus provides an incentive for thieves and may also organize, finance, and direct their operations. In her research on fences, Walsh (1977: 13) found that about 13 percent of the fences she studied were part of organized crime: "For these individuals fencing appeared to be just another enterprise in a varied and totally illegal business portfolio." In addition to fencing, she notes, these persons were active in loansharking and gambling, and some were enforcers. In the Genovese Family, for example, Anthony ("Figgy") Ficcorata (or Ficcarata) forced jewel thieves to deal only with certain fences, from whom Ficcorata would receive a commission (Abadinsky 1983). In Chicago, eight "independent" burglars "were murdered for refusing to dispose of their loot through syndicate-connected fences" (Nicodemus and Petacque 1981: 5). Because of his connection with criminals (and otherwise) legitimate businessmen, the wiseguy is in a unique position to arrange for the disposition of stolen goods.

THE BUSINESS OF SEX

Organized crime's involvement in sex as a money-maker has changed with the times. House prostitution (whorehouses or bordellos) was an important social phenomenon during the days of large-scale immigration; immigrants were most often unattached males, single or traveling without their wives (Light 1977). Commercial sex, usually confined to infamous vice ("red-light") districts in urban areas, was a target of social and religious reformers. The campaign against this activity became known as the war on the "white slavery" trade, which at the turn of the century was an international problem. In a book titled *White Slavery* (Bell 1909: 48), Edwin W. Sims, U.S. Attorney for Chicago, states that "The recent examination of more than two hundred 'white slaves' by the office of the United States district attorney at Chicago has brought to light the fact that literally thousands of innocent girls from the country districts are every year entrapped into a life of hopeless slavery and degradation because parents in the country do not understand conditions as they exist and how to protect their daughters from the 'white slave' traders who have reduced the art of ruining young girls to a national and international system."

In 1904 an international treaty was signed in Paris by all of the governments of Western Europe and Russia. The respective governments, as the treaty preamble states, were "desirous to assure to women who have attained their majority and are subjected to deception or constraint, as well as minor women and girls, an efficacious protection against the criminal traffic known under the name of trade in white women (*Traite des Blanches*)."[8] The treaty was ratified by the U.S. Senate in 1908. In 1910 the "White Slave Act," called the Mann Act after its sponsor, Congressman James R. Mann of Illinois, prohibited the interstate transportation of women "for the purpose of prostitution, or debauchery or for any other immoral purpose." Nevertheless, the practice flourished.

In the United States, there was an elaborate system for procuring and transporting women between New York, Milwaukee, St. Louis, and Chicago (Landesco 1968). The constant transfer of women provided "new faces" and was good for business. The syndicates that dominated the trade included one headed by Big Jim Colosimo and Johnny Torrio in Chicago. Madams opened brothels, attracted prostitutes and customers, and secured protection from the police. The most famous of these establishments was owned and operated by the Everleigh sisters, who left their brutal husbands in Kentucky and traveled to the Windy City at the turn of the century. In 1900 the two sisters opened the lavish Everleigh Club in the downtown area. Despite the high cost of political protection, the establishment netted $10,000 a month. The club was closed in a flush of reform in 1911 (Washburn 1934). The madam also acted as

---

[8]In chapters 7, 9, and 10, it is noted that a variety of transnational criminal organizations are involved in global trade in sex workers, a situation paralleling that which led to the Paris treaty of 1904.

Chicago Historical Society

Prostitution and the white slave trade flourished in several cities at the turn of the century, but nowhere as profitably as in Chicago. The Everleigh Club, the city's most famous brothel, netted $10,000 a month before it closed in 1911.

a "housemother," preventing quarrels and providing advice; she was both friend and employer: "Her work made it almost inevitable that she would assume traditionally maternal functions" (Winick and Kinsie 1971: 98).

Organized crime's interest in prostitution waned during Prohibition because money could be made more easily in bootlegging. With Prohibition drawing to a close, and with the advent of the Great Depression, OC groups began looking for new areas of income. In many cities, they "organized" independent brothels: the madams were forced to pay OC middlemen for protection from the police and from violence. Gangsters such as David ("Little Davey") Betillo, a member of the Luciano crime Family, organized previously independent brothels in New York, which, as noted in Chapter 4, eventually resulted in Luciano's imprisonment. The normalization of the gender ratio—immigrants were predominantly male—and changes in sexual mores led to a reduction in the importance of house prostitution. The brothel industry reached its peak in 1939. During World War II, and more significantly after 1945, the importance of brothels as a source of income for OC steadily declined but did not entirely disappear (Winick and Kinsie 1971). OC members may organize or finance or be involved in an extortionate relationship with the proprietors of commercial sex establishments, ranging from brothels to bars that feature sexually explicit entertainment. In some of the Chicago suburbs, such establishments pay "street taxes" to the Outfit for the privilege of operating. And there is also pornography.

The pornography business, like prostitution, apparently suffers from a great deal of "amateur" involvement. Pornography, which at one time was under the almost exclusive control of organized crime, is widely available throughout the United States. Liberal court decisions have virtually legalized pornography, and legitimate entrepreneurs have entered the market. OC involvement today may simply be parasitic—extorting "protection" money. In Los Angeles, the entire hierarchy of the Dragna crime Family was convicted of, among other crimes, extorting money from the owners of porno shops. Since they were no longer illegitimate entrepreneurs, porno operators in Los Angeles were able to go to the authorities and complain about the extortion attempt.

The International Sex Industry

As noted in chapters 7, 9, and 10, international trafficking in women for the sex industry has been a characteristic of modern transnational organized crime. Italian, Albanian, Russian, Chinese, and Japanese criminal groups have been at the center of a global trade that often enslaves female adults and (sometimes male) children for sale. In the states of the former Soviet Union and the volatile Balkans region, women are recruited for lawful foreign employment only to find themselves in the hands of criminals who force them into the sex trade. As part of a nefarious web that spreads across the Balkans and into Western Europe, "tens of thousands of women have been caught up by the traffickers and have suffered rape, extreme violence and slavery at the hands of criminal groups renowned for their brutality and greed" (Gall 2001: 1). Even traditional enemies such as Albanians and Slavs readily deal with one another in this trade. Women are recruited through ads in newspapers, in magazines, and on the Internet offering employment as dancers, waitresses, maids, and babysitters in nonspecified western countries.

People in the Balkans find it inherently attractive to travel abroad, and although the women in general are aware that the offers for certain types of work abroad in reality mean prostitution, an unspecified number of the women are nevertheless misled. The women aware that they are going to work as prostitutes consider present living conditions and earning potential as considerably poorer than the prospects held out to them (Task-Force on Organized Crime in the Baltic Sea Region 2001). Thus, even in the absence of deception and physical coercion, "trafficking must be seen as part of the world-wide feminization of poverty and of labour migration. When women are structurally denied access to the formal and regulated labour market, they are increasingly pushed into unprotected or criminalized labour markets, such as sexual and exploitive domestic work" (International Organization for Migration 1998: 14). And at the center of this exploitation is organized crime.

INTERNET CONNECTIONS

Organized crime topics: **faculty.ncwc.edu/toconnor**

New Jersey State Commission of Investigation: **www.state.nj.us/sci**

International Organization for Migration: **www.iom.int**

United Nations criminal justice: **uncjin.org**

REVIEW QUESTIONS

1. In addition to providing "goods and services" that happen to be illegal, what important criminal activity is part of the business of organized crime? How does this activity operate?
2. How does the concept of *rispetto* enable a member of organized crime to act as an arbitrator?
3. Why is it often important for a professional criminal to have ties to organized crime?
4. How can traditional organized crime act as a catalyst for a great deal of conventional crime?
5. What are the various roles of organized crime in bookmaking?
6. In sports betting, what is the "line"?
7. What was the role of organized crime in Las Vegas?
8. What factors led to the heavy involvement of organized crime in loansharking?
9. Why has OC involvement in the sex industry in the United States waned in recent years?
10. What is the nature of the international trade in women for the sex industry?

♠

CHAPTER 12

ORGANIZED CRIME IN LABOR AND BUSINESS

Labor racketeering is the infiltration, domination, and use of a union for personal benefit by illegal, violent, and fraudulent means. Ronald Goldstock points out that the "sometimes bewildering array of labor rackets assume three basic forms: the sale of 'strike insurance' in which the union threatens a walkout and the employer pays to assure a steady supply of labor; the 'sweetheart deal' in which management pays the labor representative for contract terms unobtainable through arm's-length bargaining; and the direct or indirect siphoning of union funds" (PCOC 1985b: 658). An employer may be tempted into a corrupt relationship with labor unions because "he may hope that through a payment to the union officers he can persuade them not to organize his shop, thereby allowing for payment of less than the going union wage. Such an arrangement is particularly beneficial when his competitors are organized." If he cannot stifle organization, "he may at least be able to get a lenient 'sweetheart' agreement with the union." Furthermore, the "union itself can be used for the benefit of the employer through the limitation of competition. Competition can be limited by

the union in several ways—either through the refusal to work on goods or by directly enforcing price agreements" (Newell 1961: 79). Although labor and related business racketeering can be conducted by anyone, the history of the labor movement shows that the most substantial corruption of unions is conducted by organized crime.

Labor and business racketeering distinguish *traditional* organized crime from other forms, making traditional OC more influential than the others. Irish, Jewish, and Italian organized crime groups helped shape the economic life of the United States. The rise of organized labor and the subsequent reaction of American business generated a conflict that provided fertile ground for the seeds of racketeering and organized crime. The leaders of organized crime provided mercenary armies to unions that were willing to use violence to organize workers and thwart strikebreakers. In the spirit of ideological neutrality, they also provided private violence to business for use in its efforts against organized labor and also its dealings with the demanding competition of a capitalistic marketplace.

ORGANIZED LABOR IN AMERICA

The Civil War led to the dramatic industrialization of America. War profiteers accumulated large amounts of capital, enabling them to invest in the trusts: oil, coal, iron, steel, sugar, and railroads. Congress imposed protective tariffs, and industry blossomed during the Gilded Age of the robber barons: "Within twenty-five years of the assassination of Abraham Lincoln, America had become the leading manufacturing nation in the world" (Brooks 1971: 39).

At the bottom of this industrial world was labor, often immigrants who spoke English with foreign accents, if they spoke English at all. Children of both sexes often labored twelve hours a day, six days a week, under conditions that threatened life and limb. Labor's struggle for better working conditions and wages resulted in what Sidney Lens calls *The Labor Wars* (1974: 4): "The labor wars were a specific response to a specific set of injustices at a time when industrial and financial capitalism was establishing its predominance over American society. In a sense the battles were not different from the hundreds of other violent clashes against social injustices, as normal as the proverbial apple pie in the nation's annals."

During the first half of the nineteenth century until the Civil War, criminal conspiracy statutes were used against labor's efforts to organize and strike. This approach was replaced by the use of equity—a civil procedure—in the form of injunctions restraining unions from striking. The unions sought relief from Congress, but in 1908 the Supreme Court declared that Congress had no power with respect to union activities (*Adair v. United States*, 208 U.S. 161). It was not until the Great Depression that Congress stripped the federal courts of their power to issue injunctions in labor disputes (the 1932 Norris–La Guardia Act). In 1935 the Wagner (National Labor Relations) Act gave explicit protection to the rights of workers to organize and engage in collective bargaining.

From the earliest days of our republic until the passage of the Wagner Act, labor confrontations with employers often took on a particular scenario: company spies, often from the Pinkerton Private Detective Agency, would identify union leaders, who were then fired by management. The guard force would be increased and strikebreakers secured. Company lawyers would secure injunctions from friendly judges prohibiting a strike. The union would organize "flying squadrons" to guard against the influx of strikebreakers and plan for mass picketing. If the guard force proved inadequate, hired thugs, deputy sheriffs, policemen, the National Guard, and even U.S. Army troops would be used to deal with strikers.

LABOR RACKETEERING: IN THE BEGINNING . . .

The first step away from union democracy was a response to power wielded by employers. In order to avoid the problem of company spies reporting to management, some unions employed the "walking delegate" or business agent, who was empowered to call a strike without any formal vote by the union membership. As an employee of the union, he was immune from management intimidation, and his power enabled the union to strike quickly and at the most opportune time. The men chosen for this position were usually tough, and it was this quality rather than intelligence, integrity, and commitment to labor that characterized business agents. Before long, some of these men began abusing their power, calling needless strikes and engaging in extortionate practices (Seidman 1938). In 1928, for example, two racketeers set up the United Lathing Company and hired the Lathers Union walking delegate. He would appear at job sites and issue a strike order. When contractors asked for an explanation, he would refer them to the United Lathing Company, where, for a fee, the strike would be called off (Nelli 1976). These types of racketeers intimidated union members and employers but were usually not connected to a syndicate (Newell 1961).

In the early days, labor unions provided their own "muscle" from the ranks of their membership to deal with Pinkerton agents and strikebreakers.

In the first decade of the twentieth century, however, a need arose for a more systematic and professional approach. Enter Benjamin Fein (known as "Dopey Benny" because an adenoidal condition made him look sleepy). Fein became an integral part of the Jewish labor movement (Joselit 1983: 109). Whenever a strike was called under the auspices of the umbrella organization called United Hebrew Trades (UHT), "Dopey and his men were given union cards as pickets and union delegates." They protected fellow pickets against management goons—strong-arm personnel who were employed by licensed detective agencies.

Fein formed alliances with New York street gangs such as the Hudson Dusters, assigning territories and working out businesslike arrangements and patterns of operation. He also assisted the union in keeping its members in line. However, it soon became clear that it was easier to hire gangsters than it was to fire them (Seidman 1938). Racketeers such as Lepke Buchalter and Gurrah Shapiro came to dominate many of the industries into which they were invited (see Chapter 4): "The introduction of armed hoods as 'finks' (strikebreakers) or as 'nobles' (armed guards) by industry, facilitated the entry of the Arnold Rothsteins and Capones into the lucrative business of industrial racketeering" (Brooks 1971: 147).

When Max ("the Butcher") Block tried to organize a union, the Wholesale Butcher Drivers, and called a strike, he found himself meeting with some fearsome representatives of the meat packing houses: Harry ("Pittsburgh Phil") Strauss and his fellow partners in Murder, Inc. Max the Butcher's background as an ex-con and professional boxer allowed him to "sweet talk" the "Boys from Brooklyn," and he was left alone: "So the wholesalers couldn't break the strike. They'd gone to the toughest and lost. They saw they couldn't shake us, that nobody would go against us" (Bloch and Kenner 1982: 72). The business agent for the Chicago local of the Bartenders International League (which later merged with the Hotel and Restaurant Employees Union) was not so lucky. In 1939, representatives of the Capone syndicate ordered him to step aside and appoint one of their men to the local's presidency. When he returned to his office and, after consultation with the other officers of the local, it was decided that the honest union leader's life was worth more than resisting the syndicate—he resigned (Newell 1961).

Labor racketeers "didn't target steel mills and auto factories and foundries, the giant pool of workers who truly needed the protection of a collective bargaining agreement." Instead, they "picked on small, vulnerable mom-and-pop operations such as dry cleaners, taverns, and bakeries." Or they exploited their control over labor to extort money from vulnerable businesses such as those selling wholesale fish. Because of the perishable nature of the product, seafood wholesalers depend on speed for display and delivery, which makes them vulnerable to threats of delay (Neff 1989: 20).

The Fulton Fish Market

New York's Fulton Fish Market represents a classic example of the power of organized crime to control an industry. While the market was established in 1833, the OC connection began during Prohibition, when some innovative criminals—in this case, Joseph ("Socks") Lanza—avoided bootlegging for the less competitive rewards of labor and business racketeering. At age 14, Lanza began working as a fish handler at the giant wholesale market along the East River near Fulton Street in lower Manhattan. He became a member of the crime Family of Lucky Luciano (now known as the Genovese Family), and in 1923 he organized his fellow workers into Local 359 of the United Seafood Workers' Union. As head of the local and *caporegime* in the Genovese Family, Lanza extorted money from every dealer in the market: "Lanza influenced the price of fish not only in New York but throughout much of the nation. The union served as the principal basis of Lanza's $20-million-a-year racket" (Nelli 1976: 245). He and his brother, also a Genovese captain, determined which businesses could operate in the market. Through his leadership of the union, Lanza asserted control over fishing boats because he could withhold the labor needed to unload the vessels. He also controlled the Fulton

Market's Watchmen's Protective Association: "Dealers who visited the market and failed to have a Lanza watchman look after their vehicles usually found their tires slashed" (Peterson 1983: 173).

In 1938, Lanza was convicted of racketeering (Carroll 1991). In 1943, he was convicted of extortion involving local Teamster union officials. Paroled in 1950, Lanza was arrested as a parole violator seven years later in a case that touched off a scandal. New York State parole officers recommended returning Lanza to prison as a major racketeer, but the parole board member in charge of his case released the "Fish Market Czar." A subsequent investigation revealed that high-level political pressure had led to the decision to release Lanza. The parole board subsequently overruled the decision, and Lanza was returned to prison to finish out his unexpired term. Convictions and imprisonment notwithstanding, Lanza continued to control the Fulton Market until his death in 1968, when domination passed into other Genovese Family hands (Nelli 1976).

Despite the fact that the market operated on city property, government controls remained absent for decades, creating a lawless atmosphere in which rules of operation evolved through violence and intimidation—an ideal atmosphere for organized crime (Carroll 1991). In 1988, as a result of a civil action brought by the U.S. Department of Justice, an outside administrator was appointed to monitor the market and rid it of illegal activities—U.S. Attorney Rudolph Giuliani convinced a federal judge that the market was dominated by the Genovese Family (Glaberson 1989). Two years later, however, the administrator stated that the market continued to operate "in a frontier atmosphere, in that the Fulton Fish Market is a sovereign entity where the laws of economic power and physical force, not the laws of New York City, prevail" (Raab 1990: B12).

The market is a vital economic asset to the city, generating sales of 125 million tons of seafood annually and providing about 1,000 jobs. It is the source of most seafood sold in retail outlets and served in restaurants throughout the New York region. When they come to pick up supplies, merchants are assigned parking spots by unlicensed loaders who charge a fee and retain the right to transport supplies to the purchaser's vehicle. Many firms seek to avoid the high prices at the market, shopping instead in Philadelphia and Boston, which has cost New York City $2 billion in lost sales annually (Raab 1995f, 1995g).

When the former U.S. Attorney became Mayor Giuliani, he asserted city control over the market through the power to license, regulate, and investigate who does business or works in the market. The city evicted six unloading companies allegedly affiliated with the Genovese Family and hired an outside firm to replace them. In response, a 1995 wildcat strike threw the market into chaos. The strike soon ended, and a strained sense of calm prevailed, only to be upset again in 1996 by more wildcat strikes. Reforms established by the city of New York have reduced, if not eliminated, the influence of organized crime, but this is seen as a mixed blessing by the market's wholesale dealers, who complain of rigid rules and increased overhead costs (Raab 1996a, 1996c). In 2001, the city broke ground on a $75-million indoor facility in the Bronx to replace the one on Fulton Street.

LABOR RACKETEERING AND THE "BIG FOUR"

Unions fought not only with management but also with one another. In 1938 a number of industrial unions led by John L. Lewis broke with the American Federation of Labor (AFL) and formed the Congress of Industrial Organizations (CIO). During struggles over jurisdiction and representation between the AFL and the CIO, both sides resorted to "muscle" from organized crime. But for whatever reason, whoever used OC was "playing with the devil." Many locals and some internationals were delivered into the hands of organized crime. Forty years later, a congressional committee concluded that "At least four international unions are completely dominated by men who either have strong ties to or are members of the organized crime syndicate. A majority of the locals in most major cities of the United States in the International Brotherhood of Teamsters (IBT), Hotel and

Restaurant Employees Union (HRE), Laborers International Union of North America (Laborers), and International Longshoremen's Association (ILA) are completely dominated by organized crime" (Permanent Subcommittee on Investigation 1982: 5).

Laborers International Union

Formed in 1903, the Laborers International Union of North America (LIUNA) is one of 15 unions that belong to the Building Construction Trades Department of the AFL-CIO. Representing about 800,000 laborers in hundreds of locals in the United States and Canada, LIUNA members perform the dirtiest, most strenuous, and most dangerous work associated with building construction. Control over laborers provides control over many construction sites. The Laborers Union "is classic Chicago old-time unionism. It was headed for years by Peter Fosco,[1] an Italian immigrant whose association with Capone-era hoodlums did not prevent him from winning public office and once earning an Italian-American award at a dinner addressed by Richard Nixon. . . . The Laborers' Union has always had a healthy treasury, kept brimming with hard-working workers' dues" (Kilian, Fletcher, and Ciccone 1979: 247).

In Chicago, the Laborers Union has always had close ties to the Outfit. For more than a decade, the 19,000-member Chicago District Council of the Laborers Union was headed by Ernest Kumerow, who is married to the daughter of the late Outfit boss Tony Accardo. Until his death in 1992, Accardo spent winters in a coachhouse in the rear of Kumerow's home. Street boss Vincent Solano was president of Local 1 until his death from natural causes in 1992. His son remained a LIUNA official. Street boss Alfred Pilotta was president of Local 5 until he was convicted in 1982 for his role in a kickback scheme involving the union's welfare benefit fund. In 1992, a veteran LIUNA official and Outfit boss in charge

of the southern suburbs was sentenced to 32 years for extorting money from bookmakers in northwest Indiana. His codefendant, a Laborers Union field representative, received 36 years. In 1997, the $90,000-per-year LIUNA secretary-treasurer of Local 5, a top lieutenant for the South Side Outfit boss, was charged with the 1988 murder of the owner of a pallet company who refused to pay a $100,000 juice loan—he had been shot six times. In 2000, while awaiting trial for murder, the LIUNA official died of natural causes. In 2001, John Serpico, a former international vice-president of LIUNA and reputed Outfit associate, was convicted of receiving kickbacks for using his union influence to arrange for millions of dollars in loans.

Surveillance tapes contain conversations involving New Jersey Family boss Sam DeCavalcante, during which he discussed how control of Laborers Union locals enabled him to "shake down" building contractors who wanted to avoid using expensive union labor. For much of his adult life, until he was voted out in 1992, Matthew ("Mikey") Trupiano, head of the St. Louis *Cosa Nostra*, led the Laborers Union Local 110.[2] In 1985 the President's Commission concluded that in New York, several LIUNA locals are controlled by members of the five crime Families.

In 1995 the U.S. Department of Justice reached a consent agreement with the union under which the government would monitor efforts to purge LIUNA officials connected to organized crime. As part of the agreement with the government, LIUNA agreed to hold direct elections for the union's top posts; previously, they had been chosen by delegates at the annual convention. In only one instance did an opposition candidate ever challenge the union slate, and he was physically beaten on the floor of the 1981 convention (Johnson 1996). Chicago's Bruno Caruso lost the government-monitored election to Arthur Coia.

Coia is the son of a former secretary-treasurer

---

[1] Peter Fosco was succeeded by his son Angelo in 1975. Angelo was acquitted of union corruption charges and remained president of the LIUNA until his death in 1993 at age 71.

[2] In 1997, Trupiano, at 58, died of a heart attack. The criminal organization he headed was considerably weakened by internal strife—and bombings—after the death of Trupiano's uncle, Anthony Giordano, under whose leadership the St. Louis *Cosa Nostra* was a unit of some local stature.

of LIUNA who allegedly had close ties with New England crime boss Raymond Patriarca. A native of Rhode Island, Arthur Coia first headed the Laborers local in Providence and later throughout New England. He admitted knowing Raymond Patriarca, Jr., who took over the crime Family after his father died of natural causes in 1984. Coia has also admitted that he met with mob figures in Chicago—he denied knowing they were connected to the Outfit. He stated that he was told to meet with them in order to get permission to take the top spot in the union (Greenhouse 1997, 2000a).

Under an arrangement with the Department of Justice, the union conducted an internal investigation led by a former federal OC prosecutor. As a result, the Justice Department dropped a 1995 civil complaint that sought to remove Coia and place the union under receivership. One of those suspended in the subsequent union purge was the president of the Chicago LIUNA Local 225, who, in 1999, was convicted of syndicated gambling—accepting $200,000 in sports wagers over a three-week period—for which he was placed on probation. In 1999 the president of LIUNA Local 2 in Chicago was removed for his alleged role in the Outfit's North Side crew (see Chapter 5). In 2001 a federal hearing officer removed the business managers of Locals 1001 and 1006 in Chicago; according to the government, the brothers Bruno and Leo Caruso, along with Outfit members, rigged union elections (Possley 2001). The Caruso brothers are the sons of Frank ("Skids") Caruso, for many years the Outfit boss of Chinatown, who died in 1983, and nephews of a convicted First Ward (see Chapter 5) alderman.

A civil RICO action (discussed in Chapter 14) was taken to rid the Buffalo, New York, LIUNA local of organized crime control. In 1996 the government concluded that 11 Buffalo LIUNA officials were made members of the Buffalo crime Family, and they were barred from the union. The Buffalo local was subsequently placed in trusteeship under the provisions of RICO (Office of Inspector General 2000).

In 2000 a hearing officer cleared Coia of associating with members of organized crime but fined

him $100,000 for buying a $450,000 Ferrari with help from a supplier to the union. The hearing officer's ruling was criticized by the Department of Justice, union dissidents, and Republican lawmakers (Greenhouse 1999; Franklin 1999; Kaiser 1999). Under Coia, the union was one of the three biggest contributors to President Clinton's 1997 inauguration. The union has also been one of the biggest contributors to the Democratic Party, and (now senator) Hillary Rodham Clinton has spoken before the LIUNA convention (Greenhouse 1997). On the first day of 2000, Coia, after agreeing to pled guilty to defrauding Rhode Island of about $100,000 in taxes, retired as LIUNA president (Greenhouse 2000a). Later that year, the Justice Department agreed to relax its oversight of LIUNA—this after the union removed 220 corrupt officials from union positions, 127 of them found to be members or associates of organized crime (Office of Inspector General 2000).

Hotel Employees and Restaurant Employees International Union (HEREIU)

HEREIU was established in Chicago in 1891: "At first, only workers from pubs and restaurants were represented. Yet as America's cities began to grow so did the international, and soon hotel workers as well as food and beverage workers were represented. Thwarted only by prohibition in the 1920s, the international became the fastest growing union in the United States in the 1930s. By 1941, the international was the seventh largest union in North America" (Permanent Subcommittee on Investigations 1982: 4). Today the international is the largest service union in the United States, with about 260,000 members in 235 locals in 48 states and 8 Canadian provinces.

HEREIU charters often provided the basis for extortion from restaurants in Chicago, as U.S. Senator John L. McClellan explained (1962: 141–42):

If an owner knew what was good for him, he agreed to have his place unionized upon the first visit of the organizer. The workers were not consulted in this organizing drive; they rarely knew it was going on. The restaurant owner was told that the union wasn't greedy, a compromise figure would always be accepted. If the owner had forty employees, then twenty memberships would be given to the union. The owner paid the initiation fees and the dues for twenty names that he gave the organizer. That arrangement usually continued for years. It didn't make any difference to anyone concerned in the deal that, after a period of time, possibly ten or more of the twenty union members may no longer be employees. . . . Dues continued to be collected for twenty names.

In return, there "were no sudden fires in the middle of the night, no beatings, no sugar poured into gas tanks, no tires slashed, no vandalism" (1962: 142). The restaurant owners did not have to worry about workers' salaries or working conditions, conditions of employment that are the concerns of legitimate unions.

Many of the HEREIU locals were/are reputed to be under the domination of organized crime. Local 450 in Chicago was chartered in 1935 by Joey ("Doves") Aiuppa, a top leader in the Outfit. For 40 years, the Outfit wielded power in Chicago-area HEREIU locals and the joint executive board: "Their actions took on national proportions when Edward Hanley [a former bartender from Chicago's West Side], who began his career in Local 450 as a business agent in 1957, was elected to the HEREIU presidency in 1973" (PCOC 1986b: 73). When Hanley, who has never been convicted of any crime, appeared before a U.S. Senate investigating committee, he refused to answer any questions, invoking the Fifth Amendment 36 times (Franklin 1995a). In Illinois the 40,000-member union local has made significant political contributions, and Hanley has been feted by the Cook County Democratic organization.

Local 54 in New Jersey has about 22,000 members, most of them employed in the Atlantic City casino business. The local has been controlled by the Philadelphia crime Family once headed by Angelo Bruno. As a result, Bruno Fam-

ily members have been able to force hotels in Atlantic City to buy supplies and provisions from companies they own. In 1980, when the president of the Philadelphia Roofers Union Local 30 attempted to organize bartenders in Atlantic City—even though they belonged to Local 54—he was murdered at his home. Two union officials were convicted of ordering the murder and are serving life sentences. In 1981 the New Jersey Casino Control Commission concluded that Local 54 was controlled by Philadelphia crime boss Nicky Scarfo, and their legal action eventually forced the local's president to resign. In 1991 the local was placed in government receivership, which has since been lifted.

In New York, HEREIU Locals 6 and 100 have long been under the control of organized crime. The locals were used to dictate the way in which restaurants "could do business in New York. In return for payoffs, restaurant owners could pay reduced wages and pension and welfare fund contributions, or buy a lease on a restaurant shut down because it owed money to the union, or hire and fire without regard to grievance procedures, or operate without regard to union work rules" (PCOC 1986b: 83–84). At one point, there appeared to be a jurisdictional dispute between the two locals, something that is not unusual in organized labor. However, intercepted conversations between union officials and important OC figures revealed that the split was in fact "a market allocation of New York's entire restaurant business between the Colombo and Gambino crime families" (PCOC 1986b: 84).

In 1995, as the result of a settlement of a civil RICO lawsuit, the U.S. Department of Justice placed the HEREIU under supervision and appointed a monitor with disciplinary and oversight authority (Franklin 1995a). In 1998, faced with another federal investigation, Edward Hanley, who ran the union for 25 years, was forced to retire—with a guaranteed $267,000-per-year salary for the rest of his life. In 2000, at age 67, Hanley was killed in a traffic accident. The government-appointed monitor expelled 17 union officials, and at the end of 2000, the Justice Department agreed to end five years of intensive monitoring—

according to the government, the union has been largely purged of its ties to organized crime (Greenhouse 2000b).

International Longshoremen's Association (ILA)

New York City's premier position as a commercial capital is due in large part to its deep-water harbor, the finest in North America. The New York waterfront encompasses over 700 miles of wharves and shoreline and 1,900 piers. With government regulation absent, organized crime was able to assert control over this lucrative piece of geography.

With the able assistance of men such as Antonio Vaccarelli, better known as Paul Kelly, the ILA was organized in the 1890s and gained complete control over the waterfront by 1914 (Nelli 1976). Kelly, leader of the notorious Five Points Gang (discussed in Chapter 4), became vice president of the International Longshoremen's Association. Until the twentieth century, about 95 percent of the longshoremen in the New York City area were Irish. By 1912, Italians made up about 35 percent, and by 1919, they accounted for about 75 percent of the area's longshoremen. The Irish controlled the notoriously violent West Side ("Hell's Kitchen") docks, while the Italians dominated the East Side, Brooklyn, and New Jersey docks.

For poorly educated and often illiterate immigrants, the waterfront provided attractive employment opportunities. It was also attractive to racketeers for its lucrative illegal opportunities. The "shape-up," vividly portrayed in the Academy Award-winning film *On the Waterfront*, provided corrupt officials with kickbacks from workers eager for a day's wage. Loansharking, large-scale pilfering, smuggling, and deals with employers eager for "labor peace" profited the criminals who dominated the waterfront. The "necessity for speed, plus the lack of rail connections to the piers, gave rise to the coveted 'loading' racket, which involved moving cargo from the pier floor to waiting trucks. Since demand for cargo loading was inelastic and dependent upon immediate need when ships arrived, loading generated extraordinary profits, and

was a principal incentive for organized crime to infiltrate the ILA" (PCOC 1986b: 33). Whoever controls waterfront labor controls the waterfront.

While Paul Kelly led an influx of criminals to the waterfront, it was under Joseph P. Ryan that OC control of the waterfront became complete (Nelli 1976). Ryan—a strident anti-Communist—served as ILA president from 1927 to 1953. On the West Coast, Australian-born Alfred Reuton ("Harry") Bridges withdrew from the ILA and organized the International Longshoremen and Warehousemen's Union (ILWU), which became part of the rival CIO. Bridges, who was born in 1901 and came to the United States as a merchant seaman in 1920, went to work as a longshoreman in San Francisco. He reactivated a dormant ILA local in 1933 and led a successful strike in 1934, a strike opposed by ILA president Joe Ryan. Ryan attacked Bridges for his leftist views and close association with Communists (Lens 1974). During the 1940s, the House of Representatives voted to have Bridges deported as an undesirable alien, an order that was overturned by the Supreme Court. In marked contrast to the ILA, always a strongly anti-Communist union, the ILWU has been free of OC influence. Nevertheless, the ILWU was expelled from the CIO in 1950 for "following the communist line." A variety of unions, including the Teamsters, unsuccessfully attempted to raid the ILWU membership (Kimeldorf 1988). Bridges headed the ILWU until his retirement in 1977. He died in 1990 (Saxon 1990).

Once in control of the union, organized crime found the shipping industry an attractive and easy target for the more traditional types of racketeering (PCOC 1986b: 34–35): "When a ship docks, it must be emptied quickly. The cargo may include perishable foodstuffs, and in any event, the owner gathers no return for his capital investment—the ship—while it is in port. Ship turnaround time is thus a crucial key to profitability." Pier bosses regularly shook down shippers by threatening walkouts: "Time pressures also encouraged owners to maintain an oversupply of labor so that all ships, even on the busiest days, could be unloaded at once. The lucrative and commonly used 'kickback' racket also arose from time pressures. Because the number of ship arrivals fluctuated, the hiring boss (usually a union officer) selected the necessary number of workers from the surplus of men at the daily 'shape up.' The criterion for selection on many piers was the willingness, evidenced by a prearranged signal, such as a toothpick by the ear, to 'kickback' a part of the day's wages to the boss."

Other traditional rackets ran rampant on the ILA-controlled waterfront: gambling, loansharking, and cargo theft. OC-corrupted port employees provided "access to cargo shipments and storage areas, security for the movement of contraband, such as narcotics, falsification of invoices and shipping documents in insurance scams, and collusion in the expropriation of stolen property, such as luxury vehicles and construction equipment" (PCOC 1986b: 35).

In 1953 the AFL convention voted to revoke the ILA charter because of rampant corruption. Shortly afterward, under indictment for misappropriating union funds, Ryan stepped down and William Bradley was elected president. The AFL attempted to wrest control of longshoremen from the ILA by setting up a rival union, the International Brotherhood of Longshoremen (IBL). In 1955 the AFL and CIO merged into the AFL-CIO. And, in 1959, after a series of often physical battles between the rival longshoremen's unions, the IBL and ILA merged. Shortly afterward, the ILA was admitted to the AFL-CIO.

Bradley, however, failed to cooperate with OC, and taped conversations between leading waterfront racketeers indicate that he "was visited by mob members who told him he'd have to give up his position to Teddy Gleason or he'd be killed" (Permanent Subcommittee on Investigations 1981b: 447). In 1963, after Bradley declined to run for reelection, Thomas W. ("Teddy") Gleason was unanimously elected president of the ILA, a post he held until his retirement in 1987; he stepped down from the 110,000-member union at age 87 because of poor health. Gleason died of natural causes in 1992. Without any opposition, the post went to his associate and ILA executive vice president, John Bowers.

In 1952 it was revealed that organized crime, using its control of the ILA, "had for years been levying the equivalent of a 5 percent tax on all general cargo moving in and out of the harbor" (Goddard 1980: 35). The outrage that was generated led to the 1953 establishment of the Waterfront Commission, which was given subpoena power and investigative authority in New York and New Jersey. The commission employs investigators who possess full police powers in both states. The commission is authorized to regulate waterfront employees and license stevedoring operations that contract with shipping companies to unload their ships. The stevedoring firms own or rent the heavy equipment needed and hire longshoremen who provide the labor. The commission banned persons with serious criminal records from the docks, and the notorious "shape-up" was eliminated. Convicted criminals are prohibited from holding office in waterfront unions, and the commission audits the books and records of the licensed stevedore firms to guard against illegal payoffs and other violations of law.

In 1953, Michael Clemente, president of ILA Local 856 in Manhattan and a member of the Genovese Family, was convicted of extorting money from waterfront employers and perjury before the New York State Crime Commission (PCOC 1986b). Upon his release from prison, however, Clemente resumed his control of the Manhattan waterfront. Another Genovese Family member, Tino Fiumara, exercised similar control on the New Jersey side. In 1963, Anthony Scotto, a *caporegime* in the Gambino Family, took over Local 1814 in Red Hook, Brooklyn, when his father-in-law, Anthony ("Tough Tony") Anastasio, a member of the Gambino Family (and brother of crime Family boss Albert Anastasia), died of natural causes.

As a result of more stringent law enforcement efforts in the port of New York and New Jersey, notes Donald Goddard (1980: 66), "the ILA racketeers moved operations to Florida, where they plundered the booming Port of Miami." The ILA shifted from exploiting its 90,000 members to "carving up the cargo traffic among the port's stevedores and 'taxing' them on their shares." The ILA used its domination of the port to establish a system whereby competition among stevedoring companies and other waterfront firms was significantly reduced. Goddard points out that ship owners, agents, stevedores, contractors, and service companies were caught up in a web of corrupt practices with the ILA—and few wanted to escape: "They only had to pay their 'rent' in order to enrich themselves with guaranteed profits." As Louis J. Freeh of the FBI noted before a congressional committee (Permanent Subcommittee on Investigations 1981b: 183), "You do not have extortion, you do not have threats, you do not have violence. What you have is a businessman who is as corrupt as the ILA official who he pays looking for additional business, looking for an advantage against his competitors and using his organized crime connection . . . to have that union official contact another businessman to extend an economic advantage."

The FBI's UNIRAC investigation (1975–1979) was accomplished with the help of stevedore Joe Teitelbaum, who was approached by ILA officials for a $3,000 payoff as a down payment for continuing to do business in Miami. When he declined to pay, shipping clients began to receive calls from the union officials indicating Teitelbaum was having labor problems, and he could not guarantee that he could provide longshoremen when their cargo needed offloading in Miami. Teitelbaum went to the FBI and agreed to serve in an undercover capacity. The investigation resulted in 117 convictions, including that of Tino Fiumara,[3] Michael Clemente, and Anthony Scotto. (This did not stop New York's governor and two former New York City mayors from acting as character witnesses at Scotto's trial.)

The investigation revealed that ports along the East Coast from New York to Florida had been divided between the Genovese and Gambino Families into spheres of interest. Scotto and the others were convicted of a number of corrupt practices, including the following:

- Payoffs in lieu of employer contributions to ILA pension and welfare plans.

- Payoffs to secure "labor peace" and avoid adhering to costly ILA rules that amounted to "featherbedding."
- Payoffs by businessmen to secure union contracts that were necessary to qualify for maritime work in ports under ILA control.
- Payoffs to help firms secure new business and to keep the business they had without competitive bidding.

The relationship between racketeers and employers has frequently been mutually beneficial: "Convicted union officers have gone back to the ports working for industries closely associated with the port, thus enabling them to circumvent the provisions of the Landrum–Griffin Act," which bars them from holding union office (PCOC 1986b: 44). In 2001 the imprisoned acting boss of the Genovese crime Family was indicted for laundering money that he siphoned from the ILA benefit fund (Rashbaum 2001b).

International Brotherhood of Teamsters (IBT)

The IBT is the largest labor union in the United States, representing more than 1.4 million truckers, delivery drivers, warehouse workers, flight attendants, and other workers.[4] In 1899 the Team Drivers International Union, headquartered in Detroit, received a charter from the AFL for its membership of 1,200 drivers. In 1902, Chicago members of the Team Drivers established a rival Teamsters National Union with 18,000 horse handlers. The following year, Samuel Gompers, president of the AFL, arranged for a merger of the two, which became the IBT. The union was marked by violence from its inception. When the Teamsters went on strike, the public suffered and therefore supported efforts against the drivers. As Allen Friedman, IBT vice-president and former strongarm for the union, reports, the Teamsters' "answer was to fight back, sending their own men to do

---

[3]When Fiumara was released from prison in 1994, he became the head of the Genovese Family's New Jersey operations. In 1999, at age 57, he was returned to prison for parole violation.

[4]The union has lost considerable membership since the 1970s, when it represented 2.2 million workers.

battle with baseball bats, knives, guns, blackjacks, and any other weapon they owned or could make. They also teamed up with local gangsters who enjoyed being paid to break heads for either side." Unfortunately, the influx of neighborhood gangsters marked a major change in the Teamsters: "Suddenly there were men involved who had neither loyalty nor ideology. They began changing the face of organized labor in many communities, taking control and becoming extortionists" (Friedman and Schwartz 1989: 9).

Although the Teamsters remained a relatively weak union, by 1933 they had about 125,000 members who were concentrated in industrial centers such as Detroit and Chicago. In 1907, Dan Tobin became IBT president and served without major scandal until 1952. He was succeeded by Dave Beck of Seattle, who controlled the Western Conference of Teamsters. Because of the support he received from Jimmy Hoffa, head of the Teamsters in Detroit, Beck awarded Hoffa with an IBT vice presidency. In 1957, before a U.S. Senate (McClellan) Committee, Beck took the Fifth Amendment 142 times. That year he was convicted of state charges and in 1959 of federal charges—embezzling union funds and income tax violations—for which he received a five-year prison sentence. Beck died at the end of 1993, at age 99.

At the 1957 IBT convention in Miami, James R. Hoffa, who had been accused of dozens of improper activities by the McClellan Committee (see Chapter 2), was elected president. That same year, the IBT was expelled from the AFL-CIO (Moldea 1978). In 1987 the AFL-CIO readmitted the IBT to its ranks. At the time, the Teamsters were struggling against a Justice Department effort to place them under the control of a court-appointed trustee under provisions of the Racketeer Influenced and Corrupt Organizations (RICO) statute.

Jimmy Hoffa   James Riddle Hoffa was born in Brazil, Indiana, in 1913 and moved to Detroit with his family in 1924. A high school dropout, Hoffa eventually became a warehouse worker and developed a reputation as a tough street fighter who always stood up for his fellow workers against man-

agement. Because of this, Hoffa was fired from his warehouse job and hired as an organizer for Local 299 of the IBT, a troubled local—misuse of funds, rigged elections—that had to be taken into receivership by the IBT. He and other IBT organizers battled management goons in their organizing efforts throughout Detroit. Hoffa also used OC connections to shake down an association of small grocery stores, leading to his first criminal conviction, for which he paid a fine. After he had risen to a leadership position in Local 299, Hoffa continued to work with OC in Detroit, using the threat of labor trouble to force businesses to use a mob-controlled overalls supply firm (Friedman and Schwarz 1989).

In 1941, Hoffa found himself in a battle with the CIO that began a "raid" to represent Detroit's teamsters. The CIO action was backed by a small army of goons, and the AFL-affiliated IBT was literally being beaten in the streets of Detroit. Hoffa turned to his friends in the Detroit underworld and secured the assistance of the powerful Meli crime Family: "The CIO raiders were defeated by the end of the year. And considering the new players on Hoffa's team, it was a miracle that the CIO survived at all in Detroit" (Moldea 1978: 38). The victory was not without cost: "The CIO's defeat, brought about by Hoffa's ringers, became the major factor in his rapid plunge from union reformer to labor racketeer. His pact with the underworld, no matter how tenuous at the time, took him out of the running as a potentially great leader of the Teamsters' rank and file" (1978: 38).

Hoffa's road to power and the presidency of the IBT was strewn with scandal—for example, his alliance with Anthony Provenzano: "The Hoffa–Provenzano alliance was typical of the bargains Hoffa struck with gangsters around the country; they helped push him to the top, and he helped them use their union posts for a series of money-making schemes: extortion from employers, loan-sharking, pension-fund frauds, and anything else that control of union muscle and money offered" (Brill 1978: 125).

Tony Provenzano and Local 560   Born in 1917, Anthony ("Tony Pro") Provenzano was one of six sons of a Sicilian immigrant couple living on the Lower East Side of New York. He dropped out of school at age 15 to become a truck helper and later a driver. He had aspirations of becoming a professional boxer, and his reputation for violence brought him to the attention of a next-door neighbor, Anthony Strollo ("Tony Bender," born in 1899). Bender was a *caporegime* in the Genovese Family and a powerful waterfront racketeer. As a result of Bender's patronage, Provenzano became a member of the Genovese Family and an organizer for IBT Local 560 in New Jersey. By 1941, Provenzano was a shop steward. In 1959, with the help of Jimmy Hoffa, Provenzano was elected president of the local. In 1960, Hoffa appointed Provenzano to fill a vacancy among IBT vice presidents. He also rose in the ranks of the Genovese Family, reportedly becoming a *caporegime* (McFadden 1988).

Union opponents of Provenzano found themselves subjected to threats, beatings, or (in at least two instances) murder. In 1961 a rival was beaten and garroted by mob executioners led by the infamous ex-fighter Harold ("Kayo") Konigsberg (Konigsberg 2001). In 1963, another Provenzano rival was shot to death in Hoboken, New Jersey. By 1963, Provenzano's union salaries totaled $113,000—at the time, he was the highest paid union official in the world. That same year, he was convicted of extorting $17,000 from a trucking company to end a discipline problem the firm was having with its union employees. During the 4.5 years he was in prison and the five years he was disqualified from holding union office (as per the 1959 Landrum–Griffin Act), his brothers Salvatore ("Sammy") and Nunzio headed the local while Tony ran its affairs. In 1978, Tony Pro was convicted of the 1961 murder and sentenced to life imprisonment.

In 1981, Nunzio Provenzano, president of Local 560, was sentenced to 10 years' imprisonment. He was convicted of accepting $187,000 from four interstate trucking companies to ensure "labor peace," and he permitted the companies to avoid contract rules for hiring Local 560 drivers. Brother "Sammy Pro" became president of Local 560. In 1984, Sammy Pro went to prison, and a close Provenzano aide, Michael Sciarra, became interim president; Tony Pro's daughter became the secretary-treasurer at a salary of $71,000. That same year, the federal government invoked the civil racketeering provision of the RICO statute, and a federal judge in New Jersey removed Local 560's executive board and put the local into trusteeship "until such time as the membership can freely nominate and elect new officers" (PCOC 1986b: 123).

After more than two years under government trusteeship, the members of Local 560 voted in the local's first contested election in 25 years. Sciarra was barred from seeking his former position as the local's president after a federal judge released tapes indicating that Matthew ("Matty the Horse") Ianiello, a *caporegime* in the Genovese Family, wanted Sciarra to head the local. In 1988, when the mailed ballots were counted by government monitors, Danny Sciarra—running as a surrogate for his brother Michael—won by a vote of 2,842 to 1,535 (Sullivan 1988). Four days later, at age 71, Anthony Provenzano died of a heart attack in a California hospital near the federal prison where he was incarcerated. At the end of 1998, a former truck driver running on a reform platform was elected president of the 4,400-member local, and the following year Local 560 was released from a court-ordered federal trusteeship (McFadden 1999).

John Dioguardi and Anthony Corallo Elections were scheduled to be held in 1956 to choose officers for the IBT's Joint Council 16 in New York City. If Jimmy Hoffa could affect the outcome of the Joint Council 16 elections, it would enable him to win control of the IBT national presidency. Accordingly, in 1955 Hoffa had seven new Teamster charters issued to his friend John ("Johnny Dio") Dioguardi.

Born on the Lower East Side in 1914, Dioguardi was the nephew of James Plumeri (better known as "Jimmy Doyle"), a *caporegime* in the Lucchese Family. Dioguardi also became a member of that crime Family and in 1937 was convicted for extorting money from the trucking industry. In 1956, Dioguardi was indicted for ordering the acid-throwing attack that blinded labor reporter Victor Reisel—Reisel had been critical of union racketeering. The charges were dropped when a witness refused to testify. In 1967, Dioguardi received a five-year sentence for bankruptcy fraud ("scam"). When he finished that term, he was convicted of stock fraud involving a car-leasing company and died in prison in 1979 (Kihss 1979).

Along with Anthony ("Tony Ducks") Corallo, also a member of the Lucchese Family, Dioguardi filled the IBT locals for which he had charters with a number of gangsters who could then vote in the 1956 union election. Five of the seven locals did not have a single legitimate member—they were "paper locals." Corallo had already gained control of five other Teamster locals, although he held office in only one. Dioguardi and Corallo brought into the newly chartered locals 40 men with an aggregate record of 178 arrests and 70 convictions. Corallo was subsequently described by Robert F. Kennedy (1960: 84) as "an underworld figure of great influence whose unusual nickname stems from his reputation for 'ducking' convictions in court cases in which he is arrested. Tony Ducks, whose police record includes drug and robbery charges and who is on the Treasury Department's narcotic list, lost only one bout with the law." In 1941 he was sentenced to six months for unlawful possession of narcotics. In 1962, Corallo received a two-year sentence for bribing a judge in a fraudulent bankruptcy case. In 1968 he was convicted for his part in a kickback scheme that involved a New York City water commissioner; Corallo received a three-year sentence. He subsequently became boss of the Lucchese Family.

While Hoffa was interested in winning over the locals and their votes in his quest for the IBT presidency, Dioguardi and Corallo were interested in the financial rewards that control of the locals promised. The newly "elected" officers would approach various nonunion employers with an offer they could not easily refuse: pay the union initiation fees and membership dues for your employees (who usually did not even know they were members of a union), and you keep your business free of all labor problems, including demands by legitimate unions; fail to pay, and labor problems, or worse, will result. By the time Hoffa gained control of the IBT in New York, 25 of the men "Dio" and "Ducks" brought into their locals had already been convicted of crimes, including bribery, extortion, perjury, and forgery (Sheridan 1972; Brill 1978). According to the federal government, Lucchese crime Family control over IBT Local 295 continued into the 1990s. In 1992 a special trustee was appointed by a federal judge to monitor the local's activities (Fried 1992).

An important part of Hoffa's Teamster legacy involves his connection to Allen Dorfman and the looting of the IBT pension fund.

Allen Dorfman Born in 1923, Dorfman was awarded the Silver Star during his World War II service with the Marine Corps. In 1948, he was a physical education teacher at the University of Illinois, earning $4,000 a year; by 1953, he was a millionaire. Allen's stepfather, Paul ("Red") Dorfman, was a professional boxer and a close friend of Chicago crime boss Tony Accardo. In 1928, Red Dorfman was indicted for rigging election ballots and using terrorist tactics in a local election, although there is no record of the case's disposition. In 1940 the founder and secretary-treasurer of the Chicago Waste Handlers Union was murdered. Red Dorfman, who had never been a member of the union or a waste handler, showed up at a union meeting, paid his dues, and on the same night became the new secretary-treasurer. In 1942 he was arrested as the result of a dispute with the chairman of the waste handlers employers' association—the two disagreed over wages to be paid to men in Dorfman's union. Using brass knuckles concealed in a glove, Dorfman severely beat the man in his office. The charges were dropped when the victim refused to prosecute. In 1949, Red Dorfman assisted Jimmy Hoffa by introducing him to important people in the Outfit and gaining their help in Hoffa's organizing drive for the Teamsters (Brill 1978).

Allen Dorfman established an insurance

agency, and in 1950 and 1951, Hoffa successfully maneuvered the insurance business of the Teamsters health and welfare funds to Red and Allen Dorfman. Subsequently, the Dorfmans, with absolutely no experience in the insurance field, "received more than $3 million in commissions and service fees on Teamsters insurance over an eight year period" (Permanent Subcommittee on Investigations 1983b: 83).

In 1955, Jimmy Hoffa negotiated the IBT's first pension plan, into which each employer was to contribute $2 per week per Teamster employee: the Central States, Southeast and Southwest Areas Pension Fund and Health and Welfare Fund (usually referred to simply as the Central States Pension Fund). Allen Dorfman was appointed as a consultant to the fund's board of trustees and turned it into "a bank for the underworld and their cronies in the 1960s and early 1970s" (Frantz and Neubauer 1983: 1). Dorfman had the trustees lend millions of dollars to Las Vegas casinos, OC-connected resorts, and speculative hotel and land ventures, projects that conventional lending institutions would not finance. Investments in Las Vegas casinos were directed by OC bosses in Chicago, Kansas City, Milwaukee, and Cleveland, who were then able to skim casino profits.

In 1972, as a result of the FBI's PENDORF investigation, Dorfman was convicted of taking $55,000 in kickbacks to secure a $1.5-million loan from the pension fund, and he served ten months in federal prison. In 1974, he was indicted along with Irwin Weiner and Outfit members Joey Lombardo and Anthony Spilotro on charges of fraud in connection with another pension fund loan. They were subsequently acquitted after the chief government witness was gunned down outside his business establishment. In 1977, the federal government forced the trustees of the Central States Pension Fund to relinquish financial control to an independent management firm (Frantz and Neubauer 1983).

On December 15, 1982, Dorfman, Lombardo, and Teamster president Roy L. Williams were found guilty of attempting to bribe U.S. Senator Howard Cannon of Nevada in return for his help in delaying legislation that would substantially deregulate the trucking industry. Dorfman, Lombardo, and Williams were scheduled for sentencing on February 10, 1983.[5] On January 20, 1983, Dorfman was walking with Irwin Weiner in a parking lot in suburban Lincolnwood, just outside Chicago. Two men approached from behind. One carried a sawed-off shotgun under his coat, and the other drew a .22 caliber automatic with a silencer attached and fired five shots, point blank, into Dorfman's head. Weiner ducked down between two cars, and the gunmen made no effort to harm him. The two men then pulled on ski masks and fled in a car driven by a third person.

Hoffa Versus Kennedy

During the 1950s, the activities of the Teamsters Union gained the attention of the U.S. Senate—in particular, the Permanent Subcommittee on Investigations, which for many years was chaired by John L. McClellan of Arkansas. However, IBT officials refused to cooperate with the committee. They "would not produce records; they repeatedly challenged the jurisdiction of the Permanent Subcommittee to probe the inner workings of the union; they exerted considerable and constant pressure upon members of Congress in both houses to have Teamster activities rest in the traditionally gentle hands of the Senate's Labor Committee" (McClellan 1962: 14).

"The response of the Senate," notes Senator McClellan (1962: 19), "was prompt and decisive." With a unanimous vote, on January 30, 1957, an eight-member bipartisan Senate Select Committee on Improper Activities in the Labor or Management Field was established. The senator wrote of his experiences with the IBT in a 1962 book titled *Crime Without Punishment*. Robert Kennedy, who was chief counsel to the committee, also authored a book on his experiences with the committee: *The Enemy Within* (1960). The first IBT target of the committee was its president, Dave Beck of Seattle. The committee spotlight shone very

---

[5]In 1982, Senator Cannon was defeated in his bid for a fifth term; Williams received a ten-year sentence and was paroled in 1989.

AP/Wide World Photos

Teamster president Jimmy Hoffa talks with Robert Kennedy, chief counsel for the Senate Rackets Commitee. When Kennedy later became attorney general, he made the Labor and Racketeering Unit in the Department of Justice his personal "Get Hoffa Squad."

brightly on Beck, and within months of his appearance he was convicted of embezzling union funds and income tax violations. The spotlight then turned to James R. Hoffa.

Subpoenaed to appear before the Select Committee, Jimmy Hoffa was sometimes blunt, sometimes evasive in his testimony (McClellan 1962). At times, the Teamster leader referred to Kennedy as "Bob" or "Bobby" and as "nothing but a rich man's kid." Law professor Monroe Freedman states that "From the day that James Hoffa told Robert Kennedy that he was nothing but a rich man's kid who never had to earn a nickel in his life, Hoffa was a marked man" (quoted in Navasky 1977: 395).

In 1957, FBI surveillance cameras recorded Hoffa giving $2,000 in exchange for confidential McClellan Committee documents to a New York attorney who was cooperating with the government. Hoffa had recruited the attorney to serve as a plant on the committee. When FBI agents arrested Hoffa the following day, he had confidential committee reports on him. Nevertheless, Hoffa was acquitted in a jury trial. The following year, Hoffa was tried for illegally wiretapping the phones of some Teamster officials. The first trial resulted in a hung jury, the second in an acquittal.

In 1960, John F. Kennedy was elected president of the United States. He appointed his brother attorney general, and Robert Kennedy made the Labor Racketeering Unit of the Criminal Division his personal "Get Hoffa Squad." The unit was headed by former FBI special agent Walter Sheridan, who was actually on the attorney general's payroll as a "confidential assistant" (Navasky 1977). Sheridan subsequently wrote a book, *The Fall and Rise of Jimmy Hoffa* (1972), on the IBT and the government's efforts to prosecute Hoffa.

Soon federal grand juries across the country began investigating the IBT. Several important convictions were secured, including that of Anthony Provenzano. In 1962, Hoffa was charged with a conflict-of-interest violation of the Taft–Hartley Act—a misdemeanor. Victor Navasky (1977: 417) comments that "Never in history had the government devoted so much money, manpower, and top-level brainpower to a misdemeanor case." The trial lasted two months and ended in a hung jury—seven to five for acquittal. Hoffa was subsequently accused of trying to bribe jurors in the first trial. In 1964 he was convicted of jury tampering and sentenced to eight years' imprisonment.

In 1971, Hoffa was released from prison after President Richard Nixon approved his application for executive clemency—the IBT had supported Nixon for president. By 1975, Hoffa was actively seeking the Teamster presidency, and IBT officials loyal to him were holding fund-raising dinners to prepare for the campaign. Hoffa began attacking Frank Fitzsimmons, the man who had replaced him as IBT president. Ironically, Hoffa criticized Fitzsimmons as a tool of organized crime. On July 30, 1975, Hoffa arrived at a suburban Detroit restaurant to meet with several persons, including his friend Anthony ("Tony Jack") Giacalone, a *caporegime* in the Detroit crime Family, and Anthony Provenzano. Giacalone had arranged the meeting ostensibly to mediate differences between Provenzano and Hoffa over Hoffa's quest for the IBT presidency.[6] None of the principals were at the restaurant, and Hoffa has not been seen since. Fitzsimmons died of natural causes in 1981.

OC Families maneuvered behind the scenes to ensure that Roy L. Williams of Kansas City, Missouri, would become the new IBT president. At the same time, "the Senate Permanent Subcommittee on Investigations rushed out a report spotlighting William's LCN [*La Cosa Nostra*] ties. The senators revealed a portion of the Justice Department's evidence that Williams was getting kickbacks of cash skimmed from Las Vegas casinos bought with Teamster pension loans, kickbacks funnelled through Nick Civella's Kansas City Mafia family" (PCOC 1985b: 42).

Nevertheless, the IBT executive board chose Williams to fill the unexpired term of Frank Fitzsimmons, and the Teamster convention subsequently elected him to a full term. After his 1982 conviction, Williams testified before the President's Commission on Organized Crime that his election had been engineered by OC bosses and that he himself was under the control of Kansas City boss Nick Civella. When Williams resigned, Jackie Presser of Cleveland was chosen to head the IBT, despite (or because of) his close ties to organized crime.

Jackie Presser   Born in Cleveland in 1926, Jackie Presser learned about organized labor at an early age from his father, Bill Presser, a Teamster Union official and close associate of the Cleveland crime Family. Large for his age, Jackie was an unruly, brawling student who dropped out of school at age 16 and joined the navy; he was honorably discharged in 1947. As expected, Jackie went into the union business, securing a position with the Teamsters. He was joined by his uncle, Allen Friedman,

an ex-convict and juice-loan collector. Jackie soon showed that he lacked the tact necessary for successful labor racketeering: his threats, shakedowns, and embezzlements attracted so much attention that he had to temporarily bow out of union activities. Using IBT pension fund loans, Jackie opened up several bowling alleys, but they failed due to mismanagement, and the Teamster money was lost.

Nevertheless, Bill Presser had a new IBT local chartered for his son, and Jackie teamed up with two relatives, Allen Friedman and his brother Harry—both stalwart union organizers and ex-convicts—to organize warehouse workers for the IBT. With Bill Presser's help, they raided other IBT locals, and Jackie's local prospered, moving beyond warehousemen and adding other workers to Local 507's membership. Part of local's success was due to the sweetheart contract: employers fearful of other (legitimate) unions organizing their workers agreed to recognize the local and signed a contract with Jackie.

When Jimmy Hoffa went to prison and Frank Fitzsimmons became acting president of the IBT, Bill Presser filled a vacancy on the executive board, becoming a union vice president. Bill organized a political action committee called DRIVE to raise money and support political candidates, and Jackie was given a major role in DRIVE's efforts. Jackie Presser was astute enough to recognize the value of good public relations. He began a major effort to clean up the image of the IBT, hiring a public relations firm and personal publicist. However, he continued to cheat his union members.

When Bill Presser fell seriously ill, Jackie replaced him as an IBT vice president. When IBT president Fitzsimmons became terminally ill, Roy Williams became acting president. Williams's conviction in the PENDORF case cleared the way for Jackie Presser to become IBT president. Jackie was supported by leaders of Cleveland's organized crime Family, who lobbied OC chieftains in Chicago and New York on Presser's behalf (Neff 1989).

With Jackie's backing, DRIVE and the IBT supported Ronald Reagan's successful candidacy for president. After the election, Allen Friedman

---

[6]At the time of his death in 2001, Giacalone, 82, was awaiting trial for racketeering and extortion.

reports that his brother-in-law, Bill Presser, "handed me a briefcase he said was filled with cash and told me to take it to [Attorney General] Edwin Meese in Washington. This was back in late November or early December after Ronald Reagan became president. I don't know how much was in that case; Bill knew I would never open it. But after Reagan got in, he named Bill's son, Jackie Presser, to his transition cabinet. Then he wanted to make Jackie undersecretary of labor, though I guess cooler heads prevailed. Jackie's presence would have been just one more scandal for the administration. After all, though Jackie never did time in jail as Bill and I did, that was only because his father and I covered his ass, not because he was ever an honest man" (Friedman and Schwarz 1989: 3).

Jackie Presser died of cancer in 1988. In 1989, as part of a RICO case against the IBT, court records revealed that he had been providing information to the FBI for nine years (Serrin 1989). Two Chicago OC figures informed Anthony ("Fat Tony") Salerno, boss of the Genovese Family, that Presser was an informant, but Salerno refused to believe them.

In 1988, William J. McCarthy became IBT president, and the following year he reached an agreement with the Department of Justice to settle a RICO suit against the union. McCarthy became the last Teamster president chosen at a national convention by delegates from the various locals; he died of natural causes in 1998. In 1991, for the first time, the union's international officials were elected by the rank and file in a secret ballot supervised by the government; Ronald R. Carey was elected president.

Carey has headed the United Parcel Service local in Long Island City, New York, and is a longtime IBT dissident. Despite his reform credentials, Carey was criticized in 1992 by a federal judge overseeing the consent decree that helped elect him; the judge accused the IBT of dragging its feet on reform. Fifteen months after taking office, Carey suspended six of the top officers of the 14,000-member IBT Local 705 in Chicago—the local has long been linked to organized crime—and appointed trustees to run the local. In 1995 he

brought a lawsuit against the former officers, alleging that they had defrauded the local (Franklin 1993, 1995b). He also placed more than two dozen locals in the New York City area under trusteeship control.

Carey's enemies in the union alleged that he had ties to organized crime and had engaged in improper financial deals. These accusations were supported by a former acting boss of the Lucchese crime Family ("Gaspipe" Casso), who became a government witness. However, a three-member panel created by a federal court order found no evidence to support the allegations (Raab 1994c).[7] But Carey's most serious challenge came from Jimmy Hoffa, Jr., son of the missing Teamster leader and five years younger than Carey. Hoffa, Jr., a labor lawyer with backing from much of the union's "old guard," challenged Carey for the union's presidency in 1996, but lost. Carey was reelected to a second five-year term with about 52 percent of the vote.

The following year, the election was declared invalid because Carey had received more than $220,000 in illegal contributions. He was subsequently barred from running in the new election—a rematch against Jimmy Hoffa, Jr.—because it was discovered that he had backed a plan to divert union funds for his campaign. A court-appointed review board subsequently expelled Carey from the Teamsters Union, and a new election in 1998 pitted Hoffa against a leader of the reformist wing of the IBT. Hoffa, who was never been a truck driver or laborer, easily beat the reform candidate.

BUSINESS RACKETEERING[8]

As we have already seen with respect to the waterfront, there is no hard-and-fast line separating labor racketeering from business racketeering—one is often an integral part of the other. In many

[7]Jeffrey Goldberg (1995) presents a less flattering portrait of Carey and the report that cleared him.
[8]For a look at case studies involving organized crime infiltration of legitimate business, see Kelly (1999).

Union Weakness

Union membership has fallen from approximately 35 percent of the work force in 1954 to less than 14 percent in 1999, even though union membership has increased to more than 16.2 million. Unionization among private-sector workers is a mere 11 percent (Franklin 1999; Palley 1996): "In part this decline reflects the declining size of those industries in which unions historically have been strongest. But it also reflects the antagonism that many American nonunion workers feel toward unions, which have come to be viewed as just another special interest, without any particular moral standing" (Palley 1996: 55).

---

schemes involving corrupt union officials, "legitimate" businessmen have willingly cooperated in order to derive benefits such as decreased labor costs, inflated prices, or increased business in the market (PCOC 1986b). Jonathan Kwitny (1979) describes the machinations of racketeer-extraordinaire Moses ("Moe") Steinman, who dominated the wholesale meat industry in New York City. Because of his connections with important OC figures such as John Dioguardi and Paul Castellano, Steinman was able to deal with racketeer-controlled unions and thus affect labor relations in the meat industry. This ability secured him a position as a supermarket chain executive who led industry-wide negotiations with meat industry unions. Using under-the-table payments to the union leaders, Steinman determined from whom the supermarkets purchased their meat. Supermarket officials bought from firms recommended by Steinman, overpaying for their beef; they were rewarded with kickbacks. Steinman was paid handsome commission fees by the beef companies for these sales.

Steinman's greatest achievement was his relationship with the founder of Iowa Beef, the largest meat processing firm in the world. The patrician midwestern businessman and the hard-drinking, inarticulate New York racketeer had something in common—greed. In return for opening up New York markets for Iowa Beef and assisting the company with "labor relations," Iowa Beef gave millions of dollars to Steinman and his friends and relatives (Kwitny 1979). Two former FBI agents (O'Brien and Kurins 1991) allege a similar relationship between Gambino Family boss Paul Castellano and chicken tycoon Frank Perdue.

Certain industries and their associated businesses are more attractive and, thus, more vulnerable to organized crime. These are relatively easy businesses to enter—they do not require a large cash investment—and highly competitive. Other characteristics include an intense need for timely action—for example, businesses that deal with perishable foods and industries where any disruption of work or deliveries can be quite costly, such as in the construction industry. Organized crime is drawn to labor-intensive industries that provide an opportunity to control related component businesses through a "choke point strategy." For example, domination of the concrete business provides influence over widely divergent construction activities dependent on a steady and predictable delivery of concrete supplies. Or control over the supply of labor—though control of a union local—enables domination of an industry dependent on a predictable supply of workers (Edelhertz and Overcast n.d.). The role of trucking in New York's garment center provides an example.

The Garment Center

Extensive business racketeering in New York's garment industry dates back to the days of Lepke Buchalter (see Chapter 4). Its more contemporary manifestation centered on the ability of racketeers to control local trucking, for whoever controls trucking controls the industry. The fast-paced nature of the fashion industry cannot countenance even short delays in shipping garments: "In New York City, garment manufacturers do not, as a rule, actually cut cloth and sew it into a dress, shirt, or other garment. They design clothes, order cloth, and arrange for the cutting and sewing to be done in smaller shops, called contractors. As a result, cloth is constantly being shipped by truck from manufacturer to contractor, from contractor to contractor, and from contractor back to manufacturer" (Mass 1991: 38–39).

Until 1992, control over garment-center trucking was exercised by the multi-millionaire sons of Carlo Gambino, Thomas and Joseph. Crime Family boss Gaetano Lucchese had been introduced to the garment center by Lepke Buchalter himself, and Thomas Gambino is Lucchese's son-in-law. Residing in an 1881 mansion in the exclusive Lenox Hill neighborhood, Thomas Gambino, a graduate of Manhattan College, is known for his charitable contributions; he is also known as a *caporegime* in the crime Family that bears his father's name.

The Gambino brothers owned Consolidated Carriers, the major garment-center cartage firm. Together with a trucking firm owned by a Lucchese Family member, they divided manufacturers and contractors among a limited number of truckers and assigned one to each shop: "None of these truckers will carry garments for a shop not assigned to him. If a shop uses a gypsy trucker and is caught, it is required to pay its regular trucker for the goods shipped, just as if the assigned trucker had carried them. Elaborate rules govern the trading of shops among the cartel members and the allocation of a trucker to a company leasing space that was formerly occupied by another company serviced by a cartel member" (Mass 1991: 39). Manufacturers and contractors knew who they were dealing with, which was usually enough to ensure compliance with the allocation scheme.

Because there was an absence of competition, trucking prices remained high, while service remained poor. Some companies fled the garment center, and others refused to move in. The number of people employed in the industry declined substantially. This state of affairs negatively affected the New York City economy.

Evidence against the Gambinos was compiled through an elaborate sting operation orchestrated by investigators from the office of Manhattan District Attorney Robert M. Morgenthau. First, an undercover state police officer drove around Chinatown posing as a gypsy trucker soliciting business from companies that had been serviced by the Gambino cartel. He quickly found that no matter how competitive his prices, he could not secure any accounts. One manufacturer whispered the reason: "the Mafia." Another undercover officer succeeded in being hired by Consolidated Carriers.

On Halloween night 1989, investigators disguised as Consolidated Edison workers broke into the Gambino trucking company headquarters and planted a court-authorized "bug." State police investigators opened up their own garment manufacturing firm, which was the ultimate weapon in the Gambino sting. In 1992, in exchange for not being imprisoned, the Gambino brothers pled guilty to restraint-of-trade violations and agreed to quit New York City's garment center and pay a fine of $12 million (Mass 1991; Blumenthal 1992). After three years without the Gambino brothers, shipping costs in the garment center fell dramatically, taking about 7 percent off the price of a finished garment. The fine paid by the Gambinos has financed a government-appointed monitor for the garment center, provided funds for the district attorney's office and the state police, and paid for compensation to several overcharged companies (Raab 1995c). In 1993, Thomas Gambino, at 64, was found guilty of racketeering charges stemming from his control of a Connecticut gambling operation and sentenced to five years' imprisonment. He entered a federal prison in 1996 and was released in 2000.

The end of Gambino brothers' operations did not end racketeering in the garment center. In 1998 the acting boss of the Lucchese Family and eleven others, including members of the Gambino and Genovese Families, were indicted for an extortion scheme that netted $30,000 to $40,000 a month. In return for payments, garment makers (sewing, cutting, and dyeing plants) were given "protection" and guaranteed labor peace; if they weren't unionized, they were allowed to remain so (Weiser 1998a). Most of the defendants subsequently pled guilty.

Restraint of Trade

While organized crime may aid in the policing of illegal contracts, OC involvement in a restraint-of-trade scheme may simply be through the use of private resources for coercion and violence, something relatively easy to accomplish, since the participants are operating outside of the law and cannot easily complain to the authorities. In New Jersey, for example, the organizer of a waste haulers association that had effectively restrained competition found himself being pushed out by an emissary from Gerardo ("Jerry") Catena, who ran New Jersey operations for the Genovese Family. The head of the association described his response: "I had a feeling, fear, that if I did not just put my tail between my legs and allow myself to be pushed out, they would find another way to get me out" (Abadinsky 1981a: 30).

Organized crime is not necessarily a crucial element in restraint-of-trade schemes. The pattern of racketeering may precede the involvement of organized crime and would likely continue in its absence. In 1980, 37 manufacturers were accused of being part of an 18-year nationwide conspiracy to fix the prices of corrugated containers and sheets, a multi-billion-dollar scheme. They settled out of court. In 1991, Pet, Inc., pled guilty to conspiring with other companies to rig bids on school milk contracts. Pet agreed to pay a $3.5-million fine (Associated Press, August 26, 1991). From May 1983 through June 1992, the U.S. Department of Justice initiated 102 prosecutions for price fixing involving 100 corporations: of these, 96 pled guilty or were found guilty after trial (Ross 1992). In 1993, it was revealed that in at least 20 states, executives of the nation's largest dairy companies had conspired, some for decades, to rig bids on milk products sold to schools and military bases. Dozens of dairy executives pled guilty (Henriques, with Baquet 1993). In 1996, Archer Daniel Midlands (ADM), one of the world's leading grain processors, with about $13 billion in annual sales, pled guilty to price fixing and agreed to pay $100 million, the largest fine ever in a federal antitrust case (Millman 1996).

In 1999, two major vitamin manufacturers pleaded guilty to price fixing and bid rigging. According to the Department of Justice, the firms convened a summit meeting every year during the 1990s to carve up the world market: they set production quotas, drafted a budget, and specified how the expanding global market would be divided. The companies were fined $755 million, and one executive agreed to serve a four-month prison term. In a class-action lawsuit related to the conspiracy, seven vitamin companies agreed to settle for $1.1 billion (Bendavid 1999; Labaton and Barboza 1999; Barboza 1999). Price-fixing collusions that have become public in recent years have included two major auction houses and dynamite and ammonium nitrate companies, whose products are used in the coal and metal mining industries (Labaton 2001).

As discussed at the beginning of Chapter 11, organized crime is sometimes a provider of illegal goods and services—helping to arrange and enforce collusive bidding arrangements, for example—while at other times it is simply a predator imposing itself on those involved in such activities. With this in mind, we will examine business racketeering in the construction and private waste hauling industries.

The Construction Industry

Construction is both a lucrative and a highly competitive industry. While competition is advantageous to the builder, it reduces the profits of construction firms. Organized crime can play a crucial role in limiting competition by enforcing a system of collusive bidding. As the President's Commission reports, "Participating construction contractors, with the guidance of union officials and LCN family members, allocate construction jobs among themselves and exclude non-cartel contractors whose entry into the New York market might threaten the stability, predictability and control of construction work that the cartels offer their members. Under such a system, the participant companies are beneficiaries, not victims, since the benefits of the cartel may totally offset the increased costs it imposes" (PCOC 1986b: 219).

The construction industry in New York City is huge and fragmented, "with over one hundred thousand workers, many hundreds of specialty subcontractors, hundreds of general contractors, and dozens of major developers. There are also a large number of one-time or infrequent builders ranging from large corporations to small entrepreneurs" (New York State Organized Crime Task Force 1988: 3—hereafter, NYSOCTF). Construction businesses range from those building private single-family dwellings to those putting up shopping centers and high-rise buildings. Construction workers are organized into approximately 100 building trades local unions, which engage in collective bargaining with the approximately 50 employer associations formed by contractors in the same type of construction work.

"Traditionally, unions have had a great deal of leverage in high-rise construction because they have had a monopoly over the skilled workers needed to carry out this highly complex type of building" (NYSOCTF 1988: 44). Through collective bargaining agreements, construction unions typically control access to skilled labor: "Some pre-hire contracts contain clauses requiring contractors to hire all or part of their employees from union hiring halls. Even where there is no hiring hall provision, the union's designation as exclusive bargaining agent gives its elected officials control over who works for that contractor" (NYSOCTF 1988: 45–46). Through control over labor unions, racketeers are able to offer benefits to or impose prohibitive costs on contractors. The ability to assign (or not assign) workers to jobs is a powerful tool that can be used against union members who might wish to challenge racketeer leadership. There is also the very real threat of violence.

The New York State Organized Crime Task Force reported that the industry's structure creates fragmentation and fragility: "An organized crime syndicate can use its network of relationships throughout the construction industry to reduce uncertainties and promote needed stability. For example, if more than one union has a jurisdictional claim over a particular construction task, an organized crime syndicate in return for a payoff can work out a reasonable arrangement between the contractor and the affected unions. In this role, the syndicate serves the same functions, albeit by

criminal means, as a highly effective, legitimate labor consultant" (1988: 66).

Writing in 1985, the President's Commission reported that in "New York City organized crime controls all construction contracts of a half-million dollars or more extending up to amounts of approximately $100 million. . . . The prime source of influence and the prime point of contact for organized crime are the 20 or so largest contractors in New York City who from time to time, through collusive bidding, decide among themselves who will get a particular project." After the rigged bid, an emissary of organized crime or a union official approaches the general contractor and informs him "who his suppliers will be, who his subcontractors will be, from whom he will purchase materials, and at what price those materials will be purchased, and, on occasion, designating to the general contractor which unions he will use during the course of the construction of the building and other construction jobs in the New York City area" (PCOC 1985b: 71–72).

Ralph Scopo, a member of the Colombo Family and president of the Cement and Concrete Workers District Council of the Laborers Union, was at the center of a "contractors' club" that received payments for allocating bids on construction jobs. Jobs under $2 million required "one point" (1 percent); "two points" were required for jobs over $2 million. In 1987, Scopo and a *caporegime* in the Colombo Family were convicted of racketeering. (Scopo died in 1993 while serving a 100-year sentence.) In 1988, ten union officials and contractors were convicted in Brooklyn federal court for accepting or extorting payoffs from contractors in return for labor peace and rigging bids on projects to reward companies that paid bribes and to punish those that did not (Rangel 1988). In 1991, a federal jury convicted the *consiglieri* of the Genovese and Colombo Families for heading a 12-year bid-rigging scheme involving contracts for installing windows in New York City Housing Authority projects (Lubasch 1991b). In 1996, a major New York City contractor who had designed and helped build scores of Manhattan skyscrapers, in addition to working on the Javits Convention Center and a new federal courthouse, admitted to being a *caporegime* in the Colombo crime Family. In the courthouse he helped build, the 62-year-old contractor pled guilty to being the Colombo Family representative on the mob council that oversaw activities in the construction industry ("Contractor Admits Double Life" 1996). Nevertheless, racketeering continued in the construction industry, as evidenced by a 2000 indictment of 38 persons, including the acting boss of the Lucchese Family, for bid rigging and associated crimes (Rashbaum 2000a).

Payments to OC may be direct, or by making a racketeer (or one of his relatives) a business partner, or by employing "ghost employees," names of persons on a construction payroll who receive salaries but do not work. When two construction workers began complaining about ghost employees on the payroll of a contractor helping to build the World Trade Center in New York, one of the "ghosts," the boss of the Genovese Family, referred the problem to his private "police force," headed by Anthony ("Figgy") Ficarotta, a former professional boxer:

Figgy, Joey, Louie and me went over to the Twin Towers construction site. The building was up about eleven stories and there were no walls, just the frames and concrete floors. The elevator was in an open shaft, and that's how the workers got up and down. We went up to the top floor and Figgy sees these two guys working. "Follow me," he says and we start walking around the floor. Figgy is telling the other workers: "Why don't youse go to lunch, go ahead." One of the workers says: "Who are you? We take our orders from Phillie." "Well I'm over Phillie," Figgy says, "so just go down and when you see him tell him who sent you—a short guy with the funny nose."

We walked around telling guys to go downstairs until we got to the two guys and they start to walk toward the elevator shaft. "You guys goin' to lunch?" Figgy asks. They are standing by the shaft for the lift to come back and Figgy picks up a two-by-four and pushes it under the chin of this guy. The guy

grabs onto the shaft to keep from fallin' in: "So you want a fuckin' check too, huh? Well it's waitin' for you on the ground. I'm gonna see that you get it—in a hurry." The guy is hanging on for his life and Figgy keeps pushing him further into the shaft. The second guy doesn't know what to do—there's nowhere to run. Joe and Louie start backing him up—and there's nowhere to go except down eleven stories.

The guy with Figgy is yelling: "No, no, please, I don't want no check." "Why? You been bitchin' about some checks and I'm gonna send you down to get one." "Please no. I don't want no check." Joey and Louie back the other guy up to the edge and he yells out: "I don't want no check either." "Then just do your fuckin' work and shut the fuck up. Or we'll be back." Figgy threw the piece of wood down and we went onto the lift. There was no further trouble. (Abadinsky 1983: 131)

In New Jersey, firms owned by Philadelphia crime boss Nicky Scarfo and his underboss were able to gain lucrative construction contracts because of their influence over a few key labor unions, particularly Concrete Workers Local 33 and Ironworkers Local 350. Contractors subcontracting work to the Scarfo firms were guaranteed labor peace, and the two firms were able to underbid rivals by violating the union contract with respect to pension and other benefits (New Jersey State Commission of Investigation 1987). In fact, the construction industry is quite inefficient, characterized by various unions having overlapping jurisdictions and a great deal of featherbedding: "The existence of so much inefficiency provides a strong incentive to pay off union officials not to press their jurisdictional claims or to reach out to racketeers who can dictate accommodations between competing unions" (NYSOCTF 1988: 50).

Private Solid Waste Carting

If there is an activity that conjures up an image of organized crime, it is the private collection of solid

Policing Illegal Contracts, International Style

"Whether in the United States, Italy, Russia, or Japan, trust is not always sufficient to enforce illegal agreements and to avoid individuals exiting from the covert exchanges. Coercion provided by organized crime may be needed as an additional resource to punish 'lemons,' 'free riders,' or those who threaten to denounce the corrupt system" (della Porta and Vannucci 1999: 22).

waste—it's the business of "Tony Soprano." Back in 1931, Walter Lippman (1962: 61) noted that "racketeering in many of its most important forms tends to develop where an industry is subjected to exceedingly competitive conditions." Companies "faced with the constant threat of cutthroat competition are subject to easy temptation to pay gangsters for protection against competitors." Peter Reuter (1987) offers additional insight into an industry's attractiveness to OC. When the entrepreneurs have a low-status (for example, limited education) background, and the enterprises are small, local, and family based, the industry is vulnerable to OC infiltration. The solid waste collection industry meets these criteria. It is characterized by numerous, relatively small competing firms that are often family based. It is an easy-entry enterprise, requiring only some trucks and a willingness to work hard. Competition for a customer's business drives down profits until, at some point, with or without help from OC, an association is formed. Association members divide up the industry, usually allocating geographic areas (territories) or specific customers. The members (illegally) agree not to compete for another member's business. Each is thereby free to charge whatever the market will bear for its services (State Commission of Investigation 1989).

Organized crime may become involved if there is a need to police the (illegal) agreements. In 1956, New York City began requiring all commercial enterprises to arrange for their own garbage collection services. Within months, restraint-of-trade cartels were in place, formed around waste-hauling trade associations (Behar 1996). A made guy would sit on the grievance committees that settle disputes between members of the associations, "using the basic rule that whoever serviced the site first has continuing rights to any customer that occupies the site. While there is little evidence of either threats or actual violence, it seems reasonable to infer that the racketeers provide a credible continuing threat of violence that ensures compliance with the ruling of the committee" (Reuter et al. 1983: 11). James ("Jimmy Brown"—partial to brown clothes) Failla, a *caporegime* in the Gambino Family, headed the Association of Trade Waste Removers of Greater New York for 30 years, organizing and enforcing restraint-of-trade agreements (Fried 1993b). In 1999, Failla, 80, died while serving a seven-year sentence for his role in the 1985 murder of Paul Castellano.

In New York City, about 300 trash haulers were servicing 250,000 businesses. In 1995, four waste-hauling associations (as well as individual firms and their owners) affiliated with the Gambino and Genovese Families were accused of having "carved out a system of property rights: a carter 'owns' the building where his customer is located. If the customer leaves or goes out of business, the carter has the right to service the new customer. If the carter loses a stop to another carter, the 'owner' of the stop has the right to be compensated for his loss either by receiving a stop of comparable value or through the payment of a multiple of the monthly charges the 'owner' had charged. The multiple is frequently '40 to 1' or more, meaning 40 times the monthly fee charged by the 'owner.' Disputes over which carter has the 'right' to service a particular stop are mediated by the associations" (District Attorney of New York County and the New York City Police Department 1995: 2). Carters not belonging to the associations—"outlaws"—faced economic and physical intimidation if they attempted to compete with association members.

The investigation that broke this cartel began when the Manhattan district attorney received a complaint from the second-largest waste-hauling company in the country, Browning-Ferris Industries (BFI) of Houston.[9] The company was attempting to compete in the New York market but found it virtually impossible to win and maintain customers despite submitting lower bids. Company officials were subjected to intimidation—one received the freshly severed head of a German shepherd with a note reading "Welcome to New York." In the ensuing investigation, a detective worked three years undercover as an executive for an "outlaw" firm—one that refused to join the cartel. His role began inadvertently. Detective Richard Cowan was investigating the arson of an empty garbage truck. As he was interviewing the owner, two thugs burst in and threatened the trash firm's owner, who said the detective was his cousin. As the "cousin," Detective Cowan successfully infiltrated the trash-hauling industry and helped break the OC-dominated cartel. His work led to the conviction of 14 persons, including its two leaders, a *caporegime* in the Genovese Family and a soldier in the Gambino Family—both headed trash-collecting trade associations (Raab 1997c, 1997d).

As a result of these efforts, cartel customers who (often with great trepidation) switched to BFI saved as much as 60 percent on their trash-hauling contracts (Behar 1996). With the cartel broken, members scrambled to keep customers, lowering their fees to become more competitive. One of the largest privately owned buildings in Manhattan had been paying $1.2 million for garbage pickup; BFI bid $120,000. In 1996, New York put a cap on what businesses could be charged for waste hauling and created a Trade Waste Commission, which can deny a license to any firm with ties to organized crime (Goozner 1996). Dozens of persons were convicted of restraint-of-trade-related charges, and dozens of small firms were driven out of business.

While organized crime appears to have been eliminated from this industry in New York, there are problems. Steep price cuts for trash removal engineered by national firms are driving the remaining small companies out of business, significantly limiting competition. While OC-orchestrated trade restraints have been eliminated, a market dominated by five national firms may result in steep price increases for trash removal (Raab 1998c). By 2001, this possibility was coming closer to reality. With a stranglehold on the city's private waste-collection business, the three major national firms, acting in concert, demanded an end to any price restraints under the threat of abandoning the city (Lipton 2001a, 2001b).

ORGANIZED CRIME AND LEGITIMATE BUSINESS

In addition to their illegal business activities, persons involved in organized crime often own or invest in legitimate enterprises. One popular activity of government officials has been to decry the "infiltration" of organized crime into legitimate business. Michael Maltz (1975: 83) states that the "alternative to penetration of legitimate business is the reinvestment of the ill-gotten gains into some criminal enterprises, which may cause greater social harm." However, Annelise Anderson (1979: 77) points out that funds from illegal business activities cannot easily "be profitably reinvested in illegal market enterprises without aggressive expansion of the territory controlled by the group." Thus, OC members may have an oversupply of illegally derived funds that cannot be profitably used to expand their illegal activities. Maltz (1975) concludes that the penetration of OC into legitimate business can be viewed as the equivalent of the legitimation of family fortunes by the robber barons, discussed in Chapter 2.

However, Mark Moore (1987: 51) points out that it is the features of the organized crime group, rather than the substantive offenses committed, that make it a societal menace: "What is bad about organized crime is that the criminal groups seem resistant to law enforcement mea-

---

[9]BFI has been accused of price fixing in several markets and has paid millions of dollars in fines for such activities (Myerson 1995).

sures, that they seem to become rich as a result of their crimes, that they coolly calculate how best to make money without worrying about whether a planned enterprise is illegal and violent, and that they threaten additional criminal activity in the future even if their current conduct is tolerable." In other words, OC groups would pose a threat to society "even if they were engaged largely in legitimate activities and even if their criminal activities produced relatively insignificant levels and kinds of victimization" (1987: 52). Moore suggests that the OC group should be viewed as a business firm pursuing profit with a portfolio that encompasses illicit as well as licit enterprises and that poses a serious societal threat. Activities of a Genovese Family crew in New Jersey provide an example of Moore's observations. In addition to more traditional activities—gambling, loansharking, and labor racketeering—the Hoboken-based crew controlled a firm that arranged managed group health care for employers and locals of the Teamsters, Laborers, and Hotel Workers unions. According to the New Jersey attorney general, the firm increased its profit margin by coercing plan administrators into approving inflated fees for service (Raab 1996d).

Anderson provides six reasons for organized criminal involvement in legitimate business:

1. *Profit.* For persons in organized crime, profit provides motivation; not all members of organized crime are able to make a "respectable" income from illicit activities. In an intercepted conversation, New Jersey underboss Anthony Russo complained to boss Sam de Cavalcante that the *amici nostri* could not even support themselves. In another incident, de Cavalcante arranged for the removal of a local union official, who was also a *caporegime* in his crime Family, because the official was not providing *legitimate* employment to the *amici nostri* as construction laborers. Jimmy Fratianno's biography, *The Last Mafioso* (Demaris 1981), contains very little discussion of his business activities. Indeed, it appears that Fratianno's most successful enterprise was a legitimate trucking firm that he owned in California.

2. *Diversification.* A legitimate business provides the OC member with security of income. While it

may be subject to market and other business conditions, a legitimate enterprise is usually not a target of law enforcement efforts. (As will be discussed in Chapter 14, since Anderson wrote her book in the late 1970s, federal and local governments have become increasingly active in the civil seizure of criminal assets, including those derived from legitimate businesses.)

3. *Transfer.* Illegitimate enterprises are difficult, if not impossible, to transfer to dependents (particularly if they are female). Investing in legitimate enterprises such as a business or real estate venture ensures that an estate can be legally inherited.

4. *Services.* An OC member with a legitimate business is in a position to act as a patron for a person in need of legitimate employment—for example, persons on probation or parole, or relatives he wants to shield from the stigma and risks associated with criminal enterprises.

5. *Front.* A legitimate business can provide a front or a base of operations for a host of illegal activities: loansharking, gambling, and drug trafficking, to name a few.

6. *Taxes.* A legitimate business can provide a tax cover, thereby reducing the risk of being charged with income tax evasion. Funds from an illegitimate enterprise can be mixed with those from the legitimate business, particularly if it is a "cash" business.

Obviously, these categories are not mutually exclusive. It is quite likely that OC involvement in legitimate business involves a combination of these six reasons. Persons in organized crime may also use a legitimate business as part of a scam.

The Scam

The scam is a bankruptcy fraud that victimizes wholesale providers of various goods and sometimes insurance companies. The business used as the basis for a scam may be set up with that scheme as its purpose, or it may be an established business that has fallen into OC control as a result of gambling or loanshark debts. Scam operations are popular in industries with merchandise that has a high turnover potential, is readily transportable, and is not easy to trace. There are three basic variations (De Franco 1973: 5–7).

The Three-Step Scam   A new corporation is formed and managed by a front man, or "pencil," who has no prior criminal or bankruptcy record. This person may owe money to a loanshark and may participate in the scam to help pay off the debt. A large bank deposit, known as the "nut," is made to establish credit. This money, plus other money subsequently deposited, is later withdrawn. A large store is rented, and orders for merchandise are placed with as many companies as possible. The size of these orders appears to indicate a successful operation to the suppliers. The owners then proceed with the three steps:

1. Smaller orders are placed during the first month, and such orders are paid for in full. During the second month, larger orders are placed, and about a quarter of the balance due on such orders is paid.

2. During the third month, using credit established as a result of the payments made for the previous orders, very large orders are placed. Items easily converted into cash, such as jewelry and appliances, usually constitute a large proportion of these orders. Thereafter, merchandise is converted into cash through a fence or a surplus-property operator, normally one with a sufficiently large legitimate inventory to easily intermix the scam merchandise into the normal inventory.

3. The company is then forced into bankruptcy by creditors because, according to plan, all cash has been appropriated by the scam operators.

The One-Step Scam   Since the three-step scam requires several months for completion, the more rapid one-step scam may be used. A successful business with good credit references is purchased or falls into the hands of a loanshark. No notice of the change in management is provided to Dun and Bradstreet or other credit agencies, thus enabling the new management to trade on the previous owner's reputation for good credit. Manufacturers are approached in person or at trade shows to arrange for the purchase of merchandise. The orders are usually large, and suppliers that did not sell to the company before are very politely informed by the scam operator that if they do not want to fill the order, some other company will be glad to do so. This technique is known as the "sketch." Orders then include many items not previously purchased by the company. After the orders have been received, the merchandise is sold, as in the three-step scam. The money is milked from the business, and the company is forced into bankruptcy.

The Same-Name Scam   In a variation of the one-step scam, a company is organized with a name deceptively similar, and often almost identical, to that of a successful company in the same area. Large orders are placed with suppliers, who fill them assuming the legitimacy of the company based on the similarity in firm names. The merchandise is then sold in the same fashion as with the other types of scam.

A popular time for the scam operator is just before a seasonal increase in the popularity of particular merchandise, when rush deliveries are commonplace and thorough credit checks are often overlooked. In some scams, arson is the final step: the business is "torched" for the insurance instead of declaring bankruptcy.

Stock Fraud

The entry of organized crime into the stock market is not new. It was noted earlier that John Dioguardi, who died in prison in 1979, was convicted of stock fraud involving a car-leasing company. Chapter 11 points out that whenever the volume of securities being traded increases, it becomes more difficult for brokerage houses and banks to keep track of the paperwork, thus providing an opportunity for criminals to convert stolen securities for their own uses.

Stolen securities can be transferred to a country with strict bank secrecy laws, such as Panama. The securities are deposited in a bank, which issues a letter of credit that is used to secure loans, which are eventually defaulted. Letters of credit can also be used as collateral for bank loans from "cooperative" loan officials or "rented" to legitimate businesspeople in need of collateral for instant credit. Panama's strategic location between the Atlantic and Pacific oceans and between North and South America, its dollar-based economy, and its modern international trade and financial sectors make the country a magnet for such schemes.

More recently, the OC foray into the stock market has added elements—intimidation and violence—to widely known scams. With the entry of organized crime, the "boiler room" and "pump and dump," in addition to the financial dangers to unsuspecting customers, can now entail physical dangers. In 2000 the federal government accused 120 persons throughout the United States, including members of the Colombo and Bonanno Families, of involvement in a Manhattan brokerage and investment bank that bilked investors of at least $50 million. The indictment alleged that brokers who refused to cooperate were assaulted. Some of the principals in the case were part of a defunct brokerage, one of whose officers was found dead in his New Jersey mansion in 1999. His body was found with that of another broker, both of whom had been shot execution style.

Brokers for the firm used traditional high-pressure—"boiler room"—tactics to sell worthless stocks, created phony stock trades, and bribed brokers from other firms to push the stock in an effort to inflate the price. The wiseguy stock would then be sold off for enormous profits. Brokers who had a change of heart or refused further cooperation in the scheme were threatened with violence or assaulted (Sullivan and Berenson 2000; Roane 2000).

In 2001, another indictment alleged that 20 persons working with members of the Gambino Family bilked thousands of investors of more than $50 million; two victims lost at least $12 million. Investors identified from lists of retirees and businesspersons would receive a "cold call" from a broker promoting shares in several companies. The brokers would then drive up the price—the "pump"—and demand that the victims hold on to their stocks, refusing to execute sell orders and threatening some with violence if they did anything that could drive the price down. The brokers would then sell off their shares of the stocks—the "dump"—at huge profits (Christian 2001).

MONEY LAUNDERING

Money laundering is "to knowingly engage in a financial transaction with the proceeds of some unlawful activity with the intent of promoting or carrying on that unlawful activity or to conceal or disguise the nature, location, source, ownership, or control of these proceeds" (Genzman 1988: 1). Ever since Al Capone was imprisoned for income tax evasion, financially successful criminals have sought ways to "launder" their illegally secured "dirty" money. The practice has developed its own lexicon: "Getting currency into the bank, around the reporting system, at home or abroad, is called *placement*. Once the money is in the form of a bank entry, the launderer hides its criminal origins through a series of complex transactions. Police call it *layering*. The launderer then makes the proceeds available to the criminals in an apparently legitimate form. The term for this is *integration*" (Blum 1999: 59).

Some use a cash business, such as a vending machine firm, to mingle cash from illegitimate sources with legally earned money. Some criminals use casinos for the same purpose or to convert cash from small denominations to $100 bills. In New Jersey, one drug-trafficking ring opened a casino account for $118,000, stayed several days, but did not gamble. They then left the hotel with checks payable to third parties, who deposited the checks in a securities firm. The money was later withdrawn—"laundered" (PCOC 1984c). In 1991, several men from Lebanon and Argentina were convicted of laundering $1 billion in Colombian drug profits through the purchase and sale of gold, using jewelry companies in Houston, Miami, Los Angeles, and New York City as fronts.

In elaborate money-laundering schemes, the first step is to convert large quantities of cash into one or more cashier's checks. In addition to being

Modern Money Laundering

"Modern financial systems permit criminals to transfer instantly millions of dollars through personal computers and satellite dishes. Money is laundered through currency exchange houses, stock brokerage houses, gold dealers, casinos, automobile dealerships, insurance companies, and trading companies. The use of private banking facilities, offshore banking, free trade zones, wire systems, shell corporations, and trade financing all have the ability to mask illegal activities. The criminal's choice of money laundering vehicles is limited only by his or her creativity" (U.S. Department of State 1999: 3).

easier to carry—450 bills weigh about one pound—cashier's checks are difficult to trace because they do not bear the receiver's name or address. Transactions involving the proceeds of drug trafficking often consist of large amounts of cash in small denominations. In such instances, the first step is to convert the small bills into hundreds—$1 million in $20 bills weighs 110 pounds; in $100 bills, it weighs only 22 pounds. To avoid IRS reporting requirements under the Bank Secrecy Act, transfers of cash to cashier's checks or $100 bills must take place in amounts under $10,000 or through banking officials who agree not to fill out a Currency Transaction Report (CTR). A CTR is required for each deposit, withdrawal, or exchange of currency or monetary instruments in excess of $10,000. It must be submitted to the IRS within 15 days of the transaction. In 1984, tax amendments extended the reporting requirements to anyone who receives more than $10,000 in cash in the course of a trade or business. A CMIR (Currency and Monetary Instrument Report) must be filed for cash or certain monetary instruments exceeding $10,000 in value that enter or leave the United States. Federal Reserve regulations require banks to file suspicious-activity reports when they suspect possible criminal wrongdoing in transactions. Attempts to strengthen these regulations met vigorous opposition from the banking industry (Wahl 1999a). In the wake of the September 11, 2001, terrorist attacks, however, money-laundering regulations have been strengthened.

In 1985 it was revealed that the Bank of Boston, the city's oldest and biggest bank, had helped launder money for the underboss of the Patriarca Family. From 1979 to 1983, Jerry Angiulo and his brothers would convert paper bags stuffed with tens of thousands of dollars in small bills into $100 bills and more than $7 million in cashier's checks. None of the transactions were reported to the IRS. Two real estate companies controlled by the Angiulos in the Italian neighborhood of Boston's North End had been placed on the "exempt" list, so their cash transactions in excess of $10,000 did not have to be reported to the IRS. The only businesses legally entitled to such exemptions are retail outlets such as supermarkets that do a great deal of business in large amounts of cash on a daily basis. Money launderers may use car dealerships, whose managers accept cash for automobile purchases and fail to file the required CTRs.

Currency exchanges (*casas de cambio*) have sprouted up along the Texas–Mexico border. These poorly regulated enterprises accept (illegally) large amounts of cash. They pool many customers' funds into one account and deposit the money in a domestic or foreign bank, keeping records on what is owed to each customer. When a foreign drug trafficker wants to send money to his own country, the *casa* operator wires the funds from the bank to the trafficker's foreign account(s). Even when a U.S. bank completes a CTR, it names the *casa* as the owner of the funds, not the actual owner. In the Houston area, in addition to *casas*, there are *giro* (wire) houses. In general, the *giros* move drug money to Colombia, while the *casas* move Mexican drug money (Webster and McCampbell 1992).

Elmhurst–Jackson Heights, a Colombian section of the New York City borough of Queens, has

"We Don't Need No Stinkin' Offshore Bank!"

In 2001, seven persons, including the underboss of the Bonanno Family, were indicted for being in control of a Long Island bank that was used for money laundering and loansharking. One debtor who was late with his payments was beaten in the bank's conference room (Feuer 2001).

many storefront shops that wire money outside of the country. In response to their use for money laundering, the U.S. Treasury Department imposed a $750-per-transaction limit on 12 firms with 1,600 outlets suspected of wiring drug money. If they wish to avoid the transaction limit, customers must provide picture identity cards, which have to be copied by the store and submitted to the Treasury Department (McFadden 1997).

In some schemes, money launderers use dozens of persons (called "smurfs") to convert cash into money orders and cashier's checks that do not specify payees or that are made out to fictitious persons. Each transaction is held to less than $10,000 to avoid the need for a CTR. One ring operating out of Forest Hills, New York, employed dozens of persons who used about 30 banks in New York and New Jersey to launder about $100 million a year for the Cali cartel. The checks were pasted between the pages of magazines and shipped to Cali; from there, the money was transferred to banks in Panama. In 1989, 16 persons were indicted when one of the banks became suspicious of the unusual number of cash transactions and reported them to federal authorities (Morgan 1989). "Smurfing" has now been made a federal crime, and increased bank scrutiny has made tellers suspicious of cash transactions just under $10,000. In response, smurfs have reduced transactions to as low as $5,000 and often make dozens of transactions in a day, typically in banks that do not usually have long lines (Walter 1990).

One ring working for the Cali cartel was centered in a small New York City law firm that specialized in international banking. It used a number of persons, including the owner of a trucking firm, a firefighter, a police officer, and two rabbis. Whenever $1 million in street sales had been accumulated, the law firm would be notified and a courier sent to pick up the money. The couriers would take the money to a bank, which wired the money on behalf of the firm to Zurich (Treaster 1994). Other legitimate companies have been involved in money laundering. In 1994 a banking arm of American Express paid the federal government $32 million to settle a money-laundering case involving the drug organization of Juan Garcia Abrego (discussed in Chapter 8). In response, the government agreed not to seek criminal charges against the corporation (Myerson 1994). Two American Express employees were convicted of playing a role in the scheme ("Bank Officer Is Convicted of Laundering" 1994).

Money laundering has been greatly enabled by advances in banking technology. It has become increasingly difficult for the government to effectively monitor banking transactions: "An alternative to physically removing money from the country is to deposit the cash, then transfer the funds electronically to other domestic and foreign banks, financial institutions, or securities accounts. Swiss law enforcement officials report that when money is transferred by wire to Switzerland, it seldom comes directly from the country of origin; rather it is 'prewashed' in a third country such as Panama, the Bahamas, the Cayman Islands, or Luxembourg" (Webster and McCampbell 1992: 4). The sheer volume of wire transfers makes accounting difficult—one major bank in New York handles about 40,000 wires each business day.

A customer can instruct his or her personal computer to direct a bank's computer to transfer money from a U.S. account to one in a foreign bank. The bank's computer then tells a banking clearinghouse that assists in the transfer—no person talks to another. Although depositing more than $10,000 in cash into an account requires the filing of a CTR, the government receives more

A Complex Island Laundry

As the result of an undercover money-laundering investigation, in 1998 federal agents seized $1.8 million from several Citibank accounts in New York City. The accounts were held by a Cayman Islands bank that never had an office in that country; its listed corporate headquarters in Uruguay were actually an accounting firm that processed its correspondence. Despite the seizure, for almost two years an additional $300 million moved through the accounts. Part of the money wired into the accounts was paid out in cash in Argentina to a local real estate agent reputed to be a representative of Mexican drug traffickers (Golden 2001).

---

than 12 million such reports annually and is hopelessly behind in reviewing them.

The Internet has also made money laundering easier. A launderer establishes a company—the Abadinsky Computer Co.—offering high-end products over the Internet. The launderer purchases products from Abadinsky over the Internet, using credit cards. Abadinsky invoices the credit card company, which, in turn, forwards payment for the purchases: "The credit card company, the Internet service provider, the Internet invoicing service, and even the bank from which the illegal proceeds begin this process would likely have no reason to believe there was anything suspicious about the activity, since they each only see one part of it" (Financial Action Task Force on Money Laundering 2001: 4).

In 1989 a Panamanian bank pled guilty to money-laundering charges in the largest such case to end in a conviction. Although the bank (*Banco de Occidente*) had no operations in the United States, it held several accounts in Continental Illinois Bank's New York branch that were used to launder money. Drug dealers in New York, Miami, Houston, and Los Angeles distributed money from cocaine sales to bogus jewelry firms that acted as fronts. The cash was sent by Wells Fargo armored truck to other phony jewelry operations in Los Angeles, where it was counted by high-speed machines. The cash was then shipped by armored courier to Los Angeles banks, which were told it was being used to purchase gold bullion, something common in the jewelry business. The Los Angeles banks made an electronic transfer to New York, and from there the funds were electronically transferred to Europe or directly to Latin America, eventually winding up in Colombia. The operators were paid 7 percent of the funds they laundered. The scheme ended when Wells Fargo became suspicious and informed federal authorities of the unusually large amounts of cash that were being deposited—$25 million in three months (Labaton 1989a).

As part of an overseas laundering scheme, a lawyer acting on behalf of a client creates a "paper" (or "boilerplate") company in any one of a number of countries that have strict privacy statutes—for example, Panama. In 2001, Panama had 373,701 registered offshore banks and companies (James 2001). The funds to be laundered are transferred physically or wired to the company's account in a local bank. The company then transfers the money to the local branch of a large international bank. The paper company is then able to borrow money from the United States (or any other) branch of this bank, using the overseas deposit as security (Walter 1990). Or an employment contract is set up between the launderer and his or her "paper" company for an imaginary service for which payments are made to the launderer. In some cases, the lawyer may also establish a "boilerplate bank"—like the company, this is a shell. Not only does the criminal get his money laundered, but he also earns a tax write-off for the interest on the loan. Under the Bank Secrecy Act, however, wiring or physically transporting cash or other financial instruments out of the country in excess of $10,000 must be reported to the Customs Service. Once the money is out of the United States, however, it may be impossible for the IRS to trace it.

The Cayman Islands

Located south of Cuba, an easy flight from either Florida or Colombia, this small West Indian island is only 100 miles square and has a population of only 23,400. Yet there are 570 banks and 20,000 registered companies on the Cayman Islands. The Georgetown financial district has the highest density of banks and fax machines in the world. Most banks are simply "plaques" or box offices—no vaults, tellers, or security guards—with transactions recorded by Cayman booking centers. In 1984 the United States and Great Britain signed an agreement that gives American officials investigating drug cases information about secret bank accounts in the Cayman Islands. The Caymans, which are administered by Britain, can maintain secrecy in all other cases unless there is proof of an offense under Cayman law. Virtually anyone can still "establish his or her own shell company for a few thousand dollars in legal fees, open a local bank account and, because the required disclosure is minimal and business operates behind a wall of strict secrecy, no one need know about the company or what funds are stashed there. The few slips of paper that constitute the company records may be held in the office of a Cayman lawyer" (Lohr 1992: 28; Silverstein 2000).

Another method of laundering funds without actually moving cash out of the country involves otherwise legitimate companies that import goods from the United States. Representatives of the Cali cartel in the United States paid for imported goods with dollars that went to the exporters. In return, the participating companies paid the cartel in Colombia at slightly less than the true exchange rate (Krauss and Frantz 1995). Or drug proceeds are used to purchase easily sold goods such as expensive liquor or electronic products. These are shipped to Colombia and sold at a 20 to 30 percent discount (Sanger 1995). In a more elaborate scheme, a currency exchange broker in the United States receives—at 30 to 40 percent below the actual market rate—dollars in exchange for pesos. He promises to deliver the money to the trafficker's accounts in Colombia—the broker's life provides collateral. The broker's "smurfs" deposit the cash into hundreds of U.S. bank accounts in amounts below $10,000. The dollars are sold to businessmen in Colombia for pesos at a 20-percent discount. The pesos are transferred to the trafficker's accounts. The Colombian businessmen use the dollars to import American goods (Leonhardt and Whitaker 2000).

Chinese criminals are aided by an underground banking system operating through gold shops, trading companies, commodity houses, travel agencies, and money changers, managed in many countries by the same extended Chinese family: "The method of moving money is the *chop*, which is in effect a negotiable instrument. A *chop* can be cashed in Chinese gold shops or trading houses in many countries. The value and identity of the holder of the *chop* is a secret between the parties. The form of *chop* varies from transaction to transaction and is difficult to identify. In effect, the *chop* system allows money to be transferred from country to country instantaneously and anonymously" (Chaiken 1991: 495). For example, cash to finance a heroin deal is deposited in a San Francisco Chinatown gold shop in return for a *chop*. The *chop* is sent by courier to Hong Kong and is cashed. The owner of the *chop* receives his money from the original issuer, who is fronting for the drug deal.

A similar system, the *hawala*, is used in South Asia, where the size of the underground economies is estimated to be 50 to 100 percent the size of the documented economies. An ancient system, the *hawala* was the primary money transfer mechanism used in South Asia prior to the introduction of Western banking: "Hawala operates on trust and connections ('trust' is one of the several meanings associated with the word 'hawala'). Customers trust hawala 'bankers' (known as hawaladars) who use their connections to facilitate

The Western and South Pacific

The Western Pacific islands of Cook, the Marshalls, Nauru, Niue, Samoa, and Vanuatu have seen the development of offshore financial centers (OFCs). Together, these tiny entities have more than 18,000 registered banks and companies (James 2001). Naura, with a population of about 12,000, has 450 banks registered to a single post office box: "These islands have a laissez-faire approach to their banking rules and regulations. This regulatory philosophy was created especially to prevent effective oversight of the offshore sector. As a result, governments in most of these nations have little or no control over their OFCs.

"Isolated as they are, these OFCs demonstrate the globalization of international finance. Via the Internet and wire transfer, many U.S.-based Asians are now using banking facilities of Nauru's OFC. There is significant use by Russian organized crime of the OFCs of Vanuatu, Samoa and Nauru. One increasingly common scheme is to employ non-Russian middlemen to open accounts or charter shell banks or shell companies (all with the same post office box in Nauru) to give the impression of legitimate business with non-Russian entities" (U.S. State Department 1999: 11).

money movement worldwide. Hawala transfers take place with little, if any, paper trail, and, when records are kept, they are usually kept in code" (U.S. Department of State 1999: 22). In Pakistan, for example, $100,000 (plus a transaction fee) is given to an hawaladar who provides a code term. Via the Internet, the hawaladar informs his broker in the Cayman Islands, where someone who provides the code term is given $100,000 to deposit in an island account.

Taking advantage of bank secrecy laws to avoid disclosure of ownership has drawbacks, however: it may be difficult, if not impossible, to pass on these assets to one's heirs.

In the next chapter, we examine organized crime and the business of drugs.

INTERNET CONNECTIONS

NY–NJ Waterfront Commission: **wcnynj.org/index.html**

U.S. Department of State: **state.gov/index.cfm**

Global Organized Crime Project: **csis.org/goc**

REVIEW QUESTIONS

1. What are all of the possible advantages for an employer that enters into a corrupt relationship with a labor union?
2. What were the historical factors that led to the entry of organized crime into labor unions?

3. How did "Dopey" Benny Fein rationalize labor's relationship with criminals?
4. What four international unions have reputedly been under the control of organized crime?
5. Why were stevedoring firms often willing partners in corruption with organized labor?
6. What are "paper locals," and how were they used by labor racketeers?
7. How is labor leasing used by union racketeers?
8. How does business racketeering differ from labor racketeering?
9. What are the elements that make a particular industry, such as private waste hauling, susceptible to racketeering?
10. How did the election of John F. Kennedy lead to the demise of Jimmy Hoffa?
11. What is a scam, and how is it used by organized crime figures?
12. What are the six reasons for OC involvement in legitimate business?
13. What is the typical role of OC in a restraint-of-trade agreement?
14. What is money laundering, and how can it be accomplished?
15. What is a Currency Transaction Report (CTR)?
16. What are the advantages of using offshore banking facilities for money laundering?
17. What are the similarities between the *chop* and the system of *hawala*?

♠

CHAPTER 13

ORGANIZED CRIME AND DRUGS

In order to fully appreciate the relationship between drug trafficking and organized crime, it is necessary to examine the history of how drug trafficking, like bootlegging during the Prohibition era, became an important criminal enterprise. Since concern over opium products—morphine and heroin—led to the most important piece of drug legislation, the Harrison Act, our historical review will center on that substance. We will then move to other drugs—in particular, cocaine.

HISTORICAL BACKGROUND

The earliest "war against drugs" (other than Prohibition) in the United States was in response to opium, an analgesic (pain reliever) and central nervous system depressant that can provide relief from stress. Its source is the *Papaver somniferum*, or opium poppy, of which there are many species. There is some dispute as to when opium was first used. Wherever the poppy plant is found, the young leaves have been used as potherbs and in salads; its small, oily seeds are high in nutritional value. The seeds can be eaten. They can be pressed to release an edible oil, baked into cakes, and ground into flour, and the oil may also be burned in lamps. As a source of vegetal fat, "the seed oil could have been a major factor attracting early human groups to the opium poppy" (Merlin 1984: 89). Wherever it was found, opium was used both medicinally and recreationally.

Explaining the popularity of opium is easy when we realize that the chief end of medicine up to the beginning of the nineteenth century was to relieve pain, and therapeutic agents were directed at symptoms rather than cause. Therefore, "it is not difficult to understand the wide popularity of a drug which either singly or combined so eminently was suited to the needs of so many medical situations" (Terry and Pellens 1928: 58). At a time when the practice of medicine was quite primitive, opium became the essential ingredient in innumerable remedies dispensed in Europe and America for the treatment of diarrhea, dysentery, asthma, rheumatism, diabetes, malaria, cholera, fevers, bronchitis, insomnia, and pain of any kind (Fay 1975).

As the primary ingredient in many "patent" medicines—actually, secret formulas that carried no patent at all—opiates were readily available in the United States until 1914. Doctors and others prescribed them for general symptoms as well as for specific diseases. The smoking of opium was popularized by Chinese immigrants who brought the habit with them to California, which in 1848 became part of the United States. During the latter part of the nineteenth and early twentieth centuries, Chinese immigrants also operated commercial "opium dens" that often attracted the attention of the police not because of the use of drugs but because they became gathering places for criminals.

Around the turn of the eighteenth century, a German pharmacist poured liquid ammonia over opium and obtained an alkaloid, a white powder that he found to be many times more powerful than opium. He named the substance *morphium* after Morpheus, the Greek god of sleep and dreams. Ten parts of opium can be refined into one part of morphine (Bresler 1980). However, it was not until 1817 that the publication of articles in scientific journals popularized the new drug, resulting in its widespread use by doctors. Quite incorrectly, as it turned out, the medical profession viewed morphine as an opiate without negative side effects.

By the 1850s, morphine tablets and a variety of morphine products were readily available without prescription. In 1856, the hypodermic method of injecting morphine directly into the bloodstream was introduced to American medicine. The popularity of morphine rose dramatically during the Civil War, when it was used intravenously in an indiscriminate manner to treat battlefield casualties (Terry and Pellens 1928). Following the war, the increase in morphine use was so marked among ex-soldiers as to give rise to the term "army disease": "Medical journals were replete with glowing descriptions of the effectiveness of the drug during wartime and its obvious advantages for peacetime medical practice" (Cloyd 1982: 21). Hypodermic kits became widely available, and the use of unsterile needles by many doctors and laypersons led to abscesses or disease (Morgan 1981).

In the 1870s, morphine was exceedingly cheap, cheaper than alcohol. Pharmacies and general stores carried preparations that appealed to a wide segment of the population. Physicians commonly prescribed morphine for any complaint, from a toothache to tuberculosis (Latimer and Goldberg 1981), and widely abused the substances themselves. Until the late 1870s, the concept of addiction was not widely known or understood (Morgan 1981). While it eventually became associated with the underworld elements of urban America, morphine abuse in the latter part of the nineteenth century was apparently most prevalent in rural areas (Terry and Pellens 1928). At the turn of the century, diacetylmorphine was synthesized, creating the most powerful of the opiates—*heroin*—marketed as a non-habit-forming analgesic to take the place of morphine (Bresler 1980; Nelson et al. 1982). Opiates, including morphine and heroin, were readily available in the United States until 1914. In 1900 alone, 628,177 pounds of opiates were imported into the United States (Bonnie and Whitebread 1970).

China and the Opium Wars

The American response to drugs in the twentieth century is directly related to international affairs and trade with China. Until the sixteenth century, China was a military power whose naval fleet surpassed any that the world had ever known. A fifteenth-century power struggle ultimately led to a regime dominated by Confucian scholars. In 1525 they ordered the destruction of all oceangoing ships and set China on a course that would lead to poverty, defeat, and decline (Kristoff 1999b). In 1626 a British warship appeared off China, and its captain imposed his will on Canton with a bombardment. In response to the danger posed by British ships, the emperor opened the city of Canton to trade.

The British East India Company enjoyed a government-granted monopoly over the China trade. Shipments of tea to England were particularly important. By the 1820s, a trade imbalance existed between England and China. While the British consumer had an insatiable appetite for

Chinese tea, few English goods were desired by the Chinese. The exception was opium (Beeching 1975). Poppy cultivation had been an important source of revenue for the Mogul emperors (Muslim rulers of India, 1526–1857). When the Mogul empire fell apart, the British East India Company salvaged and improved upon the system of state control of opium. In addition to controlling the domestic market, the British supplied Indian opium to China.

Opium was first prohibited by the Chinese government in 1729, a time when only small amounts of the substance were reaching China. Ninety years earlier, tobacco had been similarly banned as a pernicious foreign good. Opium use was strongly condemned in China as a violation of Confucian principles, and for many years the imperial decree against opium was supported by the population (Beeching 1975). In 1782 an attempt by a British merchant ship to sell 1,601 chests of opium resulted in a total loss, for no purchasers could be found. By 1799, however, a growing traffic in opium led to an imperial decree banning the trade.

The ban was not successful (official corruption was endemic in China). As consumption of imported opium increased and the method of ingestion shifted from eating to smoking, official declarations against opium increased, as did smuggling: "When opium left Calcutta, stored in the holds of country ships and consigned to agents in Canton, it was an entirely legitimate article. It remained an entirely legitimate article all the way up to the China Sea. But the instant it reached the coast of China, it became something different. It became contraband" (Fay 1975: 45).

Opium provided the British with the silver needed to buy tea. Since opium was illegal in China, however, its importation—smuggling—brought China no tariff revenue. Prior to 1830, opium was transported to the coast of China, where it was offloaded and smuggled inland by the Chinese themselves. The outlawing of opium by the Chinese government led to the development of an organized underworld. Gangs became secret societies—Triads (discussed in Chapter 10)—that continue to smuggle heroin to destinations all over

the world (Latimer and Goldberg 1981). The armed British opium ships were safe from Chinese government intervention, and the British were able to remain aloof from the actual smuggling.

In the 1830s, the shippers grew bolder, entering Chinese territorial waters with their opium cargo. The British East India Company, now in competition with other opium merchants, sought to flood China with cheap opium and drive out the competition (Beeching 1975). In 1837 the emperor ordered his officials to move against opium smugglers, but the campaign was a failure, and the smugglers grew even bolder. In 1839, in a dramatic move, Chinese authorities laid siege to the port city of Canton, confiscating and destroying all opium awaiting offloading from foreign ships. The merchants agreed to stop importing opium into China, and the siege was lifted. The British merchants petitioned the Crown for compensation and retribution. However, the reigning parliamentary Whig majority was very weak, and compensating opium merchants was not politically or financially feasible. Instead, the cabinet, without Parliament's approval, decided to wage a war that would result in the seizure of Chinese property (Fay 1975).

In 1840 a British expedition attacked the poorly armed and organized Chinese forces. The emperor was forced to pay $6 million for the opium that his officials had seized and $12 million as compensation for the war, and Hong Kong became a crown colony. Opium was not mentioned in the peace (surrender) treaty, but the trade resumed with new vigor. By the mid-1840s, in a remarkable reversal of the balance of trade, China had a significant opium debt (Latimer and Goldberg 1981). In the wake of the First Opium War, China was laid open to extensive missionary efforts by Protestant evangelicals, who, although they opposed the opium trade, viewed saving souls as their primary goal. Christianity, they believed, would save China from opium (Fay 1975).

The Second Opium War began in 1856, when the balance of payments once again favored China. A minor incident between the British and Chinese governments was used as an excuse to force China into making further treaty concessions. This time, the foreign powers seeking to exploit a militarily weak China included the French, Russians, and the Americans. Canton was sacked, and a combined fleet of British and French warships sailed right up the Grand Canal to Peking and proceeded to sack and burn the imperial summer palace. The emperor was forced to indemnify the British in an amount more than enough to offset the balance of trade that had actually caused the war. A commission was appointed to legalize and regulate the opium trade (Latimer and Goldberg 1981).

In the 1870s, the British opium monopoly in China was challenged by opium imported from Persia and cultivated in China itself. Because British colonial authorities were heavily dependent on a profitable opium trade, they increased the output of Indian opium. This caused a decline in prices, driving the competition out of business. This oversupply resulted in an increase in the amount of opium entering the United States for the Chinese population.

The "Chinese Problem" and the American Response

Chinese workers were originally encouraged to emigrate to the United States in 1848 to labor in the gold mines, doing the dangerous work refused by most white men, such as blasting shafts, putting beams in place, and laying track lines in the mines. Chinese immigrants also helped build the Western railroad lines at "coolie wages"—pay that few whites would accept. After their work was completed, the Chinese were often banned from the area. By the 1860s, they were clustering in Pacific Coast cities, where they established Chinatowns— and smoked opium.

Beginning in 1875, there was an economic depression in California, and the first significant piece of prohibitionary drug legislation in the United States was enacted by the city of San Francisco: "The primary event that precipitated the campaign against the Chinese and against opium was the sudden onset of economic depression, high unemployment levels, and the disintegration of working-class standards of living" (Helmer 1975: 32). The San Francisco ordinance prohib-

ited the operation of opium dens—commercial establishments for the smoking of opium—"not because of health concerns as such, but because it was believed that the drug stimulated coolies into working harder than non-smoking whites" (Latimer and Goldberg 1981: 208). Depressed economic conditions and xenophobia led one western state after another to follow San Francisco's lead and enact anti-Chinese legislation that often included the prohibition of smoking opium.

Anti-Chinese efforts were supported and advanced by Samuel Gompers (1850–1924) as part of his effort to establish the American Federation of Labor. The Chinese served as a scapegoat for organized labor—the "yellow devils" were accused of undercutting wages and breaking strikes. Anti-opium legislation was also fostered by stories of Chinese men seducing white women into prostitution—"white slavery"—through the use of opium. In 1882 the Chinese Exclusion Act banned the entry of Chinese laborers into the United States. Not until 1943, when the United States was allied with China against Japan in World War II, were citizenship rights extended to Chinese immigrants, and China was permitted an annual immigration of 105 persons.

In 1883, Congress raised the tariff on the importation of smoking-grade opium. In 1887, Congress responded to obligations imposed on the United States by a Chinese-American commercial treaty by banning the importation of smoking opium by Chinese subjects. Americans were still permitted to import the substance, and many did so, selling it to both Chinese and U.S. citizens (PCOC 1986c). The typical American opiate addict during the nineteenth century was a middle-aged white woman of the middle or upper class (Courtwright 1982). As opposed to the Chinese, however, this addict did not smoke opium but ingested it as medicine. During the nineteenth century, opiates were not associated in the public mind with crime. While opium use may have been frowned upon by some as immoral, employees were not fired for addiction. Children were not taken from their homes and lodged in foster homes or institutions because one or both parents were addicted: "Addicts continued to participate fully in the life of the community. Thus, the nineteenth century avoided one of the most disastrous effects of current narcotic laws and attitudes—the rise of a deviant addict subculture, cut off from respectable society and without a 'road back' to respectability" (Brecher 1972: 6–7).

THE TWENTIETH CENTURY

Domestic anti-Chinese legislation raised the ire of China against the United States. In an effort to increase American influence in China, and thus improve its trade position, the United States supported the anti-opium efforts of the International Reform Bureau (IRB). A temperance organization representing over 30 missionary societies in the Far East, the IRB sought a ban on opiates, which was also the position of the Chinese government. In 1901, Congress enacted the Native Races Act, which prohibited the sale of alcohol and opium to "aboriginal tribes and uncivilized races." The provisions of the act were later expanded to include "uncivilized elements" in the United States proper: Indians, Eskimos, and Chinese (Latimer and Goldberg 1981).

In 1898, as a result of the Spanish-American War, the Philippines were ceded to the United States. At the time of Spanish colonialism, opium smoking was widespread among Chinese workers on the islands. The Reverend Charles Henry Brent (1862–1929), a supporter of the IRB, arrived in the Philippines as the Episcopal bishop. His arrival coincided with a cholera epidemic that began in 1902 and that reportedly led to an increase in the use of opium. As a result of his efforts, in 1905 Congress banned the sale of opium to Filipino natives except for medicinal purposes and three years later banned sales to all Philippines residents: "Reformers attributed to drugs much of the appalling poverty, ignorance, and debilitation they encountered in the Orient. Opium was strongly identified with the problems afflicting an apparently moribund China. Eradication of drug abuse was part of America's white man's burden and a way to demonstrate the New World's superiority" (Morgan 1974: 32).

The Reverend Brent proposed the formation of an international opium commission to meet in Shanghai in 1909. This plan was supported by President Theodore Roosevelt, who saw it as a way to assuage Chinese anger at the passage of the Chinese Exclusion Act (Latimer and Goldberg 1981). The International Opium Commission, chaired by Brent and consisting of representatives from 13 nations, convened in Shanghai on February 1. Brent successfully rallied the conferees around the American position that opium was evil and had no use outside of medical applications. The commission unanimously adopted a number of vague resolutions (Terry and Pellens 1928).

Only the United States and China, however, were eager for future conferences, and strong anti-opium legislative efforts in the United States following the conference were generally unsuccessful. Southerners distrusted federal enforcement, and the drug industry was opposed to any new regulations. Attempts to gain southern support for antidrug legislation focused on the alleged abuse of cocaine by blacks, which reputedly made them "uncontrollable." On February 14, 1914, a *New York Times* headline screamed: "Negro Cocaine 'Fiends' Are a New Southern Menace." This caused many southern police departments to change from .32 caliber revolvers to more powerful .38 caliber revolvers (Kinder 1992).

A second conference was held in The Hague in 1912, with representatives from the United States, China, and ten other nations. A number of problems stood in the way of an international agreement: Germany wished to protect its burgeoning pharmaceutical industry and insisted on a unanimous vote before any action could be agreed upon; Portugal insisted on retaining the Macao opium trade; the Dutch demanded to maintain their opium trade in the West Indies; Persia and Russia wanted to continue growing opium poppies. Righteous American appeals to the delegates were rebuffed with allusions to domestic usage and the lack of laws in the United States (Latimer and Goldberg 1981). Nevertheless, the conference resulted in a patchwork of agreements known as the International Opium Convention, which was ratified by Congress in 1913. The signatories committed themselves to enacting laws designed to suppress the abuse of opium, morphine, and cocaine, as well as any drugs prepared or derived from these substances (PCOC 1986c). In 1914 the Harrison Act was approved by President Woodrow Wilson, representing the U.S. attempt to carry out the provisions of The Hague convention.

The Harrison Act

The Harrison Act provided that persons in the business of dealing in drugs covered by the act—including opium derivatives and cocaine—were required to register yearly and to pay a special annual tax of $1. The statute made it illegal to sell or give away opium or opium derivatives and coca or its derivatives without a written order on a form issued by the Commissioner of Internal Revenue. Persons who were not registered were prohibited from engaging in interstate drug trafficking, and anyone who possessed drugs without first registering and paying the tax faced a penalty of up to five years' imprisonment and a fine of up to $2,000. Rules promulgated by the Treasury Department permitted only medical professionals to register, and they had to maintain records of the drugs they dispensed. Within the first year, more than 200,000 medical professionals registered, and the small staff of treasury agents could not scrutinize all the prescription records generated (Musto 1973).

Concern over federalism—constitutional limitations on the police powers of the central government—led Congress to use the taxing authority rather than the police authority of the federal government to respond to the problem of drug control. At the turn of the century, federal authority to regulate narcotics and the prescription practices of physicians was generally thought to be unconstitutional (Musto 1973). In 1919, however, the use of taxing authority to regulate drugs was upheld by the U.S. Supreme Court in *United States v. Doremus* (249 U.S. 86).

The Harrison Act was supported by the American Medical Association (AMA), which by that time "was well on its way to consolidation of American medical practitioners" (Musto 1973:

56), and by the American Pharmaceutical Association, which, like the AMA, had grown more powerful and influential in the first two decades of the twentieth century. The medical profession had been granted a monopoly over the dispensing of opiates and cocaine. The Harrison Act also effectively imposed a stamp of illegitimacy on most narcotics use, fostering an image of the degenerate "dope fiend" with immoral proclivities (Bonnie and Whitebread 1970). At this time, there were an estimated 300,000 opiate addicts in the United States (Courtwright 1982).

But the addict population was already changing. The medical profession had, by and large, abandoned its liberal use of opiates. Imports of medicinal opiates declined dramatically during the first decade of the twentieth century. The public mind came to associate heroin with urban vice and crime. Unlike the (often female and) "respectable" opiate addicts of the nineteenth century, opiate users of the twentieth century were increasingly male habitués of pool halls and bowling alleys, denizens of the underworld. As in the case of minority groups, this marginal population was an easy target of drug laws and drug-law enforcement.

The Commissioner of Internal Revenue was in charge of upholding the Harrison Act. In 1915, 162 collectors and agents of the Miscellaneous Division of the Internal Revenue Service were given the responsibility of enforcing drug laws. In 1919, a narcotics division was created within the Bureau of Prohibition, with a staff of 170 agents and an appropriation of $270,000. However, the narcotics division suffered from its association with the notoriously inept and corrupt Prohibition Bureau and from a corruption scandal of its own: there was "public dissatisfaction with the activities of the Narcotics Division, which was tainted by its association with the country's anti-liquor laws" (PCOC 1986c: 204).

In 1916 the Supreme Court ruled in favor of a physician who had provided maintenance doses of morphine to an addict (*United States v. Jin Fuey Moy*, 241 U.S. 394). Three years later, however, the Court ruled (*Webb v. United States*, 249 U.S. 96) that a prescription for morphine that was issued to an habitual user who was not under a physician's care and that was intended not to cure but to maintain the habit was not a prescription and thus violated the Harrison Act. Private physicians found it impossible to handle the sudden upsurge in their drug clientele: they could do nothing "more than sign prescriptions" (Duster 1970: 16). In *United States v. Behrman* (258 U.S. 280, 289, 1922), the Court ruled that a physician was not entitled to prescribe large doses of proscribed drugs for self-administration *even if* the addict was under the physician's care. The Court stated that "prescriptions in the regular course of practice did not include the indiscriminate doling out of narcotics in such quantity as charged in the indictments." In 1925 the Court limited the application of *Behrman* when it found that a physician who had prescribed small doses of drugs for the relief of an addict did not violate the Harrison Act (*Linder v. United States*, 268 U.S. 5).

The powers of the Narcotics Division were clearly limited to the enforcement of registration and record-keeping regulations: "The large number of addicts who secured their drugs from physicians were excluded from the Division's jurisdiction." Furthermore, the public's attitude toward drug use "had not much changed with the passage of the Act—there was some opposition to drug use, some support of it, and a great many who did not care one way or the other. The Harrison Act was actually passed with very little publicity or news coverage" (Dickson 1977: 39). Richard Bonnie and Charles Whitebread (1970: 976) note similarities between the temperance and antinarcotics movements: "Both were first directed against the evils of large scale use and only later against all use. Most of the rhetoric was the same: These euphoriants produced crime, pauperism, and insanity." However, "the temperance movement was a matter of vigorous public debate; the antinarcotics movement was not. Temperance legislation was the product of a highly organized nationwide lobby; narcotics legislation was largely ad hoc. Temperance legislation was designed to eradicate known evils resulting from alcohol abuse; narcotics legislation was largely anticipatory."

Writing in 1916, Pearce Bailey (1974: 173–74) noted that the passage of the act spread dismay among heroin addicts. The price of heroin soared 900 percent, and heroin was sold in adulterated form, putting it beyond the easy reach of the majority of users. Beginning in 1918, narcotic clinics opened in almost every major city. Information about them is sketchy (Duster 1970), and there is a great deal of controversy surrounding their operations. While they were never very popular with the general public, most clinics were well run and under medical supervision (Morgan 1981).

Following World War I and the Bolshevik Revolution, xenophobia and prohibitionism began to sweep the nation. The United States severely restricted foreign immigration, and alcohol and drug use were increasingly associated with an alien population. In 1922, federal narcotics agents closed the drug clinics and began to arrest physicians and pharmacists who provided drugs for maintenance. At issue was section eight of the Harrison Act, which permitted the possession of controlled substances if prescribed "in good faith" by a registered physician, dentist, or veterinarian in accord with "professional practice." The law did not define "good faith" or "professional practice." Under a policy developed by the federal narcotics agency, thousands of persons, including many physicians, were charged with violations: "Whether conviction followed or not mattered little as the effects of press publicity dealing with what were supposedly willful violations of a beneficent law were most disastrous to those concerned" (Terry and Pellens 1928: 90). However, "After this initial burst of arrest activity directed against registrants, the Narcotics Division turned its attention to closing clinics that had been established to conduct research and treat large numbers of addicts who could not afford private care" (PCOC 1986c: 202). These clinics were declared illegal by the drug agency and were closed down (Terry and Pellens 1928).

The medical profession stopped dispensing drugs to addicts, forcing them to look to illicit sources and giving rise to an enormous illegal drug business. Those persons addicted to opium smoking eventually found their favorite drug unavailable—the bulky opium used for smoking was difficult to smuggle—and they turned to the more readily available heroin, which was prepared for intravenous use (Courtwright 1982). The criminal syndicates that resulted from Prohibition added heroin trafficking to their business portfolios. When Prohibition was repealed in 1933, profits from bootlegging disappeared accordingly, and drug trafficking remained an important source of revenue for organized criminal groups.

THE BUSINESS OF HEROIN

The opium poppy,[1] *Papaver somniferum*, requires a hot, dry climate and very careful cultivation (Wishart 1974). Poppy seeds are scattered across the surface of freshly cultivated fields. Three months later, when the poppy is mature, the green stem is topped by a brightly colored flower. Gradually the flower petals fall off, leaving a seedpod about the size of a small egg. Incisions are made in the seedpod just after the petals have fallen but before it is fully ripe. A milky-white fluid oozes out and hardens on the surface into a dark brown gum—raw opium. The raw opium is collected by scraping the pod with a flat, dull knife—a labor-intensive process.

The raw opium is dissolved in drums of hot water and lime (calcium oxide). Fertilizer is added, precipitating out organic wastes and leaving morphine suspended near the surface. After residual waste is removed, the morphine is transferred to other drums, where it is heated and mixed with concentrated ammonia. The morphine solidifies and falls to the bottom of the drum, where it is filtered out in the form of chunky white kernels. In this form, morphine weighs about one-tenth as much as the original raw opium. To produce 10 kilograms (1 kilogram = 2.2046 pounds—hereafter, kilo) of almost pure heroin, the chemist mixes 10 kilos of morphine and 10 kilos of acetic

anhydride and heats it at exactly 185 degrees for 6 hours, producing an impure form of heroin. While this step is not complex, it can be dangerous: "If the proportion of morphine to acetic acid is incorrect or the temperature too high or too low the laboratory may be blown up." Acetic acid is also highly corrosive, attacking both skin and lungs (Lamour and Lamberti 1974: 17).

Next, the solution is treated with water and chloroform until the impurities precipitate out. The heroin is drained off into another container, to which sodium carbonate is added until crude heroin particles begin to solidify and drop to the bottom. The particles are filtered out and purified in a solution of alcohol and activated charcoal. This mixture is heated until the alcohol begins to evaporate, leaving granules of almost pure heroin at the bottom. In the final step, the granules are dissolved in alcohol, and ether and hydrochloric acid are added to the solution. Tiny white flakes begin to form. These flakes are filtered out under pressure and dried in a special process, the result being a powder between 80 and 99 percent pure, known as *No. 4 heroin*.

For street sale, the white crystalline powder (the Mexican product contains impurities that give it a thick oily "black tar" appearance or a more refined brown powder color) is typically diluted ("stepped on" or "cut") with any powdery substance that dissolves when heated, such as lactose, quinine, flour, or cornstarch. Until the 1990s, consumer-available heroin prepared for intravenous use usually had a purity of less than 5 percent. In recent years, purity levels of retail heroin sold in parts of New York City have approached 90 percent, revealing that heroin is being subjected to little if any cutting before it reaches the consumer level. Increased purity makes smoking and sniffing feasible. The increased purity and the concern about AIDS have caused a shift from injecting to smoking and sniffing among heroin users (Epstein and Gfroerer 1997; Adrade, Sifaneck, and Neaigus 1999). Heroin can be sniffed like cocaine and even smoked. When smoked—"chasing the dragon"—heroin is heated and the fumes inhaled, usually through a small tube.

Most of the heroin smuggled into the United

---

[1]The sale of poppy seeds for cultivation, not culinary use—they often appear on bagels—has been illegal in the United States since 1970. The Drug Enforcement Administration has been conducting an ineffectual campaign against the cultivation of the pretty red flower, which looks elegant when dried (Vest 1997).

FIGURE 13.1 *Major Asian Opium Regions*

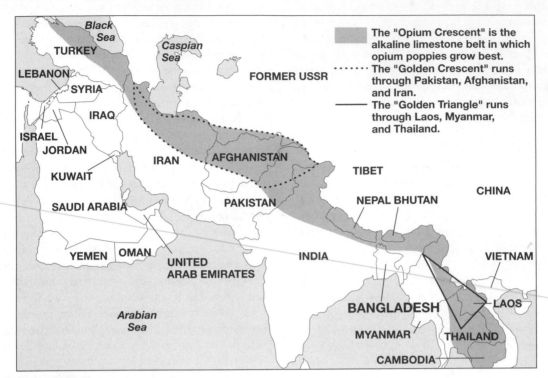

Source: Levins (1980: 115).

States originates in areas where the opium poppy thrives—parts of Asia known as the Golden Triangle and the Golden Crescent, Mexico, and, more recently, Colombia. (See Figure 13.1.)

The Golden Triangle

The Golden Triangle of Southeast Asia encompasses approximately 150,000 square miles of forested highlands, including the western fringe of Laos, the four northern provinces of Thailand, and the northeastern parts of Myanmar (Burma)—Myanmar accounts for about 90 percent of the total heroin production of the Golden Triangle. Colonial officials, particularly the French, set paramilitary organizations and indigenous tribes against various insurgent groups, particularly those following a Marxist ideology. As support for overseas colonies dwindled at home, French offi-

cials in Southeast Asia used the drug trade to finance their efforts. Golden Triangle opium was shipped to Marseilles, where the Corsican underworld processed it into heroin for distribution in the United States—the "French Connection." The French withdrew from Southeast Asia in 1955, and several years later the United States took up the struggle against Marxist groups—the Vietnam War is part of this legacy. The U.S. Central Intelligence Agency waged its own clandestine war. Again, heroin played a role, for many of the indigenous tribal groups recruited and armed by the CIA cultivated opium. In Laos and South Vietnam, corrupt governments were heavily involved in heroin trafficking, making the substance easily available to American GIs (McCoy 1972, 1991). The long-standing tradition of using drugs to help finance military efforts continues in this part of the world.

At the end of colonial rule, countries emerged with relatively weak central governments, their rural areas inhabited by bandits and paramilitary organizations such as the Kuomintang.

Kuomintang With the defeat of the Chinese Nationalist forces in 1949, the Third and Fifth Armies of Chiang Kai-shek, stationed in the remote southern province of Yunnan, escaped over the mountainous frontier into Burma's Shan States. While part of this army dispersed and became integrated with the local population, "more than six thousand of them remained together as a military entity, their numbers being swollen by indigenous tribesmen" (Lamour and Lamberti 1974: 94). By 1952, the Kuomintang (KMT), numbering about 12,000, became the de facto power in the eastern part of the Shan States. In 1951 and 1952, with support from the United States, the KMT was rearmed and resupplied and, with additional troops from Taiwan and recruits from the Hmong hill tribesmen—poppy cultivators—attempted to invade China. When the attempts failed, U.S. interest and support waned, and the KMT settled permanently in Burma. For several years the Burmese military attempted to evict the KMT and finally succeeded in 1954, forcibly escorting them to the Thai border, from which the Nationalist government evacuated about 6,000 troops to Taiwan. Nevertheless, the strength of the KMT grew, through secret reinforcements from Taiwan and/or through recruitment among indigenous tribes, to about 10,000 troops.

In 1961 a resentful government in Rangoon, perhaps with assistance from the People's Republic of China, finally drove the KMT into the Thai portion of the Golden Triangle (Lamour and Lamberti 1974), where it sold its military skills to a joint Central Intelligence Agency and Thai Army command fighting Communist insurgents in the Shan States. This force tried to prevent the Laotian Communist Pathet Lao from linking up with local insurgents. In 1961 and 1969, U.S.-backed airlifts of KMT troops to Taiwan were the last official contacts between the KMT remnants on the mainland and Chiang Kai-shek's government, but unofficial ties remained strong (Lamour and Lam-

berti 1974). The remaining troops, about 4,000, became known as the Chinese Irregular Forces (CIF). While the KMT had always dabbled in opium, it now became the sole support of the CIF. Despite this fact, the CIF was tolerated on the Thai border as a barrier against Communist insurgents. In Mae Salong, Thailand, a KMT general ruled a heroin empire, collected taxes, and drafted boys as young as 13 into his army. In 1965 an opium war broke out between the CIF and the indigenous Shan United Army (SUA), and the CIF drove SUA leader Khun Sa into Laos. Khun Sa returned and in 1981 defeated the CIF.

The Shan United Army/Mong Tai Army The Shan States, an area somewhat larger than England, lie on a rugged, hilly plateau in the eastern part of central Myanmar, flanking the western border of China's Yunnan Province. They contain an array of tribal and linguistic groupings. The largest group is the Shans, who speak Thai and thus have more in common with their neighbors in Thailand than with Myanmar. The Shans are lowland rice cultivators, but hill tribes on the mountain ridges around them cultivate opium. During British colonial rule (1886–1948), the Shan States were administered independently from Burma, and the Shan princes enjoyed a great deal of autonomy. Burma won independence in 1948: the Shans, with great misgivings, agreed to join the Union of Burma in return for statehood and guarantees of a number of ministry posts. As a final incentive, the Shans were given the right to secede after 1957.

A nation slightly smaller than Texas, with a population of more than 47 million, Burma has been dominated by a repressive military dictatorship since a coup in 1962. In 1989 the country changed its name to Myanmar. Brutality against ethnic minorities and collaboration with drug trafficking continue. The government's heavy-handed approach to the Shan States set the stage for revolution. Official Burmese financial policies were devastating to many hill farmers, who turned more and more to poppy cultivation as a cash crop outside of central government control (Delaney 1977). Shan princes (known as *sawbwas*) "had been encouraged to introduce the opium poppy to their fiefdoms by the British as far back as 1866 and opium shops had been opened throughout to retail the narcotics to licensed addicts" (Bresler 1980: 67). In later years, the British made a number of efforts to abolish opium cultivation in the Shan States, although they were never completely successful (McCoy 1972). In any event, many Shans blamed their princes for accommodating the central government, and traditional systems of authority deteriorated.

Originally known as the Shan United Army (SUA), the Mong Tai Army (MTA), under the leadership of Chang Chifu, who is half-Chinese, half-Shan, and better known as *Khun Sa*, resorted to opium trafficking in order to purchase arms and support its independence movement (Delaney 1977). The SUA/MTA came to dominate the opium trade along the Thai–Burma border, where about 400,000 hill tribesmen had no source of income other than heroin (Permanent Subcommittee on Investigations 1981a). The SUA/MTA was able to control both the shipments of opium and the production of heroin in its laboratories.

In the 1980s, the Thai government succeeded in driving the MTA out of Thailand and back into Burma, but the group continued to dominate opium traffic, taxing drug caravans crossing their territory. In 1990 the Shans suffered significant setbacks: Khun Sa was indicted for drug trafficking by a federal grand jury, and the United States offered a $3-million reward for his capture and conviction in an American court. And his Mong Tai Army suffered defeats by the primitive but ferocious Wa tribesmen (Schmetzer 1990).

In 1994 a joint U.S./Thai operation ("Tiger Trap") closed the Thai/Myanmar border in areas where the MTA operated. This cut off Khun Sa's ability to move heroin into Thailand and curtailed purchase of supplies for his forces. Later that year, Thai police arrested 13 major MTA brokers who had been indicted by a federal grand jury in New York. The squeeze was complete when, in 1995, the Myanmar army moved against Khun Sa, whose forces were low on food, ammunition, and medical treatment for their wounded. Shortly afterward, ethnic strife broke out: the rank-and-file ethnic Shans mutinied against the MTA, whose

top officers are ethnic Chinese (Shenon 1996). Khun Sa began secret negotiations with Myanmar, and in 1996 a deal was made. In front of reporters from Thailand, the 61-year-old Khun Sa submitted his resignation—he was retiring to raise chickens, he told them—disbanded the MTA, and closed the MTA laboratories. As a result, the amount of Southeast Asian heroin entering the United States dropped dramatically (replaced by heroin from Colombia). The Myanmar government refused to extradite him, and until his health deteriorated, Khun Sa regularly golfed with the generals against whom he fought a protracted guerrilla war (Wren 1998b).

The United Wa State Army Until 1989, another formidable private army in the Golden Triangle served the Burmese Communist Party (BCP). The BCP force had in the past received support from the People's Republic of China. After Beijing cut off this aid in order to improve relations with Burma, the BCP, following a long-established precedent in the region, went into the opium business. The BCP controlled much of the poppy-producing area and received opium as a form of tax and tribute from local farmers, which it then refined into heroin in its own laboratories.

In 1989 its ethnic rank-and-file Wa tribesmen—fierce warriors whose ancestors were headhunters—rebelled, and the BCP folded as an armed force (Haley 1990). Most Wa political groups reached an accommodation with the Myanmar ruling junta, while one faction of the Wa organized as the United Wa State Army (UWSA). Headquartered on the border of China's Yunnan Province, the UWSA uses heroin—and more recently methamphetamine—trafficking as a means of funding efforts against Burmese control (Witkin and Griffen 1994). There are nearly one million Wa who straddle the border between Myanmar and China, and the UWSA has an estimated strength of 15,000 to 20,000 men, well-armed with ground-to-air missiles and modern communications equipment. In 1997 a Myanmar military patrol of 30 men stumbled onto a Wa drug caravan smuggling methamphetamine into Thailand and was wiped out. For the Wa, profits from methamphetamine production and smuggling have surpassed heroin. Ironically, the Wa routinely execute anyone caught dealing drugs for local use (Wren 1998d): "Since the surrender of the SUA/MTA, the USWA has reigned supreme in narcotics production in Burma," the world's largest producer of heroin (*NNICC Report* 1998: 50).

In 2000 the Wa reached an accommodation with Myanmar and China. In return for sophisticated weapons and expertise from China, the Wa moved their people, their army, and their drug laboratories into the Thai–Myanmar border area known as Doi Lang. The Chinese were concerned with their own drug problem and preferred the Wa to be a Thai rather than a Chinese problem. But the situation has grown complex and volatile. Thailand supports the Shans—also drug traffickers—who are in rebellion against Myanmar. Myanmar supports the Wa, who police the border against Shan incursions. China supports Myanmar and the Wa, while the United States supports Thailand. In 2001 the United States moved about 5,000 troops into northern Thailand, where Myanmar and Thailand have exchanged threats and artillery shells along their Doi Lang border (Schmetzer 2001).

Thailand Whether the source is CIF, MTA, BCP, or UWSA, opium in the form of morphine base or of almost pure heroin is usually brokered in Thailand, which has modern communications and transportation systems. A nation of 50 million persons, Thailand is almost as large as France. A staunch anti-Communist ally of the United States, Thailand sent troops to fight alongside American soldiers in Korea and Vietnam. In addition to its role in drug trafficking, Thailand, with an estimated 50,000 active brothels, has a reputation of being the "world's biggest whorehouse" (Schmetzer 1991b). In 1991 a military coup—one of 17 since 1932—overthrew the democratically elected Thai government.

At the center of much of Thai drug trafficking are ethnic Chinese organizations such as the Triads, discussed in Chapter 10. They dominate a major part of the world heroin market: "In Southeast Asia, not only did the British and French

opium monopolies create massive addict populations, but they also inadvertently formed a smuggling network that was crucial to the post-World War II heroin epidemic. Although the colonial administrations reaped huge profits, they never became involved in the drug's distribution and sale. That work was left to each colony's licensed opium merchant. Invariably they were Chinese" (Posner 1988: 66). Bangkok has a large population of Thai-born Chinese, called *Haw*, who are known by Thai names but maintain close ties with compatriots in Hong Kong, Yunnan Province,[2] Amsterdam, and British Columbia. From Bangkok, Chinese criminal organizations have flooded their "China White" into major cities of Europe, Canada, and the United States.

The Golden Crescent

The Golden Crescent of Southwest Asia includes parts of Iran, Afghanistan, and Pakistan. The region has limestone-rich soil, a climate and altitude ideal for poppy cultivation, and, like the Golden Triangle, a ready abundance of cheap labor for the labor-intensive production of opium. Afghan opium is processed into heroin in local laboratories or shipped—generally aboard donkeys, but sometimes aboard jeeps bought with United States funds—to processing plants in Pakistan (Burns 1990; *NNICC Report* 1998). In Pakistan the typical poppy farmer lives in semiautonomous northern tribal areas outside the direct control of the central government in Islamabad. The Pakistani authorities have little control in these areas and must appeal to tribal leaders to move against the region's dozens of illegal processing laboratories.

In northwest Pakistan's Karakorum Mountains, one acre of poppies yields about a dozen kilos of opium gum; ten kilos of opium gum can be

---

[2]Because it is located next to the Golden Triangle, China's Yunnan ("south of the clouds") Province, with a population that includes 20 of the country's minority groups, has been a center for drug trafficking. High-quality heroin passes easily over borders that were opened for trade more than a decade ago, supported by rampant corruption among the police and other officials. The traffickers are well armed, gunfights are frequent, and the army has been used extensively to combat the drug gangs (Tyler 1995).

Fighting the Drug Trade in Pakistan

With the knowledge of Pakistan authorities, the 43-year-old Pakistani had been working as a U.S. agent and interpreter for the small DEA office in the American Embassy in Islamabad. In 1997 he participated in a sting operation that netted two Pakistani Air Force pilots, who were arrested for smuggling heroin. Within days of the operation, he was arrested by the military-run intelligence, injected with drugs, tortured with electric shocks, and finally sentenced to 10 years' imprisonment by a military court for inducing a military officer to commit a crime (Golden 1997b). In response to U.S. pressure, he was released from custody in 1998.

converted into one kilo of base morphine. The wholesaling is accomplished in lawless border towns such as Landi Kotal, which is about three miles from the Afghan border. Much of the heroin trade in and from Pakistan is controlled by a consortium of three Quetta-based families, referred to as the Quetta Alliance. Quetta, a border city of more than one million persons, is filled with Afghan refugees, poverty, and drug addicts. Although these groups appear to be independent, they cooperate with one another when such cooperation is to their mutual benefit. Extensive corruption efforts shield them from law enforcement, and many family members hold provincial-level political offices (*NNICC Report* 1998).

Unlike Southeast Asia, Afghanistan's rugged terrain and the martial tradition of its tribes kept it free of colonialism. Western interest in this nation of about 27 million was limited until the Soviet invasion. The Pashtuns, a tribal group that populates Pakistan's Northwest Frontier Province, make up about 40 percent of the inhabitants of Afghanistan. The border dividing the Pashtuns in Pakistan from their tribal brethren in Afghanistan was drawn by the British more than a century ago, and is generally ignored—there are few border patrols in the region (Ahmed-Ullah 2001).

Known as exceptional warriors, the Pashtuns are also the major drug traffickers in the region. Along with other Islamic groups, many Pashtuns fought a guerrilla war against the Soviet-backed regime in Kabul. In late 1979, the Soviets rolled their tanks into the opium provinces of Afghanistan: "Suddenly, the tribes which had spent the last decade maneuvering their heavily armed drug caravans past the increasingly troublesome patrols of the U.S. Drug Enforcement Administration's agents found themselves flung into the limelight as the new anti-communist 'crusaders'" (Levins 1980: 201).

U.S. anti-Soviet efforts in Afghanistan were orchestrated by the CIA, which adopted a benign attitude toward drug trafficking. As the conflict wound down, the United States became increasingly concerned with rebel drug activity. Opium is the cash crop that has traditionally enabled feuding tribes in Afghanistan and in Pakistan's Northwest Frontier Province to purchase weapons and ammunition. In 1991, U.S. officials announced that they would no longer provide military assistance to Afghan rebels. Prior to its disintegration, the Soviet Union also agreed to stop aiding the Afghan government. The following year, *mujahedin* forces entered Kabul without encountering any resistance, and the war officially ended, but warfare between rebel groups continued, supported by heroin. By 1998, the Islamic fundamentalist Taliban movement, made up primarily of Pashtuns, controlled most of the country, and Afghanistan became one of the world's largest producers of heroin (Wren 1998c; Department of State 1998). Until 2001, the country was the world's second largest grower of the opium poppy, producing about one-third of the heroin entering the United States and about 80 percent of the heroin consumed in Europe. Despite the severe economic ramifications, in 2001 the Taliban leadership banned the growing of poppies as a sin

Afghani drug dealers unpack opium for sale. Cash from the sale of opium is used by feuding tribes in Afghanistan and the Northwest Frontier Province of Pakistan to buy weapons and ammunition.

against the teachings of Islam. Compliance was immediate and thorough (Bearak 2001). However, a United Nations report offered a cynical explanation for the new policy: the Taliban were stockpiling opium and heroin, suggesting that production was halted to keep heroin prices from plummeting (Lederer 2001). In any event, in the wake of the September 11, 2001, terrorist attacks and U.S. military action, the Taliban government told farmers they were once again free to grow the opium poppy. With the collapse of the Taliban, the poppy once again became an indispensable crop in parts of Afghanistan: "There is no other way to survive," notes one farmer. Raw opium can be sold for $100 or more a pound, more than one hundred times what fruits and vegetables will bring (Weiner 2001b; also Torriero 2002; Waldman 2002).

The United States has pressured Pakistan to move against poppy cultivation, but the infusion of hundreds of thousands of Afghan tribesmen into Pakistan has made this difficult, if not impossible. Tribesmen in Pakistan are now armed with rocket-propelled grenade launchers and automatic weapons to protect miles of poppy plants, pledging to die fighting rather than give up their best cash crop. Furthermore, there is a growing domestic market for heroin in Pakistan: while most poppies now grow on the Afghan side of the border and are shipped to Europe and America in the form of powdered heroin, Pakistan's heroin-smoking population has grown, with estimates as high as one million users.

Iran has been fighting a deadly battle against heavily armed Afghan traffickers and has lost several thousand men in the effort. The traffickers, equipped with anti-aircraft missiles, night-vision goggles, and satellite telephones, are better armed than their opponents in Iranian law enforcement (Moore 2001). Turkey, which serves as a land bridge to markets in the West for heroin from the Golden Crescent, is fighting a similar battle. Kurdish separatists and Turkish criminal groups (*babas*) have important connections in the Western drug market. They move heroin across the highways of Turkey and into Europe, where other criminal organizations, in particular Mafia and Camorra groups, distribute the drug throughout the European market.

The nations of Central Asia that surround Afghanistan, such as Tajikistan, have a predominantly young, rapidly growing, and poverty-stricken population. Add heroin to this mix, and you get an expanding addict population and drug organizations taking advantage of porous borders and easily bribed officials: "The drug business sustains up to 50 percent of the Tajik economy and props up its currency, if only because of the great number of people it employs" (Orth 2002: 168). For many of the warlords who are part of the post-Taliban Afghan government, heroin was the way they supported their armed followers. Islamic terrorist groups also operate in this region, and heroin provides them with an invaluable source of funds. And the corruption–drug connection reaches into the highest ranks of the Russian military (Orth 2002).

Mexico

Mexico is the source of "brown heroin," which gained a foothold in the American drug market after the demise of the "French Connection." In the five years after the collapse of the French connection, Mexico became the major source of U.S. heroin: "Mexico's rise was logical: the country contains extensive regions suitable for both opium cultivation and refining and shares a lightly guarded 2,000 mile border with the United States. Mexicans could manufacture heroin and smuggle it into the United States with little risk of detection. This simplified trafficking system resulted in increased

Mexican heroin availability in the United States" (PCOC 1986c: 107).

Mexico is the source of "black tar" and brown heroin, less-refined but more-potent—and very popular—forms of the substance. The conversion of the opium gum to black tar—No. 3—heroin is more convenient and requires only simple equipment, which can be readily dismantled if law enforcement is detected in the area. In addition, almost anyone can be trained to perform the conversion process, making it unnecessary to pay the higher salaries that would most certainly be demanded by skilled chemists. The process is more rapid and more economical than that required to produce the higher purity—No. 4—white heroin (Drug Enforcement Administration 1991a). While white heroin from the Golden Triangle and the Golden Crescent can approach 100 percent purity, Mexican black tar or brown generally ranges from 65 to 85 percent pure.

The poppy is not native to Mexico but was brought into the country at the turn of the century by Chinese laborers who were helping to build the railroad system. Chinese immigrants dominated heroin trafficking until anti-Chinese riots and property confiscations during the 1930s caused the trade to pass into Mexican hands (Lupsha 1991).

Poppy fields are generally small and difficult to detect, although larger fields cultivated by more sophisticated growers have been discovered. The poppies are grown in remote areas of the Sierra Madre states of Durango, Sinaloa, and Chihuahua, as well as Sonora (the Mexican state just south of Arizona). Opium gum is then transported to nearby villages. *Acaparadores*, or gatherers, travel around the countryside buying large quantities of opium gum, which is flown to secret laboratories owned and operated by major heroin organizations.

The conversion process for Mexican heroin takes about three days (although with special equipment and trained personnel, it can be accomplished in one day). Once the chemists are finished, the heroin is moved to large population centers. From there, Mexican couriers transport the heroin to members of the trafficking organization in the United States (PCOC 1986c).

The drug trade is big business in poverty-wracked Mexico. Large traffickers (discussed in Chapter 8) have traditionally received protection from the highest levels of government and law enforcement. Indeed, some important traffickers have backgrounds in law enforcement. As Peter Lupsha notes, "For some of Mexico's top enforcement officials entrance into drug trafficking has simply been a lateral transfer" (1990: 12). This ugly facet of the drug trade was dramatically revealed when several Mexican law enforcement officers were implicated in the torture-murder of a U.S. drug agent. They were acting on orders from drug kingpin Rafael Caro Quintero. When Quintero and other members of his Guadalajara cartel were arrested, they were carrying credentials identifying them as agents of the Dirección Federal de Seguridad, the Mexican equivalent of the FBI. Sicilia Falcón, another leading Mexican trafficker, carried similar credentials (Lupsha 1991). In Rafael's hometown of Sinaloa, just south of Arizona, he and other members of the Caro Quintero clan are revered and are even the subjects of songs and legends (Bowden 1991). As noted in Chapter 8, Mexican organizations are now transporting cocaine into the United States for Colombian traffickers.

The vast and remote 1,933-mile border between Mexico and the United States makes patrolling very difficult and aids the transportation of drugs into Texas, California, Arizona, and New Mexico. Drugs are also secreted in a variety of motor vehicles and smuggled past official border entry points. Private aircraft make use of hundreds of small airstrips that dot the U.S.–Mexican border and dozens of larger airstrips on the Yucatán Peninsula to move heroin north.

Colombia

As noted in Chapter 8, since the 1980s Colombia has become a major poppy grower, and Colombians have become major heroin wholesalers. On the mountain slopes of Colombia's Andean rain forests, guerrillas and drug traffickers have become major poppy growers (McGuire 1993). While coca is a lowland crop, the poppy thrives in the Andes. On the hillsides of a reservation in the south-

ern Colombian state of Cauca, 9,000 feet high, Guambiano Indians cultivate their most precious crop—gum from their poppies brings about $115 a pound and represents the difference between food and hunger. Nine other states are known to have poppy plantations (Tamayo 2001).

At the end of 1991, police raids in Colombia disclosed thousands of acres of poppy plants ("Colombian Heroin May Be Increasing" 1991). By 1998, Colombian heroin accounted for more than 50 percent of the drug smuggled into the United States. The purity level of Colombian heroin—it passes through fewer hands from "the farm to the arm" than the Asian variety—enables ingestion by sniffing and smoking, methods much safer than injection, which is the only way to gain a potent high with weaker versions of the drug. By 1999, Colombia was believed the source of 70 percent of the heroin sold on the East Coast. In New York, Colombians caused a glut on the heroin market, with declining prices and street-sale purity as high as 90 percent—in the early (pre-Colombian) 1980s, it was barely 5 percent (Wren 1999a).

COCAINE

Cocaine is an alkaloid found in significant quantities only in the leaves of two species of coca shrub. One species grows in the Andes of Ecuador, Peru, and Bolivia; the other is found in the mountainous regions of Colombia, along the Caribbean coast of South America, on the northern coast of Peru, and in the dry valley of the Marañon River in northeastern Peru. The practice of chewing coca leaves has been carried on by Indians in Peru for at least 20 centuries. The leaves are used as a poultice for wounds and to brew a tea, *mate de coca*, said to cure the headaches of tourists bothered by the 12,000-foot altitude of La Paz. While cash crops raised on the mountain slopes of Peru require a great deal of care—the nutrient-poor soil needs continuous fertilization—coca is a hardy jungle plant with abundant seeds and needs little or no fertilizer: "Once a coca field is planted, it will yield four to five crops a year for thirty to forty years, needing little in return but seasonal weeding" (Morales 1989: xvi).

Spanish explorers observed indigenous people chewing coca leaves during their colonization of South America, although they did not adopt the practice. In the middle of the nineteenth century, scientists began experimenting with the substance, noting that it showed promise as a local anesthetic and had an effect opposite that of morphine. At first, cocaine was used to treat morphine addiction, but the result was often a morphine addict who also became dependent on cocaine (Van Dyke and Byck 1982): "Throughout the late nineteenth century, both coca itself (that is, an extract from the leaf including all its alkaloids) and the pure chemical cocaine were used as medicines and for pleasure—the distinction was not always made—in an enormous variety of ways" (Grinspoon and Bakalar 1976: 19). By the late 1880s, a feel-good pharmacology based on the coca plant and its derivative, cocaine, was promoted for everything from headaches to hysteria. However, the most famous beverage containing coca was first bottled in 1894 (Helmer 1975). Coca-Cola continues to use nonpsychoactive residue from the coca plant for flavoring.

After the first flush of enthusiasm for cocaine in the 1880s, there was a decline in its use. While it continued to be used in a variety of notions and tonics, cocaine did not develop a separate appeal as did morphine and heroin (Morgan 1981). Indeed, it gained a reputation for inducing bizarre and unpredictable behavior. After the turn of the century, cocaine, like heroin, became identified with the urban underworld. From 1930 until the 1960s, there was limited demand for cocaine and, accordingly, only limited supply. Cocaine use was associated with deviants—jazz musicians and the denizens of underworld—and supplies were typically diverted from medical sources.

During the late 1960s and early 1970s, attitudes toward recreational drug use became more relaxed, a spinoff of the wide acceptance of marijuana. Cocaine was no longer associated with deviants, and the media played a significant role in shaping public attitudes: "By publicizing and glamorizing the lifestyle of affluent, upper-class drug dealers and the use of cocaine by celebrities and athletes, all forms of mass media created an effective advertising campaign for cocaine, and many people were taught to perceive cocaine as chic, exclusive, daring, and nonaddicting. In television specials about cocaine abuse, scientists talked about the intense euphoria produced by cocaine and the compulsive craving that people (and animals) develop for it. Thus, an image of cocaine as being extraordinarily powerful, and a (therefore desirable) euphoriant was promoted" (Wesson and Smith 1985: 193).

Cocaine soon became associated with a privileged elite. The new demand was sufficient to generate new refining and marketing networks outside of medical channels (Grinspoon and Bakalar 1976) and the development of the international cocaine organizations discussed in Chapter 8. This situation led to greater availability of cocaine, with a corresponding increase in use. Enormous profits accrue at each level of the cocaine business. These profits have proved so alluring that criminal organizations which have traditionally avoided direct involvement in drug trafficking have become involved in the cocaine business.

The Business of Cocaine

Coca is a flowering bush or shrub that in cultivation stands three to six feet tall. Each shrub yields at most four ounces of waxy, elliptical leaves that are about 1 percent cocaine by weight. Pulverized leaves of the coca bush are soaked and shaken in a mixture of alcohol and benzol (a petroleum derivative). The liquid is then drained, sulfuric acid is added, and the solution is again shaken. Sodium carbonate is added, forming a precipitate, which is washed with kerosene and chilled, leaving behind crystals of crude cocaine known as coca paste. Between 200 and 500 kilos of leaves are made into 1 kilo of paste; 2.5 kilos of coca paste are converted into 1 kilo of cocaine base—a malodorous, grainy, greenish yellow powder of more than 66 percent purity. Cocaine base is converted into cocaine hydrochloride by being treated with ether, acetone, and hydrochloric acid. One kilo of cocaine base is synthesized into one kilo of cocaine hydrochloride, a white crystalline powder that is about 95 percent pure.

In the United States, cocaine hydrochloride is cut for street sale by adding sugars such as lactose, inositol, or mannitol, or talcum powder, borax, or other neutral substances, and local anesthetics such as procaine hydrochloride (novocaine) or lidocaine hydrochloride. (Novocaine is sometimes mixed with mannitol or lactose and sold as cocaine.) After cutting, the cocaine typically has a consumer sale purity of less than 20 percent. More recently, however, huge increases in the availability of cocaine have resulted in consumer sale purity levels as high as 50 percent—and a concomitant increase in the number of emergency room admissions for cocaine overdose.

The most common method of using cocaine is "snorting"—inhaling it into the nostrils through a straw or rolled paper or from a "coke spoon." Some abusers take it intravenously, which is the only way to ingest 100 percent of the drug. When the drug is inhaled, its effects peak in 15 to 20 minutes and disappear in 60 to 90 minutes. Intravenous use results in an intense feeling of euphoria that crests in 3 to 5 minutes and wanes in 30 to 40 minutes. Cocaine causes the release of the natural substance adrenaline: "In essence the cocaine-stimulated reactions in the body are mimicking a natural physiological stress response." The body prepares for "fight" or "flight," but the brain sends the message that everything is better than fine (Gold et al. 1986: 38). In small doses, cocaine will bring about a sensation of extreme euphoria and indifference to pain, along with illusions of increased mental and sensory alertness and physical strength. At higher doses, the drug has the potential "to produce megalomania and feelings of omnipotence in most individuals" (Gold et al. 1986: 44).

Cocaine has limited medical use. It constricts blood vessels when applied topically, the only local anesthetic that has this effect. Because of this quality, cocaine is used during surgery of the mucous membranes of the ear, nose, and throat, and for procedures that require the passage of a tube through the nose or throat (Van Dyke and Byck 1982).

For many decades, coca leaf was converted to cocaine base in Bolivia and Peru, and smuggled by small aircraft or boat into Colombia, where it was refined into cocaine in jungle laboratories. Laboratories have relocated to cities far from cultivation sites to be closer to sources of precursor chemicals and also because improved law enforcement methods make it easier to find jungle laboratories. Precursor chemicals are usually manufactured in the United States and Germany, and Panama and Mexico serve as a major transit sources. Colombian cartels, using dummy companies and multiple suppliers, pay up to ten times the normal prices for these chemicals.

Some Colombian traffickers have set up laboratories in other Latin American countries and even in the United States in response to increased law enforcement in Colombia and the increasing cost of ether, sulphuric acid, and acetone in Colombia. While sulphuric acid and acetone has wide industrial use in Colombia, ether does not, and each kilo of cocaine requires 17 liters of ether. The cost of these chemicals has increased as a result of controls imposed by the Colombian government on their importation and sale and of U.S. Drug Enforcement Administration efforts to disrupt the supply of chemicals essential in the cocaine refinement process. Acetone, sulphuric acid, and ether are widely available for commercial purposes in the United States (Hall 2000).

In the past, because the quality of Colombian coca was significantly less than that grown in Peru and Bolivia, Colombia had not been a major coca producer. Success in eradicating coca in Bolivia and Peru[3] led to a major increase in Colombian coca cultivation, and in 1998, Colombia became the world's leading producer (Goering 1998; Krauss 2000). Colombian traffickers have achieved extraordinary levels of efficiency in extracting cocaine from their coca crops (*International Narcotics Control Strategy Report* 2000). About three-quarters of the coca is grown in six rural provinces about the size of Kansas, southwest of Bogatá, with a population of about six million persons. The area is desperately poor and plagued by left- and right-wing paramilitary groups (Forero 2001a). Indeed,

[3]By 2002, coca was making a comeback in Peru, driven by a combination of poverty and soaring prices for coca (Forero 2002).

Colombia is the only country in Latin America still fighting a major guerrilla insurgency (Howe 2000).

The government has conceded an area in central Colombia about the size of Switzerland to the main Marxist guerrilla group, the Revolutionary Armed Forces of Colombia (FARC), with about 18,000 fighters. FARC acts as a "labor organizer in the coca fields, keeping the price of a bushel up while taking a hefty percentage from the farmers" (Howe 2000: 38). In FARC-controlled areas, the economy is built on coca, and coca paste often serves as the local currency. Since paper currency is in short supply, "it is not unusual for people to be paid for their work in coca. They, in turn, pay for the necessities with the paste, which is soft and powdery like flour" (Forero 2001f: Sec. 4:12). The traffickers buy the paste, process it into cocaine, and ship it by the ton to the United States, while FARC taxes the trade: "To prevent narcotraffickers from ripping off farmers, the rebels set a minimum price for a kilo of coca paste. They also tax the traffickers for protection of smuggling routes, the use of clandestine runways, the importation of cocaine-processing chemicals, and the export of every kilo of refined cocaine shipped from the region" (Semple 2001a: 61).

Contesting the FARC and other leftist militias are right-wing paramilitaries, which often receive assistance from wealthy landowners, ranchers, and the Colombian military (Forero 2001h). They are part of a loose-knit coalition called the United Self-Defense Forces of Colombia (AUC)—about 11,000 strong and still growing—that is fighting Marxist guerrillas for control of poppy- and coca-producing regions. One group is headed by 35-year-old Carlos Castaño, whose 8,000 uniformed, well-trained, and well-armed men regularly do battle against leftist guerrillas. The group's methods are characterized by their nickname, "The Headcutters." Victims—anyone believed collaborating with leftists—are frequently kidnapped and usually found decapitated. Castaño finances his operation through drug trafficking and is believed to be an associate of the Montoya brothers, major cocaine traffickers in the Northern Valle de Cauca region. Ranchers who had been under siege from

the guerrillas helped transform this small group of outlaws into a formidable army (Forero 2001h). In 2001, Castaño announced on the AUC web site that he had resigned to oversee the group's political wing (Forero 2001a).

Operating out of the foothills of the Sierra Nevadas is another paramilitary headed by Hernán Giraldo, whose group, *Los Chamizos* (Charred Tree), numbers about 400. His men routinely kill suspected leftists, including university professors, student activists, and trade unionists—in 2000, at least 130 Colombian trade unionists were murdered (Forero 2001g). Giraldo is reputed to control a drug syndicate that exports more than $1 billion worth of cocaine to the United States and Europe, although he is not adverse to other means of raising money. In 1995 his men kidnapped a wealthy local businessman and demanded a $1-million ransom. After the money was delivered, the victim was shot and his body carved up with chain saws. Three years later, his men abducted the victim's widow and demanded a ransom of $5 million. After the money was delivered, she met the same fate as her husband.[4] Despite his notorious reputation, port authorities, police officials, and politicians are often eager to secure his largess, which has enabled him to elude capture (Hammer 1997; Schemo 1997b; Contreras 2001; Goering 2001; Wilson 2001).

The militias have proven more effective against the guerrillas than government forces, and this has endeared them to elements of the population at risk. They have reinforced this support by building roads and schools in the areas from which they have driven the guerrillas (Forero 2001h).

Distribution

The organizers who arrange for the importation and wholesale distribution of heroin and cocaine typically avoid physical possession: "The key figures in the Italian heroin establishment never

---

[4]Kidnapping is a major source of funds for both right- and left-wing groups in Colombia, as well as common criminals. In 2000 there were 3,076 reported kidnappings and many others hidden from authorities (Semple 2001b).

touched heroin. Guys who were in the business for twenty years and had made millions off it had never seen it. After all, does a commodities trader on Wall Street have to see hog bellies and platinum bars?" (Durk and Silverman 1976: 49). Importation often entails little or no risk of arrest—heroin or cocaine can be secreted in a variety of imported goods, and possession cannot be proven. Furthermore, while a single shipment may be detected and confiscated, smugglers often divide their supplies so that other shipments arrive unimpeded. Colombian dealers have been known to offer to insure their shipments through a joint arrangement. The cost of insurance is passed on to the import buyer, who is then financially protected in the event of interdiction by American authorities.

After importation, heroin is sold in 10-to-50-kilo quantities to wholesalers—"kilo connections." The heroin is then "stepped on" or diluted several times. The wholesaler, basically a middleman, arranges for the cutting (diluting) of the almost-pure heroin. The actual work is often done by women brought together for the task. Between 10 and 20 women cut from 10 to 50 kilos in an apartment rented for this purpose. Under guard, often working without any clothes on (as a precaution against theft of the precious powder), and wearing surgical masks to avoid inhaling heroin dust, they mix the heroin with quinine, lactose, and dextrose, usually four or five parts of the dilutant to one part of heroin. They work through the night and receive several thousand dollars each, making the risk and embarrassment worthwhile.

When the cutting is complete, jobbers—"weight dealers"—who have been waiting for a telephone call arrive with the necessary cash, which they exchange for two to five kilos of the cut heroin. The jobbers move it to wholesalers, who cut it again. From there, it moves to street wholesalers, then to street retailers, and finally to consumers. At each step of the process, profits increase as the kilo of pure heroin increases in bulk, the result of further cutting.

The enormous profits that accrue in the business of drugs are part of a criminal underworld where violence is always a reality. Transactions must be accomplished without recourse to the for-mal mechanisms of dispute resolution that are usually available in the world of legitimate business. This reality leads to the creation of private mechanisms of enforcement. The drug world is filled with heavily armed and dangerous persons in the employ of the larger cartels, although even street-level operatives are often armed. These private resources for violence serve to limit market entry, to ward off competitors and predatory criminals, and to maintain internal discipline and security within an organization.

Below the multi-kilo wholesale level, cocaine or heroin is an easy-entry business, requiring only a source, clientele, and funds. A variety of groups deal heroin and cocaine, including street gangs in many urban areas. In several parts of the country, particularly New York City and Los Angeles, the relatively stable neighborhood criminal organizations that dominate the heroin and cocaine trade have found new competitors: youthful crack dealers. Crack requires only a small investment for entry to the trade. Street gangs or groups of friends and relatives have entered the market, often touching off explosive competitive violence that frequently involves the use of high-powered handguns and automatic weapons. The sharp decline in murder in some major cities such as New York is believed related to a stabilizing of the crack market, much as post-Prohibition organized-crime-related murder dipped significantly in Chicago in the absence of competition.

The sale of heroin and cocaine/crack is carried out by thousands of small-time operators who dominate particular local markets—a public housing complex, a number of city blocks, or simply a street corner. Control is exercised through violence. For most participants at the street level, however, the net profits are rather modest. While dealers typically work long hours and subject themselves to substantial risk of violence and incarceration, their incomes generally range from $1,000 to $2,000 a month. Less successful participants eke out a living that rivals minimum wage. Many are there to support their own drug habits, to supplement earnings from legitimate employment, or both. In the crack business, young men often work for less than minimum wage—for

Crack

While cocaine hydrochloride cannot easily be smoked, freeing the alkaloid from the hydrochloride attachment produces purified crystals of cocaine base that can be crushed and smoked in a special glass pipe or sprinkled on a tobacco or marijuana product. Cocaine hydrochloride powder is easily converted into crack by cooking it in a mixture of sodium bicarbonate (baking soda) and water, then removing the water. The soaplike substance is then cut into bars or chips, sometimes called "quarter rocks," and smoked. It is generally sold on the street in small glass vials. The nickname "crack" comes from the crackling sound the drug makes when it is smoked in a glass pipe. Smoking crack produces a short but very powerful euphoria that lasts 10 to 15 minutes.

example, $30 a day for acting as a lookout or 50 cents for each vial of crack sold. They can expect $100 to $200 per week for working long hours under unpleasant conditions and are without unemployment insurance, medical insurance, or any of the other usual benefits of legitimate employment.

Many retail operators sell more than one drug—they are often "walking drugstores." The lower down on the distribution chain, the more likely that the person or organization will be involved in the sale of more than one substance. And the business of drugs includes substances other than heroin and cocaine/crack.

METHAMPHETAMINES

Amphetamines are synthetic drugs, and their effects are similar to cocaine's. They mimic the naturally occurring substance adrenaline and cause a biochemical arousal—being "turned on"—without the presence of sensory input to cause such arousal. The body becomes physiologically activated. Because they ward off sleep, amphetamines have proven popular with college students cramming for exams and with long-haul truck drivers.

First synthesized in 1887, amphetamines were introduced into clinical use in the 1930s (Smith 1979) and eventually offered as a "cure-all" for just about every ailment. Between 1932 and 1946, there were 39 generally accepted medical uses, including the treatment of schizophrenia, morphine addiction, low blood pressure, and caffeine and to-

bacco dependence. It was believed that the substance had no abuse potential (*Drug Abuse and Drug Abuse Research* 1987). Since amphetamines appear to act on the hypothalamus to suppress the appetite, at one time they were widely prescribed to treat obesity. As opposed to more natural forms of dieting, however, the appetite returns with greater intensity after withdrawal from the drug. Only as a "last resort" is methamphetamine hydrochloride (Desoxyn) used to treat obesity as one component of a weight-reduction regimen, and even then the treatment is limited to only a few weeks.

Legally produced amphetamine is taken in the form of tablets or capsules. Some abusers crush the substance, dissolve it in water, and ingest it intravenously. Illegally produced amphetamines are often available in powdered form (called "ice") and are sometimes smoked. There are three basic types of amphetamines. Methyl-amphetamines have the greatest potential for abuse because they are fast-acting and produce a "rush." Methamphetamine hydrochloride, one of the methyl group, is a widely abused drug known on the street simply as "meth"; in liquid form, it is often referred to as "speed." As with cocaine, in small doses amphetamines will bring about a "rush," a sensation or euphoria often described in sexual terms, along with indifference to pain and illusions of increased mental and sensory alertness, and physical strength.

The main active ingredient in methamphetamine, phenyl-2-propanone, referred to as P2P, is widely available in Europe, and bulk shipments of

P2P from Germany are often the source of illegal methamphetamine produced in the United States. But the dynamics of illicit methamphetamine production and trafficking have been changing, with P2P as the primary precursor being replaced by ephedrine. Mexican manufacturers typically produce the drug in three phases, using such precursor chemicals as ephedrine, pseudoephedrine, red phosphorus, and hydriodic acid. Canada has been the source of pseudoephedrine, which is imported in powder form, mostly from China, as a decongestant. Because of lax government controls, the substance is diverted for the U.S. market (Krauss 2002).

Although most of the chemicals needed are easily obtained or manufactured clandestinely, they also present numerous hazards both during the production process and after, when they are discarded due to their caustic, flammable, or reactive nature. The danger of chemical fires and explosions extends beyond manufacture. After producing the finished methamphetamine, clandestine lab workers are typically left with 5–6 pounds of hazardous waste for each pound of the finished drug produced. Most of this waste consists of corrosive sodium hydroxide solution often discarded in Freon cans, which may become a hazard due to temperatures and internal pressure. In addition, traces of red phosphorous will likely remain on discarded materials and equipment, presenting a flammable hazard for three to four decades.

The illegal activities associated with methamphetamine production and hazardous waste encompass more than the clandestine lab cooks and workers. Just as legitimate industries generate secondary services, clandestine lab site "brokers," property owners, and "oil barons" support and profit from the manufacture of methamphetamine, with the first two negotiating or allowing the use of property and the third recycling hazardous waste material.

Even when law enforcement is able to arrest and prosecute the individuals involved, there can be staggering costs associated with removing the containers, contaminated apparatus, and chemical waste. Depending on the extent of the contamination and whether the area affected is a structure, soil, or water, costs can range from thousands of dollars to do the initial cleanup to hundreds of thousands of dollars to cleanse a water supply or make a dwelling rehabitable. Undetected contaminated areas will continue to do incalculable damage to the environment (Nieves 2001).

As noted in Chapter 1, the distribution of methamphetamine has been a main staple of outlaw bikers. In recent years, there has been an increase in the involvement of Mexican gangs operating in southern California, where they produce methamphetamine in unpopulated desert areas. Mexican organizations have saturated the Western market with high-purity methamphetamine, so even outlaw motorcycle clubs "are finding it more cost effective to purchase this stimulant from Mexican sources" (Drug Enforcement Administration 1995a: 1). By using previously established networks, Mexican organizations are producing and distributing d-methamphetamine, a drug that is twice as potent as its predecessor (dl-methamphetamine) and that offers a longer lasting high than cocaine.

As Mexican d-methamphetamine producing and trafficking organizations seek to further expand their controlling interest in this emerging, lucrative market, the incidence of clandestine lab and dump sites has increased, although this remains primarily a West Coast phenomenon. In the 17 counties of California's Central Valley area—Bakersfield to Sacramento—there are vast, unpopulated areas with ready access to interstate roads, while chronic unemployment in the area makes recruiting drug workers relatively easy, despite the hazards of methamphetamine production. Mexican organizations have set up laboratories throughout the area. Labs that are discovered are easily replaced, as are the workers who are arrested—they are viewed as a "renewable resource" (Nieves 2001).

CANNABIS/MARIJUANA

The biggest influence on marijuana legislation has been racism. State laws against marijuana were often part of a reaction to Mexican immigration (Bonnie and Whitebread 1970). By 1930, 16 states with relatively large Mexican populations had enacted anti-marijuana legislation: "Chicanos in the Southwest were believed to be incited to violence by smoking it" (Musto 1973: 65). Because of marijuana's association with suspect marginal groups—Mexicans, artists, intellectuals, jazz musicians, bohemians, and petty criminals—it became an easy target for regulation (Morgan 1981). By 1931, 22 states had marijuana legislation, often part of a general purpose statute against narcotics (Bonnie and Whitebread 1970). In 1937, Congress passed the Marijuana Tax Act, which put an end to lawful recreational use of the substance. Despite being outlawed, marijuana was never an important issue in the United States until the 1960s: "It hardly ever made headlines or became the subject of highly publicized hearings and reports. Few persons knew or cared about it, and marihuana laws were passed with minimal attention" (Himmelstein 1983: 38).

The source of marijuana, the hemp plant, grows wild throughout most of the tropical and temperate regions of the world, including parts of the United States. It has been cultivated for several useful products: the tough fiber of the stem is used to make rope, the seed is used as part of feed mixtures, and the oil is used as an ingredient in paint. The psychoactive part of the plant is a substance called Delta9THC or simply THC. It is most highly concentrated in the leaves and resinous flowering tops of the plant. The THC level of marijuana cigarettes varies considerably: domestic marijuana typically has had less than 0.5 percent, since the plants were originally introduced to produce hemp fiber. However, more recently developed strains exhibit considerably higher levels, the result of careful cross-breeding by outlaw horticulturalists. The domestic cultivation of marijuana has spawned a significant market in horticultural equipment. These suppliers advertise in *High Times*, a magazine devoted to marijuana use.

Jamaican, Colombian, and Mexican marijuana ranges from 0.5 to 4.0 percent THC. The most select product, sinsemilla (from the Spanish *sin semilla*, "without seed"), is prepared from the unpollinated female cannabis plant. Sinsemilla has been found to have as much as 8.0 percent THC. Hashish, which is usually imported from the Middle East, contains the drug-rich resinous secretions of the cannabis plant, which are collected, dried, and then compressed into a variety of forms—balls, cakes, or sheets. It has a potency as high as 10 percent. Hashish is usually mixed with tobacco and smoked in a pipe. "Hashish oil" is a dark, viscous liquid, the result of repeated extractions of cannabis plant materials. It has a THC level as high as 20 percent. A drop or two on a cigarette has the effect of a single marijuana cigarette. Marijuana prepared for street sale may be diluted with oregano, catnip, or other ingredients and may also contain psychoactive substances such as LSD.

In the United States, marijuana is usually rolled in paper and smoked. The user typically inhales the smoke deeply and holds it in the lungs for as long as possible. This tends to maximize the absorption of the active THC, about one-half of which is lost during smoking. The psychoactive reaction occurs in one to ten minutes and peaks in about ten to thirty minutes, with a total duration of three to four hours. The most important variables with respect to the drug's impact are the individual's experiences and expectations and the strength of the marijuana ingested. Thus, the first-time user may not experience any significant reaction. In general, low doses tend to induce restlessness and an increasing sense of well-being and gregariousness, followed by a dreamy state of relaxation; hunger, especially a craving for sweets, frequently accompanies marijuana use. Higher doses may induce changes in sensory perception—heightening the senses of smell, sight, hearing, and taste—which may be accompanied by subtle alterations in thought formation and expression.

There is little or no pattern to marijuana trafficking in the United States, although some areas have apparently gotten hooked on the business. In Kentucky, most cultivation takes place in the eastern region: the mountainous and inaccessible Appalachia. This impoverished region has a high unemployment rate. In the region's rugged hills, poverty—and thus incentive—is widespread.

While the rest of the nation prospered amid record economic growth at the end of the last century, the region's endemic poverty and ideal growing climate fed the industry. Appalachia's rugged terrain also provides a natural camouflage for marijuana. Much of the cultivation occurs on federal lands to avoid forfeiture laws (discussed in Chapter 14). In Boone National Forest, in 1999, 192,685 plants worth $384 million were eradicated. The marijuana business has a positive impact on the legitimate economy supported by the region's cultivators—everything from grocery stores to car dealerships depends on marijuana (Hefling 2000).

BARBITURATES

There are about 2,500 derivatives of barbituric acid and dozens of brand names for these derivatives. Lawfully produced barbiturates are found in tablet or capsule form. Illegal barbiturates may be found in liquid form for intravenous use because lawfully produced barbiturates are poorly soluble in water. According to the *Physicians' Desk Reference,* "Barbiturates depress the sensory cortex, decrease motor activity, alter cerebralar function, and produce drowsiness, sedation, and hypnosis" (1987: 1163). They inhibit seizure activity and can induce unconsciousness in the form of sleep or surgical anaesthesia. Unlike opiates, barbiturates do not decrease one's sense of pain. They can produce a variety of mood alterations, ranging from mild sedation to hypnosis and deep coma. A high dosage can induce anesthesia, and an overdose can be fatal. Barbiturates are used primarily as sedatives for the treatment of insomnia and as anticonvulsants (Mendelson 1980), although in some persons they produce excitation (*Physicians' Desk Reference* 1988). The euphoria that follows barbiturate intake makes them appealing as intoxicants (Wesson and Smith 1977).

Barbiturates are classified according to the speed with which they are metabolized (broken down chemically) in the liver and eliminated by the kidneys: slow, intermediate, fast, and ultrafast. The fast-acting forms—the best-known is sodium pentothal—are used to induce unconsciousness in a few minutes. At relatively high dosages, they are used as anesthetics for minor surgery and to induce anesthesia before the administration of slow-acting barbiturates. In low dosages, barbiturates may actually increase a person's reaction to painful stimuli. It is the fast-acting barbiturates, particularly Nembutal (sodium pentobarbital), Amytal (amobarbital sodium), Seconal (secobarbital sodium), and Tuinal (secobarbital sodium and amobarbital sodium combined), that are abuse risks (O'Brien and Cohen 1984).

There is no apparent pattern to the illegal market in barbiturates, and traffickers may sell them as part of their portfolio.

METHAQUALONE

Methaqualone was first synthesized in 1951 in India, where it was introduced as an antimalarial drug but found to be ineffective. At the same time, its sedating effects resulted in its introduction in Great Britain as a safe, nonbarbiturate sleeping pill. The substance subsequently found its way into street abuse: a similar sequence of events occurred in Germany and Japan. In 1965, methaqualone was introduced into the United States as the prescription drugs Sopors and Quaalude. It was not listed as a scheduled (controlled) drug. By the early 1970s, "ludes" and "sopors" were part of the drug culture. Physicians overprescribed the drug for anxiety and insomnia, believing that it was safer than barbiturates. The supplies for street sales came primarily from diversions of legitimate sources.

Eight years after it was introduced into the United States, the dangers of methaqualone became evident. The drug was placed on Schedule II—high potential for abuse, limited medical use—in 1973. Although the drug is chemically unrelated to barbiturates, methaqualone intoxication is similar to barbiturate intoxication. Addiction develops rapidly, and an overdose can be fatal. However, while similar to barbiturates in its effects, methaqualone produces an even greater loss of motor coordination, which explains why it is sometimes referred to as a "wallbanger."

Methaqualone is now illegally manufactured in Colombia and smuggled into the United States.

PHENCYCLIDINE (PCP)

Phencyclidine is reported to have received the name PCP—"peace pill"—on the streets of San Francisco. The drug was reputed to give illusions of everlasting peace. Frequently referred to as "angel dust," PCP was first synthesized in 1956 and found to be an effective surgical anesthetic when tested on monkeys. Experiments on humans were carried out in 1957, and while PCP proved to be an effective surgical anaesthetic, it had serious side effects. Some patients experienced agitation, excitement, and disorientation during the recovery period. Some male surgical patients became violent, while some females appeared to experience simple intoxication (Linder, Lerner, and Burns 1981): "When PCP was subsequently given to normal volunteers in smaller doses, it induced a psychotic-like state resembling schizophrenia. Volunteers experienced body image changes, depersonalization, and feelings of loneliness, isolation, and dependency. Their thinking was observed to become progressively disorganized" (Lerner 1980: 14).

There are more than 100 variations (analogs) of the substance. Unlike other anesthetics, PCP increases respiration, heart rate, and blood pressure, qualities that make it useful for patients endangered by a depressed heart rate or low blood pressure. In the 1960s, PCP became commercially available for use in veterinary medicine as an analgesic and anesthetic, but diversion to street use led the manufacturer to discontinue production in 1978. It is now produced easily and cheaply in clandestine laboratories in tablet, capsule, powder, and liquid form and sometimes sold as LSD. Its color varies, and there is no such thing as a standard dose. As with any drug sold on the street, PCP is often mixed with other psychoactive substances. Most commonly, PCP is applied to a leafy vegetable, including marijuana, and smoked: "Street preparations of phencyclidine have continuously changed in name, physical form and purity" (Lerner 1980: 15).

A moderate amount of PCP produces a sense of detachment, distance, and estrangement from one's surroundings within 30 to 60 minutes of ingestion: the effects last up to five hours. Numbness, slurred speech, and a loss of coordination also occur. These symptoms are often accompanied by feelings of invulnerability: "A blank stare, rapid and involuntary eye movements, and an exaggerated gait are among the more common observable effects" ("Drugs of Abuse" 1979: 30). Users may also experience mood disorders, acute anxiety, paranoia, and violent behavior. Some reactions are similar to LSD intoxication—auditory hallucinations and image distortion, similar to fun-house mirror images: "PCP is unique among popular drugs of abuse in its power to produce psychoses indistinguishable from schizophrenia" ("Drugs of Abuse" 1979: 30).

Like methamphetamine, PCP has been distributed by outlaw motorcycle clubs.

ECSTASY

Ecstasy, the common name for 3, 4-Methylene-DioxyMethAmphetamine or MDMA, is a synthetic drug with a chemical structure similar to the stimulant methamphetamine and the hallucinogen mescaline (Grob et al. 1996). It was used by some therapists in the 1970s to help patients explore their feelings for one another. In a controlled setting, it was reputed to promote trust between patients and physicians (Karch 1996). In 1985, scheduling hearings on MDMA were conducted, and the administrative law judge expressed his view that there was sufficient evidence for safe use under medical supervision and recommended Schedule III status. He was overruled by the director of the Drug Enforcement Administration, who placed MDMA in Schedule I—high potential for abuse, no medically accepted use.

MDMA is usually ingested orally in tablet or capsule form. It is also available as a powder and is sometimes snorted and occasionally smoked. It was not until its "rediscovery" in the late 1970s that ecstasy received a great deal of attention because of its purported ability to produce profound pleasurable effects: acute euphoria and long-lasting positive changes in attitude and self-confidence, with some symptoms resembling those caused by LSD but without the severe side effects typically associated with methamphetamine.

According to Jerome Beck and Marsha Rosenbaum, "The effects of MDMA usually become apparent twenty to sixty minutes following oral ingestion of an average dose (100–125 milligrams) on an empty stomach. The sudden and intense onset of the high experienced by many users is commonly referred to as the 'rush' (also the 'wave' or 'weird period')." This phase is often (particularly during initial use) experienced with a certain degree of trepidation, tension, stomach tightness, and/or mild nausea. Discomfort is generally transitory and melts away into a more relaxed state of being: "Although novice users occasionally experienced some apprehension during this initial onset, anxiety levels typically decreased with subsequent use, allowing for increased enjoyment" (1994: 63). The total effects last from three to six hours.

The drug's rewarding effects vary with the individual taking it, the dose and purity, and the environment in which it is taken. In high doses, ecstasy may cause the body's temperature to markedly increase (malignant hyperthermia), leading to muscle breakdown and kidney and cardiovascular system failure, which in some cases has proven fatal. While drinking water does not reduce the effects of ecstasy, it prevents dehydration. However, drinking too much water may lead to serious health complications in some people. Ecstasy may also produce a hangover effect: loss of appetite, insomnia, depression, and muscle aches. It can also make concentration difficult, particularly on the day after ecstasy is taken. Higher doses of ecstasy can produce hallucinations, irrational behavior, vomiting, and convulsions. Some evidence suggests that long-term use of ecstasy may cause damage to the brain, heart, and liver.

Although the vast majority of MDMA/ecstasy consumed domestically is produced in Europe—primarily the Netherlands and Belgium—a limited number of MDMA labs operate in the United States. In recent years, Israeli crime syndicates, some composed of Russian émigrés associated with Russian organized crime syndicates, have forged relationships with Western European traffickers and gained control over a significant share of the European market. The Israeli syndicates are currently the primary source for U.S. distribution (Keefe 2001b).

Overseas ecstasy trafficking organizations smuggle the drug in shipments of 10,000 or more tablets via express mail services, couriers aboard commercial airline flights, or air freight shipments from several major European cities to cities in the United States. The drug is sold in bulk quantity at the mid-wholesale level in the United States for approximately eight dollars per dosage unit. The retail price of MDMA sold in clubs in the United States is 20 to 30 dollars per dosage unit. Ecstasy traffickers use brand names and logos as marketing tools and to distinguish their product from that of competitors. The logos are produced to coincide with holidays or special events. Among the more popular logos are butterflies, lightning bolts, and four-leaf clovers.

LYSERGIC ACID DIETHYLAMIDE (LSD)

In 1949, LSD was introduced into the United States as an experimental drug for treating psychiatric illnesses, but until 1954 it remained relatively rare and expensive, because its ingredients were difficult to cultivate. In that year, the Eli Lilly Company announced that it had succeeded in creating a totally synthetic version of LSD (Stevens 1987). LSD affects the body in a variety of ways. The visual effects range from blurring to a visual field filled with strange objects; three-dimensional space appears to contract and enlarge, and light appears to fluctuate in intensity. Auditory effects occur but to a lesser degree. All of these changes are episodic throughout the "trip." Temperature sensitivity is altered, and the environment is perceived as being abnormally cold or hot. Body images are altered—out-of-body-experiences are common, and body parts appear to float. Perceptions of time are affected: sometimes time is perceived as running fast-forward or -backward.

There are "good acid trips" and "bad acid trips." This phenomenon appears to be controlled by the attitude, mood, and expectations of the user and often depends on suggestions of others at the time of the trip. Favorable expectations produce "good trips," while excessive apprehension is likely to produce the opposite. Since the substance appears to intensify feelings, the user may feel a magnified sense of love, lust, and joy, or anger, terror, and despair: "The extraordinary sensations and feelings may bring on fear of losing control, paranoia, and panic, or they may cause euphoria and even bliss" (Grinspoon 1979: 13). Ingesting LSD unknowingly can result in a highly traumatic experience, because the victim may feel that he or she has suddenly "gone crazy" (Brecher 1972), and it takes only .01 milligram to have an effect.

LSD is colorless, odorless, and tasteless, and it is relatively easy to produce. One ounce contains about 300,000 human doses (Ray 1978). Although LSD has been used experimentally to treat a variety of psychological illnesses, it currently has no accepted medical use. It may be taken orally in a pure form as a white powder, mixed with a number of other substances, or absorbed on paper ("blotter acid"), sugar, or gelatin sheets ("windowpanes"). A trip begins between 30 to 60 minutes after ingestion, peaks after 2 to 6 hours, and fades out after about 12 hours.

LSD was popular for a time during the 1960s, when it became part of the "hippie" culture. Current use appears limited, and distribution patterns are not well-known.

ANALOGS AND DESIGNER DRUGS

There are many chemical variations, or analogs, of the drugs discussed in this chapter—for example, semisynthetic opiates such as hydromorphine, oxycodone, etorphine, and diprenorphine, as well as synthetic opiates such as pethidine, methadone, and propoxyphene (Darvon). The synthetic drug fentanyl citrate, which is often used intravenously in major surgery, works exactly like opiates: it kills pain, produces euphoria, and, if abused, leads to addiction. The substance is easily produced by persons skilled in chemistry. Fentanyl compounds are often sold as "China White," the street name for the finest Southeast Asian heroin, to addicts who cannot tell the difference. Those who know the difference may actually prefer fentanyl because it is usually cheaper than heroin, and some users believe it contains less adulterants than heroin (Roberton 1986). In fact, fentanyl compounds are quite potent and hence difficult for street dealers to cut properly, a situation that can lead to overdose and death. Fentanyl has been used (illegally) to "dope" race horses, because the substance is very difficult to detect in urine or blood.

Synthetic substances chemically similar to cocaine, such as lidocaine and procaine (novocaine), will eliminate all feeling when applied topically, as dental patients recognize. Single small doses of lidocaine, when taken intranasally by experienced cocaine users, produced the same euphoric response as cocaine—they could not distinguish between the two substances (Van Dyke and Byck 1982). Other tests indicate that laboratory animals will work as hard for procaine as they will for cocaine. Since the passage of the Antidrug Abuse Act of 1986, all analogs of controlled substances have themselves become controlled substances.

In Chapter 14, we will review statutes designed to deal with the problem of drug trafficking and organized crime.

INTERNET CONNECTIONS

Office of National Drug Control Policy: **whitehousedrugpolicy.gov**

International Narcotics Control Board: **www.kincb.org**

United Nations Office for Drug Control and Crime Prevention: **undcp.org**

Drug Enforcement Administration: **www.usdoj.gov/dea/index**

REVIEW QUESTIONS

1. Up until they were made illegal in the United States, why were opium and opiates so popular?
2. Why were attempts to produce domestic opium unsuccessful in the United States?
3. What was the real cause of the opium wars?
4. How did the Chinese opium problem affect the United States?
5. What was the relationship between Chinese immigrants and the legislation against opium?
6. What was the relationship between the efforts against opiates and the temperance movement?
7. What was the direct cause of the passage of the Harrison Act?
8. How did Supreme Court rule with respect to the Harrison Act?
9. How did the federal drug enforcement agency respond to the Harrison Act?
10. What are the similarities and differences between trafficking in alcohol during Prohibition and drug trafficking after the Harrison Act?
11. Why is it difficult, if not impossible, for an organized crime unit to control the drug market?
12. What elements are required to produce opium profitably?
13. What political elements result in the enormous production of Golden Triangle heroin?
14. Why has it been difficult to curtail the cultivation of poppies and the manufacturing of heroin in the Golden Crescent?
15. What led to the widespread popularity of cocaine during the late 1960s and early 1970s?
16. What characteristics of the substance have made crack cocaine popular among young persons?
17. What led to the decrease in violence in the crack business?
18. What is the connection between anti-Mexican attitudes and marijuana laws in the United States?
19. What are designer drugs?
20. What is the pattern of manufacture and distribution of ecstasy (MDMA)?

CHAPTER 14

ORGANIZED CRIME STATUTES

Before we examine specific statutes in this chapter and examine law enforcement in Chapter 15, we need to consider three constraints on law enforcement efforts in general and organized crime law enforcement in particular: constitutional restraints, jurisdictional limitations, and the intertwining problems of corruption and informants.

CONSTITUTIONAL RESTRAINTS

Law enforcement in the United States operates under significant constitutional constraints. Important protections against government, while they protect individual liberty, also benefit the criminal population: the right to remain silent (Fifth Amendment), the right to counsel (Sixth Amendment), the right to be tried speedily by an impartial jury (Sixth Amendment), and the right to confront witnesses (Sixth Amendment). Particularly important for organized crime law enforcement are the Fourth Amendment and the exclusionary rule. The Fourth Amendment provides that "the right of the people to be secure in their

persons, houses, papers and effects, against unreasonable searches and seizures shall not be violated, and no Warrants shall issue, but upon probable cause, supported by Oath or affirmation, and particularly describing the place to be searched, and the persons or things to be seized." In practice, information sufficient to justify a search warrant in organized crime cases is difficult to obtain; unlike conventional crimes such as robbery and burglary, there are usually no innocent victims to report the crime. The *exclusionary rule* provides that evidence obtained in violation of the Fourth Amendment cannot be entered as evidence in a criminal trial (*Weeks v. United States*, 232 U.S. 383, 1914; *Mapp v. Ohio*, 357 U.S. 643, 1961), although there are a number of exceptions that are beyond the scope of this book.

Intercepting confidential information is a prerequisite to moving against organized crime. However, the Fourth Amendment and Title III of the Omnibus Crime Control and Safe Streets Act of 1968 (18 U.S.C. Sections 2510–2520) place restrictions on the ways that the government can secure this information. In order to surreptitiously intercept conversations by wiretapping telephones or using electronic ("bugging") devices, a court order must be secured. Like a search warrant, it must be based upon information sufficient to prove the legal standard of probable cause. When an order to intercept electronic communications is secured (generally referred to as a Title III), it is quite limited and requires extensive documentation, and the persons monitored must be notified after the order expires. These requirements make electronic surveillance quite expensive (in terms of personnel hours expended) and difficult to accomplish. (Electronic surveillance is discussed in Chapter 15.)

JURISDICTIONAL LIMITATIONS

The Constitution provides for a form of government in which powers are diffused horizontally and vertically. There are three branches—legislative, judicial, and executive—and four levels of government—federal, state, county, and municipal. Although each level of government has responsibilities for responding to organized criminal activities, there is little or no coordination among them—each level of government responds to the problem largely independent of the others. Federalism was part of a deliberate design to help protect us against tyranny; it also provides us with a level of inefficiency that significantly handicaps efforts to deal with organized criminal activity.

On the federal level, a host of executive branch agencies, ranging from the military to the Federal Bureau of Investigation, have responsibility for combating organized crime. There is also a separate federal judicial system that is responsible for trying OC cases and a legislative branch responsible for enacting OC legislation and allocating funds for federal enforcement efforts. The jurisdiction of many federal enforcement agencies overlaps, and efforts are often competitive rather than cooperative (see Dannen 1992a). At the local level, there are about 20,000 police agencies. Each state has state-level enforcement agents (state police or a similar agency), and the state is responsible for operating prisons and the parole system (if

Plainclothes police officers break down the door of a suspected crack house in the Bronx. Only in larger cities do plainclothes and detective units include specialties such as vice and drug enforcement.

one exists). County government usually has responsibility for prosecuting defendants, and a county-level agency, typically the sheriff, is usually responsible for operating jails. The county may also have a department with general policing responsibilities, independent of or part of the sheriff's office. Almost every municipality has a police department, whose officers enforce laws involving organized criminal activity. Each of these levels of government has taxing authority and allocates resources with little or no consultation with other levels of government. The result is a degree of inefficiency that surpasses that of most democratic nations.

American efforts against drug trafficking are limited by national boundaries: cocaine and heroin originate where U.S. law enforcement has no jurisdiction. The Bureau of International Narcotics Matters, within the U.S. Department of State, is the primary agency responsible for coordinating international programs and gaining the cooperation of foreign governments in antidrug efforts. But the bureau has no authority to force governments to act in a manner most beneficial to U.S. efforts in dealing with cocaine or heroin. The State Department collects intelligence on policy-level international drug developments, while the Central Intelligence Agency collects strategic narcotics intelligence and is responsible for coordinating foreign intelligence on narcotics. However, the CIA has often shielded drug traffickers who have provided foreign intelligence information useful to that agency. U.S. efforts against drug trafficking are often sacrificed to foreign policy (Sciolino and Engelberg 1988; Golden 1995b). For example, the U.S.-backed contras in Nicaragua trafficked in cocaine, allegedly with the knowledge if not the assistance of the Central Intelligence Agency (Harmon 1993). Similar relationships in Southeast Asia are discussed in Chapter 13.

CORRUPTION

Two basic strategies are available to law enforcement agencies—reactive and proactive—and many use a combination of both. *Reactive law enforcement* has its parallel in firefighting: firefighters remain in their stations, equipment at the ready, until a call for service is received. Reactive law enforcement encourages citizens to report crimes; the agency then responds. This type of law enforcement is used for dealing with conventional crimes such as murder, rape, assault, robbery, burglary, and theft—crimes that are likely to be discovered by or reported to the police. (However, it should be noted that with the exception of murder and auto theft, studies indicate that most of these crimes do not come to the attention of the police.) *Proactive law enforcement* requires officers/agents to seek out indications of criminal behavior, a necessity when the nature of the criminal violation includes victim participation: examples are gambling, prostitution, and drugs. These crimes are often referred to as "victimless" because the victims are unlikely to report the crime.

In order to seek out criminal activity in the most efficient manner possible, proactive law enforcement officers must conceal their identities and otherwise deceive the criminals they are stalking. James Q. Wilson (1978: 59) points out that both reactive and proactive law enforcement officers are exposed to opportunities for graft but that the latter are more severely tested: the reactive law enforcement officer, "were he to accept money or favors to act other than as his duty required, would have to conceal or alter information about a crime already known to his organization." However, the proactive enforcement agent "can easily agree to overlook offenses known to him but to no one else or to participate in illegal transactions (buying or selling drugs) for his own rather than for the organization's advantage." Undercover officers pretending to be criminals are difficult to supervise; the agency for which they work often knows about their activities only to the extent that the agents inform it.

In 1996, prosecutors in New York City had to throw out cases against 98 drug defendants because the police officers involved in their cases were from the Uptown Manhattan 30th Precinct, where 33 officers were convicted of drug corruption charges (Kocieniewski 1997). The following year, prosecutors in Chicago had to drop charges in 120 drug cases because police officers involved in the cases were indicted for taking payoffs and extorting money from drug dealers (Warnick 1997). In 1998, 44 officers from five law enforcement agencies in the Cleveland area were charged with taking bribes to protect cocaine dealers in northern Ohio (Belluck 1998).

There is also the problem of corruption in foreign countries that grow, process, or serve as transshipment stations for illegal substances. "The corrupt official," notes the President's Commission on Organized Crime (1986c: 178), "is the *sine qua non* of drug trafficking." The commission concluded that "corruption linked to drug trafficking is a widespread phenomenon among political and military leaders, police and other authorities in virtually every country touched by the drug trade. The easily available and enormous amounts of money generated through drug transactions present a temptation too great for many in positions of authority to resist."

Nick Mitola, Jr.—Informant

Raised in middle-class circumstances and college educated, Nick Mitola, Jr., became a career criminal at an early age. He moved from gambling to credit card scams to drugs and, after being convicted for drug trafficking, to informer. In return for his freedom, Mitola worked for the FBI, developing evidence against a crew from the New Jersey branch of the Lucchese Family headed by *caporegime* Anthony ("Tumac") Accetturo. At the same time—without the knowledge of his FBI handler—Mitola continued in the drug business. In this capacity, he began dealing with a DEA informant: "Not only was an undercover FBI informant dealing with an undercover DEA informant without either agency realizing that the other was an informant, but the DEA informant was cheating the DEA. In the spirit of true American entrepreneurs, the DEA informant claimed to be buying drugs from Mitola at a higher price than Mitola was actually selling them and, apparently, pocketing the difference" (Rudolph 1992: 341). In 1991, Mitola, who had entered the Witness Protection Program, was imprisoned for the stabbing death of an Iranian immigrant (Possley 1996).

A problem related to proactive law enforcement and corruption involves the use of informants.

Informants

The "snitch" or confidential informant (CI) comes in two basic categories, the "good citizen" and the "criminal." The former is so rare, particularly in OC law enforcement, that we will deal only with the criminal informant, an individual who provides help to law enforcement in order to further his or her own ends. These include financial rewards, vengeance, an effort to drive competition out of business, and, most frequently, "working off a beef"—securing leniency for criminal activities that have become known to the authorities.

Typically, "while serving as informers, suspects are unofficially allowed to engage in illegal activity" (Goldstein 1982: 37). The more involved is the informer in criminal activity, the more useful is his or her assistance. This raises serious ethical and policy questions. Should the informant be given immunity from lawful punishment in exchange for cooperation? If so, who is to make that determination—the agent who becomes aware of the informant's activities, his or her supervisor, the prosecutor who is informed of the situation, or a trial judge? Should a murderer be permitted to remain free because he or she is of value to OC law enforcement efforts?

Los Angeles intelligence detective Mike Rothmiller (1992: 89–90) points to a problem with using informants. He was sharing an informant with a DEA agent. On one occasion, he arranged to meet the DEA agent at the informant's home. When the detective walked in, he found the informant in the living room with at least a pound of cocaine on a glass table, dividing it up into sale packages—as the DEA agent looked on. Rothmiller motioned the agent into another room.

"What's going on here?" he said. The federal agent explained that his informant was helping him take down some other dealers and that he also claimed to have information on a major hydroponic marijuana-growing operation in Colorado. "You gotta do what you gotta do," the agent shrugged apologetically.

There are other dangers: "Given the number of law enforcement agencies and given their heavy dependence on intelligence, it is inevitable that there are informants who inform on other informants, who are probably informing on them. A consequence of that is selective prosecution: arbitrary decisions made by police officers and agents as to who will go to jail and who will be allowed to remain on the street. Given the vast amounts of money at stake in the drug business, selective prosecution raises the specter of corruption" (Eddy, Sabogal, and Walden 1988: 85).

This raises the problem of informant veracity. With strong incentives to produce information, how reliable is an informant? Journalist Jack Newfield (1979) quotes an FBI agent who specialized in OC cases: "I once had an informant who told me all sorts of stories. Later on I found out the guy was simultaneously an informant to the New York City Police Department, only I didn't know. What he was telling the police was completely different than what he was telling the bureau. And we were both paying him for his bullshit." In Chicago the FBI paid an informant $10,000 a month for his work in ferreting out corrupt union officials. Unfortunately, the money was wasted and, in at least one case, an innocent union official was framed by the informant. In 1999 the informant was convicted of lying to a grand jury and sentenced to 2.5 years in prison (M. O'Connor 1999b). In 1989 an informant in Los Angeles admitted that he had committed perjury in several cases and suggested that some men may have gone to death row based, at least in part, on his false testimony. The informant said he received prison furloughs, a recommendation for parole, a reduction of bail, and $2,700 for his efforts ("Jail Informer's Admissions Spur Inquiry" 1989; Reinhold 1989). One high school dropout began working as a paid informant for the DEA in 1984, after a hitch in the Marines. Despite the fact that the DEA was aware that he had compromised dozens of prosecutions by falsely testifying under oath and concealing his own arrest record, the agency continued to use—and pay—him until 2000, by which time he had earned $1.8 million (Thompson 2001).

Furthermore, working closely with informants is a potentially corrupting influence. The informant helps the agent enter an underworld filled with danger—and great financial rewards. Under such circumstances, there is always concern that the law enforcement agent may become something else to the informer—a friend, an employee, an employer, or a partner. The rewards can be considerable: the agent can confiscate money and drugs or receive payment for not arresting gamblers or traffickers and at the same time improve his or her work record by arresting competing or unaffiliated criminals. It is often only a small step from using criminals as informants to entering into business with them.

In 1982, FBI special agent Daniel A. Mitrione, an eleven-year veteran of the bureau, was assigned to an undercover operation involving drug trafficking. In his undercover role, the agent began working with an informant. As Arnold Trebach (1987: 343) reports, "In a familiar scenario that sometimes seems to flow naturally from the dynamics of the situation, one day the informer asked for the privilege of being a real dealer on the side while he was acting like one for the government. Agent Mitrione allowed the man to take a small load of cocaine to Miami and simply failed to tell his FBI supervisors about it. For this small initial courtesy, the appreciative informant-trafficker gave him $3,500 and a $9,000 Rolex watch. Over the next few years, the agent received more than $850,000 and eventually a ten-year prison term."

Criminal informants who testify against former colleagues present problems for any prosecutor. These persons typically have serious criminal histories that may equal or surpass those of the defendants. They are almost invariably provided with significant incentives to provide testimony. Acquittals occur in such cases when the informant is key to successful prosecution and juries do not accept the credibility of the witness.

One of the more bizarre agent–confidential informant relationships involves the case of Gregory Scarpa of the Colombo crime Family and his FBI handler. Known as the "Grim Reaper" because of his penchant for violence, Scarpa was a wealthy man who ran an important Colombo crew out of his social club in Bensonhurst, Brooklyn. Although arrested ten times from 1950 to 1985, his only jail time was 30 days for attempting to bribe a police officer.

After a six-week jury trial in 1995, two Colombo captains and five soldiers were acquitted of murder and firearms charges. Their defense centered on the relationship between Scarpa and his FBI handler, who was accused of giving the CI information to help his faction of the Colombo Family track down its opponents in a mob war.

Defense attorneys argued that the FBI agent used Scarpa to foment the war between rival factions of the crime Family that led to 10 dead and 14 wounded. The defendants claimed that their actions were an effort to avoid being killed (Raab 1994b, 1995a).

Scarpa's colleagues occasionally suspected his close relationship with the FBI. As one crew member recalls (Connolly 1996: 50), "We all suspected something, but a few days later we were in the club with Greg and a guy he hated. We're talking and joking, and out of nowhere, Greg whips out a piece and shoots the guy in the head. . . . [T]he guy's brains were all over me! My ears were ringing from the gunshot. Cool as he can be, he told us to roll the body in the rug and get rid of it. Nobody distrusted Greg after that day."

Scarpa's bizarre relationship with the FBI actually dates back to 1964. In that year, reportedly at the behest of J. Edgar Hoover, he traveled to Mississippi, where the FBI had been unable to solve the disappearance of three young civil rights workers. The Bensonhurst wiseguy quickly got to the heart of the case—he kidnapped a Philadelphia, Mississippi, Klansman and placed a gun in his mouth while starting to cut off the man's penis. Within 72 hours, the FBI had uncovered the three bodies and seven men had been arrested, including a deputy sheriff who had originally arrested the three young men (Robbins and Capeci 1994; Dannen 1996).

The potential dangers of involvement with criminal informants is exemplified by the actions of the FBI in Boston.

Boston Until the 1930s, much of organized crime in Boston was dominated by the Irish Gustin Gang. When they attempted to move into territory in the Italian North End, three of the gang were gunned down. The Irish eventually made their peace with the Italians, whose leader, Raymond Patriarca, operated out of Providence, Rhode Island. Despite the power of the Italians, local Irish-led gangs continued to have a presence in the Boston area, and one, the Winter Hill gang—Winter Hill is a neighborhood in the Boston suburb of Somerville—maintained a close working relationship with the Patriarca Family.

From "Southie," as the insular Irish neighborhood of South Boston is known, emerged the Bulger brothers, who grew up in a public housing project. William M. Bulger was president of the state senate for longer than anyone in history, until he stepped down to assume the presidency of the University of Massachusetts. Brother James ("Whitey") Bulger (b. 1929) was the vicious and widely feared crime boss of Southie. A delinquent in his youth, at 27 Whitey was serving federal time for bank robbery. When he returned home in 1965, to satisfy the conditions of his parole he took a political job as a courthouse custodian. His parole completed, Bulger became an enforcer and debt collector for a local bookmaker. When his boss became embroiled in a dispute with Howie Winter, head of the Winter Hill gang, Bulger abandoned him and allied himself with the predominantly Irish gang. With the backing of Howie Winter, Whitey became the leading gangster in Southie (Lehr and O'Neil 2000).

In 1976, in one of the more bizarre episodes in organized crime, Whitey Bulger became a government informant. Unbeknownst to Whitey at the time, his partner, Steve ("The Rifleman")[1] Flemmi (b. 1934)—who had declined an invitation to become a made guy in the Patriarca Family—had already been providing information to the FBI. According to Sean Flynn (1998), this arrangement resulted from an attempt by Jerry Angiulo, Patriarca Family underboss in charge of Boston, to use law enforcement authorities to take out the Winter Hill group—they were too dangerous for a more violent approach. Bulger and Flemmi succeeded in turning the tables—helping the FBI take out Angiulo. But, for the government, it was a bargain with the devil.

FBI field offices were under pressure to wage an effective war against the Italian mob, known in New England as the "Office." So, in return for informing on the Patriarca Family, Bulger and Flemmi were given virtually unbridled freedom to conduct their criminal business, safe in the

---

[1]Flemmi served as a paratrooper during the Korean War.

knowledge that they were protected by the FBI. If Bulger's victims complained to the FBI, his case agent would see to it that nothing happened, as when vending machine executives complained that Bulger and Flemmi were shaking them down. When the husband and wife owners of a liquor store complained that Bulger and Flemmi had threatened to kill them if they would not sell it to the pair at a "bargain" price, the FBI asked the frightened couple to wear a wire—and tipped off Bulger. Other victims who insisted on action were told of the need to testify and enter the Witness Protection Program. When the Massachusetts State Police conducted its own investigation, which included electronic surveillance, Bulger and Flemmi were tipped off by the FBI. They were also tipped about DEA and local police attempts at electronic surveillance.

Emboldened by their FBI protection, Bulger and Flemmi engaged in a systematic shakedown of independent bookmakers and loansharks in the south Boston area. Howie Winter was imprisoned in 1978, and Bulger took over the Winter Hill gang. When cocaine become popular in the 1980s, Bulger and Flemmi extended their shakedowns to include drug dealers. And then there were murders. In 1981, to protect an embezzling accountant, Bulger had the notorious Winter Hill hit man John Martorano kill a business executive in Tulsa, Oklahoma. Martorano was then sent to Florida, and the accountant was found stuffed into the trunk of a car at the Miami airport. In 1982, Bulger was the executioner of a Winter Hill member who had turned informant (Butterfield 1997; Lehr and O'Neil 2000).

Raymond Patriarca was indicted in 1980—for labor racketeering—and in 1981—for ordering a double execution. In 1984, while charges were still pending, he died of natural causes. Raymond Patriarca, Jr., claimed the position and, with the approval of the New York Families, became boss of the Office. By 1989, Junior's reign was in trouble. Information being provided by Bulger and Flemmi and electronic bugs led to the convictions of almost every member of the Boston branch of the Office. Replacements chosen by Junior irritated the Providence branch, and a war broke out.

In an effort to restore peace, an initiation ceremony was staged in 1989 to allow four new members, three from Boston, one from Providence, to be made. The ceremony was recorded by two electronic eavesdropping devices placed in the basement ceiling of a house in a Boston suburb. It was the first time that the FBI had been able to record a Mafia initiation. In 1991, Patriarca pleaded guilty to racketeering and was sentenced to eight years. Another two years were added as the result of a government appeal of the original sentence. He was released on parole in 1998. Further prosecutions decimated the New England crime Family.

In 1995, Bulger and Flemmi were indicted by a federal grand jury for racketeering and extortion; the Rifleman was arrested, and Whitey became a fugitive. In 1999, during his trial, Flemmi's attorney argued that the federal government cannot prosecute crimes that it effectively authorizes informers to commit (Goldberg 1999; especially *United States of America v. Stephen J. Flemmi*, U.S. Court of Appeals for the First Circuit, No. 99–2292 [2000]). The chief witness against him was John Martorano, 62, who admitted to 20 murders in return of a sentence of 10–12.5 years. Since Bulger and Flemmi were informants, it is believed that Maratorano felt he had no obligation to be loyal to them. In 2001, in exchange for a plea of guilty, Flemmi was sentenced to 10 years for extortion and money laundering. He still faces several murder charges.

The success of the FBI in prosecuting the Patriarca Family was marred by revelations concerning the activities of some of its agents. In 1999 a federal grand jury indicted a retired FBI agent on charges of conspiring with Bulger and Flemmi, receiving gifts, and protecting their criminal activities. As a result of disclosures from this case, it was revealed that in order to protect their informants, the FBI allowed three men to be convicted and imprisoned for a murder they did not commit. Furthermore, the FBI knew of the murder plan and did not intervene. One of the three falsely convicted died in prison; another had his sentence commuted and was released from prison in 1997; the third had his conviction vacated and was released from prison in 2001 after serving more than

33 years, 4 of them on death row (C. Goldberg 2001).

STATUTES

The business of organized crime involves the violation of numerous laws. Many of these statutes are routinely enforced by municipal police departments, including laws against gambling, drugs, prostitution, assault, and murder. However, the investigation and prosecution of organized crime per se have largely been the responsibility of the federal government, which has a number of specialized statutes to carry out this purpose. Chief among them are the Internal Revenue Code, the Controlled Substances Act, the Hobbs Act, the Racketeer Influenced and Corrupt Organizations (RICO) statute, the Continuing Criminal Enterprise statute, the Consumer Credit Protection Act, statutes against conspiracy, and the anti-money-laundering provision of Title 18.

The Internal Revenue Code

In 1927 the U.S. Supreme Court decided the case of *United States v. Sullivan* (274 U.S. 259), which denied the claim of self-incrimination as an excuse for failure to file income tax on illegally gained earnings. This decision enabled the federal government to successfully prosecute Al Capone and members of his organization. Because persons in organized crime have obligations as taxpayers, they can be prosecuted for several acts:

1. Failing to make required returns or maintain required business records
2. Filing a false return or making a false statement about taxes
3. Willful failure to pay federal income tax or concealment of assets with intent to defraud
4. Helping others evade income taxes
5. In gambling operations, failing to file a "Special Tax Return and Application for Registry-Wagering"

"Acts which do not comprise a violation or attempt to violate any of these substantive sections may be punishable as part of a conspiracy 'to impair, defeat, and obstruct the functions of the Commissioner of Internal Revenue' by concealing matters relevant to collection of federal taxes" (Johnson 1963: 17). An employer can be prosecuted for not complying with Social Security withholding requirements relative to employees. Thus, the manager of an illegal enterprise—a gambling operation, for example—could be prosecuted for such evasions.

The Internal Revenue Service of the Department of the Treasury employs special agents in the Criminal Investigation Division (CID). While the primary role of the IRS is collection of revenue and compliance with tax codes, the CID seeks evidence of criminal violations for prosecution by the Department of Justice. In particular, the agents seek out information relative to income that has not been reported: "Additional income for criminal purposes is established by both direct and indirect methods. The direct method consists of the identification of specific items of unreported taxable receipts, overstated costs and expenses (such as personal expenses charged to business, diversion of corporate income to office-stockholders, allocation of income or expense to incorrect year in order to lower tax, etc.), and improper claims for credit or exemption. The advantage of using this method is that the proof involved is easier for jurors and others to understand" (Committee on the Office of Attorney General 1974: 49–50).

Persons in organized crime have devised methods for the successful evasion of taxes—dealing in cash, keeping minimal records, and setting up fronts. This is countered by the indirect method known as the *net-worth theory:* "The government establishes a taxpayer's net worth at the commencement of the taxing period [which requires substantial accuracy], deducts that from his or her net worth at the end of the period, and proves that the net gain in net worth exceeds the income reported by the taxpayer" (Johnson 1963: 17–19). In effect, the Internal Revenue Service reconstructs a person's total expenditures by examining the person's actual standard of living and comparing it with reported income. The government

Antidiversion Legislation

The principal statute to control the diversion of precursor and essential chemicals for the manufacture of drugs is the Chemical Diversion and Trafficking Act, Subtitle A of the Anti-Drug Abuse Amendments of 1988. The act established record-keeping requirements and enforcement standards for more than two dozen precursor and essential chemicals. State and federal statutes make the unauthorized trade in any of the listed substances equivalent to trafficking in the actual illegal drugs. There are three basic requirements for all manufacturers and distributors:

1. They must keep retrievable records of the distribution, receipt, sale, importation, or exportation of any of the chemicals or machines on a special list prepared pursuant to the act.
2. They must report certain unusual or suspicious orders for these substances to the DEA.
3. They must obtain proof of identity for customers, whether individuals or companies.

The DEA is authorized to stop the import or export of precursor and essential chemicals if their use cannot be shown to have legitimate medical, scientific, or commercial purposes (DeWitt 1993).

---

can then maintain that the taxpayer did not report his or her entire income. The government does not have to show a probable source of the excess unreported gain in net worth. Earl Johnson (1963: 18) points out that the Capone case taught many criminals a lesson: "management-level persons in organized crime scrupulously report their income—at least the part of it that they spend."

In 2002 a federal judge ruled that money paid to organized crime—$1.7 million per year to a captain in the Gambino Family—for protection of coin-operated video pornographic booths was not a deductible business expense. The judge found that although such payments might qualify as ordinary and necessary payments in this industry, the defendant had attempted to hide the payments from the IRS, and the judge ruled that this disqualified the deduction (Johnston 2002).

The Controlled Substances Statutes

In 1914 the Harrison Act made it illegal to sell or give away opium or opium derivatives and coca or its derivatives without written order on a form issued by the Commissioner of Revenue. Persons who were not registered were prohibited from engaging in interstate traffic in the drugs, and no one could possess any of the drugs who had not registered and paid the special tax under a penalty of up

to five years' imprisonment and a fine of no more than $2,000.

By 1970, the issue of federal police authority had been largely resolved, and the Comprehensive Drug Abuse Prevention and Control Act of 1970 represented a new legal approach to federal drug policy—it was predicated not on the constitutional power to tax but on federal authority over interstate commerce. This shift had enormous implications for the way in which the federal government would approach drug enforcement in the future. The act "set the stage for an innovation in Federal drug law enforcement techniques. That innovation was the assigning of large numbers of Federal narcotic agents to work in local communities. No longer was it necessary to demonstrate interstate traffic to justify Federal participation in combating illegal drug use" (PCOC 1986c: 28). The new approach was sustained by decisions of the Supreme Court. The 1970 legislation establishes five schedules into which all controlled substances could be placed according to their potential for abuse (see Figure 14.1).

The Comprehensive Crime Control Act of 1984 supplemented the 1970 drug statute by authorizing the doubling of a sentence for drug offenders with prior domestic or foreign felony drug convictions. The Anti-Drug Abuse Act of 1986 imposes mandatory prison sentences for certain

FIGURE 14.1   *Schedules of Controlled Substances*

SCHEDULE I

A. The drug or other substance has a high potential for abuse.
B. The drug or other substance has no currently accepted medical use in treatment in the United States.
C. There is a lack of accepted safety for use of the drug or other substance under medical supervision.

SCHEDULE II

A. The drug or other substance has a high potential for abuse.
B. The drug or other substance has a currently accepted medical use in treatment in the United States or a currently accepted medical use with severe restrictions.
C. Abuse of the drug or other substances may lead to severe psychological or physical dependence.

SCHEDULE III

A. The drug or other substance has a potential for abuse less than the drugs or other substances in Schedules I and II.
B. The drug or other substance has a currently accepted medical use in treatment in the United States.
C. Abuse of the drug or other substance may lead to moderate or low physical dependence or high psychological dependence.

SCHEDULE IV

A. The drug or other substance has a low potential for abuse relative to the drugs or other substances in Schedule III.
B. The drug or other substance has a currently accepted medical use in treatment in the United States.
C. Abuse of the drug or other substance may lead to limited physical dependence or psychological dependence relative to the drugs or other substances in Schedule III.

SCHEDULE V

A. The drug or other substance has a low potential for abuse relative to the drugs or other substances in Schedule IV.
B. The drug or other substance has a currently accepted medical use in treatment in the United States.
C. Abuse of the drug or other substances may lead to limited physical dependence or psychological dependence relative to the drugs or other substance in Schedule IV.

Source: Drug Enforcement Administration.

---

drug offenses and a mandatory doubling of the minimum penalties for offenders with prior felony drug convictions. In 1988 the military's role in drug-law enforcement was substantially increased, and Congress enacted another drug abuse act that mandates greater control over precursor chemicals and devices used to manufacture drugs, such as encapsulating machinery.

The Anti-Drug Abuse Amendments of 1988 created a complex and extensive body of civil penalties aimed at casual users. These include withdrawal of federal benefits, such as mortgage guarantees, and loss of a pilot's license or stockbroker's license, at the discretion of a federal judge. Fines of up to $10,000 can be imposed for illegal possession of even small amounts of controlled substances. There are special penalties for the sale of drugs to minors. The statute permits imposition of capital punishment for murders committed as part of a continuing criminal enterprise or for the murder of a law enforcement officer during an arrest for a drug-related felony. The statute also established an Office of National Drug Policy, headed by a director appointed by the president. The director is charged with coordinating federal drug supply reduction efforts, including international control, intelligence, interdiction, domestic law enforcement, treatment, education, and research.

The Hobbs Act

The earliest statutes designed to deal with "racketeering" are collectively known as the Hobbs Act

(18 U.S.C. Sections 1951–55). Since 1946, they have been amended several times. The Hobbs Act makes it a federal crime to engage in criminal behavior that interferes with interstate commerce:

> Whosoever in any way or degree obstructs, delays, or affects commerce or the movement of any articles or commodity in commerce, by robbery or extortion or attempts or conspires to do so, or commits or threatens physical violence to any person or property in furtherance of a plan or purpose to do anything in violation of this section shall be fined not more than $10,000 or imprisonment for not more than twenty years or both.

The statute has been broadly interpreted so as to permit the successful prosecution of more than 60 Chicago police officers for extorting payoffs from the owners of saloons. The six-year investigation (1970–1976) by the U.S. Department of Justice was based on the part of the Hobbs Act that makes extortion that in any way affects interstate commerce a federal crime: federal attorneys "reasoned that because taverns sold beer and liquor, much of which was either delivered from or manufactured in states other than Illinois, extortion of a tavern owner would be a violation of the Hobbs Act" (Biegel and Biegel 1977: 7).

The Hobbs Act also prohibits foreign or interstate travel or the use of interstate facilities, such as the mails or telephones, to advance illegal activities such as gambling, drug trafficking, extortion, and bribery. This permitted the federal government to prosecute corrupt officials and lawyers in Cook County, Illinois—"Operation Greylord"— in the late 1980s and early 1990s. Section 1954 defines as criminal a union official who misuses an employee benefit plan: "An official who receives or agrees to or solicits any fee, kickback, commission, gift, loan, money, or thing of value because of or with intent to be influenced with respect to, any of the actions, decisions, or other duties relating to any question or matter concerning such plan or any persons who directly or indirectly gives or offers, or promises to give or offer, any fee, kickback, commission, gift, loan, money, or thing of value

prohibited by this section, shall be fined not more than $10,000 or imprisoned for not more than three years, or both."

Conspiracy

The United States does not criminalize participation in a criminal organization as such, since to do so might violate constitutional prohibitions against measures inhibiting freedom of association. However, both at the federal level and in most of the states, conspiracies to commit offenses are punishable. Under the laws of the United States and in most of the states, conspiracy is defined as an agreement to do an act that is unlawful or to do an act that is lawful by unlawful means. For someone to be convicted of violating the general conspiracy statutes of federal law in the United States, it is necessary that the prosecution prove that two or more persons agreed to commit an offense and that one or more of these persons did at least one act to carry out the agreement.

To prove a conspiracy, it is not necessary to show that the offense was actually committed. Conspiracy is an agreement between two or more persons to commit a criminal act; it is the *agreement* that becomes the *corpus* (body) of the crime. Conspiracy requires proof (beyond a reasonable doubt) that two or more persons planned to violate the law and, in most but not all instances, that at least one overt act[2] in furtherance of the conspiracy was made by a conspirator, such as the purchase of materials to aid in the transportation or dilution of drugs. Conspiracy statutes provide valuable tools for prosecuting persons in organized crime:

- Intervention can occur prior to the commission of a substantive offense.
- A conspirator cannot shield himself or herself from prosecution because of a lack of knowledge of the details of the conspiracy or

---

[2]Federal drug conspiracy laws do not refer to *overt acts*, and in 1994 the Supreme Court (*United States v. Shabani*, 115 S.Ct. 382) ruled that conspiring to violate federal drug laws can be a crime even in the absence of an overt act.

the identity of co-conspirators and their contributions.

- An act or declaration by one conspirator committed in furtherance of the conspiracy is admissible against each co-conspirator (an exception to the hearsay rule).
- Each conspirator is responsible for the substantive crimes of his or her co-conspirators; even late joiners can be held liable for prior acts of co-conspirators if the agreement by the latecomer is made with full knowledge of the conspiracy's objective.

The charge of conspiracy, which federal prosecutors generally include whenever a case involves multiple defendants (Campane 1981a), is particularly effective against upper-echelon OC figures: "The fundamental essence of a conspiracy obviates the necessity of establishing that the organization leader committed a physical act amounting to a crime or that he even committed an overt act in furtherance of the object of the conspiracy. It is sufficient if he can be shown to have been a party to the conspiratorial agreement" (Johnson 1963: 2). Its usefulness can be seen in the following incident:

> Two young men entered an Italian restaurant and approached the table of an elderly gentleman who was sipping anisette with a large, burly individual. After he acknowledged them, the two sat down at the table. They were members of the Genovese crime Family; the older man was the boss. The young men explained that they had just discovered a large-scale gambling operation that was not tied to OC—an "outlaw" game. They wanted to "license" the operation and asked for his approval. The boss gestured with his hands and face, saying nothing, but conveying approval. The two young men excused themselves and left. With several other members of the Family, they proceeded to assault and threaten to kill the owner of the gambling operation, extorting several thousand dollars from him. They returned and shared the money with their boss, who knew nothing of the details of what had occurred.

There are three basic types of conspiracy:

1. *Wheel conspiracies.* One person at the "hub" conspires individually with two or more persons who make up the "spokes" of the wheel. For the conspiracy to be (legally) complete, the wheel needs a "rim": each of the spokes must be aware of and agree with each other in pursuit of at least one objective.

2. *Chain conspiracies.* Like the lights on a Christmas tree, each conspirator is dependent on the successful participation of every other member. Each member is a "link" who understands that the success of the scheme depends upon everyone in the chain.

3. *Enterprise conspiracies.* The RICO enterprise conspiracy avoids the practical limitations inherent in proving wheel and chain conspiracies. The statute makes it a separate crime to conspire to violate state or federal law as the result of an agreement to participate in an *enterprise* by engaging in a *pattern of racketeering activity*. Members of the conspiracy need not know one another or even be aware of one another's criminal activities. All that needs to be shown is each member's agreement to participate in the organization—the *enterprise*—by committing two or more acts of racketeering such as gambling or drug violations within a ten-year period (a pattern of racketeering). The enterprise conspiracy enables mass trials with each member of the enterprise subject to the significant penalties—20 years' imprisonment on each count—that can result from a conviction.

Prosecuting criminal conspiracy cases can be problematic. In a 1974 case (*United States v. Sperling*, 506 F.2d 1323, 1341, 2d Cir.), the court noted that "it has become too common for the government to bring indictments against a dozen or more defendants and endeavor to force as many of them as possible to trial in the same proceeding on the claim of a single conspiracy when the criminal acts could more reasonably be regarded as two or more conspiracies, perhaps with a link at the top. This creates the risk of 'guilt by association,' wherein a jury, confronted by a large number of defendants and a great volume of evidence, is unable to give each defendant the individual consideration that due process requires. In such situations, a finding of guilty brings with it the risk of being reversed on appeal." Constitutional guarantees of a fair trial "make it imperative to determine whether the evidence establishes one large conspiracy as opposed to multiple smaller ones" (Campane 1981b: 30).

Another considerable problem is that conspiracy cases usually require direct testimony of eyewitnesses; these are often participants in the conspiracy who agree to testify ("flip") against their co-conspirators in exchange for leniency or immunity from prosecution: "An investigator should therefore be prepared to locate witnesses (often immunized co-conspirators) who are willing to testify and are able to explain the complicated or intricate nature of the unlawful activity, and as a consequence, the stake in the venture or mutual dependence each participant has with each other" (Campane 1981b: 29).

RICO

The *Racketeer Influenced and Corrupt Organizations* statute (18 U.S.C. Sections 1961–68), usually referred to as RICO, is the most important single piece of legislation ever enacted against organized crime. Part of the Organized Crime Control Act of 1970, RICO defines racketeering in an extremely broad manner, and it includes many offenses that do not ordinarily violate any federal statute: "any act or threat involving murder, kidnapping, gambling, arson, robbery, bribery, extortion, or dealing in narcotic or other dangerous drugs, which is chargeable under State law and punishable by imprisonment for more than one year." In addition, there is a "laundry list" of federal offenses that are defined as "racketeering":

- Hobbs Act violations
- Bribery
- Sports bribery
- Counterfeiting
- Embezzlement from union funds
- Loansharking
- Mail fraud
- Wire fraud

- Obstruction of (state or federal) justice
- Contraband cigarettes
- White slavery (Mann Act violations)
- Bankruptcy fraud (scam)
- Drug violations
- Obscenity (added in 1984)

RICO has provided the federal government with jurisdiction that heretofore had been exclusively that of state and local law enforcement, which are often ineffective in dealing with organized crime. As a result, the FBI became the lead agency in organized crime law enforcement.

Under traditional conspiracy statutes, prosecution for engaging in "organized crime" requires agreement among the participants about the specific crime(s). Given the diverse and often unrelated crimes committed by members of organized crime, the use of conspiracy statutes proved difficult. The thrust of RICO is to prove a pattern of crimes conducted through an organization—an *enterprise:* "any individual, partnership, corporation, association, or other legal entity, and any union or group of individuals associated in fact, although not a legal entity." In place of having to prove a series of separate conspiracies, under RICO it is a crime to belong to an enterprise—for example, an OC Family or outlaw motorcycle club—that is involved in a "pattern of racketeering," even if the "racketeering" was committed by other members: "It shall be unlawful for any person employed by or associated with any enterprise engaged in, or the activities of which affect, interstate or foreign commerce, to conduct or participate, directly or indirectly, in the conduct of such enterprise's affairs through a pattern of racketeering activity or collection of an unlawful debt." The enterprise must contain some structure distinct from the "pattern of racketeering" (Bourgeois et al. 2000).

In order for "racketeering" to be a RICO violation, there must be a "pattern," which requires the commission of at least two of the specified crimes within a ten-year period, although, in ruling against anti-abortion activists, the Supreme Court has determined that RICO does not require defendants to have an economic motive. However, isolated criminal acts do not constitute a "pattern." Instead, there must be a relationship between the two (or more) predicate crimes over a substantial period of time.

The criminal penalties for violating RICO are substantial: "Whoever violates any provision of section 1962 of this chapter shall be fined not more than $25,000 or imprisoned not more than twenty years, or both." In addition to the criminal penalties, there are civil forfeiture provisions, requiring the violator to forfeit to the government any business or property that he or she has acquired in violation of RICO. The government can also freeze a defendant's assets before trial.

Under the provisions of RICO, the government can file a petition in federal district court seeking to have a branch (local) of a labor union, or even the leadership of the union itself, removed and the entity placed in receivership. As noted in Chapter 12, this was done with Local 560 of the International Brotherhood of Teamsters (the "Tony Pro local") and Local 54 of the Hotel Employees and Restaurant Employees Union.

RICO also has provisions by which private citizens can sue for damages: "Any person injured in his business or property by reason of a violation of section 1962 of this chapter may sue therefore in any appropriate United States district court and shall recover threefold damages he sustains and the cost of the suit, including a reasonable attorney's fee." In *NOW v. Scheidler* (510 U.S. 249 [1994]), the Supreme Court ruled unanimously that abortion clinics can invoke RICO to sue violent anti-abortion protest groups for damages.[3] In 1998 a federal jury in Chicago found three leading anti-abortion activists liable under RICO and awarded $85,000 to two abortion clinics, an amount tripled by the judge as per the statute (Pallasch and Peres 1998). In an editorial, the *New York Times* noted that "The use of RICO has raised legitimate concern that this precedent could be expanded to obstruct free speech and political protest" ("Abortion Harassers as Racketeers" 1998).

While it took some time for federal prosecu-

tors to fully understand and incorporate RICO into their array of prosecutorial tools, it has become clear that the use of the statute has been quite effective. By 1990, more than 1,000 major and minor organized crime figures had been convicted and given lengthy prison sentences: "The hierarchies of the five New York LCN Families have been prosecuted, and similar prosecutions have dented the LCN hierarchies in Boston, Cleveland, Denver, Kansas City, Milwaukee, New Jersey, Philadelphia, Pittsburgh and St. Louis" (Pennsylvania Crime Commission 1990: 18). In fact, the threat of lengthy imprisonment under RICO provides a "stick" that has been used to gain the cooperation of defendants. Rudolph W. Giuliani (1987: 106), former U.S. Attorney for the Southern District of New York, who successfully used RICO in prosecuting OC cases, points out that "the federal prosecutor derives a variety of benefits from the RICO statute's definitions of enterprise and racketeering activity. For example, it is the only criminal statute that enables the Government to present a jury with the whole picture of how an enterprise, such as an organized crime family, operates. Rather than pursuing the leader of a small group of subordinates for a single crime or scheme, the Government is able to indict the entire hierarchy of an organized crime family for the diverse criminal activities in which that 'enterprise' engages. Instead of merely proving one criminal act in a defendant's life, it permits proof of a defendant's whole life in crime." Giuliani provides an example, the successful prosecution of the Colombo Family.

Criticism of RICO Four basic criticisms of RICO have been raised:

1. RICO is overreaching, leading to the prosecution of persons who, although they may have been involved in criminal behavior, are not by any stretch of the imagination connected to organized crime.
2. Invoking RICO can result in assets being frozen even before a trial begins, an action that can effectively put a company out of business. The threat of freezing

---

[3]For a discussion of this case, see Randolph (1995) and Vitielo (1995).

RICO and the Colombo Crime Family

Fourteen defendants were indicted as either leaders, members, or associates of the Colombo Family of La Cosa Nostra. In setting forth the "enterprise," the indictment identified the three "bosses" of the Family and five *capos,* who were all charged with supervising and protecting the criminal activities of the subordinates of the Family. The leadership as well as the lower-ranking members were included within the Family "enterprise" as a group of individuals associated in fact. The ongoing nature of the enterprise was demonstrated by the fact that the Family selected an acting boss to direct its criminal activities while the boss was in jail. Reliance entirely upon traditional conspiracy law without RICO would not have enabled the government to include all of these individuals within a single prosecution or to identify each of their specific roles within the enterprise.

In addition, RICO's requirement of proving a "pattern of racketeering activity" and its broad definition of "racketeering activity" allowed the prosecution to join in a single indictment the widely diverse state and federal crimes that the Colombo Family had engaged in over the past 15 years. Thus, the indictment included charges that the Family had engaged in extortion, labor racketeering, drug trafficking, gambling, loansharking, and both state and federal bribery violations. The prosecution was also able to include as predicate acts of racketeering the prior federal bribery convictions of three of the defendants.

Moreover, venue in RICO cases permits the prosecution of a continuing offense in any district in which such offense was begun, continued, or completed. Thus, the prosecution was able to include crimes committed in the Southern and Eastern Districts of New York, as well as in Florida and New Jersey.

Finally, because of RICO's broad definition of a pattern of racketeering activity, it was possible for the prosecutors to include predicate offenses in which the criminal conduct occurred at a time beyond the reach of the general federal five-year statute of limitations. In this regard, all that RICO requires is that one act of racketeering occurred after the effective date of the statute (October 15, 1970) and that the last or most recent predicate act occurred within ten years of a prior act of racketeering. Given these provisions, the prosecution was permitted to charge a 1970 heroin transaction as well as extortions that took place in 1975 (Giuliani 1987).

---

assets can induce corporate defendants to plead guilty even when they believe themselves to be innocent.

3. A RICO action brings with it the stigma of being labeled a "racketeer," which may be inappropriate given the circumstances at issue.
4. RICO permits lawsuits for triple damages when ordinary business transactions, not organized crime or racketeering, are at issue.

The Organized Crime Act (of which RICO is a part) fails to define *organized crime,* and RICO fails to define *racketeer.* This lack of precision coupled with the substantial penalties makes RICO a tempting tool for federal prosecutors to use against persons who are not connected to organized crime, no matter how widely that term is defined. In Chicago, for example, a deputy sheriff and a traffic court clerk were convicted under RICO for helping to fix parking tickets. In New York, the U.S. attorney used RICO against a small commodities firm for a transaction so commonplace that on some days, such transactions account for a third of the volume on the New York Stock Exchange (Epstein 1988a). In 1988 the government brought a RICO indictment against a securities firm, seeking $500,000 in illegal profits. However, prosecutors insisted on a bond of $24 million, forcing the company to liquidate before a trial even began (Nocera 1988).

Supporters argue that RICO has been very effective in combating corporate crime that has traditionally proven difficult to prosecute successfully (Waldman and Gilbert 1989). Illegal business practices—crimes—can certainly be defined as organized if they are sufficiently large in scale and are continuously performed by specialists, even in the absence of violence and/or corruption. For example, securities violations involving prestigious brokerage firms have been successfully prosecuted using RICO.

About 1,000 civil racketeering suits are filed each year by private plaintiffs (the government averages about 100 per year) seeking to recover triple damages from a variety of defendants—business competitors, swindlers, securities brokers, unions, and, as noted earlier, anti-abortion activists. There are so many cases that the practice has spawned its own publication: *RICO Law Reporter*.

While private cases have generally proven hard to win, critics argue that the threat of triple damages—and of being referred to as a "racketeer"—causes many defendants to settle. Furthermore, the triple-damage provision encourages contingency lawyers to sue when under ordinary circumstances the potential reward would not be worth the commitment of time. However, the courts have fined lawyers for bringing frivolous racketeering claims (Diamond 1988). One critic (O'Brien 1986) argues that in contract disputes, attorneys routinely add RICO violations, thereby removing their cases from state court and overloading federal courts. Law professor Robert Blakey (1986), author of RICO, argues that the civil sections provide a powerful tool for persons victimized by swindlers to recover their losses and also serve as a deterrent. To avoid the problem of inappropriate labeling, some recommend that the term *racketeer* be removed from the civil aspects of the statute (Waldman and Gilbert 1989).

In the first case to limit the scope of a state RICO law, the U.S. Supreme Court ruled that the inventory of a Fort Wayne, Indiana, adult bookstore could not be subjected to seizure in advance of an obscenity conviction. In a unanimous decision, the Court referred to prohibitions against "prior restraint" of publications that had not yet been judged to be obscene. In a 6–3 vote, however, the Court rejected a claim that the First Amendment prohibits the use of RICO to prosecute obscenity cases and left open the possibility that the materials could be confiscated if obscenity was proven at trial (*Fort Wayne Books, Inc. v. Indiana, et al.*, 488 U.S. 445, 1989). That same year, the Supreme Court unanimously refused to limit the scope of RICO with respect to private suits (*H.J., Inc. v. Northwestern Bell Telephone Co.*, 492 U.S. 229).

The Commission Case   Use of the RICO statute resulted in one of the most important prosecutions ever brought against organized crime in the United States. A task force of personnel from federal, state, and local law enforcement agencies targeted the commission of OC Families in New York. Electronic surveillance was used on an unprecedented scale—bugs were planted in cars, homes, and social clubs. In addition, the Bonanno Family was penetrated by an FBI agent to the point of his being proposed for membership (see Pistone 1987): "The theory of the government's case was that the Cosa Nostra commission constituted a criminal enterprise, that each defendant had committed two or more racketeering acts in furtherance of the commission's goals. According to the prosecution, the defendant's predicate racketeering acts fell into three categories: first, management of a multifamily bid-rigging and extortion scheme in the New York concrete industry; second, conspiracy to organize loansharking territories in Staten Island; and, third, the murders of Bonanno family boss Carmine Galente and two of his associates [discussed in Chapter 3] in furtherance of the commission's effort to resolve a Bonanno family leadership dispute" (Jacobs 1994: 81).

During the course of the trial, the defense admitted the existence of *Cosa Nostra* and the commission. However, they denied the commission's involvement in criminal activity, but to no avail: in 1986 all of the defendants, including Carmine Persico, boss of the Colombo Family, Anthony Salerno, boss of the Genovese Family, and Anthony Corallo, boss of the Lucchese Family, were found guilty. Charges against Paul Castellano, boss of the Gambino Family, were dropped after his murder (*United States v. Salerno*, 85 CR 139 SDNY 1985).

Continuing Criminal Enterprise

The Continuing Criminal Enterprise (CCE) statute (21 U.S.C. 848) is similar in purpose to RICO but targets only illegal drug activity. The statute makes it a crime to commit or conspire to commit a continuing series of felony violations of the 1970 Drug Abuse Prevention and Control Act when the violations are undertaken in concert with five or more persons. The courts have ruled that *series* requires three or more violations: "For conviction under this statute, the offender must have been an organizer, manager, or supervisor of the continuing operation and have obtained substantial income or resources from the drug violations" (Carlson and Finn 1993: 2). In 1999 the Supreme Court ruled (*Richardson v. United States*, No. 97–8629) that juries must agree on which specific illegal acts were committed by a defendant, rather than simply finding that he or she committed a series of drug violations without specifying which ones. The 6–3 decision will make it harder to convict persons for violating the CCE.

The Consumer Credit Protection Act (CCPA)

The 1968 Consumer Credit Act (18 U.S.C. Sections 891–94) was designed to combat loansharking. It provides a definition of a loanshark debt as any extension of credit with respect to which is the *understanding* of the creditor and the debtor at the time the loan is made that delay in making repayment or failure to make repayment could result in the use of violence or other criminal means to cause harm to the person, his or her reputation, or the property of any person. The statute chose the term *understanding*, note Ronald Goldstock and Dan Coenen (1978: 65), "in an obvious effort to catch the many loansharks who operate purely on the basis of implication and veiled suggestion." The critical element of the offense is the under-

standing that violence "could result" if repayment is not timely. The statute even provides for an alternative to direct evidence. An implied threat can be assumed: "The state must show the debtor's reasonable belief that the creditor had used, or had a reputation for using, 'extortionate means' to collect or punish nonpayment. Second, if direct evidence of this sort is unavailable (as when the victim is dead or too frightened to testify) and certain other prerequisites are met, the court may allow evidence tending to show the creditor's reputation as to collection practices to show the 'understanding' element" (Goldstock and Coenen 1978: 110–11).

The CCPA also contains a provision intended to make it possible to prosecute upper levels of the OC hierarchy who, although they may not make the loans themselves, are often the original source of funding for extortionate credit transactions made directly by underlings (18 U.S.C. Section 893): "Whoever willfully advances money or property, whether as a gift, as a loan, as an investment, pursuant to a partnership or profit-sharing agreement, or otherwise, to any person, with the reasonable grounds to believe that it is the intention of that person of making extortionate extensions of credit, shall be fined not more than $10,000 or an amount not to exceed twice the value of the money or property so advanced, whichever is greater, or shall be imprisoned not more than 20 years, or both." The same penalties hold for the loanshark actually making the loan and to those who assist in attempting to collect an extortionate extension of credit.

Forfeiture

For obvious reasons—funds available without taxation—governments have found forfeiture very attractive. In 1972, Hawaii enacted civil RICO legislation with the seizure and forfeiture provision, and by 1989, 25 other states had enacted similar legislation. Interest in forfeiture has generated several related periodicals. In 1985 the Department of Justice established the National Assets Seizure and Forfeiture Fund, which takes in about $500 million annually (Navarro 1996). The law requires that cash and proceeds from resold property be spent on the fight against drugs, so much of the money resulting from forfeiture goes back into state and local law enforcement efforts. Seized automobiles are usually transferred to law enforcement agencies for undercover use.

In addition to the civil procedures contained in RICO, Section 881 of the Comprehensive Drug Abuse Prevention and Control Act of 1970 provides for the seizure of assets under certain conditions. The reach of Section 881 was extended through amendments in 1978 and 1984: the statute now permits forfeiture of all profits from drug trafficking and all assets purchased with such proceeds or traded in exchange for controlled substances. It authorizes the forfeiture of all real property used in any manner to facilitate violations of drug statutes, including entire tracts of land and all improvements regardless of what portion of the property facilitated the illegal activities. Currency, buildings, land, motor vehicles, and airplanes have all been confiscated (Stahl 1992). The government also has the right to seize untainted assets as a substitute for tainted property disposed of or otherwise made unavailable for forfeiture (Greenhouse 1994).

A seizure can be made incident to an arrest or customs inspection or upon receipt of a seizure order. To obtain a seizure order (actually a warrant—see Figure 14.2), the government must provide sworn testimony in an affidavit spelling out the property to be seized and why there is reason to believe that it is being used to commit crimes or was acquired with money from criminal activity—the same process used in securing a search warrant. The filing of criminal charges against the owner is not required. The owner of the property has a right to contest the seizure only after it has occurred; he or she must prove that the money or property was earned through legal enterprise. In 1993 the Supreme Court (*United States v. Good Real Property*, 510 U.S. 43) ruled that the government may not seize real estate without providing the owner with a notice and opportunity to contest the proposed seizure. This decision applies only to real estate and not portable possessions.

Civil forfeiture is an *in rem* proceeding in contrast to the *in personam* proceedings used in criminal forfeiture. As such, the action is against the property, not the person, so that even an acquittal on the criminal charges does not preclude civil forfeiture. In 1996 the Supreme Court ruled in *United States v. Ursery* (518 U.S. 267) that a criminal prosecution and civil forfeiture in the same case do not violate the constitutional prohibition against double jeopardy:[4] ordinary forfeiture is not punishment but a device for denying someone the fruits of his or her criminal behavior.

Although forfeiture laws vary, two legal theories have evolved: *facilitation* and *proceeds*. The *facilitation* theory allows the government to seize property when it facilitates certain criminal conduct. For example, in drug investigations, any property involved in the manufacture, delivery, and sale of controlled substances can be subjected to seizure. This includes real estate used to store drugs, automobiles and boats used to transport drugs, and other facilitating property, such as cash and firearms. The *proceeds* theory allows the government to seize property that represents the proceeds of certain specified unlawful activities. This can be quite complex because before seizure can occur, the government must identify property and prove ownership. The government also must trace the asset to the criminal activity, and each time the subject converts the proceeds from one form to another, the more complicated this becomes (Hartman 2001).

Under federal statutes, before an order to seize property can be issued, the government must show there is a substantial connection between the property and the crime by *a preponderance of the evidence*, the legal standard of proof for civil cases. (Prior to 2000, the standard of proof was *probable cause*, a lower level of evidence such as is required for search warrants and arrests.) This is done without notice to the defendant at an *ex parte* (defendant not present) hearing. After seizure, if forfeiture is contested, there is a shift in the burden of

---

[4]The Supreme Court has long interpreted the Fifth Amendment as prohibiting multiple punishments as well as multiple prosecutions for the same offense (Greenhouse 1996).

FIGURE 14.2   *Verified Complaint for Forfeiture*

IN THE UNITED STATES DISTRICT COURT
NORTHERN DISTRICT OF ILLINOIS
EASTERN DIVISION

UNITED STATES OF AMERICA Plaintiff, v. A 1987 ROLLS-ROYCE CORNICHE VIN SCAZDO2A4HCX20937, $152,645.00 in UNITED STATES CURRENCY seized from SAFE DEPOSIT BOX 6265 at CLYDE FEDERAL, $30,040 in UNITED STATES CURRENCY seized from SAFE DEPOSIT BOX 5660 at WESTERN NATIONAL BANK, $22,400 in UNITED STATES CURRENCY seized from SAFE DEPOSIT BOX 8805–N AT OAK PARK TRUST AND SAVINGS BANK, and UNITED STATES CURRENCY in THE AMOUNT OF $120,023.00 Defendants	NO. **89C1250** FEB 15 1989 JUDGE **JUDGE NORGLE** MAGISTRATE LEFKOW

VERIFIED COMPLAINT FOR FORFEITURE

The United States of America, by its attorney, Anton R. Valukas, United States Attorney for the Northern District of Illinois for its complaint states:

1.) This is a forfeiture action under Title 21, United States Code, Section 881 (a) (6) and this Court has jurisdiction under Title 28, United States Code, Sections 1345 and 1355.

2.) The defendants named in the caption were seized on land within the Northern District of Illinois and will remain within this Court's jurisdiction throughout the pendency of this action.

3.) On February 7, 1989, a search warrant arising from a narcotics investigation of an individual known as Rufus Sims was executed at a residence at 2606 South Boeger in Westchester, Illinois. The search resulted in the seizure of a large quantity of weapons and twenty-three (23) bags containing cocaine repackaged for sale commingled with United States Currency in the amount of $4,301.00.

4.) During the execution of the warrant at the residence, the police discovered title to the defendant 1987 Rolls Royce Convertible, VIN SCAZDO2A4HCX20937. Review of records at Steve Foley Cadillac revealed that the purchase price of the car was $176,681, of which $129,461 was paid in currency and the remainder of the purchase price came from Sims' trade-in of another Rolls-Royce owned by him.

FIGURE 14.2   (Continued)

5.) During the execution of the search warrant at Sims' residence, the police discovered a number of keys to safe deposit boxes at banks in the Chicago area. One of the keys seized was for safe deposit box 2655 at the Forest Park National Bank. On February 10, 1989, police officers stopped Andrea Thomas, Sims' common-law wife, and Estelle Greenfield, Sims' mother, outside the Forest Park National Bank with $120,023.00 in United States currency which they had just taken from box 2655. Both women disavowed knowledge of the money (even though it filled a large satchel which Estelle Greenfield was carrying) and each claimed that it did not belong to them.

6.) On February 11, 1989, Magistrate Bucklo issued seizure warrants ordering the Federal Bureau of Investigation to seize the contents of the other safe deposit boxes for which keys had been found at the Sims' residence. The warrants resulted in the seizure of $152,645.00 from box 6265 at Clyde Federal, $30,040 from box 5660 at Western National Bank, and $22,400 from Box 8805–N at Oak Park Trust and Savings Bank.

7.) Rufus Sims is unemployed and has no known legitimate source of income. Although he is unemployed, he purchased a 1987 Rolls-Royce worth $176,681, owns real estate and numerous other vehicles, and had safe deposit boxes containing over $320,000.00 in cash.

8.) The affidavit of Chicago Police Sergeant Robert M. Lombardo verifying this complaint is appended hereto and incorporated herein.

9.) By reasons of the foregoing, and as detailed more specifically in the attached affidavit, the defendants constitute proceeds of narcotics trafficking and are therefore subject to forfeiture pursuant to Title 21, United States Code, Section 881 (a) (6).

WHEREFORE, for the reasons described above, the United States prays:

1.) That the defendants be proceeded against for forfeiture and condemnation;

2.) That a warrant of seizure and monition issue;

3.) That due notice be given to all interested parties to appear and show cause as to why the forfeiture should not be decreed; and,

4.) That this Court adjudge and decree that the defendants be forfeited to the United States of America, and that they be properly disposed of according to law.

---

proof, which diminishes the Fifth Amendment privilege against self-incrimination because the defendant cannot pursue the claim to seized property without explaining its ownership. The Supreme Court has refused to apply the Fifth Amendment's Double Jeopardy Clause or the Sixth Amendment's guarantee of the right to confront witnesses to *in rem* forfeiture (Stahl 1992). Since the process is quasi-criminal, however, the exclusionary rule is applicable, and evidence seized in violation of the Constitution cannot be considered (*One 1958 Plymouth Sedan v. Pennsylvania*, 380 U.S. 691, 701 [1965]).

Section 881 provides for an innocent owner's defense: the violation occurred without the owner's knowledge. The burden is on the owner to prove innocence by a preponderance of the evidence. The government can overcome claims of innocence by showing that it would be reasonable to believe that the owner was aware. In addition, some courts have required the owner to prove that he or she took all reasonable steps to prevent the violation (Stahl 1992). There is also a remission

procedure—the claimant can file a petition with the attorney general, who can order the return of property if there are mitigating circumstances. However, remission is a discretionary act. In 1996 the Court determined that property can be seized even when the owner is innocent of any wrongdoing. In this case, *Bennis v. Michigan* (517 U.S. 1163), a couple's jointly owned car was impounded after the husband used it to solicit a prostitute.

In 1988 the Supreme Court, in a 5–4 decision, ruled that under the Comprehensive Forfeiture Act, the government can freeze the assets of criminal defendants before trial (*Caplin and Drysdale, Chartered v. United States*, 491 U.S. 617; *United States v. Monsanto*, 491 U.S. 600). Legislation enacted in 2000, in addition to raising the standard of evidence, allows federal judges to release property to the owner pending trial if confiscation causes him or her substantial hardship.

Criticism of Forfeiture   A great deal of criticism has been leveled at forfeiture. The normally conservative *Chicago Tribune*, for example, in an

Get Out of Jail (Almost) Free

Forfeiture has been criticized as a plea-bargaining device for drug kingpins. They negotiate lighter sentences by promising to reveal hidden assets and not put up court challenges to their seizure. Law enforcement agencies eager for additional funds allegedly promote leniency for those at the top of the drug trafficking ladder, while those down below, without significant hidden assets, face significant penalties (Navarro 1996).

editorial (April 1, 1993) stated that while forfeiture, when used appropriately, can be an effective punishment for crime, "a growing number of innocent parties and two-bit players are being swept up in the net. And those who are unfairly trapped find that forfeiture laws turn due process on its head." In 1993 the Supreme Court ruled unanimously that the Eighth Amendment's protection against "excessive fines" requires that there be a relationship between the gravity of the offense and the value of the property seized (*Austin v. United States*, 506 U.S. 602). In 1998 the Court extended *Austin*, ruling 5–4 against the forfeiture of $357,144 in cash that was not the proceeds of crime. The money had been seized from someone who attempted to take cash out of the country to pay debts without filing a Currency Transaction Report (*United States v. Bajakajian*, 524 U.S. 321).

Until 1988, the act permitted the Department of Justice to prosecute attorneys and seize fees from tainted sources. Defense attorneys argued that this created a situation "in which a defendant cannot retain an attorney because of the government's threat of criminal and civil sanctions against any attorney who takes the case" (Weinstein 1988: 381). The defendant is left without a free choice of attorneys and dependent upon a public defender, who is not always able to defend against the often complex nature of RICO prosecutions. Supporters of this legislation argue that criminals who have grown wealthy from crime are not entitled to any greater consideration with respect to legal representation than their less successful criminal colleagues, who are often represented by a public defender. In 1988, President Ronald Reagan signed an anti-drug abuse bill that contained an amendment to 18 U.S.C. Section 1957. The amendment excluded defense attorneys' fees from the criminal money-laundering provisions. Thus, while criminal defense fees could still be subject to forfeiture, attorneys who accept tainted fees are exempt from criminal prosecution.

Money Laundering

In 1970, in response to increasing reports of people bringing bags full of illegally obtained cash into banks for deposit, Congress enacted the statute commonly referred to as the Bank Secrecy Act (BSA). (Technically, the BSA is Titles I and II of Pub.L. 91–508, as amended. Title II is also called the Currency and Foreign Transactions Reporting Act.) The BSA contains two basic sets of authorizing provisions, which are put into effect by implementing regulations. The first set authorizes the Secretary of the Treasury (and in some places, the Secretary and the Federal Reserve Board jointly) to require banks and other financial institutions to retain records to ensure that the details of financial transactions can be traced if investigators need to do so.

The second set of provisions authorizes the Secretary of the Treasury to require financial institutions and, in some cases, other businesses and private citizens to report financial transactions of certain kinds. The two most important reporting rules authorized in 1970 were the reporting by financial institutions of transactions in currency in excess of $10,000 (using the Currency Transaction Report [CTR]) and the reporting of the transportation of currency and bearer instruments (in amounts initially in excess of $5,000—now in excess of $10,000) into or out of the United States (using the Report of International Transportation of Currency or Monetary Instruments [CMIR]).[5] A specific prohibition was added to the BSA against "structuring" transactions to avoid the impact of the BSA's reporting thresholds. This system generates more than 12 million CTRs annually.

Prior to the passage of the Money Laundering Control Act of 1986, money laundering was not a federal crime, although the Department of Justice had used a variety of federal statutes to successfully prosecute money-laundering cases. The act consolidated these statutes with the goal of increasing prosecutions for this offense. Money laundering was made a separate federal offense punishable by a fine of $500,000 or twice the value of the property involved, whichever is greater, and 20 years' imprisonment (Weinstein 1988). Title 18, U.S.C. Section 981, provides for the civil confiscation of any property related to a money-laundering scheme. Legislation enacted in 1988 allows the government to file a suit claiming ownership of all cash funneled through operations intended to disguise its illegal source. The courts can issue an order freezing all contested funds until the case is adjudicated. An amendment to the Drug Abuse Act of 1988 requires offshore banks to record any U.S. cash transactions in excess of $10,000 and to permit U.S. officials to have access to the records. Offshore banks that fail to comply can be banned from holding accounts in U.S. banks and denied access to U.S. dollar-clearing and money-transfer systems.

The Annunzio–Wylie Money Laundering Act of 1992 and the Money Laundering Suppression Act of 1994 (the "MLSA") give the Treasury Department a wider variety of regulatory tools to combat money laundering. Annunzio–Wylie amends the BSA in several respects. Most important, it authorizes the Secretary of the Treasury to require financial institutions and gambling casinos to submit a "Suspicious Activity Report" relevant to a possible violation of law or regulation. The statutory suspicious transaction authorization includes a "safe-harbor" provision to protect financial institutions from civil liability to their clients and third parties that might otherwise be claimed to have arisen from the designation of transactions as suspicious by reporting institutions. Other Annunzio–Wylie provisions authorize the Secretary to require financial institutions to carry out anti-money-laundering programs and authorize special record keeping. Finally, Annunzio–Wylie makes operation of an illegal money-transmitting business a crime (information from the U.S. Department of the Treasury).[6]

Under the Currency and Foreign Transactions Reporting Act (31 U.S.C. Sec. 5311, as amended), the United States can compel other countries to maintain certain financial records similar to those required under the Bank Secrecy Act. The Treasury Department's Financial Crimes Enforcement Network (FinCen) works with bank regulators to ensure compliance with the act. FinCen is a key component of the U.S. international strategy to combat organized crime, using counter-money-laundering laws and providing intelligence and analytical case support to federal, state, local, and international investigators and regulators. Its 200 employees include intelligence analysts and criminal investigators as well as specialists in the financial industry and computer field. In addition, approximately 40 long-term detailees are assigned to FinCen from 21 different regulatory and law enforcement agencies. FinCen maintains a database in Detroit that documents every suspicious-activity report filed since they were initiated in 1996 (Wahl 1999b). If a country

---

[5]The constitutionality of the BSA has been challenged on a number of grounds. In *California Bankers Association v. Shultz*, 416 U.S. 21 (1974), the U.S. Supreme Court rejected claims that various parts of the BSA violated constitutional due process requirements, the Fourth Amendment protection against unreasonable searches and seizures, and the Fifth Amendment privilege against self-incrimination. The Court emphasized that the information sought from the reporting banks concerned transactions to which the banks themselves had been parties. A later Supreme Court decision, *United States v. Miller*, 425 U.S. 435 (1976), settled a question reserved in *California Bankers Association* by ruling that bank customers possess no privacy interests protected by the Fourth Amendment in records of their affairs maintained by the banks with which they deal.

[6]Because this statute requires proof of "willfulness," in 1994 the Supreme Court ruled that persons who structured their transactions to avoid the CTR—by keeping transactions at $9,500, for example—did not violate the law unless they *knew* such action was illegal (*Ratzlaf v. United States*, 510 U.S. 135).

fails to negotiate an acceptable records system, its financial institutions can be denied access to the U.S. banking system. There are problems with implementing this legislation: apart from developed countries with exchange control laws, few countries have legislation requiring their banks and other financial institutions to collect and report such information to a government (Chaiken 1991). Antiterrorism legislation enacted in 2001 permits the Treasury Department to impose sanctions on countries that refuse to provide information on depositors. The legislation also bars American banks from doing business with offshore ("shell") banks having no connection to any regulated banking industry.

A person is guilty of money laundering if he or she knows that the property involved represents the proceeds of some illegal activity; attempts to conceal or disguise the nature, the location, the source, the ownership, or the control of the proceeds; or attempts to avoid a transaction-reporting requirement. Furthermore, a person is guilty of money laundering if he or she transports or attempts to transport a monetary instrument or funds out of the United States with the intent to carry out an unlawful activity. If a person knows that the monetary instrument or funds involved represent the proceeds of some form of unlawful activity or attempts to conceal or disguise the nature, location, source, ownership, or control of the proceeds or to avoid a transaction-reporting requirement, he or she is guilty of money laundering.

The International Emergency Economic Powers Act allows the president to take extraordinary actions in the case of an "unusual threat to national security." In 1995, President Bill Clinton issued a directive under the act, requiring financial institutions to search for and freeze accounts held in the name of persons or companies determined by the government to assist or play a significant role in international drug trafficking. The order also forbids American businesses and officials to trade with those individuals and their front companies (Mitchell 1995).

In 1999 two of Mexico's biggest banks pleaded guilty to money laundering in an effort to stave off sanctions that would include not being able to do business in the United States; they had to forfeit millions of dollars seized by federal officials. As part of a vast undercover operation in Mexico by the U.S. Customs Service, dozens of Mexican bankers, businessmen, and suspected drug traffickers were indicted. Controversy surrounds the investigation, which drew the wrath of Mexico—U.S. agents were operating in that country without informing the Mexican government—and criticism that the Clinton administration ordered the investigation terminated early in order not to further embarrass Mexico (Golden 1999a, 1999b).

The Victims of Trafficking and Violence Protection Act of 2000

The Victims of Trafficking and Violence Protection Act of 2000, which was passed virtually unanimously by both houses of Congress, addresses issues of worker exploitation resulting from trafficking in persons. The law expands the definition of forced labor to reach modern forms of coercion. The statute:

- creates new laws that criminalize trafficking with respect to slavery, involuntary servitude, peonage, or forced labor
- permits prosecution where nonviolent coercion is used to force victims to work in the belief that they would be subject to serious harm if they did not
- permits prosecution where the victim's service was compelled by confiscation of documents such as passports or birth certificates
- increases prison terms for all slavery violations from 10 years to 20 years and adds life imprisonment when the violation involves the death, kidnapping, or sexual abuse of the victim
- requires courts to order restitution and forfeiture of assets upon conviction
- enables victims to seek witness protection and other types of assistance
- gives prosecutors and agents new tools to get legal immigration status for victims of trafficking during investigation and prosecution. (U.S. Department of Justice information)

Now that we have completed our examination of the limitations of organized crime law enforcement and relevant statutes, Chapter 15 will look at the agencies engaged in organized crime law enforcement and the techniques that they use to carry out their mission.

INTERNET CONNECTIONS

Crime topics: **faculty.ncwc.edu/toconnor**

Financial Crimes Enforcement Network: **www.ustreas.gov/fincen**

Federal Judicial Center: **www.fjc.gov**

Criminal justice links: **lawguru.com/ilawlib**

American Bar Association Criminal Justice links: **abanet.org/crimjust/links.html**

U.S. Department of Justice Links: **www.usdoj.gov/02organizations/02_1.html**

REVIEW QUESTIONS

1. How is organized crime law enforcement limited by constitutional restraints and jurisdictional limitations?
2. Why is corruption a problem associated with organized crime law enforcement?
3. What is the problem inherent in using informants in organized crime law enforcement?
4. What are the most important federal statutes used in organized crime control?
5. What historically significant changes were instituted by the drug control legislation of 1970?
6. What are the major provisions of the Hobbs Act?
7. How is the Consumer Credit Protection Act used against organized crime?
8. What is a conspiracy, and what are the three forms that a conspiracy can take?
9. How can "guilt by association" become a problem in a conspiracy prosecution?
10. Why does a conspiracy prosecution usually require an informant to testify?
11. What are the required elements for a RICO prosecution?
12. Why has RICO been criticized?
13. According to forfeiture statutes, under what conditions can the government seize property?
14. What are the levels of evidence applicable in a forfeiture proceeding?
15. What are the provisions of the anti-money-laundering statutes?
16. What is the purpose of the Victims of Trafficking and Violence Protection Act of 2000?

♠

CHAPTER 15

ORGANIZED CRIME
LAW ENFORCEMENT

In this chapter, we will examine the law enforcement agencies responding to organized crime and the techniques they use to enforce the statutes reviewed in Chapter 14. Before we turn to primary agencies of organized crime law enforcement, certain issues must be noted. General police responsibility is the function of a "full-service" municipal department—there is no national police force in the United States—while the primary responsibility of state police forces is highway traffic enforcement. Most of the resources of a municipal police department go into uniformed services such as patrol; only a small portion goes into plainclothes or detective units. In larger cities, such units include specialties such as "vice" (gambling and prostitution) and drug enforcement. In this function, local police do apprehend some of the participants in organized criminal activity. However, organized crime is rarely a priority item for a municipal department. Resources devoted to OC detract from the department's ability to respond to citizen demands for police services:

Few local departments have the luxury of developing a sophisticated organized crime control program. Obviously, the daily realities of police work at the grass-roots level militates against a well-developed execution of an organized crime control strategy. Since organized crime is often synonymous with vice enforcement—gambling, prostitution, narcotics, and loansharking—there are few incentives for a police administrator to allocate limited and valuable resources toward this particular form of criminality. Often the investment of personnel to enforce laws which govern "consensual relationships" between customer and supplier are met with judicial indifference and public apathy; and as demonstrated through numerous studies and investigations, it is highly questionable from a purely cost–benefit analysis whether the benefits outweigh the costs incurred. Accordingly, most investigative and law-enforcement efforts against OC are found at the federal level. (Dintino and Martens 1980: 67)

An important exception is in New York, where the Organized Crime Task Force has been responsible for developing important cases against persons involved in organized crime. The task force is an independent investigative agency with a mandate to investigate and prosecute multi-county organized criminal activity and to assist local law enforcement agencies in their efforts against organized crime. The task force has statewide jurisdiction with three regional offices. Each office comprises teams that are assigned to investigate a specific type of OC activity, such as labor racketeering or narcotics. Each team consists of an attorney, an accountant, an investigative analyst, and a senior investigator, who supervises investigations using personnel from the state police. Other states, such as New Jersey and New Mexico, have established investigating or crime commissions in response to organized criminal activity.

Because the police are the most visible agents of governmental power, and because Americans have historically distrusted government in general and the federal government in particular, there has never been serious consideration of a federal police force. Over the decades, however, necessity led to the creation of a number of specialized federal enforcement agencies in an unplanned and uncoordinated manner. Thus, while they all have the same nominal boss—the president—federal law enforcement is fragmented. The result is a confusing number of agencies in several departments—Justice, Treasury, Transportation, Labor, and Defense—whose responsibility for OC law enforcement lacks systematic coordination.

THE DEPARTMENT OF JUSTICE (DOJ)

Clearly the most important federal department dealing with organized crime, the Department of Justice is headed by the attorney general, a member of the president's cabinet. Each of the 94 federal judicial districts has a U.S. attorney appointed by the president for a period of four years. The U.S. attorneys and about 2,000 assistant U.S. attorneys prosecute cases for all federal enforcement agencies. Within the DOJ is the Organized Crime and Racketeering Section (OCRS), which is re-

sponsible for coordinating and developing nationwide programs for responding to organized crime.

The Federal Bureau of Investigation (FBI)

The FBI is the closest thing to a federal police force in the United States. Its origins date back to the establishment of the Department of Justice in 1870. Until 1908, the department used private detectives or borrowed men from the Secret Service. In that year, President Theodore Roosevelt directed the attorney general to develop an investigative unit within the Justice Department; it was named the Bureau of Investigation. In 1935 Congress renamed it the Federal Bureau of Investigation.

After World War I, the bureau was involved in a great deal of "antiradical" activity at the direction of Attorney General A. Mitchell Palmer. The FBI conducted raids and arrested thousands of people in what became known as the "Red Scare of 1919." The "Palmer Raids" were the subject of a congressional investigation and were strongly defended by the bureau's assistant director, John Edgar Hoover, who was appointed director in 1924 and remained head of the FBI until his death in 1972.

Over the years, the bureau was given responsibility for investigating interstate shipment of stolen vehicles, kidnapping, bank robbery, interstate fugitives, espionage, and sabotage. After World War II, FBI resources were directed toward the perceived threat posed by domestic Communism, while the problem of organized crime was left unattended—in 1956, there were four agents assigned to the New York office to investigate "Crime, Organized" (Volkman 1998). Stanford Ungar (1975: 391) argues that "the Director was simply clever enough to steer clear of the toughest problems—the ones less likely to produce prompt and stunning results, that might test conflicts of loyalty among agents, or that would require them to be exposed to the seamier side of life (and, as with many policemen, tempt them into corruption)."[1] This changed when President John F.

---

[1] Anthony Summers (1993) presents a more sinister set of explanations for Hoover's lack of activity against organized crime.

Kennedy appointed his brother Robert as attorney general.

The FBI has since become the major law enforcement agency combating organized criminal activity and the lead agency in using the RICO statute (discussed in Chapter 14). In 1982 its broad investigative mandate was expanded when the FBI was given concurrent jurisdiction with the Drug Enforcement Administration for drug law enforcement and investigation.

The Drug Enforcement Administration (DEA)

In 1919 a Narcotics Division was created within the Bureau of Prohibition, with a staff of 170 agents and an appropriation of $270,000. The Narcotics Division was tainted by its association with the country's anti-liquor laws: "Public dissatisfaction intensified because of a scandal involving falsification of arrest records and charges relating to payoffs by, and collusion with, drug dealers" (PCOC 1986c: 204). Responding in 1930, Congress removed drug enforcement from the Bureau of Prohibition and established the Federal Bureau of Narcotics (FBN) as a separate agency within the Department of the Treasury: "Although the FBN was primarily responsible for the enforcement of the Harrison Act and related drug laws, the task of preventing and interdicting the illegal importation and smuggling of drugs remained with the Bureau of Customs" (PCOC 1986c: 205). In 1973, responsibility for enforcing federal drug statutes was given to the DEA, which was placed in the Department of Justice.

The DEA is a single-mission agency responsible for enforcing federal statutes dealing with controlled substances by investigating alleged or suspected major drug traffickers. The DEA is also responsible for regulating the legal trade in controlled substances such as morphine, methadone, and barbiturates. Diversion agents conduct accountability investigations of drug wholesalers, suppliers, and manufacturers. They inspect the records and facilities of major drug manufacturers and distributors, and special agents investigate instances where drugs have been illegally diverted

from legitimate sources. DEA special agents are also stationed in other countries, where their mission is to gain cooperation in international efforts against drug trafficking and to help train foreign enforcement officials.

The basic approach to DEA drug-law enforcement is the "buy and bust" or the "controlled buy." Typically, a drug agent is introduced to a seller by an informant. The agent arranges to buy a relatively small amount of the substance and then attempts to move further up the organizational ladder by increasing the amount of drugs purchased: "The agent prefers to defer an arrest until he can seize a large amount of drugs or can implicate higher-ups in the distribution system or both" (Wilson 1978: 43). When arrests are made, DEA agents attempt the "flip"—convince a defendant to become an informant, particularly if the person has knowledge about the entire operation so that a conspiracy case can be effected. As discussed in Chapter 14, however, the use of informants is problematic. The DEA, usually with the aid of customs agents and state and local enforcement agencies, monitors airports in an effort to interdict drugs being smuggled by "mules."

Mule Skinning   DEA special agents, working with state and local police agencies, monitor airports at key junctures for drugs entering the United States. In addition to primary ports of entry, such as South Florida, Los Angeles, and New York, they also cover secondary routes such as Atlanta and Chicago, where travelers frequently change planes. Using a drug courier profile, which has been developed over the past 15 years, the agents look for specific clues (primary and secondary characteristics) that have been shown to distinguish persons most likely to be carrying wholesale quantities of illegal substances ("mules"). There are seven primary characteristics:

1. Arrival from or departure to an identified foreign source country, such as Colombia, or a domestic source city, such as Miami
2. Carrying empty suitcases or little or no luggage

3. Unusual travel patterns, such as short turnaround times for lengthy airplane trips
4. Use of an alias
5. Possession of large amounts of currency
6. Purchase of airline tickets with small bills
7. Unusual display of nervousness

And there are four secondary characteristics:

- Exclusive use of public transportation, particularly cabs, to and from the airport
- A phone call made immediately after deplaning
- Providing a phony telephone number when purchasing airline tickets
- Excessive travel to a source country or a distribution city or cities

While these primary and secondary traits can be consistent with lawful behavior, they characterize a person who should be questioned. Passengers meeting enough profile characteristics may be approached and questioned—asked for identification and travel documentation. Agents are particularly interested in signs of excessive nervousness. If such signs are observed, agents will ask the passenger to consent to a search for drugs. A refusal, which is rare, can result in detention and the securing of a drug-sniffing dog and/or search warrant. At times the agents discover large amounts of cash that cannot be accounted for; it is seized until its "lawful" owner appears to claim it, a highly unlikely event. If a courier is arrested, efforts are made to "flip" the mule in order to implicate the person picking up the drugs (Hedgepeth 1989).

Although its use is rather controversial, the "profile" permits drug agents to act in the absence of specific information. The use of the profile and any evidence discovered as a result has been upheld by the courts as a legitimate law enforcement tool, the Fourth Amendment notwithstanding. In 1989 the U.S. Supreme Court, in a 7–2 decision, ruled that the profile provides a "reasonable basis" to suspect that a person is transporting drugs. The case involved Andrew Sokolow, who in July of 1984 flew from Honolulu to Miami and then returned to Hawaii after 48 hours. Dressed in a black jumpsuit with gold jewelry, Sokolow purchased two airline tickets in Miami for $2,100 in cash, taken from a roll of $20 bills containing about twice that amount. He was traveling under a name that did not match his telephone listing. Sokolow did not check any luggage and appeared quite nervous. After stopping him in Honolulu, drug agents, with the help of a drug-sniffing dog, discovered 1,063 grams of cocaine in Sokolow's carry-on luggage.

Writing for the Court, Chief Justice William H. Rehnquist stated that "While a trip from Honolulu to Miami, standing alone, is not a cause for any sort of suspicion, here there was more: surely few residents of Honolulu travel from that city for 20 hours to spend 48 hours in Miami during the month of July." However, the Court did not base its decision on the existence or use of the DEA drug profile. According to the decision, agents must justify stopping a suspect on the basis of their own observations and experience (Elsasser 1989; Greenhouse 1989b).

The Immigration and Naturalization Service (INS)

The primary role of the INS is to prevent the illegal entry of persons into the United States and to apprehend those who have entered illegally. This is particularly important in the fight against OC when illegal aliens are used to strengthen the ranks and operations of criminal organizations. Uniformed Border Patrol officers check suspicious persons within 100 miles of border areas most likely to be used as illegal crossing points, and they often arrest persons transporting drugs. At airports, the INS works closely with Customs, alerting Customs agents to visitors who should be subjected to scrutiny.

The Marshals Service

The Marshals Service is the oldest federal law enforcement agency, dating back to 1789. During the period of westward expansion, the U.S. marshal played a significant role in the "Wild West," where he was often the only symbol of law and order. In the past, marshals have also been used in civil disturbances as an alternative to military intervention. Today, they provide security for federal court facilities; transport federal prisoners; serve civil writs issued by federal courts, which can include the seizure of property under the provisions of RICO; and investigate and apprehend certain federal fugitives. However, their most important task relative to organized crime is responsibility for administering the *Witness Protection Program*.

The Witness Protection Program Because of the potentially undesirable consequences for a witness who testifies in an organized crime case, efforts have been made to protect such witnesses from retribution. The Witness Protection Program was authorized by the Organized Crime Control Act of 1970:

> The Attorney General of the United States is authorized to rent, purchase, modify or remodel protected housing facilities and to otherwise offer to provide for the health, safety, and welfare of witnesses and persons intended to be called as Government witnesses, and the families of witnesses and persons intended to be called as Government witnesses, in legal proceedings instituted against any person alleged to have participated in an organized criminal activity whenever, in his judgment, testimony from, or a willingness to testify by, such a witness would place his life or person, or the life or person of a member of his family or household, in jeopardy. Any person availing himself of such an offer by the Attorney General to use such facilities may continue to use such facilities for as long as the Attorney General determines the jeopardy to his life or person continues.

The program was given over to the U.S. Marshals Service to administer, an arrangement designed to enhance the value of witness testimony: "Law enforcement officers wanted the protecting and relocating agency to be in the criminal justice system but to be as far removed as possible from both investigating agents and prosecution. That

way the Government could more readily counter the charge that cooperating witnesses were being paid or otherwise unjustifiably compensated in return for their testimony" (Permanent Subcommittee on Investigations—hereafter, PSI, 1981c: 54).

However, the Marshals Service was not prepared for these new responsibilities—its typical duties were related to support of the judicial system. Moreover, the educational requirements and training of deputy U.S. marshals were not rigorous. This has changed. Marshals Service personnel are better trained, and a new position, that of inspector, was created specifically for the Witness Protection Program. Nevertheless, officials had not anticipated the number of persons who would enter the program. They had expected about two dozen annually, and not the more than 500 principals brought into the program each year—by the end of 1996, 6,500 witnesses and 15,000 dependents (Sabbag 1996).

Some critics of the program have charged that the Marshals Service shields criminals not only from would-be assassins but also from debts and lawsuits. In an attempt to remedy this, an amendment to the 1984 Comprehensive Crime Control Act directs the Justice Department to stop hiding witnesses who are sued for civil damages and to drop from the program participants linked to new crimes. But the program still provides career criminals with "clean" backgrounds that they can use to prey on or endanger an unsuspecting public.

The problem is obvious: "The marshals are often dealing with men and women who have never done an honest day's work in their lives. Many of them were skilled criminals—burglars, embezzlers, arsonists, physical enforcers—accustomed to lucrative financial rewards and a high standard of living" (PSI 1981c: 53–54), a standard that is not going to be duplicated by the program, which typically provides about $2,000–$3,000 monthly for 17 months; participants may also receive help with job training. Once the immediate physical danger has passed, some of these protected witnesses begin to yearn for the excitement and, for some, the status and financial rewards that crime brought to their lives. Government witness Sammy Gravano, former underboss of the Gam-

Wayward Witnesses

- Charles J. McDonald, in order to "work off a beef," spent two years as an FBI undercover operative, taping conversations with his associates in the Colombo Family. He and his family were provided with new Social Security cards, phony job records, a military service record, references from nonexistent employers, and school records for his children. The 300-pound career criminal emerged as Charlie Bertinelli and, with his associates, posed as Teamster Union pension officials, bilking legitimate businessmen in the United States and Canada out of an estimated $1.5 million (Coates 1986).

- Arthur Katz, in order to avoid imprisonment for insurance fraud, provided information in a Philadelphia OC case. He subsequently entered the Witness Protection Program and emerged as Arthur Kane. When he lost $6 million in the October 1987 stock market crash, Kane shot and killed the local Merrill Lynch brokerage manager and badly wounded another broker before turning the gun on himself ("Insurer Won't Pay on Federal Witness" 1987).

- Vito Arena was a vicious 300-pound hitman for the Gambino crime Family who delighted in dismembering victims. He was placed in the program for his testimony against Paul Castellano. In 1991, Arena was killed trying to hold up a supermarket in Houston (Coffey and Schmetterer 1991).

- Cecil O'Connor testified against Jamaican drug gangs operating in Florida and New York. Despite admitting to participation in nine murders, he was granted immunity from prosecution and entered the Witness Protection Program. A decade later, as Charles Miller, operating out of St. Kitts and Nevis, the smallest country in the Western hemisphere—population 46,000—O'Connor surfaced as the most dangerous and powerful drug trafficker in the Caribbean (Rohter 1998b).

bino Family, was relocated to Arizona. He soon grew bored with his new life and, while keeping his new name, told neighbors his real identity and signed autographs for people who stopped him on the street. In 2000, Gravano was arrested for involvement in an ecstasy drug ring that also included his son, who apparently introduced his father to the trade (Murr 2000). Having few if any noncriminal skills, it is not surprising that some of these protected witnesses return to criminal activity even if it places both their freedom and their lives, and the lives of their families, at risk. While about 30 witnesses who left the program have been murdered, none following program guidelines have been harmed (Sabbag 1996).

In some cases, estranged spouses have been unable to visit their own children. This was dramatically portrayed in the 1980 movie *Hide in Plain Sight*, starring James Caan. In 1983 the government relocated the ex-wife and young daughter of Anthony Prisco to a secret location. His ex-wife was married to a drug trafficker who became a government witness. Prisco hired a private investigator, who found out that she and their daughter were in the Witness Protection Program. In 1984, Congress amended the law to provide greater rights to parents in such cases. They permit Prisco monthly visits monitored by marshals, but he has no input into his daughter's upbringing (Tulsky 1987).

THE DEPARTMENT OF THE TREASURY

The primary responsibility of the Department of the Treasury is the collection of revenues due the federal government. In carrying out these responsibilities, the Treasury Department employs law enforcement personnel in several agencies. Three of these have important roles in dealing with organized crime.

The Internal Revenue Service (IRS)

The mission of the IRS is to encourage and achieve the highest possible degree of voluntary compliance with tax laws and regulations. When such compliance is not forthcoming or not feasible, as in the case of persons involved in organized criminal activity, the Criminal Investigation Division (CID) receives the case. CID special agents examine bank records, canceled checks, brokerage accounts, property transactions, and purchases, compiling a financial biography of the subject's lifestyle in order to prove that proper taxes have not been paid (according to the net-worth theory, discussed in Chapter 14). As a result of the excesses revealed in the wake of the Watergate scandal during the presidency of Richard Nixon, Congress enacted the Tax Reform Act of 1976. The act reduced the law enforcement role of the IRS and made it quite difficult for law enforcement agencies other than the IRS to gain access to income tax returns. Amendments in 1982 reduced the requirements and permit the IRS to better cooperate with the efforts of other federal agencies investigating organized crime, particularly drug traffickers.

The Bureau of Alcohol, Tobacco and Firearms (ATF)

The ATF traces its origins to 1791, when a tax was placed on alcoholic spirits. Eventually, the Prohibition Bureau evolved. With the repeal of Prohibition, this became known as the Alcohol Tax Unit. In 1942 the bureau was given jurisdiction over federal firearms statutes and, in 1970, over arson and explosives. ATF agents are empowered to seize and destroy contraband and illegal liquor production facilities, and they are responsible for combating contraband cigarette smuggling from a low-tax state to a high-tax state—North Carolina to New York, for example—and the bootlegging of untaxed tobacco products, activities often engaged in by persons in OC, who, through their extensive networks, have readily available outlets for such products. Because of enforcement of federal firearms and explosives statutes and regulations, ATF has been involved in the investigation of outlaw motorcycle clubs. The

Anti-Arson Act of 1982 increased the bureau's jurisdiction over arson. (The FBI has jurisdiction in arson or bombings that occur at federal buildings or other institutions that receive federal funds and in incidents that fit the Department of Justice's definition of terrorism.) ATF's National Response Teams investigate cases of arson and bombings in conjunction with state and local agencies. Each team is composed of special agents, a forensic chemist, and an explosives specialist, and is equipped with sophisticated, state-of-the-art equipment.

The Customs Service

The Customs Service was established in 1789 to collect duties on various imports. Customs inspectors examine cargoes and baggage, articles worn or carried by individuals, and vessels, vehicles, and aircraft entering or leaving the United States. Special teams of inspectors and canine enforcement officers concentrate on cargo and conveyances determined to be high risk. In 1981 the Customs Service established an Office of Intelligence to better manage information and target suspects. The service participates in several multiagency programs designed to combat organized drug trafficking. The service works with commercial carriers, often signing cooperative agreements, to enhance the carriers' ability to prevent their equipment from being used to smuggle drugs. Special agents of the Customs Service are responsible for carrying out investigations involving drug smuggling and currency violations as part of laundering schemes.

The Customs Service is not hampered by Fourth Amendment protections that typically restrain domestic law enforcement. Customs agents do not need probable cause or warrants to engage in search and seizure at ports of entry; a variety of degrees of suspicion will suffice. The typical Customs case is a "cold border bust," the result of an entry checkpoint search. Since it is impractical, if not impossible, to subject most vehicles and persons entering the United States to a thorough search, Customs agents have developed certain techniques for minimizing inconvenience to legitimate travelers and shippers while targeting those most likely to be involved in smuggling activity. The agents are vigi-

Record Haul

In the biggest seizure in maritime history, the Coast Guard captured 13 tons of cocaine aboard a fishing boat 1,500 miles south of San Diego. The 152-foot vessel with a crew of ten—eight Ukrainians and two Russians—aroused suspicion because it lacked operable fishing equipment. The cocaine was apparently destined for the Tijuana Cartel/Arellano-Félix drug trafficking organization, whose territory is close to where the ship was operating (Fox 2001).

lant for any signs of nervousness and incongruities. In addition to various cues that act as tipoffs, officials at border crossing points have computers containing information about known or suspected smugglers, such as license plate numbers and names. Persons arrested by the Customs Service become targets for plea bargaining deals in an effort to gain their cooperation for follow-up enforcement efforts by the Drug Enforcement Administration—they are pressured to become informants in return for some form of leniency: "Customs cases almost always began with a seizure. If the smugglers were amateur, bringing in the stuff for their own use, or to finance their vacation or mortgage arrears, then the buck usually stopped there. But if they were professional couriers, the specialized skill and the standard procedure of the Customs agent was to flip them . . . and carry out a controlled delivery with a view toward arresting their employers, and perhaps moving on from there, widening the net, to pull in the whole operation, from source to final customer" (Goddard 1988: 158).

THE DEPARTMENT OF LABOR

The Office of the Inspector General (OIG), Office of Investigations, Division of Labor Racketeering, conducts investigations in three general areas: employee benefit plans, labor–management relations, and internal union affairs. Within this broad investigative area, top priority is given to traditional organized crime domination of labor unions and/or employee benefit plans. Second priority is given to organized crime influence or manipulation of labor unions and/or employee benefit plans. The OIG employs special agents to carry out these responsibilities (OIG information).

THE DEPARTMENT OF TRANSPORTATION/COAST GUARD

The Coast Guard, part of the Department of Transportation, is responsible for drug interdiction on the seas. Its vessels conduct continuous surface patrols and frequent surveillance flights over waters of interest, and its personnel board and inspect suspect vessels at sea. Coast Guard personnel are law enforcement officers who do not have to establish probable cause prior to boarding a vessel: "The Coast Guard conducts both continuous surface patrols and frequent surveillance flights over waters of interest, and boards and inspects vessels at sea. In the past major Coast Guard resources have been concentrated in the 'choke points' traditionally transversed by traffickers. Cutters now more frequently patrol the Bahamas, the eastern passes of the Caribbean, and the Gulf, Atlantic and Pacific coastal areas" (PCOC 1986c: 313).

A typical seizure beings with the sighting of a suspect plane by a Coast Guard radar plane 250 miles away. The radar plane informs an intelligence center, where the suspect plane's flight track is compared with flight plans submitted to the Federal Aviation Administration. If a flight plan has not been filed, a two-engine Coast Guard tracking plane is dispatched. The tracking plane picks up the suspect plane on radar and then turns the radar off to avoid being detected by a "fuzz-buster." The tracker follows behind and above the suspect aircraft, maintaining surveillance with an infrared device that

Corrupting the Navy

In 1996, 21 American sailors were arrested in Italy by the Naval Criminal Investigative Service, whose agents were able to infiltrate a Nigerian drug ring that paid the defendants to carry bags of cocaine and heroin across European borders. A lieutenant commander was the highest-ranking member of the group ("Navy Holds 21 Sailors in Italy in Smuggling Case" 1996).

senses heat but does not send out an electronic beam. When the suspect plane prepares to land, the tracker notifies officers aboard a waiting helicopter, and they move in to make arrests. If the plane makes a drop at sea for pickup by boat, a Coast Guard helicopter or patrol boat makes the seizure. Coast Guard personnel are sometimes assigned to U.S. Navy ships assigned to drug interdiction, because military personnel are prohibited from making arrests of civilians by the Posse Comitatus Act.

The Coast Guard and the Customs Service are hampered by the need to patrol more than 12,000 miles of international boundary, over which more than 420 billion tons of goods and 270 million persons cross each year.

THE DEPARTMENT OF DEFENSE (DOD)

The primary role of the Department of Defense is obviously to protect the security of the United States from hostile military activities of foreign powers. In more recent decades, however, it has been drawn into the fight against drug trafficking, and this role is quite controversial. In the wake of the Reconstruction era, when the Union Army occupied the states of the Confederacy, Congress enacted the 1878 Posse Comitatus Act, which prohibits the U.S. Army from performing civilian law enforcement. In 1956, Congress added the Air Force to the Posse Comitatus Act, while the Navy and Marines promulgated administrative restrictions.

The prohibiting of military involvement in domestic law enforcement, particularly drug en-forcement, is based on fear that DOD involvement could

- compromise American security by exposing military personnel to the potentially corrupting environment of drug trafficking; in 1993, for example, Army personnel were accused of smuggling hundreds of pounds of cocaine from Panama into the United States via military transport.
- impair the strategic role of the military.
- present a threat to civil liberties: "The very nature of military training precludes any considerations of due process or civil rights" (Marsh 1991: 63).

Until 1981, the DOD limited its involvement in law enforcement to lending equipment and training civilian enforcement personnel in its use. In that year, as part of a new "war on drugs," Congress amended the Posse Comitatus Act, authorizing a greater level of military involvement in civilian drug enforcement, particularly the tracking of suspect ships and airplanes and the use of military pilots and naval ships to transport civilian enforcement personnel. As a result of this legislation, the DOD provides surveillance and support services, using aircraft to search for smugglers and U.S. Navy ships to tow or escort vessels seized by the Coast Guard to the nearest U.S. port. The 1981 legislation authorized the military services to share information collected during routine military operations with law enforcement officials and to make facilities and equipment available to law enforcement agencies.

Further amendments to the 1981 legislation led to the use of military equipment and personnel

Hi-tech devices, including night vision gear and thermal imaging, are used in patrolling the U.S.–Mexican border. Here a U.S. Border Patrol officer wears a binocular-equipped helmet to scout for illegal immigrants.

in interdiction efforts against cocaine laboratories in Bolivia. These amendments permit the use of such personnel and equipment if the secretary of state or the secretary of defense and the attorney general jointly determine that emergency circumstances exist—that the scope of specific criminal activity poses a serious threat to the interests of the United States. Combined operations involving U.S. Army Special Forces, DEA agents, U.S. Border Patrol officers, and Bolivian police and military officers have been successful in destroying hundreds of coca-paste laboratories in the coca-growing Champare region. The U.S. Department

of State uses former military pilots to fly helicopter gunships, transport planes, and cropdusters used by U.S. and foreign drug agents in countries where U.S. military operations are barred.

Until 1988, federal efforts against airborne drug smuggling were coordinated by the Customs Service and the Coast Guard, with the DOD using radar to help detect smugglers. The following year, Congress designated the DOD as the lead agency in these efforts, but a report by the General Accounting Office stated that the equipment used was costly, operated poorly in bad weather, and required frequent maintenance. Furthermore, airborne smugglers responded to the DOD activities by switching airports and finding other ways of entering the country (Berke 1989).

DOD support roles include air and ground observation and reconnaissance, environmental assessments, intelligence analysts and linguists, transportation, and engineering support. Mobile training teams teach civilian law enforcers such skills as combat lifesaving, advanced marksmanship, and tactical police operations that can be used in counterdrug operations.

Using night vision gear and thermal imaging equipment, U.S. service members staff observation posts and patrol the rugged terrain along the 2,000-mile border between the United States and Mexico. Their job is to watch and listen; if they spot suspicious activity, they radio for the Border Patrol or local law enforcement. Since November 1989, U.S. forces have helped law officers in their counterdrug activities in Texas, New Mexico, Arizona, and California, an area covering about 580,000 square miles. By the end of 1995, the mission expanded to provide support throughout the continental United States, Puerto Rico, and the U.S. Virgin Islands (American Forces Information Service information).

U.S. military officials have traditionally opposed involvement of the armed forces in law enforcement: it was viewed as inappropriate because the goal of military operations is to kill and destroy, and law enforcement could potentially undermine its primary mission. Other fears include a threat to civil liberties and the potentially corrupting

Call Out the Marines

In 1997, camouflaged U.S. Marines were on an anti-drug/immigrant smuggling patrol near the Texas–Mexico border when they spotted an armed man. He was an 18-year-old tending a herd of goats near his home; the .22 rifle was for snakes and wild dogs. The young man had no criminal record and was not a suspect in drug trafficking. He probably never saw the Marines, but their noise startled him, and he readied his rifle. A shot from an M-16 ended his life. The government agreed to pay the victim's family $1.9 million. In 1999 the Pentagon issued an order ending the routine use of ground troops for anti-drug missions along the Mexican border (Holt 1999).

influence of drug traffickers on the military. Furthermore, civilian casualties ("collateral damage") are often a by-product of military operations (Marsh 1991). Despite this fear, legislation was overwhelmingly approved in 1988 to dramatically expand the role of the military and allow the arrest of civilians under certain circumstances.

OTHER FEDERAL ENFORCEMENT AGENCIES

In addition to the agencies already discussed, a number of other federal agencies have an investigative or law enforcement role that at times may involve its personnel with organized crime. The *Secret Service* in the Treasury Department, in addition to its primary role of providing executive protection, is responsible for investigating the counterfeiting of money and credit cards, and the *Postal Inspection Service* has the responsibility of ensuring the integrity of the mails, and in this role investigates the use of the mails to further racketeering or for the unlawful shipment of controlled substances.

INTERPOL

The International Police Organization, known by its radio designation INTERPOL, assists law enforcement agencies with investigative activities that transcend national boundaries. It was founded in 1923 through the efforts of the police chief of

Vienna. The organization became dormant during World War II but was reorganized at a conference in Brussels in 1946. A stormy relationship existed between the director of the FBI and leaders of INTERPOL, and in 1950 the FBI withdrew from participation. The Treasury Department, anxious to maintain international contacts to help with its drug enforcement responsibilities, continued an informal liaison with INTERPOL.

Until 1968, "INTERPOL meant very little to the United States law enforcement community and was virtually unknown" (Fooner 1985: 19). In that year, Iran announced that it was going to end its ban on opium production. At the same time, there appeared to be an epidemic of drug use in the United States. A U.S. National Central Bureau (NCB) with a connection to INTERPOL was quickly activated in Washington, and by 1970 the NCB was handling about 300 cases a year. In the mid-1970s, a turf battle ensued between the Treasury Department and the Justice Department: the attorney general, after decades of neglect, decided that he wanted the United States to be part of INTERPOL, but the Treasury Department resisted. An agreement—a memorandum of understanding—was effected between the two departments in 1977; they would share the responsibility of representing the United States to INTERPOL and of operating the NCB.

There are currently more than 175 INTERPOL members. A country merely announces its intention to join in order to become a member. In each country, there is an NCB that acts as a point of contact and coordination with the General Secretariat in Lyon, France. INTERPOL has a head-quarters staff of about 250, about 60 of whom are law enforcement officers from nearly 40 different countries. There is a large communications facility that links 72 of the member countries into a radio network; other nations use telex or cable facilities. INTERPOL is under the day-to-day direction of a secretary general; it is a coordinating body and has no investigators or law enforcement agents of its own. INTERPOL's headquarters maintain databases containing records of people linked to international crime (Imhoff and Cutler 1998).

The USNCB receives more than 12,000 requests for assistance from federal, state, and local law enforcement agencies each year. They are checked and coded by technical staff and entered into the INTERPOL Case Tracking System (ICTS), a computer-controlled index of persons, organizations, and other crime information items. The ICTS conducts automatic searches of new entries, retrieving those that correlate with international crime. The requests are forwarded to senior staff members who serve as INTERPOL case investigators, usually veteran agents from a federal agency whose experience includes work with foreign police forces. Each investigator is on loan from his or her principal agency, and each state, the District of Columbia, Puerto Rico, territories, and New York City has a designated liaison office through which state and local agencies can connect to NCBs throughout the world (Imhoff and Cutler 1998).

Requests for investigative assistance range "from murder, robbery, narcotics violations, illicit firearms traffic, and large frauds, to counterfeiting, stolen works of art, bank swindles, and locating fugitives for arrest and extradition. The bureau also receives investigative requests for criminal histories, license checks, and other ID verifications. Sometimes locations of persons lost or missing in a foreign country are also requested" (Fooner 1985: 6). The Financial and Economic Crime Unit at INTERPOL headquarters aids in the exchange of information stemming from credit card fraud, airline ticket counterfeiting, computer crime, offshore banking, commodity futures, and money-laundering schemes. The monitoring of this type of activity can sometimes lead to the identification of suspects involved in drug trafficking or other types of organized crime who had previously escaped detection.

INVESTIGATIVE TOOLS IN ORGANIZED CRIME LAW ENFORCEMENT

Enforcing the law against organized criminal activity requires highly trained agents and prosecutors using sophisticated investigative and enforcement tools. In this section, we will examine these tools—their advantages, disadvantages, and limitations.

Intelligence

The collection of information about organized crime—its evaluation, collation, analysis, reporting, and dissemination—is referred to as "intelligence" (Dintino and Martens 1983). It is laborious and usually unexciting work that requires a great deal of expertise. The *American Heritage Dictionary* (2000) defines *intelligence* as the work of gathering secret information about an actual or potential enemy. Justin Dintino and Frederick Martens (1983: 9) conceive of intelligence as "(1) a process through which information is managed which (2) will hopefully increase our knowledge of a particular problem (3) resulting in preventive and/or informed public policy."

Intelligence data are collected for two main purposes—tactical and strategic. At times, these two categories overlap (Godfrey and Harris 1971). *Tactical intelligence* is information that contributes directly to the achievement of an immediate law enforcement objective, such as arrest and prosecution. *Strategic intelligence* is information that contributes to producing sound judgment with respect to long-range law enforcement objectives and goals. The information is collected over time and put together by an intelligence analyst to reveal new (or newly discovered) patterns of organized crime activity. The information may be unsubstantiated ("raw") data requiring further investigation for confirmation—to become "hard" data.

Robert Stewart (1980: 54) notes the common sources of intelligence data:

- court records
- other public agency documents such as real estate, tax, and incorporation records
- business records
- old case records in the intelligence unit's files
- investigative and intelligence files of other law enforcement agencies
- newspapers, periodicals, books
- utility company records
- documents and items recovered during searches or subpoenaed by grand juries, administrative agencies, and legislative committees
- electronic surveillance
- information and material produced voluntarily by citizens
- statements and/or testimony obtained from accomplices, informants, victims, and law enforcement personnel

This material can be collected overtly or covertly. Covert collection involves the accumulation of information from subjects who are unaware that they are being observed or overheard. Since this type of collection is usually quite expensive in terms of the personnel required, it is usually tied directly to the goal of securing evidence that can be used in prosecution; that is, it is more tactical than strategic.

Drexel Godfrey and Don Harris (1971) refer to analysis as the "heart" of the intelligence system. An analyst uses the methods of social science research, and central to this approach is the hypothesis. The analyst develops a hypothesis, an "educated guess," about the relevance of the information that has already been collected, collated, and stored. The investigators are then told to seek data that will permit "hypothesis testing." If the hypothesis does not withstand an adequate test, alternative hypotheses must be developed and tested. A hypothesis that has been supported by the data after rigorous testing becomes the basis

for an intelligence report. The report guides tactical and/or strategic law enforcement efforts.

Intelligence gathering lacks many of the exciting aspects of law enforcement—there are no television series based on the adventures of intelligence analysts. The results produced by strategic intelligence are never immediate and seldom dramatic. They fail to impress those who allocate funds for law enforcement agencies, and intelligence personnel often have little status in agencies such as the DEA. There have been abuses as well: "A basic principle in collecting information for a criminal intelligence file is that such information should be restricted to what an agency needs to know in order to fulfill its responsibility to detect and combat organized crime in its jurisdiction." Therefore, "the ethnic origin or the political or religious beliefs of any individual, group, or organization should never be the reason for collecting information on them. Criminal activities or associations must be the key factors. If associations are found not to be criminal in nature, the data collected on them should be dropped from the files" (Task Force on Organized Crime 1976: 122).

For several decades, this was not the practice. In many urban police departments and the FBI, extensive intelligence efforts were directed against political groups and personalities. In Los Angeles, this type of activity was accomplished under the cover of the Organized Crime Intelligence Division, which "maintained secret Stalinesque dossiers, some of them kept in privately rented units; there were files on virtually every mover and shaker in Southern California" (Rothmiller and Goldman 1992: 9). "Red squads" and similar units would sometimes "leak" raw data whose source was untrustworthy. However, when such data move through a respected law enforcement agency, there is a "cleansing" effect, and the now "laundered" information takes on new importance, particularly when reported by the news media. Law enforcement intelligence files frequently contain news clips whose source is the agency itself—known as "circular sourcing." Restrictions on what information may be kept in intelligence files and "freedom of information" statutes have resulted to correct such abuses.

Regional Information Sharing Systems (RISS)

Established in 1974, RISS is a multijurisdictional criminal intelligence system that supports the sharing of intelligence information among nearly 5,000 federal, state, and local agencies. Funded by the Bureau of Justice Assistance of the U.S. Department of Justice, RISS is designed to enhance the ability of state and local criminal justice agencies to identify, target, and remove criminal conspiracies and activities spanning jurisdictional boundaries. The six regional RISS centers are staffed by intelligence and analytical personnel, field representatives, and technical systems personnel. They provide controlled input and dissemination, rapid retrieval, and systematic updating of criminal justice information, as well as data analysis. Centers may also provide investigative support and technical assistance, training, and the loan of specialized equipment (*Regional Information Sharing Systems Program* 1998).

Electronic Surveillance

The great majority of law enforcement officials believe that evidence necessary to bring criminals in the higher echelons of organized crime to justice will not be obtained without the aid of electronic surveillance techniques (President's Commission on Law Enforcement and Administration of Justice 1968). The Task Force on Organized Crime (1976: 148) points out that "because of their organization and methods organization, organized crime activities require sophisticated means of evidence gathering. Often witnesses will not come forward, and members are bound by either an oath of silence or threats of violence. Often the use of informants is of limited value, and many organizations are difficult, if not impossible, for undercover agents to penetrate to the point where they can obtain useful evidence." One way to break through these conspiratorial safeguards, notes the task force, is through the use of electronic surveillance.

As the technology to accomplish electronic surveillance became increasingly sophisticated, the temptation to use it to gain information that is none of the state's business has proven quite strong. Legal definitions of just what may be part of law enforcement's business have been evolving since the first wiretap case confronted the U.S. Supreme Court in 1928. In *Olmstead v. United States* (277 U.S. 438), telephone wiretaps were used to prosecute persons involved in large-scale Prohibition violations. The interception of Olmstead's telephone line was accomplished without trespass. Chief Justice William Howard Taft, writing for the majority, determined that since telephone conversations are not tangible items, they cannot be the subject of an illegal seizure, and thus wiretapping is not prohibited by the Fourth Amendment. Shortly after the *Olmstead* decision, Congress prohibited interception of telephonic communication without judicial authorization.

The first case to reach the Supreme Court under the congressional restrictions was *Goldman v. United States* (316 U.S. 129), in 1942. The Court, consistent with *Olmstead*, ruled that a dictaphone placed against an office wall did not violate the Fourth Amendment because there was no trespass. In *Silverman v. United States* (365 U.S. 505, 1961), a foot-long spike with a microphone attached was inserted under a faceboard and into the wall until it made contact with a heating duct that ran through Silverman's house. The Court found this activity unconstitutional, not because of trespass but because of actual intrusion into "a constitutionally protected area."

In 1967 the Supreme Court ruled (*Berger v. New York*, 388 U.S. 41) that a New York State law authorizing "eavesdropping" was unconstitutional. The case involved a Chicago public relations man who was convicted of conspiracy to bribe the chairman of the New York State Liquor Authority. The

Electronic Surveillance

- *Telephone tap:* An extension hooked into a line at a telephone switching station.
- *Transmitter:* A microphone about the size of a small wooden matchbox. The batteries need to be changed every 48 hours. More-sophisticated devices can be turned on and off from a remote location using a microwave signal.
- *Telephone transmitter:* A microphone wired inside a telephone, from which it draws its power. Some devices are activated by an outside telephone call and can transmit voices as well as telephone conversations.

- *Laser interceptors:* These devices can be pointed at a window to record vibrations on the glass caused by indoor conversations. A computer converts the vibrations into conversations.
- *Satellite relays:* Some microphones can transmit by way of a space satellite to a ground receiver.
- *Fiber optics:* Microsized fiber optic filaments embedded into walls draw power from a building's electrical system and can be used to intercept conversations.

evidence consisted of conversations intercepted by bugs and wiretaps pursuant to a court order. According to the Court, the statute failed to require warrants to state the specific crime being committed and the place or the persons to be surveilled. Also, no time limits were placed on the order once incriminating conversation was secured.

Later in 1967, the case of *Katz v. United States* (389 U.S. 347) came before the Supreme Court. In violation of the Hobbs Act, Katz transmitted wagering information on the telephone (McGuiness 1981: 27):

In *Katz*, the Government, acting without a warrant or other judicial authorization, intercepted defendant's end of telephone conversations by means of two microphones attached by tape to the top of two adjoining public telephone booths from which Katz regularly made calls. Katz was subsequently prosecuted for the interstate transportation of wagering information by telephone in violation of a Federal statute, and tape recordings of the intercepted telephone calls were introduced in evidence over his objection. The Government argued that since no physical intrusion was made into the booth and since it was not a "constitutionally protected area" (the defendant having no possessory interest as such in the booth), a search for

Fourth Amendment purposes did not occur. In holding that there was a search, the Court stated that it was erroneous to resolve questions of Fourth Amendment law on the basis of whether a constitutionally protected area is involved, "[f]or the Fourth Amendment protects people, not places." This being the case, the reach of the "Amendment [also] cannot turn upon the presence or absence of a physical intrusion into any given enclosure." The Court thus concluded that the Government's activities "violated the privacy upon which [the defendant] justifiably relied while using the telephone," and hence a search within the meaning of the Fourth Amendment had taken place.

The keys to understanding *Katz* and subsequent decisions concerning surveillance and the Fourth Amendment are the phrases "reasonable expectation of privacy," "legitimate expectation of privacy," and "justifiable expectation of privacy" (McGuiness 1981). As Kimberly Kingston (1988: 22–23) notes, the Supreme Court "redefined the term 'search' to include any governmental action which intrudes into an area where there is a reasonable expectation of privacy." However, as she points out (1988: 24), it is not the subjective expectation of privacy that is protected but rather "only those that society as a whole is willing to recognize and protect." Thus, while a drug trafficking defendant may have had a subjective expectation that his trash was private, it was not an expectation of privacy that society was willing to recognize and protect—the defendant had exposed his garbage to the public, and that included the police (*California v. Greenwood*, 107 S.Ct. 3260, 1987).

During the 1960s, the FBI used electronic surveillance extensively, often without the benefit of judicial authorization: "Numerous Congressional committees and criminal court judges in the 1960s found that the FBI and local police had for decades used illegal electronic surveillance to supplement their investigations. And, worse, they had used taps and bugs to spy on and disrupt the activities of law-abiding citizens and organizations. Civil rights leader Martin Luther King, Jr., for one, was the subject of extensive electronic surveillance in the 1960s" (Krajick 1983: 30). Furthermore, private wiretapping received greater coverage in the press: "The publicity continued to grow, and by the mid-1960s there were regular exposures of industrial espionage and of electronic surveillance operations by private detectives" (National Commission for the Review of Federal and State Laws Relating to Wiretapping and Electronic Surveillance 1976: 39—hereafter, Wiretap Commission).

As a result of this activity, and in order to bring some uniformity into the use of electronic surveillance, Congress enacted Title III of the Omnibus Crime Control and Safe Streets Act in 1968 (18 U.S.C. Sections 2510–20). It was the first time in history that Congress had sanctioned electronic surveillance (Lapidus 1974): "Pressures had been mounting on Congress to enact legislation regulating electronic surveillance, but the scope of the controls could not be agreed to. *Berger* and *Katz* not only forced some legislative action by ruling out law enforcement use of electronic microphones without judicial warrant, but also outlined the scope of the privacy which was protected by the Fourth Amendment and sketched the guidelines for adequate warrant protection" (Wiretap Commission 1976: 38).

Title III bans all private eavesdropping and authorizes federal officials and prosecutors in states whose laws conform to the federal statute to petition for court authorization to intercept wire or oral communications, provided that

1. There is probable cause for belief that an individual is committing, has committed, or is about to commit a particular offense that is enumerated in Title III.
2. There is probable cause for belief that particular communications concerning that offense will be obtained through such interception.
3. Normal investigative procedures have been tried and have failed, or reasonably appear unlikely to succeed if tried, or are too dangerous.
4. There is probable cause for belief that the facilities in which, or the place where, the oral communications are to be intercepted is being used, or is about to be used, in conjunction with the commission of such offense, or is leased to, listed in the name of, or commonly used by persons believed to commit such offenses.

The Title III judicial order terminates in 30 days or less, unless extended by the issuing judge:

No order entered under this section may authorize or approve the interception of any wire or oral communication for any period longer than necessary to achieve the objective of the authorization, nor in any event longer than thirty days. Extensions of an order may be granted, but only upon the application for an extension made in accordance with subsection (1) of this section [essentially the four points listed earlier]. . . . The period of extension shall be no longer than the authorizing judge deems necessary to achieve the purposes for which it was granted and in no event for longer than thirty days. Every order and extension thereof shall contain a provision that the authorization to intercept shall be executed as soon as practicable, shall be conducted in such a way as to *minimize the interception of communications not otherwise*

"Double Jeopardy"

In 1982 the FBI bugged the home of Angelo Ruggiero, a Gambino soldier in the crew headed by then-*caporegime* John Gotti. The tapes implicated Ruggiero in drug trafficking—which Family boss Paul Castellano had "outlawed"—and he was recorded being critical of Castellano's leadership and impugning his manhood. The FBI subsequently placed a bug in Castellano's home, and he was heard referring to the Gotti faction as a bunch of brainless gorillas. Legal procedure requires that the results of electronic surveillance be made available to all defendants prior to trial. Castellano, who was awaiting trial, would have access to the Ruggiero comments. Before they could be revealed, however, the Gotti faction, fearing retribution from their boss, assassinated Castellano (O'Brien and Kurins 1991).

subject to interception under this chapter; and must terminate upon attainment of the authorization objective, or in any event in thirty days [emphasis added].

The *minimization* noted above requires that great care be taken to avoid intercepting conversations that are not relevant to the judicial order. In order to ensure that an unauthorized interception does not occur, the eavesdropping equipment must be monitored at all times. Each time a conversation is intercepted, the agent is permitted to listen only briefly, long enough to establish whether the nature of the conversation is within the scope of the judicial order. If the monitoring agent should hear a privileged conversation between doctor and patient or attorney and client or a personal conversation between husband and wife unrelated to the judicial order, he or she must discontinue the interception by hitting the DNR (dialed number recorder) button. The recorder stops, and an audible tone starts; the DNR prints out the time and date that the minimization occurred and whether the monitor went back to the conversation or the conversation ended in the minimization mode. A monitoring agent who allows the recording of a privileged conversation jeopardizes the results of the investigation.

Judges and prosecutors are required to file reports on their use of Title IIIs with the Administrative Office of the United States Courts (AOUSC) in Washington, D.C., and the AOUSC must submit an annual report on Title III with Congress. Title III requires that the target(s) of the judicial order be notified that their conversations have been intercepted within 90 days after termination of the order.

Although Title III regulates the interception of wire and oral communications, Congress did not explicitly provide any authority for the surreptitious placement of a listening device ("bug") to intercept oral communication—a "black bag job." Federal courts remained in conflict over the issue until *Dalia v. United States* (441 U.S. 238, 1979). FBI agents pried open a window in the New Jersey office of Lawrence Dalia in order to install a bug in his ceiling. As a result of the intercepted conversations, Dalia was convicted of violating the Hobbs Act by receiving property stolen from an interstate shipment. The Supreme Court concluded that a Title III warrant for eavesdropping implicitly grants authority for covert entry. Amendments to Title III in 1986 authorize "roving surveillance" of suspects using a number of different telephones or sites.

Title III is sometimes criticized by law enforcement officials because of the extensive investigation and documentation required to secure a warrant, although there are emergency exceptions built into the statute:

> Any investigative or law enforcement officer, specially designated by the Attorney General, or by the principal prosecuting attorney of any State or subdivision thereof acting pursuant to a statute of that State, who reasonably determines that (a) an emergency situation exists with respect to conspiratorial

activities threatening the national security interests or to conspiratorial activities characteristic of organized crime that requires a wire or oral communication to be intercepted before an order authorizing such interception can with due diligence be obtained, and (b) there are grounds which an order could be entered under this chapter to authorize such interception may intercept such wire or oral communication if an application for an order approving the interception is made in accordance with this section within forty-eight hours after the interception has occurred, or begins to occur.

Any wire or oral communication may be intercepted legally by federal agents (while some states, such as Illinois, have local restrictions) without a court order if one of the parties to the communication gives prior consent. Thus, law enforcement officers and informants may be "wired" to secure incriminating conversation without a court order. In 1979 the U.S. Supreme Court (by a 5–3 vote) ruled that the police do not need a search warrant to record the numbers dialed from a particular telephone—there is an absence of a "reasonable expectation of privacy" because the telephone company routinely maintains such information for billing purposes. In *Smith v. Maryland* (442 U.S. 735), the Court affirmed the robbery conviction of a man linked to the crime by a pen register, which, when installed at a telephone company switching station, can record the numbers dialed from a particular phone.

Since Title III was enacted in 1968, more than 30 states have passed statutes permitting electronic surveillance, although some place restrictions beyond those contained in the federal statutes. Some states rarely make use of the law, and cost is a major reason. In addition to the investigative costs of securing the order, monitoring ties up at least two law enforcement officers over three shifts for 30 days or more on a continuous basis, at an average cost in excess of $40,000. There have been cases in which the cost exceeded $2 million—and less than 20 percent of all electronic surveillance actually produces incriminating evidence. Persons in orga-

nized crime frequently limit conversations that could be subjected to interception to code phrases. As John Gotti, boss of the Gambino Family, was recorded as advising a young associate about telephone conversations, "Don't ever say anything you don't want played back to you some day"—advice that he frequently disregarded (Mustain and Capeci 1988: 115). Conversations may be in a foreign language, so monitors have to be fluent in that language, or the conversation may be in a dialect or contain colloquial expressions that are difficult for outsiders to translate.

Material from electronic bugs often must be enhanced by specialists to reduce background noise from radios or televisions. The conversations must then be transcribed, and usually only the monitoring agents are familiar enough with the subjects' manner of speech to be able to accomplish this tedious task, which can take months of effort.

In addition to the wire and oral communications covered in Title III, the Electronic Communications Privacy Act (ECPA) of 1987 created a third category, "electronic communications," governing conversations over a broader array of technology, including cellular (but not cordless) telephones and electronic (e-) mail. The ECPA also regulates the use of pen registers (devices that can record the phone numbers of outgoing calls) and trap-and-trace devices that can record the numbers of incoming calls—they are usually used in tandem. A simplified court order is required to install these devices (Colbridge 2000).

In recent years, electronic surveillance has been complicated by technological advances in communications. For example, conversations via high-capacity digital lines (human voices translated into numbers) and fiber optic lines (using pulses of light) cannot be intercepted using conventional wiretap equipment. Advances in encryption technology allow for communication virtually impossible for eavesdroppers to decipher; they would need access to the code (or an impossible expenditure of time—years). Inexpensive computer programs and hardware can now scramble telephone calls and e-mail. In response, the Department of Justice (DOJ) has requested a

More Than One Way . . .

In 1999, federal agents seized a computer from Nicodemo S. Scarfo, Jr., son of the imprisoned Philadelphia crime boss. However, they were unable to access information because it was stored in an encrypted file. The agents subsequently requested another search warrant (but not a Title III wiretap order) to install a "key logger," a device that records the keys pressed on a computer keyboard. This enabled the FBI to figure out the password and, thereby, decrypt Scarfo's files, which allegedly contained records of gambling and loansharking operations (Salkowski 2001; Schwartz 2001).

weakening of the systems so they can be subjected to law enforcement surveillance. Authority for this is based on a DOJ interpretation of the 1994 Communications Assistance for Law Enforcement Act intended to help law enforcement agencies intercept telephone calls. This has engendered strong opposition from many members of Congress and from telephone companies. They argue that making communication devices more susceptible to FBI surveillance would also make them more vulnerable to illegal penetrations while retarding advances in communications technology. In 1998 the Federal Communications Commission moved the deadline for complying with the law. The September 11, 2001, terrorist attacks will undoubtedly lead to greater authority to intercept electronic communications.

In the meantime, additional methods for avoiding electronic surveillance have surfaced, such as the use of anonymous remailers. Messages sent over the Internet are received by the remailer, which automatically strips off all traces of the sender's identity and forwards the message to an electronic mailbox (or to other remailers to further bury the identity of the source). Since messages are remailed in a random sequence different from the order in which they arrive, anyone monitoring the remailer cannot match outgoing messages with incoming messages to identify who sent which message (Lohr 1999).

Additional problems arise with the widespread use of cellular phones. Based on the 1994 Communications Assistance for Law Enforcement Act, the DOJ requires the installation of devices that will make it easier for the government to intercept cellular calls. The cellular industry is resisting and has filed suit to avoid compliance. When used by criminals, drug traffickers in particular, cellular phones are often clones of those used by innocent persons. A criminal can aim a scanner at a car in a heavily trafficked location and illegally record phone identification numbers that are transmitted every time a call is made. Then, using special software, the stolen numbers are transferred to a microchip in a new telephone. Phones and numbers are changed frequently, making interception and tracing difficult. There is further controversy over the use of devices to track cellular callers—cellular companies have been installing them to be able to locate callers in the event of emergencies—which would be an aid to law enforcement. Should the caller have control over giving out his or her location? In addition, there are readily available radios that can hop frequencies—"spread spectrum"—and are nearly impossible to track.

THE GRAND JURY

In the federal system, a grand jury is a body of 23 citizens empowered to operate with a quorum of 16 and requiring 12 votes for an indictment. In the state system, the minimum number of jurors varies considerably, although nowhere does the maximum number of grand jurors exceed 23. While some states adhere to the federal rule of 12 for an indictment, in others the range is anywhere from 4 to 9. Like those serving on a petit or trial jury, grand jurors are usually selected from the voting rolls; however, they meet in secret to consider evidence presented by the prosecutor.

Since the members of a grand jury are not agents of the government—they act as direct representatives of the citizenry—the extensive due process rights typically enjoyed by a criminal defendant are not necessarily relevant to grand jury proceedings. Their activities are secret, and only 16 states permit the subject of a grand jury inquiry to have an attorney present, and then only to give advice. In the remaining states and the federal system, an attorney is not even permitted to accompany his or her client at a grand jury hearing. There is no right to present evidence or to cross-examine adverse witnesses. While the subject can refuse to answer any questions whose answers may be incriminating, he or she can be granted immunity and required to testify under the threat of being jailed for contempt.

The grand jury can receive virtually any type of information, even that which would not be admissible at a trial, such as certain types of hearsay and evidence that was secured in violation of the Fourth Amendment—the exclusionary rule does not apply to the grand jury (*United States v. Calandra*, 414 U.S. 338, 1974). In every state and in the federal system, the grand jury may be used for investigative purposes, and when so used it has broad investigative authority, including the power to subpoena persons and documents. In those states where statutes permit and in the federal system, the grand jury is used to investigate the operations of law enforcement and other government agencies, particularly when corruption is suspected, and to investigate the activities of organized crime.

The Organized Crime Control Act of 1970 requires that a special grand jury be convened at least every 18 months in federal judicial districts of more than one million persons. It can also be convened at the request of a federal prosecutor. Its typical life, 18 months, may be extended to 36 months. The special grand jury and grand juries of several states have the power to publish reports at the completion of their terms on certain types of noncriminal misconduct by public officials. While such reports cannot command any particular ac-

tion, the widespread publicity they typically enjoy usually encourages action by government officials.

According to Robert Stewart (1980: 124), the investigative grand jury is:

> the single most useful tool by which to attack the traditional forms of organized crime. For example, convicted drug pushers, bookmakers, numbers writers and runners, prostitutes, weapons offenders and petty thieves can be summoned before the grand jury, immunized and questioned about the higher-ups in a particular enterprise or activity. If the witness is not already under charges, there is little likelihood that the grant of immunity will jeopardize any prosecution. If the witness testifies truthfully, that witness will be ostracized from the criminal community and thereby neutralized as an organized crime operative. Moreover, the defection of one member of an organization may serve as a catalyst which forces others within the organization to defect and cooperate with the state. Whenever any appreciable number of lower-level offenders are summoned before an investigative grand jury, the higher-ups in the organized crime structure can never be sure what, if anything, is being said. This alone is sufficient to generate severe tensions within the organized crime structure.

IMMUNITY

The Fifth Amendment to the U.S. Constitution provides that no person "shall be compelled in any criminal case to be a witness against himself." This is an important protection for the individual against the coercive powers of the state, and it can be partially neutralized by a grant of immunity. There are two types of immunity:

1. *Transactional immunity* provides blanket protection against prosecution for crimes about which a person is compelled to testify.
2. *Use immunity* prohibits the information provided by a person from being used

against him or her, but the person can still be prosecuted using evidence obtained independently of his or her compelled testimony.

In many states and the federal system, the court or the prosecutor may grant immunity to reluctant witnesses. Legislative or administrative bodies investigating criminal activity can also request a grant of immunity. A witness who, after being granted immunity, refuses to testify can be subjected to civil or criminal contempt:

> The *civil contempt* proceeding is summary in nature and relatively simple. First the witness is immunized. Upon refusing to answer in the grand jury [or other authorized body,] the witness appears before the court. The prosecutor makes an oral application and the court instructs the witness to testify. The witness returns to the grand jury room; and, if recalcitrant, is directed to reappear before the court. The prosecutor then makes an oral application for the court to enforce its previous order, which the witness has disobeyed. The prosecutor explains what has occurred before the grand jury, and the foreperson or reporter testifies about these facts. The witness is given an opportunity to be heard; and thereafter the court decides whether the witness is in contempt and should be remanded. (Stewart 1980: 239)

"The remand order normally specifies that the witness shall remain confined until he offers to purge himself of the contempt by agreeing to testify or for the life of the grand jury, whichever is shorter" (Stewart 1980: 240). The term of a grand jury is usually 18 months. Legislative committees and administrative bodies, of course, have indefinite terms. In 1970, as a result of his refusal to testify before a New Jersey investigating committee after being immunized, Jerry Catena (then acting boss of the Genovese Family) was imprisoned for contempt. He remained imprisoned for five years, never testifying.

The *criminal contempt* proceeding is quite different, since it requires a formal trial, and the witness is entitled to the full array of due process rights enjoyed by any criminal defendant. However, being found guilty of criminal contempt can result in a substantial sentence of imprisonment: "The purpose of the remand is coercive [to compel testimony], while the purpose of the criminal contempt sentence is punitive and deterrent" (Stewart 1980: 246). Of course, a witness, whether immunized or not, is subject to the laws against perjury.

In 1972 the Supreme Court decided the case of *Kastigar v. United States* (406 U.S. 441), which involved several persons who had been subpoenaed to appear before a federal grand jury in California in 1971. The assistant U.S. attorney, believing that the petitioners in *Kastigar* were likely to assert their Fifth Amendment privilege, secured from the federal district court an order directing them to answer all questions and produce evidence before the grand jury under a grant of immunity. Nevertheless, the persons involved refused to answer questions, arguing that the "scope of the immunity provided by the statute was not coextensive with the scope of the privilege against self-incrimination, and therefore was not sufficient to supplant the privilege and compel their testimony."

The Supreme Court, in upholding the immunity order, quoted from the federal immunity statute: "The witness may not refuse to comply with the order on the basis of his privilege against self-incrimination; but no testimony or other information compelled under the order (or any information directly or indirectly derived from such testimony or other information) may be used against the witness in any criminal case, except a prosecution for perjury, giving a false statement, or otherwise failing to comply with the order." The Court concluded that since the statute prohibited the prosecutorial authorities from using the compelled testimony in any respect, it therefore ensured that the testimony could not lead to the infliction of criminal penalties on the witness. In a dissenting opinion, Justice Thurgood Marshall pointed to the possibility of using the testimonial information for investigative leads designed to secure evidence against the witness. The Court majority stated that the statute barred such use of the testimony.

However, civil action against a criminally immunized witness is possible and has been upheld by the appellate courts (Rhodes 1984). In addition, a grant of immunity does not protect the witness from a loss of social status, employment, and, most important, revenge from those against whom he or she is forced to testify. Rufus King (1963: 651) raises additional issues:

> The immunity bargain is a somewhat unsavory device per se, inaccurate and potentially very unfair; it should be used only sparingly and where it is absolutely required. Immunity grants are always exchanges, a pardon for crimes that would otherwise be punishable, given in return for testimony that could otherwise be withheld. In every case the interrogating authority must enter into a special "deal" with a wrongdoer to buy his testimony at the price of exoneration for something [for which] he would otherwise deserve punishment.
>
> Such bargains are always somewhat blind. Ordinarily the witness will be hostile, so that his examiners cannot be sure in advance exactly what value the withheld testimony will have. And at the same time, especially in broad legislative or administrative inquiries, it is impossible to tell beforehand just what crimes are likely to be exonerated. Conceivably, the witness may have a surprise ready for his questioners at every turn of the proceedings.

Because of the potentially undesirable repercussions, some prosecutors have developed guidelines for consideration when making an immunity decision. The following guidelines are from the New Jersey Division of Criminal Justice (quoted in Committee on the Office of Attorney General 1978: 27):

- Can the information be obtained from any source other than a witness who wants to negotiate immunity?
- How useful is the information for the purposes of criminal prosecution?
- What is the likelihood that the witness can successfully be prosecuted?
- What is the relative significance of the witness as a potential defendant?
- What is the relative significance of the potential defendant against whom the witness offers to testify? In other words, is the witness requesting immunity more culpable than those against whom she or he is agreeing to testify? Are they in a position to provide evidence against the witness or superior evidence against others?
- What is the value of the testimony of the witness to the case (is it the core evidence upon which the prosecution is based)?
- What impact will immunity have on the credibility of the witness at trial? Are the terms of the immunity agreement so favorable to the witness that the jury will not accept the testimony?
- What impact will immunity have on the prosecutor's personal credibility and that of his or her office?

However, Rhodes notes "that a grant of immunity has a favorable impact on a jury. It makes a defendant's testimony more credible. A prosecutor can point to the witness with a sordid record and say to the jury, 'What reason does Mr. X have to lie? His immunity is assured and if he lies he will be prosecuted for perjury!'" (1984: 193).

Following this chapter, "In Conclusion" will provide an overview of organized crime and its future.

INTERNET CONNECTIONS

Bureau of Alcohol, Tobacco and Firearms: **atf.treas.gov**

U.S. Customs Service: **www.customs.ustreas.gov**

Federal Bureau of Investigation: **www.fbi.gov**

Law enforcement agencies/international links: **www.copnet.org/index.html**

Drug Enforcement Administration: **www.usdoj.gov/dea**

U.S. Coast Guard: **www.uscg.mil**

U.S. Marshals Service: **www.usdoj.gov/marshals**

Federal law enforcement links: **state.gov/www/global/narcotics_law/sites.html**

REVIEW QUESTIONS

1. Why does most organized crime law enforcement take place at the federal level?
2. What are the two primary responsibilities of the Drug Enforcement Administration?
3. What agencies of the Department of Justice are responsible for organized crime law enforcement?
4. What agencies of the Department of the Treasury have responsibilities for organized crime law enforcement?
5. What unusual powers are enjoyed by Customs Service agents?
6. What are the responsibilities and special powers of the Coast Guard?
7. Why is the use of military personnel to fight drug trafficking controversial?
8. What is meant by "intelligence" in law enforcement, and what are the two types of intelligence?
9. What does federal law (Title III) require with respect to electronic surveillance?
10. What are the advantages of using the grand jury to investigate organized crime?
11. What are the advantages and disadvantages of using immunity in OC cases?
12. Why is the Witness Protection Program both necessary and controversial?
13. What is the role of the grand jury in responding to organized crime?

IN CONCLUSION. . .

Responding in a rational manner to organized crime requires a sense of proportion and an appreciation of American history. Organized crime in America can be conceived of as one stage along a continuum. Our colonial forebears exhibited many of the activities currently associated with organized crime: bribery, usury, and monopoly, not to mention seizure of land by force, indentured servitude, and slavery. Early American adventurers cheated and killed Native Americans, and chartered pirates—privateers—plundered the high seas. During the War of 1812, and later during the Civil War, profiteers accumulated fortunes while the less fortunate suffered and died. The range wars in the West and the frauds, bribery, violence, and monopolistic practices of the "robber barons" are all part of the context in which we must understand modern forms of organized crime. The cost of organized crime must be measured against the cost of corporate crime, which has the potential to harm far more persons, both financially and physically (see, for example, Clinard et al. 1979; Mokhiber 1988; Tillman and Pontell 1995).

Organized crime has provided economic opportunity for certain groups, allowing them to move into legitimate society on a level that would otherwise not be readily available. There are, of course, ethical and moral objections to "blasting" or "thieving" into the middle or upper strata, even though this has been a feature of U.S. history from the earliest days. Very few management-level members of OC have been able to escape either assassination or significant prison terms. Indeed, law enforcement efforts against organized crime are impressive, constrained as they are by the requirements of a democratic system that provides a great deal of legal protection to even its criminal citizens. With this in mind, we should proceed with a

great deal of caution when contemplating changes in policy with respect to organized crime.

Organized crime evolved out of moralistic laws that created opportunity for certain innovative actors. As circumstances changed, so did available opportunity, and organized crime exhibited great flexibility. Beginning as essentially a provider of "goods and services," it entered racketeering and legitimate business, adapting to changing laws and social and economic conditions. Policy for responding to organized crime must be based on an appreciation of history, an understanding of the "side effects" of proposed policy changes, and the realization that organized crime has proven to be a dynamic phenomenon.

In the future, we can expect that in the Darwinian world of organized crime, weaker components will either die either literally or figuratively, while the survivors will improve on their style of organization and the sophistication of their operations. Affecting this process will be government, helping to "trim the herd" while occasionally dealing shattering blows to organized criminals and their organizations. We can expect that *Cosa Nostra* will continue indefinitely, at times limping along, while others, such as Russian organized crime, will become more structured—and more threatening. Organized crime differs in many significant ways from the nonorganized variety. Organization permits a scope of activities unavailable to conventional criminals, while providing a vehicle for criminal interaction and coordination on a regional, national, and international level. For these reasons, organized crime, like threatening diseases, will always be part of the global community, requiring vigilance and international cooperation to limit its destructive power.

REFERENCES

Abadinsky, Howard
  1983 *The Criminal Elite: Professional and Organized Crime.* Westport, CT: Greenwood.
  1981a *The Mafia in America: An Oral History.* New York: Praeger.
  1981b *Organized Crime.* Boston: Allyn and Bacon.

Abel, Ernest L., ed.
  1978 *The Scientific Study of Marijuana.* Chicago: Nelson-Hall.

"Abortion Harassers as Racketeers"
  1998 *New York Times* (April 23): 20.

Abrahamson, Mark
  1996 *Urban Enclaves: Identity and Place in America.* New York: St. Martin's Press.

Adrade, Xavier, Stephen J. Sifaneck, and Alan Neaigus
  1999 "Dope Sniffers in New York City: An Ethnography of Heroin Markets and Patterns of Use." *Journal of Drug Issues* 22(2): 271–98.

Afro-Lineal Organized Crime
  1990 New Jersey State Commission of Investigation.

Agence France-Press
  1997 "Japan Fears Reprisals After Mob Boss Is Slain." *New York Times* (August 29): 5.

Ahmed-Ullah, Noreen S.
  2001 "Pashtun Identity Defies Colonial Line." *Chicago Tribune* (November 6): 15.

Aichhorn, August
  1963 *Wayward Youth.* New York: Viking Press.

Albanese, Jay S.
  1996 *Organized Crime in America,* 3d ed. Cincinnati, OH: Anderson.
  1995 *Contemporary Issues in Organized Crime.* Monsey, NY: Criminal Justice Press.
  1988 "Government Perceptions of Organized Crime: The Presidential Commissions, 1967 and 1987." *Federal Probation* 52 (March): 58–63.

Albini, Joseph L.
  1971 *The American Mafia: Genesis of a Legend.* New York: Appleton-Century-Crofts.

Albini, Joseph L., R. E. Rogers, Victor Shabalin, Valery Kutushev, and Vladimr Moiseev
  1995 "Russian Organized Crime: Its History, Structure and Function." *Journal of Contemporary Criminal Justice* 11 (December): 213–43.

Alexander, Herbert E. and Gerald E. Caiden
  1985 *The Politics and Economics of Organized Crime.* Lexington, MA: D.C. Heath.

Alexander, Shana
  1988 *The Pizza Connection: Lawyers, Money, Drugs, Mafia.* New York: Weidenfeld and Nicolson.

Allen, Frederick
  1998 "American Spirit." *American Heritage* (May/June): 82–92.

Allsop, Kenneth
  1968 *The Bootleggers: The Story of Prohibition.* New Rochelle, NY: Arlington House.

Allum, P. A.
  1973 *Politics and Society in Post-War Naples.* Cambridge: Cambridge University Press.

American Heritage Dictionary, 4th edition
  2000 Boston: Houghton Mifflin.

Anastasia, George
  1998 *The Goodfella Tapes.* New York: Avon.
  1991 *Blood and Honor: Inside the Scarfo Mob—The Mafia's Most Violent Family.* New York: William Morrow.

Anbinder, Tyler
  2001 *Five Points: The 19th-Century Neighborhood That Invented Tap Dance, Stole Elections, and Became the World's Most Notorious Slum.* New York: Free Press.
  1992 *Nativism and Slavery: The Northern Know-Nothings and the Politics of the 1850s.* New York: Oxford University Press.

Anderson, Annelise Graebner
  1979 *The Business of Organized Crime: A Cosa Nostra Family.* Stanford, CA: Hoover Institution Press.

Andrews, Edmund L.
  1995 "The Mob's Truly Sorry: Killing Upsets the Police." *New York Times* (September 6): 4.

Andrews, Wayne
  1941 *The Vanderbilt Legend.* New York: Harcourt, Brace.

"Anti-Drug Efforts Encounter Resistance in Colombia"
  1995 *New York Times* (December 12): 4.

Arax, Mark and Tom Gorman
  1995 "The State's Illicit Farm Belt Export." *Los Angeles Times* (March 13): 1, 16, 17.

Argentine, Adolfo Beria di
1993 "The Mafias in Italy." Pages 19–30 in *Mafia Issues*, edited by Ernesto U. Savona. Milan, Italy: United Nations.

Arlacchi, Pino
1993 *Men of Dishonor: Inside the Sicilian Mafia*. New York: William Morrow.
1986 *Mafia Business: The Mafia Ethic and the Spirit of Capitalism*. London: Verso.

Aronson, Harvey
1978 *Deal*. New York: Ballantine Books.
1973 *The Killing of Joey Gallo*. New York: Putnam's.

Asbury, Herbert
1950 *The Great Illusion: An Informal History of Prohibition*. Garden City, NY: Doubleday.
1942 *Gem of the Prairie: An Informal History of the Chicago Underworld*. Garden City, NY: Knopf.
1928 *Gangs of New York*. New York: Knopf.

Associated Press
1998a "Italy Arrests Scores of Mafia Suspects." *New York Times* (June 27): 4.
1998b "12 Convicted in Prison Plot to Control Drug Gangs." *New York Times* (May 31): 8.
1997 "'Wino Willic' Forkner; Inspired 'The Wild One.'" *Chicago Tribune* (June 26): Sec. 2: 10.
1996 "Hell's Angels Center Explodes in Denmark." *New York Times* (October 7): 4.

"At a Mafia Grave, Violent Death"
1996 *New York Times* (August 28): 6.

Audett, James Henry
1954 *Rap Sheet: My Life Story*. New York: William Sloane.

Bailey, Pearce
1974 "The Heroin Habit." Pages 171–76 in *Yesterday's Addicts: American Society and Drug Abuse, 1865–1920*, edited by Howard Wayne Morgan. Norman: University of Oklahoma Press.

Baker, Russell
1996 "Taking the Saps." *New York Times* (June 15): 11.

"Bank Officer Is Convicted of Laundering"
1994 *Chicago Tribune* (June 3): 10.

Barboza, David
1999 "$1.1 Billion to Settle Suit on Vitamins." *New York Times* (November 4): C1.

Barboza, Joe and Hank Messick
1976 *Barboza*. New York: Dell.

Barger, Ralph "Sonny" with Keith and Kent Zimmerman
2000 *Hell's Angels*. New York: William Morrow.

Barnum, Art and Ray Gibson
2000 "Indicted Man's Wife Said to Aid Theft Probe." *Chicago Tribune* (October 21): 6.

Barzini, Luigi
1977 "Italians in New York: The Way We Were in 1929." *New York* (April 4): 34–38.
1972 *The Italians* (paperback ed.). New York: Bantam.
1965 *The Italians*. New York: Atheneum.

Bearak, Barry
2001 "At Heroin's Source, Taliban Do What 'Just Say No' Could Not." *New York Times* (May 24): 1, 12.

Beck, Jerome and Marsha Rosenbaum
1994 *Pursuit of Ecstasy: The MDMA Experience*. Albany, NY: State University of New York Press.

Beeching, Jack
1975 *The Chinese Opium Wars*. New York: Harcourt Brace Jovanovich.

Behan, Tom
1996 *The Camorra*. London: Routledge.

Behar, Richard
1996 "How Bill Ruchelshaus Is Taking on the New York Mob." *Fortune* (January 15): 91–100.

Bell, Daniel
1964 *The End of Ideology*. Glencoe, IL: Free Press.
1963 "The Myth of the Cosa Nostra." *The New Leader* 46 (December): 12–15.

Bell, Ernest A., ed.
1909 *War on the White Slave Trade*. Chicago: Thompson.

Belluck, Pam
1998 "44 Officers Are Charged After Ohio Sting Operation." *New York Times* (January 22): 14.

Belsamo, William and George Carpozi
1995 *Under the Clock: The Mafia's First Hundred Years*. Far Hills, NJ: New Horizon Press.

Bendavid, Naftali
1999 "Vitamin Price-Fixing Draws a Record $755 Million in Fines." *Chicago Tribune* (May 21): 3.

Bennett, David H.
1988 *The Party of Fear: From Nativist Movements to the New Right in American History*. Chapel Hill: University of North Carolina Press.

Bequai, August
1979 *Organized Crime: The Fifth Estate*. Lexington, MA: D.C. Heath.

Berger, Meyer
1957 "Anastasia Slain in a Hotel Here: Led Murder, Inc." *New York Times* (October 26): 1, 12.

1944 "Lepke's Reign of Crime Lasted Over 12 Murder-Strewn Years." *New York Times* (September 21): 1, 20.

1940 "Gang Patterns: 1940." *New York Times Magazine* (August 4): 5, 15.

1935 "Schultz Reigned on Discreet Lines." *New York Times* (October 25): 17.

Bergreen, Laurence
1994 *Capone: The Man and His Era.* New York: Simon and Schuster.

Berke, Richard L.
1989 "U.S. Attack on Airborne Drug Smuggling Called Ineffective." *New York Times* (June 9): 10.

Bey, Lee
1995 "Police Don't Buy Hoover's Reform." *Chicago Sun-Times* (September 1): 23.

Biegel, Herbert and Allan Biegel
1977 *Beneath the Badge: A Story of Police Corruption.* New York: Harper & Row. "Biker Club House Blasted in Norway"
1997 *New York Times* (June 5): 5.

Black, Donald W. with C. Lindon Larson
1999 *Confronting Antisocial Personality Disorder.* New York: Oxford University Press.

Blakey, G. Robert
1986 "RICO's Triple Damage Threat: The Public's Secret Weapon vs. Boesky." *New York Times* (December 7): F3.

Blakey, G. Robert, Ronald Goldstock, and Charles H. Rogovin
1978 *Rackets Bureau: Investigation and Prosecution of Organized Crime.* Washington, DC: U.S. Government Printing Office.

Blau, Peter M.
1964 *Exchange and Power in Social Life.* New York: Wiley.

Bloch, Max with Ron Kenner
1982 *Max the Butcher.* Secaucas, NJ: Lyle Stuart.

Block, Alan A.
1991 *The Business of Crime: A Documentary Study of Organized Crime in the American Economy.* Boulder, CO: Westview.
1979 *East Side–West Side: Organizing Crime in New York, 1930–1950.* Swansea, Wales: Christopher Davis.
1978 "History and the Study of Organized Crime." *Urban Life* 6 (January): 455–74.

Block, Alan A. and Frank R. Scarpitti
1985 *Poisoning for Profit: The Mafia and Toxic Waste.* New York: William Morrow.

Blok, Anton
1974 *The Mafia of a Sicilian Village, 1860–1960: A Study of Violent Peasant Entrepreneurs.* New York: Harper and Row.

Blount, William E. and H. Roy Kaplan
1989 "The Impact of the Daily Lottery on the Numbers Game: Does Legalization Make a Difference?" Paper presented at the Annual Meeting of the Academy of Criminal Justice Sciences, March 29, Washington, DC.

Blum, Howard
1993 *Gangland: How the FBI Broke the Mob.* New York: Pocket Books.

Blum Jack A.
1999 "Offshore Money." Pages 57–84 in *Transnational Crime in the Americas,* edited by Tom Farer. New York: Routledge.

Blumenthal, Ralph
1992 "When the Mob Delivered the Goods." *New York Times Magazine* (July 26): 22–23, 31–34.
1988a *Last Days of the Sicilians: At War with the Mafia; the FBI Assault on the Pizza Connection.* New York: Times Books.

Bohlen, Celestine
1999 "To Sicilians, Russia Has No Mafia. It's Too Wild." *New York Times* (January 19): WK 5.
1998 "Russian Lawmaker's Killing Stirs Anger." *New York Times* (November 22): 14.
1997 "Officially, Sicily Is Desperately Short of Jobs, But Sub Rosa, Things Are Rosier." *New York Times* (June 17): 6.
1996a "Italian Police Arrest a Top Mafia Boss in Sicily." *New York Times* (May 22): 1, 6.
1996b "Italy Treats a Mafia Leader's Repentance with Caution." *New York Times* (August 24): 5.
1996c "Tell-All, Forgive-All Mood of Mafia Disturbs Italians." *New York Times* (October 23): 4.
1996d "Italy's North–South Gap Widens, Posing Problem for Europe Too." *New York Times* (November 15): 1, 8.
1995a "Uffizi Blast 2 Years Ago Laid to Mafia." *New York Times* (August 7): 2.
1995b "Vatican Draws Criticism for Embrace of Andriotti." *New York Times* (December 20): 7.
1995c "As Omerta Crumbles, the Mafia Changes the Rules." *New York Times* (October 11): 3.
1995d "Killings in Sicily Raise Fears of Mafia Campaign." *New York Times* (March 9): 4.
1994 "Graft and Gangsterism in Russia Blight the Entrepreneurial Spirit." *New York Times* (January 30): 1, 6.

1993 "Russia [sic] Mobsters Grow More Violent and Pervasive." *New York Times* (August 16): 1, 4.

Boissevain, Jeremy
1974 *Friends of Friends: Networks, Manipulators and Coalitions.* Oxford: Basil Blackwell.

"Bomb Kills 1 at Biker Gang Headquarters"
1997 *Chicago Tribune* (June 6): 14.

Bonanno, Bill
1999 *Bound by Honor: A Mafioso's Story.* New York: St. Martin's Press.

Bonanno, Joseph with Sergio Lalli
1983 *A Man of Honor: The Autobiography of Joseph Bonanno.* New York: Simon and Schuster.

Bonavolonta, Jules and Brian Duffy
1996 *The Good Guys: How We Turned the FBI 'Round—And Finally Broke the Mob.* New York: Simon and Schuster.

Bonner, Raymond
1999 "Russian Gangsters Exploit Capitalism to Increase Profits." *New York Times* (July 25): 1, 4.

Bonner, Raymond and Christopher Drew
1997 "Cigarette Makers Are Seen as Aiding Rise in Smuggling." *New York Times* (August 25): 1, C12.

Bonner, Raymond and Timothy L. O'Brien
1999 "Activity at Bank Raises Suspicions of Russia Mob Tie." *New York Times* (August 19): 1, 6.

Bonnie, Richard J. and Charles H. Whitebread II
1970 "The Forbidden Fruit and the Tree of Knowledge: An Inquiry into the Legal History of American Marijuana Prohibition." *Virginia Law Review* 56 (October): 971–1203.

Booth, Martin
1990 *The Triads: The Growing Global Threat from the Chinese Criminal Societies.* New York: St. Martin's Press.

Bopp, William J.
1977 *O. W. Wilson and the Search for a Police Profession.* Port Washington, NY: Kennikat Press.

Borger, Julian
2001 "Bodies Pave the Way to Jamaican Polls." *Guardian* (July 12): 6.

Bourgeois, Richard L., Jr., S. P. Hennessey, Jon Moore, and Michael E. Tschupp
2000 "Racketeer Influenced and Corrupt Organizations." *American Criminal Law Review* 37 (Spring): 879–91.

Bowden, Charles
1991 "La Virgen and the Drug Lord." *Phoenix* (March): 96–103.

Bowden, Mark
2001 *Killing Pablo: The Hunt for the World's Greatest Outlaw.* New York: Atlantic Monthly Press.
1987 *Doctor Dealer.* New York: Warner Books.

Boyd, Kier T.
1977 *Gambling Technology.* Washington, DC: U.S. Government Printing Office.

Brant, Martha
1997a "Most Wanted Kingpin?" *Newsweek* (March 10): 36.
1997b "Liposuctioned to Death." *Newsweek* (July 21): 43.

Brashler, William
1981 "Two Brothers from Taylor Street." *Chicago* (September): 150–56, 194.
1977 *The Don: The Life and Death of Sam Giancana.* New York: Harper & Row.

Brecher, Edward M. and the Editors of *Consumer Reports*
1972 *Licit and Illicit Drugs.* Boston: Little, Brown.

Brenner, Marie
1990 "Prime Time Godfather." *Vanity Fair* (May): 109–15, 176 81.

Bresler, Fenton
1980 *The Chinese Mafia.* New York: Stein and Day.

Briley, Ron
1997 "Hollywood and the Rebel Image in the 1950s." *Social Education* (October): 352–58.

Brill, Steven
1978 *The Teamsters.* New York: Simon and Schuster.

Bristow, Edward J.
1982 *Prostitution and Prejudice: The Jewish Fight Against White Slavery 1870–1939.* New York: Schocken Books.

Brodt, Bonita
1981a "'Royal Family' Are Kings of Killing." *Chicago Tribune* (September 6): 5.
1981b "'Royal Family' Boss Gets Death Sentence for Killing." *Chicago Tribune* (September 10): 14.

Brooke, James
1995a "Colombia Marvels at Drug Kingpin: A Chain-Saw Killer, Too?" *New York Times* (June 21): 7.
1995b "Drug Arrests in Colombia Lead to New York Killings." *New York Times* (November 25): 1, 6.
1995c "A Drug Crackdown in Colombia Puts the Cali Cartel on the Run." *New York Times* (June 27): 1, 4.
1995d "Colombia's Rebels Grow Rich from Banditry." *New York Times* (July 2): 1, 4.
1993 "In a 'Dirty War,' Former Drug Allies Are Terrorizing Escobar." *New York Times* (March 4): 4.

1992a "Trafficker Is Still Feared in Colombia." *New York Times* (January 21): 5.

1992b "How Escobar, a Rare Jailbird, Lined His Nest." *New York Times* (August 5): 1, 2.

1991a "Colombia's Rising Export: Fake U.S. Money." *New York Times* (April 21): 4.

1991b "Cali, the 'Quiet Cocaine Cartel,' Profits Through Accommodation." *New York Times* (July 14): 1, 6.

1990 "In the Capital of Cocaine, Savagery Is the Habit." *New York Times* (June 7): 4.

Brooks, Thomas R.
1971 *Toil and Trouble: A History of American Labor.* New York: Dell.

Buenker, John D.
1973 *Urban Liberalism and Progressive Reform.* New York: Scribner's.

"Bugs Moran Dies in Federal Prison"
1957 *New York Times* (February 26): 59.

Bullough, Vern L.
1965 *The History of Prohibition.* New Hyde Park, NY: University Books.

Burnett, Stanton H. and Luca Mantovani
1998 *The Italian Guillotine.* Lanham, MA: Rowman and Littlefield.

Burns, John F.
1990 "Afghans: Now They Blame America." *New York Times Magazine* (February 4): 23–29, 37.

Buse, Renee
1965 *The Deadly Silence.* Garden City, NY: Doubleday.

Butterfield, Fox
1997 "Use of Informants May Taint FBI Cases." *New York Times* (June 16): 8.

"By Order of the Mafia"
1888 *New York Times* (October 22): 8.

Byck, Robert, ed.
1974 *Cocaine Papers: Sigmund Freud.* New York: Stonehill.

Campane, Jerome O.
1981a "Chains, Wheels, and the Single Conspiracy: Part 1." *FBI Law Enforcement Bulletin* (August): 24–31.

1981b "Chains, Wheels, and the Single Conspiracy: Conclusion." *FBI Law Enforcement Bulletin* (September): 24–31.

Campbell, Rodney
1977 *The Luciano Project.* New York: McGraw-Hill.

Candeloro, Dominic
1981 "Suburban Italians." Pages 180–209 in *Ethnic Chicago*, edited by P.A. Jones and M. G. Holli. Grand Rapids, MI: W.B. Eerdman's.

Cantalupo, Joseph and Thomas C. Renner
1990 *Body Mike.* New York: Saint Martin's Press.

Caparella, Kitty
1999 "Mob–Pagan Pact: Joey's Bid for Philly Crime Boss Fueled by Link with Biker Gang." *Philadelphia News* (March 11): 3.

Capeci, Jerry
1999a "Another Persico Problem." *Gang Land Column* (February 22): Internet.

1999b "Bonanno Capo Killed." *Gang Land Column* (March 22): Internet.

1998a "Junior Pays for Dad's Deeds." *New York Daily News* (February 9): Internet.

1998b "The Gangster." *New York Daily News* (November 9): Internet.

1978 "Tieri: The Most Powerful Mob Chieftain." *New York* (August): 22–26.

Capeci, Jerry and Gene Mustain
1996 *Gotti: Rise and Fall.* New York: Onyx.

Caputo, David A.
1976 *Organized Crime and American Politics.* Morristown, NJ: General Learning Press.

Cardwell, Diane
2001 "Fugitive Gang Enforcer Arrested in Push-in Robberies." *New York Times* (March 2): Internet.

Carlson, Kenneth and Peter Finn
1993 *Prosecuting Criminal Enterprises.* Washington, DC: Bureau of Justice Statistics.

Carroll, Brian
1991 "Combatting Racketeering in the Fulton Fish Market." Pages 183–98 in *Organized Crime and Its Containment: A Transatlantic Initiative*, edited by Cyrelle Fijnaut and James Jacobs. Deventer, Netherlands: Kluwer.

Carter, Hodding, IV
1991a "King of the Jungle." *M Inc.* (March): 84–91.

1991b "Day of the Triads." *M Inc.* (June): 68–73.

Cashman, Sean Dennis
1981 *Prohibition.* New York: Free Press.

Catanzaro, Raimondo
1992 *Men of Respect: A Social History of the Sicilian Mafia.* New York: Free Press. Translated by Raymond Rosenthal.

Center for Strategic and International Studies (CSIS)
1997 *CSIS Task Force Report: Russian Organized Crime.* Internet.

Chafetz, Henry
1960 *Play the Devil: A History of Gambling in the United States from 1492 to 1955.* New York: Clarkson Potter.

Chaiken, David A.
1991 "Money Laundering: An Investigatory Perspective." *Criminal Law Forum* 2 (Spring): 467–510.

Chalidze, Vallery
1977 *Criminal Russia: Crime in the Soviet Union.* New York: Random House.

Chambliss, William
1975 "On the Paucity of Original Research on Organized Crime: A Footnote to Galliher and Cain." *American Sociologist* 10 (August): 36–39.
1973 *Functional and Conflict Theories of Crime.* New York: MSS Modular Publications.

Chapman, Stephen
1991 "Prohibition—From Alcohol to Drugs—Is a Costly Failure." *Chicago Tribune* (September 1), Sec. 4: 3.

Chernow, Ron
1990 *House of Morgan.* New York: Atlantic Monthly Press.

Chicago Crime Commission (CCC)
1997 *The New Faces of Organized Crime, 1997.* CCC.
1990 *Organized Crime in Chicago: 1990.* Chicago: CCC.

Chin, Ko-lin
1995 "Triad Societies in Hong Kong." *Transnational Organized Crime* 1 (Spring): 47–64.
1990 *Chinese Subculture and Criminality: Non-Traditional Crime Groups in America.* Westport, CT: Greenwood.

Chin, Ko-lin, Robert J. Kelly, and Jeffrey Fagan
1994 "Chinese Organized Crime in America." Pages 213–43 in *Handbook of Organized Crime in the United States,* edited by Robert J. Kelly, Ko-lin Chin, and Rufus Schatzberg. Westport, CT: Greenwood.

Chin, Ko-lin, Sheldon Zhang, and Robert J. Kelly
1998 "Transnational Chinese Organized Crime Activities: Patterns and Emerging Trends." *Transnational Organized Crime* 4 (Autumn/Winter): 127–154.

"Chinatown's New Enforcer"
1995 *New Yorker* (April 3): 36.

Christain, Nichole M.
2001 "Officials Say Stock Scheme Raised Money for the Mob." *New York Times* (March 9): 19.

Christian, Shirley
1992 "Why Indulge Drug Lord? Colombia Pressed to Tell." *New York Times* (July 29): 3.

Chubb, Judith
1982 *Patronage, Power, and Poverty in Southern Italy.* Cambridge: Cambridge University Press.

Cilluffo, Frank J. and George Salmoiraghi
1999 "And the Winner Is . . . the Albanian Mafia." *The Washington Quarterly,* 22 (Autumn): 21–25.

Clarke, Donald Henderson
1929 *In the Reign of Rothstein.* New York: Grosset and Dunlap.

Clinard, Marshall B., Peter C. Yeager, Jeanne Brissette, David Petrashek, and Elizabeth Harries
1979 *Illegal Corporate Behavior.* Washington, DC: Government Printing Office.

Cloward, Richard A. and Lloyd E. Ohlin
1960 *Delinquency and Opportunity.* New York: Free Press.

Cloyd, Jerald W.
1982 *Drugs and Information Control: The Role of Men and Manipulation in the Control of Drug Trafficking.* Westport, CT: Greenwood.

Coates, James
1986 "Another Bad Apple Spoils Witness Protection Image." *Chicago Tribune* (March 2): 4.

Cocaine in Japan
1994 Washington, DC: Drug Enforcement Administration.

Coffey, Joseph and Jerry Schmetterer
1991 *The Coffey Files: One Cop's War Against the Mob.* New York: St. Martin's Press.

Coffey, Thomas A.
1975 *The Long Thirst: Prohibition in America: 1920–1933.* New York: Norton.

Cohen, Mickey
1975 *Mickey Cohen: In My Own Words.* Englewood Cliffs. NJ: Prentice-Hall.

Cohen, Stanley
1977 *The Game They Played.* New York: Farrar, Straus and Giroux.

Colbridge, Thomas D.
2000 "Electronic Surveillance: A Matter of Necessity." *FBI Law Enforcement Bulletin* (February): 25–32.

Collins, Randall
1975 *Conflict Sociology.* New York: Academic Press.

"Colombian Heroin May Be Increasing"
1991 *New York Times* (October 27): 10.

Commission on the Review of the National Policy Toward Gambling
1976 *Gambling in America.* Washington, DC: U.S. Government Printing Office.

Committee on Law Reform of the New York County Lawyers Association
1987 *Advisory Reports. Part I: Why Cocaine and Her-*

oin Should be Decriminalized. Part II: Why Cocaine and Heroin Should Not Be Decriminalized. New York: Photocopied.

Committee on the Office of Attorney General

1978 *Witness Immunity.* Raleigh, NC: National Association of Attorneys General (NAAG).

1977 *State Grand Juries.* Raleigh, NC: NAAG.

1974 *Prosecuting Organized Crime.* Raleigh, NC: NAAG.

Comptroller General

1989 *Nontraditional Organized Crime: Law Enforcement Officials' Perspectives on Five Criminal Groups.* Washington, DC: U.S. Government Printing Office.

Conklin, John E., ed.

1977 *The Crime Establishment.* Englewood Cliffs, NJ: Prentice-Hall.

Connable, Alfred and Edward Silberfarb

1967 *Tigers of Tammany: Nine Men Who Ruled New York.* New York: Holt, Rinehart and Winston.

Connolly, John

1996 "Who Handled Who?" *New York* (December 2): 46–49.

Constantine, Thomas A.

1999a "Statement Before the U.S. Senate Subcommittee on the Western Hemisphere, Peace Corps, Narcotics, and Terrorism." February 26.

1999b "Statement Before the U.S. Senate Drug Caucus." February 24.

1999c "Statement Before the Subcommittee on Criminal Justice, Drug Policy and Human Resources." March 4.

"Contractor Admits Double Life"

1996 *New York Times* (May 2): 13.

Contreras, Joseph

2001 "War Without End." *Newsweek* (May 21): 38–39.

Cook, Fred J.

1979 "Shaking the Bricks at the FBI." *New York Times Magazine* (March 25): 31–40.

1973 *Mafia!* New York: Fawcett.

1972 "Purge of the Greasers." Pages 89–109 in *Mafia, U.S.A.*, edited by Nicholas Gage. New York: Dell.

Courtwright, David T.

1982 *Dark Paradise: Opiate Addiction in America Before 1940.* Cambridge, MA: Harvard University Press.

Cowell, Alan

1994 "Gunmen Linked to the Mafia Kill a Priest in Italy." *New York Times* (March 20): 3.

1993a "Heroin Pouring Through Porous European Borders." *New York Times* (February 9): 3.

1993b "Busting the Mafia: Italy Advances in War on Crime." *New York Times* (June 27): 3.

1992a "Inquiry into Sicilian Slaying Looks for Mafia Link to Colombia Drug Cartel." *New York Times* (June 21): 3.

1992b "A Top Sicilian Politician Is Slain; Pre-Election Mafia Warning Seen." *New York Times* (March 12): 2.

1992c "Mafia Throws the Gauntlet in Italy's Face." *New York Times* (July 21): 5.

1992d "Sicilian Symbolizes Mob's Survival." *New York Times* (August 2): 8.

1992e "Italians Defying Shakedowns Pay with Lives." *New York Times* (November 12): 5.

Crack Cocaine

1994 Washington, DC: Drug Enforcement Administration.

Cressey, Donald R.

1972 *Criminal Organization: Its Elementary Forms.* New York: Harper & Row.

1969 *Theft of the Nation.* New York: Harper & Row.

1967a "The Functions and Structure of Criminal Syndicates." Pages 25–60 in *Task Force on Organized Crime.* Washington, DC: U.S. Government Printing Office.

1967b "Methodological Problems in the Study of Organized Crime as a Social Problem." *Annals* 374 (November): 101–12.

Criminal Intelligence Service Canada (CISC)

1999 "Outlaw Motorcycle Gangs." CISC web site.

1998 *Annual Report on Organized Crime in Canada.* Ottawa: CISC.

Crouse, Russel

1947 "The Murder of Arnold Rothstein: 1928." Pages 184–200 in *Sins of New York*, edited by Milton Crane. New York: Grosset and Dunlap.

Daley, Dave

2000 "Biker Is Convicted of '93 Killings of Richmond Couple." *Chicago Tribune* (June 16): Sec. 2: 3.

Daley, Robert A.

1978 *Prince of the City.* Boston: Houghton Mifflin.

Dannen, Federic

1996 "The G-Man and the Hit Man." *New Yorker* (December 16): 68–81.

1995 "Hong Kong Babylon." *New Yorker* (August 7): 30–38.

1992a "The Untouchable? How the FBI Sabotaged Competing Prosecution Teams in the Race to Nail Alleged Mob King John Gotti." *Vanity Fair* (January): 27–44.

1992b "Revenge of the Green Dragons." *New Yorker* (November): 76–99.

David, John J.
1988 "Outlaw Motorcycle Gangs: A Transnational Problem." Paper presented at the Conference on International Terrorism and Transnational Crime, Chicago, August.

Davis, John H.
1993 *Mafia Dynasty: The Rise and Fall of the Gambino Crime Family.* New York: HarperCollins.

Decker, Scott, Tim Bynum, and Deborah Weisel
1998 "A Tale of Two Cities: Gangs as Organized Crime Groups." *Justice Quarterly* 15 (September): 395–425.

De Franco, Edward J.
1973 *Anatomy of a Scam: A Case Study of a Planned Bankruptcy by Organized Crime.* Washington, DC: U.S. Government Printing Office.

Defus, R. L.
1928 "The Gunman Has an Intercity Murder Trade." *New York Times* (July): XX 3.

de Gennaro, G.
1995 "The Influences of Mafia Type Organizations on Government, Business and Industry." *Trends in Organized Crime* 1 (Winter): 36–42.

de la Garza, Paul
2000 "Mexico Striking Back at Top Drug Cartel." *Chicago Tribune* (June 1): 4.

1998 "With Drug War, Anarchy Reigns in Mexican City." *Chicago Tribune* (October 31): 4.

1997a "The Scent of Scandal Has Church Scrambling." *Chicago Tribune* (October 6): 8.

1997b "In Tijuana, War on Drugs Is Lost." *Chicago Tribune* (March 31): 1, 13.

de Lama, George
1988a "For Colombian Officials, Nowhere Is Safe." *Chicago Tribune* (November 21): 1, 12.

1988b "Besieged Colombia Becoming the Lebanon of Latin America." *Chicago Tribune* (November 20): 5.

Delaney, William P.
1977 "On Capturing an Opium King: The Politics of Law Sik Han's Arrest." Pages 67–88 in *Drugs and Politics*, edited by Paul E. Rock. New Brunswick, NJ: Transaction Books.

della Porta, Donatella and Alberto Vannucci
1999 *Corrupt Exchanges: Actors, Resources, and Mech-* *anisms of Political Corruption.* New York: Walter de Gruyter.

Dellios, Hugh
1998 "Once Just a Supplier, Nigeria Develops Heroin Woes." *Chicago Tribune* (July 29): 4.

Demaris, Ovid
1981 *The Last Mafioso: The Treacherous World of Jimmy Fratianno.* New York: Bantam.

1969 *Captive City: Chicago in Chains.* New York: Lyle Stuart.

Department of Justice
1975 *Report on the National Conference on Organized Crime.* Washington, DC: U.S. Government Printing Office.

Department of Justice and Department of Transportation
1972 *Cargo Theft and Organized Crime.* Washington, DC: U.S. Government Printing Office.

Department of State
1998 *International Narcotics Control Strategy Report.* Washington, DC: U.S. Department of State.

de Tocqueville, Alexis
1966 *Democracy in America.* Translated by George Lawrence. New York: Harper and Row.

DeWitt, Charles B.
1993 *Controlling Chemicals Used to Make Illegal Drugs: The Chemical Action Task Force and the Domestic Chemical Action Group.* Washington, DC: National Institute of Justice.

Diamond, Stuart
1988 "Steep Rise Seen in Private Use of Federal Racketeering Law." *New York Times* (August 1): 1, 15.

Diapoulos, Peter and Steven Linakis
1976 *The Sixth Family.* New York: Dutton.

Dickson, Donald T.
1977 "Bureaucracy and Morality: An Organizational Perspective on a Moral Crusade." Pages 31–52 in *Drugs and Politics*, edited by Paul E. Rock. New Brunswick, NJ: Transaction Books.

Dillon, Sam
1999a "Mexico's Troupadors Turn from Amor to Drugs." *New York Times* (February 19): 4.

1999b "Ruling Party, at 70, Tries Hard to Cling to Power in Mexico." *New York Times* (March 4): 1, 12.

1998a "Mexico Arrests Two Accused of Flooding the U.S. with 'Speed.'" *New York Times* (June 3): 7.

1998b "Mexico Drug Trafficker Slain; Major Figure Near U.S. Border." *New York Times* (September 12): 3.

1998c "Gunmen Kill 3 Families in Mexico Over Drugs." *New York Times* (September 18): 6.

1998d "Mexico Jails 2 Drug Agents and U.S. Sees Graft." *New York Times* (September 25): 12.

1998e "Mexico Says Rivalry Between Gangs Led to Mass Murders." *New York Times* (November 11): 10.

1997 "Mexico Editor Hurt in Ambush; His Bodyguard and Gunman Die." *New York Times* (November 28): 5.

1996a "Mexico Arrests a Top Suspect in Drug Trade." *New York Times* (January 16): 1, 2.

1996b "Mexican Trafficker Plans to Cooperate in FBI's Inquiries." *New York Times* (January 20): 1, 5.

1996c "Mexican Drug Gang's Reign of Terror." *New York Times* (February 4): 24.

1996d "Canaries Are Singing, But Uncle Juan Won't." *New York Times* (February 9): 4.

1996e "Mexicans Tire of Police Graft as Drug Lords Raise Stakes." *New York Times* (March 21): 3.

1996f "Bribes and Publicity Mark Fall of Mexican Drug Lord." *New York Times* (May 12): 1, 6.

1996g "Mexican Aide's Millions; U.S. Charges Drug Link." *New York Times* (November 12): 5.

1995 "Speed Carries Mexican Drug Dealer to the Top." *New York Times* (December 27): 6.

Dillon, Sam and Craig Pyes
1997a "Court Files Say Drug Baron Used Mexican Military." *New York Times* (May 24): 1, 4.

1997b "Drug Ties Taint 2 Mexican Governors." *New York Times* (February 23): 1, 4.

Dintino, Justin J, and Frederick T. Martens
1983 *Police Intelligence Systems and Crime Control.* Springfield, IL: Charles C. Thomas.

1980 "Organized Crime Control in the Eighties." *Police Chief* (August): 66–70.

District Attorney of New York County and the New York City Police Department
1995 "Press Release, June 22." New York: Photocopied.

Dobyns, Fletcher
1932 *The Underworld of American Politics.* New York: Fletcher Dobyns.

Dorsett, Lyle W.
1968 *The Pendergast Machine.* New York: Oxford University Press.

Douglas, Paul H.
1974 "Introduction." *Bosses in Lusty Chicago,* by Lloyd Wendt and Herman Kogan. Bloomington: Indiana University Press.

Draffen, Duayne
1998 "Members of Motorcycle Gang Are Charged in Extortion Case." *New York Times* (April 8): Internet.

Dretzka, Gary
2001 "Rolling the Dice on Internet Gambling." *Chicago Tribune* (June 15): Sec. 5: 1, 3.

Drew, Christopher
1998 "RJR Subsidiary Pleads Guilty to Smuggling." *New York Times* (December 23): 1, 25.

Drug Abuse and Drug Abuse Research
1987 Rockville, MD: National Institute on Drug Abuse.

"Drug Crackdown Said to Sap Colombia's Economy"
1995 *New York Times* (November 24): 4.

Drug Enforcement Administration (DEA)
1995a *Illegal Drug Price/Purity.* Washington, DC: DEA.

1995b *LSD in the United States.* Washington, DC: DEA.

1994a *Crack Cocaine.* Washington, DC: DEA.

1994b *Colombian Opiate Assessment.* Washington, DC: DEA.

1993 *Worldwide Cocaine Situation.* Washington, DC: DEA

1991a *Worldwide Heroin Situation.* Washington, DC: DEA.

1991b *Worldwide Cocaine Situation.* Washington, DC: DEA.

1988 *Crack Cocaine Availability and Trafficking in the United States.* Washington, DC: DEA.

"Drug Smugglers Used Cuban Base for U.S. Shipment, Jury Charges"
1988 *New York Times* (February 27): 6.

"Drugs of Abuse"
1979 *Drug Enforcement* (July), entire issue.

Dubocq, Tom and Manny Garcia
1997 "'Redfellas': Cops Say Strip Club was Hangout for Russian Mob." *Miami Herald* (February 8): 1, 6.

Duggan, Christopher
1989 *Fascism and the Mafia.* New Haven, CT: Yale University.

Durk, David and Ira Silverman
1976 *The Pleasant Avenue Connection.* New York: Harper & Row.

Durkheim, Emile
1951 *Suicide.* New York: Free Press.

Duster, Troy
1970 *The Legislation of Morality: Law, Drugs, and Moral Judgment.* New York: Free Press.

Duzán, Maria Jimena
1994 *Death Beat: A Colombian Journalist's Life Inside the Cocaine Wars.* New York: HarperCollins.

Earely, Pete and Geral Shur
2002 *Inside the Federal Witness Protection Program.* New York: Bantam.

Eaton, Leslie
1997 "Russian Émigrés Run Afoul of Stock Regulators." *New York Times* (January 14): C1, 7.

Edberg, Mark C.
2001 "Drug Traffickers as Social Bandits." *Journal of Contemporary Criminal Justice* 17 (August): 259–77.

Eddy, Paul, Hugo Sabogal, and Sara Walden
1988 *The Cocaine Wars.* New York: Norton.

Edelhertz, Herbert and Thomas D. Overcast
n.d. *The Business of Organized Crime.* Loomis, CA: Palmer Press.

"Editorial"
1995 *Chicago Tribune* (January 2): 12.

Ehrenfeld, Rachel
1990 *Narco-Terrorism.* New York: Basic Books.

Eichenwald, Kurt
2002 "White-Collar Defense Stance: The Criminalless Crime." *New York Times* (March 3): WK 3.

Elliott, Delbert S., David Huizinga, and Suzanne S. Ageton
1985 *Explaining Delinquency and Drug Use.* Beverly Hills, CA: Sage.

Elliott, Dorinda
1992 "Russia's Goodfellas: The Mafia on the Neva." *Newsweek* (October 12): 50, 52.

Elsasser, Glen
1989 "Suspicion Is Ruled Ample Basis for Drug Search." *Chicago Tribune* (April 4): 3.

Engelmann, Larry
1979 *Intemperance: The Lost War Against Liquor.* New York: Free Press.

English, T. J.
1995a *Born to Kill.* New York: William Morrow.
1995b "Where Crime Rules." *New York Times* (June 26): 11.
1990 *The Westies: Inside the Hell's Kitchen Irish Mob.* New York: Putnam's.

Epstein, Edward Jay
1988a "Marrying the Mob to Wall Street." *Manhattan, Inc.* (October): 43–47.
1988b "The Dope Business." *Manhattan, Inc.* (July): 25–27.

Epstein, Joan F. and Joseph C. Gfroerer
1997 *Heroin Abuse in the United States.* Substance Abuse and Mental Health Services Administration. Internet.

Epstein, Leon D.
1986 *Political Parties in the American Mold.* Madison: University of Wisconsin Press.

Erie, Steven P.
1988 *Rainbow's End: Irish-Americans and the Dilemmas of Urban Machine Politics, 1840–1985.* Berkeley: University of California Press.

Eskridge, Chris
1998 "The Mexican Cartels: A Challenge for the 21st Century." *Criminal Organizations* 12 (1 & 2): 5–15.

Faison, Seth
1995a "Charges Against President Threaten Chinatown Tong." *New York Times* (June 1): 16.
1995b "U.S. Indicts 2 Businessmen as Gang Lords in Chinatown." *New York Times* (September 10): 11.
1993 "How Betrayal Snagged a Chinatown Gang Leader." *New York Times* (August 31): 12.

Farrell, Ronald A. and Carole Case
1995 *The Black Book and the Mob.* Madison: University of Wisconsin Press.

Fay, Peter Ward
1975 *The Opium War: 1840–1842.* Chapel Hill: University of North Carolina Press.

"FBI Says Los Angeles Gang Has Drug Cartel Ties"
1992 *New York Times* (January 10): 8.

Federal Bureau of Investigation
1988 "Debriefing of Gerald H. Scarpelli." Investigative File # CG183B–2272.

Feinberg, Alexander
1959 "Genovese Is Given 15 Years in Prison in Narcotics Case." *New York Times* (April 18): 1, 15.
1950 "A Who's Who of New York's Gambling Inquiry." *New York Times* (October 29): IV 6.
1944 "Lepke Is Put to Death, Denies Guilt to Last; Makes No Revelation." *New York Times* (March 5): 1, 30.

Ferkenhoff, Eric and Heather Vogell
2001 "Cops Seize $2 Million in Goods." *Chicago Tribune* (February 24): 5.

Feuer, Alan
2001 "Reporter's Notebook: Violent Testimony in Staccato Language." *New York Times* (May 13): Internet.

Fijnaut, Cyrelle and James Jacobs, eds.
1991 *Organized Crime and Its Containment: A Transatlantic Initiative.* Deventer, Netherlands: Kluwer.

Financial Action Task Force on Money Laundering (FATF)
2001   *Report on Money Laundering Typologies, 2000–2001.* Paris: FATF.

Financial Crimes Enforcement Network
2000   *A Survey of Electronic Banking, and Internet Gambling.* U.S. Department of the Treasury: Internet.

Finckenauer, James O. and Yuri A. Voronin
2001   *The Threat of Russian Organized Crime.* Washington, DC: National Institute of Justice.

Finckenauer, James O. and Elin J. Waring
2001   "Challenging the Russian Mafia Mystique." *NIJ Journal* (April): 2–7.
1999   *Russian Mafia in America: Immigration, Culture, and Crime.* Boston, MA: Northeastern University Press (advance page proofs).

Finkelstein, Katherine Eban
1998   "The Brighton Beach Swindle." *New York* (February 2): 39–43, 78.

Finley, M. I., Denis Mack Smith, and Christopher Duggan
1987   *A History of Sicily.* New York: Viking.

Fiorentini, Gianluca and Sam Peltzman, eds.
1995   *The Economics of Organized Crime.* Cambridge: Cambridge University Press.

Fisher, Ian
1993   "In New York City's Underworld: A Window on Immigrant Crime." *New York Times* (June 17): 13.

Fisher, Sethard
1975   "Review of the 'Black Mafia.'" *Contemporary Sociology* 4 (May): 83–84.

Flinn, John J.
1973   *History of the Chicago Police.* New York: AMS Press. Originally published in 1887.

Flynn, Kevin
1998   "Charity's Ties to Mobster Snarl It in Investigation." *New York Times* (December 12): 16.

Flynn, Sean
1998   "Good Guy, Bad Guy." *Boston Magazine* (Internet).

Fogelson, Robert M.
1977   *Big City Police.* Cambridge, MA: Harvard University Press.

Foglesong, Todd S. and Peter H. Solomon, Jr.
2001   *Crime, Criminal Justice, and Criminology in Post-Soviet Ukraine.* Washington, DC: National Institute of Justice.

Fong, Mak Lau
1981   *The Sociology of Secret Societies: A Study of Chinese Secret Societies in Singapore and Peninsular Malaysia.* Oxford, England: Oxford University Press.

Fooner, Michael
1985   *A Guide to Interpol.* Washington, DC: U.S. Government Printing Office.

Forero, Juan
2002   "Farmers in Peru Are Turning Again to Coca." *New York Times* (February 14): 3.
2001a "New Challenge to the Bogotá Leadership." *New York Times* (May 6): 8.
2001b "No Crops Spared in Colombia's Coca War." *New York Times* (January 31): 1, 8.
2001c "In the War on Coca, Colombian Growers Simply Move Along." *New York Times* (March 17): 1, 5.
2001d "Europe Expands as Market for Colombian Cocaine." *New York Times* (May 29): 1, 9.
2001e "Rightist Chief in Colombia Shifts Focus to Politics." *New York Times* (June 7): Internet.
2001f "Where a Little Coca Is as Good as Gold." *New York Times* (July 8): Sec. 4: 12.
2001g "Union Says Coca-Cola in Colombia Uses Thugs." *New York Times* (July 26): 6.
2001h "Ranchers in Colombia Bankroll Their Own Militia." *New York Times* (August 8): 1, 6.

"$4,000,000 in Narcotics Seized Here Tied to Rothstein Ring."
1976   *New York Times* (December 19): 1.

Fox, Ben
2001   "Record Cocaine Cache Seized." *Chicago Tribune* (May 15): 9.

Fox, Mike
2001a "Quebec's Biker Gangs on Trial." *BBC News* (February 19): Internet.
2001b "Jury Selection Begins in Biker Trial." *BBC News* (February 20): Internet.

Fox, Stephen
1989   *Blood and Power: Organized Crime in the Twentieth Century.* New York: William Morrow.

"Frank Costello Dies of Coronary at 82; Underworld Leader."
1972   *New York Times* (February 19): 1, 21.

Franklin, Stephen
1999   "Laborers' President Cleared by Union." *Chicago Tribune* (March 10): Sec. 3: 1, 3.
1995a "Hotel Workers' Union, U.S. Reach Oversight Accord." *Chicago Tribune* (August 20): Sec. 3: 1, 4.
1995b "Teamsters Aim at Corruption." *Chicago Tribune* (February 10): Sec. 3: 1, 3.

1993 "Teamsters Move on Local." *Chicago Tribune* (June 17): Sec. 2: 1, 2.

Franks, Lucinda
1977 "An Obscure Gangster Is Emerging as the New Mafia Chief in New York." *New York Times* (March 17): 1, 34.

Frantz, Douglas and Chuck Neubauer
1983 "Teamster Pension Fund Just Fine After Surgery." *Chicago Tribune* (May 29): 1, 10.

Frantz, Douglas with Vivian S. Toy
1995 "Portrait of Man as Mobster Stirs Community's Disbelief." *New York Times* (July 11): 1, B15.

Franzese, Michael and Dary Matera
1992 *Quitting the Mob*. New York: Harper Paperbacks.

Freeman, Ira Henry
1957 "Anastasia Rose in Stormy Ranks." *New York Times* (October 26): 12.

French, Howard W.
2001 "Even in Ginza, Honor Among Thieves Crumbles." *New York Times* (October 10): 4.

Freud, Sigmund
1933 *New Introductory Lectures on Psychoanalysis*. New York: W. W. Norton.

Fried, Albert
1980 *The Rise and Fall of the Jewish Gangster in America*. New York: Holt, Rinehart and Winston.

Fried, Joseph P.
1995 "Civic Pillar Pleads Guilty in Slaying Plot." *New York Times* (October 31): B15.
1993a "Government Sues to Seize Gotti's Remaining Assets." *New York Times* (January 15): 16.
1993b "Indictment Links the Mafia to Trash-Hauling Industry." *New York Times* (April 20): B16.
1992 "Inside Man for U.S. Oversees Union at Kennedy in War on Airport Rackets." *New York Times* (May 17): 21.

Friedman, Allen and Ted Schwarz
1989 *Power and Greed: Inside the Teamsters Empire of Corruption*. New York: Watts.

Friedman, Robert I.
2000 *Red Mafia: How the Russian Mob Has Invaded America*. Boston: Little, Brown.
1998 "The World's Most Dangerous Mobster." *Village Voice* (May 20–26): Internet.
1996 "The Money Plane." *New York* (January 22): 25–33.
1994 "The Organizatsiya." *New York* (November 7): 50–58.

Friel, Frank and John Gunther
1990 *Breaking the Mob*. New York: Warner Books.

Frisby, Tanya
1998 "The Rise of Organised Crime in Russia: Its Roots and Social Significance." *Europe–Asia Studies* 50 (January): 27–50.

Gage, Nicholas
1975 "Carlo Gambino Dies in His Long Island Home at 75." *New York Times* (October 16): 26.
1974 "Questions Are Raised on Lucky Luciano Book." *New York Times* (December 17): 28.
1971a *The Mafia Is Not an Equal Opportunity Employer*. New York: McGraw-Hill.
1971b "Gallo–Colombo Feud Said to Have Been Renewed." *New York Times* (June 29): 21.

Gage, Nicholas, ed.
1972 *Mafia, U.S.A.* New York: Dell.

Gall, Carlotta
2001 "Macedonia Village Is Center of Europe Web in Sex Trade." *New York Times* (July 28): 1, 6.

Gall, Carlotta and Thomas de Waal
1998 *Chechnya: Calamity in the Caucasus*. New York: New York University Press.

Gallagher, James P.
1995a "Corruption Touches Many Lives in Russia." *Chicago Tribune* (August 13): 15, 18.
1995b "In Chechnya, Vendetta Is a Way of Life, Death." *Chicago Tribune* (March 5): 1, 12.
1994 "Russian Gangs Send the Dead Out in Style." *Chicago Tribune* (November 20): 29.
1992a "As Law Enforcement Crumbles, Russian Crime, Gangs Proliferate." *Chicago Tribune* (September 2): 6.
1992b "Chechens Stir Bloody Cauldron in Caucasus." *Chicago Tribune* (January 10): 20.

Galliher, John F. and James A. Cain
1974 "Citation Support for the Mafia Myth in Criminology Textbooks." *American Sociologist* 9 (May): 68–74.

Gallo, Patrick J.
1981 *Old Bread, New Wine: A Portrait of the Italian-American*. Chicago: Nelson-Hall.

Galvan, Manuel
1982 "Capone's Yacht Sails Calmer Seas Today." *Chicago Tribune* (February 16): Section 2: 1.

Gambetta, Diego
1993 *The Sicilian Mafia: The Business of Private Protection*. Cambridge, MA: Harvard University Press.

Gambino, Richard
  1977   *Vendetta.* Garden City, NY: Doubleday.
  1974   *Blood of My Blood: The Dilemma of the Italian-American.* Garden City: Doubleday.
"Gamblers Hunted in Rothstein Attack"
  1928   *New York Times* (November 6): 1.
Gambling Commission. See Commission on the Review of the National Policy Toward Gambling.
"Gang Kills Suspect in Alien Smuggling"
  1931   *New York Times* (September 11): 1.
"Gang Linked to Union Charged at Trial"
  1934   *New York Times* (January 31): 8.
"Gangster Shot in Daylight Attack"
  1928   *New York Times* (July 2): 1.
Gardiner, John A.
  1970   *The Politics of Corruption: Organized Crime in an American City.* New York: Russell Sage Foundation.
Garvin, Glenn
  2001   "U.S. Missionary Plane Strafed in Peru; 2 Die." *Chicago Tribune* (April 21): 4.
Gately, William and Yvette Fernandez
  1994   *Dead Ringer.* New York: Donald I. Fine.
Genzman, Robert W.
  1988   "Press Release." October 11.
Giancana, Antoinette and Thomas C. Renner
  1985   *Mafia Princess: Growing Up in Sam Giancana's Family.* New York: Avon.
Giancana, Sam and Chuck Giancana
  1992   *Double Cross: Inside Story of the Mobster Who Controlled America.* New York: Warner Books.
Giuliani, Rudolph W.
  1987   "Legal Remedies for Attacking Organized Crime." Pages 103–30 in *Major Issues in Organized Crime Control*, edited by Herbert Edelhertz. Washington, DC: U.S. Government Printing Office.
Glab, Michael G.
  1997   "Gang Green." *Chicago Reader* (November 14): 1, 16–34.
Glaberson, William
  1989   "U.S. Loses Round in Bid to Curb Mob at Fish Market." *New York Times* (January 25): 12.
Goddard, Donald
  1988   *Undercover: The Secret Lives of a Federal Agent.* New York: Times Books.
  1980   *All Fall Down.* New York: Times Books.
  1978   *Easy Money.* New York: Farrar, Straus and Giroux.
  1974   *Joey.* New York: Harper & Row.

Godfrey, E. Drexel, Jr. and Don R. Harris
  1971   *Basic Elements of Intelligence.* Washington, DC: U.S. Government Printing Office.
Godson, Roy and William J. Olson
  1995   "International Organized Crime." *Society* (January/February): 18–29.
Goering, Laurie
  2001   "Colombia Caught in a Struggle for Power." *Chicago Tribune* (May 27): 1, 12.
  1998   "In Peru, Battle Against Flow of Drugs Moves to Amazon River Maze." *Chicago Tribune* (June 30): 6.
Gold, Mark S., Charles A. Dackis, A. L. C. Pottash, Irl Extein and Arnold Washton
  1986   "Cocaine Update: From Bench to Bedside." *Advances in Alcohol and Substance Abuse:* 5.
Goldberg, Carey
  2001   "An Innocent Man Goes Free 33 Years After Conviction." *New York Times* (February 2): 12.
Goldberg, Jeffrey
  1999   "The Don Is Done." *New York Times Magazine* (January 31): 24–31, 62–66, 71.
  1995   "Hoffa Lives!" *New York* (July 31): 27–35.
Golden, Tim
  2001   "The Citibank Connection: Real Money, Shadow Banks." *New York Times* (February 27): 6.
  2000a   "Mexican Gang Still on Loose Despite Search." *New York Times* (January 10): 1, 9.
  2000b   "Killing Raises Doubts on Mexico's War on Drugs." New York Times (June 5): 3.
  1999a   "2 Mexican Banks to Plead Guilty in Laundering Case." *New York Times* (March 30): 3.
  1999b   "Top Mexican Off-Limits to U.S. Drug Agents." *New York Times* (March 16): 1, 10.
  1998a   "In Breakthrough, Mexican Official Testifies in Texas." *New York Times* (July 15): 1, 6.
  1998b   "Elite Mexican Drug Officers Said to Be Tied to Traffickers." *New York Times* (September 16): 1, 10.
  1998c   "Salinas Brother Is Tied by Swiss to Drug Trade." *New York Times* (September 19): 1, 6.
  1998d   "Saying Salinas Aided Traffickers, Swiss Seize $90 Million." *New York Times* (October 21): 3.
  1997a   "Mexico and Drugs: Was the U.S. Napping?" *New York Times* (July 11): 1, 10.
  1997b   "Pakistan's Jailing of a Drug Agent Sours U.S. Ties." *New York Times* (November 17): 1, 10.
  1995a   "Mexican Connection Grows as Cocaine Supplier to U.S." *New York Times* (July 30): 1, 8.
  1995b   "To Help Keep Mexico Stable, U.S. Soft-Pedaled Drug War." *New York Times* (July 31): 1, 4.

Goldstein, Joseph
   1982   "Police Discretion Not to Invoke the Criminal Process." Pages 33–42 in *The Invisible Justice System: Discretion and the Law*, 2d ed., edited by Burton Atkins and Mark Pogrebin. Cincinnati, OH: Anderson.

Goldstock, Ronald and Dan T. Coenen
   1978   *Extortionate and Usurious Credit Transactions: Background Materials*. Ithaca, NY: Cornell Institute on Organized Crime.

Gootman, Elissa
   2002   "Investigators Call Attack on Hells Angels Event a Clash Over Long Island Turf." *New York Times* (February 25): 19.

Goozner, Merrill
   1996   "New York Trying to Trash Mob Hold on Waste-Hauling." *Chicago Tribune* (December 6): 1, 16.
   1992   "Thugs Avenge a Movie's Insults." *Chicago Tribune* (June 4): 4.

"Gorden Made by Dry Era."
   1933   *New York Times* (December 2): 6.

"Gorden Says He Got Up to $300 a Week."
   1933   *New York Times* (December 1): 14.

Gordon, Michael R.
   1996   "Key Russian Legislator Accuses Leading Military Officers of Graft." *New York Times* (July 10): 1, 4.

Gosch, Martin and Richard Hammer
   1974   *The Last Testament of Lucky Luciano*. Boston: Little, Brown.

Gosnell, Harold
   1977   *Machine Politics: The Chicago Model*. Chicago: University of Chicago. Originally published in 1937.

Gottfried, Alex
   1962   *Boss Cermak of Chicago*. Seattle: University of Washington Press.

"Gotti Associate Among 3 Guilty of Fraud"
   1995   *New York Times* (May 27): 7.

Gove, Walter R., Michael Geerken, and Michael Hughes
   1979   "Drug Use and Mental Health Among a Representative Sample of Young Adults." *Social Forces* 58 (December): 572–90.

Graham, Fred
   1977   *The Atlas Program*. Boston: Little, Brown.

Graham, Hugh Davis and Ted Robert Gurr, eds.
   1969   *The History of Violence in America: A Report to the National Commission on the Causes and Prevention of Violence*. New York: Bantam.

Grant, Madison and Charles S. Davison, eds.
   1930   *The Alien in Our Midst: Or Selling Our Birthright for a Mess of Pottage*. New York: Galton Publishing Co.

Greenberg, Norman
   1981   *The Man with a Steel Guitar: Portrait of Desperation, and Crime*. Hanover, NH: University Press of New England.

Greenhouse, Linda
   1996   "Justices Uphold Civil Forfeiture as Anti-Drug Tool." *New York Times* (June 25): 1, 8.
   1994   "Supreme Court Supports the U.S. on Seizures in Drug Cases." *New York Time* (November 8): 13.
   1989a "In Spotless Switzerland, Dirty Money Is Washed." *New York Times* (April 4): 6.
   1989b "High Court Backs Airport Detention Based on 'Profile.'" *New York Times* (April 4): 1, 10.
   1989c "Racketeering Law Limited in Pornography Cases." *New York Times* (February 22): 12.

Greenhouse, Steven
   2000a "Ex-Union Leader to Admit Ferrari Fraud." *New York Times* (January 28): 10.
   2000b "U.S. Is Easing Close Scrutiny of Hotel Union." *New York Times* (December 3): 31.
   2000c "Union Cleanup Praised; U.S. Oversight Is Eased." *New York Times* (January 21): 20.
   1999   "Laborers' Union President Is Cleared of Links to Mob." *New York Times* (March 10): 9.
   1997   "An Overseer Bars Teamster Leader from Re-election." *New York Times* (November 18): 1, 16.

Grinspoon, Lester
   1979   *Psychedelic Drugs Reconsidered*. New York: Basic Books.

Grinspoon, Lester and James B. Bakalar
   1976   *Cocaine: A Drug and Its Social Evolution*. New York: Basic Books.

Grob, Charles S., Russell E. Poland, Linda Chang, and Thomas Ernst
   1996   "Psychobiologic Effects of 3,4-methylenedioxymethamphetamine in Humans: Methodological Considerations and Preliminary Observations." *Behavioral Brain Research* 73: 103–107.

Grutzner, Charles
   1969   "Genovese Dies in Prison at 71; 'Boss of Bosses' of Mafia Here." *New York Times* (February 15): 1, 29.

Gugliotta, Guy and Jeff Leen
   1989   *Kings of Cocaine: Inside the Medellin Cartel—An*

Astonishing True Story of Murder, Money, and International Corruption. New York: Simon and Schuster.

Gunst, Laurie
1996 *Born Fi' Dead: A Journey Through the Jamaican Posse Underworld*. New York: Henry Holt and Company.

Gusfield, Joseph R.
1963 *Symbolic Crusade: Status Politics and the American Temperance Movement*. Urbana: University of Illinois Press.

Haberman, Clyde
1985 "TV Funeral for Japan's Slain Godfather." *New York Times* (February 1): 6.

Haley, Bruce
1990 "Burma's Hidden Wars." *U.S. News & World Report* (December 10): 44–47.

Hall, Kevin G.
2000 "Drug Chemicals Difficult to Target." *Chicago Tribune* (November 23): 36.

Haller, Mark H.
1991 *Life Under Bruno: The Economics of an Organized Crime Family*. Conshohocken, PA: Pennsylvania Crime Commission.
1990a "Illegal Enterprise: A Theoretical and Historic Interpretation." *Criminology* 28 (May): 207–35.
1990b "Policy Gambling, Entertainment, and the Emergence of Black Politics: Chicago from 1900 to 1940." *Journal of Social History* 24: 719–38.
1985a "Bootleggers as Businessmen: From City Slums to City Builders." Pages 139–57 in *Law, Alcohol, and Order: Perspectives on National Prohibition*, edited by David E. Kyvig. Westport, CT: Greenwood.
1985b "Philadelphia Bootlegging and the Report of the Special Grand Jury." *Pennsylvania Magazine of History and Biography* 109 (April): 215–33.
1974 "Bootlegging in Chicago: The Structure of an Illegal Enterprise." Paper presented at the annual meeting of the American Historical Association, Chicago, December 28.
1971–72 "Organized Crime in Urban Society: Chicago in the Twentieth Century." *Journal of Social History* 5: 210–34.

Hamilton, Don
1998 "For Motorcyclists, It's the Black Hills or Bust." *Chicago Tribune* (July 26): Sec. 12: 1, 7.

Hamm, Richard F.
1995 *Shaping the 18th Amendment*. Chapel Hill: University of North Carolina Press.

Hammer, Joshua
1997 "'Headcutters' at War." *Newsweek* (June 2): 42–43.

Hammer, Richard
1975 *Playboy's Illustrated History of Organized Crime*. Chicago: Playboy Press.

Handelman, Stephen
1995 *Comrade Criminal: Russia's New Mafiya*. New Haven, CT: Yale University Press.
1993 "Inside Russia's Gangster Economy." *New York Times Magazine* (January 24): 12–15, 30–31, 34, 40, 50.

Hanley, Charles J.
1993 "Drug Bust May Signal Colombia–Russia Link." *Chicago Tribune* (May 14): 31.

Hapgood, Norman and Henry Moskowitz
1927 *Up from the Streets: Alfred E. Smith*. New York: Harcourt, Brace.

Harker, R. Phillip
1978 "Sports Bookmaking Operations." *FBI Law Enforcement Bulletin* (September); FBI reprint.
1977 "Sports Wagering and the 'Line.'" *FBI Law Enforcement Bulletin* (November); FBI reprint.

Harmon, Dave
1993 "Ex-Agent: Drug Sales Aided Contras." *Chicago Tribune* (January 26): 3.

Hartman, Victor E.
2001 "Implementing an Asset Forfeiture Program." *FBI Law Enforcement Bulletin* (January): 1–7.

Hayner, Don
1990 "Chinatown Gambling: Inside Story." *Chicago Sun-Times* (September 2): 1, 20–21.

Hazarika, Sanjoy
1993 "Indian Heroin Smugglers Turn to New Cargo." *New York Times* (February 21): 8.

Hedgepeth, William
1989 "Mule Skinner." *Atlanta* (March): 61–62, 93–101.

Hefling, Kimberly
2000 "Pot Crop Thrives in Appalachia." Associated Press (May 14): Internet.

Helmer, John
1975 *Drugs and Minority Oppression*. New York: Seabury Press.

Henriques, Diana B. with Dean Baquet
1993 "Investigators Say Bid-Rigging Is Common in Milk Industry." *New York Times* (May 23): 1, 12.

Herion, Don
  1998 Director of the Vice Enforcement Unit of the Cook County (IL) Sheriff's Police Department. Personal interviews.

Hersh, Seymour M.
  1994 "The Wild East." *Atlantic Monthly* (June): 61–85.

Hess, David, Kenneth Meyers, Michele Gideon, Sal E. Gomez, and John Daly
  1999 "Italian Organized Crime and Money Laundering." Pages 345–405 in *Organized Crime: Uncertainties and Dilemmas,* edited by Stanley Einstein and Menachem Amir. Chicago, IL: Office of International Criminal Justice of the University of Illinois at Chicago.

Hess, Henner
  1973 *Mafia and Mafiosi: The Structure of Power.* Lexington, MA: D.C. Heath.

Hibbert, Christopher
  1966 *Garibaldi and His Enemies.* Boston: Little, Brown.

Hill, Henry, with Douglas S. Looney
  1981 "How I Put the Fix In." *Sports Illustrated* (February 16): 14–21.

Himmelstein, Jerome L.
  1983 *The Strange Career of Marijuana: Politics and Ideology of Drug Control in America.* Westport, CT: Greenwood.

Hirsch, Michael and Hideo Takayama
  1997 "Big Bang or Bust?" *Newsweek* (September 1): 44–45.

Hirschi, Travis
  1969 *Causes of Delinquency.* Berkeley: University of California Press.

"History of Antagonism, A"
  1994 *New York Times* (December 13): 3.

Hobsbawm, Eric J.
  1976 "Mafia." Pages 90–98 in *The Crime Society,* edited by Francis A. J. Ianni and Elizabeth Reuss-Ianni. New York: New American Library.
  1971 *Bandits.* New York: Dell.
  1969 "The American Mafia." *The Listener* 82 (November): 685–88.
  1959 *Social Bandits and Primitive Rebels.* Glencoe, IL: Free Press.

Hockstader, Lee
  1995 "Crime Atop Chaos: In Post Communist Russia, the Strong Arm of the Mafiya is Everywhere." *Washington Post,* National Weekly Edition (March 20–26): 6–9.

Hoffman, Paul
  1976 *To Drop a Dime.* New York: Putnam's.

Hofstadter, Richard
  1956 *The Age of Reform: From Bryan to F.D.R.* New York: Knopf.

Hofstadter, Richard and Michael Wallace, eds.
  1971 *American Violence: A Documentary History.* New York: Vintage.

Hohimer, Frank
  1975 *The Home Invaders.* Chicago: Chicago Review Press.

Holbrook, Stewart H.
  1953 *The Age of Moguls.* Garden City, NY: Doubleday.

Holt, Douglas
  1999 "Pentagon Halts Routine Use of Troops for Anti-Drug Border Patrols." *Chicago Tribune* (January 29): 13.

Homans, George C.
  1961 *Social Behavior: Its Elementary Forms.* New York: Harcourt, Brace and World.

Homer, Frederic D.
  1974 *Guns and Garlic.* West Lafayette, IN: Purdue University Press.

Hopton, Isobel
  1996 "On the Triad Trail." *CJ International* 12 (July–August): 5–6.

Horne, Louther
  1932 "Capone's Trip to Jail Ends a Long Battle." *New York Times* (May 8): IX1.

Howe, Benjamin Ryder
  2000 "Out of the Jungle." *nn* (May): 32–38.

Humphries, Drew and David F. Greenberg
  1981 "The Dialectics of Crime Control." Pages 209–54 in *Crime and Capitalism,* edited by David F. Greenberg. Palo Alto, CA: Mayfield.

Hundley, Tom
  2001 "Italy Can't Put a Face on Mafia Fugitive." *Chicago Tribune* (March 20): 1, 16.
  1998a "Anti-Mafia Sweep Helps Sicilian Capital Clean Up Its Act." *Chicago Tribune* (April 22): 7.
  1998b "Sicilian Women Lift Past Veil to Take Charge." *Chicago Tribune* (September 20): 5.
  1998c "Euro Conversion Could Be Mafia's Big Chance." *Chicago Tribune* (November 8): 4.
  1997 "Violence Tempers Naples' Return to Glory." *Chicago Tribune* (March 1): 7.

Ianni, Francis A. J.
  1974 *The Black Mafia: Ethnic Succession in Organized Crime.* New York: Simon and Schuster.
  1972 *A Family Business: Kinship and Social Control in*

Organized Crime. New York: Russell Sage Foundation.

Iannuzzi, Joseph
1993 *Joe Dogs: The Life and Crimes of a Mobster*. New York: Simon and Schuster.

Ibrahim, Youssef M.
1997 "Sweden's Courteous Police Spoil a Hell's Angels Party." *New York Times* (March 3): 1, 6.

Imhoff, John J. and Stephen P. Cutler
1998 "INTERPOL: Extending Law Enforcement's Reach Around the World." *FBI Law Enforcement Bulletin* (December): 10–16.

Inciardi, James A.
1975 *Careers in Crime*. Chicago: Rand McNally.

"Insurer Won't Pay on Federal Witness"
1987 *Chicago Tribune* (December 9): 10.

Intelligence Bulletin Colombia
1995 Washington, DC: Drug Enforcement Administration.

International Narcotics Control Strategy Report, 1999
2000 Bureau for International Narcotics and Law Enforcement Affairs, U.S. Department of State. Washington, DC, March 2000.

International Organization for Migration (IOM)
1998 *Information Campaign Against Trafficking in Women from Ukraine*. IOM.

Irey, Elmer L. and William T. Slocum
1948 *The Tax Dodgers*. Garden City, NY: Doubleday.

Iwai, Hiroaki
1986 "Organized Crime in Japan." Pages 208–33 in *Organized Crime: A Global Perspective*, edited by Robert J. Kelly. Totowa, NJ: Rowman and Littlefield.

Jackson, David
1990 "Bad Company." *Chicago* (February): 91–95, 109–10.

Jacobs, James B. with Colleen Friel and Robert Raddick
1999 *Gotham Unbound: How New York City Was Liberated from the Clutches of Cosa Nostra*. New York: New York University Press.

Jacobs, James B. with Christopher Panarella and Jay Worthington
1994 *Busting the Mob: United States v. Cosa Nostra*. New York: New York University Press.

Jacobson, Mark
2000 "The Return of Superfly." *New York* (August 14): 36–45.

"Jail Informer's Admissions Spur Inquiry"
1989 *New York Times* (January 3): 10.

James, Frank
2001 "Tax Havens an Evasive Issue." *Chicago Tribune* (July 22): Sec 5: 1, 6.

Jamieson, Alison
2000 *The Antimafia: Italy's Fight Against Organized Crime*. New York: St. Martin's.

Jenkins, Philip and Gary W. Potter
1985 *The City and the Syndicate: Organizing Crime in Philadelphia*. Lexington, MA: Ginn Custom Publishing.

Jennings, Dean
1967 *We Only Kill Each Other*. Englewood Cliffs, NJ: Prentice-Hall.

Joe, Karen
1992 "Chinese Gangs and Tongs: An Exploratory Look at the Connection on the West Coast." Paper presented at the annual meeting of the American Society of Criminology, New Orleans, November 4–7.

"Johnny Torrio, Ex-Public Enemy 1, Dies; Made Al Capone Boss of the Underworld"
1957 *New York Times* (May 8): 32.

Johnson, Earl, Jr.
1963 "Organized Crime: Challenge to the American Legal System." *Criminal Law, Criminology, and Police Science* 54 (March): 1–29.

Johnson, Kirk
1996 "Laborers' Union Agrees to Open Up Elections." *New York Times* (February 2): 12.
1986 "Manhattan Gang Is Tied to 30 Unsolved Killings." *New York Times* (December 17): 19.

Johnson, Malcolm
1972 "In Hollywood." Pages 325–38 in *Mafia, U.S.A.*, edited by Nicholas Gage. New York: Dell.

Johnston, David
1993 *Temples of Chance: How America Inc. Bought Out Murder Inc. to Win Control of the Casino Business*. Garden City, NY: Doubleday.

Johnston, David Cay
2002 "Loophole Is Too Small for an Ex-Convict." *New York Times* (March 17): 8.

Johnston, Michael
1982 *Political Corruption and Public Policy in America*. Monterey, CA: Brooks/Cole.

Jones, Mark
1993 "Nigerian Crime Networks in the United States." *International Journal of Offender Therapy and Comparative Criminology* 37: 59–73.

Jordon, Mary and Kevin Sullivan
1999 "Exploiting Weakness, Japanese Mobsters Go Mainstream." *Philadelphia Inquirer* (April 25): 17.

Joselit, Jenna Weissman
1983 *Our Gang: Jewish Crime and the New York Jewish Community, 1900–1940*. Bloomington: Indiana University Press.

Josephson, Matthew
1962 *The Robber Barons*. New York: Harcourt, Brace and World. Originally published in 1934.

Kaban, Elif
1998 "Russian Mafia Suspect Goes on Swiss Trial." Reuters (November 30): Internet.

Kaiser, Rob D.
1999 "Laborers Union Ousts Local Chief." *Chicago Tribune* (May 18): Sec. 3: 1, 2.

Kalfus, Ken
1996 "Far From Normal: Scenes from the New Moscow." *Harper's* (December): 53–62.

Kamm, Henry
1982a "A Modern Mafia Stirs Rage and Fear." *New York Times* (September 12): E3.
1982b "Pope Begins Visit to Mafia Stronghold." *New York Times* (November 21): 3.
1982c "Gang War in Naples Laid to Jailed Chief." *New York Times* (April 4): 11.

Kaplan, David
1998 "Yakuza, Inc." *U.S. News & World Report* (April 13): 40–47.

Kaplan, David E. and Alec Dubro
1986 *Yakuza: The Explosive Account of Japan's Criminal Underworld*. Reading, MA: Addison-Wesley.

Karch, Steven B.
1996 *The Pathology of Drug Abuse*, 2nd edition. Boca Raton, FL: CRC Press.

Katcher, Leo
1959 *The Big Bankroll: The Life and Times of Arnold Rothstein*. New York: Harper and Brothers.

Katel, Peter
1996 "Handing Off a Hot Case." *Newsweek* (January 29): 41.
1995 "Justice: The Trouble with Informants." *Newsweek* (January 30): 48.

Katz, Leonard
1973 *Uncle Frank: The Biography of Frank Costello*. New York: Drake Publishers.

Keefe, Joseph D.
2001a "Testimony Before the U.S. House of Representatives Committee on Government Reform Subcommittee on Criminal Justice, Drug Policy and Human Resources," July 12.
2001b "Testimony Before the U.S. Senate Governmental Affairs Committee," July 30.

Kefauver, Estes (Special Committee to Investigate Organized Crime in Interstate Commerce)
1951a *Third Interim Report*. Washington, DC: U.S. Government Printing Office.
1951b *Crime in America*. Garden City, NY: Doubleday.

Kelly, Robert J.
1999 *The Upperworld and the Underworld: Case Studies of Racketeering and Business Infiltrations in the United States*. Hingham, MA: Kluwer.
1986 *Organized Crime: An International Perspective*. Totowa, NJ: Rowman and Littlefield.

Kelly, Robert J., Ko-lin Chin, and Jeffrey A. Fagan
1993 "The Dragon Breathes Fire: Chinese Organized Crime in New York City. *Crime, Law and Social Change* 19: 245–69.

Kelly, Robert J., Ko-lin Chin, and Rufus Schatzberg, eds.
1994 *Handbook of Organized Crime in the United States*. Westport, CT: Greenwood.

Kennedy, David M.
1999 "Victory at Sea." *Atlantic Monthly* (March): 51–76.

Kennedy, Frances
2001 "Caught After Two Years on the Run, the Woman Who Heads Naples' Mafia." *Independent Digital* (UK) Ltd (June 18): Internet.

Kennedy, Randy
1996 "Drugs Stir Neighborhood Worries." *New York Times* (October 3): B12.

Kennedy, Robert F.
1960 *The Enemy Within*. New York: Popular Library.

Kerr, Peter
1988a "Chinese Criminals Move to Broaden Role in U.S." *New York Times* (January 4): 1, 12.
1988b "Cocaine Ring Holding Fast in Colombia." *New York Times* (May 21): 1, 5.

Kessler, Robert E.
1999 "Biker Gang VP Admits Beatings." *Newsday* (January 8): 36.
1998 "29 Bikers Busted: Pagans Charged with Racketeering." *Newsday* (April 8): 5.

Kidner, John
1976 *Crimaldi: Contract Killer*. Washington, DC: Acropolis Books.

Kihss, Peter
1979 "John Dioguardi (Johnny Dio), 64, a Leader in Organized Crime, Dies." *New York Times* (January 16): B6.

Kilian, Michael
    2002 "Seizure of Drugs at Sea Soaring." *Chicago Tribune* (March 18): 9.
Kilian, Michael, Connie Fletcher, and Richard P. Ciccone
    1979 *Who Runs Chicago?* New York: St. Martin's Press.
Kimeldorf, Howard
    1988 *Reds or Rackets? The Making of Radical and Conservative Unions on the Waterfront.* Berkeley: University of California Press.
Kinder, Douglas Clark
    1992 "Shutting Out the Evil: Nativism and Narcotics Control in the United States." Pages 117–42 in *Drug Control Policy: Essays in Historical and Comparative Perspective*, edited by William O. Walker. University Park: Pennsylvania State University.
King, Rufus
    1969 *Gambling and Organized Crime.* Washington, DC: Public Affairs Press.
    1963 "The Fifth Amendment Privilege and Immunity Legislation." *Notre Dame Lawyer* 38 (September): 641–54.
Kingston, Kimberly A.
    1988 "Reasonable Expectation of Privacy Cases Revive Traditional Investigative Techniques." *FBI Law Enforcement Bulletin* (November): 22–29.
Kinzer, Stephan
    1996a "Biker Wars in the Land of Vikings." *New York Times* (May 6): 5.
    1996b "In Germany, Vietnamese Terrorize Vietnamese." *New York Times* (May 23): 4.
Kirk, Donald
    1981 "Death of Japan Crime Boss Breeds Fear." *Miami Herald* (July 27): 17.
    1976 "Crime, Politics and Finger Chopping." *New York Times Magazine* (December 12): 60–61, 91–97.
Klatt, Wayne
    1983 "The Unlucky Love of King Mike McDonald." *Chicago Reader* (September 23): 8–9, 30–34.
Klein, Malcolm, Cheryl L. Maxson, and Lea C. Cunningham
    1991 "'Crack,' Street Gangs, and Violence." *Criminology* 29 (November): 623–50.
Klein, Maury
    1986 *Life and Times of Jay Gould.* Baltimore, MD: Johns Hopkins University Press.

Kleinfield, N. R.
    1995 "Chinatown Officers Said to Forge a Partnership of Vice and Greed." *New York Times* (June 19): 1, B12.
Kleinknecht, William
    1996 *The New Ethnic Mobs: The Changing Face of Organized Crime in America.* New York: Free Press.
Klepper, Michael, Robert Gunther, Jeanette Baik, Linda Barth, and Christine Gibson
    1998 "The American Heritage 40." *American Heritage* (October): 56–60.
Klockars, Carl B.
    1974 *The Professional Fence.* New York: Free Press.
Knapp, Whitman et al.
    1972 *Report of the Commission to Investigate Alleged Police Corruption.* New York: Braziller.
Kobler, John
    1971 *Capone: The Life and World of Al Capone.* Greenwich, CT: Fawcett.
Kobrin, Solomon
    1966 "The Conflict of Values in Delinquency Areas." Pages 151–60 in *Juvenile Delinquency: A Book of Readings*, edited by Rose Giallombardo. New York: Wiley.
Kocieniewski, David
    1997 "New York Pays a High Price for Police Lies." *New York Times* (January 5): 1, 16.
Konigsberg, Eric
    2001 "Blood Relation." *New Yorker* (August 6): 46–59.
Koziol, Ronald and Edward Baumann
    1987 "How Frank Nitti Met His Fate." *Chicago Tribune* (June 29): Sec. 5: 1, 7.
Koziol, Ronald and George Estep
    1983 "Fresh Insight into February 14 Killings." *Chicago Tribune* (February 14): 13.
Koziol, Ronald and John O'Brien
    1992 "Reputed Mob Boss Accardo Dies." *Chicago Tribune* (May 28): Sec. 2: 1, 8.
Krajick, Kevin
    1983 "Should Police Wiretap?" *Police Magazine* (May): 29–32, 36–41.
Kramer, Jane
    1992 "Letter from Europe." *New Yorker* (September 21): 108–24.
Krane, Jim
    1999 "Russian Mobsters Kick Down World's Doors." *APBnews.com* (March 7): Internet.
Krauss, Clifford
    2002 "U.S. Moves to Close Canadian Drug Route for Illegal Stimulant." *New York Times* (March 5): 5.

2000   "Bolivia Wiping Out Coca, at a Price." *New York Times* (October 23): 10.

1995   "Colombia Arrests Raise Price of Cocaine in New York City." *New York Times* (September 15): 1, 12.

Krauss, Clifford and Douglas Frantz
1995   "Cali Drug Cartel Using U.S. Business to Launder Cash." *New York Times* (October 30): 1, 13.

Kristoff, Nicholas D.
1999   "A Sexy Economic Feud of No Interest to the I.M.F." *New York Times* (June 17): 4.

1995a   "Mob Takes a Holiday as V.I.P.'s Tour Osaka." *New York Times* (November 19): 6.

1995b   "The Quake That Hurt Kobe Helps Its Gangs Get Richer." *New York Times* (June 6): 1, 4.

1995c   "Japanese Outcasts Better Off Than in Past But Still Outcast." *New York Times* (November 30): 1, 8.

Kurtz, Howard
2001   "Made-Up Murder Has Philly Editors Chagrined." *Washington Post* (April 20): C1.

Kwitny, Jonathan
1979   *Vicious Circles: The Mafia in the Marketplace.* New York: Norton.

Labaton, Stephen
2001   "The World Gets Tough on Price Fixers." *New York Times* (June 3): Sec. 3: 1, 7.

1997   "100 Are Arrested as Drug Ring with 'Speed' Is Broken Up." *New York Times* (December 6): 7.

1989a   "Bank to Plead Guilty to Laundering Drug Money." *New York Times* (August 11): 1, 10.

1989b   "Banking's Technology Helps Drug Dealers Export Cash." *New York Times* (August 14): 1, 10.

Labaton, Stephen and David Barboza
1999   "U.S. Outlines How Makers of Vitamins Fixed Global Prices." *New York Times* (May 21): 1, C6.

Lacey, Robert
1991   *Little Man: Meyer Lansky and the Gangster Life.* Boston: Little, Brown.

Lamour, Catherine and Michael R. Lamberti
1974   *The International Connection: Opium from Growers to Pushers.* New York: Pantheon.

Landesco, John
1968   *Organized Crime in Chicago.* Chicago: University of Chicago Press. Originally published in 1929.

1933   "The Life History of a Member of the '42' Gang." *Journal of Criminal Law, Criminology, and Police Science* 23: 964–98.

Lanfranchi, Marian
1976   "A Political History of Chicago Heights." Unpublished ms., Chicago, Governors State University.

Langlais, Rudy
1978   "Inside the Heroin Trade: How a Star Double Agent Ended Up Dead." *Village Voice* (March 13): 13–15.

Lapidus, Edith J.
1974   *Eavesdropping on Trial.* Rochelle Park, NJ: Hayden Book Co.

Lardner, James and Thomas Reppetto
2000   *NYPD: A City and Its Police.* New York: Henry Holt.

Lasswell, Harold D. and Jerimiah B. McKenna
1972   *The Impact of Organized Crime on an Inner-City Community.* New York: Policy Sciences Center.

Latimer, Dean and Jeff Goldberg
1981   *Flowers in the Blood: The Story of Opium.* New York: Franklin Watts.

Lavigne, Yves
1996   *Hells Angels: Into the Abyss.* New York: HarperCollins.

1987   *Hells Angels: Taking Care of Business.* Toronto, Canada: Deneua and Wayne.

Leapman, Ben
2001   "Met Team to Fight Crime in Jamaica." Associated Newspapers (July 30): Internet.

Lederer, Edith M.
2001   "Taliban a Heroin Trader, UN Panel Says." *Chicago Tribune* (May 27): 6.

LeDuff, Charlie
1998   "'Common Folk' Put Up Homes for Mob Suspect." *New York Times* (October 18): 30.

Ledwith, William E.
2000   "Testimony Before the House of Representatives Subcommittee on Criminal Justice, Drug Policy, and Human Resources," February 15.

Lee, Henry
1963   *How Dry We Were: Prohibition Revisited.* Englewood Cliffs, NJ: Prentice-Hall.

Lehmann, Daniel J. and Tom McNamee
1995   "Gang Busted." *Chicago Sun-Times* (September 1): 1, 22.

Lehr, Dick and Gerard O'Neil
2000   *Black Mass: The Irish Mob, the FBI, and a Devil's Deal.* New York: Public Affairs.

Leitsinger, Miranda
2001 "Alleged Drug Boss Arrives in U.S." *Chicago Tribune* (September 9): 14.

Lens, Sidney
1974 *The Labor Wars.* Garden City, NY: Doubleday.

Leonard, John
1996 "Bandit King." *New York* (August 19): 55–56.

Leonhardt, David with Barbara Whitaker
2000 "U.S. Companies Tangled in Web of Drug Dollars." *New York Times* (October 10): 1, 20.

Lerner, Steven E.
1980 "Phencyclidine Abuse in Perspective." Pages 13–23 in *Phencyclidine Abuse Manual*, edited by Mary Tuma McAdams, Ronald L. Linder, Steven E. Lerner, and Richard Stanley Burns. Los Angeles: University of California Extension.

Lev, Michael A.
1997 "Meeting Protection Racket Snares Mitsubishi." *Chicago Tribune* (October 24): Sec. 3: 1, 2.

Levine, Edward M.
1966 *The Irish and Irish Politicians.* Notre Dame, IN: University of Notre Dame Press.

Levine, Gary
1995 *Jack "Legs" Diamond: Anatomy of a Gangster.* Fleishmanns, NY: Purple Mountain Press.

Levine, Michael
1990 *Deep Cover.* New York: Delacorte.

LeVine, Steve, Betsy McKay, and Natasha Lebedeva
1993 "A Long Bloody Summer." *Newsweek* (August 30): 38–39.

Levins, Hoag
1980 "The Kabul Connection." *Philadelphia* (August): 114–20.

Levy, Clifford J.
1995 "Russian Emigre's Are Among 25 Named in Tax Fraud in Newark." *New York Times* (August 8): 1, 8.

Lewis, Norman
1964 *The Honoured Society.* New York: Putnam's.

Liddick, Don
1998 *The Mob's Daily Number: Organized Crime and the Number's Gambling Industry.* Lanham, MD: University Press of America.

Lieven, Anatol
1998 *Chechyna: Tombstone of Russian Power.* New Haven, CT: Yale University Press.

Light, Ivan
1977 "The Ethnic Vice Industry, 1880–1944." *American Journal of Sociology* 42 (June): 464–79.

Lindberg, Richard C.
1991 *To Serve and Collect: Chicago Politics and Police Corruption from the Lager Beer Riot to the Summerdale Scandal.* New York: Praeger.

Linder, Ronald L., Steven E. Lerner, and R. Stanley Burns
1981 *PCP: The Devil's Dust.* Belmont, CA: Wadsworth.

Lippman, Walter
1962 "The Underworld as Servant." In *Organized Crime in America*, edited by Gus Tyler. Ann Arbor: University of Michigan Press. Article originally published in 1931.

Lipton, Eric
2001a "Trash Haulers Threaten to Leave City if Fees Do Not Rise." *New York Times* (January 13): 21.
2001b "Even with Mob Gone, Trash Haulers Have Muscle in New York City." *New York Times* (January 29): 21.

Liu, Jainhong, Dengke Zhou, Allen E. Liska, Steven F. Messner, Marvin D. Krohn, Lening Zhang, and Zhou Lu
1998 "Status, Power, and Sentencing in China." *Justice Quarterly* 15 (June): 289–300.

Lloyd, Henry Demerest
1963 *Wealth Against Commonwealth.* Edited by Thomas C. Cochran. Englewood Cliffs, NJ: Prentice-Hall.

Logan, Andy
1970 *Against the Evidence: The Becker–Rosenthal Affair.* New York: McGraw-Hill.

Lohr, Steve
1999 "Privacy on Internet Poses Legal Puzzle." *New York Times* (April 19): C4.
1992 "Where the Money Washes Up: Offshore Banking in the Cayman Islands." *New York Times Magazine* (March 29): 26–29, 32, 46, 52.
1985 "Taiwan Trial: Verdict, But No Motive." *New York Times* (April 10): 6.

Lombardo, Robert M.
1994a "The Organized Crime Neighborhoods of Chicago." Pages 169–87 in *Handbook of Organized Crime in the United States*, edited by Robert J. Kelly, Ko-Lin Chin, and Rufus Schatzberg. Westport, CT: Greenwood.
1994b "The Social Organization of Organized Crime in Chicago." *Contemporary Criminal Justice* 4 (December): 290–313.
1979 "Organized Crime and the Concept of Community." Unpublished paper, Department of Sociology, University of Illinois at Chicago.

Lonardo, Angelo
  1988   Testimony Before the Permanent Subcommittee on Investigations of the Senate Committee on Government Affairs, April 4, 1988.
Longstreet, Stephen
  1973   *Chicago 1860–1919.* New York: McKay.
Lorch, Donatella
  1990   "Mourners Shot Back at Funeral." *New York Times* (July 30): 9.
Loth, David
  1938   *Public Plunder: A History of Graft in America.* New York: Carrick and Evans.
Lubasch, Arnold H.
  1993   "Gambino Trial Opens with Focus on Witnesses Defense Calls Liars." *New York Times* (February 2): C19.
  1992a "Death Penalty Sought at a Trial in Brooklyn." *New York Times* (April 14): 16.
  1992b "U.S. Moves to Break Up Trash Cartel." *New York Times* (August 18): B12.
  1992c "U.S. Prosecutors Say That Gotti Is Still a Functioning Crime Boss." *New York Times* (September 16): 18.
  1992d "Mobster Testifies of Bribing Juror." *New York Times* (November 5): 13.
  1991a "Ex-Mob Leader Tells Court of Killings." *New York Times* (April 26): 16.
  1991b "Jury in Windows Trial Convicts 3 of Lesser Charges and Acquits 5." *New York Times* (October 19): 12.
Luft, Kerry
  1995a "For Bogota's Street Children, Death Is Just Around the Corner." *Chicago Tribune* (January 15): 12.
  1995b "Colombia's Vow: Eradicate the Drug Crop." *Chicago Tribune* (February 9): 4.
Lupsha, Peter A.
  1995   "Transnational Narco-Corruption and Narco Investment: A Focus on Mexico." *Transnational Organized Crime* 1 (Spring): 84–101.
  1991   "Drug Lords and Narco-Corruption: The Players Change But the Game Continues." *Crime, Law and Social Change* 16: 41–58.
  1990   "The Geopolitics of Organized Crime: Some Comparative Models from Latin American Drug Trafficking Organizations." Paper presented at the annual meeting of the American Society of Criminology, Baltimore, MD, November.
  1987   "The President's Commission on Organized Crime." *Corruption and Reform* 2: 279–91.
  1983   "Networks Versus Networking: Analysis of an Organized Crime Group." Pages 59–87 in *Career Criminals,* edited by Gordon P. Waldo. Beverly Hills, CA: Sage.
  1981   "Individual Choice, Material Culture, and Organized Crime." *Criminology* 19: 3–24.
Lupsha, Peter A. and Kip Schlegel
  1980   "The Political Economy of Drug Trafficking: The Herrera Organization (Mexico and the United States)." Unpublished paper, Department of Political Science, University of New Mexico at Albuquerque.
Maas, Peter
  1997   *Underboss: Sammy the Bull Gravano's Story of Life in the Mafia.* New York: HarperCollins.
  1968   *The Valachi Papers.* New York: Putnam's.
MacDougall, Ernest D., ed.
  1933   *Crime for Profit: A Symposium on Mercenary Crime.* Boston: Stratford.
Maltz, Michael D.
  1990   *Measuring the Effectiveness of Organized Crime Control Efforts.* Chicago: Office of International Criminal Justice, University of Illinois.
  1976   "On Defining 'Organized Crime.'" *Crime and Delinquency* 22 (July): 338–46.
  1975   "Policy Issues in Organized and White Collar Crime." Pages 73–95 in *Crime and Criminal Justice,* edited by John A. Gardiner and Michael A. Mulkey. Lexington, MA: D.C. Heath.
"Man Loses Federal Appeal in Internet Gambling Case"
  2001   *New York Times* (August 1): 16.
Manca, John and Vincent Cosgrove
  1991   *Tin for Sale: My Career in Organized Crime and the NYPD.* New York: William Morrow.
Mangione, Jerre
  1985   *A Passion for Sicilians: The World Around Danilo Dolci.* New Brunswick, NJ: Transaction Books.
Mangione, Jerre and Ben Morreale
  1992   *La Storia: Five Centuries of the Italian American Experience.* New York: HarperCollins.
Mann, Arthur
  1965   *La Guardia Comes to Power: 1933.* Philadelphia: Lippincott.
Márquez, Gabriel García
  1997   *News of a Kidnapping.* New York: Knopf.
Marriott, Michel
  1992   "A Mob Witness Describes Murder as a Business Tool." *New York Times* (May 28): 13.

Marsh, Harry L.
1991 "Law Enforcement, the Military, and the War on Drugs: Is the Military Involvement in the War on Drugs Ethical?" *American Journal of Police* 10: 61–75.

Marshall, Donnie
2001 "Testimony Before the U.S. House of Representatives Committee on the Judiciary Subcommittee on Crime," March 29.

1999 "Testimony Before the U.S. House of Representatives Committee International Relations Subcommittee on the Western Hemisphere," March 3: 1–11.

Marshall, Eliot
1978 "State Lottery." *New Republic* (June 24): 20–21.

Martin, Andrew
1996 "Even with Leaders in Jail, Gang's Drug Business Is Flourishing." *Chicago Tribune* (January 29): 1, 13.

Martin, Andrew and John O'Brien
1996 "Alleged Drug Hub Didn't Fit the Area." *Chicago Tribune* (October 13): 1, 21.

Martin, Andrew and Matt O'Connor
1996a "Jeff Fort's Son Faces Drug Charges." *Chicago Tribune* (September 4): Sec. 2: 1, 2.

1996b "Gang 'Prince' Stakes Claim to the Throne." *Chicago Tribune* (September 21): 1, 12.

Martin, Raymond V.
1963 *Revolt in the Mafia.* New York: Duell, Sloan, and Pearce.

Martinez, Michael
1995 "Hells Angels Pay Their Last Respects to Slaying Victim." *Chicago Tribune* (March 8): Sec. 2: 1, 4.

Marx, Gary
1991 "Drug Lord, or Ghost, Stalks Colombian Town." *Chicago Tribune* (July 28): 4.

Mass, Robert
1991 "Law Enforcement Approaches to Organized Crime Infiltration of Legitimate Industry." Pages 37–47 in *Organized Crime and Its Containment: A Transatlantic Initiative*, edited by Cyrelle Fijnaut and James Jacobs. Deventer, Netherlands: Kluwer.

McAlary, Mike
1998 "Breaking the Code." *New York* (April 13): 31–35, 74.

McCaffrey, Lawrence J.
1976 *The Irish Diaspora in America.* Bloomington: Indiana University Press.

McClellan, John L.
1962 *Crime Without Punishment.* New York: Duell, Sloan, and Pearce.

McConaughy, John
1931 *From Cain to Capone: Racketeering Down the Ages.* New York: Brentano's.

McCormick, John
1999 "Winning a Gang War." *Newsweek* (November 1): 46–49.

McCoy, Alfred W.
1991 *The Politics of Heroin: CIA Complicity in the Global Drug Trade.* Brooklyn, NY: Lawrence Hill.

1972 *The Politics of Heroin in Southeast Asia.* New York: Harper and Row.

McFadden, Robert D.
1999 "Teamsters' Unit Regains Control." *New York Times* (February 26): 19.

1997 "Limits on Cash Transactions Cut Drug-Money Laundering." *New York Times* (March 11): 1, 11.

1988 "Anthony Provenzano, 71, Ex-Teamster Chief, Dies." *New York Times* (December 13): 22.

1983 "Meyer Lansky Is Dead at 81; Financial Wizard of Organized Crime." *New York Times* (January 16): 21.

McGraw, Dan
1997 "The National Bet." *U.S. News & World Report* (April 7): 50–55.

McGuinness, Robert L.
1981 "In the Katz Eye: Use of Binoculars and Telescopes." *FBI Law Enforcement Bulletin* (June): 26–31.

McGuire, Michael
1993 "Airborne Police Wage Losing Battle in Colombia Poppy Fields." *Chicago Tribune* (April 4): 6.

McGuire, Phillip C.
1988 "Jamaican Posses: A Call for Cooperation Among Law Enforcement Agencies." *Police Chief* (January): 20–27.

McKinley, James C., Jr.
1990 "17 Charged in Raids of Brooklyn 'Posse' Linked to Deaths." *New York Times* (December 8): 1, 7.

McMahon, Colin
1996 "Top Drug Suspect Seized in Mexico." *Chicago Tribune* (January 16): 4.

1995 "Mexicans Make Their Mark in Drug Game as Middlemen." *Chicago Tribune* (September 18): 1, 14.

1992   "Illegal Wagers Now Are Safer Than Ever." *Chicago Tribune* (November 15): 1, 17.

McPhaul, Jack
1970   *Johnny Torrio: First of the Gang Lords.* New Rochelle, NY: Arlington House.

Melzack, Ronald
1990   "The Tragedy of Needless Pain." *Scientific American* 262 (February): 27–33.

Mendelson, Wallace B.
1980   *The Use and Misuse of Sleeping Pills: A Clinical Guide.* New York: Plenum.

Merlin, Mark David
1984   *On the Trail of the Ancient Opium Poppy.* Rutherford, NJ: Fairleigh Dickinson University Press.

Mermelstein, Max
1990   *The Man Who Made It Snow.* New York: Simon and Schuster.

Merriam, Charles Edward
1929   *Chicago: A More Intimate View of Urban Politics.* New York: Macmillan.

Merton, Robert
1967   *On Theoretical Sociology.* New York: Free Press.
1964   "Anomie, Anomia, and Social Interaction." Pages 213–42 in *Anomie and Deviant Behavior,* edited by Marshall B. Clinard. New York: Free Press.
1938   "Social Structure and Anomie." *American Sociological Review* 3: 672–82.

Meskil, Paul
1977   "Meet the New Godfather." *New York* (February 28): 28–32.
1973   *Don Carlo: Boss of Bosses.* New York: Popular Library.

Messick, Hank
1973   *Lansky.* New York: Berkley.
1967   *The Silent Syndicate.* New York: Macmillan.

Millman, Nancy
1996   "$100 Million Fine in ADM Guilty Plea." *Chicago Tribune* (October 16): 1, 27.

Mills, James
1986   *The Underground Empire: Where Crime and Governments Meet.* New York: Dell.

Mitchell, Alison
1995   "U.S. Freezes Assets of Cartel in New Effort Against Drugs." *New York Times* (October 23): 5.
1992   "Russian Emigres Importing Thugs to Commit Contract Crimes in U.S." *New York Times* (April 11): 1, 18.

Mokhiber, Russell
1988   *Corporate Crime and Violence: Big Business Power and the Abuse of the Public Trust.* San Francisco: Sierra Club Books.

Moldea, Dan E.
1978   *The Hoffa Wars.* New York: Charter Books.

Moody, John
1991   "A Day with the Chess Player." *Time* (July 1): 34–36.

Moore, Mark H.
1987   "Organized Crime as a Business Enterprise." Pages 51–64 in *Major Issues in Organized Crime Control,* edited by Herbert Edelhertz. Washington, DC: U.S. Government Printing Office.

Moore, Molly
2001   "Iranians Wage War on Afghan Drugs." *Chicago Tribune* (July 19): 10.

Moore, Richter H., Jr.
1995   "Motor Fuel Tax and Organized Crime: The Russian and the Italian-American Mafia." Pages 189–200 in *Contemporary Issues in Organized Crime,* edited by Jay Albanese. Monsey, NY: Criminal Justice Press.

Moore, Robin with Barbara Fuca.
1977   *Mafia Wife.* New York: Macmillan.

Moore, William Howard
1974   *The Kefauver Committee and the Politics of Crime.* Columbia: University of Missouri Press.

Morales, Edmundo
1989   *Cocaine: White Gold Rush in Peru.* Tucson: University of Arizona Press.

Morello, Celeste A.
1999   *Before Bruno: Book 1—1880–1931.* Self-published.

Morgan, Howard Wayne
1981   *Drugs in America: A Social History, 1800–1980.* Syracuse, NY: Syracuse University Press.

Morgan, Howard Wayne, ed.
1974   *Yesterday's Addicts: American Society and Drug Abuse, 1865–1920.* Norman: University of Oklahoma Press.

Morgan, John
1985   *Prince of Crime.* New York: Stein and Day.

Morgan, Thomas
1989   "16 Charged in Scheme to Launder Millions." *New York Times* (May 14): 24.

Mori, Cesare
1933   *The Last Struggle with the Mafia.* London: Putnam's.

Moriarity, Tom
1998 Special Agent, Criminal Investigation Division, Internal Revenue Service. Personal interview.

Moseley, Ray
1997 "Biker War Revving Up in Denmark." *Chicago Tribune* (July 3): 1, 14.

Murr, Andrew
2000 "Corralling Sammy 'The Bull.'" *Newsweek* (March 6): 36–37.

Murray, George
1975 *The Legacy of Al Capone.* New York: Putnam's.

Mustain, Gene and Jerry Capeci
1992 *Murder Machine: A True Story of Murder, Madness, and the Mafia.* New York: Dutton.
1988 *Mob Star: The Story of John Gotti, the Most Powerful Criminal in America.* New York: Franklin Watts.

Musto, David
1973 *The American Disease: Origins of Narcotic Control.* New Haven, CT: Yale University Press.

Mydans, Seth
1995 "Racial Tensions on the Rise in Los Angeles Jail System." *New York Times* (February 6): 8.

Myers, Gustavus
1936 *History of Great American Fortunes.* New York: Modern Library.

Myers, Willard H., III
1995 "Orb Weavers—The Global Webs: The Structure and Activities of Transnational Ethnic Chinese Groups." *Transnational Organized Crime* 1 (Winter): 1–36.

Myerson, Allen R.
1995 "The Garbage Wars: Cracking the Cartel." *New York Times* (July 30): F1, 11.
1994 "American Express Bank Unit Settles U.S. Laundering Case." *New York Times* (November 22): 1, C8.

Nash, Robert J.
1981 *People to See.* New Brunswick, NJ: New Century.

National Advisory Commission on Causes and Prevention of Violence
1969 *Staff Report: Crimes of Violence.* Washington, DC: U.S. Government Printing Office.

National Association of Attorneys General
1977 *Organized Crime Control Units.* Raleigh, NC: Committee on the Office of Attorneys General.

National Commission on Law Observance and Enforcement
1931 *Report on Police.* Washington, DC: U.S. Government Printing Office.

National Commission for the Review of Federal and State Laws Relating to Wiretapping and Electronic Surveillance
1976 *Electronic Surveillance.* Washington, DC: U.S. Government Printing Office.

National Police Agency of Japan
1996 "Promotion of Measures Against Organized Crime Groups." Excerpted in *Trends in Organized Crime* 1 (Spring): 49–57.

Navarro, Mireya
1998 "Upgraded Drug Traffic Flourishes on Old Route." *New York Times* (May 31): 14.
1997 "Russian Submarine Surfaces as Player in the Drug World." *New York Times* (March 7): 1, 9.
1996 "When Drug Kingpins Fall, Illicit Assets Buy a Cushion." *New York Times* (March 19): 1, C19.
1995 "Colombia's Heroin Couriers: Swallowing and Smuggling." *New York Times* (November 2): 1, 12.

Navasky, Victor S.
1977 *Kennedy Justice.* New York: Atheneum.

"Navy Holds 21 Sailors in Italy in Smuggling"
1996 *New York Times* (May 29): 13.

Needler, Martin C.
1995 *Mexican Politics: The Containment of Conflict,* 3d ed. Westport, CT: Praeger.

Neely, Richard
1982 "The Politics of Crime." *Atlantic Monthly* (August): 27–31.

Neff, James
1989 *Mobbed Up: Jackie Presser's High Wire Life in the Teamsters, the Mafia, and the F.B.I.* New York: Atlantic Monthly Press.

Nelli, Humbert S.
1976 *The Business of Crime.* New York: Oxford University Press.
1969 "Italians and Crime in Chicago: The Formative Years: 1890–1920." *American Journal of Sociology* 74 (January): 373–91.

Nelson, Jack E., Helen Wallenstein Pearson, Mollie Sawyers, and Thomas J. Glynn
1982 *Guide to Drug Abuse Research Terminology.* Rockville, MD: National Institute on Drug Abuse.

Neumeister, Larry
2000 "Landmark Conviction in Web Gambling." Associated Press (February 28): Internet.

"New Gang Methods Replace Those of Eastman's Days"
1923 *New York Times* (September 9): Sec. 9: 3.

New Jersey State Commission of Investigation (NJSCI)
  1987 *Report and Recommendations on Organized Crime-Affiliated Subcontractors at Casino and Public Construction Sites.* Trenton, NJ: NJSCI.
New York State Commission of Investigation (NYSCI)
  1978 *A Report on Fencing: The Sale and Distribution of Stolen Property.* New York: NYSCI.
  1970 *Racketeer Infiltration into Legitimate Business.* New York: NYSCI.
New York State Organized Crime Task Force
  1988 *Corruption and Racketeering in the New York City Construction Industry.* Ithaca, NY: Cornell University School of Labor and Industrial Relations.
Newell, Barbara Warne
  1961 *Chicago and the Labor Movement: Metropolitan Unionism in the 1930s.* Urbana: University of Illinois Press.
Newfield, Jack
  1979 "The Myth of Godfather Journalism." *Village Voice* (July 23): 1, 11–13.
Nicodemus, Charles and Art Petacque
  1981 "Mob Jewel Fencing Investigated." *Chicago Sun-Times* (November 29): 5, 76.
Nieves, Evelyn
  2001 "Drug Labs in Valley Feed Nation's Habit." *New York Times* (May 13): 1, 18.
Nigerian Advance Fee Fraud
  1997 U.S. Department of State publication.
NNICC
  1998 *The Supply of Illicit Drugs to the United States.* Washington, DC: National Narcotics Intelligence Consumers Committee (NNICC).
Nocera, Joseph
  1988 "Drexel: Hanged Without a Trial." *New York Times* (December 30): 19.
O'Brien, Edward I.
  1986 "RICO's Assault on Legitimate Business." *New York Times* (January 5): F2.
O'Brien, John
  1996b "Chicago at Heart of Heroin Case." *Chicago Tribune* (October 12): 1, 9.
  1993 "James J. D'Antonio, 65, Mob Driver." *Chicago Tribune* (December 15): Sec. 2: 11.
  1988 "Car-Theft Figure Slain at His Home." *Chicago Tribune* (August 16): Sec. 2: 3.
  1983 "Gambling Boss Ken Eto Tells of Mob Murder and Intrigue." *Chicago Tribune* (May 16): Sec. 2: 1.
O'Brien, John and Jan Crawford Greenburg
  1996 "Raids Reveal How Little Guys Climb the Drug Ladder." *Chicago Tribune* (May 3): 1, 21.

O'Brien, John, Matt O'Connor, and George Papajohn
  1995 "U.S. Goes Behind Bars to Indict 39 Gang Leaders." *Chicago Tribune* (September 1): 1, 12.
O'Brien, Joseph F. and Andris Kurins
  1991 *Boss of Bosses: The FBI and Paul Castellano.* New York: Dell.
O'Brien, Robert and Sidney Cohen
  1984 *Encyclopedia of Drug Abuse.* New York: Facts on File.
O'Connor, Anne-Marie
  1999 "10 Alleged Leaders of Drug Ring Arrested." *Los Angeles Times* (February 2): Internet.
O'Connor, Len
  1984 "Give Me That Old-Time Politics." *Chicago Magazine* (February): 114–19.
O'Connor, Matt
  2000 "Gang Member Is Sentenced to 100 Years." *Chicago Tribune* (December 14): Sec. 2: 5.
  1999a "3 Who Succeeded Hoover Get Life Terms." *Chicago Tribune* (January 9): 5.
  1999b "When a Bribe Isn't a Bribe: FBI Mole Lands Prison Term." *Chicago Tribune* (October 15): 1, 14.
  1998 "Raiders Net Millions, Ton of Cocaine." *Chicago Tribune* (May 28): Sec. 2: 7.
  1997 "Hoover, 6 Others Convicted; Seen as Blow to Gang." *Chicago Tribune* (May 10): 1, 12.
  1996a "Hoover Files to Be Used Against Him." *Chicago Tribune* (January 4): 1, 17.
  1996b "Turncoat Lifts Veil of Gang Vengeance." *Chicago Tribune* (February 1): Sec. 2: 3.
  1996c "Gambling Manager for Mob Pleads Guilty to Racketeering." *Chicago Tribune* (September 25): Sec. 2: 3.
  1994a "On Leong, Moy Plead Guilty to Running Longtime Casino." *Chicago Tribune* (February 12): 5.
  1994b "Sentencing of 'Chinatown Mayor' Closes On Leong Case." *Chicago Tribune* (May 16): Sec. 2: 1, 4.
O'Connor, Richard
  1962 *Gould's Millions.* Garden City, NY: Doubleday.
  1958 *Hell's Kitchen.* Philadelphia, PA: Lippincott.
O'Day, Patrick
  2001 "The Mexican Army as Cartel." *Journal of Contemporary Criminal Justice* 17 (August): 278–95.
Office of Inspector General
  2000 *Semiannual Report to the Congress: October 1, 1999–March 31, 2000.* Washington, DC: U.S. Department of Labor.

Okada, Daniel W.
1992 "Asian Gangs: What Are We Talking About?" Paper presented at the annual meeting of the American Society of Criminology, New Orleans, November.

O'Malley, Pat O. and Stephen Mugford
1991 "The Demand for Intoxicating Commodities: Implications for the 'War on Drugs.'" *Social Justice* 18 (Winter): 49–75.

O'Neill, Gerard and Dick Lehr
1989 *The Underboss: The Rise and Fall of a Mafia Family.* New York: St. Martin's Press.

Oppenheimer, Andres
1996 *Bordering on Chaos: Guerillas, Stockbrokers, Politicians, and Mexico's Road to Prosperity.* Boston: Little, Brown.

Orlando, Leoluca
2001 *Fighting the Mafia and Renewing Sicilian Culture.* San Francisco, CA: Encounter Books.

O'Rourke, John J.
1997 Special Agent, Federal Bureau of Investigation, retired. Personal interview.

Orth, Maureen
2002 "Afghanistan's Deadly Habit." *Vanity Fair* (March): 150–52, 165–77.

Overly, Don H. and Theodore H. Schell
1973 *New Effectiveness Measures for Organized Crime Control Efforts.* Washington, DC: U.S. Government Printing Office.

Packer, Herbert L.
1968 *The Limits of the Criminal Sanction.* Stanford, CA: Stanford University Press.

Pallasch, Abdon and Judy Peres
1998 "Abortion Foes Suffer a Big Setback." *Chicago Tribune* (April 21): 1, 8.

Palley, Thomas I.
1996 "The Forces Making for an Economic Collapse." *Atlantic Monthly* (July): 44–45, 58.

Palsey, Fred D.
1971 *Al Capone: The Biography of a Self-Made Man.* Freeport, NY: Books for Libraries Press. Originally published in 1931.

Pantaleone, Michele
1966 *The Mafia and Politics.* New York: Coward and McCann.

Paoli, Leticia
1994 "An Underestimated Criminal Phenomenon: The Calabrian 'Ndrangheta." *European Journal of Crime, Criminal Law and Criminal Justice* 2 (3): 212–38.

Papajohn, George and Tracy Dell'Angela
1995 "Indictments Open Door for Next Gang." *Chicago Tribune* (September 3): 1, 16.

Passell, Peter
1991 "Coca Dreams, Cocaine Reality." *New York Times* (August 14): C2.

Patterson, Orlando
2001 "The Roots of Conflict in Jamaica." *New York Times* (July 23): 21.

PCOC. See President's Commission on Organized Crime.

Pennsylvania Crime Commission (PCC)
1992 *Racketeering and Organized Crime in the Bingo Industry.* Conshohocken, PA: PCC.
1991 *1991 Report.* Conshohocken, PA: PCC.
1990 *Organized Crime in Pennsylvania: A Decade of Change, 1990 Report.* Conshohocken, PA: PCC.
1989 *1989 Report.* Conshohocken, PA: PCC.
1988 *1988 Report.* Conshohocken, PA: PCC.

Permanent Subcommittee on Investigations (PSI)
1984 *Profile of Organized Crime: Great Lakes Region.* Washington, DC: U.S. Government Printing Office.
1983a *Crime and Secrecy: The Use of Offshore Banks and Companies.* Washington, DC: U.S. Government Printing Office.
1983b *Organized Crime in Chicago* (March 4). Washington, DC: U.S. Government Printing Office.
1983c *Profile of Organized Crime: Mid-Atlantic Region* (February 15, 23, 24). Washington, DC: U.S. Government Printing Office.
1983d *Staff Study of Crime and Secrecy: The Use of Offshore Banks and Companies.* Washington, DC: U.S. Government Printing Office.
1982 *Hotel Employees and Restaurant Employees International Union: Part I* (June 22, 23). Washington, DC: U.S. Government Printing Office.
1981a *International Narcotics Trafficking.* Washington, DC: U.S. Government Printing Office.
1981b *Waterfront Corruption.* Washington, DC: U.S. Government Printing Office.
1981c *Witness Security Program.* Washington, DC: U.S. Government Printing Office.
1980a *Organized Crime and the Use of Violence: Part I.* Washington, DC: U.S. Government Printing Office.
1980b *Organized Crime and the Use of Violence: Part II.* Washington, DC: U.S. Government Printing Office.
1978 *Organized Crime Activities: South Florida and*

United States Penitentiary, Atlanta Georgia (August 1, 2, 3, 9, 10): Part I. Washington, DC: U.S. Government Printing Office.

1971 *Organized Crime and Stolen Securities: Part I.* Washington, DC: U.S. Government Printing Office.

Petacco, Arrigo
1974 *Joe Petrosino.* New York: Macmillan.

Petacque, Art and Hugh Hough
1983 "'Banker' Holds Lansky Secrets." *Chicago Sun-Times* (January 23): 9.

Peterson, Robert E.
1991 "Legalization: The Myth Exposed." Pages 324–55 in *Searching for Alternatives: Drug Control Policy in the United States,* edited by Melvyn B. Krauss and Edward P. Lazear. Stanford, CA: Hoover Institution.

Peterson, Virgil
1983 *The Mob: 200 Years of Organized Crime in New York.* Ottawa, IL: Green Hill Publishers.

1969 *A Report on Chicago Crime for 1968.* Chicago Crime Commission.

1963 "Chicago: Shades of Capone." *Annals* 347 (May): 30–39.

1962 "Career of a Syndicate Boss." *Crime and Delinquency* 8 (October): 339–49.

Physicians' Desk Reference
1988 Oradell, NJ: Medical Economics Co.
1987 Oradell, NJ: Medical Economics Co.

Pileggi, Nicholas
1995 *Casino.* New York: Pocket Books.

1990 *Wise Guy: Life in a Mafia Family.* New York: Pocket Books.

1982 "There's No Business Like Drug Business." *New York* (December 13): 38–43.

Pistone, Joseph D.
1992 *The Ceremony: The Mafia Initiation Tapes.* New York: Dell.

1987 *Donnie Brasco: My Undercover Life in the Mafia.* New York: New American Library.

Pitkin, Thomas Monroe and Francesco Cordasco
1977 *The Black Hand: A Chapter in Ethnic Crime.* Totowa, NJ: Littlefield, Adams.

Plate, Thomas and the Editors of *New York,* eds.
1972 *The Mafia at War.* New York: New York Magazine Press.

"Police Tackle London's Yardies"
1999 *BBC News* (July 20): Internet.

Pomfret, John
2001 "Made Man in China Has Gangland Ties, Party Pals." *Seattle Times* (January 21): Internet.

Pooley, Eric
1992 "Cop Stars." *New York* (March 16): 43–49.

Popiano, Willie with John Harney
1993 *Godson: A True-Life Account of 20 Years Inside the Mob.* New York: St. Martin's Press.

Porrello, Rick
1995 *The Rise and Fall of the Cleveland Mafia.* Ft. Lee, NJ: Barricade Books.

Posner, Gerald L.
1988 *Warlords of Crime: Chinese Secret Societies—The New Mafia.* New York: McGraw-Hill.

Possley, Maurice
2001 "Union Ousts 3 Leaders for Mob Ties." *Chicago Tribune* (January 12): Sec. 2: 1, 5.

1996 "U.S. Will Help Mole Set Up His New Digs." *Chicago Tribune* (January 22): 1, 16.

Possley, Maurice and Rick Kogan
2001 *Everybody Pays: Two Men, One Murder, and the Price of Truth.* New York: Putnam.

Post, Henry
1981 "The Whorehouse Sting." *New York* (February 2): 31–34.

Potter, Gary
1994 *Criminal Organizations: Vice, Racketeering, and Politics in an American City.* Prospect Heights, IL: Waveland.

Powell, Hickman
2000 *Lucky Luciano: The Man Who Organized Crime in America.* Ft. Lee, NJ: Barricade Books. (Originally published in 1939.)

Powis, Robert E.
1992 *The Money Launderers.* Chicago: Probus.

Prall, Robert H. and Norton Mockridge
1951 *This Is Costello.* New York: Gold Medal.

President's Commission on Law Enforcement and Administration of Justice
1968 *The Challenge of Crime in a Free Society.* New York: Avon.

President's Commission on Organized Crime (PCOC)
1986a *The Impact: Organized Crime Today.* Washington, DC: U.S. Government Printing Office.

1986b *The Edge: Organized Crime, Business, and Labor Unions.* Washington, DC: U.S. Government Printing Office.

1986c *America's Habit: Drug Abuse, Drug Trafficking, and Organized Crime.* Washington, DC: U.S. Government Printing Office.

1985a *Organized Crime and Labor–Management Racketeering in the United States.* Washington, DC: U.S. Government Printing Office.

1985b *"Materials on Ethical Issues for Lawyers Involved with Organized Crime Figures." Paper.*

1984a Organized Crime and Cocaine Trafficking. Washington, DC: U.S. Government Printing Office.

1984b *Organized Crime of Asian Origin.* Washington, DC: U.S. Government Printing Office.

1984c *The Cash Connection: Organized Crime, Financial Institutions, and Money Laundering.* Washington, DC: U.S. Government Printing Office.

"Press Release"

1999 "Operation Impunity Dismantles Nationwide Drug Trafficking Operation." U.S. Department of Justice, September 22.

Preston, Julia

1999 "Rights Report on Mexico Says Widespread Abuses Continue." *New York Times* (January 15): 7.

Preston, Julia and Craig Pyes

1997 "Mexican Tale: Drugs, Crime, Torture and the U.S." *New York Times* (August 18): 1, 5, 6.

"Profaci Dies of Cancer, Led Feuding Brooklyn Mob."

1962 *New York Times* (June 8): 32.

PSI. See Permanent Subcommittee on Investigations.

Puente, Teresa and Paul de la Garza

1999 "Fear, Loathing and Drugs in Mexico." *Chicago Tribune* (December 5): 6.

Pulley, Brett

1999 "Living Off the Daily Dream of Winning a Lottery Prize." *New York Times* (May 22): 1, 12–13.

1998 "Those Seductive Snake Eyes; Tales of Growing Up Gambling." *New York Times* (June 16): 1, 23.

Putnam, Robert D.

1993 *Making Democracy Work: Civic Traditions in Modern Italy.* Princeton, NJ: Princeton University Press.

Quinney, Richard

1974 *Critique of the Legal Order.* Boston: Little, Brown.

Raab, Selwyn

2000 "A Mafia Family's Second Wind." *New York Times* (April 29): 11.

1998a "Facing Leadership Vacuum, Mob Family Is Seen Promoting Old Hands." *New York Times* (July 26): 24.

1998b "Mob's 'Commission' Believed Defunct." *New York Times* (April 27): 1, 16.

1998c "Cheaper Trash Pickup with New York's Crackdown on Mob Cartel." *New York Times* (May 11): C19.

1997a "Simone DeCavalcante, 84, Former Crime Figure in New Jersey." *New York Times* (February 12): 18.

1997b "FBI Agent Runs Brooklyn Club to Sting Mafia Stolen Goods Ring." *New York Times* (January 24): 1, 18.

1997c "Arson Case Led to Inquiry of Mob Cartel." *New York Times* (June 23): 13.

1997d "Two Convicted as Masterminds of Mob's Hold on Private Garbage Collection." *New York Times* (October 22): 19.

1996a "Walkout Disrupts Fish Market." *New York Times* (January 3): B12.

1996b "Gotti Files 2d Appeal and Authorities Call It a Power Play." *New York Times* (January 21): 18.

1996c "Crackdowns on Mob Seen as Mixed Blessing by Merchants of Fulton Fish Market." *New York Times* (March 31): 18.

1996d "New Jersey Officials Say Mafia Infiltrated Health-Care Industry." *New York Times* (August 21): 1, C19.

1995a "The Thin Line Between Mole and Manager." *New York Times* (July 2): 15.

1995b "With Gotti Away, the Genoveses Succeed the Leaderless Gambinos." *New York Times* (September 3): 1, 12.

1995c "Crackdown on Mob Aids Garment Makers." *New York Times* (June 12): B12.

1995d "Brother of Mob Turncoat Is Gunned Down." *New York Times* (October 6): 8.

1995e "Jury Convicts Philadelphia Mob Leader." *New York Times* (November 22): 8.

1995f "Mayor Seeks Fulton Fish Market Takeover." *New York Times* (February 1): 16.

1995g "New York Bookies Go Computer Age But Wind Up Being Raided Anyhow." *New York Times* (August 25): 6.

1994a "New Groups of Russian Gangs Gain Foothold in Brooklyn." *New York Times* (August 23): 1, 3.

1994b "Court Disclosures Expose Mobster Who Died of AIDS as F.B.I. Mole." *New York Times* (November 20): 19.

1994c "Panel Clears Teamsters' Chief of Mob Ties." *New York Times* (July 12): C20.

1993 "FBI Arrests a Mafia Boss in New Jersey." *New York Times* (January 20): B1, B6.

1992a "Mafia Family in New York Linked to Newspaper Fraud." *New York Times* (July 8): C3.

1992b "'Most Dangerous Mafioso' Left at Helm of

Lucchese Crime Family." *New York Times* (November 28): 14.

1992c "Top Member of Colombo Crime Family Is Ambushed in Brooklyn." *New York Times* (December 30): 13.

1990 "Racketeering Held to Persist at New York's Fish Market." *New York Times* (August 9): B12.

"Racket Chief Slain by Gangster Gunfire."

1931 *New York Times* (April 16): 1.

Rakove, Milton L.

1975 *Don't Make No Waves, Don't Back No Losers.* Bloomington: Indiana University Press.

Randolph, Jennifer G.

1995 "RICO—The Rejection of an Economic Motive Requirement." *Journal of Criminal Law and Criminology* 85 (Spring): 1189–222.

Rangel, Jesus

1988 "10 Are Convicted for Corruption." *New York Times* (November 20): 25.

Rashbaum, William K.

2001a "Mob Soldier Faces a Return to Jail for Parole Violations." *New York Times* (July 18): Internet.

2001b "Two Are Charged in Money-Laundering Scheme." *New York Times* (July 18): Internet.

2000a "38 Charged in Control of Building Projects by Mafia and Unions." (September 7): 27.

2000b "A Smuggling Operation with a Russian Twist." *New York Times* (August 9): 1, 15.

Rawlinson, Patricia

1997 "Russian Organized Crime: A Brief History." Pages 28–52 in *Russian Organized Crime: The New Threat?* edited by Phil Williams. London, England: Frank Cass.

Ray, Oakley

1978 *Drugs, Society, and Human Behavior.* St. Louis: Mosby.

Reagan, Ronald

1986 "Declaring War on Organized Crime." *New York Times Magazine* (January 12): 26, 28, 47, 55–57, 62, 65, 84.

Reece, Jack

1973 "Fascism, the Mafia, and the Emergence of Sicilian Separatism." *Journal of Modern History* 45 (June): 261–76.

Reedy, George E.

1991 *From the Ward to the White House: The Irish in American Politics.* New York: Scribner's.

Regional Information Sharing Systems Program

1998 Washington, DC: Bureau of Justice Statistics.

Reid, Ed

1970 *The Grim Reapers.* New York: Bantam.

Reid, Ed and Ovid Demaris

1964 *The Green Felt Jungle.* New York: Cardinal Paperbacks.

1953 *The Shame of New York.* New York: Random House.

Reinhold, Robert

1989 "California Shaken Over an Informer." *New York Times* (February 17): 9.

Remnick, David

1995 "In Stalin's Wake." *New Yorker* (July 24): 46–62.

Repetto, Thomas A.

1978 *The Blue Parade.* New York: Free Press.

Reuter, Peter

1995 "The Decline of the American Mafia." *The Public Interest* (Summer): 89–99.

1987 *Racketeering in Legitimate Industries: A Study in the Economics of Intimidation.* Santa Monica, CA: RAND Corporation.

1983 *Disorganized Crime.* Cambridge, MA: MIT Press.

Reuter, Peter and Carol Petrie, eds.

1999 *Transnational Organized Crime: Summary of a Workshop.* Washington, DC: National Academy Press.

Reuter, Peter, Jonathan Rubinstein, and Simon Wynn

1983 *Racketeering in Legitimate Industries: Two Case Studies. Executive Summary.* Washington, DC: U.S. Government Printing Office.

Reuters (News Service)

1999 "Italian Police Capture Calabrian Mafia Boss." (March 11): Internet.

1996 "Hells Angels Convicted In Denmark Slaying." *New York Times* (December 21): 7.

Rey, Guido M. and Ernesto U. Savona

1993 "The Mafia: An International Enterprise?" Pages 69–80 in *Mafia Issues,* edited by Ernesto U. Savona. Milan, Italy: United Nations.

Reynolds, Marylee

1995 *From Gangs to Gangsters: How American Sociology Studied Organized Crime, 1918–1994.* Albany, NY: Harrow and Heston.

Rhodes, Robert P.

1984 *Organized Crime: Crime Control vs. Civil Liberties.* New York: Random House.

Richtel, Matt

2002 "A Credit Crisis for Web Casinos." *New York Times* (January 21): C1, 5.

Riding, Alan
  1987a "Colombian Envoy Shot in Budapest." *New York Times* (January 14): 5.
  1987b "Colombia Effort Against Drugs Hits Dead End." *New York Times* (August 20): 4.

Risley, Raymond
  1998 Commander, Organized Crime Division, Chicago Police Department. Personal interview.

Roane, Kit R.
  2000 "The Mob Goes Downtown." *U.S. News & World Report* (June 26): 16–17.

Robb, Peter
  1996 *Midnight in Sicily.* Boston: Faber and Faber.

Robbins, Tom and Jerry Capeci
  1994 "Wiseguy Helped: Civil Rights Killings Solved by Snitch." *New York Daily News* (June 21): 12–13.

Roberton, Robert J.
  1986 "Designer Drugs: The Analog Game." Pages 91–96 in *Bridging Services: Drug Abuse, Human Services and the Therapeutic Community*, edited by Alfonso Acampora and Ethan Nebelkopf. New York: World Federation of Therapeutic Communities.

Robinson, Linda
  1998a "Is Colombia Lost to Rebels?" *U.S. News & World Report* (May 11): 38–42.
  1998b "Land for Peace in Colombia." *U.S. News & World Report* (November 23): 37.

Robinson, Louis N.
  1933 "Social Values and Mercenary Crime." Pages 13–31 in *Crime for Profit: A Symposium on Mercenary Crime*, edited by Ernest D. Mac-Dougall. Boston: Stratford Company.

"ROC" 1996. See "Russian Organized Crime in the United States."

Rockaway, Robert A.
  1993 *But—He Was Good to His Mother: The Lives and Crimes of Jewish Gangsters.* Jerusalem, Israel: Gefen Publishing House.

Roemer, William F., Jr.
  1995 *Accardo: The Genuine Godfather.* New York: Donald I. Fine.
  1994 *The Enforcer, Spilotro: The Chicago Mob's Man Over Las Vegas.* New York: Ivy Books.

Rohter, Larry
  1998a "Haiti Paralysis Brings a Boom in Drug Trade." *New York Times* (October 27): 1, 4.
  1998b "A Turncoat Now Turning on Americans in Caribbean." *New York Times* (August 23): 11.

  1991 "A Cocaine Baron's Tales of Intrigue and Greed Liven Up Noriega's Trial." *New York Times* (November 24): E3.
  1989a "Bandit Wears a Halo in an Unsaintly City." *New York Times* (May 11): 7.
  1989b "Mexico Captures Top Drug Figure and 80 Policemen." *New York Times* (April 11): 1, 6.

Rohter, Larry and Clifford Krauss
  1998a "Dominicans Allow Drugs Easy Sailing." *New York Times* (May 10): 1, 6.
  1998b "Dominican Drug Traffickers Tighten Grip on the Northeast." *New York Times* (May 11): 12, 17.

Rome, Florence
  1975 *The Tattooed Men.* New York: Delacorte.

Romoli, Kathleen
  1941 *Colombia.* Garden City, NY: Doubleday, Doran.

Rosen, Charles
  1978 *Scandals of '51: How the Gamblers Almost Killed College Basketball.* New York: Holt, Rinehart and Winston.

Rosenberg, Matthew J.
  2000 "Jamaica Struggles with Cocaine." Associated Press (February 10): Internet.

Rosenthal, Andrew
  1988 "Inquiry Raises Questions on Anonymous Sources." *New York Times* (June 27): 9.

Rosner, Lydia S.
  1995 "Preface" to "Organized Crime IV: The Russian Connection." *Contemporary Criminal Justice* 11 (December): vi–viii.
  1986 *Soviet Way of Crime.* South Hadley, MA: Bergin and Garvey.

Ross, Irwin
  1992 *Shady Business: Confronting Corporate Corruption.* New York: Twentieth Century Fund Press.
  1980 "How Lawless Are the Big Companies?" *Fortune* (December 1): 57–58, 62–64.

Rothmiller, Mike and Ivan G. Goldman
  1992 *L.A. Secret Police: Inside the LAPD Elite Spy Network.* New York: Pocket Books.

Rubinstein, Jonathan and Peter Reuter
  1978a "Fact, Fancy, and Organized Crime." *Public Interest* 53 (Fall): 45–67.
  1978b "Bookmaking in New York." New York: Policy Sciences Center. (Preliminary unpublished draft).
  1977 "Numbers: The Routine Racket." New York: Policy Sciences Center. (Preliminary unpublished draft).

Rudolph, Robert
  1992   *The Boys from New Jersey.* New York: William Morrow.
Ruggiero, Vincenzo
  1993   "The Camorra: 'Clean' Capital and Organised Crime." Pages 141–61 in *Global Crime Connections: Dynamics and Control,* edited by Frank Pearce and Michael Woodiwiss. Toronto, Canada: University of Toronto Press.
Rugoff, Milton
  1989   *America's Gilded Age: Intimate Portraits from an Era of Extravagance and Change, 1850–1890.* New York: Henry Holt.
"Russian Organized Crime in the United States"
  1996   Hearing Before the U.S. Senate Permanent Subcommittee on Investigations, May 15. Washington, DC: Committee on Governmental Affairs.
Ryan, Patrick J. and George E. Rush, eds.
  1997   *Understanding Organized Crime in Global Perspective: A Reader.* Thousand Oaks, CA: Sage.
Sabbag, Robert
  1996   "The Invisible Family." *New York Times Magazine* (February 11): 33–39.
Salerno, Joseph and Stephen J. Rivele
  1990   *The Plumber.* New York: Knightsbridge.
Salerno, Ralph and John S. Tompkins
  1969   *The Crime Confederation.* Garden City, NY: Doubleday.
Salkowski, Joe
  2001   "Encryption on Wrong Side of Law, Officers Say." *Chicago Tribune* (January 29): Sec. 4: 2.
Salopek, Paul
  1998   "Indians Grow It; Cartels Rake It In." *Chicago Tribune* (February 19): 6.
Sandoval, Ricardo
  1998   "19 Mexicans Slain; Drug Feud Is Blamed." *Chicago Tribune* (September 18): 10.
Saney, Parviz
  1986   *Crime and Culture in America: A Comparative Perspective.* New York: Greenwood.
Sanger, David E.
  1997   "Japanese Near Pact with U.S. on Threat to Bar Their Ships from American Ports." *New York Times* (October 18): 5.
  1995   "Money Laundering, New and Improved." *New York Times* (December 24): E4.
  1992   "Top Japanese Party Leaders Accused of Links to Mobsters." *New York Times* (September 23): 1, 4.

Sann, Paul
  1971   *Kill the Dutchman: The Story of Dutch Schultz.* New York: Popular Library.
Sante, Luc
  1991   *Low Life.* New York: Vintage.
Sawyers, June
  1988   "A 'King' Who Had Us in His Pocket." *Chicago Tribune Magazine* (October 2): 10.
  1987   "Hinky Dink and Bathhouse John's 'Carnival of Evil.'" *Chicago Tribune Magazine* (January 25): 7.
Saxon, Wolfgang
  1990   "Harry Bridges, Docks Leader, Dies at 88." *New York Times* (March 31): 11.
Scaramella, Gene
  1998   Investigator, Cook County (IL) Sheriff's Police. Personal interview.
Schatzberg, Rufus
  1994   "African American Organized Crime." Pages 189–212 in *Handbook of Organized Crime in the United States,* edited by Robert J. Kelly, Ko-lin Chin, and Rufus Schatzberg. Westport, CT: Greenwood.
  1993   *Black Organized Crime in Harlem: 1920–1930.* New York: Garland.
Schatzberg, Rufus and Robert J. Kelly
  1996   *African-American Organized Crime: A Social History.* New York: Garland.
Schelling, Thomas C.
  1971   "What Is the Business of Organized Crime?" *American Scholar* 40 (Autumn): 643–52.
Schemo, Diana Jean
  1999   "Bogotá Sees Drug War as Path to Peace." *New York Times* (January 6): 11.
  1997a "Players Are Main Danger in Noisy Colombian Game." *New York Times* (December 26): 10.
  1997b "Heroin Is Providing a Growth Industry for Colombia." *New York Times* (March 30): 3.
  1996   "With Its Drug Binge Over, Cali Returns to Old Values." *New York Times* (December 4): 12.
Schemo, Diana Jean and Tim Golden
  1998   "Bogotá Aid: To Fight Drugs or Rebels?" *New York Times* (June 2): 1, 12.
Schmetzer, Uli
  2001   "U.S., China Take Sides in Border Skirmish." *Chicago Tribune* (May 19): 1, 6.
  1991a "'Nigerian Connection' Ties Chicago to Asian Drugs." *Chicago Tribune* (December 21): 1, 11.

1991b "Slave Trade Survives, Prospers Across Asia." *Chicago Tribune* (November 15): 1, 18.

1990 "'Prince of Death' Is a Wanted Man." *Chicago Tribune* (March 21): 21.

1988 "Sicily: Artist Packs 'Em in Despite His Many Brushes with the Law." *Chicago Tribune* (January 13): 16.

1987 "Godfather's Shadow Still Darkens Town Notorious for Death." *Chicago Tribune* (December 28): 14.

1985 "A City Whose Kids Are Hired to Kill." *Chicago Tribune* (October 13): 4.

1982 "Naples Mafia—Slaughter with a Vengeance." *Chicago Tribune* (March 7): Sec. 3: 1.

Schmidt, John R.
1989 *The Mayor Who Cleaned Up Chicago*. DeKalb, IL: Northern Illinois University Press.

Schoenberg, Robert J.
1992 *Mr. Capone*. New York: William Morrow.

Schorr, Mark
1979 "The .22 Caliber Killings." *New York* (May 7): 43–46.

"Schultz Aide Slain; 7th in Five Months"
1931 *New York Times* (June 22): 2.

"Schultz Product of Dry Law Era"
1933 *New York Times* (January 22): 23.

"Schultz Succumbs to Bullet Wounds Without Naming Slayers"
1933 *New York Times* (October 25): 1.

Schwartz, John
2001 "U.S. Declines to Release Data in Trial." *New York Times* (August 25): B1, 2.

Sciascia, Leonard
1963 *Mafia Vendetta*. New York: Knopf.

Sciolino, Elaine and Stephen Engelberg
1988 "Narcotics Effort Foiled by U.S. Security Goals." *New York Times* (April 10): 1, 10.

Scott, W. Richard
1981 *Organizations: Rational, Natural, and Open Systems*. Englewood Cliffs, NJ: Prentice-Hall.

Seedman, Albert A.
1974 *Chief!* New York: Arthur Fields.

Seidman, Harold
1938 *Labor Czars: A History of Labor Racketeering*. New York: Liveright.

Semple, Kirk
2001a "Colombia's Cocaine Frontier." *Mother Jones* (November/December): 58–63.

2001b "The Kidnapping Economy." *New York Times Magazine* (June 3): 46–50.

Serao, Ernesto
1911a "The Truth About the Camorra." *Outlook* 98 (July 28): 717–26.

1911b "The Truth about the Camorra: Part II." *Outlook* (August): 778–87.

Serio, Joseph
1992a "Organized Crime in the Soviet Union and Beyond." *Low Intensity Conflict and Law Enforcement* 1 (Autumn): 127–51.

1992b "Shunning Tradition: Ethnic Organized Crime in the Former Soviet Union." *CJ International* 8 (November–December): 5–6.

Serrin, William
1989 "Jackie Presser's Secret Lives Detailed in Government Files." *New York Times* (March 27): 1, 11.

Servadio, Gaia
1976 *Mafioso: A History of the Mafia from Its Origins to the Present Day*. Briarcliff Manor, NY: Stein and Day.

1974 *Angelo LaBarbera: The Profile of a Mafia Boss*. London: Quartet Books.

Sexton, Joe
1995 "3 Men Accused of Running Chinatown Organized Crime." *New York Times* (June 2): 1, 16.

Seymour, Christopher
1996 *Yakuza Diary*. New York: Atlantic Monthly Press.

Shannon, Elaine
1991 "New Kings of Coke." *Time* (July 1): 29–33.

1988 *Desperados: Latin Drug Lords, U.S. Lawmen, and the War America Can't Win*. New York: Viking.

Shannon, William V.
1989 *The American Irish: A Political and Social Portrait*. Amherst: University of Massachusetts Press.

Shaw, Clifford and Henry D. McKay
1972 *Juvenile Delinquency and Urban Areas*. Chicago: University of Chicago Press. Originally published in 1942.

Shawcross, Tim and Martin Young
1987 *Men of Honour: The Confessions of Tommaso Buscetta*. London: Collins.

Shelley, Louise I.
2001 "Corruption and Organized Crime in Mexico in the Post-PRI Transition." *Journal of Contemporary Criminal Justice* 17 (August): 213–31.

1997 "Post-Soviet Organized Crime: A New Form of Authoritarianism." Pages 122–38 in *Russian*

Organized Crime, The New Threat? edited by Phil Williams. London: Frank Cass.

Shenon, Philip
1996 "Opium Baron's Rule May End with Surrender in Myanmar." *New York Times* (January 6): 4.
1986 "U.S. Crime Panel: Discord to the End." *New York Times* (April 6): 9.

Sheridan, Michael
1997 "Triads Move on Hong Kong." *London Times* (July 13): 19.

Sheridan, Walter
1972 *The Fall and Rise of Jimmy Hoffa*. New York: Saturday Review Press.

Sherman, Lawrence W.
1978 *Scandal and Reform: Controlling Police Corruption*. Berkeley: University of California Press.
1974 *Police Corruption: A Sociological Perspective*. Garden City, NY: Doubleday.

Shipp, E. R.
1985 "Former Chief of Teamsters Ordered to Jail Next Month." *New York Times* (April 25): 12.

Short, James F., Jr., ed.
1968 *Gang Delinquency and Delinquent Subcultures*. New York: Harper & Row.

Siciliano, Vincent
1970 *Unless They Kill Me First*. New York: Hawthorn Books.

Siebert, Renate
1996 *Secrets of Life and Death: Women and the Mafia*. London: Verso.

"Siegel, Gangster, Is Slain on Coast."
1947 *New York Times* (June 22): 1.

Silverstein, Ken
2000 "Trillion-Dollar Hideaway." *Mother Jones* (November/December): 38–45, 94–96.

Sims, Calvin
2000a "Feeling Pinch, Japan's Mobs Struggle for Control." *New York Times* (April 2): 6.
2000b "Gangster Shootout in Tokyo Violates an Unspoken Pact." *New York Times* (August 9): 6.

Sinclair, Andrew
1962 *The Era of Excess: A Social History of the Prohibition Movement*. Boston: Little, Brown.

Skolnick, Jerome H., Theodore Correl, Elizabeth Navarro, and Roger Rabb
1990 "The Social Structure of Street Drug Dealing." *American Journal of Police* 9: 1–41.

Sloane, Arthur A.
1992 *Hoffa*. Cambridge, MA: MIT Press.

Sly, Liz
1999 "In a Hail of Bullets, Island of Macau Awaits a New Master." *Chicago Tribune* (February 18): 8.

Smith, Alson J.
1962 "The Early Chicago Story." Pages 138–46 in *Organized Crime in America*, edited by Gus Tyler. Ann Arbor: University of Michigan Press.

Smith, David E., ed.
1979 *Amphetamine Use, Misuse, and Abuse*. Boston: G. K. Hall and Co.

Smith, Dwight C., Jr.
1982 "Paragons, Pariahs, and Pirates: A Spectrum-Based Theory of Enterprise." *Crime and Delinquency* 26 (July): 358–86.
1978 "Organized Crime and Entrepreneurship." *International Journal of Criminology and Penology* 6: 161–77.
1974 *The Mafia Mystique*. New York: Basic Books.

Smith, Dwight C., Jr., and Ralph Salerno
1970 "The Use of Strategies in Organized Crime Control." *Journal of Law, Criminology and Police Science* 61: 101–11.

Smith, John L.
1998 *The Animal in Hollywood: Anthony Fiato's Life in the Mafia*. New York: Barricade Books.

Smith, Peter H.
1999 "Semiorganized International Crime: Drug Trafficking in Mexico." Pages 193–216 in *Transnational Crime in the Americas*, edited by Tom Farer. New York: Routledge.

Smith, Richard Norton
1982 *Thomas E. Dewey and His Times*. New York: Simon and Schuster.

Smith, Sherwin D.
1963 "35 Years Ago Arnold Rothstein Was Mysteriously Murdered and Left a Racket Empire Up for Grabs." *New York Times Magazine* (October 27): 96.

"Smoking Gun, The"
1998 *New York* (November 22): 16.

Snedden, Christopher and John Visser
1994 *Financial and Organised Crime in Italy*. Commonwealth of Australia.

Sniffen, Michael J.
2000 "Mexico–Jamaica Drug Ring Broken." Associated Press (April 13): Internet.

Sondern, Frederic, Jr.
1959 *Brotherhood of Evil: The Mafia*. New York: Farrar, Straus and Cudahy.

Song, John Juey-Long
1996 The Asian Factor: Methodological Barriers to the Study of Asian Gangs and Organized Crime." *American Journal of Criminal Justice* 21 (1): 27–41.

Spadolini, Giovanni
1993 "Foreword." Pages 7–9 in *Mafia Issues*, edited by Ernesto U. Savona. Milan, Italy: United Nations.

Special Committee to Investigate Organized Crime in Interstate Commerce
1951 *Kefauver Crime Report*. New York: Arco.

Spector, Michael
1995 "Old-Time Boss for Russia's Showcase Port." *New York Times* (August 28): 1, 2.
1994 "New Moscow Mob Terror: Car Bombs." *New York Times* (June 10): 4.

Spergel, Irving
1964 *Racketville, Slumtown, Haulberg*. Chicago: University of Chicago Press.

Spiering, Frank
1976 *The Man Who Got Capone*. Indianapolis, IN: Bobbs-Merrill.

"Spotlight"
1981 *Chicago Crime Commission Searchlight* (October): 8.

Stahl, Marc B.
1992 "Asset Forfeiture, Burdens of Proof and the War on Drugs." *Journal of Criminal Law and Criminology* 83: 274–337.

Stanley, Alessandra
2001 "Where Hit Men Better Mean It When They 'Yes Ma'am' the Boss." *New York Times* (January 11): 11.
1998 "The Army Is Leaving But the Mafia Probably Isn't." *New York Times* (June 26): 4.
1994 "Where Politicians Sometimes Tote Assault Rifles." *New York Times* (May 10): 4.

Starks, Carolyn
1999 "Witness Offers Inside Look at Biker Battle." *Chicago Tribune* (April 6): Sec. 2: 1, 4.

State Commission of Investigation
1989 *Solid Waste Regulation*. Trenton: New Jersey State Commission of Investigation.

Steffens, Lincoln
1957 *The Shame of the Cities*. New York: Hill and Wang. Originally published in 1904.
1931 *The Autobiography of Lincoln Steffens*. New York: Chautauqua Press. Reprinted by Harcourt, Brace and World, 1958.

Steinberg, Alfred
1972 *The Bosses*. New York: New American Library.

Sterling, Claire
1990 *Octopus: The Long Reach of the Sicilian Mafia*. New York: Simon and Schuster.

Sterngold, James
1995 "Organized Crime Puts Its Talent to Helping and Tokyo to Shame." *New York Times* (January 22): 7.
1994 "Gangster Ties to Banks Hurt Japan's Financial Recovery." *New York Times* (October 18): C1, C14.
1992a "Japan Takes on Mob, and the Mob Fights Back." *New York Times* (June 15): 1, 6.
1992b "Mob and Politics Intersect, Fueling Cynicism in Japan." *New York Times* (October 21): 1, 4.
1992c "Corporate Japan's Unholy Allies." *New York Times* (December 6): 3: 1, 6.

Stevens, Jay
1987 *Storming Heaven: LSD and the American Dream*. New York: Atlantic Monthly Press.

Stewart, Robert C.
1980 *Identification and Investigation of Organized Criminal Activity*. Houston, TX: National College of District Attorneys.

Stille, Alexander
1995a *Exquisite Cadavers: The Mafia and the Death of the First Italian Republic*. New York: Pantheon.
1995b "Letter from Sicily: The Fall of Caesar." *New Yorker* (September 11): 68–83.
1993 "Letter from Palermo: The Mafia's Biggest Mistake." *New Yorker* (March 1): 60–73.

Stocckers, Sally W.
2000 "The Rise in Human Trafficking and the Role of Organized Crime." Transnational Crime and Corruption Center, American University. Internet.

Stolberg, Mary M.
1995 *Fighting Organized Crime: Politics, Justice, and the Legacy of Thomas E. Dewey*. Boston: Northeastern University Press.

Stone, Michael
1992 "After Gotti." *New York* (February 3): 23–30.

Stutman, Robert M. and Richard Esposito
1992 *Dead on Delivery: Inside the Drug Wars, Straight from the Street*. New York: Warner.

Sullivan, John and Alex Berenson
2000 "Brokers Charged with Crime Figures in Complex Scheme." *New York Times* (June 15): 1, C27.

Sullivan, Joseph F.
1991 "Casino Union Yields Power as Its Leaders Accept Curbs." *New York Times* (April 13): 7.

1988   "New Jersey Teamster Local Elects Slate Tied to the Mob." *New York Times* (December 8): 16.

Summers, Anthony
1993   *Official and Confidential: The Secret Life of J. Edgar Hoover.* New York: Putnam's.

Supreme Court of the State of New York
1942   *A Presentment Concerning the Enforcement by the Police Department of the City of New York of the Laws Against Gambling.* New York, reprinted by Arno Press, 1974.

Sutherland, Edwin H.
1973   *Edwin H. Sutherland: On Analyzing Crime.* Edited by Karl Schuessler. Chicago: University of Chicago Press.
1972   *The Professional Thief.* Chicago: University of Chicago Press. Originally published in 1937.

Suttles, Gerald D.
1968   *The Social Order of the Slum.* Chicago: University of Chicago Press.

Swanberg, W. A.
1959   *Jim Fisk: The Career of an Improbable Rascal.* New York: Scribner's.

Taft, Philip and Philip Ross
1969   "American Labor Violence: Its Causes, Character, and Outcome." Pages 281–395 in *The History of Violence in America*, edited by Hugh Davis Graham and Ted Robert Gurr. New York: Bantam.

Tagliabue, John
1994   "Live by the Rules? An Italian Haven for Cigarette Smugglers Is Fuming." *New York Times* (March 7): 4.

Takahashi, Sadahiko and Carl B. Becker
1985   *Organized Crime in Japan.* Osaka, Japan: Kin'ki University, unpublished paper.

Talese, Gay
1971   *Honor Thy Father.* New York: World Publishing.
1965   *The Overreachers.* New York: Harper & Row.

Talmadge, Eric
1999   "Japanese Mob Raising Fears, Concern." Associated Press, April 20. Internet.
1988   "All Is Not Well Within Japan's Underworld." *Southtown Economist* (December 15): Sec. 2: 4.

Tamayo, Juan O.
2001   "Colombia's Heroin Trade Is Flourishing." *Chicago Tribune* (August 24): 6.

Task Force on Organized Crime
1976   *Organized Crime.* Washington, DC: U.S. Government Printing Office.

1967   *Task Force Report: Organized Crime.* Washington, DC: U.S. Government Printing Office.

Task-Force on Organized Crime in the Baltic Sea Region (TFOCBSR)
2001   *Report on the Fact-Finding Mission Conducted in November 2000 by the National Commissioner of Police for the Baltic Countries Regarding Trafficking in Women.* TFOCBSR: Internet.

Tayler, Jefferey
2001   "Russia Is Finished." *Atlantic Monthly* (May): 35–52.

Taylor, Ian, Paul Walton, and Jock Young
1973   *The New Criminology.* New York: Harper and Row.

Tendler, Stewart
2000   "Yardie Gangs Move into the Provinces." *London Times* (August 3): 4.

Teresa, Vincent, and Thomas C. Renner
1973   *My Life in the Mafia.* Greenwich, CT: Fawcett.

Terry, Charles E. and Mildred Pellens
1928   *The Opium Problem.* New York: The Committee on Drug Addictions, in collaboration with the Bureau of Social Hygiene, Inc.

Thomas, Jerry
1994a   "Bombings in Chicago, Rockford Linked to Motorcycle Gang Merger." *Chicago Tribune* (November 9): Sec. 2: 4.
1994b   "Biker War Erupts in Illinois." *Chicago Tribune* (November 20): Sec. 2: 1, 2.

Thompson, Cheryl W.
2001   "DEA Shielded Tainted Informant." *Washington Post* (July 19): 1.

Thompson, Craig and Allan Raymond
1940   *Gang Rule in New York.* New York: Dial.

Thompson, Hunter S.
1966   *Hell's Angels: A Strange and Terrible Saga.* New York: Random House.

Thoumi, Francisco E.
1995   "The Size of the Illegal Drug Industry." Pages 77–96 in *Drug Trafficking in the Americas*, edited by Bruce M. Bagley and William O. Walker, III. New Brunswick, NJ: Transaction.

Thrasher, Frederic Milton
1968   *The Gang: A Study of 1,313 Gangs in Chicago*, abridged. Chicago: University of Chicago Press. Originally published in 1927.

Tillman, Robert and Henry Pontell
1995   "Organizations and Fraud in the Savings and Loan Industry." *Social Forces* 73 (June): 1439–63.

Tindall, George Brown
 1988 *America: A Narrative History*, vol. 2. New York: Norton.

Toby, Jackson
 1958 "Hoodlum or Businessman: An American Dilemma." Pages 542–50 in *The Jews: Social Patterns of an American Group*, edited by Marshall Sklare. Glencoe, IL: Free Press.

Tomass, Mark
 1998 "Mafianomics: How Did Mob Entrepreneurs Infiltrate and Dominate the Russian Economy?" *Journal of Economic Issues* 32 (June): 565–75.

Torriero, E. A.
 2002 "Afghan Officials Struggle to Stop Opium Bonanza." *Chicago Tribune* (March 3): 6.

Touhy, Roger
 1959 *The Stolen Years*. Cleveland, OH: Pennington.

Toy, Calvin
 1992 "A Short History of Asian Gangs in San Francisco." *Justice Quarterly* 9 (December): 647–65.

Train, Arthur
 1922 *Courts and Criminals*. New York: Scribner's.
 1912 "Imported Crime: The Story of the Camorra in America." *McClure's Magazine* (May): 83–94.

Treaster, Joseph B.
 1994 "U.S. Arrests Drug 'Laundry.'" *New York Times* (December 1): 1, 18.
 1993a "A Dozen Killings Tied to Colombia." *New York Times* (May 16): 1, 10.
 1993b "U.S. Says Top Trafficker Is Seized in Puerto Rican Connection." *New York Times* (June 5): 7.
 1992a "Nigerian Connection a New Threat in Heroin War." *New York Times* (February 15): 1, 10.
 1992b "Jailbreak Dramatizes Drug-Policy Failures." *New York Times* (July 26): E3.
 1991a "New York City's Top Cocaine Smugglers Are Arrested in Raids, Police Say." *New York Times* (December 7): 10.
 1991b "Cocaine Is Again Surging Out of Panama." *New York Times* (August 13): 1, 4.
 1991c "U.S. Seizes Suspect in New York in 40 Colombian Drug Slayings." *New York Times* (September 27): 1, 7.
 1989a "A Nice Place (Just Ask Drug Barons)." *New York Times* (May 23): 6.
 1989b "In Bolivia, U.S. Pumps Money into the Cocaine War, But Victory Is Elusive." *New York Times* (June 11): 10.

Trebach, Arnold S.
 1987 *The Great Drug War: Radical Proposals That Could Make America Safe Again*. New York: Macmillan.

Tricarico, Donald
 1984 *The Italians of Greenwich Village*. Staten Island, NY: Center for Migration Studies of New York.

Tri-State Joint Soviet Émigré Organized Crime Project
 1997 "An Analysis of Russian Émigré Crime in the Tri-State Region." Pages 177–210 in *Russian Organized Crime, The New Threat?* edited by Phil Williams. London: Frank Cass.

Tucker, Richard K.
 1991 *The Dragon and the Cross: The Rise and Fall of the Ku Klux Klan in Middle America*. Hamden, CT: Archon Books.

Tuite, James
 1978 "Would Benefits of Legalized Betting on Sports Outweigh the Drawbacks?" *New York Times* (December 19): B21.

Tullis, LaMond
 1995 *Unintended Consequences: Illegal Drugs and Drug Policies in Nine Countries*. Boulder, CO: Lynne Reinner.

Tully, Andrew
 1958 *Treasury Agent: The Inside Story*. New York: Simon and Schuster.

Tulsky, Frederic N.
 1987 "U.S. Witness Protection Program Hides a Daughter from Her Father." *Chicago Tribune* (March 5): Sec. 5: 3.

Turbiville, Graham H., Jr.
 1995 "Organized Crime and the Russian Armed Forces." *Transnational Organized Crime* 1 (Winter): 57–104.

Turkus, Burton and Sid Feder
 1951 *Murder, Inc.: The Story of the Syndicate*. New York: Farrar, Straus and Young.

Turner, Wallace
 1984 "U.S. and Nevada Agents Crack Down on Casinos." *New York Times* (January 28): 1, 7.

Tyler, Gus
 1975 "Book Review of 'The Black Mafia.'" *Crime and Delinquency* 21 (April): 175–80.

Tyler, Gus, ed.
 1962 *Organized Crime in America*. Ann Arbor: University of Michigan Press.

Tyler, Patrick E.
 1995 "China Battles a Spreading Scourge of Illicit Drugs." *New York Times* (November 15): 1, 7.

Ungar, Sanford
  1975   *The FBI*. Boston: Little, Brown.
"Unger Indicted in Drug Conspiracy"
  1928   *New York Times* (December 11): 1.
United States General Accounting Office
  1981   *Stronger Federal Effort Needed in Fight Against Organized Crime*. Washington, DC: U.S. Government Printing Office.
United States of America v. Carlisi, 92Cr 1064 F2d, 1990.
United States Senate Subcommittee on Administrative Practice and Procedure
  1978   *Hearings on Oversight of the Witness Protection Program*. Washington, DC: U.S. Government Printing Office.
U.S. Department of State
  2001   *The Caribbean*. Bureau for International Narcotics and Law Enforcement Affairs. Internet.
  1999   *Money Laundering and Financial Crimes*. Washington, DC: Bureau for International Narcotics and Law Enforcement Affairs.
"Usury Racket Stirred Gang War"
  1935   *New York Times* (October 25): 17.
Van Devander, Charles W.
  1944   *The Big Bosses*. New York: Howell, Soskin.
Van Duyne, Petrus and Alan A. Block
  1995   "Organized Cross-Atlantic Crime: Racketeering in Fuels." *Crime, Law and Social Change* 22: 127–47.
Van Dyke, Craig and Robert Byck
  1982   "Cocaine." *Scientific American* 246 (March): 139–41.
Van Natta, Don, Jr.
  1998   "U.S. Indicts 26 Mexican Bankers in Laundering of Drug Funds." *New York Times* (May 19): 6.
  1996   "19 Indicted on U.S. Charges in Blow to Genovese Family." *New York Times* (June 12): B12.
Varese, Federico
  2001   *The Russian Mafia: Private Protection in a New Market Economy*. Oxford, United Kingdom: Oxford University Press.
Vest, Jason
  1997   "DEA to Florists: The Poppies Are Unlovely." *U.S. News & World Report* (March 17): 49.
Vigil, Michael S.
  2000   Special Agent in Charge. Caribbean Field Division, Drug Enforcement Administration, Before the U.S. House of Representatives Subcommittee on Criminal Justice Oversight, May 9.

Villano, Anthony
  1978   *Brick Agent*. New York: Ballantine.
Violante, Luciano
  2000   "Foreword." Pages ix–xi in Alison Jamieson, *The Antimafia: Italy's Fight Against Organized Crime*. New York: St. Martin's Press.
Vitielo, Michael
  1995   "Has the Supreme Court Really Turned RICO Upside Down? An Examination of *Now v. Scheidler*." *Journal of Criminal Law and Criminology* 85 (Spring): 1223–57.
Volkman, Ernest
  1998   *Gangbusters: The Destruction of America's Last Mafia Dynasty*. Boston: Faber and Faber.
Volkov, Vadim
  2000   "The Political Economy of Protection Rackets in the Past and the Present." *Social Research* 67 (Fall): Internet.
Voronin, Yuriy A.
  1997   "The Emerging Criminal State: Economic and Political Aspects of Organized Crime in Russia." Pages 53–62 in *Russian Organized Crime, The New Threat?* edited by Phil Williams. London: Frank Cass.
Waldman, Michael and Pamela Gilbert
  1989   "RICO Goes to Congress: Keep the Teeth in the White-Collar Law." *New York Times* (March 12): F2.
Wahl, Melissa
  2000   "Surge Puts Payday Loans Under Scrutiny." *Chicago Tribune* (May 7): 1, 11.
  1999a   "Hitting a Wall of Opposition." *Chicago Tribune* (February 4): Sec. 3: 1, 4.
  1999b   "Suspicions Mount About Secrecy Act." *Chicago Tribune* (March 26): Sec. 3: 1, 4.
  1999c   "Payday Loans Hit Pay Dirt." *Chicago Tribune* (November 18): 1, 6.
Waldman, Amy
  2002   "A Village at Source of Heroin Trade Fears the Eradication of Its Poppies." *New York Times* (March 12): 12.
Walker, Samuel
  1980   *Popular Justice: A History of American Criminal Justice*. New York: Oxford University Press.
Wallance, Gregory
  1982   *Papa's Game*. New York: Ballantine.
Walsh, Marilyn E.
  1977   *The Fence*. Westport, CT: Greenwood.
Walston, James
  1986   "See Naples and Die: Organized Crime in Campania." Pages 134–58 in *Organized Crime:*

A Global Perspective, edited by Robert J. Kelly. Totowa, NJ: Rowman and Littlefield.

Walter, Ingo
1990 *Secret Money: The World of International Financial Secrecy*. New York: Harper Business.

Warnick, Mark S.
1997 "City Cop Scandals Dash Drug Trials." *Chicago Tribune* (December 25): Sec. 2: 1, 2.

Washburn, Charles
1934 *Come into My Parlor: Biography of the Aristocratic Everleigh Sisters of Chicago*. New York: Knickerbocker Publishing Co.

"Washington Talk"
1986 *New York Times* (January 18): 8.

Webster, Barbara and Michael S. McCampbell
1992 *International Money Laundering: Research and Investigation Join Forces*. Washington, DC: National Institute of Justice.

Webster, Donovan
1994 "Chips Are a Thief's Best Friend." *New York Times Magazine* (September 18): 54–59.

Weiner, Tim
2002 "Drug Kingpin, Long Sought, Is Captured by Mexicans." *New York Times* (March 10): 15.
2001a "Mexican Jail Easy to Flee: Just Pay Up." *New York Times* (January 29): 5.
2001b "With Taliban Gone, Opium Farmers Return to Their Only Cash Crop." *New York Times* (November 26): B1, 4.

Weinstein, Adam K.
1988 "Prosecuting Attorneys for Money Laundering: A New and Questionable Weapon in the War on Crime." *Law and Contemporary Problems* 51 (Winter): 369–86.

Weiser, Benjamin
1999 "Indictments Said to Show Reach of New Jersey Crime Family." *New York Times* (December 3): C25.
1998a "Reputed Crime Family Head Indicted in Extortion Case." *New York Times* (April 29): Internet.
1998b "14 Charged in Internet Betting in the First Case of Its Kind." *New York Times* (March 5): 1, 23.
1999a "2 Linked to Mob Admit Role in Stock Manipulation Scheme." *New York Times* (January 22): 25.
1999b "City Hall to Pay Hells Angels in Settlement." *New York Times* (April 3): 12.

Weisman, Alan
1989 "Dangerous Days in the Macarena." *New York Times Magazine* (April 23): 40–48.

Weisman, Steven R.
1991 "Is Business Too Cozy with the Mob?" *New York Times* (August 29): 11.

Weiss, Murray and Jim Nolan
1993 "Scrub Out! Top Mobster Nabbed in the Shower." *New York Post* (January 20): 7.

Wendt, Lloyd and Herman Kogan
1974 *Bosses in Lusty Chicago: The Story of Bathhouse John and Hinky Dink*. Bloomington: Indiana University Press. Originally published in 1943.

Werner, M. R.
1928 *Tammany Hall*. Garden City, NY: Doubleday, Doran.

Wesson, Donald R. and David E. Smith
1985 "Cocaine: Treatment Perspectives." Pages 193–203 in *Cocaine Use in America: Epidemiologic and Clinical Perspectives*, edited by Nicholas J. Kozel and Edgar H. Adams. Rockville, MD: National Institute on Drug Abuse.
1977 *Barbiturates: Their Use, Misuse, and Abuse*. New York: Human Sciences Press.

Wethern, George and Vincent Colnett
1978 *A Wayward Angel*. New York: Marek Publishers.

Whalen, David C.
1995 "Organized Crime and Sports Gambling: Point-Shaving in College Basketball." Pages 19–34 in *Contemporary Issues in Organized Crime*, edited by Jay Albanese. Monsey, NY: Criminal Justice Press.

"Who Are the Yardies?"
1999 *BBC News* (June 19): Internet.

"Who Took the Stone of Alphonse Capone?"
1981 *Chicago Tribune Magazine* (September 6): 6.

Whymant, Robert
2001 "Crime Bosses Killed in Funeral Attack." *London Times* (September 20): Internet.

Whyte, William Foote
1961 *Street Corner Society*. Chicago: University of Chicago Press.

Williams, Phil
1997 "Introduction: How Serious a Threat Is Russian Organized Crime?" Pages 1–27 in *Russian Organized Crime, The New Threat?* edited by Phil Williams. London: Frank Cass.
1995a "The New Threat: Transnational Criminal

Organizations and International Security." *Criminal Organizations* 9 (3 and 4): 3–19.

1995b "The Geopolitics of Transnational Organized Crime." Paper presented at the annual meeting of the American Society of Criminology, Boston, November.

Williams, T. Harry
1969 *Huey Long*. New York: Bantam.

Wilson, James Q.
1978 *The Investigators*. New York: Basic Books.
1975 *Thinking About Crime*. New York: Basic Books.

Wilson, Scott
2001 "Colombia's War Reaches Colleges." *Chicago Tribune* (June 1): 3.

Wilson, Theodore
1975 "The Kefauver Committee, 1950." Pages 353–82 in *Congress Investigates: 1792–1974*, edited by Arthur M. Schlessinger, Jr., and Robert Burns. New York: Chelsea House.

Winick, Charles and Paul M. Kinsie
1971 *The Lively Commerce*. Chicago: Quadrangle.

Wiretap Commission. See National Commission for the Review of Federal and State Laws Relating to Wiretapping and Electronic Surveillance.

Wishart, David
1974 "The Opium Poppy: The Forbidden Crop." *Journal of Geography* 73 (January): 1425.

Withers, Kay
1982 "Cardinal Leads Drive to Crush Sicily's Mafia." *Chicago Tribune* (September 29): 5.

Witkin, Gordon
1991 "The Men Who Created Crack." *U.S. News & World Report* (August 19): 44–53.

Witkin, Gordon with Jennifer Griffen
1994 "The New Opium Wars." *U.S. News & World Report* (October 10): 39–44.

Witt, Howard
1996 "For Russians, Mafia Part of Everyday Life." *Chicago Tribune* (November 24): 1, 14.
1994 "Welcome to Vladivostok, Where Crime Is King." *Chicago Tribune* (November 21): 1, 19.

Woetzel, Robert K.
1963 "An Overview of Organized Crime: Mores Versus Morality." *Annals* 347 (May): 1–11.

Wolf, Daniel R.
1991 *The Rebels: A Brotherhood of Outlaw Bikers*. Toronto: University of Toronto Press.

Wolf, Eric R.
1966 "Kinship, Friendship, and Patron–Client Relations in Complex Societies." Pages 1–22 in *The Social Anthropology of Complex Societies*, edited by Michael Banton. London: Tavistock.

Wolfgang, Marvin E. and Franco Ferracuti
1967 *The Subculture of Violence: Toward an Integrated Theory in Criminology*. London: Tavistock.

"Woman, 2 Men, Slain as Gang Raids Home in Coll Feud"
1932 *New York Times* (February 2): 1.

Woodham-Smith, Cecil
1962 *The Great Hunger: Ireland 1845–1849*. New York: Old Town Books. Originally published by Harper and Row.

Woodiwiss, Michael
1988 *Crime, Crusades and Corruption: Prohibitions in the United States, 1900–1987*. Totowa, NJ: Barnes and Noble.
1987 "Capone to Kefauver: Organized Crime in America." *History Today* 37 (June): 8–15.

Wren, Christopher S.
1999a "Pipeline of Poor Smuggling Heroin." *New York Times* (February 21): 28.
1999b "U.S. Gives Colombia and Mexico Nod on Drugs." *New York Times* (February 27): 6.
1998a "Drug Officials Sense a Shift in Dominicans." *New York Times* (August 14): 16.
1998b "Road to Riches Starts in the Golden Triangle." *New York Times* (May 11): 8.
1998c "Afghanistan's Opium Output Drops Sharply, U.N. Survey Shows." *New York Times* (September 27): 11.
1998d "Where Opium Reigned, Burmese Claim Inroads." *New York Times* (April 19): 8.
1997 "29 Held in Drug Smuggling to New York from Mexico." *New York Times* (August 12): C23.
1996 "Mexican Role in Cocaine Is Exposed in U.S. Seizure." *New York Times* (May 3): C19.

Wright, Michael
1979 "Phenix City, Ala., Leaves Ashes of Sin in the Past." *New York Times* (June 18): 14.

WuDunn, Sheryl
1996 "Uproar Over a Bad Debt Crisis." *New York Times* (February 14): C1, 4.

Wyman, Mark
1984 *Immigrants in the Valley: Irish, Germans, and Americans in the Upper Mississippi Country, 1830–1860*. Chicago: Nelson-Hall.

Yates, Ronald E.
1985 "Lawmen's Dispute on Gangs Rages Over Pacific." *Chicago Tribune* (December 8): 5.

Zalisko, Walter
  2001   "Russian Organized Crime, Trafficking in Women, and Government's Response." PMC International Inc. (April): Internet.

Zilg, Gerard Colbykiik
  1974   *DuPont: Behind the Nylon Curtain.* Englewood Cliffs: NJ: Prentice-Hall.

Zimmermann, Tim and Alan Cooperman
  1995   "Special Report." *U.S. News & World Report* (October 23): 56–67.

Zorbaugh, Harvey
  1929   *The Gold Coast and the Slum.* Chicago: University of Chicago Press.

AUTHOR INDEX

SUBJECT INDEX

PHOTO CREDITS